STATE HOUSE AT ANNAPOLIS IN 1789

# THE
# GENERAL ASSEMBLY
# OF
# MARYLAND
## 1634 - 1776

by

## CARL N. EVERSTINE

THE MICHIE COMPANY

*Law Publishers*

CHARLOTTESVILLE, VIRGINIA

To Barbara

# TABLE OF CONTENTS

CHAPTER                                                    Page

Preface ........................................... ix

1. The Legislative Heritage from England .......... 1

   The Period of Invasions — The Common Law —
   Magna Carta — The Early Parliaments —
   Commons and Lords — The Speaker — Bills —
   Money Bills — Procedure and Rules — Journals
   — Committees — The Tudors — The Stuarts —
   Political Parties — American Developments —
   "Mother of Parliaments"

2. The Establishment of Legislative Power in
   Maryland, 1634-1638 ......................... 23

   The Charter — St. Mary's — A Plan of
   Government — The General Assembly —
   Rules and Procedure in 1637/8 — Governing the
   Province — The Legislation of 1637/8

3. Developing Powers and Procedures, 1638/9-1649    55

   Calling the Third Session — The Session of
   1638/9—The Legislation of 1638/9—The Session
   in October, 1640 — The Session of August, 1641
   —The Session of March, 1641/2—The Session of
   July 18, 1642 — The Sessions of 1642 and 1644/5
   — The Sessions of 1646 and 1647 — The
   12th Session, in 1649

4. The Puritan Regime and Restoration, 1650-1668    83

   The Session in April, 1650 — The Sessions during
   the 1650s — The Early 1660s — The Middle
   1660s — Legislative Billingsgate

CHAPTER                                           Page

5.  A Time of Adjustment and Questioning, 1669-1687  107

The Nicholett Episode — Control and Conflict —
The Impeachment of Major Thomas Truman —
"Grievances" of the Lower House — Prerogatives
of the Lower House — Laws Effective for Three
Years — Uncertainties of Jurisdiction —
Procedure and Protocol — Legislation in the
1670s and 1680s — The New State House

6.  Maryland as a Royal Colony, 1688-1715 ........ 149

The Session of 1688 — Taking the Oath — The
Associators' Assembly — The Early 1690s — The
Move to Annapolis — The New State House —
The Late 1690s — Compensation of Public
Officials — Legislative Privileges and
Prerogatives — Into the Eighteenth Century —
Problems of Annapolis — Non-Legislative
Powers — The State House Fire of 1704 —
Legislative Contention — Procedures and
Policies — The Restoration

7.  The Proprietary Restored, 1716-1732 ........... 213

The Reinstatement of Lord Baltimore — Revision
of the Laws — Relationships with Lord Baltimore
and the Governor — Legislative Routine —
Compensation of the Council of State — Other
Legislative Controversies — English Statutory
and Common Law — Procedures and Jurisdiction
— A Century of Progress

8.  Into the Second Century, 1733-1748 ............ 265

Members Holding Two Offices — Compensation
for Council of State — Taxes and Finance —
Other Controversies — Operations and Privileges

CHAPTER Page

— Troubles with an Indian Treaty — Fines, Forfeitures, and Revenues — The Late 1740s

9. Deepening Confrontation with Lord Baltimore, 1749-1756 ................................. 313

Appointment of the House Clerk — Election Disputes — The Seamy Side of Politics — Holding Two Public Employments — The Province at Mid-Century — Taxes, Fees, Fines, and Forfeitures — The Supply Bill — Revenue and Finance

10. Legislative Operations and Privilege, the 1750s 353

Compensation of Legislators — Procedures and Operations — Legislative Privilege — The Ridout Affair — Abolition of the Upper House — The Supply Bill — Power over the Militia

11. Toward the Final Break with England, 1757-1764 383

Supply and Assessment Bills — The Tax Bill from the House of Delegates — Other Efforts for a Supply Bill — Financial Powers of the House of Delegates — Dignity and Decorum — House Rules and Procedures — Jonas Green, Printer — Bacon's Laws — The Impending Stamp Act

12. The Stamp Act, 1765-1767 .................... 417

Protest in Maryland — Daniel Dulany the Younger — Preparation for the Stamp Act Congress — Distribution of Stamps — The Stamp Act Congress — Repeal of the Stamp Act — Other Problems of 1765 — Compromise on Disputed Issues — Procedures

CHAPTER                                   Page
13. The Townshend Acts, 1768-1772 ............... 453

Enactment and Provisions — Reaction in
Maryland — Prerogatives, Procedures, and
Decorum — "Treating" the Voters — The Steuart
Case — Legislative Problems and Issues — Rules
and Petitions — The New State House — The Eve
of Revolution

14. The Tea Act, 1773-1774 ...................... 449

Enactment and Response — Matters of Routine
— "First Citizen" and "Antillon" — The Burning
of the *Peggy Stewart* — Jonathan Boucher and
William Eddis — The End of the Provincial
Assembly

15. Government by Convention, 1774-1776 ......... 517

The Convention Format — The Convention of
June 22, 1774 — The Convention of
November 21, 1774 — The Convention of
December 8, 1774 — The Convention of April 24,
1775 — The Convention of July 26, 1775 — The
Convention of December 7, 1775 — The
Convention of May 8, 1776 — The Departure of
Governor Eden — The Convention of June 21,
1776 — The Constitutional Convention of August
14, 1776 — The End of an Era — The Constitution
of 1776

Index .......................................... 571

# PREFACE

This volume is a history of the General Assembly of Maryland from the beginnings of the Province of Maryland in 1634 to the start of the American Revolution in 1776. Its source material is heavily and primarily from the *Journals* of the Upper House (Senate) and the Lower House (House of Delegates). The *Journals* are printed verbatim in the monumental and invaluable *Archives of Maryland,* published in seventy-two volumes by the Maryland Historical Society, from 1883 to 1972.

The book does not purport in any sense to be a general history of the Province of Maryland, except as that history is reflected in the proceedings and actions of the General Assembly. The general history of Maryland is covered in a number of standard references, supplemented by dozens of articles and commentaries on separate topics.

With the limited exception of the sketchy and non-analytical publications of Elihu S. Riley, some seventy-five years ago, the other publications do not emphasize the text of the legislative *Journals* and the workings of the General Assembly. This volume is grounded upon the proceedings as published in the *Journals,* and to a lesser degree upon the Acts of Assembly as contained in the *Archives* and in Kilty's *Laws.*

The aim has been to cover matters of legislative philosophy, organization, and procedure, the *how* of the legislative processes rather than the *what* of their accomplishments. Acts of Assembly are described and quoted mainly for the insight they give in explaining the political and social philosophies of the seventeenth and eighteenth centuries and the reactions of legislators; and both the strengths and the frailties of the legislators are included.

The development and evolution of legislative processes in Maryland also are related to the foundations built in England for centuries prior to 1634 and to the continuing development and growth of parliamentary government during many decades following 1776.

In the use of the *Archives,* to avoid a multiplicity of footnotes, precise page references usually are not given. Instead, either the actual date of the occurrence or a mention of the session involved is provided in the text. Page references for the *Archives* are used only for those volumes not directly involving the proceedings of the General Assembly.

In quotations from printed documents, usually either the *Journals* or the text of laws, abbreviations have been expanded into full words. Otherwise, original spellings have been retained, and without the use of *sic.* Original capitalization and punctuation also have been retained. "Old Style" letters in the quotations have been modernized.

Both Old Style and New Style dates are provided in the text, as 1634/5. This usage continues until the enactment of the English New Style Calendar Act of 1750, effective in 1752.

Generous words of thanks and indebtedness are expressed to Dr. Morgan H. Pritchett and his staff in the Maryland Room of the Enoch Pratt Free Library in Baltimore; and to Miss Alice Hester Rich and her staff in the library of the Maryland Historical Society, also in Baltimore. Both groups have contributed freely of their knowledge and energies; and both libraries are valuable adjuncts to a study and understanding of Maryland's past.

My deep thanks and appreciation go also to my wife, Barbara, for her unfailing support and perceptive awareness of the refinements of grammar, syntax, and style.

C. N. E.

# Chapter 1

## THE LEGISLATIVE HERITAGE FROM ENGLAND

The General Assembly of Maryland first convened in 1635, less than a year after the settlement at St. Mary's. It claimed at once the legislative prerogative in the new colony, a role it now has continued for nearly 350 years, throughout the Provincial and Colonial period and for two centuries of statehood.

If ever there was an unlikely spot for the development and growth of democratic and parliamentary government, it was the tiny settlement in Southern Maryland. Some two or three hundred persons landed from the Ark and the Dove, separated from England by a long and arduous journey and not knowing what manner of reception they might have from the native Indians. It was a time and a place for rule of the strong man.

The settlers had their problems, in truth, yet they held to legal institutions, established and maintained a legislature, and went forward to the democratic and republican precepts of the American states.

Why, and how?

Original cause is a difficult concept in history, but here one can hardly avoid linking the success of the Maryland colonists with the life, progress, and traditions from whence they came.

England in the early seventeenth century was nearing the culmination of a thousand years of what, in retrospect, seems an inexorable (if uneven) drive toward self-government and parliamentary rule. When Maryland was settled in 1634, however, the home country was going into a particularly difficult period. The English Civil War, the execution of Charles I, the Commonwealth, and the Protectorate were but a few years in the future. England in 1634 was already in the throes of the controversies which led to the dramatic

1

climaxes of the 1640s and 1650s. It was still a half-century before the Peaceful Revolution of 1688, which finally assured the primary place of the Parliament and the secondary place of the Crown in the workings of English government.

So much that was "English" became also "American" and "Anglo-American" in Maryland, and in other American colonies, that the connection is direct and clear.

Indeed, the organization and procedures of legislative bodies throughout the world, and perhaps the very fact that there can be an effective legislative process, stem directly from early beginnings in England. The story of their development runs as a thread throughout those thousand years of English history and spreads into many other nations which share the English tradition. John Bright's "England is the mother of parliaments" states the debt owed to Great Britain.

Why the English legislative system should have developed so much earlier and better than systems elsewhere is one of the unanswered questions of history. One need not claim any inherent superiority of the English people over others; those we call "English" today, and for many centuries past, are the product of successive waves of Germanic invasions from the Continent, engrafted upon the earlier Celtic people who seem to have been the original inhabitants of the British Isles. Nor can one claim inherent superiority for the immigrants from the Continent; the Germanic peoples who remained at home have not so highly distinguished themselves in the art of government.

Perhaps the tight little English Channel was a sufficient deterrent to invasion and conquest to set England somewhat apart from the turmoil and frictions on the Continent. Not since 1066 has there been a successful invasion of Britain from the Continent; one may speculate that the English people were less embroiled than their neighbors on the

Continent with constant threats of foreign domination, and so better able to indulge in the luxury of legislative and parliamentary government.

## The Period of Invasions

For centuries in the early Christian era, however, England did undergo a continuing series of invasions from abroad, most of them violent in the manner of the times. The first one in historical periods was that of the Romans, from the first century B.C. to the fifth century A.D. It was largely a military conquest, leaving the original Celts little changed when the Romans withdrew.[1] In the fifth and sixth centuries, waves of Angles, Saxons, and Jutes crossed the English Channel. These invasions were mass migrations, with the warriors accompanied by their families; the surviving Celts were pushed into the uplands in the north and west of England. The institutions today called "English" may be traced back to these Germanic invaders.

By the end of the seventh century, the land was divided politically into seven small and independent kingdoms. Another set of invaders in the eighth century, the Danes, brought the English together for their own protection. By the end of that century, England was loosely united under one king. This was the first of the events, perhaps fortuitous, which in later centuries seem to be landmarks in a developing English polity.

The Danes invaded again in the early ninth century. Their temporary defeat at the hands of Alfred the Great (871-899) brought to the fore an English king who may be called a second landmark in the history and constitutional growth of the English nation. Alfred, in addition to having substantial military achievements, was a promoter of law and a patron

---

1. *See generally, Roman Britain, 55 B.C. — A.D. 409*, 6 British History Illustrated, (1979).

3

of learning. He compiled a code of laws, encouraged scholars to come from abroad, and improved local government in the shires; and he fostered a sense of nationalism in the "English" peoples.

There were other invasions in the tenth and early eleventh centuries, culminating in the last successful thrust from the Continent, the Norman Conquest in 1066.

In the five hundred years of Anglo-Saxon government, the country was ruled by the king and his council, the latter known as the "witan." The king was selected by the witan, generally being taken from members of the ruling house. His powers were limited, partly by the traditions of localism and also by his dependence on the witan for making decisions. This body, also called the "witanagemot," comprised about a hundred of the leading men of the realm.

The invading Normans were from the Duchy of Normandy, in northwest France; but they were the product of earlier raids by the Vikings, and, hence, originally a Nordic and Germanic people. Their rule was concentrated in the king and his curia regis, or king's court. After a bloody and complete military conquest, the Norman King William was master of England as no man before him.[2]

William continued and developed the feudal system that he found in England, and that came to have constitutional importance in Magna Carta. It was a close system of land tenure, combining obligations of service and allegiance with the ownership and occupation of land. All ownership came ultimately from the king, with the concepts of use and service descending through a hierarchy to end in the vassals. Obligations of service gave a political overtone to what basically was an economic system.

The curia regis in Norman government was composed of the king's chief tenants. Under the king, it handled all

---

2. *See generally, England under the Normans, 1066-1154*, 5 BRITISH HISTORY ILLUSTRATED, (1978).

legislative, executive, and judicial functions of government. In their administration of local government, the Normans largely continued the earlier Anglo-Saxon system. The counties, the office of sheriff, and the courts continued as before, giving the Norman kings wide contacts throughout the country.

## THE COMMON LAW

King Henry II (1154-1189) gets a major share of the credit for developing the concept of the English common law, certainly another landmark in the evolution of parliamentary and constitutional government. He improved, without actually beginning, the system of itinerant justices. They represented the king and tried to follow precedents established by their fellow justices. Ultimately they created a system of jurisprudence "common" to all England. While this accomplishment was mainly judicial and not legislative, it improved the quality of "the law" and gave it a degree of acceptability among the English people.

## MAGNA CARTA

Magna Carta came during the reign of the "bad" King John (1199-1216). His participation was reluctant and deceitful, as befitted his general character, but it brought John a degree of immortality.[3] It was the feudal system that caused his downfall, forcing John to operate with a set of strong nobles and barons. He tried to play one against the other, to strengthen the weak and weaken the strong, and to make promises he never intended to keep. Finally, by sheer force of military potential, the barons brought him to the

---

3. *See generally,* SIDNEY PAINTER, THE REIGN OF KING JOHN (Baltimore, 1949).

5

famous meadow at Runnymede, outside London, and required his acquiescence in Magna Carta on June 15, 1215.

Magna Carta has been glamorized as containing a whole new philosophy of government, but it hardly reached that importance. It was in purpose only a set of concrete remedies for specific complaints, all grounded in the feudal system. It contained, as such, no statement of abstract principles of government; it was mainly a landlord-tenant document, an effort to get the King to observe his side of the feudal contract.

Whatever their purpose, however, the barons put into Magna Carta a number of provisions which have been immortalized into the political concepts of the Anglo-American tradition. No. 39 read that "no freeman shall be taken, or imprisoned, or disseised, or outlawed, or exiled, or in any way destroyed, nor will we go upon him, nor will we send upon him, except by the legal judgment of his peers or by the law of the land." No. 40 said that "to no one will we sell, deny, or delay right or justice." No. 20 provided that amercements were to be in accordance with the measure of the offense, and not so heavy as to deprive any man of his means of livelihood. In a number of clauses there was the concept that one's property should not be taken for public use without his consent.[4]

The impact of Magna Carta has been indirect. Its unmistakable thrust was that the king is not above the law. In time, it became England's (and America's) justification for asserting the liberties of the subject against the Crown and the government and for the principle that the powers of the king and of the government are limited. No subsequent king of England was ever allowed to forget that John had granted Magna Carta; later kings reaffirmed its principles thirty

---

4. *See generally,* J. C. HOLT, MAGNA CARTA (Cambridge University Press, 1965); WILLIAM F. SWINDLER, MAGNA CARTA: LEGEND AND LEGACY (New York, 1965).

times or more.[5] As a document of state, it has had a deep and persistent influence on the course of history.

## THE EARLY PARLIAMENTS

Another great constitutional development of the thirteenth century was the beginning of parliamentary government in the modern sense, a change from the old Anglo-Saxon witan and the later Norman curia regis to a more representative assembly.

The English mark this change as dating from 1265. At the instigation of Simon de Montfort (the brother-in-law of Henry III and leader of the insurgents who had reduced the King to a puppet's role), a summons was issued for knights of the shire and to "discreet, lawful and upright citizens and burgesses" (*i.e.,* freemen of cities and boroughs) to meet for consultation. The ostensible reason was to give an appearance of legality to de Montfort's actions. Whatever the background, the year 1265 usually is given for the "birth" of the Parliament.

Actually, there were several prior meetings of a representative body, all earlier in the thirteenth century. The first one, ironically enough, involved "bad" King John.

In the year 1213, John sent writs to the sheriffs of all the counties, directing them to have at Oxford, on a specified date, four knights from each shire "to deliberate with us concerning the affairs of our kingdom." Here was a beginning of the representative body known as the House of Commons, the lower house of the English Parliament. The curia regis, or king's court, led into the upper house of the Parliament, the House of Lords. Other such summons were issued to knights of the shires in 1254 and 1261. However, the

---

5. "Sir Edward Coke reaches 32 instances when the Charter was solemnly ratified." J. MOSS IVES, THE ARK AND THE DOVE — THE BEGINNINGS OF CIVIL AND RELIGIOUS LIBERTIES IN AMERICA 81 (New York, 1936).

division of the Parliament into two houses was not to come for many years.

The knights of the shire who were summoned in 1213, 1254, 1261, and 1265 were clearly supposed to be cooperative in voting "aid" to the king. In 1254, for example, the writs sent to the sheriffs to have "Lawful and discreet" knights elected in each county contained a directive to the sheriffs that "to the knights and others . . . you yourself shall explain the needs and urgency of our business, and you shall persuade them to render us effective aid."

Probably all these changes in government in the thirteenth century stemmed from friction between the kings and the barons.[6] In the process, the barons became critical of the membership of the great council which for centuries had advised the king on his major decisions. At the same time, England was in a period of increasing wealth and social change, and it was realized that the knights and the burghers of the towns must also be considered. The new "councils," then, had a wider membership than the traditional select council; and the use of the term "Parliament," meaning "discussion," showed its function. Gradually, the governing body of the king in council became the king in council in Parliament. Legislation which formerly had been the will of the king, with the consent of his great council, came to be introduced by the king in council in Parliament, and it had a new formality when it emerged as a written statute embodying the will of the Parliament.

---

6. The civil commotion in the 1260s, under Simon de Montfort, is known as the Barons' War. *See* SIR MAURICE POWICKE, THE THIRTEENTH CENTURY, 1216-1307, at 170 (Oxford, 1954).

## Commons and Lords

Separation of the Parliament into a bicameral body, with a House of Lords and a House of Commons, dates from the fourteenth century. The members of the council (the Anglo-Saxon witan and the Norman curia regis) became the "upper" house or House of Lords; and all the knights of the shire and burghers from the towns comprised the House of Commons. The two groups, when meeting together, were too large and heterogeneous an assembly for smooth functioning. One reason undoubtedly was the wide difference among them in education and social background. The split at first was informal; the groups would meet separately to discuss issues and then come together for a final decision. Later, two separate houses were created and, by the latter part of the fourteenth century, they were meeting apart as a matter of course. Even prior to the separation, the two sets of legislators were mentioned as such. An enacting clause in 1318, for example, spoke of "the assent of the prelates, earls, barons, and the commonalty of the realm."

The value of the two houses generally is said to be in the enforced brake, machinery for delay, and means of additional deliberation. Lord Lyndhurst, in the House of Lords in 1770, had this (and more) in mind when he spoke of "the inconsiderate, rash, hasty, and undigested legislation of the other House." Legend has it that George Washington illustrated the need for a second chamber by pouring a cup of hot liquid into a saucer and allowing it to cool. A very old tradition is that the ancient Goths made a practice of twice debating every issue, once while sober and once while drunk; the sober debate was to give them discretion, and the debate while drunk was to bring vigor to their councils.

The early development of the bicameral system in England perhaps was almost one of chance, though that is not too satisfying an answer for such an important result. A primary reason, certainly, was the recurring need of the kings for money, for "an aid," and the strategy to invite in representatives of "the people" in order to make the request palatable. Once the knights of the shire and the burghers from the towns appeared in the Parliament, the break into two houses might have been expected.

## THE SPEAKER

The office of Speaker of the House of Commons was an early development. From the very beginning, the idea was that he would speak for the House of Commons, as its representative. Before the separation into two Houses, when the groups were meeting separately for their deliberations, the lower group, or Commons, would appoint a "speaker" to report back to the council. He would preface his report with a "protestation" that what he had to say was not said on his own initiative, but by the initiative, assent, and express will of those he represented. He was, that is, a spokesman.

This is the English doctrine that "a speaker hardly ever speaks"; meaning, of course, that he is to speak for the Commons and not for himself. It was sometimes more an ideal than an actuality in the early centuries of the speakership, for the kings early discovered the value of imposing their own nominee upon the Commons, where he could become the king's agent for managing the Commons. There were a number of notable clashes over the dual concepts of the position, with the king supposing the speaker to be *his* agent in the Commons, while the House of Commons regarded him as *its* representative and spokesman.

One such clash occurred while Sir John Finch was Speaker, in 1627-1628. Without denying to the Commons that he represented the King, he stoutly insisted to them that "I am not less the King's servant for being yours."

Another occasion was in 1640, when King Charles I entered the chamber of the House of Commons with a band of troops in search of five members whom he wished to arrest. The King pressed the Speaker as to whether the five were present, evoking from Speaker William Lenthall the classic reply, "May it please your majesty, I have neither eyes to see nor tongue to speak in this place, but as the House doth direct me, whose servant I am." This is the ideal of the English speakership.

The same idea had been expressed earlier by Queen Elizabeth I, in the 1560s, although she gave it a different twist. A delegation of the House of Commons had approached the Queen concerning the urgency of a marriage, in order to assure a successor to the throne. Some members of the group thought the Speaker should be present. The Queen told them this would not be appropriate, for, she said, he was "not there to speak."

## BILLS

The device of legislative "bills" grew from the much-used practice of submitting petitions to the king for the redress of grievances. Petitions were an old practice, and the right to present them was one of the privileges protected in Magna Carta. The legislators came slowly to realize that they might combine a petition with a royal request for "an aid," and thus be more likely to get a favorable answer to the petition. The Parliament in 1309 seemed to make its consent to a tax bill conditioned upon a favorable reply to a petition. The legislators came into a bargaining procedure, whereby the king had his taxes and they had the redress of a grievance. From here it was only a step from changing the petition to a bill, plus informally insisting upon "grievances before supply."

## Money Bills

The change from petitions to bills, and the doctrine of "grievances before supply," led next into the constitutional principle that the king could not levy a tax without a properly constituted representative assembly. This concession was made by Edward III (1327-1377). He consented that all "aids" should be granted only in the Parliament, while accepting collective petitions from the Commons as preliminary bases for statutes. A later king, Henry IV (1399-1413), refused for a time to accept the Parliamentary doctrine of "grievances before supply," but he was so in need of funds that he did not press the matter of principle.

The next financial development was that the Parliament began to follow the expenditures of the monies it voted, and to require and receive accounts from administrative officials, including the king's household. Thus, the Commons resented the constant demands for funds coming from Henry V (1413-1422), and it accused the King of inefficiency and extravagance. As a condition of further grants, it appointed auditors to study the spending of public funds; in so doing it was concerned with the expenditures of the royal household as well as all other tax monies.

## Procedure and Rules

Other matters of procedure also are known from the early Parliaments. The meeting took place at the convenience of the king, of course. When in London it usually was in the Great Hall of the king's palace. The king would sit on the throne at one end, surrounded by the important officers of state. He would explain why a Parliament had been summoned, and then the Lords and Commons would withdraw to consider the matters of concern. Later, they reassembled to report their decisions.

In the very early days there were no standing orders and few rules of procedure. In the year 1376, the Commons agreed to speak frankly about the matters before the House, to keep its discussions secret, and to take an oath of loyalty to each other. Anyone who wanted to speak went to the reading desk in the center.

Before the time of mechanical printing, a bill was usually read each time it was discussed in the Parliament. Each stage became a "reading", and from about the year 1500 each bill normally was read three times before final passage. Why there were three readings and not two or four (or even one) must be a matter of conjecture. The only certainty was that the state of the art in printing made full reading a practical necessity.[7]

By the sixteenth century, some simple rules of debate were well established, and some of them have persisted into the twentieth century:

1. Members who wished to speak rose in their places, and in case of doubt the speaker would indicate which member had the floor. When the Commons moved to St. Stephen's Hall in 1547, the members began to speak from their places rather than to go to the reading desk in the center.

2. "Every man speaketh as to the Speaker ... It is also taken against the order to name him you do confute but by circumlocution ... No reviling or nipping words must be used."

3. If no bill or formal motion was before the House, it was left to the speaker to formulate a motion to embody "the sense of the House," which could be adopted, perhaps after amendment. By the seventeenth century the practice was for formal, written motions to be filed by members from the floor.

---

7. The American colony of South Carolina is said once to have required six readings in each house for the passage of a bill.

4. There was no method of limiting debate by moving for cloture. Members could speak as frequently and at such length as they liked.

Henry VIII was responsible, in 1532, for the first public division in the House of Commons. Before then the votes had not been public. Henry was trying to steer the Annates Bill (concerning papal finances, a part of the effort against the Roman Catholic Church) through the Commons. He conceived the plan of having the members vote by standing on one side or the other of the House. Some of those called upon to vote publicly were afraid of the King's displeasure if they opposed him. Following the division, the bill passed; and, by the seventeenth century, divisions became a usual way of voting.

## JOURNALS

The early secrecy in voting also resulted in the complete absence of anything like a modern journal of proceedings. Until the sixteenth century, the only accounts of proceedings and debates in the Parliament were in diaries and other private writings.

When the journals were begun in the sixteenth century, they were a personal record of the clerks and not kept by instruction from the two houses. Until the early nineteenth century, however, the debates were not published, and as late as 1809 there were two criminal convictions against private reporters and printers who published accounts of the debates. Even in 1868 there was a suit for libel against the London *Times* for printing a portion of a petition presented in the House of Lords, but the court held for the *Times* and for freedom of the press.

## COMMITTEES

The early beginnings of the committee system are uncertain, but it was given a considerable impetus in the early seventeenth century, as part of the long-running struggle between the Parliament and James I. Members of the House of Commons who opposed the King discovered that friends of the King could exert less influence in committee than in concerted action on the floor of the House. They began to transact much of the important business in committee, and some of the important bills were introduced by a committee. Along with the use of committees, the House of Commons about this time discovered also the effective use of "the committee of the whole house."

Somewhat later, the House of Commons began to appoint five committees at the beginning of each Parliament. They were Privileges and Elections, Religion, Grievances, Courts of Justice, and Trade.

## THE TUDORS

By the fifteenth century, there was a bicameral Parliament, with apparently a solid right to enact legislation. Early in the century, indeed, the House of Commons felt so sure of its place that it was claiming (incorrectly) that no statute had ever been enacted without its consent; and it was demanding (without success) that its bills should not be amended without its assent. The Tudors, and after them the Stuarts, held the Parliament to a more modest role in the legislative scheme of things. During part of the Tudor period, the kings were able to secure revenues from sources other than taxes and thus did not have to call the Parliament into session. In one 12-year period, for example, Henry VII (1485-1509) had to call only one session.

Henry VIII (1509-1547) and Elizabeth I (1559-1603) also called as few sessions as possible, but they were singularly successful in securing the legislation they desired from a cooperative Parliament. Both of them spent more money than they had available and had to ask frequently for "an aid." Henry VIII made much use of the Parliament at the time he was engaged in his contest with the Roman Catholic Church. At several sessions of the Reformation Parliament, from 1529 to 1532, he called upon the legislators to pass a total of 137 statutes. They complied, though the process was made easier by their agreeing with what he sought.

At the beginning of every session of the Parliament during the later years of the Tudor period, it was customary for the House of Commons to ask for assurances of freedom from arrest, freedom of speech, and freedom of access; the latter was the right, through the Speaker, to have an audience with the king or queen. A court case in 1512 had vindicated the idea of freedom of speech for members of the Parliament.

The House of Commons increased considerably in size during the sixteenth century. The basis for representation remained the same (two members for every county and two for each city and borough), but the number of these units grew rapidly. New counties were added, with their towns; and Wales was incorporated into the English representative system. As a consequence, the size of the Commons increased by half.

## THE STUARTS

James I (1603-1625) had been the King of Scotland. He little understood the mood of the House of Commons; but having inherited the debts of Elizabeth I, he had to request "an aid" early in his reign. He was a strong exponent of the divine right of kings, and took little heed of popular opinion or of the wish of the Commons to participate in matters of policy. The very first session of the Parliament under James I drew up a declaration, called an Apology, to remind him

16

that the liberties of the Parliament included free elections, free speech, and freedom from arrest during sessions.

After years of argument between the King and the Parliament on issues of absolute versus limited monarchy, James I dissolved the Parliament in 1611. Another was called in 1614 and shortly dissolved. While in session, however, that Parliament composed a famous document known as the Protestation. It declared that "the liberties, franchises, privileges and jurisdictions of Parliament are the ancient and undoubted birthright and inheritance of the subjects of England." Continuing, "every member of the House of Parliament hath, and of right ought to have, freedom of speech." The Protestation was entered in the *Journal* of the House of Commons. The King immediately sent for the *Journal* and tore out the offending pages. Disputes between the King and the Parliament continued to the time of the death of James I in 1625.

He was succeeded by his son, Charles I (1625-1649). Charles called the Parliament into session in 1625 and asked for tax moneys. He was given a small grant and was asked for his plans in spending the remainder; Charles then dissolved the Parliament. He called another session in 1626, asked for money, and was answered by a petition for redress of grievances. Again the Parliament was dissolved.

When the Parliament was back in session in 1628, it drew up a lengthy Petition of Right, which is second only to Magna Carta in importance in English history. The Petition of Right specified that no tax could be imposed without the consent of the Parliament; and Charles did not receive his tax money until he assented to the Petition. But, during an ensuing debate over the scope of the Parliament's power to tax, Charles prorogued the body.

It was called back in 1629 and soon dissolved. This time Charles went for 11 years without calling it into session; and during this time he imprisoned nine leaders of his

17

Parliamentary opposition. He brought the body back in 1640, but the members wanted to air their grievances before voting taxes. That Parliament was dissolved after three weeks. It has been dubbed the Short Parliament. Another session was called late in 1640, to be styled the Long Parliament. Charles I soon outraged its sensibilities, in June of 1642, by invading the Parliamentary chambers and demanding papers belonging to five members of the House of Commons.[8]

The Long Parliament established procedures for having the body called into session at least once every three years, even without a summons from the king. It also provided that the Parliament could not be dissolved without its own consent. Civil war broke out in 1642, culminating in the execution of the King in 1649. For a time, England was governed by a Parliamentary Council of State and then under the Protectorate of Oliver Cromwell. The monarchy was reestablished in 1660, under Charles II (1660-1685).

The execution of Charles I by Cromwell and his associates was a legislative victory of sorts, but in the end it did not at all advance the hopes for parliamentary government. Parliament had justified its long campaign against the Stuart kings as an effort to achieve a constitutional and limited monarchy, but it came in 1649 only to naked and unbridled power. When firmly established in the Protectorate, Cromwell chose the members of and then convened the Parliament and later disbanded it. He ruled the Parliament as had no king for centuries before; and he narrowly declined to accept the kingship itself.

The restoration in 1660 left the King and Parliament about equal in power. Contention between the two continued for

---

8. The incident is described in MARY PATTERSON CLARKE, PARLIAMENTARY PRIVILEGE IN THE AMERICAN COLONIES 1 (New Haven, 1943).

years, but without the violence of the 1640s.[9] Finally, in 1688, the Parliament deposed James II (who had succeeded to the throne when Charles I died in 1685) and invited William and Mary of Orange to accept the throne. Here the Parliament clearly had made a king; thereafter it held primary power within the framework of English government. Within the Parliament itself, the House of Commons held the balance of power.

## POLITICAL PARTIES

The political party in the modern sense was one element of legislative life missing during the formative centuries in England. Its full development came later, and partly from America. Even so, the traditional English names for the two major parties there date from the 1680s. As part of the waning religious disputes, there were two groups in the Parliament known for a time as the Petitioners and the Abhorrers. These two clumsy names had to give way; and the groups styled each other (both being terms of opprobrium) as "Whigs" and "Tories." The names are no longer used formally, but for two centuries they were the political parties in England.

A typically English development of parties is seen in calling the minority party "Her Majesty's Opposition," or sometimes "Her Majesty's Loyal Opposition." It has the idea that opposition will never be carried to the extreme of

---

**9.** "In part because Parliament itself had been so obviously guilty of abusive use of governmental power during the Civil War and Interregnum and in part because Parliament's existence no longer appeared to be in jeopardy, the conditions under which Charles II returned to the throne created strong pressures toward cooperation between King and Parliament." Jack P. Greene, *Political Mimesis: A Consideration of the Historical Roots of Legislative Behavior in the British Colonies in the Eighteenth Century,* 75 AMERICAN HISTORICAL REVIEW 342 (1969).

changing the basic form of government. With the same idea, since 1937, the leader of the opposition has been paid a special salary from public funds.

## AMERICAN DEVELOPMENTS

The main lines of parliamentary and legislative government were charted in England by 1688. This extensive background was transferred to the American colonies and subsequently to the national and state governments formed in America. They have made some significant changes in the English model.

One was that of the formal and written constitution. America and its colonies were the product of revolution. They could ill afford the long process needed to develop constitutional procedures in the informal and unwritten English style.

Another area of change was in the doctrine of separation of powers. Much of the credit for this came from the familiarity of the constitutional draftsmen in America with the writings of Locke and Montesquieu. John Locke has been called the philosopher of the Revolution of 1688. Montesquieu was the French political philosopher of the mid-eighteenth century. The latter wrote extensively of English government and of the three separate functions of government. The format of having three separate and distinct branches became the prevailing one in all the new American constitutions.

A corollary to the separation of powers into separate legislative, executive, and judicial branches in the American constitutions has been the doctrine of checks and balances. It was to give each branch of government some restraint over one or both of the others. Thus, while the legislative body would be given a power to pass laws, that power (in the national government and in most of the state governments) was balanced by a right of executive veto; and that right, in turn, was balanced by a legislative right of overriding the veto with an extraordinary majority.

Another of the checks and balances was in the power of the executive and of the Senate to appoint judges to the courts comprising the judicial system. Also, the right of the legislative branch to impeach members of the other two branches was a check against them. Another, and in some respects perhaps the most important of the checks and balances, was devised in America by the judiciary itself, in the ruling that the judiciary as part of its judicial function could declare an act of the legislature to be unconstitutional and therefore invalid.

A final modification of the English system was in the change of political parties to the modern American style, giving them a much more important and vital part in the administration of government than had been true earlier in England. As one example, the American development completely changed the non-partisan and selective intent of the Electoral College for the choice of a President of the United States. Another application of political parties in America has been the "team" concept. By combining a chief executive and a legislative majority, all from the same party, the doctrine of separation of powers has been blurred.

## "MOTHER OF PARLIAMENTS"

It yet remains that the national government and all the state governments in the United States, as well as such members and former members of the English commonwealth as Canada, Australia, New Zealand, and South Africa, today have governmental systems strongly reminiscent of, and in their origins closely dependent upon, the developing political and parliamentary institutions of England. The origins trace backward for a thousand years or more. England was truly "the mother of parliaments," and legislative development in the Province and State of Maryland stems directly from the mother country.

## Chapter 2

# THE ESTABLISHMENT OF LEGISLATIVE POWER
# IN MARYLAND

## 1634-1638

The legislative heritage in England brought full parliamentary government to that country in the late seventeenth century. In contrast, when Maryland was settled earlier in the century, in 1634, there were many uncertainties about prospects for the new Province in America.

The English Civil War and the Parliamentary victories of 1649 and 1688 still were in the future. John Locke's *Two Treatises of Government,* which was to give an excellent philosophical basis for modern democracy, still was a half-century ahead.

It was only a few years past, in 1603, that King James I of England had declared that "As it is atheism and blasphemy to dispute what God can do; so it is presumption and high contempt in a subject to dispute what a king can do, or say that a king cannot do this or that." At the middle of the seventeenth century, the monarchy was glorified in *The Leviathan* of Thomas Hobbes, in the doctrine that "where the public and the private interest are most closely united, there is the public most advanced."

In the 1630s both the confused situation in England and the insecurity of prospects in America cast doubt upon the success of the venture in Maryland.

The new colony was distinctly the creation of George Calvert, who for long had had an interest in the colonization of America. After receiving both Bachelor's and Master's degrees from Oxford, Calvert served in a variety of public posts, including Clerk of the Privy Council, emissary on a number of diplomatic missions, twice a member of the Parliament, and Secretary of State.

23

He was closely familiar with the settlements of the Virginia Company at Jamestown, the New England Company in Massachusetts, and the ill-fated colony on Roanoke Island. He tried at one time to acquire the latter site for the Province of Maryland. In 1621, Calvert sent colonists to settle upon a tract in Newfoundland. Twice he visited "Avalon," as the settlement there was named. Ultimately, by the late 1620s, the severe winters caused Avalon to be abandoned.[1] As Lord Baltimore (Calvert had been elevated to the peerage in 1625), he visited Jamestown and, for a time, sought another grant of land south of the James River.[2]

Finally, with the approval of Charles I, Lord Baltimore received a grant north of the Potomac River. Tradition has it that the King himself took part in naming the new colony, and that he proposed naming it for Queen Henrietta Marie. "Mariana" was discussed as a name, with the King finally proposing "Terra Mariae." In English that became Mary Land.[3]

George Calvert, Lord Baltimore, died on April 15, 1632. He left three sons who were to have close connections with the colony, Cecil, Leonard, and George.

Maryland was established as a proprietary government, as distinguished from the other two forms of colonial

---

1. See Thomas M. Coakley, *George Calvert and Newfoundland: "The Sad Face of Winter,"* 71 MARYLAND HISTORICAL MAGAZINE 1-18 (1976).

2. For details of the life and ancestry of the Calvert family, *see* Mrs. Arthur Barneveld Bobbins, *The English Beginnings in Maryland,* 28 MARYLAND HISTORICAL MAGAZINE 283-308 (1931). *See also* James W. Foster, *George Calvert and His Yorkshire Boyhood,* 55 MARYLAND HISTORICAL MAGAZINE 261-74 (1960).

3. For a biographical sketch of the Queen, *see* Milton Rubincam, *Queen Henrietta Marie: Maryland's Royal Namesake,* 54 MARYLAND HISTORICAL MAGAZINE 131-48 (1959).

government, charter and royal. Charter governments had powers of self-government granted by charter. Royal governments, on the other hand, were directly under the king, subject to whatever power and authority were vested in the monarch. In the proprietary form, the sovereign power of the king was given to either one or a number of proprietaries.[4] Some of the colonies which started off under this arrangement ran into trouble and later became royal governments. Of the several proprietary governments, only Maryland and Pennsylvania remained such at the time of the American Revolution. During the interim in Maryland, the proprietary status was interrupted for a temporary period as a royal government, from 1688 to 1715; and the rule of the Lord Proprietary was suspended during the time of Cromwell and the Commonwealth, in the late 1640s and 1650s.

## THE CHARTER

The Charter of Maryland was confirmed on June 20, 1632. It was granted to Cecil Calvert (1606-1675), eldest son of the late George Calvert. Cecil Calvert inherited his father's title also, as the second Lord Baltimore. The Charter constituted "the now Baron of Baltimore, and his heirs, the true and absolute lords and proprietaries" of the new colony,

> to have, hold, possess and enjoy the aforesaid region, islands, islets, and other the premises, unto the aforesaid now Baron of Baltimore, and to his heirs and assigns, to the sole and proper behoof and use of him, the now Baron of Baltimore, his heirs and assigns, for ever. To hold of us, our heirs and successors, kings of England, as of our castle of Windsor, in our county of Berks, in free and common socage, by fealty only for all services,

---

4. *See* JOHN V. L. MCMAHON, AN HISTORICAL VIEW OF THE GOVERNMENT OF MARYLAND 139-41 (Baltimore, 1831).

and not *in capite,* nor by knight's service, yielding therefore unto us, our heirs and successors, two Indian arrows of those parts, to be delivered at the said castle of Windsor, every year, on Tuesday in Easterweek; and also the fifth part of all gold and silver ore, which shall happen from time to time, to be found within the aforesaid limits.

The grant was made in feudal terms, with the land to be held "in free and common socage." This type of feudal obligation was based upon a fixed and determinate service, it being here two Indian arrows annually and one-fifth of all gold and silver found in the colony.[5] The obligation for Maryland was distinguished from military tenure or villenage, requiring respectively indefinite amounts of military service or work and labor. Elsewhere in the Charter the proprietary was given the powers of a palatinate which, in the usage of the time, carried with it virtually all powers which the king himself might have exercised within the Province.

In spelling out the practically unlimited and strongly monarchical authority given to the Proprietary, the Charter gave him power to establish courts and appoint judges and magistrates, enforce all laws, confer titles, erect towns, pardon all offenses, found churches, call out the fighting population and wage war, impose martial law, convey or lease the land, and levy duties and tolls.

The legislative powers of the colony were a possible exception to the almost unlimited powers conferred upon the Proprietary; they were specified with two main provisions. First, the Proprietary was given the right to make all laws,

---

5. For a synoptical analysis of tenancies and estates in early English law, *see* EDWARD COKE, THE FIRST PART OF THE INSTITUTES (London, 1789). Socage is particularly discussed on pp. vii and 85-93. *See also* Lawrence C. Wroth, *Two Indian Arrows of These Parts,* 12 MARYLAND HISTORICAL MAGAZINE 253-61 (1917).

with the assent of the freemen of the Province. Secondly, he was given the right to promulgate ordinances (not impairing life, limb, or property) without their consent. The exact division of the legislative power was set out in some detail, in sections 7 and 8 of the Charter:

VII. And forasmuch as we have above made and ordained the aforesaid now Baron of Baltimore, the true Lord and Proprietary of the whole province aforesaid, know ye therefore further, that we, for us, our heirs and successors, do grant unto the said now Baron, (in whose fidelity, prudence, justice, and provident circumspection of mind, we repose the greatest confidence) and to his heirs, for the good and happy government of the said province, free, full, and absolute power, by the tenor of these presents, to ordain, make and enact laws, of what kind soever, according to their sound discretions, whether relating to the public state of the said province, or the private utility of individuals, of and with the advice, assent, and approbation of the free men of the same province, or of the greater part of them, or of their delegates or deputies, whom we will shall be called together for the framing of laws, when, and as often as need shall require, by the aforesaid now Baron of Baltimore, and his heirs, and in the form that shall seem best to him or them, and the same to publish under the seal of the aforesaid now Baron of Baltimore and his heirs .... Which said laws, so to be published as abovesaid, we will, enjoin, charge, and command, to be most absolute and firm in law, and to be kept in those parts by all the subjects and liege-men of us, our heirs and successors, so far as they concern them, and to be inviolably observed under the penalties therein expressed, or to be expressed. So nevertheless, that the laws aforesaid be consonant to reason, and be not repugnant or contrary, but (so far as conveniently may be) agreeable to the laws, statutes, customs and rights of this our kingdom of England.

VIII. And forasmuch as, in the government of so great a province, sudden accidents may frequently happen, to which it will be necessary to apply a remedy,

27

before the freeholders of the said province, their delegates, or deputies, can be called together for the framing of laws; neither will it be fit that so great a number of people should immediately on such emergent occasion, be called together. We, therefore, for the better government of so great a province, do will and ordain, and by these presents, for us, our heirs and successors, do grant unto the said now Baron of Baltimore; and his heirs, by themselves, or by their magistrates and officers, thereunto duly to be constituted as aforesaid, may, and can make and constitute fit and wholesome ordinances from time to time, to be kept and observed within the province aforesaid, as well for the conservation of the peace, as for the better government of the people inhabiting therein, and publicly to notify the same to all persons whom the same in any wise do or may affect. Which ordinances, we will to be inviolably observed within the said province, under the pains to be expressed in the same. So that the said ordinances be consonant to reason, and be not repugnant nor contrary, but (so far as conveniently may be done) agreeably to the laws, statutes, or rights of our kingdom of England; and so that the same ordinances do not, in any sort, extend to oblige, bind, charge, or take away the right or interest of any person or persons, of, or in member, life, freehold, goods or chattels.

These sections of the Charter, thus, established two forms of legislative power. The first was the law-making power, which was vested in the Proprietary, subject to the "advice, assent, and approbation" of the freemen of the Province. The second was an ordinance-making power, to supplement the laws and to meet emergencies; it was vested in the Proprietary alone, but was limited in that it could not affect adversely the life, limb, or property of any person. Both the laws and the ordinances were to be "consonant to reason" and agreeable to the laws, statutes, and rights of England.

The Charter also had a grant of supportive background privileges, in that the English subjects in Maryland and their

28

descendants were to have the "Privileges Franchises and Liberties" of native-born Englishmen. The colonists were frequently to use this assurance as a grant of substantive and interpretive powers to them and their legislature. This grant was esteemed so highly as to be argued with vehemence during all the years of Provincial government and to be stated in explicit detail in the Constitution of 1776, at the end of the Provincial period and the beginnings of the State of Maryland.

It is evident that strong powers were given to the Lords Baltimore, conferred by a monarch believing in the divine right of kings and lesser only in degree from the powers of the king. It could be argued with some force that Lord Baltimore was empowered by the Charter to control legislative activity along with his other authority.

With all its trappings of royalty, however, the Charter *did* require that laws be made with the assent of the freemen of the Province; that the freemen be called together when necessary for the framing of laws; that the laws and ordinances be reasonable and not repugnant to those of England; and that the Proprietary's ordinance-making powers could not affect life, limb, or property. Building from this base, much of the history of the Province for many years touched two main aspects of the legislative process, that of broadening the jurisdiction of the General Assembly as the exclusive legislative body and that of increasing the relative powers of the Lower House in contrast to those of the Upper House. These strivings and the consequent changes over the years helped to maintain public support for Maryland's government all through the colonial period.

All this was for the future. In late March, 1634, with the Charter provisions as a sort of basic constitution, the little colony settled at St. Mary's.[6]

6. For an account of the development of the town during the early decades, including maps, *see* REGINA COMBS HAMMETT, HISTORY OF ST.

## St. Mary's

The voyage to America began at Cowes, on the Isle of Wight, on November 22, 1633. An earlier part of the trip had begun at Gravesend, on the Thames below London. Direction of the voyage was entrusted to Leonard Calvert, a brother of the Proprietary. A younger brother, George, also was aboard. About 20 "gentlemen of very good fashion" and some two or three hundred laboring men were on the two ships, named the Ark and the Dove.[7] Some of the "laboring men" are thought to have been persons of rank or position, perhaps including adventurous younger sons with no prospects of succeeding to family estates.

The ships put in at the Canary Islands about Christmastime. From early January until early February they made a number of stops at islands in the West Indies, and they finally arrived off Old Point Comfort, Virginia, on February 27, 1633/4.[8] Passing up Chesapeake Bay and into the

---

MARY'S COUNTY, MARYLAND 12-27 (Ridge, Maryland, 1977). *See also* JAMES WALTER THOMAS, CHRONICLES OF COLONIAL MARYLAND 19-68 (Cumberland, 1913).

There is an excellent account of the origin and development of St. Mary's, and of its virtual demise, in Lois Green Carr, *"The Metropolis of Maryland: A Comment on Town Development Along the Tobacco Coast"* 69 MARYLAND HISTORICAL MAGAZINE 124-45 (1974).

7. On August 23, 1633, three months before the voyage began, a delivery to the Ark included "12 pipes of Canary wine at 14.10 the pipe," for a total cost of 174 pounds; and there was a delivery to the Ark and the Dove of "one hundred five tonne of Beare," at a cost of 6 pounds, 19 shillings. *See* J. Moss Ives, *The Ark and Dove,* 1 MARYLAND HISTORICAL MAGAZINE 352-54 (1906).

✳ 8. Care must be used in citing and understanding dates in English and American history, up to the year 1752. It was not until that year that Great Britain changed from the Old Style to the New Style calendar. The New Style or Gregorian calendar was promulgated in 1582 by Pope Gregory

Potomac River, they landed at St. Clement's Island on March 25, the first day of the year under the Old Style calendar. Later, after having concluded an agreement with the native Indians, and in order to provide themselves more space, the settlers sailed downstream to the St. Mary's River [9] and established their permanent settlement on that site. They were fortunate in the treatment they received from the Indians,[10] with the colonists being given land, growing crops, and crude huts.

About 11 months later, on February 26, 1634/5, the colonists first assembled for legislative action. If any records

XIII, but for many years in the early life of the colony in Maryland the Old Style calendar was followed in England and its possessions. Under the Old Style, the first day of the new year was on March 25, rather than January 1. Also, from 1582 to 1700 there was a difference of ten days between the Old Style and the New Style, so that the fifth day of a month Old Style was the 15th day New Style. From 1700 to 1752 this difference was 11 days. The English Calendar (New Style) Act of 1750 took effect in 1752, with the day following September 2 becoming September 14; and the year 1753 began on the following January 1. The dates used for references to the General Assembly of Maryland are taken from the *Journals* and other primary and original sources which, until 1752, followed the Old Style calendar. For clarity of citation, both the Old Style and New Style years are included. Thus, "March 1, 1648/9" means 1648 Old Style and 1649 New Style. References to the days of the month are taken from the original sources without change and with no attempt to adjust them to the New Style calendar. For the text of the English Calendar Act of 1750, *see The Maryland Gazette* (Annapolis), January 2, 1752.

9. The present St. Mary's River was first known as the St. George's River. *See* J. Louis Kuethe, *A Gazetteer of Maryland, A.D. 1673*, 30 MARYLAND HISTORICAL MAGAZINE 322 (1935).

10. For a general account of the Indians in this area, *see* James E. Hancock, *The Indians of the Chesapeake Bay Section*, 22 MARYLAND HISTORICAL MAGAZINE 23-40 (1927). For Indian life and customs in the St. Mary's area, *see* REGINA COMBS HAMMETT, HISTORY OF ST. MARY'S COUNTY, MARYLAND 8-12 (Ridge, Maryland 1977).

were made and preserved they have never been recovered, so very little is known about this first session of the General Assembly of Maryland. It is supposed that all the freemen of the colony attended, giving a town-meeting atmosphere to the proceedings. A later Maryland act provides the information that "among other wholesome laws" they enacted that "the offenders in all murders and felonies should suffer such pains, losses, and forfeitures as they should or ought to have suffered in the like crimes in England."

The fragments of information concerning the meeting of the General Assembly in 1635 do furnish a clue to what must have been its most significant feature: It was the Legislature which proposed the laws, and not the Proprietary. The Charter clearly vested in the executive the initiative in proposing and propounding legislation, yet 11 months after landing in Maryland the freemen sought this as a legislative function. Lord Baltimore accordingly vetoed the entire set of laws when they were presented for his sanction.

Legislatively, then, the colony after the 1634/5 session was in the same posture as before, with no specific Maryland laws for its governance and control. Presumably it reacted as in a similar situation two years later, when the Assembly decided that in the absence of other laws the colony should be governed by "the lawes of England." The "lawes of England" included the English common law; and that great body of case law would have provided a ready control of the day-to-day relationships among the settlers. A frame of mind, as well as a body of law, the common law had the stabilizing influence necessary to keep the colony on an even keel while its Charter and statutory powers were being determined.

Cecil Calvert, second Lord Baltimore and Proprietary, had not accompanied the colonists on the voyage to Maryland in 1633 and 1634. He sent his brother Leonard to be in active charge of the expedition, as the Lieutenant General or Governor of the Province.[11]

## A PLAN OF GOVERNMENT

The first organized and detailed plan of government for the new colony dates from April 15, 1637. On that day, Lord Baltimore executed a commission to his brother Leonard, defining his powers, stating his functions, and specifying the offices he was to fill.[12] Lord Baltimore also announced officially his dissent from the laws proposed by the Assembly of the freemen in 1634/5, and added that he intended to submit a further set of laws and ordinances to the next meeting of the General Assembly.

The commission executed by Lord Baltimore in 1637 enjoined all the inhabitants of the colony to acknowledge Leonard Calvert as "our lieutenant general, admiral, chief captain and commander of all our said province." He was further constituted as "our chancellor, chief justice, and chief magistrate within our said province." With all these titles, Leonard Calvert obviously had all executive and judicial power vested within his office.

---

11. The terms may be used interchangeably during the early years in Maryland, although "Lieutenant General" perhaps had primary reference to the military establishment of the Province. He sometimes also was referred to as "President of the Assembly," this term having an obvious meaning.

12. "The proprietary governor of Maryland had a dual position: he was the centre of all local administration, the chief executive of the province; and he was the agent of a higher authority, the guardian of the interests of the proprietor. In addition to his political functions, he was the manager of an essentially commercial enterprise." CHARLES JAMES ROHR, THE GOVERNOR OF MARYLAND — A CONSTITUTIONAL STUDY 37 (Baltimore, 1932).

The commission went on to name "our well beloved Jerome Hawley, esqr., Thomas Cornwaleys, esqr., and John Lewger, gent." to be a Council to advise Leonard Calvert. Finally, it gave the Lieutenant General authority to appoint a deputy in case of his own absence from the colony; and it gave the Council power to appoint a successor to the Lieutenant General, if that should be necessary.

Lord Baltimore referred to this commission issued in 1637 as an "ordinance," and presumably he considered he was promulgating it under the ordinance-making power given to him in the Charter. So far as it concerned the legislative lines of power, it contained several main provisions: First, the Proprietary summoned a meeting of the Assembly, to be composed of all the freemen or their deputies. Secondly, Lord Baltimore formally announced his dissent from the laws propounded by the Assembly of 1634/5; and he declared his intention of submitting another set of proposals to the forthcoming second meeting of the Assembly. Thirdly, he gave to the Lieutenant General a blanket authority to convene other meetings of the Assembly at his discretion, and to dissolve and adjourn any meeting. Finally, the Proprietary delegated to the Lieutenant General the authority to promulgate ordinances, so long as they conformed to the Charter's injunction not to carry penalties affecting life, limb, or property.

In sum, then, the commission submitted by Lord Baltimore vested executive and judicial power in the Lieutenant General, who was appointed by the Proprietary and held office at his pleasure. He was to be assisted in both functions by the Council, sometimes known as the Council of State and appointed in the same manner. Members of the Council occasionally in the future would be sent out from England, but more frequently they were influential colonists. Together with the Lieutenant General or Governor, the Council cared for the Proprietary's interests; and it acted as an advisory group to assist the Governor. At the same time, the members of the Council sat in the Assembly. Ultimately, they were the nucleus of a separate Upper House; but even from the first their position, education, and conservatism gave them an influence beyond their comparative numbers.

The Council also constituted the Provincial Court, which during the early years was the chief judicial body of the Province; the Governor during these early years served as presiding judge and chancellor in the Provincial Court. Finally, members of the Council usually held other positions in the administrative hierarchy, leading to protracted and sometimes acrimonious arguments about whether they were to be compensated for these other duties from the revenues of Lord Baltimore or from "public" funds.[13]

Other officers in the executive branch included the Secretary of the Province, the Attorney General, and the Surveyor General.

## THE GENERAL ASSEMBLY

Pursuant to the commission issued by Lord Baltimore to Leonard Calvert as Governor of the Province, the latter issued warrants directing the attendance of the freemen of the Province at the second meeting of the Assembly. The warrant sent to Captain George Evelyn, Commander of the Isle of Kent, was "to will and require you (all excuses sett apart) to make your personal repaire to the ffort of St maries on the said five and twentieth day of January, then and there

---

13. Members of the Council "received the most lucrative public offices to insure their loyalty to the Proprietor." DAVIS CURTIS SKAGGS, ROOTS OF MARYLAND DEMOCRACY, 1753-1776, at 15 (Westport, Conn., 1973).

Also, the plan of government made no provisions for any elected officials in the counties that would be formed in the future. "The whole structure of Maryland government . . . was calculated to cultivate loyalty to the Proprietor." Id.

to consult and advise of the affaires of this Province." He was further instructed to "assemble" all the freemen of Kent and to "proclaime the said generall Assembly." A final instruction was to "perswade such and so many of the said freemen as you shall thinke fitt to repair personally to the said assembly . . . and to give free power & liberty to all the rest of the said freemen" either to be present or to elect persons to be "the deputies or burgesses for the said freemen, in their name and steed to advise and consult of such things as shalbe brought into deliberation in the said assembly."

The warrant made it optional whether individual freemen attended in person or by deputy; to the extent that proxies were used, this Assembly was beginning its role as an institution of representative government.[14]

The word "freeman" subsequently was defined, during discussions in the Assembly about the membership of that body. This occurred in 1642, when a freeman was determined to be a citizen of the Province above the age of 21 years, if not held to personal service. One of the settlers at that time, evidently anxious to avoid participation in the Legislature, argued that as he held no land and had no "certain dwelling-house", he was not a freeman. The Assembly decided, however, that even without holding real property he was included as a freeman and had to appear, either in person or by proxy.

One item in the warrant for the session of 1637/8 was a forerunner of what was to become an established piece of constitutional practice in Maryland. It specified that the Assembly was "to enter all the severall votes and suffrages vpon record," beginning the custom and later requirement of roll call votes for the passage of laws.

14. For a discussion and explanation of the proxy system in the early years of the Assembly, *see* Susan Rosenfeld Falb, *Proxy Voting in Early Maryland Assemblies,* 73 MARYLAND HISTORICAL MAGAZINE 217-23 (1978).

This second meeting of the General Assembly of Maryland convened on January 25, 1637/8. Leonard Calvert, the Lieutenant General, "taking his place, came and appeared personally." His "place," of course, was as presiding officer. The three members of the Council appeared and took seats as ordinary members, despite the fact that they were also to act as an advisory group for the Lieutenant General. One of the members of the Council, John Lewger, acted as Secretary for the session.

The *Journal* of the Assembly proceedings lists all the men who appeared either in person or by proxy at the first day's session. In addition to the Lieutenant General and the three members of the Council, there were listed as present eight gentlemen ("gent"), 13 planters, a constable, a sheriff, a carpenter, and a marshal, for a total of 29 present. Three gentlemen were summoned to appear "by vertue of writts to them directed," but their absence was excused by reason of sickness.

Somewhat more than the number of those present were represented by proxies. Twenty-five planters, a cooper, a brickmason, and a carpenter sent proxies, which were exhibited by the holders. "The freemen of the Ile of Kent" also were represented by proxy.[15] Seven planters were listed by name as not having appeared, either in person or by proxy. "Then was proclaymed," the *Journal* continues, "that all freemen omitted in the writts of summons, that would clayme a voice in this general assembly, should come & make their clayme. Whereupon clayme was made by John Robinson, carpenter & was admitted."

---

15. Mereness lists the combination of delegates and proxies at this session as comprising 19 persons and 69 votes. *See* NEWTON D. MERENESS, MARYLAND AS A PROPRIETARY PROVINCE 195 (1901, reprinted in 1968).

Two of the "gentlemen" were listed as from the Isle of Kent. Among the addresses of the others, it is evident that the Province already had been formed into the old English divisions called "hundreds." Of those who appeared either in person or by proxy, 24 were listed as from St. Mary's Hundred, 12 were from St. George's Hundred, and eight were from Mattapanient. St. Mary's Hundred was at the site of the original settlement, on the easterly bank of the St. Mary's River; St. George's Hundred was on the westerly bank of the St. Mary's River (then known as the St. George's River); Mattapanient, created as a hundred in 1638, was on the southerly shore of the Patuxent River, about six miles upstream from the mouth of the river.[16] The Isle of Kent (Kent Island) was considered as a hundred within St. Mary's County. St. Mary's was established as a county in 1637; and Kent, in 1640.

## Rules and Procedures in 1637/8

"Then were certaine orders established by generall consent, to be observed during the Assembly. *viz*

Orders. Imprimis, the Lieutenant General, as President of the Assembly, shall appoint and direct all

---

16. *See* J. Louis Kuethe, A Gazetteer of Maryland, A.D. 1673 (Baltimore, 1935). This is a reprint from 30 Maryland Historical Magazine 310-13. This gazetteer was compiled from Augustine Herrmann's map of Virginia and Maryland, published in London in 1673. See also The Maryland Directory and State Gazetteer, 1887 at 490 (Baltimore, 1887). The latter source describes Mattapany as having a population of 25 persons and being located 15 miles from Leonardtown and near Millstone.

*See also* Henry J. Berkley, *The Proprietary Manors and Hundreds of St. Mary's, Old Charles, Calvert, New Charles, and Prince George's Counties,* 29 Maryland Historical Magazine 237-45 (1934); Frederic Arnold Kummer, 1 The Free State of Maryland — A History of the State and its People, 1634-1941, at 39 (Baltimore, 1941).

things that concerne forme and decency to be observed in the same; and shall command the observance thereof as he shall see cause vpon paine of imprisonment or fine as the house shall adiudge.

Item every one that is to speake to every matter, shall stand vp, and be vncovered and direct his speech to the Lieutenant General as President of the Assembly. And if two or more stand vp to speake together, the Lieutenant General shall appoint which shall speake.

Item no man shall stand vp to speake to any matter vntill the partie that spake last before, have sate downe, nor shall any one speake above once to any bill or matter at one reading nor shall refute the speech of any other with any vncivil or contentious termes, nor shall name him but by some circumloquution. And if any one offend to the contrary, the Lieutenant General shall command him to silence.

Item the house shall sitt every day at eight of the clock in the morning, and at two of the clock in the afternoone.

Item the freemen assembled at any time to any number above ten persons, at the houres aforesaid, or within one houre after, shalbe a house to all purposes.

Item every one propounding any matter to the house shall digest it first into writing and deliver it to the Secretary to be read vnto the house.

And it was ordered by the house that these Orders shall be sett vp in some publique place of the house, to the end all men might take notice of them.

Here, in 1637/8, was the first recorded set of rules adopted by the General Assembly of Maryland. It makes convincing evidence of the continuity of the legislative process in Maryland, for a number of its provisions remained in the twentieth century as familiar requirements of legislative decorum. The presiding officer was given charge of the House chamber; the House was given a power to punish its offending members; members desiring to speak were to rise and be "uncovered," and were to direct their remarks through the presiding officer; personal or derogatory references to other members were prohibited;

the member having the floor was not to be interrupted, but he could not obtain the floor a second time on the same reading of a bill; a quorum of the House was established. The one provision in these rules of 1637/8, which was to sound distant and outmoded three centuries later, was that "the House shall sitt every day at eight of the clock in the morning."

With the adoption of the rules, the House ended its first day's session in January, 1637/8. It met the following day, "betweene the houres of eight and nine in the morning." Twenty-one persons assembled, including the Lieutenant General and the three members of the Council. A number of absentees were "summoned." Some sent proxies, which were exhibited. In the case of three of those summoned, "Robt Clerke made answere for them that they desired to be excused from giving voices in this Assembly, and was admitted." Then the *Journal* listed ten names, with the notation that they were "amerced for not appearance." Just a few lines below, however, there was this further record:

> Then it was ordered that any member of the house not appearing at the houres appointed, should be amerced 20 lbs. of tobacco for every default. But for this present meeting, such as did appear though tardie should be pardoned the amercement, but for the rest which appeared not it should stand.

At the afternoon session on January 26, 1637/8, some of the absences of the morning were explained. For three of those missing earlier, "it was answered for them, that they could not come, for want of passage over St. George's river. & was admitted." For a fourth, "it was answered for him that he was absent out of the Province in Virginia." His amercement was remitted.

"Likewise the amercement was remitted to William Bretton, Thomas Nabbs, John Davis; for the same reason; as the first.

"Likewise vpon petition made by Thomas Stente, and Thomas Baldridge, alledging the necessity of important businesse, the amercement was remitted for non appearance in the morning." Only one person was fined for not appearing at this afternoon session.

The important work of this meeting of the General Assembly was begun at the morning session on this second day, with the set of bills proposed by Lord Baltimore being submitted to the House. In the words of the *Journal,* "then was read out the draught of Lawes transmitted by the Lord Proprietor, the first twelve Acts of the said draught: and were severally debated by the House." This discussion continued in the afternoon; "then were the Acts read throughe, & severally debated in the reading. And the Lieutenant General adiorned the house vntil Monday morning at 8 of the clock."

When the House met on the third day of the session, it being January 29, 1637/8, the proceedings were between one and two hours late in commencing. "Then was proposed," it is recorded in the *Journal,* "whether the Lawes formerly read should be read again in the house; or putt to the vote without further reading."[17] Here there was a sharp split of opinion. Captain Cornwaleys, a member of the Council, and five others, representing with their proxies a total of 18 voices, voted to have them read again. There were 33 votes, including proxies, for voting immediately on the bills without a further reading of them. Included in this latter group were Leonard Calvert, the presiding officer; Captain Evelyn, commander of the Isle of Kent; and John Lewger, Secretary of the Assembly and a member of the Council. It having been determined not to read the bills again, the House could proceed to a vote on the bills themselves.

---

17. The word "reading" here obviously applies to the physical act of reading the text of the proposed laws, and not to the later use of the word as a legislative colloquialism to apply to the actual vote.

41

"Then were the Lawes putt to the question, whether they should be received as Lawes or no." On this vote, only the President and Mr. Lewger were recorded in the affirmative, although with their proxies they represented 14 votes. The question was "denied" by all the rest of the Assembly, with a total of 37 votes.

Thus, on the third day of the session of 1637/8, the Assembly rejected the entire program of bills submitted by the Proprietary. Here again was an unexpected twist to the exercise of legislative power. The Charter gave to the Proprietary "free, full and absolute power ... to ordain, make and enact laws ... of and with the advice, assent, and approbation of the free men" of the Province. The Charter was silent as to what would happen if the Assembly refused to grant its consent to the bills proposed.

## GOVERNING THE PROVINCE

Once the Assembly had rejected the bills proposed by Lord Baltimore, the first thought was to consider by what system of laws they could be governed. As the discussion was described in the *Journal:*

> Then question being moved what Lawes the Province should be governed by it was said by some that they might doe well to agree vpon some lawes till we could heare from England againe. The President denying any such power to be in the house, Capt: Cornwalers propounded the lawes of England. The President acknowledged that the Commission gave him power in civill causes to proceed by the lawes of England; and in criminal causes likewise not extending to life or member. but in those he was limited to the lawes of the Province, there could be no punishment inflicted on any enormous offendors, by the refusall of these lawes.
>
> wherevpon the Commission was produced and examined, & vpon the reading of it it appeared that there

was no power in the province to punish any offence deserving losse of life or member, for want of lawes. To this they answered, that such enormous offences could hardly be committed without mutinie & then it might be punished by martiall law.

By this ingenious application of the provisions of the Charter, they were able to contrive a set of laws to cover their elementary needs. The Charter gave to the Lieutenant General a power to proceed by the laws of England in ordinary civil affairs; it also gave him power to mete out criminal punishments, so long as they did not affect life, limb, or property. To fill the apparent gap in the power of the Province to govern itself, it was agreed that any offense deserving such a drastic penalty would amount to mutiny, with which the Lieutenant General also was empowered by the Charter to deal. If the reasoning was a little strained, there was a will for orderly government.

Although Leonard Calvert had denied there was any power in the General Assembly to propose laws for the approval of the Lord Proprietor (the Charter clearly gave to Lord Baltimore the right to initiate the passage of laws), the House went ahead to formulate a program of legislation. "Then was propounded that the house would consider of some lawes to be sent vp to the Lord Proprietor," it was reported in the *Journal*. "And the President advised that they would chuse some Committees to prepare the draft of them, and then the house might meete for confirming of them; & in the mean time every one might follow their other occasions." It was agreed that they should elect five persons to comprise the legislative drafting committee. Every person present then voted for five members of the committee. Ten persons in all received votes, but those who were elected on the committee were Leonard Calvert, the President of the Assembly, Captain Cornwaleys and Captain Wintour, both members of the Council, Captain Evelyn, commander of the

Isle of Kent, and Mr. Snow.[18] The House then adjourned until the tenth day following, on February 8, 1637/8.

A fundamental question of legislative immunity arose during these first three days of the session of 1637/8. The question was whether freemen who either were or had a right to be in the Assembly should have immunity from arrest during the time the Assembly was in session. It was decided that they should have such immunity, until enough time had elapsed after the meeting for them to return home. As described in the *Journal:*

> Vpon occasion of some warrants granted out against some freemen that had made proxies; a question was moved in the house whether freemen having made proxies during the assembly might be arrested before the Assembly were dissolved. And Captain Cornwaleys and James Baldridgẽ were of opinion that they might: but the rest of the house generally concurred that after the writts issued for summoning the Assembly, no man having right to repaire vnto the Assembly, might be arrested, until a convenient space of time after the dissolution of the said Assembly, for his repaire home.

The question came up again on January 29, just before the House adjourned to February 8, in order to give its committee time to draft a series of bills. The Assembly then decided that "because the Court was to be held in the meane time that is to say, on the 3d of ffebruary; that therefore the privilege of parliament should be void vntil the Court were past; & all freemen might be arrested as if no assembly were." Here the privilege of legislative immunity was construed strictly, so as not to interfere with the administration of justice.

---

18. This was probably Justinian Snow, a planter of St. Mary's Hundred. A Marmaduke Snow, likewise a planter of St. Mary's Hundred, also was a member of the Assembly. On this particular day the *Journal* records that Marmaduke was absent and among those summoned to appear, with the note "essoined by his brother, & admitted."

When the House met again on February 8, 1637/8, the committee appointed to submit a draft of laws to the General Assembly reported that "they thought fitt to read the former draught of lawes again, and to putt them to the vote the second time, in regard there was found a great deale of misvnderstanding of them among the freemen which made them to refuse them." The reference evidently was to the set of bills proposed by Lord Baltimore, which, in the view of the committee, was rejected by the Assembly through misunderstanding. It was accordingly put up to the House whether these bills would be read a second time, with the vote being 48 to 21 in favor of the reading.

The bills submitted by Lord Baltimore then were read the second time, and immediately afterwards 20 bills proposed by the committee were read the first time. Some of the committee's bills were not completed, however, so the President of the Assembly suggested that it adjourn again, "till the lawes which they would propound to the Lord Proprietor were made ready, which some would take care of, & in the meanetime the company might attend their other businesses &c."

Captain Cornwaleys replied to this suggestion "that they could not spend their time in any businesse better than in this for the countries good; and one of the planters demanded the reason why it should be adiorned, & said they were willing to leave their other businesse to attend it." To this the President stated firmly that he was accountable to no man in his right to declare the General Assembly adjourned. Captain Cornwaleys then moved that another committee be chosen to take charge of preparing the bills. This motion was carried, with the committee to be elective and to have three persons on it; of the three highest, Captain Cornwaleys received 56 votes; the President, 46 votes; and Captain Evelyn, 44 votes. The President then adjourned the House until February 26, 1637/8.

Again for this interval, it was decided that the privilege of Parliament should be suspended. It was at this session on February 8, also, that the Assembly adopted two basic and time-honored pieces of Anglo-American legislative procedure. The first was a requirement that no bill should become a law unless read on three separate days. "There was an order made by generall consent of the house," said the *Journal,* "that all bills propounded to the house for lawes, should be read 3 times on 3 several daies afore they should be putt to the vote." Soon afterwards, "Captain Cornwaleys desired it might be putt to the vote of the house, whether these Lawes at the third reading should be voted severally, or the whole body of them altogether. And that they should be voted altogether was affirmed by thirty two voices, denied by 37." Here was the beginning in Maryland of the familiar three readings for the passage of every bill, and of the separate vote on every bill for its final passage.

Between the meetings of the Assembly on February 8 and Feburary 26, Leonard Calvert made a trip from St. Mary's to the Isle of Kent. Before leaving, he executed an instrument against the contingency that some accident might hinder his return to St. Mary's, declaring that, in such event, power to hold and continue the Assembly, and to adjourn it, should vest in John Lewger, Secretary of the Province. The Lieutenant General seems in fact to have been delayed, for he was not present when the Assembly reconvened on February 26. The Assembly transacted no business and adjourned to March 5. Again, on that day, the Lieutenant General was not present, and the Assembly adjourned until March 12. On both occasions the Assembly formally ordered that the privilege of Parliament should be suspended until the next meeting.

## THE LEGISLATION OF 1637/8

The President was back for the meeting on March 12, at which time the 20 bills first read on February 8 were read the second time. These were the bills which probably were drafted by the legislative committee of five, between January 29 and February 8. On March 13, 14 other bills were read the first time, and these bills evidently were drafted by the committee of three selected on February 8. The 14 bills are listed in the *Journal,* and here for the first time is broad evidence of the subjects of primary interest to the new colony in Maryland.[19] As recorded simply and succinctly in the *Journal* for March 13, 1637/8, "Then were read the first time fourteene Bills, that is to say

1 ordering the payment of tobaccos
2 for services to be performed for manors and freeholds
3 for assurance of titles
4 for the liberties of the people
5 for swearing allegeance to our Sovereigne Lord the King
6 for descending of land
7 for succession to the goods of the deceased intestate
8 for publique Ports
9 touching general Assemblies
10 for the Probate of wills
11 for civill causes
12 for payment of debts contracted out of the Province
13 for limiting the times of service
14 for punishment of ill servants."

---

**19.** Bozman has covered in close detail the legislation in the young colony, from the first meeting of the Assembly through 1658. He has learned and intensive commentaries upon the laws enacted during this early period, probing into their derivation and application, individual terms, and obscure language. In the process he ranges widely through the law of nature, Roman civil law, English statutory and common law, and the scholarship of legal writers. *See generally,* JOHN LEEDS BOZMAN, THE HISTORY OF MARYLAND (Baltimore, 1837, reprinted in 1968).

Every one of these 14 bills touched upon the elementary needs of a new community. Those for services to be performed for manors and freeholds, for limiting the times of service, and for the punishment of ill servants (the "ill" probably meaning ill-tempered or unruly), concerned work and labor within the Province. Those for the assurance of titles to land, the descent of land, the succession to the goods of a deceased intestate, and the probate of wills all related to property rights and testamentary affairs. There was another concerning debts contracted out of the Province, and one for civil actions in the courts. The bill for the payment of tobaccos could have been either a tax bill or one controlling contracts, as that commodity was fast becoming the medium of exchange.

The bill "for the liberties of the people" went to the heart of a basic tenet of political philosophy in the new colony of Maryland. It was a claim for the rights of the settlers as Englishmen; and it was one to which they would return time after time, until finally it was written into the Constitution of 1776. The inhabitants of the Province, said the bill, "shall have and enjoy all such Rights, Liberties, Immunities, Privileges and Free Customs, within this Province, as any natural Born subject of England hath, or ought to have or enjoy in the Realm of England, by force and virtue of the Common Law or Statute Law of England, saving in such Cases as the same are or may be altered or changed by the Laws and Ordinances of this Province; and shall not be imprisoned or disseized or dispossessed of their Freehold, Goods or Chattels, or be outlawed, exiled, or otherwise destroyed, forejudged, or punished, than according to the Laws of this Province . . . ."

Questions were to arise in the future whether the "rights" and "liberties" included the guarantees of Magna Carta, but there seems little doubt of the colonists' intent that these guarantees were among the rights and liberties of any

natural born subject of England, and thus fully transferred to the "Englishmen" in Maryland. This bill, however, was one of the entire group later vetoed by Lord Baltimore and thus may be cited only to show legislative intent.

The Assembly came back to Magna Carta during the session of February-March, 1638/9, declaring in another "Act for the liberties of the people" a virtual repetition of what was in the bill of 1637/8. This bill also failed, being included in a general memorandum applying to bills which "were engrossed to be read the third time but were never read nor passed the house."

On the afternoon of March 14, 1637/8, the Assembly participated briefly in what was clearly judicial work, in considering two indictments for piracy. The colony was hampered in its enforcement of laws, as has been said, because both the Assembly and the Lord Proprietor had refused to give assent to laws proposed by the other, which, among other things, would have set up a system of courts. Yet they were specially empowered by the Charter to deal with barbarians, other enemies, pirates, and ravagers, and also to quell rebellion, sudden tumult, and sedition. Also, despite the fact that no laws had been agreed upon, and evidently upon the premise that, in the absence of other laws, those of England were in effect, two courts met at St. Mary's during February of 1637/8. One was a court of testamentary causes, composed of the Governor and Council, in which letters of administration were granted on the estates of several deceased persons. The other was called a county court; a grand jury was impanelled and sworn, and it considered two bills of indictment for piracy and murder. Both were found to be true bills.

These were the two matters brought before the House on March 14. One concerned the deaths of four persons who "feloniously and as pirates and robbers" assaulted Captain Cornwaleys and his company; they had been slain by the defenders, and the House determined that Captain Cornwaleys and his company caused the deaths "lawfully & in their owne necessary defence." The other indictment was against one Thomas Smith, for piracy. He was found guilty by the House, 18 votes to one, with three members abstaining because of not having heard the presentation of all the evidence. The President then pronounced a sentence of death by hanging. On the three succeeding days, a bill confirming the sentence against Thomas Smith was given three readings in the House.

Another affair of possible criminal import is recorded in the *Journal* for March 15, 1637/8. Thomas Baldridge was fined 40 pounds of tobacco for striking Isaac Edwards; whether this was for an infraction committed on the floor of the House or elsewhere is not specified.[20]

The *Journal* for March 15, 16, and 17 contains references to a number of bills as they received their successive readings. At one place, more than a dozen bills are listed by title as having passed "by general consent not one vote dissenting." The roll calls are not given for this group of bills; it must remain conjecture whether they were passed by a seventeenth-century "fast roll call" or as a consent calendar. Any negative votes on the bills considered during these days were recorded, but the affirmative votes are not listed by name.

A small incident recorded briefly in the *Journal* of March 17, 1637/8, deserves mention as perhaps a "first" in the history of the General Assembly of Maryland. "Then upon a question moved," one reads, "touching the resting of servants on Satturdaies in the afternoone, it was declared by the house no such custom was to be allowed." Here was the

---

20. Isaac Edwards was not listed as a member of the Assembly in the *Journal* for the 1637/8 session. In the *Journal* for the 1638/9 session, he is listed as an elector (not a delegate) from St. George's Hundred.

first simple resolution, that popular device for expressing the sentiments of the members on all and sundry questions.

This notable session of the Assembly ended on March 24, 1637/8. The bills which had been passed were engrossed and then signed by the presiding officer and all the members. As the event was described in the *Journal,* "In the morning one part, and in the afternoon the residue of the Lawes as they were fair ingrossed were read in the house; and after the reading of them; the Governor signed them, & so did the rest of the house: And so the house dissolved."

Forty-two bills were passed at this session of the Assembly in 1637/8, but the text of only one is available. This was "An act for the attainder of William Cleyborne gent," declaring his possessions and goods to be forfeited to the Province. Clayborne had led armed resistence to the Proprietary, from Kent Island,[21] but by this time he had fled from Maryland. This bill, incidentally, is listed as having been read "the fourth time."

Despite the passage of these 42 bills, one large question remained unanswered. The Charter of Maryland specifically vested in the Proprietary the initiative in the legislative process; he was given the right to make all laws, with the assent of the freemen of the Province. Already at its session of 1634/5, the General Assembly had sought this initiative only to have Lord Baltimore veto the bills it passed. In 1637/8, the Assembly itself refused to pass the program of bills proposed by the Lord Proprietary. An impasse was developing between the executive and legislative branches of government, but it was broken during the summer of 1638 by an act of rare statesmanship on the part of Lord Baltimore.

---

21. For an account of the early settlements on Kent Island, *see* Erich Isaac, *Kent Island,* 52 MARYLAND HISTORICAL MAGAZINE 93-119 (1953).

Writing from London on August 21, 1638, the Proprietary gave to his brother, Leonard Calvert, as Governor and Lieutenant General of the Province, power "to give assent unto such laws as you shall think fit and necessary" for the good government of Maryland. The laws were required to be "agreeable & not Contrary" to the laws of England, and Lord Baltimore reserved a right to veto anything approved by the Governor. His statement was as follows:

> I do hereby give you full Power and Authority from time to time in every General Assembly Summoned by you in the Province of Maryland in my name to give assent unto such Laws as you shall think fit and necessary for the Good Government of the said Province of Maryland and which shall be Consented unto and approved of by the Freemen of that Province or the Major Part of them or their deputies assembled by you there from time to time for the enacting of Laws within that Province. Provided, that the said Laws so to be assented unto be as near as conveniently may be Agreeable & not Contrary to the Laws of England; every which Law so to be assented unto by you in my name, & consented unto and approved of by the Freemen as aforesaid I do hereby declare shall be in force within the said Province till I or my heirs shall signify in me or their disassent thereunto, under the Great Seal of the said Province and no Longer unless after the transmission thereof unto us and due Consideration had thereupon I or my heirs shall think fitt to Confirm the same. Given under my hand & Seal at London in the Realm of England the 21st of August 1638.

By 1638, then, the lines of legislative power were staked out. There was a General Assembly, with an uncertain power to initiate legislation. All of its members were in one House, but the dual presence of members of the Council and the elected delegates in the same body foreshadowed the change to a bicameral legislature. All freemen in the Province were members of this early Assembly, but the indirect presence of some by proxy was the beginning of representative government. There was a veto power in the executive, but with no right of overriding. There were rules of legislative decorum; there was a *Journal;* and the familiar rule that a bill must be read on three separate days was already observed. The General Assembly had taken the first steps toward becoming the legislative power in Maryland.[22]

---

22. *See also,* Carl N. Everstine, *The Establishment of Legislative Power in Maryland,* 12 MARYLAND LAW REVIEW 99-121 (1951); BERNARD C. STEINER, BEGINNINGS OF MARYLAND, 1631-1639 (Baltimore, 1903).

## Chapter 3

## DEVELOPING POWERS AND PROCEDURES
### 1639-1649

The sessions from the late 1630s to the end of the 1640s produced a broad development of procedures and possibilities for the new Legislature. Its rules were restated and expanded; amending processes were devised; expense money was furnished to the burgesses; the veto powers of the Governor and Lord Baltimore were clarified; and the Assembly felt itself free to tender unsolicited advice to Lord Baltimore on the proper handling of his job. There was a developing application of principles of representative government and a seeking of bicameralism in the Assembly. Among a great variety of laws considered by the Assembly, one of the most famous of all Maryland statutes, the Act of Religious Toleration of 1649, was enacted into law.

### CALLING THE THIRD SESSION

The session of February 25, 1638/9 was called by Lieutenant General Leonard Calvert, to meet at St. Mary's and "to advise and Consult upon the enacting of Laws and other serious affairs of the Province." He sent out formal writs of election to require that burgesses or delegates be chosen to represent the several parts of the Province. The writ sent to the commander of the Isle of Kent instructed him that at some convenient time he should "assemble at Kent ffort, all the freemen inhabitating within the Isle of Kent and then and there to propound to the Said ffreemen to chuse from amongst themselves two or more discreet honest men to be their deputies or Burgesses during the next assembly." Furthermore, it was specified, if the freemen of Kent Island "agree not in the election," the commander was to return as elected "the names of Such two or more persons upon whom the Major part of the ffreemen Soe assembled Shall consent."

There was an innovation in this writ of election, in that it made provision for paying the expenses of the deputies or burgesses while attending the Assembly at St. Mary's. The directive to the commander of the Isle of Kent included a provision that he should require "the ffreemen So assembled to agree upon a Certain Contribution for the defraying of the Charges which Such Burgesses Shall Sustain by the repairing to the assembly."

Similar writs went to Mattapanient, St. Michael's Hundred, St. Mary's Hundred, and St. George's Hundred, except that nothing was said in these several summons about providing for the expenses of the burgesses. The *Journal* of the Assembly then gives the text of a number of memoranda written by John Lewger, Secretary, attesting to the choices made for burgesses. Seven freemen from Mattapanient chose one of their number as burgess. Fourteen from St. Michael's Hundred chose two burgesses. Two were chosen also by 17 freemen from St. Mary's Hundred; and 20 freemen from St. George's Hundred picked one of their number to be a burgess. The freemen of the Isle of Kent divided into two groups to elect burgesses, with each set of 24 electing one person to represent it. The number of burgesses had been left to the discretion of each set of electors, and from the relative number of their selections it is evident they made no effort to vie among themselves in having the most representatives. On the contrary, the notable fact is that in this first full application of the principle of representative government in Maryland, the voters achieved only an unbalanced and inequitable representation.[1] This was to be a familiar thread in the history of the General Assembly.

---

1. There were instances later in the seventeenth century when a small number of delegates was preferred, because of the lesser expense involved for the county.

At the same time that writs of election were sent to the several civil divisions of the Province, special writs or summons were sent individually to Captain Thomas Cornwaleys and to Giles Brent, both councillors; and to Fulk Brent, Thomas Greene, and John Boteler, Gentlemen, requiring in each instance "that all excuses and delays sett apart you repair in person to the said Assembly at the time and Place prefixed there to advise and Conseult with us touching the important affairs of our Province." This Assembly, as would prevail until the Revolution, was to be a combination of elected representatives and members specially summoned by writ.

## THE SESSION OF 1638/9

The session met in the morning of February 25, 1638/9. According to the *Journal,* there assembled at the fort at St. Mary's the Lieutenant General, Captain Cornwaleys, Fulk Brent, Giles Brent, the Secretary (John Lewger), and Thomas Greene. The others, all elective, were styled for the first time in the *Journal* as "Delegates." They immediately removed the Assembly to meet at St. John's, a nearby home.

The first business was to read the letter sent by Lord Baltimore in August, 1638, in which he accepted (implicitly, at least) the power of the Assembly to initiate legislation and gave to the Lieutenant General authority to give tentative approval to laws passed by the Assembly.

The letter from Lord Baltimore to Leonard Calvert [2] gave him "full Power and Authority from time to time in every General Assembly Summoned by you in the Province of Maryland in my name to give assent unto such Laws as you shall think fit and necessary for the Good Government of the said Province of Maryland and which shall be Consented to and approved of by the Freemen of that Province or the

2. Quoted extensively near the end of Chapter 2.

Major Part of them or their deputies . . . provided that the said Laws so to be assented unto be as near as conveniently may be Agreeable & not contrary to the Laws of England." Every such law, he said, should be in force in the Province "till I or my heirs signify in my or their disassent thereto under the Great Seal of the said Province and no longer unless after the transmission thereof unto us and due Consideration had thereupon I or my heirs shall think fit to Confirm the same."

On the first day of the session, a bill was passed to settle the composition of the General Assembly. Its purpose was partly to validate the manner of selecting the members of the present Assembly, so it was passed by the Assembly and approved by the Lieutenant General at the very outset of the session.[3] The bill attempted to confirm the principle of representative government for future sessions of the Assembly:

> The said Severall Persons so elected and returned as aforesaid shall be and be called Burgesses and shall supply the places of all the freemen consenting or subscribing to such their election in the same manner and to all the same intents and purposes as the Burgesses of any burrough in England in the Parliament of England useth to Supply the place of the Inhabitants of the Burroughe whereof he is Elected Burges and that the said Gentlemen and Burgesses and such other Freemen (not haveing Consented to any the Elections as aforesaid) as now are or shall be at any time Assembled or any twelve or more of them whereof the

---

3. As printed in the *Archives* (vol. 1, at 81-82), this bill includes notations that "The freemen have assented to this Bill that it be engrossed and published under the great Seale" and "The Leiutenant Generall in the behalf of the Lord proprietarie willeth that this be a Law." However, it also is included with a number of other bills under the general "Memorandum that these bills were engrossed to be read the third time but were never read nor passed the house." This latter memorandum was marked as having been signed by John Lewger, Secretary of the Province.

Leiutenant Generall and Secretary of the Province to be allwaies two) shall be called the house of Assembly; and that all Acts and ordinances assented unto and approved by the said house or by the Major part of the Persons assembled and afterward assented unto by the Leiutenant Generall in the name of the said Lord proprietarie and shall be adjudged and established for laws to all the same force and effect as if the said Lord proprietary and all the freemen of this Province were personally present and did assent to and approve of the same.

Two freemen in the Province took advantage of the provision in the bill permitting those who had not consented to the election of one of the deputies to attend the Assembly in person. As noted in the *Journal,* "Cuthbert Fennick claimed a Voice as not assenting to the Election of Saint Marys Burgesses and was admitted Robert Clerke Similiter."

A new set of rules was adopted, similar in many respects to those adopted during the session of the previous year:

## ORDERS DEVISED AND PUBLISHED BY THE HOUSE OF ASSEMBLY TO BE OBSERVED DURING THE ASSEMBLY

The Lieutenant General shall be called President of the Assembly and shall appoint & direct all things that Concern Form and decency to be used in the house and shall Command Observance thereof as he shall see Cause upon pain of imprisonment or fine as the house shall adjudge The Burgesses shall take Precedence according to this Order

When any one of the house is to speak to any Bill he shall stand up and be Bareheaded and direct his speech to the President only and if two or more stand up to speak together the President shall appoint who shall speak

3

No man shall stand up to speak to any Bill until the Party that last spake have sat down nor shall any One refute another with any nipping or vncivil terms nor shall name another but by some Circumloquation as the Gentlemen or Burgess that spake last or that argued for or against this Bill or the Bill

4

The house shall sit every day holy days excepted unless it be adjourned at eight of the Clock in the morning at the furthest and at two of the Clock in the afternoon & if any Gentlemen or Burgess not appearing upon call at such time as the President is set at or after either of the said hours shall be amerced 20 pounds of Tobacco to be forthwith paid to the use of the house

5

After any Bill hath been once read in the house the Bill shall be read [illegible]
ingrossed or utterly rejected and upon any day or day appointed for a Session all Bills engrossed shall be put to the question and such as are assented to by the Greater part of the house and if the Votes are equal that shall be judged the Greater part which hath the Consent of the Lieutenant General shall be undersigned by the Secretary in these words the freemen have assented and after that the President shall be demanded his assent in the name of the Lord proprietary and if his assent be to the Bill, the Bill shall be undersigned by the said Secretary in these words the Lord Proprietary willeth that this be a Law

Since part of one line in Rule 5 is illegible, it is uncertain what the rule called for following the first reading of a bill. From the procedure followed, however, it is evident that it was to be read a second time and, unless rejected, ordered engrossed. The routine of later years was indicated, when bills were ordered to be printed for third reading after having passed second reading.

## THE LEGISLATION OF 1638/9

When the Assembly met on the afternoon of February 25, 1638/9, bills were read for the first time

For the planting of corn
For Publick Ports
For restraint of Liquors
For weights & measures
For limiting the time of Servants
For Swearing allegiance to the King
For erecting a Court of Admiraltie
    County Court
    Court of Chancery
    Pretorial Court
For the Government of the Isle of Kent
For the electing of certain Officers
For the Liberties of the People.

When the Assembly met again, on February 28, bills were read the first time

For the descending of land
For Succession to Goods
For Church Liberties
For assuring titles to Land
For Treasons
For Felonies
For Allowing Book to certain Felonies
For enormious offences
For Justices of Peace
For trade with the Indians
For enrolling of Grants
For accounts upon oath
For Peopling of the Province.

In the afternoon of the same day, another series of bills was given first reading:

For swearing of Judges
What Persons shall be called to an Assembly
The time of calling Assemblies

> For Building of a Town house
> Military Discipline
> For Fees
> For a ferry upon St. George's River.

On the third day of the session, March 1, one of the gentlemen and two councillors were fined for being tardy, agreeably to the rule. They were Captain Cornwaleys and Giles Brent, members of the Council, and Thomas Greene, Gentleman, who according to the brief note in the *Journal* were "amerced for tardie."

One of the bills read on March 7 was for trade with the Indians. All but three members voted against it, though the three comprised the President, Captain Cornwaleys, and Secretary Lewger. Despite the rejection, the bill was read again on the same day. There was an immediate objection that this bill already had been before the Assembly, and defeated. "The Secretary replied that it was a new Bill though the former title and that the House could not judge whether it were to be read again or no afore they heard it read the Gentlemen objected that it was against the Form & Order the Secretary replied that the Order spake of utterly rejecting a Bill but this was not utterly rejected by the house in reguard divers assented to it and therefore it Could not be put to the house to Vote the passing of it till the third reading and accordingly with the Consent of the House the Secretary proceeded to read it as the first time of reading." Those who opposed the bill evidently construed the rules to mean that a bill once rejected should not again be brought before the House. The Secretary with some resourcefulness argued two fine parliamentary distinctions: that the House could not judge whether or not the bill was to be read unless the members heard it read, and that the former bill had not been "utterly" rejected when three members voted in favor of it.[4]

---

4. Bozman devotes a long paragraph to questioning the parliamentary propriety of this ruling. "It must be confessed," he wrote, "that the

The bill subsequently was read a second time and ordered to be engrossed, but it was not finally passed.

The General Assembly in this session of 1638/9 considered more than 30 bills, passing many of them through second reading and ordering them to be engrossed for third reading. Most of them, however, were printed in the *Journal* under a "memorandum that these bills were engrossed to be read the third time but were never read nor passed the house." One of them, already mentioned, was the bill to validate the manner of selecting the members of that Assembly. All persons elected, it said, "shall be and be called Burgesses and shall supply the places of all the freemen consenting or subscribing to such their election in the same manner and to all the same intents and purposes as the Burgesses of any burrough in England in the Parliament of England . . . ."

A second of the bills under the Memorandum was "An Act what persons shall be called to every Generall Assembly." It would have provided membership in the Assembly for all members of the Council, "any other Gentleman of able judgment and quality Summoned by Writt," and "the Lord of every Mannour within this Province after Mannours be erected." Also, "some one, two or more able and Sufficient men" for every hundred were to be members. A third bill under the Memorandum was that "concerning the calling of Generall Assemblies." It would have required that the freemen of the Province be summoned at least once every

---

secretary's reasoning here does not appear quite satisfactory. It can hardly be supposed, that the words — 'utterly rejected,' — were meant as being synonymous to 'unanimously rejected'; for, according to parliamentary usage, then as well as at this day, a majority of voices always decided at any reading of a bill; and, as it seems, if the opposition succeeds at either of the readings, the bill must be dropped for that session." Bozman cites Blackstone's *Commentaries* on this point and proceeds to a further discussion of bills differing in substance and the effect of the title in such instances. *See* JOHN LEEDS BOZMAN, A HISTORY OF MARYLAND 114-15 (Baltimore, 1837, reprinted in 1968).

three years to consult "of the affairs and publique good of this province and for the enacting of Laws & ordinances for the better Government of the same." Once assembled, the freemen were to have the same powers in Maryland as the House of Commons in England.

Still another important bill of 1638/9, included under the Memorandum, was "An Act for the liberties of the People." It provided that "all the Inhabitants of this Province being Christians (Slaves excepted) Shall have and enjoy all such rights liberties immunities priviledges and free customs within this Province as any naturall born subject of England hath or ought to have or enjoy in the Realm of England by force or vertue of the common law or Statute Law of England (saveing in such Cases as the same are or may be altered by the Laws and ordinances of this Province)." This claim was to persist through the entire legislative history of the Province, being settled finally by a provision to such effect in the Constitution of 1776.

Finally, under the Memorandum in 1638/9, there was a sort of omnibus bill with clauses declaring that "Holy Churches within this province shall have all her rights and liberties, All inhabitants of this province shall take an oath of Allegiance to his Majestie, the Lord Proprietarie shall have all his rights and prorogatives, the Inhabitants of this Province shall have all their rights and liberties according to the Great Charter of England." Other sections in this omnibus bill concerned jurisdiction in civil, criminal, and testamentary cases; and there were provisions concerning the military, public fees and charges, the settlement of private debts, and an export tax on tobacco.

The several bills under the Memorandum, whether or not effective, are revealing for their insight into the thinking and philosophies of the freemen in Maryland barely five years after the Province was settled.

## The Session in October, 1640

About a year and a half later, the General Assembly met again, from October 12 to 24, 1640. Summons went out in August, some directed to the freemen of the several hundreds, to hold elections for burgesses; and others were directed to individual members of the Council. These writs were returned during September and early October, with the names of those chosen as burgesses. The session was called at St. John's, on the edge of St. Mary's.

The first item of business at this fourth session of the General Assembly was a review of the bases of its authority. "First was read that part of the Commission which Concerns the holding of Assemblys." This would have been the Commission executed by Lord Baltimore to his brother, Leonard Calvert, on April 15, 1637. It had set up an organized and detailed plan of government for the new colony. "Then was read his Lordships Proxy to the Governor for giving his assent." This would have been Lord Baltimore's letter of August 21, 1638, giving to Governor Calvert power to give assent in the name of the Proprietary to laws passed in Maryland. Next, "then was read that part of the act of last Assembly which Ordained the house of Assembly." Here was the act passed by the Assembly (but evidently not enacted) on February 25, 1638/9, providing for the manner of choosing members of the General Assembly. Finally, "then were read certain Orders made the last Assembly and respited till next day." These were the rules formerly adopted for the government of the Assembly.

A new set of rules was adopted on the next day, "13th October 8 Clock in the morning," as follows:

> 1. The Lieutenant General shall be called the President of the Assembly and shall appoint and direct all things that concern form and decency of speech and behaviour to be used in the house and shall Command observance thereof as he shall see cause upon pain of imprisonment or fine as the house shall adjudge.

2. Ten members of the house whereof the Lieutenant General to be always one at any time assembled with the Clerk of the Assembly shall be a full house except that on the Session day it shall not be a full house under the number of twelve as afore.

3. The house shall sit every morning holy days excepted unless it be adjourned by the President and any member of the house not being present at that time shall forfeit 30 pounds tobacco to the use of the house.

4. Every Bill shall be read three several days in the house (one day between every of those days being interposed) afore it may be voted for a Law but if it be rejected at the second reading by the greater part of the house it shall not be propounded again the same Assembly but if the Substance of the Bill be not amiss it may be amended and after the second reading the Bill shall be fairly engrossed.

5. Notice shall be Given of the day of Session nine days before and at the Session all the Bills engrossed shall be read and severally Voted and such Bills as are assented unto by the Greater part of the Gentlemen and Burgesses shall be presented to the Lieutenant General and when he hath signed the Bill it shall be recorded and published under the Great Seal of the Province and if the votes of the Gentlemen or Burgesses be equal the Bill may not pass.

The second of these rules provided generally that ten members of the House (including the Lieutenant General) when assembled with the Clerk should be a "full house," or quorum. There was an innovation in the fourth rule, to the effect that a day must be interposed between any two on which a bill received its readings.[5] The further provision in the fourth rule that a bill rejected on second reading "shall not be propounded again the same Assembly" was a mild form of the famous "clencher" of later years.

---

5. The earlier rule had specified separate days, but had not mentioned another day interposed.

There were other innovations in this meeting of the Assembly in October, 1640. One was a provision for compensation for employees of the House. The first order was that the Clerk of the Assembly should receive five shillings per day, and for every "private draught," 12 shillings. This seems to have been a new office; John Lewger, the Secretary of the Province, was a member of the Assembly and still carried the title of "Mr. Secretary," but he seems not to have handled the legislative duties. A few days later the Clerk was ordered to be paid 50 pounds of tobacco daily, in lieu of the sum of five shillings. The Clerk at this session was William Bretton.

The other provision as to compensation was that a Sergeant of the Assembly should have a fee of 12 shillings every day, "and for serving any warrant the usual fee." This unfortunate official, some days following, was to see the allowance of 12 shillings cut in half. The latter order also specified that the burgesses were to charge to their counties the amounts paid both to the Clerk and to the Sergeant.

The additional compensation provided for the Clerk, 12 shillings for every "private draught," evidently meant that he was the officer who, for compensation, would draft bills as requested by the members.

On October 16 of this session, "Mr. Thomas Adams for some indecent speeches touching the Lord Proprietary was censured to ask forgiveness of the Lieutenant General, which he did."

The most unusual action of this fourth session of the General Assembly was the issue of a proclamation clearly designed to have the effect of law, yet without any of the formalities attendant upon the enactment of a law. It was a simple proclamation "by the house of Assembly" and signed by William Bretton, the Clerk, prohibiting anyone from going aboard a ship to trade before "libertie of trade" had been proclaimed at the fort. It also forbade anyone from trading at a higher or greater rate than should be permitted. Governor Calvert immediately issued an order to the Sheriff of St. Mary's County, for a specific enforcement of the legislative proclamation.

As required by the rules, there was a separate roll-call on the final passage of each bill at this session. The roll-calls were journalized in brief form, however, with a bare caption for each bill to indicate its subject and no lists of names except for the nay votes. Thus,

> Triall of Causes passed by all except President
> Lesser causes not passed as afore except [John] Abbott
> Warning Jurys passed by all except President
> Ordinary Court days passed by all except ut Supra
> Chusing of Sheriffs passed by all except supra
> Publick charges passed except
> > Francis Gray
> > John Abbott
> > George Pye
> > George Allen
> > Lieut Vaughan
> > Mr Thompson
> > Fennick
> > Greene
> Uncertain Goods passed by all
> Customs passed by all except President
> Assemblys passed by all except President
> Suddain Arrests passed by all
> Securing Ground passed by all
> Exportation of Corn passed by all
> Planting of Corn passed by all. . . .

## THE SESSION OF AUGUST, 1641

The fifth session of the General Assembly was a short one, beginning in August, 1641. Prior to the session, it was declared in a certificate of election returned by the freemen of St. Clement's Hundred that they had chosen Thomas Gerard as their burgess. Following this certificate in the *Journal* is the further notation:

Whereupon Robert Vaughan (then appearing for the said hundred) was discharged of his Voice and Seat and demanding to have voice in his own person was Refused.

The refusal indicated the approaching end of the right of any freeman to appear in the Assembly, and a beginning of purely representative government.[6] The first meeting of the Assembly in 1634/5 had been like a town meeting, with all the freemen having a right of attendance. The second session, in 1637/8, was attended mainly by deputies but also by freemen in their own right. In the third session, in 1638/9, it was enacted as a general rule for the future that the several elected burgesses should represent those freemen "consenting or subscribing to such their election," and that any freeman who did not consent to the election of a burgess might himself appear. It was this rule which apparently was invoked by Robert Vaughan in 1641, only to meet a refusal by the House.

After several days in session in August, 1641, "The House Prorogued by the Lieutenant General in Audience of the house till the next Monday after twelfth day which shall be in the year 1642."[7] This prorogation was "anticipated" a few weeks later, with the Assembly "for certain weighty reasons" being called to meet on October 29 (of 1641). Twice thereafter, the Secretary of the Province, in the absence of the Lieutenant General, continued the prorogation. The sixth

---

6. Note that the proclamation for the session of January, 1646/7, required every inhabitant of the Province to be present either in person or by proxy.

7. Twelfth Day, the religious festival of the Epiphany, is 12 days after Christmas. Note that under the Old Style calendar then in effect, the reference to Twelfth Day in 1642 would have meant that the Assembly was not to meet again for nearly 18 months; the date would have been 1643 under the New Style calendar.

session of the Assembly did not commence until March 21, 1641/2.

## THE SESSION OF MARCH, 1641/2

The series of prorogations and the "anticipation" of prorogation evidently left their mark upon the members. Early in this session, the *Journal* notes "It was declared by the house that the house of Assembly may not be adjourned or Prorogued but by and with the Consent of the house." The declaration by the Assembly was not effective, of course; the Charter rather clearly gave to the Governor a right of calling and proroguing the Assembly.[8] Later, on September 13, 1642, there was a protest, but nothing more, over the power of prorogation.

The Assembly was continuing during this period to hear and determine judicial matters. In 1638/9, civil cases included one for possession of a beaver and one for rent.

---

8. The claim of the Assembly ignored the distinction between an adjournment and a prorogation. Adjournment was a continuation from day to day during a session. A prorogation was the ending of a session, comparable to adjournment *sine die* when the General Assembly later was given the right to end its sessions. Even this distinction was blurred during these early years of the Assembly, for, at times, the members were adjourned as well as prorogued by the Lieutenant General. For most of the Provincial period, however, the distinction was clearly and well observed, so that the members adjourned by their own action and were prorogued by the Governor.

The Charter specifically gave to the Governor a right to call the Assembly into session, and just as clearly it required that all actions by the Assembly be agreeable to the statutes and common law of England. The combination added up to a power vested in the Governor to prorogue as well as to call a session. Perhaps the claim of the Assembly during this session stemmed from a claim by the Parliament in 1641, during the throes of its long dispute with Charles I, that a right of prorogation was vested in the Parliament. *See* JOHN LEEDS BOZMAN, THE HISTORY OF MARYLAND 196-97 (Baltimore, 1837, reprinted in 1968).

There was also a criminal charge against a servant charged with unlawfully carrying away the goods of his master. When the delegates were polled for their verdicts in the latter case, several were for whipping ("very severely," in the words of one), and another delegate voted for hanging the accused.

A case brought before the House of Assembly in March, 1642/3, concerned one of the burgesses, Thomas Gerard. A petition was presented in the name of "the Protestant Catholicks of Maryland," charging Gerard with taking the keys of the chapel and removing some books therefrom. The House found him guilty of a misdemeanor and levied a fine against him. The trial showed a commentary on the concept of representative government held by those who had been elected as burgesses. All but one stated formally that in voting on Gerard's guilt they voted as individuals and not as representatives of others. After briefly describing the charges against Thomas Gerard and the action of the House, the *Journal* notes that "All that had Proxies expressed themselves that they voted in their own Behalfs except Jo Worthy who Voted for all his Voices." The members evidently considered their function as being, in this instance, a judicial jury of individuals, rather than a legislative body of representatives.

Immediately before adjourning at this session of March, 1641/2, the Assembly may have attempted to fix the date for its next session, a power which even three centuries later would be beyond ordinary legislative competence. The *Journal* records that "Another Assembly was appointed to begin on the first of June next." It is possible that the Lieutenant General simply was announcing the date in advance, for early in April he issued the necessary summons for the election of burgesses. However, for reasons which the *Journal* does not explain, this seventh session did not begin until July 18, 1642.

71

## THE SESSION OF JULY 18, 1642

There were stirrings in 1642 toward splitting the General Assembly to make it a bicameral body, but they failed for the time. Soon after this session convened on July 18, the question was raised by Robert Vaughan, a burgess from Kent County.[9] As recorded in the *Journal*:

> Robert Vaughan in the name of the rest desired that the house might be Seperated & the Burgesses to be by themselves, and to have a negative but it was not granted by the Lieutenant General.

The purpose of the proposal by Burgess Vaughan was to establish within the Assembly a separate house for the members appointed by the Governor and Lord Baltimore.

The same question came up in different form later in the session, on August 1. Thomas Greene, a burgess from St. Mary's Hundred, objected that a bill passed by the Assembly had not received a majority of the votes of those members who were burgesses; part of the majority vote, that is, evidently came from the non-elective members. As described in the *Journal*:

> Then Mr Greene excepted against the voting of this bill that it was not by the major part of Burgesses as it ought to be whereupon the act was read made in the beginning of this Assembly and it was found that the Company present was a house and in this house every one present whether by personal writt or as Burgess had a voice and that the major part of such voices present and such as they were to be Proxies for was judged the vote of the house.

---

9. At the session in August, 1641, a Robert Vaughan attempted to appear in his individual right from St. Clement's Hundred. The *Journal* for March 4, 1647/8, showed burgesses of this name from both Kent and St. Mary's counties.

The holding was, that is, that the elected burgesses and the other members selected by writ all held a common membership, with equal voting rights.

Several "firsts" appear in the records of this session in July and August, 1642. One was the custom of printing amendments in the *Journal*. The amendments were not prepared with the meticulous detail familiar to legislators in the twentieth century, for the bills had neither codified section numbers nor line numbers to aid in localizing the changes. All that was done in 1642 was to place the entire matter either added or deleted within brackets. Thus, several amendments were made to a bill concerning execution upon crops of corn or tobacco:

> Upon the question whether these words [in one Court] should be put out it was voted that they should
> Upon another question it was voted that these words [Landlords rents] should be incerted
> Upon another question it was voted that this word [Recognisance] should be incerted and in another place the word again in the plural number [Recognisances]

Similarly, a bill concerning succession to land was amended in this fashion:

> Upon the question these words [of freehold] were altered into these [of land in fee]
> Likewise that these words should be added [and to the mansion house to hold it during her widowhood]

Another "first" during this summer of 1642 was the beginning of the committee system in the General Assembly of Maryland; [10] and there was the added feature that the one committee appointed seemed to have something of the nature of a rules committee. The historic event thus was laconically described in the *Journal*:

---

10. A legislative drafting committee was appointed to serve during an interim period in the session of 1637/8.

Then the house appointed a Committee to meet every afternoon at 3 of the Clock at the place appointed by Captain Cornwalleys (who is to have the chair) the Committee to Consider all Bills fit to be propounded to the house and all petitions and to make Report to the house.

Finally, immediately before this session adjourned on August 1, 1642, there was an event which to many is one of the really vital legislative landmarks in the history of Maryland. Provision was made for the payment of per diem compensation to the members of the Assembly; and at the same time there were systematic and detailed arrangements made for collecting the necessary funds from the freemen of the Province (with the "funds" being in pounds of tobacco and not in currency). The per diem compensation was in addition to the expense money provided for some of the delegates in 1638/9.

Each burgess was to be paid at the rate of 40 pounds of tobacco for one day's attendance. This session ran from July 18 to August 1, for a total of 15 calendar days. They were paid for 13 days, although according to the *Journal* they were in session only on 12 of those days. There were two Sundays during this period on which the House did not meet, and it also did not meet on the Monday following the first Sunday.

Two years earlier, in October, 1640, the House had specified payments to be made to its Clerk and to a Sergeant, without any positive procedure for levying the tobacco. This time, however, a committee of the House was appointed, with power to assess the necessary amounts upon the freemen of every hundred.

When the committee met, the burgesses of St. Mary's Hundred asked to be allowed 140 pounds of tobacco for part payment of the Clerk of the Assembly, ten pounds of tobacco for part payment of the drummer, and 1040 pounds for their own compensation; the latter was to be at the rate of 40 pounds daily for each burgess. The committee accordingly levied the amount of 1260 pounds of tobacco upon the Hundred, to give what was sought and also some extra as a margin of safety for the "charge & hazard of Collecting it." The committee also listed the freemen in the Hundred and noted the share due from each.

Similarly, the committee levied 2944 pounds of tobacco upon Kent County, 1316 pounds upon St. George's Hundred, 750 pounds upon St. Clement's Hundred, 1344 pounds upon St. Michael's Hundred, and 726 pounds upon Mattapanian Hundred.[11] Each sub-division was to pay part of the expense of the clerk and the drummer. The burgesses of Kent County were allowed also one hundred pounds of tobacco for the hire of a boat for three days, and six hundred pounds for the hire of a servant and for his "diett" for 20 days.

---

11. Later in the seventeenth century, St. Mary's County was completely divided into hundreds. East of the St. Mary's (then St. George's) River, St. Mary's Hundred was around the site of the original settlement. Harvey Hundred lay to the north; and to the south, St. Inigoes and St. Michael's Hundreds. St. George's Hundred was on the west bank of the River. Beyond that, from north to south, were Resurrection, Newtown, and Poplar Hill Hundreds. Still farther west were St. Clement's and Chaptico Hundreds. Mattapanian Hundred was near the mouth of the Patuxent River.

*See* REGINA COMBS HAMMETT, HISTORY OF ST. MARY'S COUNTY, MARYLAND 44 (Ridge, Maryland, 1977).

A "hundred" was a civil division, originating in the governmental organization of Saxon England and beyond that among ancient Germanic peoples. In England it initially was a grouping of ten families, probably on the theory that the members and servants of one family would aggregate ten persons. Among the Saxons each hundred had its own constable and its own court.

Many accounts have been written about the hundreds in the counties of Maryland. They include: Henry J. Berkley, *The Proprietary Manors and Hundreds of St. Mary's, Old Charles, Calvert, New Charles, and Prince George's Counties,* 29 MARYLAND HISTORICAL MAGAZINE 237-45 (1934); Louise Joyner Hienton, *The Hundreds of Prince George's County,* 65

THE GENERAL ASSEMBLY OF MARYLAND

The colony went into an unsettled period during the 1640's. There was trouble with the Indians during these years, and for about two years the rebellions led by Claiborne and Ingles gained the ascendancy. The Proprietary government was overthrown, and Governor Calvert took refuge in Virginia. It was near the end of 1646 when he returned to St. Mary's and won back control of the government.

## THE SESSIONS OF 1642 AND 1644/5

The troubles were apparent at the session held from September 5 to 13, 1642. Several times there were discussions of the rights of the colonists to leave the Province without the consent of the Lieutenant Governor, winning from him the assurance that it was "the Common right of all inhabitants to depart out of the Province at their Pleasure unless indebted or obnoxious to Justice." One of the acts passed at this session was for the safety of the colony. It authorized the Lieutenant Governor "to presse or take any vessells, men, provisions, armes ammunition or other things necessary for defence, at the most usual rates of the country at that time, and the price or hire thereof to charge vpon the inhabitants of the Province."

For two years and more following the session held in September of 1642, a number of proclamations were issued for meetings of the Assembly. The proclamations either were rescinded or not observed; and the next session was not held until February 11, 1644/5. It passed only one reported act, concerning the defense of the Province.

MARYLAND HISTORICAL MAGAZINE 55-67 (1970); Jeffrey A. Wyand, *The Hundreds of Washington County,* 67 MARYLAND HISTORICAL MAGAZINE 302-06 (1972); Edwin W. Beitzell, *Newtown Hundred,* 51 MARYLAND HISTORICAL MAGAZINE 125-39 (1956); Oswald Tilghman, 1 HISTORY OF TALBOT COUNTY, MARYLAND, 1661-1861, at 5-6 (Baltimore, 1967); REGINA COMBS HAMMETT, HISTORY OF ST. MARY'S COUNTY, MARYLAND 44 (Ridge, Maryland, 1977).

## The Sessions of 1646 and 1647

The *Journal* lists a meeting at St. Inigoes Fort, beginning on December 29, 1646. It is perhaps uncertain whether to include it as a formal session,[12] although one act is shown as "assented unto by the Freemen and enacted by the Governor." The main interest, however, is the indication of order restored to the Province and of the coming split into two houses:

> In the vpper house . . . the Burgesses being sent for, and all appearing, the Gouvernor declared to them that they weare called hither as freemen to treat and advise in assembly touching all matters as freely and boldly without any awe or feare and with the same liberty as at any assembly they might have done heretofore . . . .

The one act passed at this session was a short one "touching Judicature":

> All Justice as well Civill as Criminall shall bee administered by the Governor or other Chiefe Judge in Court according to the Lawes of the province and in defect of Lawe, then according to the sound discretion of the said Governor or other Chiefe Judge and such of the Councell as shall bee present in Court or the Major parte of them And if the Votes of the Councell differ equally the vote of the Governor or other Chiefe Judge in Courte shall cast it

---

12. Riley lists as one session what seem to be separate sessions of December 29, 1646-January 2, 1646/7 and January 7, 1647/8-March 4, 1647/8. *See* ELIHU S. RILEY, A HISTORY OF THE GENERAL ASSEMBLY OF MARYLAND, 1635-1904 (1905, reprinted in 1972). However, the two sessions were a year apart, were called and convened separately, and were not a single session.

The fort at St. Inigoes was near the mouth of the St. Mary's (then the St. George's) River. It was built about 1637. *See* Fanny C. Gough, *Fort St. Inigoes,* 40 MARYLAND HISTORICAL MAGAZINE 54-59 (1945).

In calling the session, the Governor simply had proclamations published declaring "unto all persons whom it may concerne that I doe intend to hold a general Assembly." No writs or summons were issued either to the sheriffs or to individual members. The proclamation further required every inhabitant of the Province to be present, either by personal appearance or by proxy. It was not said in the proclamation that membership would be limited to freeholders.

Recognizing the confusion as to the membership of the Assembly, those who met in 1646 quickly passed an act declaring that the Council and the 16 burgesses named, or any ten of them, together with the Governor and the Clerk, should constitute a House of Assembly.

It was at this session that Mrs. Margaret Brent appeared and requested a vote, both in her own right and as the administratrix of Leonard Calvert's estate. Over Mrs. Brent's protests, the Governor denied her a vote in the House. Mrs. Brent had come under some criticism for serving as executrix of the estate, but, in a letter to Lord Baltimore, the Assembly came to her defense. "We do Verily Believe and in Conscience report," wrote the Assembly, "that it was better for the Collonys safety at that time in her hands than in any mans else in the whole Province after your Brothers death for the Soldiers would never have treated any other with that Civility and respect." [13]

---

13. Margaret Brent was "by far the most conspicuous and the most professional" of all the women attorneys-in-fact in colonial history. Between 1642 and 1650, her name appeared 124 times in the records of the Provincial Court. She and her sister came to Maryland in 1638, and for years they operated and sub-let the grant of land they received. Governor Leonard Calvert frequently consulted her on political matters, and, following his death in 1647, she was executrix and residuary legatee of his estate. Much of the criticism of Margaret Brent came when she sold some of the land and cattle belonging to the estate in order to pay a band of

More than a year later, on January 29, 1647/8, the Assembly issued a declaration that the act passed at the session in St. Inigoes was not validly enacted, since no summons had been issued to all the inhabitants of the Province. This was the session which began on December 29, 1646, soon after Governor Leonard Calvert returned from Virginia. He had permitted persons who opposed him to sit in the Assembly, thus bringing on the criticism from the later Assembly. Governor Thomas Greene vigorously defended the legality of the prior General Assembly and of its enactment.

## THE 12TH SESSION, IN 1649

The General Assembly which met from April 2 to 21, 1649, is distinguished in history chiefly for the enactment of the famous Act of Religious Toleration. While the act "concerning Religion" was passed at St. Mary's in 1649, it was not confirmed by the Lord Proprietor until August 26, 1650. Its "tolerance" was directed more to religion than to irreligion; blasphemy and denial of the Trinity were punishable by death and the confiscation or forfeiture of all lands and goods. "Reproachful" words or speeches concerning the Virgin Mary and the "holy Apostles or Evangelists" were subject to lesser penalties; and profaning the Sabbath day was prohibited.

The core of the Act of Religious Toleration was the assurance, distinctly unusual for its day, that persons professing to believe in Jesus Christ were not to be troubled, molested, and discountenanced for or in respect of their religion or be compelled against their consent to exercise any other religion.

soldiers the Governor had hired from Virginia to put down a local rebellion. Lord Baltimore was one of those objecting to the sales, and it was in response to his criticism that the Assembly answered in her defense. *See* Sophie H. Drinker, *Women Attorneys in Colonial Times,* 56 MARYLAND HISTORICAL MAGAZINE 349-50 (1961).

There is some thought that Lord Baltimore's support for the Toleration Act was an effort at meeting in advance possible criticism from the parliament operating under the Commonwealth. The Commonwealth was strongly Protestant in its sympathies; and the Toleration Act gave assurances to the Protestants in the Province (who by this time outnumbered the Catholics) that they would not meet religious discrimination from the Catholic Proprietary.[14] From Lord Baltimore's point of view the Toleration Act also had the advantage of protecting the minority Catholics from the majority Protestants.[15]

The 1649 Legislature made two suggestions for legislative changes in the Province, both contained in a long letter addressed to Lord Baltimore in England and signed by all members of the Council and all the burgesses.

The letter indicates, first, that Lord Baltimore had sent a set of proposed laws for the enactment of the General Assembly, following his power under the Charter to initiate legislation in this fashion. The colonists protested, however, that they were illiterate and void of the understanding and

---

14. Aubrey C. Land, *Provincial Maryland,* MARYLAND — A HISTORY, 1632-1974, at 12, edited by Richard Walsh and William Lloyd Fox (Baltimore, 1974).

*See also,* Bernard C. Steiner, *Maryland's Religious History,* 21 MARYLAND HISTORICAL MAGAZINE 1-20 (1926).

15. Doubts have been expressed whether the Act of Religious Toleration deserves all the accolades it had received, particularly from Maryland historians. Citing the death penalty provided in the Act for those denying the divinity of Jesus, it has been said that the Toleration Act "sanctioned less toleration than had previously existed in the settlement, but it did extend a cloak of protection to the uneasy Catholic minority." THOMAS A. BAILEY, THE AMERICAN PAGEANT — A HISTORY OF THE REPUBLIC 18 (Boston, 2nd ed. 1966). Lord Baltimore originally had permitted unusual freedom of worship, hoping he would thus secure toleration for his own fellow worshippers; but by the late 1640s, a heavy influx of Protestants threatened to submerge the Catholics. *Id.*

comprehension necessary "for a mature and wise discussion of such a Body of Laws." They had earnestly read over, perused, and debated the proposals, they added, but "finding them so long and tedious containing withal so many Branches and Clauses that in prudence we cannot as yet with safety to ourselves and our Posterity (being they are to be perpetual) concurr to the enacting of them as laws . . . requiring a far more serious and longer discussion of them than at this point we are able to allow thereto for the necessary employment we are forced upon in a Crop at this time of the year most of us having no other means of subsistence than the same. . . . We do humbly request your Lordship to send us no more such Bodies of Laws which serve to little other end then to fill our heads with suspitious Jealousies and dislike of that which verily we understand not. Rather we shall desire your Lordship to send some short heads of what is most desired and then we do assure your Lordship of a most forward willingness in us to give to your Governor all just Satisfaction that can be thought reasonable by us . . . ."

The members of the Assembly also wrote into their letter to Lord Baltimore some pointed advice as to the multiplicity of oaths he was requiring from the officers and inhabitants of the Province. "We do farther humbly request your Lordship," they said, "that hereafter such things as your Lordship may desire of us be done with as little Swearing as Conveniently may be. Experience teaching us that a great Occasion is given to much Perjury when swearing becometh common."

Even from his distance of three thousand miles, Lord Baltimore understandably had no difficulty in evaluating the elaborate self-abasement from the members of the Assembly. Their long letter obviously desired a release from executive controls. He replied in a detailed and spirited "declaration" dated from London on August 26, 1649, and published in the legislative *Journal* of April 6, 1650. The wording of the proposed laws was clear, he maintained, with no intention to "enslave" the colonists. In skillful wording he said that those who opposed his bills "had other Secrett reasons why they opposed those lawes, than those pretended ones on the Peoples behalfe." Accordingly, he concluded, "wee doe therefore hereby Protest against the said Remonstrance as Seditious and apparently vniust and tending to deprive vs of divers Essentiall parts of our vndoubted Jurisdiction and Rights in that Province.... And wee now hope that the Inhabitants there will unite themselves in their affection and fidelity to vs, And as well avoid all factions, and divisions among themselves."

## Chapter 4

## THE PURITAN REGIME AND RESTORATION
### 1650-1668

During much of the period of the 1640s and 1650s, England went through the trauma and the aftermath of its Civil War. Tensions there had been building for two decades earlier. Open fighting broke out in the early 1640s, culminating in the execution of Charles I in 1649. There followed the years of Parliamentary ascendancy under the Commonwealth and Oliver Cromwell. The Restoration under Charles II came in 1660.[1]

The unsettled conditions in England had obvious effects upon the colony in Maryland. For a time the regime of Lord Baltimore was suspended, as Maryland came under the control of the Parliament.[2] That period had its own internal uncertainties; Cromwell, though nominally head of the Parliamentary group, sometimes seemed to emulate the status of the monarch he had supplanted and came very close to declaring a new "kingship" for himself. Also, there has been speculation that Cromwell was more favorably disposed toward Lord Baltimore than was the Parliament generally.

At the very beginning of this period, the Assembly became a bicameral body. It was to continue as such, though with

---

1. An unfortunate *faux pas* was committed in the name of the Province after Charles I was executed in 1649. Thomas Greene, deputy Governor and acting in the absence of Governor William Stone, proclaimed Charles II as the new king. Governor Stone repudiated the proclamation, and Lord Baltimore disavowed it, but the untimely "recognition" of the new king, during the period of full powers for the Commonwealth, gave impetus to those pressing to end Proprietary control of the Province.

2. *See generally,* BERNARD C. STEINER, MARYLAND DURING THE ENGLISH CIVIL WARS (Part I, Baltimore, 1906; Part II, Baltimore, 1907); BERNARD C. STEINER, MARYLAND UNDER THE COMMONWEALTH—A CHRONICLE OF THE YEARS 1649-1658 (Baltimore, 1911).

temporary exceptions; and perhaps it was the unfamiliar two-house arrangement that led to strains and stresses between the Upper House and the Lower House. Legislative rules continued much as before, with some additions. The oath of office to the Puritan regime troubled some who long before had taken an oath to Lord Baltimore and the Proprietary government. Problems with hostile Indians continued, yet the colony grew in population and area.[3]

The move to bicameralism in Maryland and the background of Parliamentary controls in England served to emphasize the growing importance of the lower House in Maryland's legislative development.

## The Session in April, 1650

The General Assembly met for its 13th session from April 6 to 29, 1650. Historically, it was one of the most important sessions ever held by the Maryland Legislature. It organized definitely into a bicameral body and established the two houses as they were to exist virtually without change until the time of the American Revolution.

Even before the session began, the proclamation calling for the election and attendance of the members went far in determining the final status of the Assembly as a representative body and not as a town meeting. The freemen of each hundred were directed to elect from one to three persons as their burgess or burgesses. There was an alternative provided if the freemen of any hundred did not agree to such elections. In that event, "they are all of them hereby required to appear personally, and not their proxies or delegates or burgesses."

---

3. Internal conditions in England were unsettled for decades during the early seventeenth century, providing a steady pool of persons interested in emigration. *See generally,* CARL BRIDENBAUGH, VEXED AND TROUBLED ENGLISHMEN, 1590-1642 (New York, 1968).

When the burgesses met on April 6, their first act was to choose William Bretton as "Clarke of the howse." Members were present from the hundreds of St. Inigoes, St. Michaels, St. George's, New-Town, St. Clement's, and Providence; and from the counties of St. Mary's and Kent Island.

James Coxe, of Providence (now Anne Arundel County), was elected Speaker of the House. The phrase "House of Delegates" was not then used. Individual members usually were known as "burgesses," and the entire group was known simply as "the House" or "The House of Burgesses," as distinguished from the Council. The two frequently were styled as the "Upper" and "Lower" houses. Coxe was one of the Puritans who had lately settled near the Severn River and who were to seize control of the colony for some years during the 1650s.

The two houses then unanimously passed "an act for the settling of this present Assembly" into two houses; and they adopted a set of rules to apply separately in each house. The act was one of the most important documents in the legislative history of Maryland.

It was enacted "that this present assembly during the continuance thereof bee held by way of Vpper & Lower howse to sitt in two distinct roomes a part, for the more convenient dispatch of the business therein to be consulted of...." In the Upper House, a quorum was to be the Governor, the Secretary, and at least one other member. A quorum in the Lower House would be any five or more of the 14 burgesses then attending, together with the Clerk. The two houses "shall haue the full power of, & bee two howses of Assembly to all intents and purposes." All bills "that shall bee passed by the said Two howses or the maior part of them both, & Enacted or Ordered by the Goveror shall be Lawes of the province after publication thereof, under the hand of the Governor & the Great Seale of the said province as fully to all effects in law as if they were aduised & assented unto by all the ffreemen of the province generally."

The separation of the two houses into a bicameral legislature by no means created an Assembly in a united working sense. For many years, and until the time of the American Revolution, the two houses represented distinctly different interests. The Upper House was the Council (or Council of State) of the Province; and frequently, in concert with the Lord Proprietor and the Governor, it represented the monarchical and the Proprietary interests. The Lower House expressed the interests of popular government and of increased legislative power.

The enacting clause was modified at this session to reflect the division into two houses. The bills were passed "By the Lord Proprietary, with the assent and approbation of the upper and lower houses. . . ."

The rules adopted for the two houses incorporated much that already had become standard procedure in Maryland:

1. That noe member of eyther howse shall vse reuyling speeches or name any of the members of eyther howse by his owne name but by the terme or denomination of the Gentlemen that spoke last or the like.

2. That none of eyther howse shall speake aboue once, att one reading to any Bill without license of the Governor or Speaker respectively. And if 2 persons rise vp together the Governor or Speaker respectively, shall appoynt who shall speake first, & no one shall interrupt another, or speake till the other haue ended.

3. That none shall deliuer his opinion or speake to any Bill sitting, but shall stand up bare headed, directing his speech to the Governor or Speaker respectively.

4. That Every Bill proposed to the howse, shall bee read three severall dayes, before it be voted to Ingrossment unlesse uppon urgent occasion, or in matters of lesser consequence, it bee otherwise thought fitt by both howses.

5. That none shall come into eyther of the howses whillst they are sett, with any gun or weapon upon

perill of such fine or censure as the howses shall thinke fitt.

6. Any of the 14 Burgesses (bownd to attend the Assembly) that shall bee absent from their howse att the hower & place appoynted (the Governor & Secretary or any one of the Counsell being then assembled) is censured or adiudged to pay for euery such default 50 pounds of Tobacco & cask, unles iust excuse for such absence be made appeare.

7. All Tobbackos which shall accrew bee adiudged to be payd or raysed for, or by reason of any misdemeanor, absence, or censure of any of the Burgesses during this Assembly, the Governor is pleased (& the Assembly doth thereunto consent) shall bee disposed of towards the releife of the Poore of the Province.

The device of bicameralism was sufficiently new to the members of the Assembly in 1650 that upon occasion they informally reverted into one House. Thus, on April 20, the burgesses were sent for to attend the Upper House to give their opinions upon the desire of the Clerk to be discharged from his position. The burgesses returned to the Upper House on April 25, to hear a message from the Proprietary. These brief returns to unicameralism were parallel to the Parliamentary experience in England, centuries earlier. There was a more notable departure from the two-house idea on April 29. It was the final day of the session, and perhaps it was a colonial version of the modern end-of-session "jam." As the event was recorded in the *Journal,* "the Burgesses of the Lower House being sent for, came and Joyned themselves with the Vpper House this day for the more convenient and Speedyer dispatch of all busines."

Not only did the two houses work together on that last day of the session in 1650, but the members resorted to their seventeenth-century equivalent of suspending the rules for expediting their work:

After which it was put to the Vote of both Houses whether in regard of the Long expence of time elapsed they did agree that all Bills, Acts and Orders as well such as have often been read and Voted to Ingrossment as all the rest that have been read and assented vnto by both Houses shall passe for Lawes and Orders of the Province and stand Good to all intents and purposes, without further reading though they have not been soe often read and Voted as was directed by the order of the House for that purpose, Yea or Noe. And it was in the affirmative by both Houses.

Immediately after James Coxe was chosen to be Speaker of the Lower House in 1650, "vppon the motion & desyre of the Burgessed this day assembled, the Governor appoynted Mr. Secretary to draw 2 seuerall oaths one for the Burgesses, & the other for the Clarke which was done."

Each burgess was required to swear "that I will faithfully & truly, according to my hart and conscience to the best of my understanding & ability, without fauor affection of selfe ends aduise, consult, & give my uote to all Bill and other matters wherein my aduise or uote shall be required during this Assembly. . . ." His main purpose was stated to combine the glory of God and the promotion of the Lord Proprietary: "Wherein my chiefe end & ayme shall bee the glory of God in my endeauors for the aduancement & promoting the Lord Proprietors iust rights & priueledges, & the publique Good of this province. . . ." The oath concluded with a general requirement for secrecy covering legislative matters when required or necessary.

The oath of the Clerk of the Lower House was to perform his duties "faythfully & truly, to the best of my ability & understanding. . . . The source of his employment was made evident, for he was to occupy his position "soe far as it shall please the Governor to continue mee therein." A general requirement for secrecy also was appended to the Clerk's oath.

The two oaths were at once administered to the burgesses and clerk. One burgess, Thomas Mathews of St. Inigoes Hundred, refused to take the oath. His objection was that it would have interfered with the free exercise of his religion. The House thereupon censured him and denied him a seat and a vote, after which Mathews "departed & absented himselfe accordingly."

This action of the Lower House evidently was criticised in the Upper House, for on April 10, 1650, the *Journal* records that the burgesses delivered a petition to the Upper House, "desyring vindication of their honors for certaine harsh speeches uttered by Mr. Thomas Greene against them, taxing them with iniustice for expelling Mr. Thomas Mathews." [4] In debating the petition to the Upper House, the burgesses pointed out that it was useless for them to take the oath of secrecy unless it also was taken by the members of the Council in the Upper House; and the burgesses "assented" that the members of the Upper House should have neither a seat nor a vote unless they took the oath.

On the last day of this session in April, 1650, the *Journal* records that "both houses Declare that noe further secrecy is requyred mentioned in the Oath (after this present day of Sessions) taken for that purpose neyther doe they find it in any wayes requisite."

A second burgess from St. Inigoes Hundred objected to taking the oath, questioning that it might prejudice his religion and conscience. In answer, the entire Lower House joined in a declaration that the oath was never intended to infringe liberty of conscience and religion; whereupon the burgess agreed to take the oath.

---

4. Thomas Greene was the former Governor, and at this time a member of the Council.

Meanwhile, Governor Stone and the Upper House answered the action of the burgesses in seeking vindication for expelling Burgess Mathews. Their reply was "that the Lower howse had not power of themselves to expell any member out of their howse, the Governor not being present." Any possibility for conflict was nicely resolved, however, when the Governor and the Upper House went on in their opinion to say that Mathews had expelled himself from the Lower House, "for that hee came not to demand his uoyce, after the Governor himselfe was present in the howse."

Six members of the Assembly of 1650 signed a statement of legislative intent on April 29, 1650, as to an act passed by the Assembly in 1647. Not only did they give their construction to the meaning of the earlier act, but they added their opinion that such had been the intention of the entire Assembly in 1647.

In the Governor's proclamation for holding this session in 1650, it was specified that St. Mary's Hundred should have one burgess. The freemen from this Hundred sought an additional burgess, "alleaging that hundred to be the ancientest hundred & the first seated within this province." The Governor granted their request. Later in the session, one of the acts passed was for erecting in that part of the Province called Providence, "a Shire or County by the name of Annarundell County." This was the first act of the General Assembly in creating a county. Indeed, the power to establish counties and other civil divisions was generally exercised by an Order in Council (in the executive branch) during this period; there are references in this year's session to St. Mary's and Kent as already established counties.

After 1650 there was little of note in the legislative history of the Province during the years of the early 1650s.

90

## THE SESSIONS DURING THE 1650s

The Assembly next met in March, 1650/1. There are no *Journal* records of the legislative proceedings, although two acts are included as having been enacted. A long statement in the *Journal,* directed to Governor Stone and both houses of the General Assembly, maintained that Thomas Greene had not properly taken an oath of office as Governor and that all acts and things done by him were void; this was claimed to include the acts of the Assembly of 1647.

Perhaps in expectation that the Proprietary government would soon be abolished, no burgesses were sent to this Assembly from Anne Arundel County, where probably a majority of the settlers were Puritans. Notified of the incident, Lord Baltimore wrote to Governor Stone and the General Assembly in August, 1651, taking a stern view of this defection. In case any inhabitants "refuse or neglect" to send burgesses to the Assembly, the Proprietary wrote, "we will and require all the other members of our said Assembly . . . to fine all such Refusers or Neglectors according to their demerits." Also, if the offenders "wilfully persist," they are to be declared "Enemies to the publick peace and rebell to the lawful Government thereof. . . ."

In 1652, during the interval between the sessions of 1650 and 1654, the new government of the Commonwealth in England moved to take the Province from the Proprietary and to bind the inhabitants to the Commonwealth. It was required first that "all writs, warrants and process whatsoever be issued in the name of the keepers of the liberty of England, by authority of parliament." This was in conformity with an act of the Parliament passed in 1649, shortly after the execution of Charles I.

The second requirement was that all the inhabitants of the Province "should subscribe the test, called the engagement." This reference was to another act of the Parliament requiring a new oath, to "promise and engage ourselves to

91

be true and faithful to the commonwealth of England, as it is now established, without king or house of lords."[5] The Assembly in 1654 passed an "act of recognition" as an acknowledgment of being under the "supream authority of the commonwealth of England exercised by his highness the lord protector."

The transfer of the Province from the control of Lord Baltimore to that of the Parliamentary regime occurred rather suddenly, in early 1655. On March 25 of that year, 21 years to the day after the first landing in the colony, a series of threats and counter-threats between the two factions culminated in the Battle of the Severn. The Proprietary forces under Governor Stone were decisively defeated by the Puritan forces under William Fuller.[6] The Puritans then ruled the Province for three years.

---

5. JOHN LEEDS BOZMAN, THE HISTORY OF MARYLAND 440 (Baltimore, 1837, reprinted in 1968).

6. *See* DONALD MARQUAND DOZER, PORTRAIT OF THE FREE STATE 100 (Cambridge, Maryland, 1976); ELIHU S. RILEY, THE ANCIENT CITY — A HISTORY OF ANNAPOLIS, IN MARYLAND 33-37 (Annapolis, 1887). *See generally,* WILLIAM OLIVER STEVENS, ANNAPOLIS, ANNE ARUNDEL TOWN (New York, 1937); DAVID RIDGELY, ANNALS OF ANNAPOLIS (Baltimore, 1841). Captain Fuller and the Puritan forces had only about 120 men, as compared with some 300 in the Proprietary contingent of Governor Stone. It is thought that the battle was fought on Horn's Point, adjacent to the harbor of Annapolis, on the Eastport peninsula south of Spa Creek. It has been said to be the first battle in America fought between Anglo-American forces; the first in which the Provincial flag of Maryland was used; the only battle in America in which the flag of the Commonwealth of England was shown; the first battle in America to be decided by sea power; and the first anywhere in which "dum-dum" bullets were used. *See* B. Bernard Brown, *The Battle of the Severn,* 14 MARYLAND HISTORICAL MAGAZINE 154-71 (1919); JAMES E. MOSS, PROVIDENCE — YE LOST TOWNE AT SEVERN, IN MARYLAND 329 (Washington, 1976).

The new regime called a session of the Assembly for October 20, 1654. It was held at Patuxent, meeting under a commission from the new Protectorate government in England, giving full recognition to that government, and requiring the assent of the Assembly to the new regime. Richard Preston was named as Speaker.[7] Apparently the members met as one house, abandoning temporarily the bicameral system established in 1650. Beginning with this session of 1654, all the burgesses or delegates were elected by counties, and no longer by hundreds.

Thomas Hatton and Job Chandler were elected as burgesses from the county of St. Mary's and Potomac River. They appeared at the Assembly and refused to take their seats, because they previously had taken an oath to Lord Baltimore. Following a writ of election for a second choice of burgesses, two others were chosen. Subsequently, the Sheriff of that county appeared before the Assembly to

---

7. There is some evidence that during this period the records of the Province were kept at Preston's house, and that he lived "at Patuxent." This house was still standing into the 20th century, near St. Leonard's Creek not far from the mouth of the Patuxent River, in Calvert County. The house was the subject of a full-length "biography." See HULBERT FOOTNER, CHARLES GIFT — SALUTE TO A MARYLAND HOUSE OF 1650 (New York, 1939). However, the name "Charles Gift" seems to have been bestowed informally upon this house earlier in the 20th century. The original "Charles Gift," also owned by Richard Preston, was off to the east, on a portion of Calvert Cliffs overlooking the Chesapeake Bay. It is uncertain how it received this name; Preston was a Puritan, and when the house at Calvert Cliffs was built, Charles I had been dead for three years. In the late 1970s, the chimneys and foundation of the original "Charles Gift" still could be seen on the property of the Calvert Cliffs plant of the Baltimore Gas and Electric Company.

In 1954, an informal legislative group in Maryland, under the initiative of the Legislative Council, held a mock session (in period costumes) at the "second" Charles Gift, near St. Leonard's Creek, to commemorate the session of 1654 held there, as well as the 300th anniversary of the establishment of Calvert County.

collect the expenses of the special election. The Assembly ordered, however, with evidently the same force as an enactment, that "this Charge cannot be Levied on the whole, but there where the default was made that is in the county of Maryes and Potomock, and if the fault appear not to be in the Electors but in the said Hatton & Chandler then the said County hath Liberty Granted to recover the Charge on the Delinquents."

Provision was made in 1654 for calling the General Assembly once in every three years, "not infringing the Calling of Assemblies oftener if need be." Writs were to be issued three months prior to the session, by one of the commissioners under the Protectorate, or by either the sheriff or the court of the respective counties.

The 1654 session drastically modified the Act of Religious Toleration of 1649, declaring that "none who profess and Execise the Popish Religion Commonly known by the Name of the Roman Catholick Religion can be protected in this Province by the laws of England formerly established and yet unrepealed...." At the 1654 session, also, Patuxent County was erected (from a portion of the present Calvert County), and the name of Anne Arundel County was changed back to Providence.[8]

The Assembly next met at Patuxent on September 24, 1657. This was the last session at which the authority of the Commonwealth was recognized. By the time of the next following session, held in the spring of 1658, Lord Baltimore had been reinstated in his rights as Proprietary. Included in the acts of the 1657 session was a general act of amnesty for acts performed "in relation to the late Alteration of the Government."

---

8. When Lord Baltimore resumed control of the Province, in 1657, he treated as void all laws passed during the three prior years.

The little colony in the late 1650s was completing its first quarter-century and had made remarkable progress. The two or three hundred persons who had settled at St. Mary's in 1634 had grown to a population of nearly twelve thousand, and, by the 1670s, Maryland was to have an estimated population of nearly twenty thousand persons. The settlements which had been started at St. Mary's and on Kent Island had spread along both sides of the Chesapeake Bay, up the Potomac River, and along many of the tributaries and tidal estuaries. For the General Assembly which met in 1657, writs of election were issued to four counties: St. Mary's, Kent, Calvert, and Anne Arundel. When the Assembly met two years later, in 1659/60, writs of elections also went to Charles and Baltimore counties, both at that time literally frontier areas. The Province frequently is described as a "plantation-type" colony, though a high proportion of the settlers were on single-family farms. The trend was toward a single-family economy. Only a small minority ever achieved "plantation" status, and they usually were land investors who developed themselves into a planter-merchant class. The town of St. Mary's, with perhaps 50 or 60 houses, was the only settlement of any consequence.

### THE EARLY 1660s

The Assembly again became a unicameral body for a short time during the session of 1659/60. The change was closely linked to the aspirations of Josias Fendall, the Lieutenant General, and to the efforts in the Lower House to establish a commonwealth on the English model. The Lower House was anxious to improve its own relative importance in the legislative scheme of things; it and the governor are generally supposed to have acted in concert in this message delivered to the Upper House on March 12, 1659/60:

95

That this Assembly of Burgesses iudging themselves to be a lawfull Assembly without dependence on any other Power in the Province now in being is the highest court of Judicature. And if any Objection can be made to the Contrary, Wee desire to heare it.[9]

The Upper House in reply directed several interrogatories to the Lower House, asking whether the Lower House thought itself "to be a lawful Compleate Assembly without the Governor and those other Members summoned to sitt by special writt in the Vpper howse" and also whether "they doe iudge they are wholly independent on the power of the Lord Proprietary yea or not."

The Lower House now asked for a conference, which, from the *Journal* of the Upper House, "was Condiscended vnto." It extended over two days. The Lower House flatly denied the right of the Upper House to continue as a separate body, though voicing its willingness to permit the Lieutenant General and the members of the Council to sit as part of the Lower House. On further consultation, the House agreed that the Lieutenant General should preside at the combined session; but the Lower House reserved the right to have a Speaker of its own and also to adjourn and dissolve the Assembly.

Fendall then dissolved the Upper House. He next surrendered to the Lower House the commission he had received from the Proprietary, and received a new

9. The Rump Parliament in England, in 1649, had taken the same action about the House of Lords.

"Every recalcitrant lower house appeared to be bent on pursuing 'the example of the parliament of 1641' and every leader to be 'a great Magna-Carta Man & Petition-of-Right maker' determined to persuade his fellow legislators 'to dance after the Long Parliament's pipe.' " Letter of Francis Lord Willoughby to the King, August 8, 1665, quoted in Jack P. Greene, *Political Mimesis: A Consideration of the Historical Roots of Legislative Behavior in the British Colonies in the Eighteenth Century*, 75 AMERICAN HISTORICAL REVIEW 350 (1969).

commission from the House. Fendall's rule was short-lived, however; the Proprietary's brother, Philip Calvert, soon restored the usual balance in the Province. By this time England had established Charles II as King.[10]

Although the two houses nominally held separate status, there continued to be frequent instances in which they collaborated in a fashion. On April 23, 1661, the Upper House requested the Lower House to meet with it as a grand committee to consider Indian problems. From the conference came a decision to draw up a bill empowering the Governor and Council to raise forces for an expedition against tribes that had killed settlers along the Patapsco River. A few days later, on April 26, three members of the Lower House attended the Upper House to ask two members of that body to join with them in drawing up an act concerning trials at law and costs of suit. The Upper House accordingly ordered two of its members to help as requested. Again on April 30 the *Journal* records a joint conference between the two houses.

An important conference was held on April 19 of that same year. The burgesses sent a message to the Upper House asking passage of a bill that would assure to the Lower House freedom of speech while in session, so that none would be prejudiced in either person or estate for opinions delivered on the floor of the House. Then, the *Journal* records:

> The Vpper House sent to them for a Conference, whereupon the Speaker and the whole howse comeing into the upper howse the Governor assured them that they might haue all liberty of Speech and that there was noe necessity of making such an Acte as was desired and that they should haue as much liberty as any Burgesses

---

10. Fendall had been an adherent of Lord Baltimore, having fought with the Proprietary forces during the Battle of the Severn. Lord Baltimore appointed him Governor when he regained the Province, but Fendall unaccountably turned traitor at the end of the decade.

had or haue in the Parliament of England or Magna Charta did afforde them in England with which the rest were satisfied and waved the request for the Acts.

Despite the assurances from the Governor in 1661, which evidently were well received at the time, a member of the Lower House a year later initiated a further request to widen the legislative immunity of the Assembly. In 1662, a message referred to the earlier request that members of the Assembly should have liberty of speech "in deliuering their opinion and Censures without prejudice either of themselves their persons or Estates ...." The only answer received, the message continued, was that legislators should enjoy liberty of speech "as being free borne children of England according to Magna charta." The further request in 1662 was that if "any Member transgresses in this kind and abuseing this liberty ...," he should be punishable only in the house where the offense was committed and not forced to answer in any court. "All which was granted by the Vpper howse."

The Upper House, or Council, continued to perform duties which were administrative or judicial. Petitions for naturalization were submitted to the Council and recorded in its *Journal;* on September 17, 1663, one was received from Augustine Herrmann, for himself, his children, and his brother-in-law. Petitions in legal matters also were sent to the Council; its *Journal* for the session of September, 1664, carried extensive proceedings in a defamation case.

As another indication of small concern for the doctrine of separation of powers, which was not to be formulated convincingly until decades later, the Lord Proprietor is found in his message of July 30, 1659, writing meticulous distinctions of his legislative intent in signing acts passed by the General Assembly.

When writs of election were issued to the sheriffs for the session of April, 1662, seven counties were included. Talbot County was on the list for the first time, the others being St.

Mary's, Kent, Anne Arundel, Calvert, Charles, and Baltimore.

The General Assembly at the session of April, 1662, passed a bill arranging to purchase the houses and plantation of Hannah Lee, widow, to serve as a meeting place for the Assembly in St. Mary's, including a place for court facilities and a jail. The price was to be twelve thousand pounds of tobacco. Several years after these arrangements, the *Journal* of the Upper House (April 20, 1666) speaks of the building of a new property:

### Petition of William Smith

Petitioner hath undertaken to build a Stadt House for the Accomodation of the Country. But, Tobacco proving so bad a Commodity No Workmen can be procured by your Petitioner to make good his promise they refusing to work for Tobacco . . . .. Shipping is gone out of the Country, and thereby your Petitioner damnifyed both in his Creditt & loss of Tobacco lying in his hands.

The Lower House conferred with Smith about his problems and asked if he could build a "lesser" State House.

During the session of April, 1662, the General Assembly passed a bill to provide for the expenses of the burgesses. Twenty years earlier, at the session which ended on August 1, 1642, there had been for the first time provision for a per diem payment to members of the Assembly, at the rate of 40 pounds of tobacco daily. Nothing had been said in 1642 about expenses, except that the burgesses from Kent Island, doubtless because of the distance from St. Mary's, were allowed one hundred pounds of tobacco for the hire of a boat for three weeks and six hundred pounds of tobacco for the hire of a servant for 20 days. In 1662, the requirement was that each county "shall satisfy unto their respective Burgesses all their necessary expenses for meat drink and lodging for themselves and charges of boat and hands att this next ensuing cropp." There was a payment of one thousand pounds of tobacco to Hannah Lee for "house roome." The Clerk of the Lower House, William Bretton, was paid two thousand pounds of tobacco; and the Clerk of the Upper House, John Gittings, received one thousand pounds. The final payment was for five hundred pounds of tobacco for "Mr. John Metcalfe Doore Keeper."

Evidently there was some feeling from the fact that the Clerk of the Upper House received less than the Clerk of the Lower House, for at the next session the Upper House pointedly called attention to the difference and requested that the payments be equalized.

A notable "first" received brief mention in the *Journal* of the Upper house for September 17, 1663:

> Came a Message from the lower howse to desire to know whether the booke of Lawes Entituled a Coppy of all Lawes now in force within the Province of Maryland were the bodyes of all the lawes in force or not.
>
> Ordered that the booke of Lawes now Examined by the Vpper howse be subscribed by the Clerk of this howse as all the lawes now in force within this Province.

This seems to be the first-mentioned "code" in Maryland's legal history.

Also in the Upper House, on September 27, 1663, a bill was received from the Lower House, with amendments that could have been the precursor of those famous ones in the twentieth century known as "a little ole amendment that don't do nothing":

> Was returned the Additionall Act for the advancement of Childrens Estates from the Lower howse wherein they desired the words (Handy craft, Trade) might be struck out.
>
> Ordered that answere be returned that to strike out those words (Handy craft Trade) was to destroy the very

thing Intended by the Act which was to breed up all the indigent youth of this Province to Handy craft Trade and noe other.

## THE MIDDLE 1660s

Both houses took an active and joint part in 1666 in settlement of troubles with the Indians. These problems were particularly acute during this period. In part, they stemmed from the ordinary disagreements of neighbors; and the Indians complained also of the constant pressures they received from the colonists to push them from their lands. These usual problems were aggravated by the massacre of several white settlers and the unexplained death of an Indian.

After long deliberations, and with the participation of both houses, a treaty was drafted between the Indians and the settlers. It had several main provisions: (1) the Indians acknowledged that the power of appointing the Emperor of the Piscataways was in the Lord Proprietary; (2) "if an Indian kill an Englishman he shall dye for itt"; (3) an Indian approaching within three hundred paces of an English plantation was to drop his arms and call aloud, and the penalty was death for an Englishman who killed an Indian who came unpainted and gave this notice; and (4) the privileges of hunting, crabbing, fishing, and fowling were preserved to the Indians inviolably.

After the treaty was concluded, one John Nuthall presented a claim to the Assembly for housing "for the space of a fortnight twenty Indians sometimes more and sometimes less & and hath been at great Trouble in providing for them." Nuthall claimed 6,860 pounds of tobacco for his compensation. Both houses thought this amount unreasonable and agreed to settle with him for two thousand pounds. Nuthall protested ("having provided flesh for them once a day at least"), but the two houses held firm and refused to increase their offer.

The rules adopted by the Lower House for the session of April-May, 1666, were essentially the same as in earlier sessions, with two items made more precise. First, no one was to come into the House with a sword or other weapon; and secondly, there was to be no whispering or private communication by any two or more members, concerning the debate on any bill or while the House was sitting.

This session was further enlivened by a serious breach of legislative decorum on the part of one Edward Erbery. The matter required three pages in the *Journal* of the Upper House and a lesser space in the *Journal* of the Lower House. As recounted in a message from the Lower House to the Upper House, Erbery "did call the whole howse Papists, Rogues, turdy Rogues . . . a Turdy shitten assembly . . ." and "a company of turdy fellowes (meaneing the lower howse) & were ashamed of the place from whence wee came." There was other testimony that Erbery had called Charles Calvert a rogue and had said the Assembly was a company of pitiful rogues.

It seems probable that the Erbery affair occurred in a private place and not on the floor of the Lower House or during a session. The accounts in the *Journals* made no mention of Erbery trespassing upon the House. Rather, they speak of "an abuse . . . last night . . . to the disturbance of the whole howse in their quiett & rest." The statements ascribed to him were quoted from individuals, and "the Speaker is desired to take notice of & proceed therein . . . ."

Questioned on the morning after, Erbery first said he was not drunk the night before and that he remembered all he had said. Later, when called before the House, he said he had been drunk and remembered none of these words. The House, however, "doe judge the same altogether vnsatisfactory & that noe person of full age shall take advantage by drunkennes in such case . . . ." The Lower House recounted the whole sorry episode to the Upper House and asked the latter to determine proper punishment. Erbery was speedily sentenced to be tied to the apple tree before the Assembly house and publicly whipped with 39 lashes upon the bare back.

As a sequel, Erbery was required to ask the forgiveness of both houses of the Assembly and to pay a total of 624 pounds of tobacco "for fees." Most of the "fees" went to the clerks of the two houses, but they included payment of one hundred pounds of tobacco to one Fitzallen "for Erbery's tearing of his shirt."

The *Journal* of the Lower House for May 2, 1666, contains a report from what may have been the seventeenth-century equivalent of the Protocol and Entertainment committees of later days. It was an account submitted to the committee from the town ordinary, for services rendered. Parts of it were illegible in the frayed pages from which the *Archives* were published, but these items appear (all numerals being in terms of pounds of tobacco):

|                          |     |
|--------------------------|-----|
| ffor wine per gallon     | 060 |
| ffor Brandy per gallon   | 120 |
| ffor Beere per gallon    | 18  |
| ffor Rumme per gallon    | 080 |

ffor that sort of drinke called £ per gallon 16. That is to say, ffor each pownd of sugar 10 & for Lyme water ½ a pynt (which is the quantity wee iudge may bee allowed to each gallon) 4.

ffor Beuerage with sugar in it per gallon 14.

The House went on to other business for a time, perhaps being staggered by the immensity of its calculations. Later in the session it gave further consideration to the statement from the ordinary:

Vppon debate againe of the Ordinarys Account This House is willing to allow William Smyth his Account, which hee hath charged the Burgesses this Assembly for Liquors: As Wine, Rumme, Brandy, Punch, & Liminade made with Wine. But that which hee calls

Liminade without strong drinke they will allow only 25 pounds per gallon. And as to their Dyett & Lodging they will allow what they iustly may be charged with all, & noe more.

The story may be unusual not only for the listing of the variety and quantity of the refreshments, but also for the complexity of the arithmetic in computing the cost of the "Liminade."

This session in the spring of 1666 passed two bills to assure adequate publicity to its proceedings. One was to require that all laws passed at this and subsequent sessions be fairly transcribed on parchment. The sheriffs of the several counties then were directed to publish and proclaim the acts in the places that seemed to them most convenient. A levy of two thousand pounds of tobacco was made against each county for the -xpense involved.

The second bill was to require the keeping of a *Journal* in the Lower House, though this usually had been done in the past. The task was given to the Clerk of the Lower House, and he was to transcribe the *Journal* within two months after the end of a session.

George Alsop in 1666 wrote a close description of the Province which was published as "A Character of the Province of Maryland." Alsop worked for four years on the plantation of Thomas Stockett, in Baltimore County; it is thought that the purpose of his writing was to provide information about Maryland as an inducement for servants to emigrate from England. He wrote in detail of location, climate, products, Indians, religion, and life of servants. Other accounts appear in a series of letters written by Alsop to his family and friends.[11]

---

11. CLAYTON C. HALL, NARRATIVES OF EARLY MARYLAND, 1633-1684, at 335-87 (New York, 1910).

## Legislative Billingsgate

Relationships between the two houses of the General Assembly were noticeably strained during the years of the middle 1660s, beginning a history of short tempers and exasperation, frequently descending to insult, which was to agitate and excite Maryland's legislative annals for the next century. Many of the exchanges were to be openly critical and sarcastic; and if the controversies were not settled quickly, an undercurrent of bitterness would rapidly come to the surface. Even with an allowance for legislative hyperbole, the two houses often used extreme language.

A relatively mild example appeared in the *Journal* of the Upper House for April 20, 1666. As charged by the Lower House, a message from the Lower to the Upper House was returned "scrible Scrawled & obliterated." The Lower House demanded "that needful Satisfaction as in such Cases may reasonably be required." In reply, said the Upper House, the original message had not been signed by either the Speaker or the Clerk of the Lower House, and it was not deemed to be "a paper expected by them again." It seems, though, that a member of the Lower House requested return of the original paper; and the Upper House had to admit that "it is true that when a Member of that House desired the Scribled Paper It was delivered him but not as remanded by this House."

Three days later, beginning on April 23, the two houses began an exchange of messages verging upon bitterness, and raising questions about the members' sincerity and working habits. The matter at issue was a proposal to require the temporary cessation of planting tobacco, in an effort to alleviate the problems of a one-crop economy. For a time the main problem was almost lost in the welter of personalities between the two houses.

The Lower House started the argument by inquiring if the Lieutenant General and the Upper House could signify when the current session would end. It was explained that there was a very practical reason for the inquiry; it was doubtful that the ordinary could any longer provide accommodations, its provisions "being very near spent." To this the Upper House replied that "appointing" a day for the end of a session was the sole right of the Lord Proprietary. The Upper House added that it "doth desire the Lower House" to consider the extreme poverty of the Province, and that it could not believe the Lower House "in prudence" could petition for the ending of the session until the main problem of the tobacco crop had been resolved.

Later the Upper House criticised the Lower House for a "delay to the ruin of the Province," asking that it proceed to debate two bills for trade and staple commodities. This was followed by a message from the Governor and the Upper House expressing sorrow "they are obliged to tell You they have some Reason to suspect that Businesses either are not carryed on in a due Way in your House but managed by the Artifice of a few, or else" you the lower House has neither care for the Governor's interests nor respect for him. "Wherefore as You tender the preservation of Yourselves Your Wives & Familys reassume the Debate." With this the two houses gave up with criticism and came to the substance of their problem with a one-crop economy.

# Chapter 5

# A TIME OF ADJUSTMENT AND QUESTIONING

## 1669-1687

The period from the late 1660s through the early 1680s in some ways set the tone of the Legislature for the next century. The Lower House occasionally showed continuing dependence upon both the Upper House and the Governor; but mostly the Lower House was probing and sparring for improving its relative importance, assuring equal representation for the counties, protecting its prerogatives and dignity, and expanding its demands and requests to include non-legislative matters. Changes were proposed on a variety of procedural details: impeachment, approval of bills, the committee system, enacting clauses, joint committees, and the expenses of members and officers. It was a period of development, change, and rising conflicts in government.

### THE NICHOLETT EPISODE

For the session beginning on April 13 and ending on May 8, 1669, notices to make proclamation went to the sheriffs of nine counties.[1] Each county was to choose either one, two, three, or four "discreet" burgesses or delegates. Notices for the Upper House, or Council, went to Philip Calvert, Chancellor, and four others.

---

1. The latest counties organized were Dorchester and Somerset. The boundaries of the nine counties were much different from those of today. As shown on a map by Augustine Herrmann, published in 1673, the approximate boundaries were as follows:

| *Herrmann's Map* | *Present* |
|---|---|
| Anne Arundel County | Anne Arundel County |
| Baltemore County | Baltimore and Harford counties |
| Calvert County | Calvert County |
| Cecil County | Cecil and Kent counties |

The number of delegates chosen for the Lower House varied. As listed by names on the second day of the session, there were four from each of the counties of St. Mary's, Charles, Anne Arundel, and Talbot. Three were listed from Calvert County, two each from Kent and Baltimore counties, and one each from Dorchester and Somerset counties. It appeared, however, as explained below, there were additional delegates elected in Dorchester, Kent, and Somerset counties.

The session in 1669 was particularly marked by a charge of uttering seditious words, directed against Charles Nicholett, a Presbyterian minister. There is evidence that some members of the Lower House had asked the Rev. Mr. Nicholett to "stir up" the members of that body.[2]

On April 16 of that year, the Upper House was informed that two days earlier Nicholett, in his "sermon" to the Lower House, had told the members to beware of the "sin of permission." From the account in the *Journal* of the Upper

---

| | |
|---|---|
| Charles County | Charles and Prince George's counties |
| Dorchester County | Dorchester, Somerset, Wicomico, and Worcester counties |
| Kent County | Kent Island (Queen Anne's County) |
| St. Mary's County | St. Mary's County |
| Talbot County | Talbot, Queen Anne's (less Kent Island), and Caroline counties |

*See* J. LOUIS KUETHE, A GAZETTEER OF MARYLAND, A.D. 1673 (Baltimore, 1935). Reprinted from 30 MARYLAND HISTORICAL MAGAZINE 310 (1935). Note that Somerset County, established in 1666, was not separately included on Herrmann's map of 1673.

2. NEWTON D. MERENESS, MARYLAND AS A PROPRIETARY PROVINCE 197 (Baltimore, 1901, reprinted in 1968).

House, he had begged the Lower House to "Consider the poore people for the Lord will heare their cause you are not vnsensible how heavy the Tax was vpon them the last yeare therefore let me desire of you to beware of that sin of permission for it is an old saying sett a Beggar a horseback & he will Ride, soe sett a childe a horseback & he will be afrade to guide the horse, therefore let me desire you to goe on with Courage for that you have a power of yourselves & Equall to the rest of that the people & a Liberty equal to the people of England, & that if they did not make such Laws as was agreeable to their own Conscience then this was no Liberty but a seeming Liberty & had better be without it."

Phillip Calvert directed that Nichollett be summoned to appear before the Upper House, on a charge that he "hath spoken certaine seditious Words against the Government of this Province."

Nicholett, when called before the Upper House, said first that "he was desired by some of the Members to stir up the Lower House to do their Duty." He was ordered by the Lieutenant General and the entire Upper House to name the persons who had thus spoken to him. "Whereupon," according to the *Journal,* "he immediately denyed that ever he uttered the said Words to this House." He was ordered by the Upper House to go to the Lower House "and there acknowledge his Error in his late Sermon preached to the Lower House in that he medled with Businesses relating merely to the Government & there to Crave the pardon of the Lord Proprietor, the Lieutenant General & the Assembly." He also was ordered to pay to the Clerk, as "fees," 40 shillings or the same value in tobacco.

## CONTROL AND CONFLICT

There was evidence during this period of some deep-seated animosities and conflicts of the Lower House toward the Upper House and the Governor. Part of the background was that although bicameralism had then been operating for some 20 years, the Upper House and the Governor still controlled many of the day-to-day procedures of the Lower House.

Perhaps some of this was a vestige of earlier days when there had been only one house. During the years that freemen could be represented by proxy, members of the Council always held many more proxies than did the other members and could outvote them. Whatever the reason, the *Journals* for the late 1660s and early 1670s show a number of instances of the dependence of the Lower House upon decisions made in the Upper House or by the Governor.

Thus, in the spring session of 1669, two delegates from St. Mary's County complained that while they were attending session at the place appointed by the Governor, they had been "warned" to attend in another place. This they refused to do unless they had "license" from the Governor. The Upper House agreed that the members should not attend in any other place without permission from the Governor. The members then appeared before the Governor and desired leave to meet in another place, which was granted.

All sessions still were called, of course, on the decision of the Governor, and were ended in his discretion by prorogation. Similarly, as a matter of custom, at the beginning of every session the Governor would explain to the Lower House his reasons for calling the members together. Also, at the start of every session, the Governor would give to the Lower House permission to elect a Speaker; and when the choice was made, it would be referred back to the Governor for his approval. All this occurred on schedule for the session of March 27-April 19, 1671. After it was

110

accomplished, "the Upper House of Assembly were pleased upon the humble desire and Ernest Request of the Lower House to admitt Robert Cerville their Clerk who being tendered the oath ... was accordingly sworn." Finally, the oath to the Clerk specified that "You will faithfully serve the Right honourable the Lord Proprietary of this Province in the Office of Clerk of the Lower House . . . ."

Another instance of executive domination, and to modern sensibilities an extreme one, came on March 28, 1671. The Lower House inquired of the Upper House about a number of delegates who had not appeared for the session and who also had not been summoned by writ as had all the others. The reply from the Upper House was that "the true Reason why all persons elected in Kent, Dorchester and Somersett Countys were not by particular Writts Summoned to appear at this Assembly was because the respective Sherriffs of the said Countys at the time when they made their respective Returns desired the Governour in the name of the respective Countys not to charge their poore and new erected Countys with more Delegates than formerly they used to have." The Lower House gave no public sign of being disturbed at the arbitrary action of the sheriffs and the Governor in thus limiting the size of the county delegations, unless it was indulging in a not-so-subtle piece of irony in commenting that it "gratefully owned the Governours Care and Affection to them shewn in that particular."

The Lower House deferred to the Upper in a request dated March 30, 1671, when it inquired what penalty should be imposed upon a number of members of the Lower House who voluntarily had absented themselves from its proceedings.

There were times, also, when the Lower House deferred to the Upper House or to the Governor on matters which a modern legislative body would meet directly by introducing and considering remedial legislation. Thus, at the session in May and June, 1674, the *Journal* notes a debate in the Lower

House about the unsatisfactory operation of ordinaries throughout the Province. The only action of the Lower House, however, was to send a message to the Governor, "in whom the Sole Power for graunting licenses is . . . ," to ask the Governor's pleasure as to having the House draft a bill to cure the problems.

On this matter, the suggestion to the Governor was that any person licensed to keep an ordinary should give bond with good sureties that he would keep "foure good ffeather beds for the Entertainment of Customers or four good flock beds besides his own for his Private use & in any place where the County Court is kept Eight ffeather or fflock beds at the least and ffurniture Suitable & that they shall Suffer noe drinking or gaming upon the Sabboth day & that they Shall Act nothing against the Lawes of England or this Province touching ordinary Keepers Jnneholders Alehouse Keepers or Keepers of Tipling houses." The Governor's reply was that he would see that the conditions and reservations desired by the House would be observed.

Similarly, on May 31, 1674, the Lower House sent a message to the Governor and the Upper House asking an "abridgement" of the long and tedious procedures of the Chancery Court; and on May 27, 1674, the Lower House sent a message to the Governor about the need for building a combined State House, prison, and Secretary's office.

Finally, as another piece of triviality that must have been irksome to the Lower House, it made a request to the Upper House on April 5, 1671, "that the Lower House have a Copy of the List of Acts now in force and the Book of Laws." On the next day, the Upper House sent a copy of the "Book of Laws" to the Lower House.

There were other times, however, when the Lower House would assert its prerogatives. An instance came on May 6, 1669, when the Upper House sent a messenger to the Lower House "to desire a Conference with them after dinner upon all the Bills sent from either House which are not yet passed to avoid unnecessary Expence of Time in sending messages." The Lower House acceded to the request, but it carefully set up a condition that it would not confer "about any Bill already quashed & laid aside in this House." Just the day before, on May 5, another request for a conference with the Upper House brought the sharp reply that it was "against the Privileges of their house to give their reasons in the Upper House for their disassent to any Bill."

## THE IMPEACHMENT OF MAJOR THOMAS TRUMAN

A particular controversy between the two Houses occurred during the session of May and June, 1676, involving charges against Major Thomas Truman, a member of the Council. The Houses were widely split on the question of guilt and the proper punishment.

The exact degree and sequence of the offense were uncertain. About the only part of the affair which was clear beyond question was that Major Truman, in charge of a Maryland contingent against Indians, and in collaboration with a similar group from Virginia, had participated in and was largely responsible for the killing of several supposedly friendly Indians.

The expedition was formed after a number of settlers on the frontier were killed by marauding Indians. There was suspicion that the Susquehannocks were involved, but they had a history of friendliness with Maryland and insisted that a party of Senecas was responsible. Some of the Susquehannocks, in fact, accompanied the punitive force to help locate the Senecas; and it was said in the charge against him that Major Truman promised the Susquehannocks no harm would come to them. Unfortunately, at this point additional settlers were found murdered, and there was a demand among the avenging party for quick retribution. Five of the Susquehannocks who accompanied the expedition were bound and executed.

113

The Lower House brought impeachment proceedings against Major Truman. The House charged that the Major "Comitted divers and Sundry Enormous Crimes and Offences To the Dishonor of almighty God against the law of Nations" and contrary to the instructions of the Proprietary. Three charges were listed against him, first of which was that after giving assurances for the safety of the Susquehannocks, he caused five of them to be murdered.

The impeachment was sent to the Upper House. After a hearing at which Major Truman admitted this much of the facts but pleaded extenuating and mitigating circumstances, the Upper House declared him guilty of the first charge and asked the Lower House to prepare a bill of attainder against him. Although the Lower House originally had brought the impeachment, its recommendation for punishment was much milder than the Upper House thought proper; the House bill did not call for the death penalty against the Major and seemed to exact only a pecuniary punishment.

This "soe Slender and Sleight a punnishment being noe more then what Crimes of a more Inferiour nature might have deserved," replied the Upper House in criticism, would not satisfy their Indian neighbors or clear the honor of the Province. It was termed "greatly dishonourable, as well as unsafe and dangerous To lay any fine in Such cases and Where Such horrid Crimes haue been Comitted." The Lower House persisted, however, citing the "Unanimous Consent of the Virginians and the generall Impetuosity of the Whole feild as well Marylanders as Virginians upon the Sight of the Christians murdered." The Upper House would not accept the bill passed in the Lower House: "The bill is onely an Attainder in the title not in the bodie of the Act . . . ." The Upper House, it concluded, "dare not and therefore Resolve not to proceed upon an act which onely bears the title of an act of Attainder."

There the matter rested; Major Truman was dismissed from the Council but otherwise escaped punishment; he was later to become a member of the Lower House.

A problem of procedure in impeachment cases came before the two houses at the April-May session of 1669, although certainly there were other factors which lay behind the facade of jurisdiction. In the Lower House, one Robert Morris, a non-member, filed impeachment proceedings against Delegate John Morecroft. An attorney in private life, Morecroft was appearing as such in a case in the Provincial Court; and the charge against him involved his fees for the case. When the matter came before the Upper House, it criticised the action of the Lower House on jurisdictional points.

First, said the Upper House, when the impeachment was voted by the Lower House, it should have been directed to the Upper House and not to the Speaker of the Lower House. Secondly, it said, "a single Person who is no Member of this Province & no ways Employed by the Commons of Maryland" may not prefer an impeachment in either house. Finally, and on the substance of the impeachment, the Upper House voted that as there was no law controlling attorneys' fees, Morecroft could not have been at fault on this score. Almost as an afterthought, the Upper House had an additional comment on an item which was hardly of the importance of impeachment and had not theretofore been mentioned in the *Journal:* "It is no Crime to alledge Wild Street to be in the City of St. Mary's since if it be illegally done he the said Morris may demurr or move in Arrest of Judgment or by Writt of Error."

## "GRIEVANCES" OF THE LOWER HOUSE

The persistent sparring between the two houses differed in one respect from the competition and occasional ill-feeling of later centuries. In the seventeenth century it was not simply Lower House versus Upper House, but more often Lower House versus Upper House and the Governor. He was a part of the Council, which served also as the Upper House. The Governor and the Upper House as a unit, and the Lower House by itself, represented the kind of economic and social division which had led to the original distinction, centuries earlier, between the House of Lords and the House of Commons in the English Parliament.

A general source of irritation to the Lower House was the frequency with which it was the Governor who seemed to be making the decisions. Thus, near the end of the session of April-May, 1669, the Chancellor informed the Upper House it was the Lieutenant General's "pleasure" that it should expedite its business in order that the session might be ended within a few days, and also that he wished the Upper House to notify the Lower House "of his Pleasure . . . ." The Upper House then proceeded with its work, "in obedience to the Command of the Lieutenant General for expediting of Business." Similarly, near the end of the session, in May and June of 1676, the Lieutenant General gave notice to both houses that he "purposeth" to end the session two days later.

A particularly bitter confrontation of Lower House versus Upper House and Governor occurred at the April-May session of 1669. Both groups initially took positions so strong and incompatible as not to admit of solution. The long exchange of messages gradually pointed to a settlement; and if the mutual concessions were not always logical, they showed at least an early example of the truism so popular in later centuries, that "politics is the art of compromise."

The action started on April 19, 1669, when the Lower House requested the Governor to hold a conference of the

116

two houses. The conference then appointed a joint committee to consider a set of grievances coming from the Lower House. They were seven in number, as follows:

1. That there is no Person authorized by the Lord Proprietor to Confirm our Laws

2. That it appears by the Body of Laws that the Lord Proprietary did assent to these General Laws now disassented to by the Lieutenant General saying his Lordship doth will those to be Laws, & so subscribed his name vide the Book of Laws & therefore the same ought not to be disassented to without the Consent of this House

3. The raising of the last years Levys was against the Lord Proprietor's Charter the Laws of the Province & without the Consent of the Freemen of this Province

4. That these Privileged Attorneys are one of the Grand Grievances of the Country

5. The Sherriffs taking away Merchants and other Inhabitants Tobaccos upon Pretence of seisure for publick Debts

6. That Officers are Erected which do take fees exceeding & contrary to the Acts of Assembly

7. That vexatious Informers is another publick Grievance.

The answer of the Committee of the Upper House was submitted on April 21, 1669. It was a long document, addressed individually to each of the seven grievances and covering nearly five pages in the *Journal.* The general reaction of the Upper House was to criticize and disagree with the statement of grievances from the Lower House.

On the first point, that there was no person authorized by the Lord Proprietary to confirm the laws, the reply was that he was held to the principles in his patent from the king; if he tried to do otherwise he would forfeit the patent, and it was a power which should be reserved to the Lord Proprietary.

Secondly, on the grievance that the Governor assented to the laws and there should not have been a dissent by the

Proprietary without the approval of the Lower House, the answer was that an assent from the Governor was only to the extent he was empowered to assent, and that no Governor by his assent could bind the Lord Proprietary.

Thirdly, as to raising the prior year's levy without the consent of the Lower House, the reply from the Upper House was that the Lord Proprietary did only what he was bound to do under the Charter, to defend the people of the Province. Here the Upper House added an extra barb, saying that the Lower House had been offered an account of the previous year's levy, and that the time of the Lower House "had been much better spent in auditing the Account of the Province than at Girding at the Lord Proprietor's Rights, of which he makes no Use but for the Preservation of the People."

The fourth grievance from the Lower House was that "Privileged Attorneys" are a "Grand Grievance." Here the reply from the Upper House was that these were attorneys of ability, sworn to be faithful and diligent in their work, and necessary for the people. "We cannot but wonder," said the Upper House, that such attorneys should be called a grievance.

On the fifth point, as to sheriffs wrongly executing against merchants and other inhabitants by seizing their tobacco, the Upper House was conciliatory. Any such action would be punishable, it was explained; and the Upper House said it would join in enacting a law declaring what was properly a public debt subject to execution.

Next, the Lower House had stated a grievance that new offices had been created, leading to excessive fees. The Upper House said it did not know of any such offices, but if this had been done, it was only within the power of the Lord Proprietary.

Finally, on the seventh complaint, that "vexatious informers" were a public grievance, the answer was that informers had never been authorized in the Province, and that the revealing of mutinous and seditious speeches should not be so classed. The term "informer," it was added, should be applied only to one receiving an informer's fee.

Evidently feeling that this much of its reply had been restrained, the Upper House ended on a harsh note. "We cannot but exhort you," it wrote to the committee of the House, "to desire the Lower House that sent You to proceed to the publick Affairs of the Province." As for the vote of the Lower House that it would not undertake any public business while the grievances were pending, the Upper House suggested a test vote be taken in the Lower House; and that if the earlier decision was upheld, the session of the Assembly should be ended.

From that point on, the attitudes of both houses hardened. On the next day, April 23, 1669, the Upper House called upon the Lower House "to raze the mutinous & seditious Votes contained in the paper Entitled The Public Grievances ... Before which is done this House is Resolved to treat with them no further It being adjudged in this House that it is an Arraignment of the Lord Proprietor the Governor & Council."

The reply of the Lower House was equally swift and blunt. The message received from the Upper House, it said, had been voted in the Lower House "to tend very much to the dishonour & breach of Privileges of this House." The seven grievances, it was added, were not mutinous or seditious and ought not be razed from the *Journal* of the Lower House.

On the next morning, April 29, 1669, the Upper House responded. If its language seemed to be an appeal to reason, its conclusion was no less blunt. The Upper House asked the Lower to join in a conference between the two, so that "the Chancellour do remonstrate unto them the ruin that is coming upon these rash Proceedings of theirs

1. By leaving the Province without Law

119

2. The People discontented & jealous that their just
   Libertys are denyed them, when in truth We only
   vindicate that just power in my Lord which the King
   hath given him by his Charter & is no way
   communicable to the people
3. The Province much in debt & particular Persons much
   damaged . . .
4. The hinderance of the raising this Assembly's
   Charges
5. The hinderance of Curbing the Indians."

The Upper House continued that the Lower should not
deem its privileges ran parallel to those of the House of
Commons in the Parliament of England. The Lower House,
it was said, "have no power to meet but by Virtue of my
Lords Charter; for if no Charter there is no Assembly, No
Assembly no Privileges." The power of the Lower House, it
was concluded, "is but like the common Council of the City
of London which if they act Contrary or to the overthrow of
the Charter of the City run into Sedition & the Persons
Questionable."

So, said the Upper House in summation, if the Lower "do
not raze those seditious Votes contained in the paper stiled
the seven Grievances by the Vote 23 April together with that
Vote the Governour is resolved to dissolve this Assembly on
Monday Morning."

This message from the Upper House was delivered on a
Saturday afternoon, and the Upper House then attempted to
get the Lower into a conference on that very day. The
Speaker of the Lower House said that some of his members
were absent, and that he would not schedule a conference
before Monday morning. When further pressed, the Speaker
said he could not even receive any further messages until
Monday morning. The conference finally was held on
Monday afternoon.

On that day, April 26, the Upper House made clear that its
patience had been strained by having to await Monday

morning, and then Monday afternoon, for the conference. Continuing, "We desire a good Correspondence & therefore We will put no sinister Interpretation upon your Actions . . . . if You be the men the Countys that sent You imagined You were at your Election viz prudent & seeking the common Good, you will use no further delays."

The Upper House then somewhat softened its stance. If, it said, the Lower House would modify the statement of the first three grievances, so that the Lord Proprietor's "rights" were not styled as "grievances," the Upper House would join the Lower "in a Petition of Grace and Favour (not of Right) to his Lordship" in an effort to reach a settlement on the other matters.

Next it was the Lower House which became more conciliatory, though not before it indulged in some horrendous rhetoric and manifest sarcasm:

> . . . [W]e are sorry exceeding Sorry that we are driven to Say that your Answer & Objections to the paper Entituled the publick Grievances are not Satisfactory or that by the refulgent Lustre of the Eradiations of Reason that shine & dart forth from them the weak & dim Eye of our Understandings is dazled & struck into Obscurity. We are sensible of your great Condescension in receding from former Votes & Commands & yet We would desire You to believe that we did not design by Obstinacy & Refractoryness to draw You to the same God forbid that We should stile his Lordships Rights Grievances, As to that we shall only say that We verily believe his Lordship out of his abundant Grace and Goodness will not exercise any of his just Rights & royal Jurisdictions to the Aggrievance & Oppression of the good people of his Province when he shall be given to Understand that any of them in the manner wherein now Exercised are indeed so; God forbid that We should upon meer Niceties Criticisms and formalitys of Words be found to be Accountable to God and the Country for the ill Success of this meeting . . . .

121

After thus giving vent to its feelings, the Lower House proceeded to suggest this compromise, that "We shall be willing to have our Journal Contradicted, expunged, obliterated, burnt, anything, and to have our Grievances appear in any form or dress of words most pleasing to yourselves if We might be assured that the Weight & pressure of them under which the Country groans & cryes might be removed."

"We are very glad," said the Upper House in its reply, "to see the Lower House inclinable to wave their former Proceedings." Specifically, without losing sight of its main contentions, the Upper House desired the Lower to take from its *Journal* the votes by which the first three grievances had been submitted, "together with the subsequent Votes that asserted these three Things to be Grievances This We Conceive to be your promise in the paper delivered Us." The Upper House then repeated its offer to use a joint committee to draw up legislation "to protect the people in their Lives & Estates in Case of sedition Tumults or Invasion whither foreign or domestick, which is all We desire .... Upon your Complyance herewith We doubt not of a right Understanding between the two Houses which is We heartily wish & desire."

The Lower House still would not completely yield. Its return message accepted the offer of the Upper House by joint action to consider the "pressures and Grievances by this House to them presented ... and when these Pressures are removed We will raze our Journal as by the Upper House is desired."

This last clause, the Upper House immediately complained, it "doth not understand and therefore desires the Lower House to explain it." In an equally short return message, the Lower House explained that "the Sense of this House is that till our Pressures are really redressed We cannot raze our Journal."

The rejoinder of the Upper House was to "require" the Lower House to come into the Upper House in order to know the Governor's further pleasure. The Lower House did not reply. The Governor then sent a summons to the Lower House to come into the Upper House. The Lower House acceded, but requested three hours' time "to Consider of the order sent to them this day by the Upper House, Which was Allowed."

Continuing, as related in the *Journal* of the Upper House, "Then came the Speaker and said that he had in Charge from the whole Lower House to deliver to this House, that it was the vote of the whole House that they were all Grievances and the major part of the House did Vote that they ought not to be razed." The Speaker and the other members of the Lower House who had accompanied him "had two Hours time given them to Consider." After this interval, the Upper House again sent one of its members to inquire if the Lower House had razed the first three articles of the grievances.

Finally, on April 27, 1669, eight days after the controversy began, the Lower House notified the Upper it had ordered that "the three first Articles contained in a paper Styled the publick Grievances of this Province . . . and all Votes passed in this House touching the same be Oblitterated in the Journal of this House." As one final quid pro quo, the Lower House in this message asked the Upper to obliterate in its own *Journal* the words "mutinous and seditious," which earlier had been applied to the Lower House. In final settlement of the protracted issue, the Upper House declared itself satisfied with the action of the Lower and ordered "that those Words Mutinous & seditious shall not be engrossed in our Journall."

The irony of the long episode is that three centuries later the whole record still appears in both *Journals.* Nothing has been obliterated, but whatever side pressures were applied to the Lower House never were recorded for posterity.

## Prerogatives of the Lower House

There was a short-lived controversy between the two houses during the October-November session of 1682, as a by-product of a larger dispute over a bill for electing and summoning delegates. In one of its messages to the Lower House, the Upper House suggested that the Lord Proprietor had an "undoubted" right to settle the matter and expressed the hope he would give the two houses a directive for a bill, "to be passed by him with the Consent of the Two houses (who Legally Represent the Freemen of this Province) into a Perpetuall Act."

The Lower House seized upon the parenthetical phrase about the "two" houses representing the freemen of the Province. The offending words were put to a formal vote in the Lower House, and it was resolved without dissent "that the Deputies and Delegates Chosen by the Freemen of this Province in a General Assembly are the only Representative Body of the Freemen of this Province." To drive home the point more forcefully, the Lower House also resolved "that the Publick ought not to be Charged or bear the Charges or Expences of the Members of the Upper house." The Upper House backed away from a confrontation in this instance, sending a message to the Lower House on November 10, 1682, that "This house do say that they intended not anything by those Words in their Message ... further then that they are a part of the Body Politick of this Province without whose Assent no Laws can pass and do now Vote accordingly."

Another dispute between the two houses came at the session of August-September, 1681. It involved Captain John Coode, who was an elected member of the Lower House and had been admitted to serve when the session began.

On August 18, during that session, the Upper House by message informed the Lower that Captain Coode then was charged with mutinous and seditious practices and with an attempted breach of the peace and subversion of the government. The Captain had indeed taken an active part in an attempted revolt, but he had not yet been brought to trial. The Upper House, upon the instigation of the Lord Proprietary, called upon the Lower House not to treat Captain Coode as a member until he had "purged" himself of the charges.

The Lower House immediately promised to give consideration to the message, and to provide such satisfaction as it could, "not infringing the Rights and Priviledges of this house."

A day later a more detailed message was sent from the Lower to the Upper House. It pointed out that Captain Coode had presented himself for a seat in the Lower House before it had any reason to deny him admission. Further, the charges against him were only accusations at the moment, and although of heinous matters, were too general for the Lower House to find that the Captain had incapacitated himself for membership. So, although the Lower House said it wanted to comply with the Lord Proprietor in all things, it wished to know "wherein or by what Act or Means Our said Member hath Disabled or rendered himself Incapable of having his Place in this house."

The Upper House promptly repeated its complaint, saying again that Captain Coode should not sit in the Lower House until he had purged himself of the charges. Also, said the Upper House, the particular acts comprising the breach of the peace should not be divulged until the time of trial.

The Lower House next reported, on August 26, 1681, that it had made a "diligent search" for records and authorities to indicate its rights and privileges in this case. It had found, it said, that only felony, treason, and refusing to give security for breach of the peace "Can Divest any Member of this House as a Member thereof, and not a bare breach of the Peace, much Less an Accusation only of the Breach of the Peace . . . ."

The Upper House, "by his Lordships Order," then listed in general terms the words and actions of Captain Coode of which it complained, hoping that "So Scandalous a Person and so great a Disturber" would not be accounted a member of the Lower House until cleared by the Provincial Court.[3] A day later, on August 27, the Upper House again pressed the matter, this time threatening that until it had "satisfaction" from the Lower House "this house think not Convenient to Ioin with the Lower house in any Business."

To this was added, in the *Journal* of the Upper House and in the message to the Lower House, the substance of a deposition made by William Calvert, Chancellor, concerning incidents while he and Captain Coode were on Lord Baltimore's yacht on St. Mary's River. As the *Journal* candidly discloses, the Captain had told the Chancellor that "he cared not a fart for him the said William Calvert . . . that he cared not a Turd for the Chancellor nor the Governor neither, No (he Swore by God) nor for God Almighty Neither . . . ."

The Lower House remained firm, however, not finding the Captain "disabled" and "thereby have Voted him a Place in this house." The Lower House added the hope that the Upper House and Lord Baltimore would be satisfied with the reasons already expressed "and rest assured he shall not do his Lordship any Disservice in this house So that we hope his Admission may not impede the Publick Business."

Again the Upper House repeated its arguments, desiring the Lower House "to give his Lordship Satisfaction in that

---

3. "Few disturbers of government can match his record." He was "a perennial malcontent." *See* David W. Jordan, *John Coode, Perennial Rebel,* 70 MARYLAND HISTORICAL MAGAZINE 1-28 (1975).

For a biographical sketch of Captain John Coode, *see* LOIS GREEN CARR AND DAVID WILLIAM JORDAN, MARYLAND'S REVOLUTION OF GOVERNMENT, 1689-1692, at 245-48 (Ithaca, 1974).

Particular." The affair of Captain John Coode and his membership in the Lower House seemed to subside on this inconclusive ending. The Captain was to appear again in Maryland's history.

During the session of October-November, 1682, even though the point had been covered in the rules several decades earlier, the House by separate order voted that no member would be admitted with his hat on, at any time during the sitting of the House.[4]

## LAWS EFFECTIVE FOR THREE YEARS

The two houses clashed at the November session in 1681 about the wording and effect of some of the laws and the custom of passing bills to be effective only for three years, necessitating their frequent review and renewal.

On November 7, during that session, the Upper House asked for a conference with the Lower concerning "some Doubtful words in some Acts to this Sense that there are now no perpetuall Acts but that all the Laws of this Province are Temporary." The Lower House professed that its members were "ignorant of any discourses of that Nature that are held by the Members of this House." Nevertheless, the Upper House insisted upon a conference, "lett the reason be what it will."

When the conferees met, there was mention of an act of 1678 for reviving and confirming certain laws, and that the same list again was confirmed in 1681. A 3-page list of

---

4. When the Governor made his address to the Assembly at the end of the session in April, 1684, he complained that "severall of the Lower house have this Sessions rudely presumed to come before" him "in his upper house with their hats on . . . ." He hoped they would act with more modesty and better manners thereafter, for he "would not any longer endure the same." There has been speculation the Governor's remarks were directed at Quakers.

temporary acts was submitted. The Upper House tartly commented that the list had been carelessly prepared and contained some acts which were not temporary. The Lower House was loathe to take any time for verifying the list, saying that the session was about to end and that the whole matter could go over to another session. The Lower House even engaged that it would not "take advantage of any Mistakes or Errors arising and Proceeding from over hasty passing of the former Bills of Revival."

The Upper House still argued, saying that laws which concern "Our Persons and the Property of Our Estates" should have consideration; and again the Lower House said that the session was too far advanced for any more work on temporary acts. "This house," it said, "cannot Comprehend why the Upper House presses the Matter." Nevertheless, the Upper House prevailed upon the Governor to continue the session for another day; and at the end acts were passed both for reviving temporary laws and for repealing other laws.

The matter of deciding what laws were or were not in effect at a given time was becoming difficult. Although the volume of legislation was modest in comparison with later centuries, there was nothing like a code or compilation in the modern sense. Over the years the cumulative total became confusing. The situation was not helped by the clause, usually appended to the laws, that they were to remain in effect for three years or until the end of the next following General Assembly, whichever first occurred; there was no hint of permanence in the original enactment.

A long enactment in the May-June session of 1676 attempted a review of everything enacted theretofore. Citing the "many great mischiefes Errors & inconveniencyes . . . by the many Errors that are Comitted in the severall Courts & by the severall people within this Province in not knowing what Lawes are in effect & unrepealed & by the multiplicity of Lawes to one and the same thing which many tymes interferr one with another," the Assembly went on to list those repealed and those still in effect.

The act of 1676 devotes nearly six pages in the *Archives* to a summary of the repealers, with one or two lines for each act. They were on a great variety of subjects and covered the period from 1640 to 1674. They concerned such matters as servants' clothes, court days, tobacco hogsheads, probate, servants who have bastards, sowing English grain, runaways, hog stealers, pillories, limiting servants' times, appointing a "Publick Notary," payment of debt, coroners' fees, and many others.

The short titles of the acts declared ratified and confirmed covered nearly four pages in the *Archives*. Their subjects included judicature, pagans, church liberties, Indians, an oath of fidelity to the Lord Proprietary, speedy payment of debts, deserted plantations, setting up a mint, encouraging the building of windmills, encouraging the importation of Negroes and slaves, quieting possession of land, conveyances, court days, and many others.

## UNCERTAINTIES OF JURISDICTION

The sharp differences between the Upper House and the Lower House on the matters of grievances and of temporary laws were supplemented by frequent disagreements on smaller problems, all illustrating the lack of precedents and the uncertainties of jurisdiction.

Thus, the Upper House took umbrage during the August-September session of 1681, when informed that a member of the Lower House was inquiring about the accounts of those members of the Upper House "that Lodge and Dyett" at Mr. Van Sweringen's home. This was termed "an Affront to the Upper house and Breach of their Priviledge." Upon investigation, it appeared that the member from the Lower House made some slighting remarks about the Upper House and had been told by an officer of the Province that the expenses were inordinate. Van Sweringen refused any request for information.

The Lower House made inquiry at the May-June session in 1676 about the procedure of the Lord Proprietor in approving bills passed by the Legislature. The request in effect was that the Lord Proprietor give an advance indication whether he would approve a pending bill. To this the Upper House responded that it would be "unseasonable" to request His Lordship to consent to laws in general before he received a law in particular. Here the Upper House also distinguished between the "temporary" and the "perpetual" laws. The temporary ones, it opined, could be approved by the Lord Proprietor as "probationers," with less consideration than for long-term laws. Laws designed to be perpetual, stressed the Upper House, must be studied by counsel learned in the laws of England.

Five years later, during the August-September session of 1681, the Lower House presented a petition to the Lord Proprietor on another phase of his approval of acts passed by the Legislature. This one was on the "Inconveniencies" that might happen if the Lord Proprietor were not in the Province and had not empowered anyone in his absence to give a "full and Absolute Consent to Such Laws as may then be enacted." In an extra effort to be helpful, the Lower House sent along with the petition a draft copy of "one Good and Equitable Bill" to provide for the confirmation of acts under these circumstances. However, rather than treat the problem by legislation, the Lord Proprietor in a message sent to the Upper House said that if he were in residence he would signify his assent or dissent to all acts before the conclusion of the session; and that if he were out of the Province he would "promise and engage" that within 18 months after the passing of any laws his action thereon would be published in the Province.

A seemingly trivial problem of legislative procedure runs through several pages of the *Journal* for the August-September session of 1681. It concerned messages from the Lower House to the Upper, and the manner of indicating to the Lower House the concurrence of the Upper. The Lower House wanted the note of concurrence written on the back of the original message, with the original then returned to the Lower House. The Upper House wanted to keep the original for its own *Journal* files.

After discussion and disagreement about what had been the "common custom" in the exchange of messages, the Upper House somewhat grudgingly complied with the request to return the original copy to the Lower House, with the concurrence of the Upper on the reverse side; but with the condition that the Lower House then would return the entire paper for the *Journal* files of the Upper House. There was the inevitable further message from the Lower House, to which the Upper House replied with some annoyance that it seemed "altogether Needless to have any other Paper Messages of this Nature from either House."

Even following this admonition, the Lower House sent still another message, though "heartily desiring an End to those Debates," to "present the former Message in the Same Words not knowing how to Change them into more respectful Tearms." This time the Lower House attempted to enlist the support of the Lord Proprietor. Both houses seemed finally to tire of this topic of less-than-profound impact.

One other small jurisdictional question came up at the session of August-September, 1681. It was raised in a message of the Upper House to the Lower on September 6, saying that "a Law made by the Consent of both houses and Assented to by his Lordship cannot be repealed but by the consent of both houses." The Lower House stated its agreement; but perhaps because in the context there was

131

mention of only one part of an act, the Lower House asked for assurances that the acts passed at the prior session could not be repealed or abrogated without the consent of the Lower House. To this, on September 12, the baffled Upper House could only respond that it "understands not" the meaning of the Lower House.

## Procedure and Protocol

Aside from the problems of controversy between the two houses, in the 1660s, 1670s, and 1680s, there were other matters of procedure, protocol, and punishment as the legislative processes developed.

Questions persisted about the members and the membership in the Lower House. On October 24, 1678, the Lower House propounded a series of questions about its possible membership, including whether a sheriff, the Attorney General, or any member of the Council might sit as a member of the Lower House. No one provided an answer to the questions.

The Lower House raised a more immediate question about membership during the August-September session of 1681. It sent a petition to the Lord Proprietor on August 19, stating that when it had convened on August 16 there were 13 vacancies in its membership, and that on August 17 there still were 12 vacancies. Eight of the absentees were deceased, one was on the Council, two were sheriffs and not eligible for the House, and one was out of the Province. The specific request of the Lower House was that its Speaker be empowered to issue warrants to fill the vacancies; the current practice was for the writs to be issued by the Clerk of the Province, on behalf of the Lord Proprietor.

Thence ensued another long exchange of messages. The Lord Proprietor asked first whether the House (with its vacancies) deemed it could proceed with its business, to

132

which the House answered in the affirmative. Next, the Lord Proprietor, the Lower House, and the Upper House met in a joint conference to discuss the petition.

Part of the effort on the part of the Lower House was to assure the presence of four delegates from each county. There had been occasions when four were elected and only two summoned by writ to attend. Also, in 1681, the Lord Proprietor had declared by ordinance that there should be only two delegates for each county. On this point, the Lord Proprietor answered that the law calling for four delegates already had been "disassented to."

On the possibility of permitting the Speaker of the Lower House to send out the writs of election to fill vacancies, there was much discussion about whether this was a prerogative of the Commons in England. However, the Lord Proprietor agreed to instruct the Secretary of the Province to issue writs to fill the present vacancies, "Provided the Lower house will acknowledge itt as a favour from his Lordship so doing and will enter the Same as So in their *Journal.*"

This did not entirely end the controversy. The Lower House continued to press its claim for four delegates from each county and the "undoubted Priviledge" of the Speaker to issue writs of election to fill vacancies in the Lower House. The Lord Proprietor replied that he could not but "wonder" that the Lower House assumed to itself a power that was new to him and unheard of in this Province. He called upon the House to resume its business, particularly with regard to serious problems with the Indians.

With this the Lower House compromised, promising to proceed with its business if the Lord Proprietor would issue the writs of election. As a parting shot, the House sent another long message to expound the justice of its cause, being "grieved" that the Lord Proprietor should "wonder" otherwise; and as a matter of course, to this final message there was another rejoinder from the Upper House.

At the session in October-November, 1682, the Lower House had a temporary problem of decorum. A member of the Upper House was refused admission in the Lower because he was wearing his sword. The blow was softened somewhat by the Speaker, who met the offender at the door and there accepted the message being delivered.

The practice of petitioning the Assembly was much in vogue, with some of the petitions being on non-legislative problems. There were occasions, too, when petitions were referred by the Upper House for the consideration of the Lower. By the 1690s the House created a "Comittee on Agreivances" to give initial study to the petitions.

The general committee system was becoming well established, with mention in the Lower House of a Committee on Laws, a Committee of Accounts, and special committees for particular purposes. Upon occasion the Lower House used a committee of the whole House, without so naming it. Infrequently, both houses met together as a sort of super committee of the whole, calling this the "Grand Committee" of the two houses. When the Upper House made a proposal for this committee to meet on November 24, 1688, it rhapsodized "That so Generally a Good as is thereby Designed may not dye by being Stifled for want of Air to give it Life." Use of conference committees was frequent. Here the Upper House had a problem; having already joined with the Lower House in two conference committees, it said in a message on April 15, 1684, it did not have enough unassigned members remaining to set up any other committees. It was not unusual for either house to give instructions to its conferees.

The use of joint committees quickly brought on one foreseeable problem: which house should appoint a clerk to serve the joint committee? Such a controversy arose at the November-December session in 1688, and for several pages in the *Journal* the two houses carried on a spirited argument.

All of it was couched in language based upon the highest principle; if it was simply an early struggle about "who gets the job," this was not publicly revealed. "It cannot be unknown to the Upper house," said a message from the Lower House, "That all Committee Clerks hath always been Appointed by this house or Chosen by Vote in the Committee." In equally dignified mien, the Upper House was "surprized" to see such "Groundless heats" and said that for joint committees the chairman had always appointed the clerk. Back came the Lower House, retorting that it had already appointed the clerk and that he was the most capable person to serve in that place; and that the "incapacity" of this man "would retard the Bysiness of this Assembly." The Upper House promptly declared the committee to be unlawful, "and their reputed Clerk is hereby Declared no Clerk of any Lawfully Committee of accounts." The Lower House replied; and the Upper House counter-replied; each had its own series of four propositions to solve the dilemma. Finally, as ultimately always happened in these protracted controversies, they reached a rough agreement. The Lower House suggested that the choice of the clerk be left to the chairman and members of the committee. The Upper House agreed (this was what actually already had happened), and it added the assurance that "this house do (as they always did) abhorr the very thoughts of Division."

Enacting clauses on acts during this period were "The Delegates of this present Generall Assembly doe humbly pray That itt may be Enacted and Bee itt Enacted by the Right Honorable the Lord Proprietary by and with the advice and consent of the upper and lower houses of this present Generall Assembly and the Authority of the same." A few years later, after Maryland had become a royal colony, the enacting language was changed. One of the bills in 1692 used this form: "The Governor Council and Delegates of this present Generall Assembly do humbly pray that it may be

135

Enacted, and be it Enacted by the King and Queens most Excellent Majesties by and with the advice and consent of this present Generall Assembly and the Authority of the same."

Amendments were indicated as such in the *Journals*. One usage at the time was to underscore a word added by amendment, adding "so that then it will be thus Viz," repeating the amendment within its context. The Lord Proprietor did not hesitate to have inserted in the *Journal* his own suggestions for amendment.

The original rule of the late 1630s, "that the house shall meet every day at eight of the clock in the morning," was being modified later. Many of the daily sessions were called to convene at either nine or ten o'clock. Occasionally, however, daily sessions in the 1680s and 1690s were being called for seven o'clock in the morning. At one time in May of 1692, when the Upper House was scheduling its meeting for seven o'clock, there was a pointed reminder of going to prayers at six o'clock. More often, there was a break for prayers in mid-morning, at ten o'clock.

The rules still called for requiring a bill to have three readings for passage; one day was to intervene between any two readings, except by consent of the House. The *Journals* were not always clear whether this rule was observed; sometimes the wording could indicate three readings in rapid succession. There was no requirement for a roll call on the final reading, and frequently a bill was marked as passing by the early equivalent of "without objection," *"nemine contradicente."*

Acts were signed in the presence of both houses and the Governor (or Lord Proprietor, if he were in the Province). As the process was described in the *Journal* of the Upper House for October 19, 1671, "Then the Lower House with their Speaker came into this house with all the Laws made this Assembly The Title whereof being read in the Presence of both houses His Excellency signed the Laws with this Indorsment His Lordship willeth these be Laws."

The task of furnishing copies of the laws to interested persons and officials throughout the Province continued to be troublesome. An act of the May-June session of 1676 instructed each county clerk to "transcribe & fairely write out in a booke" all the laws in force at the end of that session. In 1684 both houses petitioned the Lord Proprietor about his having had the laws transcribed since the last session; both houses said they had "perused" the laws, but their problem was to ask that he have engrossed in a separate book some omissions and errors in what he had done.

All the acts passed in 1678 received a delayed veto. The vetoes were not disclosed until April 26, 1684, when at a joint session of both houses announcement was made of the veto of all bills passed six years earlier. The Proprietary had been away from St. Mary's when the bills were passed in 1678, and they had been approved by his deputy, Thomas Notley. When the announcement was made by the Governor, he said that "severall disputes have Arisen concerning the validity of those Acts of Assembly." To prevent any questions in the future, all of those laws were vetoed.

Of all the vetoes, the most important to the Assembly was that of a bill concerning the election of members of the Lower House, and their summons to attend a session. Between the time it was passed in 1678 and vetoed in 1684, the *Journals* in both houses had many references to the subject; the Lower House was well aware that during the interval the bill had neither been signed nor vetoed by the Lord Proprietor himself.

In the background of the veto, of course, was the chronic question of comparative and unequal representation in the Lower House. It went back to the Governor's action in 1670 in cutting county representation from four to two delegates. In 1676, two years before the passage of the election bill of

1678, the Lower House directed a "humble petition" to Lord Baltimore. It began with the members "well knowing" it was the prerogative of Lord Baltimore to call what number of delegates he chose to meetings of the General Assembly. They added, however, that in all but two counties at the recent election, fewer delegates had been declared elected than called for in the proclamation; "by which meanes," concluded the Lower House, "Some of the inhabitants ... seem dissatisfied and that they have not theire free Vote." The suggestion was that Lord Baltimore should order a certain number to be elected in every county, and that every person elected should be called by writ to serve in the Assembly. Furthermore, in case of the death or removal of any member, another should be elected in his stead, so that "for the future the Members of this House may be the full Choice of the people." This was not to be for some years, however; in 1681 Lord Baltimore, by ordinance, confirmed the earlier action, and he then formally repeated the reduction to two in the number of delegates assigned to each county.

In the meantime, the Assembly had passed the controversial election bill of 1678, had it tentatively approved by the deputy, and would not be notified of the veto until 1684. In the judgment of the House, the bill was a vital part in its long campaign to improve the powers of the legislative process in general and the status of the Lower House in particular. Starting with the premise that the chief foundation of any state or commonwealth is that of providing and establishing good laws, passed with the consent of the freemen and their representatives, the bill of 1678 would have legislated into law these several stipulations: First, while leaving the exact time of calling the Assembly to the discretion of the Lord Proprietor, it specified the contents of the writs to the several sheriffs in requiring them to hold elections, and in so doing it fixed at four the number of delegates for each county. Secondly, it established property qualifications for the freemen in order to be voters, either as a freehold of 50 acres of land or a visible personal estate of 40 pounds.[5] Thirdly, these same property qualifications were placed upon those who might be elected as delegates; and here the requirement for four delegates was repeated, and the sheriffs were directed to issue authorizations of attendance to each delegate elected. Sheriffs themselves were specifically denied a right of election as delegates.

Next, and this was a novelty for representative government in Maryland, provision was made for two delegates from St. Mary's City, to be chosen by town officials.[6] Finally, the act of 1678 was to apply equally to counties, cities, or boroughs which might be established in the future. At the end of the bill it was repeated that neither

---

5. The writs of election issued in 1670 had limited the suffrage to freemen having a freehold of at least 50 acres or a visible estate of 40 pounds sterling; and the same qualifications were required of persons elected as delegates. This was done by executive order of the Governor, and it was a drastic change with respect to the electoral franchise. From the beginnings of the Province, it had been freemen, and not freeholders, who could vote and hold office. One resident had argued, in 1642, that he was not a freeman because he had no land and no "certain-dwelling," but the Assembly decided that he was a freeman and as such must appear in the Assembly either in person or by proxy. *See Archives,* I at 170 and II at 47. It may be argued that the Governor's action in 1670 was questionable under the Charter, which in its original language had used the term *liberi homines,* not *libere tenentes; i.e.,* freemen, not freeholders. *See* CHARLES M. ANDREWS, THE COLONIAL PERIOD IN AMERICAN HISTORY 339-40 (New Haven, 1936).

The Upper House had argued persuasively in 1666 (on a bill proposing a temporary cessation in the planting of tobacco), that it was the freeholder and not the freeman who was the "strength" of the Province. It is the freeholders' "persons purses & Stocks" which "must bear the Burthen of the Government ... and not Freemen who can easily abandon Us." Continuing, it is the freeholder of the Province "that hath Stock Wife & Children fixed & irremovable ...." *See Archives* II at 47.

6. A municipal charter, granted by the Proprietary in 1671, already had given St. Mary's a right to elect two delegates to the General Assembly.

a sheriff nor an under-sheriff could serve in the Lower House; and then was added the provision that an ordinary keeper within the Province could not be elected to or chosen for the General Assembly and could not serve in that body.

Despite the concern of the Lower House about having four delegates from each county, that problem was of slight interest to the Upper House. On one occasion it told the Lower House, with obvious annoyance, that the matter had been settled by the Lord Proprietor on the basis of two delegates.

At a joint session of the two houses on August 26, 1681, the Lord Proprietor told the Assembly that for the satisfaction of the people he was willing, for the current session, to call four delegates from each county; but that, for the future, he and the Council had decided there would be no more than two. He asked the Lower House for its "serious consideration" of this figure. For the moment, the Lower House acquiesced with this decision. It gave the Lord Proprietor a list of its current vacancies, "their said request having no Relation to future Assemblies."

Having lost this skirmish, the Lower House pressed on with its proposal to fix the number of delegates permanently at four for each county. The Lord Proprietor would not agree. He responded to the House on November 4, 1682, that "I cannot Deeme it Honourable Nor safe to Lodge it in the Freemen as you have desired, for it would be as reasonable for me to give away my Power of Calling and Dissolving of Assemblies, as to give that of Choosing the Number of Delegates."

The Lower House continued its efforts in 1683. It passed a new bill for electing and summoning delegates and sent it to the Upper House. On October 8, it asked the Upper House to return the bill (approved, of course). To this the Upper House replied, in one sentence, that it had the bill "under consideration." Next, the Lower House artfully inquired if the Upper House might be holding the election bill in order to assure passage of another bill of much interest, one for establishing towns and ports throughout the Province.[7] The Lower House, it wrote on October 9, had hoped the Upper House would not hold the election bill so long, observing that the Upper House seemed "to keep the said Bill with intent to exact Complyance from this house to keep the Bill for Towns thereby rendering Suspitious to this house that the Upper House doth not intent that fair Correspondence with this house as the present affairs require and this house earnestly desire."

Following this message, the *Journal* has a notation from the Upper to the Lower House, that "they cannot well perfect the Bill for Towns because there are some things that will have relation to both Bills." The Upper House also expressed surprise at the use of the word "suspitious" in the message from the Lower House. The election bill did not pass at that session of the Assembly. Six months later, the situation was clarified (if not settled, by the standards of the Lower House) by the veto, in 1684, of the election bill passed in 1678.

During these years, there was a continuing recognition of Magna Carta, so dear to the hearts of all Anglo-American legislative bodies. On September 7, 1681, the *Journal* of the Upper House spoke of "the Rights and Priviledges of a free born Englishman Settled on him by Magna Charta so often confirmed by Subsequent Parliaments."

On a less serious note, but nonetheless unusual, the *Journal* disclosed on August 24, 1681, that the Upper House adjourned its morning session and arranged to hold its afternoon session in the "arbor" at Van Sweringens.

---

7. This bill named and created many towns and port areas throughout the Province, and it had wide interest and support all over the colony.

The Lower House, in 1674, intervened in something clearly non-legislative. On February 16 of that year, the Lower House asked the Governor for clemency for one John Cowman, who had been convicted under an English statute for the capital offense of witchcraft. The Governor acceded to the request of the Lower House, but with a proviso to stamp the affair indelibly upon the culprit's mind. Cowman was to be carried to the gallows, have a rope put about his neck, and then informed "how much he is beholding to the Lower House of Assemblies for Mediating and Interceeding in his behalf."

An unusual feature of the 1680s was that for the first and only time, Lord Baltimore was in residence in the Province. He was Charles Calvert, grandson of the first Lord Baltimore and thus the third holder of that title. The *Journal* for the session of August-September, 1681, lists him as "Proprietary, in person." His son Philip was Chancellor and a member of the Council; and his son William was Secretary of the Council.

## LEGISLATION DURING THE 1670S AND 1680S

A disciplinary act was passed at the October-November session of 1678 to punish Edward Husbands "for menacing and Curseing this Assembly." In the preamble it was cited that under circumstances "strong and violent" enough to convict him, Husbands was suspected of having attempted to poison the Governor and members of both houses. Under the act, he was "utterly disabled & made incapable of ever practiseing as a Phisitian or Chirurgeon within this Province." By reason of his having "Threatned menaced & Cursed this present Assembly" he also was sentenced to be whipped with 20 lashes on the bare back.[8]

---

8. *Archives*, VII at 42-50, *passim. See also* MARY PATTERSON CLARKE, PARLIAMENTARY PRIVILEGE IN THE AMERICAN COLONIES 19 (New Haven, 1943).

There were bills notable for their similarity to legislation of later centuries. One, in 1682, was against the false packing of tobacco and prohibited unreasonable tares of hogsheads. It was made illegal to include "any Rotten frost bitten, Ground Leaves, or Seconds or worse Trash in the Middle or any part of the hogshead other than what is in the head and plain View of the Hogshead." The bill was not passed at that session, but it was the first order of business at the next session.

A bill in 1671 had an amendment added as a seventeenth-century version of "killing a bill with kindness." The Lower House passed a proposal to operate a ferry across the Patuxent River. It required that "all Persons living out of the precincts of said County shall pay to the man that keepeth the ferry six pence Sterling for every Footman that is so transported over the said River & one Shilling Sterling for every Horse & man that is transported over the said River." In the Upper House this much of the bill was approved, but it was returned to the Lower House with amendments:

> This House will consent to the Bill for Ferrys Provided a Ferry may be kept over Potapsco River from Philip Thomas's Point in Ann Arundel County to Kent County over the wading place from Kent to Talbot County over Chester River from Baltimore County over Choptank into Dorchester over Nanticoke into Somerset County .... [9]

---

9. In the absence of punctuation, the geography here is a bit difficult. The substitution of "Talbot" for "Baltimore" would be an obvious correction.

The appropriation bills passed at sessions during the 1680s were surprising in their close detail.[10] They each would total more than half a million pounds of tobacco (547,606 pounds on September 17, 1681, and 516,972 pounds in 1682), distributed through a list, pages long, to a great number of persons. The first references to payments in money were appearing. An act of 1692, listing fees of officers, for the first time gave the amounts in pounds, shillings, and pence "or" in pounds of tobacco. The transition was difficult. On one occasion the Lower House was upset with the Lord Proprietor because of his insistence on using money rather than tobacco. Appropriations to him had been made in tobacco, said to be at a rate of two pence per pound. The depressed level of tobacco prices made that commodity an uncertain one for creditors and other payees; and the House complained that the Lord Proprietor had "exacted" money sterling "to the great Agreivance and oppression of the Good People of the Province."

As part of their appropriations, the members remained concerned about the expenses of the General Assembly itself. During the session of May-June, 1676, there was an exchange of messages on how best to handle the legislators' expenses. The Lower House argued that they should be charged to "the public" (i.e., the Province), rather than to the particular counties. The reason was that there were differences in the number of delegates among the counties, and "Some Counties have Treble the number of Taxables as others." The Upper House was willing to concur in this much, provided each delegate received a maximum allowance of 150 pounds of tobacco daily, while the allowance for members of the Upper House would be 200 pounds. The feature of a daily allowance gave concern to the Lower House, saying that while it "never did Intend to Stint the expences of the Upper

10. *See generally,* John A. Kinnamon, *The Public Levy in Colonial Maryland to 1689,* 53 MARYLAND HISTORICAL REVIEW 253-74 (1958).

House" an allowance by the day would be a "great dissatisfaction to the good people of the province." In the judgment of the Lower House, a delegate would be "a gainer for his Trouble." At this point the discussion was abandoned for the session, though one member of the Lower House suggested a compromise whereby the "itinerant" charges of the members would be paid by the respective counties but that the expenses at St. Mary's would be paid by the Province. The whole subject was brought up again a year or two later, without conclusion.

In 1688, the two Houses appointed a joint committee to study their expenses. A particular problem stemmed from the bills received from the ordinaries, for the care and feeding of legislators. On November 26 of that year, the Upper House complained about the excessive cost of sessions of the Assembly; it charged the excesses were not caused by the "necessary" expenses of members, but by the "Divers frauds that are often used and practiced by the Severall Ordinary Keepers in charging more to their Accounts than ever was Expended." A few days later, on December 7, the joint Committee on Accounts objected to the billings from two ordinaries. One complaint centered on the private expenses of a member; and the other, on the bill for use of the ordinary by the Lower House and its committees. The latter bill, said the committee, was "so farr from being a hindrance . . . that it was of great Advantage to him . . . It being unreasonable to pay the expence done in his house & pay the rent for his house too . . . ."

The Lower House considered this report. Perhaps it did not react as the Upper House evidently hoped, for the decision of the Lower House was to increase the allowance for ordinaries. Its reasoning was that "the several Ordinary keepers hath been forced to purchase their Liquors and Provisions for Entertainment of the Assembly with Money or Tobacco at Extraordinary dear rates." To this the Upper

145

House objected, writing that "This house do not think fitt to Allow any Ordinary keeper more than what the Law directs." The disagreement then went to a conference committee, where the increase was approved. Some years later, in 1692, the Lower House made a halting attack upon the problem by requiring that as of every Saturday night the ordinary keepers give a particular account of the expenses of each delegate.

## THE NEW STATE HOUSE

An act of much importance during these years was for the construction of a State House. As enacted at the May-June session of 1674, the act was for building a combined State House and prison at St. Mary's. The act was notable for the close detail of its specifications. It was literally a combined architect's plan and a blueprint, in words, with itemized directions for building materials, inside construction, porches, stairways, windows, baseboards, doors, transoms, locks and latches, rafters, bars over the jail windows, and a host of other minutiae. As one example, the floors on the second story were to be of quartered plank, an inch and a quarter thick after planing, and of "either good white Oke or Pine of the Countrey sawen while the Turpentine is in them ...." The structure was to be completed by the end of 1676, and the act appropriated 330,000 pounds of tobacco for its cost.[11]

The State House and prison project had long been discussed. An earlier act for the purpose was not effective, and it was repealed in 1665. An act of 1666 had provided for a jail, with ten thousand pounds of tobacco allocated for its construction. As another indication of things to come, the

---

11. The "old State House" at St. Mary's was actually reconstructed in 1934, as a replica of the building erected in 1676.

General Assembly, at its May session in 1674, questioned whether the State House should be constructed at St. Mary's or elsewhere in the Province. The Governor's decision was to use a plot of land at St. Mary's. The builder was Captain John Quigley.

The new building seemed to be somewhat less than satisfactory. Before it was completed, on June 8, 1676, the Upper House proposed to the Lower the formation of a joint committee to inspect it, in order to prevent any defects. The *Journal* further notes that, in the fall of 1678, a committee critized the building's construction, saying for one thing that flat paving stones had not been used on the lower floor.

There was a barrage of criticism of the new State House in 1682, just six years after its completion. The Upper House declared the building to be in a "ruinous" condition, and repairs were proposed. Nothing loathe, the Lower House furnished a long list of specific needs: new tiles, brick partition in lower room, new ceiling, benches and tables, wooden shelters on the windows, and iron hooks to keep the windows open. For extra measure, the Lower House desired that the Court Crier from time to time would attend to the chore of shutting the windows. In 1684, the Upper House again was complaining about the "ruinous" condition of the building. In 1688 an act was passed for further repairs; this one covered the work in very close detail, and it spoke of the State House as having "gone very much to decay and ruine."

Dissatisfaction with the State House erected in 1676 obviously contributed to the growing question about the location and adequacy of St. Mary's for meetings of the Assembly. The session in 1683 was held at a place called the Ridge, near the present Mt. Zion in Anne Arundel County. It did not have the necessary accommodations. The next move was to Battle Creek on the Patuxent River, but this also was not satisfactory. The Assembly temporarily returned to St. Mary's.[12]

---

12. Neither "Ridge" nor "Battle Creek" appears in a gazetteer made from Augustine Herrmann's map of 1673. *See* J. Louis Kuethe, *A Gazetteer of Maryland, A.D. 1673,* 30 MARYLAND HISTORICAL MAGAZINE 310-25 (1935).

However, both locations were in or adjacent to the present Calvert County. "The Ridge, topographically, is the watershed between South River and Patuxent River." Eugenia Calvert Holland, *Anne Arundel Takes Over from St. Mary's,* 44 MARYLAND HISTORICAL MAGAZINE 42 (1949). There is a village by the same name in St. Mary's County, about 20 miles southeast of Leonardtown. *See* Polk's GAZETTEER (1891-1892).

Battle Creek is a small branch of the Patuxent River, on the Calvert County side. A gazetteer for 1887 shows a village of that name about ten miles from Prince Frederick, with a population of 25 persons. *See* HENRY GANNETT, A GAZETTEER OF MARYLAND (Baltimore, 1976); MARYLAND DIRECTORY AND STATE GAZETTEER (Baltimore, 1887).

# Chapter 6

## MARYLAND AS A ROYAL COLONY

### 1688-1715

In 1688 the English Parliament deposed King James II, a Catholic, and invited in the Protestant regime of William and Mary. It was an event variously named as the "Glorious," "Peaceful," and "Protestant" Revolution. However styled, the change was clearly the handicraft of the Parliament, and the clear ascendance of the Parliament usually is dated from 1688. Though Parliamentary forces had rather precipitously ended the career of an earlier king in 1649, then they had not also created one; and the Commonwealth they substituted was of short duration. The long-term Parliamentary break with the past was much more apparent after 1688 than after 1649.

Changes were evident in Maryland over the next few years, though all of them did not necessarily stem from the new government in England. The most important change was that of converting the Province from a proprietary to a royal colony. Charles, Lord Baltimore (1637-1715), was a member of the Church of Rome; he was a grandson of the original Lord Baltimore. He had inherited the baronetcy from his father, Cecelius Calvert, in 1675; Cecelius had been the second Lord Baltimore from 1632 to 1675.

The new Protestant regime in England quickly ended the political powers of Charles Calvert in Maryland, though there is some evidence that the proceedings of dispossession had begun under James II. Lord Baltimore was reduced to the status of a landlord, entitled only to his rents and to some imposts and duties on tobacco. He disappeared from public life, and the year of his death coincided with the restoration of the Proprietary government.

The Associators' Assembly and problems with a new form of oath, both during the 1690s, were directly connected with

149

the political changes in England. There also were "local" problems and changes during the royal period. Moving the capital to Annapolis, building a new State House and then seeing it soon destroyed by fire, the compensation of public officials, and continued debate and controversy over legislative prerogatives were all a part of continued legislative development.[1]

## THE SESSION OF 1688

The 1688 session of the General Assembly was held from November 14 to December 8. The President of the Upper House was William Joseph; and his opening address to the two houses was vastly different from anything before or since. It was partly a religious homily of fire and brimstone, more appropriate to the pulpit than to the State House. Political portions of it were ill-suited to a people that only recently had relegated to the past the theory of the divine right of kings, and who had made parliamentary government the voice of the future.

All power, he said, is derived

| | |
|---|---|
| First | In God and from God |
| Secondly | In the King and from the King |
| Thirdly | In his Lordship and from his Lordship |
| Fourthly | In Us, so the End and duty of, and for which this Assembly is now Called and met is that from those four heads . . . . |

---

1. For accounts of this period in Maryland, *see generally* Michael G. Kammen, *The Causes of the Maryland Revolution of 1689,* 55 MARYLAND HISTORICAL MAGAZINE 293-333 (1960); FRANCIS E. SPARKS, CAUSES OF THE MARYLAND REVOLUTION OF 1689 (Baltimore, 1896); LOIS GREEN CARR AND DAVID WILLIAM JORDAN, MARYLAND'S REVOLUTION OF GOVERNMENT, 1689-1692 (Ithaca, 1974); Richard A. Gleissner, *The Glorious Revolution in Maryland,* 64 MARYLAND HISTORICAL MAGAZINE 327-41 (1969).

Our duty to God, he believed, consists in the making of good and wholesome laws. Here he particularly commended to the legislators' care the utter suppression and abolition of the heinous crimes of drunkenness, adultery, swearing, and Sabbath breaking.

With this beginning, President Joseph discoursed at length and individually upon those several crimes, as part of the duties owed to God under the first heading of power. Secondly, as for kings, they are "the Lords Anointed and are by God appointed over us to Rule." Continuing, "whoso keepeth the Commandment of the King shall feel no evill thing," citing the duty of the Assembly to follow the king's commandments. Here Joseph struck a mundane note by including among these commandments an item prohibiting the bulk shipment of tobacco from the Province. Thirdly, for the power of the Lord Proprietary, the President hoped that none would be so Machiavellian as to divide the interests of the Proprietor and his people. Finally, he said, the duty of the people is to suppress public sin and scandal and to abhor all private and self-interest; and he exhorted them before they began to make laws not to start by breaking them.

Some days later, on November 26, the Upper House sent a message to the Lower House asking that bills be prepared as the House thought fit for punishing the several "enormous" crimes of drunkenness, whoredom, swearing, and Sabbath breaking, as had been proposed in the President's address. The members of the Lower House, obviously no more enthusiastic about the task than the Upper House, responded on November 28 that while they were aware of the frequent occurrence of these crimes, they thought it was from no deficiency in the present laws ("there already being several good and wholesome laws on these crimes"), but from want of proper execution of those present laws. The Lower House did promise, however, that if the Upper House could prepare any other bills on these crimes the Lower would readily concur.

151

## TAKING THE OATH

A serious dispute on the matter of taking the oath of office arose at this session of November-December, 1688. It began in a message from the Upper to the Lower House, proposing that the members of the latter take an oath of fidelity. The Lower House immediately replied that its members had not forgotten their duty and had not been unfaithful to the Lord Proprietor and the government; and that they would take the oath of fidelity when informed by the Upper House what act of Assembly imposed it upon them. The members of the Lower House, of course, had already taken an oath of office when originally admitted to their seats.

The Upper House then asked that the two houses meet together for discussion; but that seemed to the Lower House to be "great Irregularity and breach of their Priviledges" unless the Lord Proprietor were present and so commanded. Returning the compliment, the Upper House termed the message of the Lower "Irregular and unparliamentary" and "required" the Lower House "forthwith to attend this house without further Message or Delay."

This demand stirred the rhetoric in the Lower House. In the inevitable counter-message, dated November 16, 1688, it told the Upper House in sharp vein that

> This House think not their last Message Irregular or Unparliamentary in that, That if his Lordship Command them to Attend him in his Upper house they are willing and ready so to do But they dare not upon their Fidelity to own or accept any other power under any other Denomination than what his Lordship by his Writts of Election hath been pleased to Express this house being no ways under the Jurisdiction of any Upper house of Assembly, this house still protesting their readiness to attend his Lordship either in his Upper house or elsewhere when by his Lordship or his Representative the Deputy Governors thereunto Commanded.

Back came the rejoinder of the Upper House, that "his Lordship the Lord Proprietary is always present in his Upper house of Assembly." This time, however, the verb was a softer "desire" in asking the Lower House to attend. The compromise was enough to get the two houses into the same room.

Once there, they were addressed by the President, William Joseph. He succeeded only in lighting the fires anew. He demanded that the members of the Lower House take the oath of fidelity, which "may be proposed even to the house of Commons in Parliament Sitting, and the refusers are Excluded from being members or having any vote in Parliament, as if they had never bin Elected." Further, "refusing Allegiance implyes Rebellion . . . . You have no Priviledge to break, Contemn or disobey Laws . . . . The more you refuse Allegiance by so much the more the Government have Cause to Suspect your Loyalty." At this point, the Upper House attempted to placate the Lower, saying that the oath could be taken by each member individually, and not by the group as a House. However, the Upper House was firm in saying that it would not proceed with further business until members of the Lower House had taken the oath.

The Lower House ignored this last message and commented upon the address of the President. They had attended the joint meeting at the command of the Proprietary (or his deputy), they said, and they repeated their fidelity to him; but not knowing of any misbehavior by any member, they resented "Divers words and Expressions" in the President's remarks. Typically, in the elaborate custom of the times, they listed in detail a seven-point declaration of their position and arguments.

Once again, by invitation, the Lower House attended a conference with the Upper House and the President. This time the President, while regretting the "unhappy Misunderstandings," prorogued the Assembly for three days.

153

The next entry in the *Journal,* under the heading "Memorandum," noted that the President required the Speaker and all the Lower House to take the oath of fidelity to the Lord Proprietor. After "some Debates," all the members complied (except one Quaker, who had special permission). From the timing of the event, the second oath probably was taken by the members as private citizens, when they no longer were in session.

Once more, at the May-June session in 1692, a message from the Lower to the Upper House touched upon problems stemming from the oath. Several members of the Lower House felt they could not comply with the new oaths of allegiance and abhorrence, now required of all subjects. The question was whether an expedient might be found "in which case the usuall Declaration made by persons so Principled will be Satisfactory to the house, of their Loyalty to their Majestys and faithfulness to their Country." The reply from the Upper House, signed by the "Governor and Council in Assembly," was that they would like to concur but could not do so "without open Violation of the Lawes of England."

The perennial problem of taking an oath came up once more, during the September-October session of 1694. Again the difficulty was that the Parliament had changed the oath under the new regime, and the old oaths of allegiance and supremacy were discarded. Four members of the Council were appointed to swear in the burgesses. Two members of the House, one from Calvert and one from Talbot County, refused to take the new oath.

In addition to being called upon to subscribe to an altered oath, the members in 1694 were required to bind themselves to a religious test: "Wee the subscribers doe declare that wee doe believe that there is not any transsubstantiation in the Sacrament of the Lords Supper or in the Elements of bread & Wine at or after the Consecration thereof by any person whatsoever." The *Journal* for the session lists the names of the delegates, under their respective counties, as witness to their taking the test. It was dated at St. Mary's on September 21, 1694.

## THE ASSOCIATORS' ASSEMBLY

The legislative session of 1689 was a so-called Associators' Assembly. It was organized under a group formed in April of that year, known as "An association in arms, for the defense of the Protestant religion, and for asserting the right of King William and Queen Mary to the Province of Maryland and all the English dominions." The head of it was John Coode, already (in the early 1680s) found guilty of treason and rebellion. In July the group captured St. Mary's City and occupied the State House. The members issued a long "Declaration" in support of their pretensions, most of it being an alarum about a possible "Popish" uprising (although it is said that at the time the Catholic population of Maryland numbered only about 3 percent of the total). The Associators also justified taking the Province away from the Lord Proprietary by reciting complaints which the Assembly, or at least the House, had voiced for years: the failure to permit four delegates for each county, the veto of laws, and the charge of "excessive" officers' fees.

Once the Associators felt they had power in their hands, they were able to disperse their opponents and to summon their own Legislature. The session of 1689 left no *Journal* or other primary records. It made a precipitous break with the past in handing over the Province to the King and making it a royal government. The new royal governor was Lionel Copley, though he did not actually arrive in the Province until 1692.

In February, 1689/90, King William recognized the Associators. Earlier, when John Coode and the Associators issued a call for an election in the summer of 1689, they had done it in William's name, but without any legal power to do so. There was opposition to the call for a new election from those who wanted a non-Catholic government appointed by the Crown, but not a self-appointed Protestant government.[2] The Assembly returned William's favor in 1692 when it passed acts to recognize the title of William and Mary and to make the Church of England the established religion.[3]

A possible wholesale substitution of laws was discussed at the May-June session of 1692. On June 3 of that year, in the Upper House, there was consideration of a proposal to make void "all Laws in General heretofore made in this Province except what upon a Review of the Body of those Laws this present Sessions have deemed fit and Convenient for the good Government of this Province." At the same time, the Lower House was assuring the Upper that it had "carefully and dilligently perused" the "whole body of the Laws."

---

2. LOIS GREEN CARR AND DAVID WILLIAM JORDAN, MARYLAND'S REVOLUTION OF GOVERNMENT, 1689-1692, at 63-4 (Ithaca, 1974).

The establishment of royal government in Maryland in 1691 was "part of a compromise worked out by William III and Charles Calvert, third Baron Baltimore. By means of this bargain William accomplished what his predecessor had been unable to achieve by coercion: the extension of Crown authority in a key dependency and the more effective integration of the colony into the mercantile framework of the empire. For his part Calvert surrendered the provincial government but received the Crown's guarantee and protection of his soil rights and certain fiscal prerogatives. Thereby, a mutually satisfactory solution to the problems arising from the Maryland revolution of 1689 was reached which acknowledged the king's immediate political interest in Maryland without doing substantial injury to the charter...." Richard A. Gleissner, *The Revolutionary Settlement of 1691 in Maryland,* 66 MARYLAND HISTORICAL MAGAZINE 405 (1971), and sources there cited.

3. *See generally,* Lawrence C. Wroth, *The First Sixty Years of the Church of England in America,* 11-13, 15 MARYLAND HISTORICAL MAGAZINE (1916, 1917, 1918, 1920), Richard A. Gleissner, *Religious Causes of the Glorious Revolution in Maryland,* 64 MARYLAND HISTORICAL MAGAZINE 327-41 (1969).

The revisory act was passed as Chapter 84 of the Acts of 1692. It repealed all laws "heretofore" made in the Province and confirmed all the laws made during the current session. The act of 1692 in turn was repealed in 1704, when the whole subject again was reviewed.

## THE EARLY 1690s

Lionel Copley, the first royal governor, died in 1693. It had been intended since 1691 that he would be succeeded by Francis Nicholson, who had been Deputy Governor in New York and Lieutenant Governor in Virginia.[4] However, Nicholson was in England at the time Copley died, and for a time the governorship in Maryland was seized by Sir Edmund Andros, who had followed Nicholson as Lieutenant Governor in Virginia. Andros soon returned to Virginia; and when Francis Nicholson returned from England, he became Governor of Maryland. Despite the royal status of the Province, the legislative *Journals* listed Charles Calvert as Lord Baltimore and Proprietary, along with Francis Nicholson as Governor.

The colony had grown rapidly by the 1690s. It listed ten counties in the *Journal* for 1694: St. Mary's, Kent, Anne Arundel, Calvert, Charles, Baltimore, Talbot, Somerset, Dorchester, and Cecil. Prince George's County was added at the May session in 1695. Of these 11 counties, most had been formed by executive order; only Anne Arundel (1650) and Prince George's (1695) were created by legislative act.

Also, at the 1695 session, there was a bill passed to settle boundary questions concerning the counties of St. Mary's,

---

4. *See* Charles William Sommerville, *Early Career of Governor Francis Nicholson,* 4 MARYLAND HISTORICAL MAGAZINE 101-14 (1909); Annie Leakin Sioussat, *Lionel Copley, First Royal Governor of Maryland,* 17 MARYLAND HISTORICAL MAGAZINE 163-77 (1922).

Charles, Prince George's, Kent, and Talbot. In the process, Kent Island was added to Talbot County. A year later, during the April-May session of 1696, it was reported to the Upper House that residents in Somerset County could not agree upon a site for a courthouse. One solution, mentioned but not adopted, was to divide Somerset County into two counties, the "sea board Side to make one County and the Bay side the other."

In the listing of the ten existing counties in the 1694 *Journal,* each was to have four delegates, plus two from St. Mary's City.[5] The representation for the ten counties was by virtue of an act passed at the May-June session of 1692, when the delegates finally won the point they had struggled so hard for in the late 1670s and early 1680s. Also, when there were vacancies among the elected members, they now were filled by the process sought earlier; *i.e.,* the Speaker issued warrants to the Secretary of the Province, who then was required to issue writs to the sheriffs of the counties involved, for the election of other delegates. The new procedure was used for the October session in 1695.

## THE MOVE TO ANNAPOLIS

The big event of 1694 was that of moving the State capitol from St. Mary's to Annapolis. It was a change that had been

---

5. The Proprietary had granted municipal charters to St. Mary's City in 1668 and 1671. An area of one square mile had been incorporated, with a mayor, board of aldermen, and common council. The charter in 1671 had already given the freemen in the town a right to elect two delegates to the Assembly. *See* Lois Green Carr, *"The Metropolis of Maryland": A Comment on Town Development Along the Tobacco Coast,* 69 MARYLAND HISTORICAL MAGAZINE 124-45 (1974). Although the population of the village did not warrant the two delegates given to it, Charles Calvert "used this device to ensure election of a particular supporter to the assembly called that year." *Id.,* at 129.

discussed, and both recommended and opposed, for many years.[6]

On two occasions during the 1650s, the General Assembly had met in Calvert County, near St. Leonard's Creek on the Patuxent River side. These shifts were political and temporary; they occurred during the time of the Puritan regime and the Commonwealth, and they had little effect beyond that to the legislators then in office. The session in 1683 had been called at a place called the Ridge, in lower Anne Arundel County near the present Mt. Zion. Next, there was a session held at Battle Creek on the Patuxent River. Neither the Ridge nor Battle Creek was satisfactory.

An indication of the plans to move to Annapolis came as early as 1683. On October 9 of that year, in a message from the Upper to the Lower House, it was said that "his Lordship hath declared to his two houses of Assembly that at what place in Ann Arundell County there shall be Conveniencyes built fit for the Reception of his Lordship and Council Upper and Lower houses Provincial Courts and Offices for Clerks, There his Lordship his heirs and Successors Lords and Proprietaries of this Province will hold the Assemblies and Courts aforesaid for the future unless upon Occasion he or they shall think fitt that the same be removed." The message also asked that committees be established to study the change; and at the same time the Upper House suggested that the "conveniency" be located on South River.[7]

---

6. *See generally,* Euginia Calvert Holland, *Anne Arundel Takes Over from St. Mary's,* 44 Maryland Historical Magazine 42-51 (1949).

7. If the move had been made to the South River area, it perhaps would have been to Londontown, on the lower shore of South River a short distance easterly from the present State Route 2. *See generally,* Henry J. Berkley, *Londontown on South River, Anne Arundel County, Md.,* 19 Maryland Historical Magazine 134-43 (1924). Both Annapolis and Londontown had been created as ports in an act of 1683. That act, which created a number of ports throughout the tidewater area, included the "Town Land at Proctors" and "South River on Col. Burgess' land."

At the April session in 1684, some question was raised about why the Assembly was meeting at St. Mary's, and the Governor's reply was that it was for the "settling" of his private affairs.

By the 1690s, the shift obviously was imminent. At the October session in 1694, the burgesses considered a bill for the Proprietary to take up a plot of land in "Ann Arundell Towne." [8] Another bill provided that "in Ann Arundell Towne their be a place set aside for a ffortification."

The expanding geography of the Province created one ready and convincing argument for moving the capital to the north. Counties already were established as far away as Cecil and Baltimore, both bordering on what later was settled as the northern extremity of the Province (and State).

The St. Mary's community vigorously opposed the move. During the September-October session of 1694 a "humble address" was sent to Governor Nicholson by the "Mayor Recorder Aldermen Common Councill men and ffreemen" of the City. It extended nearly five pages in the *Archives* and with 16 points seriatim argued for keeping the existing site.

St. Mary's, said the petition, was "the prime and originall" settlement and the "Antient and Chiefe Seate" of the government. Its situation was "most pleasant & healthfull and naturally commodious." Its harbor would hold five hundred vessels; the State House and prison built in the 1670s had cost 330,000 pounds of tobacco; the town's inhabitants had contributed one hundred pounds of tobacco toward the cost of the Governor's dwelling; an earlier move of part of the judiciary to Anne Arundel County had not been satisfactory; the local inhabitants would be impoverished; St. Mary's was contiguous to Virginia; suggestions for the

---

8. The tiny village on the Severn River had been known variously as Proctors, Ann Arundel Towne, and Providence. The change to "Annapolis" was made in 1696.

change came from "some particular persons for their owne private Interest and Advantage"; the change would be at some hazard and expense; London in England, Boston in Massachusetts, and Jamestown in Virginia all had been retained as ancient capitals.

The petition also cited a vote by the Assembly in 1692, that holding the courts and Assembly in St. Mary's was not a "greviance." Finally, on the matter of access to St. Mary's from Calvert County, and the complaint that members of the Assembly had been forced to walk that part of their journey from the Patuxent River ferry to the capital, the St. Mary's folk in the petition promised to establish a coach or caravan route to the River, with service daily during sessions and weekly for the remainder of the year.

A shorter petition, to the same effect, went to the Governor and the Council. To all the importunities, the House of Burgesses with the concurrence of the Council returned a blunt and sometimes sarcastic refusal to stay in St. Mary's. A number of the points in the petition were lumped together and rejected in one sentence: It was not felt that proximity to Virginia was "soe great an Advantage"; St. Mary's had been "very Vnequally Rankt" with London and Boston; the records and properties of the Province could be cared for equally well in another place. For the sarcasm, coarse in the extreme, St. Mary's "has only served hitherto to cast a Blemish Upon all the Rest of the Province"; strangers "perceiving the meaness of the head must Rationally Judge" the rest of the body proportionately. Finally, on the offer of stage coach service from the Patuxent River to St. Mary's, the Lower House said that the general welfare of the Province "ought to take place of that sugar plum & of all the Mayors Coaches whoe as yet has not one."

The last Assembly called at St. Mary's was that of September 20, 1694. The next following session, in February and March, 1694/5, the legislators met in Ann Arundell

Towne, shortly to be called Annapolis. It was named in honor of Princess Anne, heiress presumptive to the throne of England.

The new capital town already had been given a number of names. First called "Providence" when originally settled by Puritans from Virginia, it had at various times also been called "Proctors" and "The Town Land at Severn." The name "Proctors" had come from Proctor's Point, at the lower end of the present Duke of Gloucester Street where the Eastport Bridge is located.[9]

A letter written from Maryland, late in the 1690s, described the town: "There are indeed several places for towns, but hitherto they are only titular ones, except Annapolis, where the governor resides. Col. Nicholson has done his endeavor to make a town of that place. There are about forty dwellings in it; seven or eight of which can afford a good lodging and accommodations for strangers. There are also a state house and a free school, built of brick, which make a great show among a parcel of wooden houses; and the foundation of a church is laid, the only brick church in Maryland. They have two market days in a week; and had Governor Nicholson continued there a few months longer, he had brought it to perfection." [10]

---

**9.** *See generally,* DAVID RIDGELY, ANNALS OF ANNAPOLIS (Baltimore, 1841); ELIHU S. RILEY, THE ANCIENT CITY — A HISTORY OF ANNAPOLIS IN MARYLAND (Annapolis, 1887); WILLIAM OLIVER STEVENS, ANNAPOLIS (New York, 1937); John William Reps, *The Annapolis of Francis Nicholson,* TIDEWATER TOWNS — CITY PLANNING IN COLONIAL VIRGINIA AND MARYLAND 117-40 (Williamsburg, 1972).

**10.** Quoted in JOHN V. L. McMAHON, AN HISTORICAL VIEW OF THE GOVERNMENT OF MARYLAND 254 (Baltimore, 1831).

## THE NEW STATE HOUSE

Having accomplished the move to Annapolis, the General Assembly's next task was to conceive and supervise the building of a new State House.[11] Here the legislators repeated the close detail and attention they had given to the planning and construction of the building in St. Mary's, twenty years earlier. During the session of April-May, 1696, the Governor, Council, and House of Burgesses inspected the foundations of the new State House. The group viewed and measured the length and breadth of the foundation and the thickness of the walls, finding everything to be according to contract. The builder was Col. Casperus Augustine Herrmann, a son of Augustine Herrmann of Bohemia Manor.

At the time of inspecting the foundations, the Council made a further series of proposals for the building and put them before the House of Burgesses for consideration. Provision should be made, it was suggested, for separate rooms for the Provincial offices, the Land Office, Commissary's office, county courts office, Council Clerk's office, and two or three jury rooms; and passages should be provided so that all offices could be private. Continuing, there should be Dutch stoves, boxes for clerks' and lawyers' papers, a "contrivance" for the Grand Jury, a seat for the Crier, a place for witnesses, and one or two galleries.

Also, paving around the building was to be with a "good store" of oyster shells, the pavement was to be graded to carry off water, and there was a directive that "several Posts be set up to Hang Horses on to contrive a Pissduit and House of Office some where near the State House." Further proposals were for the chimneys, the porches, and the

---

11. *See* MORRIS L. RADOFF, BUILDINGS OF THE STATE OF MARYLAND AT ANNAPOLIS 1-11 (Annapolis, 1954); MORRIS L. RADOFF, THE STATE HOUSE AT ANNAPOLIS (Annapolis, 1972).

shingles. At one point, the House of Burgesses made other suggestions for the building; the Governor's reply was with full dignity and protocol, that "his Excellency is pleased to say that he is sorry the Country is so Poor as not to Comply with the aforesaid Proposalls."

There were other details needing attention after moving the seat of government. An act of May, 1695, directed that the old State House in St. Mary's be used as a courthouse and church. Earlier that year another act established a ferry service across the South River, for persons having business with the Provincial Court or the Assembly. The same act set up a ferry across the Patuxent River, above Mount Pleasant (also called Mount Calvert). About the same time, the House considered an order of the Governor for transferring records from St. Mary's to Annapolis.[12] Members of both houses viewed the clay for the bricks in the new building, reporting that samples of clay had been approved.

The *Journals* in 1697 had further reference to the unfinished State House. Chapter 6 of the Acts of 1697 provided for "directing and appointing" the use of the several rooms in the building. In Chapter 19 of the Acts of 1699, after the building was constructed, it was stated formally that Annapolis was to be the place for holding Assemblies.

Even before the State House was completed, a group of good citizens of Annapolis sent a petition to the Upper House

---

12. For a vivid description of the task of moving the Provincial records from St. Mary's to Annapolis, *see* Eugenia Calvert Holland, *Anne Arundel Takes Over from St. Mary's,* 44 MARYLAND HISTORICAL MAGAZINE 46-7 (1949). The records were packed in canvas bags, secured with cords, and covered with hides. Fourteen horses were used. The cavalcade proceeded from St. Mary's to the Patuxent River ferry, and the records were taken across the river in several boats. Sentinels were posted over the records during overnight stops, and two of the guards were instructed to "lie always in the room where the records are lodged."

to suggest some special status for the new capital city. It was journalized on May 1, 1696, with these proposals, among others:

First, a market house should be built and a market conducted once a week, "on which day nobody to be arrested in Town from nine of the Clock in the morning until nine a Clock the next day." Similarly, "To have in the said Town two fairs every year and no Person coming thither to be arrested from one day before the said fair and one day after." Continuing the drastic changes in the law of arrest, it was proposed further "that no Person coming to the Port of Annapolis be arrested within that Port unless his Stay shall Exceed Forty eight Hours." Another request with a different motive was that "the Inhabitants of the Town pay no County levy nor have to do with any County Roads Clearing but what are in or about the same Town." An act was passed during the session of 1696 to hold a market once a week and a fair once a year; and, during the period of each, all persons attending were not to be subject to arrest other than for treason, murder, or felony.

The completion of the new building did not at all end the problems with the State House, and the *Journals* for several years have repeated references to continuing difficulties.

The building was struck by lightning in 1699. The *Journal* for July 13 has the story:

It pleasing Almighty God that a great Clap of Thunder & Lightening fell upon the State house the house of Delegates sitting therein which Splintered the flag Staff Strook down the Vane burnt the flagg and sett the roof of the house in a flame of fire and Strikeing through the upper Rooms shattering the Door posts & Window frames, Strook down and grieviously wounded several of the Delegates . . . and passing through the upper Room where the Comittee of Laws was sitting, strook dead Mr. Iames Crawford one of the Delegates of Calvert County & one of the said Comittee to the great Astonishment of all persons, But it so pleased God by the Active Care and

165

personall presence of his Excellency the Governor the said fire was quickly Quenched a showr of rain happening Imediately thereupon And the Records preserved as also the house with little or no Considerable Damage . . . .

This account was in the *Journal* of the Upper House. That from the House of Burgesses was essentially the same, except that the quenching of the fire was by the "Dillegence & Industry" of the Governor, with no mention of the favor of God or of the shower of rain. A few days later, the Governor and Council issued a proclamation of "the mercy of Allmighty God that the State house was not burned nor greater Damage," and a day of public thanksgiving was declared for the following August 17. The Governor and Council also recommended that four or five small water engines and 20 leather buckets be sent for, to be "ready upon any such vnhappy Occasion which God Prevent."

The next concern for the State House was for needed repairs. The House at its June session in 1702 reported the building was "leaky & out of repair & is very likely to be worse unless Speedy care be taken to prevent it." A study committee was appointed to investigate the trouble and to employ workmen as necessary. The committee reported on April 29, 1704, that the "Cubilo" where the flagstaff stood was leaking, most of the offices needed plastering and glazing, and sundry repairs were needed for windows, doors, and a stone step.

## THE LATE 1690s

The General Assembly participated in two civic enterprises in 1696, both destined to have a vital and permanent impact upon Annapolis and the entire Province. One was an act passed at the July session in that year (Chapter 17, 1696), establishing "King William's School," as a free school for the study of Latin, Greek, writing, "and the like." This school is sometimes described as the beginning of the modern St. John's College, but any connection is uncertain. The other project was to establish a group in the House as a "Committee to Inspect what Tobacco is Collected towards building a Church at Annapolis." This was the present St. Anne's Church. It was estimated the cost of the structure would be twelve hundred pounds sterling. In the judgment of the committee, "We find no means to Raise more money to carry on the same without the Assistance of Charitable well disposed Persons."

Among the legislative proposals in the middle 1690s was an extraordinary bill in the Upper House, as an amendment to the existing law setting up penalties for servant girls having illegitimate children. Evidently some of the women had charged their masters with being the fathers; and the complaints must have been embarrassing and difficult to handle in a class-conscious society. The legislative solution was to require in this circumstance "it shall be the Solemne protestation or Oath of the Woman in her paines of Travaille agreeing with other pregnant circumstances which shall be Sufficient proof not otherwise."

Another bill with a seventeenth-century air to it appeared in the May session of 1695, "To Propose a way to Restrain all Negroes from wandering about on Sundayes & to keep them from prophaneing the Sabath day in making of Rendevouze with their Drums & publick dancing as is Usual with them." It was enacted as Chapter 6 of the Acts of 1695 and expired several years later.

There was a two-day session on February 28 and March 1, 1694/5, in the nature of what future generations would call a special session. Its main purpose was the enactment of remedial legislation for the Provincial Court in St. Mary's County; the *Journal* records that the court had not been able to meet regularly during the winter, because of the "severity and sharpness" of the weather.

167

Without fanfare or particular notice, a number of legislative changes occurred quietly during the late years of the seventeenth century. One of them was in the name generally given to the lower branch of the Legislature. For many years, after the bicameral system started in the 1650s, the two houses were simply the "Upper House" and the "Lower House." Late in the century, the Lower House for a period was the "House of Burgesses," with the members sometimes called "burgesses," "delegates," or "delegates and burgesses", and on rare occasions they were called "representatives." Finally, very near the end of the century, the modern "House of Delegates" became the most usual name. The Upper House retained its traditional name, though references to it were complicated because with the Governor it served also as the "Council" or "Council of State," and occasionally it and the Governor would be called the "Board."

Changes occurred also in the legislative *Journals* in the last decade or so in the seventeenth century. Punctuation and spelling were slowly being altered to "modern" usage. The *Journals* became longer and more detailed than during the earlier years, and they are excellent sources for the actions and thoughts of the legislators.

As a part of the changes, there was talk about improving the language in the laws enacted by the Assembly. On this proposal, on March 26, 1698, the House of Delegates spoke summarily: "As to having the Laws put in apter Language, this house is well satisfyed with them and will not resolve to Imply any Lawyer to mend them."

During the September-October session of 1696, there was another of those protracted and severe contests between the two houses, with the Governor supporting the Upper House against the House of Delegates. It began on September 18, at the beginning of the session, when the Governor's representative refused to administer the oath of office to an

168

elected member of the House. The member in question was John Cood. The complaint against him was that he was a former priest or minister, and that the laws of England prohibited legislative membership for such a person.[13]

The House quickly protested. It noted that Cood for 20 years had been a member of the House, and that he had held both judicial and executive commissions in the Province. The House then moved to philosophical ground, saying that it conceived itself a proper judge of its own membership; and it added the usual threat not to proceed to business "till the House was full." The Governor and Upper House responded, again citing the law of England and further averring that there had been other "irregular proceedings" involving Cood when the Province was under Lord Baltimore.

Thus far the clash developed as had many others in the past decades, but it suddenly took a surprising and unusual turn; the question of law was submitted to the private attorneys in the community. The Governor and Upper House closed their final message by saying "it being a matter of great Moment must therefore be considered and consulted by the lawyers." To the message was appended an order "that all the Lawyers in Town be sent for to appear at this Board tonight." Accordingly, "the Gentlemen professing the Law now in Town" met with the Governor and Council, had the question explained to them, and "being separately answered" agreed "that no Person in holy Orders is qualified by Law to sit in the house of Commons and so by consequence not in the House of Burgesses here."

The House, informed of the opinion of the lawyers, remained adamant in holding that John Cood was qualified

---

13. Except for the spelling of his name, this was the same Captain Coode who had been in controversy between the two houses in the 1681 session. He had been acquitted at the conclusion of his trial for treason and was reelected to the Assembly in 1688. Beginning in 1689, he had been active for several years in the Associators' movement.

to sit in that body. To this the Governor and Council replied that the only question involved was whether or not Cood had been a deacon or priest. To them, the powers of the House did not reach to qualifying a person legally disqualified; and to this they added some personal criticism of Cood, asking "whether he has not at this present Cost the County more Tobacco then Perhaps he is worth or ever will do them good." Cood at this time was deemed an atheist, but there seemed no doubt that he had been in holy orders years earlier. In a further message, the Council was "sorry that the House should continue so stiff so many days" and included depositions supporting its personal criticism of Cood. With this the House of Delegates surrendered and reported itself ready for business; and another crisis was concluded.

Earlier in 1696, the House had another complaint against the Governor and the Council. Although not as serious as the one about Cood, it ran the same predictable course. Its origin was somewhat obscure, but it concerned a paper affixed to the door of the House chamber at the time of a public meeting on a Sunday. The House charged, in a message dated May 4, 1696, that the paper attempted to bar the House from the privacy and uninterruption it should have, and that the paper "trampled" upon the rights and privileges of the House. The Governor and Council immediately responded that there was no intent to encroach upon the privileges of the House; and that if the public notice had not been removed during the evening, the fault lay with officers of the House. This reply, said the House of Delegates, was unsatisfactory; and the House then threatened to "adjourn to some other place and proceed to no other Business" until a satisfactory answer was given.

At this point, the Governor and Council inquired whether all the members of the House were present when the complaint was voiced, and whether the vote was unanimous. This, said the House in return, was a further infringement upon its privileges. The controversy finally was settled by the Governor, who called the members of the House before him. He expressed his regrets over the delay in the business of the House, with "the Country put to a vast charge and Expense without any thing done." He presented to the Speaker a copy of a sermon by the Archbishop of Canterbury and prorogued the House until the following day. Without further comment upon the prorogation or the contents of the sermon, the House next day returned to its regular business.

Also at the spring session in 1696, on May 13, the House of Delegates stated a claim for its powers on financial matters, this time without threatening to cease its work. The incident occurred during consideration of taking security from the masters of ships in the export trade, after the Governor told the House he would have to consult on the question with the Commissioner of the Customs. In rejoinder, said the House, "as it is the undoubted right and Privilege of the Representative Body of this Province to consent to the raising of Money upon the Inhabitants so likewise it is to the same when raised."[14]

The Governor showed criticism to be a two-edged sword, in a caustic comment to the Assembly in 1696. Because he considered a pending bill too strict, he hoped the members "would consider these things and not make good the old English proverb upon themselves videlicit of being like the Cow that gives a good Pale of milk and kicks it over with her foot."

In September, 1696, the Governor passed on to the Council an instruction from the King on having a quorum present when business was to be transacted. He suggested that except in case of absolute necessity "they would do well to

---

14. The two forms of internal taxation in the late seventeenth century were the poll tax and the direct property tax. *See* John A. Kinnamon, *The Public Levy in Colonial Maryland to 1689,* 53 MARYLAND HISTORICAL MAGAZINE 253 (1958).

agree among themselves about it who should go or stay so that five might be left."

The House of Delegates, for its part, was continuing its strenuous efforts to assure the full attendance of its members. On May 1, 1696, it resolved without recorded dissent that a messenger would be sent for any member not appearing at the appointed time; and that the member would pay charges for the messenger and a fine, both as set by the House. At the same time, the House was not taking any risks with the credentials of its members. On one occasion, at the March-April session of 1697/8, the Sheriff of Baltimore County had made an insufficient return for the election of delegates. Those who attended in Annapolis certified that the delegates were regularly elected, but the House sent for the Sheriff to come to Annapolis for verification.

Although Maryland had become a royal colony and was no longer under the political control of Lord Baltimore, it was regular practice during the 1690s to include his name on the title page of the *Journals,* along with the name of the Governor:

Charles Calvert, Lord Baltimore, Proprietary
Francis Nicholson, Governor

The Assembly's public printing was put upon a regular basis in October, 1696, when William Bladen, Clerk of the House, proposed at his own expense to get a press and the necessary equipment for printing the laws enacted at each session.

## COMPENSATION OF PUBLIC OFFICIALS

Compensation of the delegates was continued at 140 pounds of tobacco each day, under an act passed at the September-October session of 1696. The payment came from the "publick leavy" (*i.e.,* the Province, and not the counties). "Itinerant" charges long had been paid by the individual counties. A proposal to change this system was made at the

October-November session in 1698. Citing the rental charges for the boats required to bring the Eastern Shore members to Annapolis, one of the delegates moved to transfer this charge also to the Province. The decision was that the traditional charge upon the counties would be continued.

There was a mark of the times, in 1704, in another proposal dealing with legislative expenses and compensation, that a portion of the per diem allowance be paid in money rather than in tobacco. It came first from the House, citing that "there is Mony in Bank and the publick Levy like to be very high and hard upon the poorer sort" and suggesting that the per diem of 140 pounds of tobacco be paid partly with money, at the rate of one penny per pound. The reaction of the Council was favorable, though there was a counter proposal to set the rate at ten shillings per one hundred pounds of tobacco.

The *Journals* for the year 1700 have a full and complete accounting for legislative expenses. The House had established at the current session a Committee to Inspect and State the Public Accounts of the Province, with three members. Most of the expenses still were stated in terms of pounds of tobacco.

First, there was an allowance of 720 pounds of tobacco for members from each of the counties of Cecil, Kent, Talbot, Dorchester, and Somerset, "for a boat." There followed an itemized list by counties of all the delegates. With some variations, because of a different number of days involved for particular individuals (with 14 days being the maximum), the usual allowances for the per diem and itinerant charges of delegates from the several counties were as follows: Baltimore, 2000 pounds; Anne Arundel, 1960; Calvert, 2280; St. Mary's, 2440; Charles, 2280; Prince George's, 2280; Cecil, 2440; Kent, 2280; Talbot, 2280; Dorchester, 2440; and Somerset, 2020. The allowance for itinerant charges being paid by the Province was a change, of course, from the decision made only two years earlier to continue the custom of having these charges paid by the respective counties.

The legislative accounts for the year 1700 then went on to list other payments approved by the committee, some of them non-legislative and others uncertain. Of those which seem to have been legislative, the Clerk of the Council (a full-time job, though later it was to be treated as an executive expense) was paid over 25,000 pounds of tobacco in salary and expenses; the Clerk of the House of Delegates, 7,120; the doorkeeper in the House, 950; and members of the Council (also claimed later to be a proper executive expense) were paid varying amounts up to 2,580 pounds. The Clerk of the House Committee on Laws received 1,800 pounds of tobacco; the Clerk of the House Committee on Accounts, 2,200; the "man" for engrossing, 400; and the "Minister of the Gospell for attending the Court and the Assembly, 3,000." A final payment in money, possibly for legislative duties, was "for Mending the Ditch and Accomodating the Men while they were at work and for Setting up the house of ease," 2 pounds and 3 shillings.

A number of matters arose during the early 1700s concerning the compensation and expenses of the Governor. Governor Blakiston started them at the April-May session in 1700, writing to the House that "Since every body receives redress from you it will be farr from a Crime in me to hinte to you how great a Sufferer I am in largeness and size" of the hogsheads of tobacco received from the Province. The problem was that the weight of the hogsheads was less than that probably intended in the appropriation. The Governor added that if no change were made, he would acquiesce in the decision of the House. Legislation was passed at that session to clarify the size of hogsheads.

The problem of the Governor's residence came up a few years later, in 1704. There was another Governor by that time, John Seymour,[15] and in his opening address on September 5 he spoke of "the Illness of my House," adding that "if you should think I deserve no better Accommodation during my abode in the Province I must acquiesce with your sentiments and endeavour to be Contented being Resolved **never to ask for or expect what at any time you Judge unreasonable.**" The House a few days later recognized the "incommodiousness" of the house and expressed its "due Concern and hearty desire to do all that in us lyes to make our Actions acceptable to so good a Governor as you approve your Self to us." The best solution that occurred to the House, however, was to ask the Queen to divert part of the tax for supplying arms and ammunition. The Governor demurred to this idea, saying he could never consent to using for his purposes funds appropriated for "so publick a Benefitt to this Province as supplying them with Arms and Ammunition of which they can never have too great a Store." A temporary solution was suggested by the Council, to give the Governor an extra 30 pounds of tobacco yearly to defray the cost of his house rent.

At the March-April session in 1697/8, the doorkeeper for the House of Delegates, James Baker, asked for a small extra fee for all petitions presented to the House. The reply of the House was one of those enigmatic decisions that regularly baffle the non-legislative mind. Baker's request was denied, but "considering his extraordinary diligence" he

---

15. *See generally,* Charles B. Clark, *The Career of John Seymour, Governor of Maryland, 1704-1709,* 48 MARYLAND HISTORICAL MAGAZINE 134-59 (1953). He would not have improved his popularity if the House of Delegates had known of a comment he made about what he conceived to be the lack of cooperation from the House: "There was not any person of liberall Education that appear'd there, it was too difficult a task for me, to graft good manners on so barren a Stock . . . ." He mentioned also the "Envious & Malicious Spiritts wanting to create heats and Iealousies among the Members of the Lower House." Seymour to Board (Council), March 10, 1709/10. *Id.,* at 157-58.

was allowed 400 pounds of tobacco over his usual allotment. This same James Baker again petitioned the Assembly at the April-May session in 1700. He averred that he "is a very ancient and Poore man very infirme and Weake and has faithfully served" the House "these nine years and upwards . . . ." He asked that the House provide a servant to assist him "and his poore weake wife who is likewise ancient." The House arranged for "a good able man Servant to be delivered him," and that the cost be met from the next public levy.

## LEGISLATIVE PRIVILEGES AND PREROGATIVES

The *Journal* for the session of October, 1695, records an invitation for a social evening for members of the Upper House. The Clerk notified them that the Governor "desires theye would walk down toward the Dark of the Evening for to drink the health of the King," and added that the Governor would "cause a bone fire to be made for the Joyfull news" of the success of the English against the French.

The House of Delegates continued its determined campaign to prove and improve its relative importance in the scheme of things governmental. Its strictures were aimed variously at the Council, the Governor, and the Governor and Council (Upper House) combined. Without anything approaching a major controversy, the *Journals* for sessions during 1697 and 1698 related a number of frictional situations.

Thus, in the May-June session of 1697, a message from the House to the Upper House complained that the Clerk of its Committee on Laws had been taken into custody by the Sheriff of Anne Arundel County, "which we humbly Conceive to be a great Breach of the Priviledges of this House." Without fanning a public controversy, the Upper House sent back verbally to the House of Delegates the information that the Clerk, William Taylard, had kept in his custody a record book of fees belonging to the Secretary's office, thus breaking an oath to deliver all public books and records to that official.

Another matter concerning legislative privilege came up at the October-November session in 1698. The House of Delegates, in a "humble address" to the Governor, complained of the case of Delegate Philip Clarke, who was held in jail on a judgment for six thousand pounds of tobacco owing to the King. The House protested that no member should be restrained from legislative service unless for treason, felony, or denying security for the peace.

Governor Nicholson made a spirited and abrasive reply, that "he Cannot but wonder at the Extravagant Humour of the House of Delegates who run headlong upon Heats and private piques not at all reguarding or intending the busieness for which they are mett." Continuing, "although Mr. Speaker had not the manners to wait upon his Excellency as it was his Duty yet he could wayte upon Clarke a person Convicted upon the Oath of a Grand and petit Jury." The Governor also "wonders" that the Speaker adjourned the House after sending the message about Clarke "and did not sitt some tyme for to receive his Answer thereto." Finally, though as a side issue, the Governor said he had depositions of "scurrilous reflection" upon the House made by Clarke, "that he could talk more sence then the whole House and that he warranted he would manage them all." The Governor's conclusion was that it would be seditious and rebellious to the King to attempt illegally to take Clarke out of prison.

On the following day, the Governor took the Clarke affair to the Council. That body recommended that very little business be placed before the House, "Inasmuch as the House of Delegates are in such heats and Divisions." The Governor then prorogued the House for two days. The House persisted, however, claiming the same privilege for its members which it said pertained to the House of Commons. The Council took that question under advisement.

The Clarke controversy finally ended when the Governor called Clarke before him and promised clemency if Clarke could produce sufficient evidence to warrant release.

During the March-April session of 1697/8, the House of Delegates handled with delicacy and circumspection the troublesome problem presented whenever the Governor attended its sessions. In a message to the Governor, the House explained that "it having fallen under the consideration of this house whether it were convenient and consonant to the rules and Methods of parliaments and Assemblyes" that the Governor should attend House sessions, "We have Resolved that the same As it had not heretofore been usuall so it ought not now to be practicable." Therefore, the House "humbly desire" that when it pleased the Governor to confer with the House, "you will order us to attend you att the Council Chamber. It being more for the Grandeur & honour of the Kings Government" that the House should attend the Governor than that "you should give your selfe the trouble to come down to us." The Governor quickly acceded; but six days later, when the Speaker suffered from an ailment which evidently left him less than ambulatory, the Governor when ordering the Speaker and House to attend him in the Council Chamber added that if the Speaker were so indisposed he could not come, he (the Governor) would come to the Speaker's chamber. The House graciously replied (as it did on a similar occasion a few days later) that "This house considering the sickness of our Speaker if your Excellency pleases to condesend so fare as to come to the Speakers chamber we shall be ready to receive your Excellency."

On a couple of occasions during the late 1690s, the Governor initiated disputes. One of them occurred after he had sought from the clerks of House committees an account of what had happened in the committees. The House protested, and the Governor in reply indicated that he was trying to locate the source of criticism directed against him. The House, said the Governor, "have attacked him in an unusual manner"; and it cannot be reasonable to think that "in the station he is in he will suffer himself to be abused without endeavoring to discover the Authors." Do the members of the House, he asked rhetorically, "desire to be despotick and above the Law so as not to be questioned?" To buttress the point, the Governor sent along a message to the House from the Attorney General, which observed that the members of the House "seem afraid of Invisible nothings .... It is plaine that you would not have your words and Actions known which is enough to Create suspicion." The House was not impressed. In adopting its rules for the session, it included a rule that prohibited anyone (specifying particularly any burgess, deputy, delegate, or clerk) from uttering "any words" or making "relation of any words spoken in the house to any bill or otherwise upon debate or Conference upon penalty of such fyne as the house shall think fitt."

Also during the spring session of 1697/8, the Governor and Council proposed new legislation "on the method of holding Assemblyes," and if that were not agreeable to the House, at least the enactment of a law confirming current procedures. The House of Delegates gave short shrift to the whole idea: "This house is particularly satisfied with the proceedings of this assembly and do not think it necessary to make any such act of confirmation."

Two matters of more serious import came from the Governor, appearing in the *Journal* for April 1, 1698. Both originated with the King, and both had an active potential for harm to the legislative process.

The first directive was that the enactment of temporary laws should be discontinued, and that all laws for the good government and support of the Province should be made "indefinite and without limitation of time," unless for a temporary purpose. A corollary was that a law once enacted should not again be enacted, "except upon very urgent occasions" with the consent of the King.

The House of Delegates immediately rejected the proposal for passing only "perpetual" laws. "In this Infant Country," it explained, "we hold it best not to enact perpetuall Laws, because we have not had sufficient Experience whether they may be or not to our advantage." The same instruction came again from King William in 1699, but the House without any public protest seemed quietly to ignore it.

The second directive from the King was that the General Assembly should not "pass any Law or do any grant, Settlement or otherwise, whereby our revenue may be expended or Impaired without our Especiall leave or Command therein." It obviously impinged upon the centuries-old efforts of the Parliament, succeeded by the Assembly, to have legislative control over the purse strings. The directive was repeated by the King in 1699, in even more drastic and explicit language: "You are not to pass any Act or Order ... for leavying money and inflicting fynes and penaltyes whereby the same shall not be reserved" to the King for public uses. Again, this directive seemed to have no impact upon the House of Delegates. Queen Anne renewed both directives in 1704.

Occasionally the critical comments that were bandied between the two Houses originated with the Upper House; and it proved it could be as adept as the House of Delegates in its barbed language. During the spring session of 1697/8, for example, when the House requested a delay in a conference on Indian matters, because of the illness of the Speaker, the Upper House termed this "an Unparliamentary way of proceeding." During the fall session of 1698, in a note to the House, the Upper House referred to "the opinion of the House which is found not to be infallible but Erroneous and some of the Members Actions Arbitrary factious & seditious as will appear by theire Journalls."

Yet with the constant jockeying for position and vying for legislative leadership, there could be surprising agreement and cooperation between the two houses. Similarly, life was not always competitive between the General Assembly and the Governor. Frequently during the 1690s, for example, prior to adjourning a daily session until the following day, the Upper House would inquire of the Lower if it had any further business "for this night; the Upper House will adjourn for the night if not."

It was standard procedure at the beginning of a session that the Speaker of the House would ask the Governor, on behalf of the House, to ratify and allow the traditional liberties and procedures of House members. In the March-April session of 1697/8, after this request was granted, the Governor gave a "goun" to the Speaker, with which he was immediately invested. The Governor on this occasion also gave a mace to the Sergeant-at-Arms, adding the explanation that he "by bearing the same should have Authority to take such persons and bring them before Mr. Speaker and the house, as Mr. Speaker and the house shall direct him."

All this by the 1690s was part of a fixed ritual for the election of a Speaker; the *Journal* for the April-May session of 1704 had it in full. The first step was that the Governor made a formal address to the General Assembly at the beginning of the session, a procedure copied from a very old custom with the king and the Parliament in England. His address completed, the Governor directed the House to withdraw and choose its Speaker. In due time, the members of the House returned and indicated whom they had elected, requesting the approval of the Governor for their choice. With studied diffidence, the prospective Speaker would protest that although he had been elected by the House, he "hoped and prayed" that the Governor would direct the House to make another choice, to get a person better qualified than he "for that weighty Trust & Service from which he desired to be excused as altogether unfitting." The Governor, in turn, would say he could not disapprove of what the House had done, "especially in this their choice of him." [16] The Speakership settled, the Speaker then would entreat the Governor that all the subjects might be supported and protected in their just rights and liberties; that members of the House might have access to the Governor on all occasions; and that there would be freedom of debate. Finally, the Speaker would say to the Governor that if there should be any mistakes or misunderstandings, he hoped the Governor would not attribute them to the House, but to him, the Speaker.

One deviation from the ritual about Speakers occurred at the October-November session in 1712. Robert Tyler, of Prince George's County, was elected Speaker and followed the script in asking the Governor to "command" the House to elect another. The Governor, still following protocol, refused. Delegate Tyler then made a second request of the Governor, and this time the Governor gave "leave" to the House to consider another. When the House returned to its deliberations, Tyler "earnestly desired" of the members that he be excused, and that Robert Ungle, of Talbot County, be elected Speaker. This action followed, and when Delegate Ungle made his plea of unworthiness to the Governor, it was not accepted. The Governor "commanded" Delegate Ungle to accept the task. The Governor had prorogued the Assembly during the one day's interval the House was without a Speaker.

---

16. The *Journal* for April 26, 1715, summarized neatly the ritual of this custom. It referred to the election of a Speaker by the House of Delegates, "who after he had disabled himself as usual was approved of by his Excellency."

182

The rules adopted for procedure in the House also were in a regular pattern, stemming directly from those first adopted by the Assembly sixty years earlier. Those for the October-November session of 1698 spelled out perhaps more clearly than before the usual rule for giving a bill only one reading on a given day and added a prohibition against smoking in the House during a session. The full set of rules as adopted in 1698 was as follows:

By the house of Delegates October the 24$^{th}$ 1698.

It is this day ordered by the Burgesses and Delegates of this Province now assembled that these Rules and Orders following be observed by the Burgesses and Delegates now assembled and by the Clerk of this house dureing this Sessions of Assembly.

1$^{st}$ That no Burges Deputy or Delegate of this house shall use any revileing Speeches, or name any one by his proper name, but by another signification vizt the Gentleman which spoke last or the like

2. That no one Speake above once at a Reading to any bill without License of the Speaker, and if two persons or more rise up together the Speaker shall appoint who shall speake first and no one may Interrupt another or Speake till the other hath ended.

3. That none shall give his opinion or Speake Sitting to any bill, but shall stand up and Reverently direct his Speach to the Speaker.

4. That every bill proposed to the house shall be read three Severall tymes before it be Engrossed and that between every reading one day shall be Intermitted unless upon very urgent occasion Mr Speaker with the consent of the house shall dispence therewith, and then one being read twice at one sitting shall be sufficient as being read two Severall tymes and days when so Entered on the Clerks Iournall.

5. That no one shall come to the house of Assembly whilst the house is sitting with a Sword or other weapon, but shall put the same into the hands of the Door keeper or other person appointed, upon penalty of a fyne as the Speaker Deputys and Delegates shall thinke fitt.

6. Any of the members bound to attend this assembly which shall be absent from this house at the tyme appointed after the number of Two and Twenty and the Speaker according to the Order for Sittling the house shall forfeit all his or their Allowance or Allowances for every such and so many dayes as he or they shall be so deficient without sufficient Excuse for the same to be allowed of by the Speaker.

7. That all Misdemeanors that shall happen within this house shall be considered and fyned by the house.

8. When any bill is presented, and no one makes objection thereunto Mr. Speaker shall appoint any one member to speake to the said bill and deliver his opinion first and so in order as Mr Speaker shall thinke fitt.

9. That dureing the Sessions of this Assembly noe one whatsoever Either Burgess, Deputy, Delegate or Clerk: shall utter any words or make relation of any words spoken in the house to any bill or otherwise upon debate or Conference upon penalty of such fyne as the house shall thinke fitt.

10. That no bill be read but in full house during this sessions of Assembly, all Committees being called into the house.

11. That no Burgess, Deputy, Delegate or Clerk dureing this Sessions of Assembly presume to smoake Tobacco in the house whilst the house is a Sitting under the penalty of being fyned and censured as the house shall thinke fitt.

The Clerk of the House was ordered to post the rules in a convenient place, for everyone to peruse. As an added resolution and not a formal rule, it was determined "that the house will every morning go to prayers at ten of the clock."

Governor Nathaniel Blakiston sent word to the Council, in March 1701/2, that for reasons of health he would be returning to England that summer. Both the Council and the House of Delegates sent him profuse notes of regret. The Council wrote of "the great Ease and Happiness we have constantly enjoyed in your just moderate & equitable Treatment"; and the House expressed thanks "from a

People, whom by your Constant Endeavour Candour & Integrity Prudence and discreet Management of Affairs you have given a compleat and Entire Satisfaction."

All this was in sharp contrast to the abrasive and critical relationships between the two houses and the prior Governor, Francis Nicholson. He was transferred to Virginia, late in 1698, to the evident relief of the Assembly. Shortly before leaving, he devised a piece of drollery of the practical-joke variety, the humor of which was completely lost upon the House of Delegates. Nicholson applied for a pardon for the Province from the English Council of Trade and Foreign Plantations, and it was granted. The House protested that it was not aware the Province suffered from any guilt or that a pardon was needed. The Governor answered with some heat that never before had he heard of a people that refused mercy from their king, but the House of Delegates persisted in refusing to accept the "pardon." Nicholson's successor, Nathaniel Blakiston, had more amiable relationships with the House than had Nicholson.

## INTO THE EIGHTEENTH CENTURY

As the Province of Maryland reached the end of the seventeenth century, it had a population estimated at 30,000 people. Perhaps three-fifths of them lived on the Western Shore, and four-fifths of them south of the Patapsco and Chester rivers. Among the several religions, it was estimated that about 3,000 were Quakers, a lesser number were Roman Catholics, and the remainder belonged to the Church of England. A minority of about 3,000 were Negroes.[17]

17. Henry F. Thompson, *Maryland at the End of the Seventeenth Century,* 2 MARYLAND HISTORICAL MAGAZINE 163-71 (1907).

The first Quakers are thought to have arrived in Maryland in 1656. They settled mainly along the Severn River and on Kent Island. Delmar Leon Thornbury, *The Society of Friends in Maryland,* 29 MARYLAND HISTORICAL MAGAZINE 101-15 (1934).

As one mark of Maryland's status as a royal colony and being subject to the directives of the English monarchy, King William, in 1699, sent a series of instructions to the Governor, to be passed on to the General Assembly. One of them, which led ultimately to a general revision of the laws of the Province, was that the Governor, with the assistance of the Council, was "to take care that all Laws now in force be revised and Considered," all to be subject to the King's "approbation or disallowance." A project of revising the laws already had been started, earlier in the 1690s. Two other instructions in 1699, already discussed, were those concerning the Assembly's powers over money bills and the enactment of temporary laws.

King William died in 1702 and was succeeded by Queen Anne.[18] The Governor, Council and Upper House, and House of Delegates joined in an address of welcome and felicitation to the new Queen. Queen Anne, in 1704, renewed the general set of instructions which had been sent earlier by King William, including those affecting revenues and the passage of permanent acts.

---

18. The change in the monarchy and the slow communications of the time figured in a legal controversy in the 1760s. The General Assembly in 1702 passed an act for the establishment of churches, which, after a long legislative history, was supplemented by another act in 1763. When the latter act expired some years after 1763, the then Governor Eden said the act of 1702 again was valid. An attorney in the Province then advanced the argument that the act of 1702 was void *ab initio*. He argued that the act of 1702 was enacted in March of that year, after King William had died on March 8. The act was assented to in the name of William, but Anne actually was on the throne at that time. The call for the session of 1702 was in William's name, and the enacting clause in the bill mentioned "the King's most excellent majesty." The Assembly in the 1760s passed a special act to quiet the controversy, but the legal question never was settled. The Revolution in the next decade probably provided a practical answer to it, but otherwise the question has remained *res non judicata*.

The Queen added a further instruction about the style of the enacting clause, saying "in the passing of Laws that the Style of Enacting the Same be by the Governour Councill & Assembly, and noe other." To this the House said it would conform. The Council, however, proposed saying "By the Queens most Excellent Majestys Governour Councill & Assembly of this Province and the Authority of the Same." It was this wording that was used in acts passed at the session in 1704.

Two bills were vetoed by the King in 1699, and the Governor announced them to the Council (Upper House) at a meeting held in Annapolis on April 4, 1700. One bill was an act of 1696 for the establishment of the Protestant religion, and the other was an act of 1699 for "ascertaining" (*i.e.,* revising) the laws of the Province.

The latter was Chapter 46 of the Acts of 1699. It provided for continuing all the acts from the sessions of 1692, 1694, 1695, 1696, and 1697, "together with the several laws made this session, and no other." All of them were to be "the body of laws of this province." Also, "all laws, heretofore made, for and in this province, of what kind soever (except laws for private purposes, and the laws mentioned in the said catalogue, and the laws made and assented to this session) are annuled, repealed and made void." To the listing of the acts not repealed there had been added a clarifying act in Chapter 7 of the Acts of 1700. This law had confirmed the list of laws retained and confirmed by Chapter 46 of the Acts of 1699 and added "saving to any person the benefit and advantage of any suit or action already commenced or sued upon any of the said repealed acts."

The veto messages for the acts of 1696 and 1699 raised questions of familiar concern to future generations of legislators. The two acts vetoed were said to be defective in breaking the rule against having two subjects in the same act and in not fairly expressing the contents of the acts in their titles. In addition, the act of 1699 suffered from being phrased as a "temporary" rather than a "permanent" law. An incidental effect of the vetoes, since there was no power for enacting laws over a veto, was that, in the King's word, the laws were "repealed" and not simply "vetoed."

As for the act of 1696, to establish the Protestant religion, said the Governor in his report to the Upper House, you have "Clogged and Loaded it with things of different Natures which I hope you will wisely Correct without the least Hesitation." On the same point, and more fully, the Commissioners of Trade and Plantations advised that "it is most irregular that soe many Laws of different kinds should all be Enacted together by one Single Act." It would have been impossible, the Commissioners added, for the King to disallow any part of it without voiding the whole. "And to this we add, that as you see now the inconveniency of Passing so many Laws of Different Kinds by one Single Act whereupon your Care hereafter must be not onely that Each Act be passed Severally, but also that different matters be not mixed in the Same Act, and that nothing be put into any Act . . . of another Nature than what is agreeable to the Title of it." [19]

The Upper House (Council) concurred at once in the wisdom of the vetoes, advising the House of Delegates to avoid the "unhappy" mistake in the act of 1699 "by Joining them alltogether." Both houses joined in a message written in abject humility, expressing "a deep sence of our oversight" and a plea to "excuse our inadvertency."

---

19. The difficulties involved in possibly having more than one subject in an enactment and in having the contents of the law adequately described in the title were to be major problems stemming from the written constitutions of the future. *See* Carl N. Everstine, *Titles of Legislative Acts,* 9 MARYLAND LAW REVIEW 197-245 (1948).

The veto of the act of 1699 for revising the laws and the general agreement that a revision was necessary combined to lead to a thorough revision of the laws in the September-October session of 1704. The legislative product of that session was long and detailed. A general repeal of former and existing laws included all but two, those being the act for religious worship and the act for rules of the port of Annapolis. Except for those two laws, everything else was "repealed and made void."

One slight practical problem arose in the plans for publication of all the new laws. The House wished all the laws to be printed on parchment. However, the supply of parchment being limited, "good" paper was used for copies of the laws to be sent to the counties.

There was a rumor in 1704 that the colony of New York was promoting a scheme to bring all the American colonies under that government. The rumor came from England. Despite its seeming implausibility, it was sufficient to stir strong opposition in Maryland.

Governor John Seymour disclosed in September, 1704, that in a letter he had from "an Eminent Merchant in London," there was mention "of a Design New York hath of making all the Colonies Tributarys to them in order to Support or rather enrich them and they seem to push the thing for the Half as to have a number to be chosen out of the Northern and Southern Governments to represent these Colonies and meet at New York instead of their own Assemblyes."

Both houses in Maryland joined in a memorial to the Queen strongly opposing the possibility of being joined with New York. Members discussed the possibility of employing an agent in London to represent the Province before the Parliament and the Queen. Securing the necessary funds would have been a problem, but one proposed answer to this difficulty was both ingenious and ironic. Two years earlier, the Assembly had voted funds for New York to assist that colony in fighting the French and the Indians; New York had never called for the money, and the proposal was to use these funds to send to England in opposing any plan for absorbing the Province of Maryland into that colony.

The new St. Anne's Church in Annapolis was nearly completed during the summer of 1704, and it was mentioned several times in the legislative *Journals.* In a message to the Governor and Council in early September, the House of Delegates declared that its members had inspected the church "and have taken notice of the place you are pleased to be made for the Burgesses and Delegates to sitt in and we do very well approve" of what had been done. A few days later, the Governor and Council invited the members of the House to ceremonies for opening the church:

> Gentlemen. By a good Providence and a cheerful Assistance of the Publick and other worthy Gentlemen The Church in this town is now in such forwardness that with the blessing of Almighty God we have proposed to have divine Service celebrated therein upon Sunday the 24th Instant at which time the Sacrament will be administered, therefore to the End we may open the said Church with the greatest Solemnity we are capable of here in this remote part of the World we desire Mr. Speaker and the House of Delegates will Concur to accompany his Excellency and this Board at the time aforesaid.

Two timely comments came from the House following the church service on September 24. On the next day, in a formal message, the House commented that "This House are very well Satisfyed with the well composed Discourse preached by the Reverend Doctor Wooton at opening the Annapolitan Church." [20] A few days later, in another message, the House

---

20. The Rev. Dr. James Wooton was the third rector of St. Anne's Church and served from 1704 to 1712. *See* EDWARD DARLINGTON JOHNSON, ILLUSTRATED HISTORY AND GUIDE BOOK TO ST. ANNE'S PARISH, ANNAPOLIS 9 (Annapolis, 1935); WALTER B. NORRIS, ILLUSTRATED HISTORY AND GUIDE BOOK OF ST. ANNE'S PARISH, ANNAPOLIS 8 (Annapolis, 1947).

inquired "whether it may not be necessary for the ornament of St. Anne's Church in Annapolis that the Pews appointed for the Delegates of Assembly may be build at the publick Charge and that flag stone be sent for out of England to lay the alleys."

A new act for electing and summoning delegates to the General Assembly (Chapter 35 of the Acts of 1704) completed the important legislation of that session. Probably it simply was a part of the general revision of the laws, for it was essentially the same as in recent years. It gave the Assembly another opportunity, in the preamble to the act, to restate and emphasize the importance of the legislative processes in the Provincial government:

> Forasmuch as the Cheifest and only ffoundation and Support of any Kingdom State or Commonwealth is the providing Establishing and Enacting good and wholesome Laws for the good rule and Government thereof and also upon any necessary and Emergent occasion to raise and Levy money for the defraying the Charges of the said Government and defence thereof neither of which according to the Constitution of this Province can be made ordain'd Establishd or raised but by and with the Consent of the ffreeman of this Province by their severall delegates and Representatives by them freely nominated Chosen and Elected to serve for their Severall Citys and Countys in a Generall Assembly. And for as much as the Safest and best rule for this Province to follow in Electing such Delegates and Representatives is the presidents of the proceedings in Parliaments in England as near as the Constitution of this Province will Admitt. . . .

The act then listed in detail the substantive and procedural details for electing delegates and for calling sessions of the General Assembly. The Governor, at a time of his choosing, was to issue writs to the several sheriffs, requiring the elections. Voters were to be the freemen of the Province having a freehold of 50 acres of land or a "Visible Estate" of 40 pounds sterling, as a minimum. Each county was to elect four delegates, with two more from St. Mary's City, all of whom were required to have the same property qualifications as voters. The delegates, without any further writ, then were to attend the next session of the Legislature "to do and Consent to those things which then by the favour of God shall happen to be ordained by the Advice and Consent of the great Councill of this Province Concerning such occasions and Affaires as shall relate to the Government State and defence of this Province." The same provisions automatically were to apply to any county erected in the future. Sheriffs were excluded from membership; and at the very end of the act, as if it were an after-thought added by amendment, was a prohibition against the membership of the keeper of any ordinary.

Again, by Chapter 5 of the Acts of 1708, the Legislature enacted a law for electing and summoning the General Assembly. The provisions of the act of 1704 were essentially repeated; but the prohibition against the membership of the keeper of an ordinary was moved upward into the main body of the bill. Eight years later, by Chapter 11 of the Acts of 1716, another similar bill was enacted. This one had two novel provisions added. The first was not actually new in substance; the allowance to members of the Assembly of a per diem in the amount of 140 pounds of tobacco, plus the itinerant charges, was placed into the membership bill for the first time.

Members of the Eastern Shore Delegation (though that term seems not to have been coined in the early eighteenth century) filed a complaint in 1709 about one aspect of the itinerant charges paid to the legislators. A member of the House moved that ". . . in as much as at the last Session the weather being so bad that some of the Gentlemen Members belonging to the Eastern Shore was a long time, and run great Difficulties going home whether they ought not to

192

have some further Allowance for their Itinerant Charges." The House agreed they should get extra compensation, but ordered each to bring in an account of his particular charge and submit it to the House for further consideration.

The second new feature in the election act of 1716 was to assess a penalty in the amount of one hundred pounds of tobacco against any person who, qualified to vote in an election for delegates, failed to appear at the election. The offending voter was to be permitted to appear at the next county court if he wished to plead extenuating circumstances. This penalty had been discussed in 1708, when the Upper House suggested to the House of Delegates that such a clause should be added to the election bill "to oblige the Freeholders to appear at Elections it having been often experienced that they are very indifferent on these Occasions." The House in reply, in 1708, was not at all enthusiastic about the idea: "this House cannot see any reason why any Clause should be inserted to oblige Freeholders to appear at Elections unless it is to draw them into snares of Fines not being customary in Great Britain." In 1716 the House agreed to the penalty for non-voting.

## PROBLEMS OF ANNAPOLIS

In another development about this time, Annapolis was given a separate right of representation in the General Assembly, as a town in its own right and not simply as a part of Anne Arundel County. The change was patterned upon the privilege long accorded to St. Mary's City. It stirred issues of political philosophy going far beyond the question of representation.

For many years during the seventeenth century, Maryland was a settlement of small farms and a few plantations. St. Mary's City, though but a village in modern concepts, was the only place that remotely could be called a town. That fact, plus its designation as the capital of the Province, seemed to justify giving it two delegates in the House, in addition to the four delegates assigned to St. Mary's County (this number being the same as for every other county). By the end of the century, Annapolis was the capital and growing rapidly,[21] so the question was raised about extra representation for it. The *Journal* of the Upper House for the September-October session of 1704 has a message from the Governor and Council inquiring "if it were not fitt to Encourage this Town being the Seat of Government with that Privilege."

Before the question of separate representation could be considered, the Governor thought it necessary that the town be incorporated, and this he proceeded to do. In granting the municipal charter, he included in it a provision that the town should have two delegates in the House. They were to be entirely apart from and in addition to the four delegates regularly alloted to Anne Arundel County. Further, the town charter provided, the two delegates from Annapolis were to be chosen by town officials; this was the same manner of selection that long had been used for St. Mary's City. In accordance with these powers, two delegates from Annapolis were present at the September-October session in 1708.

On September 30, during the session that year, the House sent a message to municipal officials "to attend this House to Morrow Morning at Nine of the Clock and bring with them the record of their Charter by which they claim to send Delegates to the Assembly." The officials attended as summoned "to answer the Objections against the Charter." The House then debated whether the Governor had power to

---

21. For a lively and spirited account of the events and personalties of early Annapolis, *see* WILLIAM OLIVER STEVENS, ANNAPOLIS (New York, 1937). *See also* DAVID RIDGELY, ANNALS OF ANNAPOLIS (Baltimore, 1841); and ELIHU S. RILEY, THE ANCIENT CITY — A HISTORY OF ANNAPOLIS, IN MARYLAND (Annapolis, 1887).

issue the charter "in Manner and fforme as it is granted," and that question was unanimously decided "No."

A message sent to the Governor a few days later explained that "several of the Freeholders and Inhabitants" of Annapolis were concerned that the town's charter deprived them of a right to take part in the election of the Annapolis delegates in the General Assembly, a right "which the Laws of England and this Province undoubtedly entitles them to as Freeman." The House then proceeded to expel the two delegates representing Annapolis.

The preliminary issue was whether or not the Governor had power to issue a municipal charter. There would have been no doubt of this power if it had been exercised by Lord Baltimore under the Provincial Charter granted to him. However, in the royal status of the colony during this period, there was no specific authorization for the office of governor under the monarchy. Next, if the question concerning power of incorporation were established in the affirmative, the second question was that of voting rights for the citizens of Annapolis in choosing the two delegates for the Assembly. The charter of Annapolis gave that power to officers of the town and not to its citizens generally.[22]

On October 4, 1708, the Governor called the entire House before him, to receive his comments on the Annapolis matters. Speaking to the members of both houses, the Governor was blunt and direct about the action of the House in expelling the delegates from Annapolis:

---

22. These two questions could have led the House to another concerning its own powers and privileges. The combination of having a municipal charter issued by the Governor, and that charter providing for the choice of delegates to the Assembly, had the effect of depriving the General Assembly of any voice in the choosing of this group of its members. The final solution of the Annapolis problem partially remedied that situation.

> ... I cannot but look upon this Action to proceed from
> an ill grounded heat and Rashness not at all becoming
> the Station you fill and since no one pretends to control
> your debates and Resolves concerning the Election of
> your Members It had been much more discretion in you
> to have wholly proceeded thereon then after the
> unwarrantable manner you have expell'd the members
> whose commission for sitting in your house is derived
> from the same fountain of Authority which admits you
> thereto

Next, and this time addressing his remarks only to the
members of the House of Delegates, the Governor continued:

> Mr Speaker
> I cannot but look on this Aukward Step as Derogatory
> to her Sacred Majestys Royal prerogative and
> therefore that the charge to the poor Country of an
> unprofitable Session may not lye at my Door you have
> this one more added to the many favourable
> concessions I have already made that I wish you to
> repair to your House and there seriously reflect on
> what you have done
> Which being ended Mr. Speaker and the whole House
> repaired to their House

The House needed no time for "seriously" reflecting upon
what it had done. A message was dispatched to the Governor
at once. The charter granted to Annapolis, said the House,
"doth deprive some of her Majestys Subjects of the Rights
and priviledges which the Laws of England and this Province
undoubtedly entitles them as Freemen as particularly their
Voting for Delegates or Representatives in the General
Assembly." The House suggested that the matter of
granting municipal charters be left "undetermined till her
Majestys pleasure therein be further known." To this the
Governor responded with continued harshness. He charged
the House had acted in "so unwarrantable and
Unparliamentary a manner ... there is no Retrieving this
Misfortune your heats have run you into." He abruptly
dissolved the Assembly and said he would issue notices for
a new election.

The new Assembly was back about seven weeks later, on November 29, 1708. The House persisted in its opposition to the Annapolis charter provisions, but the two houses in conference worked out a suitable compromise; and it was passed into law as Chapter 7 of the Acts of 1708. The title to the act described it as "Confirming and Explaining the Charter of the City of Annapolis." In the preamble to that act and in the idiom of the times, the Assembly explained its purposes:

> Whereas this Present General Assembly have taken into their Consideration the Charter lately granted to the City of Annapolis and being desirous to give all due Encouragement to Cohabitation, have Resolved to confirm the same Charter, and to explain and refrain some Clauses and Grants therein contained. . . .

The act validated the incorporation of Annapolis and the grants and powers contained in the charter, with several restrictions. One of the limitations was that the two delegates elected from Annapolis would receive only half the "wages" of other delegates. Nothing was said in the act of 1708 about the power of a royal governor in Maryland to create a municipal corporation; but by the very act of legislating in the Annapolis situation, the Assembly partly corrected the imbalance whereby members of the House could be elected under laws beyond the control of the Legislature. Later, also, the House did not hesitate to exercise general jurisdiction over its members from Annapolis. At the October-November session in 1709, it declared one of the delegates from Annapolis to be disqualified for his office, not having been an "inhabitant" of the Province for three years.

The General Assembly was making other forays into areas of "local" government. Frequently, and particularly in 1709, bills for the purpose were being introduced in response to petitions to erect towns. Another, and predictable, reaction occurred in 1711. A new courthouse for Baltimore County was under discussion, and there was mention in the House *Journal* of allowing the citizens of the county to choose its location. At the same session, however, a bill passed the Assembly to have the new courthouse located at Joppa.

## NON-LEGISLATIVE POWERS

The General Assembly was assuming and exercising powers and prerogatives in many areas, seemingly without question, which to a later generation would be deemed completely non-legislative. Upon occasion, the House alone would act with a general inquisitorial power, somewhat as the Grand Inquest of later years, but without the constitutional sanction of post-Revolutionary times.

Thus, in the May session of 1705, the House of Delegates called before it the Sheriff of Anne Arundel County, John Gresham. The House was informed, he was told, that through his neglect a number of prisoners had escaped, "by which it appeared to the House the Province was much damnified." The Sheriff was questioned and withdrew; the matter was debated; and the Sheriff brought back for more questions. The decision, completely and solely by action of the House of Delegates, was that the Sheriff should release all the imprisonment fees for the several prisoners and be discharged from further damages. He "readily consented" to this solution and "returned his most humble & hearty Thanks to the House for their Favours & so withdrew."

The Assembly as a whole passed legislative acts upon a startling variety of other matters which would be forbidden to legislative action in later years. Some of them later would come under the sophistication of doctrines of separation of powers; and others would be treated only by general law, if at all. The statute books for this period show special acts for such unlikely and individual purposes as settling title to land,

198

voiding a deed, confirming a release, confirming a will, settling an estate, cutting "the entail of a tract of land," naturalizing a citizen, banishing an offender from the Province, dividing parishes,[23] declaring an illegitimacy, authorizing a set of trustees to sell land, and adjudicating a protested bill of exchange.

## THE STATE HOUSE FIRE OF 1704

The accustomed routine of the General Assembly was broken in late 1704, when the State House was destroyed by fire. At a short session from December 5 to 9 of that year, the Governor in his address said that "The late melancholy Accident might have been prevented, for I never yet saw any publiq buildings left solely to Providence but in Maryland.... What is necessary to be done in Rebuilding your Statehouse so very necessary for the accommodation of the publiq I leave Intirely to your own Serious Debates and decision."

The House responded that "Wee ... have resolved with all the unanimity and Dispatch proper to such a Conjuncture to take all possible care proper for the preservation of the Records & Restoring the State house to its former beauty and usefulness by Rebuilding and making Good the Bricks thereof."[24] Further, "this house have resolved their Willingness to rebuild the said house in as Comodious a Manner as before." The House asked the Upper House to appoint members to a joint committee to consider details of the work.

---

**23.** *See generally,* Gerald E. Hartdagen, *The Vestry as a Unit of Local Government in Colonial Maryland,* 67 MARYLAND HISTORICAL MAGAZINE 363-88 (1972).

**24.** For descriptions of this and other public buildings in Annapolis, *see* MORRIS L. RADOFF, BUILDINGS OF THE STATE OF MARYLAND AT ANNAPOLIS (Annapolis, 1954).

An attendant problem was that some of the records were destroyed in the fire. For a few of those that had survived, the Governor and Council disclosed the informality of the times in suggesting to the House of Delegates that copies be made, and for this purpose they had arranged "to have the Bills which were read in the House sent for from the late Speakers house in Charles County."

The House arranged for its temporary quarters, securing the house of Colonel Edward Dorsey. The agreed rental was to be 20 pounds sterling "for one year certain & so for a longer Time if the House think fit at the expiration of the first year."

The joint committee for rebuilding the State House decided first that the walls of the old building were "sufficient" for use in the new building. William Bladen offered to do the work and have it completed in a short time. He said he would provide security for his work in the sum of four thousand pounds sterling; and that he was willing to receive "such Pay as they shall think fitt to agree on as Mony comes in & accrue to the Province all the other publick Buildings having gone through my hands."

A bill for the work was passed at this session in December, 1704. The work was to be done "in the same full and ample manner and forme as the said late Stadthouse was built Compleated ffinished and ffurnished at any time before it was burnt the Cubiloe or Terrett only Excepted." Bladen was to get the sum of "one thousand pounds Sterling or in Dollars or pieces of Eight at four and six pence a piece as they now pass within this Province." The builder's security was to assure the completion of the job within 18 months.

By the time of the May session in 1705, the work was already in progress and the committee had been making inspections. It reported to the House of Delegates that it had found the frame of the building done in workmanlike manner and the door cases "tolerable." But, the members said, the window frames are "bad & green Timber some with the Bark on & most sham wedged & not one squared and will when shrunk drop to pieces." The House resolved that window frames already set up should be taken down "and other good & sufficient Window Frames be set in their Roome made of well seasoned Timber."

The new building was occupied in 1706, but in 1709 the committee still found that the window frames, doors, and door cases "are very slight, and not done Workman like and are not hung with sufficient Hinges and that the House is not so well Shingled as it ought to be." The House then resolved that William Bladen should be obliged "to make good the Shingling" and to make the roof "tight and good." The new building again was the subject of change during the October-November session in 1712, though only as to rearranging the use of the rooms and making minor alterations accordingly.

**As if the recent burning of the State House were not** enough, there was a bizarre scheme in 1707 to burn a number of the public buildings in Annapolis. One Richard Clarke concocted the plan. His purpose was to be able to seize arms and to sail away as a privateer.[25]

### LEGISLATIVE CONTENTION

During these early years of the 1700s, the sparring and occasional sarcasm continued between the House of Delegates and the Upper House, with the Governor frequently included as a party because of his usual sympathies with the Upper House. At the April-May session in 1704, for example, the House was assuring the Governor, in what must have been fictitious humility, that ". . . we shall

---

25. ELIHU S. RILEY, THE ANCIENT CITY — A HISTORY OF ANNAPOLIS, IN MARYLAND 81-85 (Annapolis, 1887).

be at all times very Cearful to avoid the Entertainment of Jelouscy & Runing Ourselves into heats and misconstructions."

Two years later, at the opening of the April session in 1706, the Governor in his opening address offered some gratuitous advice to be familiar to later generations. "I am obliged to take Notice," he said, "You make Use of a very Unparliamentary Practice which is to Postpone Matters to the last Eight or tenn Hours of your rising and then things of very greate Consequence are naturally hurryed up or so procrastinated that at our next meeting they are forgott."

At the opening of the September-October session in 1708, the House of Delegates in a message to the Governor "humbly" recommended Richard Dallam for approval as Clerk of the House. The Governor and Council answered that "Tho we are well Satisfied it is her Majestys prerogative to appoint proper Officers to attend the Assembly and that you have no right to the Election of any but what shall be approved by this Board we are willing rather than the Countrys business should be delayed to admit of the Clerk nominated by you pro hac Vice (salvo Jure)[26] but resent it that you rejected the Clerk appointed by his Excellency without giving any Reason." The House, not to be found lacking in legislative niceties, duly thanked the Governor for his "favourable condescension" in approving Dallam.

During this same session, which developed into a short-lived one, lasting only one week, the Governor sharply criticised the House for its failure to pass legislation about the Provincial courts, as was recommended by the Queen. Her reign, said the Governor in his opening address on September 27, 1708, is "the most Glorious of all Monarchs . . . shall we a poor Handful of her remotest Subjects dispute or

---

26. For this one particular occasion (as an exception to the law).

boggle at what her Majesty thinks reasonable and wisely judges to be for your own good as well as the Service of the Crown? . . . Banish all flattering Whispers which advise you to swallow such a pernicious notion that you Gentlemen here Assembled are wiser than the vast Crowds of her other Dominions who unanimously with open loyal Hearts run to obey and serve her Sacred Majesty the Queen."

A few days later, on October 2, the Governor inquired of the Council "whether it be convenient or no to prorogue this present General Assembly and to what time considering how dilatory and irregular their proceedings have been since this meeting." The Council agreed the session should be prorogued and suggested November 29 of the same year for another session. Accordingly, the Governor prorogued the session. In his final message, he recounted the controversies of the session and concluded, "Wherefore since there is no Retrieving this Misfortune your heats have run you into I take the Assemblys to be discontinued."

The next session was called for November 29, 1708, and in his opening address the Governor continued in the same tenor. It would not have been necessary to hold a session so late in the season, he said, "If some sower ill natured Incendiaries had not lately used their utmost Insinuations to disturb & debauch" other well meaning subjects of the Province. To this the House responded sweetly that it was "altogether unsensible" of any such disturbing person, "but if any private or particular person should be tardy in such matters this House does assure your Excellency that they will do their utmost Endeavours to prevent them."

No reason appears in the *Journal,* and perhaps it was only legislative pique, but when the session of November 29 ended and was prorogued on December 17, 1708, to the following April 5, a memorandum from Richard Dallam, Clerk, adds "And the House prorogue themselves until the said fifth day of April next." The right of prorogation, of course, was solely and completely vested in the Governor.

The next episode came during the October-November session in 1709. The House, in a message to the Council, presented in detail a series of six grievances, all of which seemed to be on matters of administrative procedure and not directly upon legislation. They concerned the custody of the Great Seal, the practice of placing one individual in two offices, the reported sale of offices, and the jurisdiction of the Provincial Court. All related to prerogatives of the Governor. After the grievances were considered by a joint committee, the Council agreed on some points and said that corrections already had been made on others.

Two years later, at the October-November session in 1711, the House again was finding fault. This time it criticised the appointments to the Provincial Court. The Governor and Council sent back a scathing rejoinder, directed particularly at the threat of the House to leave the session without passing the appropriation bill, that "you must believe It will as little affect this Board as the members of your House." We are sorry, the Council added, that deference to the Queen's commands is taken "for a slighting your House and leading you and your Posterity into very great Inconveniencys."

A final sally from the Upper House came during the June-July session in 1714, treading closely upon the prerogatives of the House of Delegates: "Finding your House rose pretty early this morning We desire you to lett us know at what time you intend to sitt & rise this Session." However the comment was meant, the House kept its reply simple: "Finding the Hour we rose at yesterday to be inconvenient for the better expediting the Countrys Business" it resolved to meet daily from eight until eleven o'clock in the forenoon and from one to six in the afternoon.

The inadequacy, in the Governor's view, of the house he was alloted arose again as a perennial source of discord between the Governor and the House of Delegates. For years the Governor had complained, and for years the House had pleaded inadequate funds. During the March-April session of 1707, Governor Seymour was back on the subject, telling the House that without some repairs and improvements "I could expect no comfortable being." Further, he said, he had refused an extra offer of 15 pounds a year when first granted by the House, "and lett the matter rest without any reluctancy or uneasiness till we knew each other better." Now he cited the necessary expenditure of some 47 pounds, spent "without any manner of Prospect to Advantage myself or family."

Some years later, in 1715, the House sent a message to then Governor Hart about the living accommodations. The House of Delegates, it said, "well knowing that since there is no House built for a Governour the want thereof must be a considerable Charge to your Excellency ..., the Circumstances of this province are at present very low So we hope your Excellency will so far continue your tender Regard of this Province as not to insist at present on the building of an House till the Province is better Able to raise a Fund for that Purpose, and we should be very glad that your excellency would be pleased to propose to us something on that subject."

Governor Hart graciously replied that "as I am Convinced the good Inclinations of the People to me on this particular are Sincere And that their Abilitys cannot come up at this time to their kind Intentions I shall be contented to Share their present Circumstances." He did request repairs "to be made to the House I live in so as not to be exposed to the Inconveniency of all Weathers."

About the same time, however, the House of Delegates temporized on another matter of public finance somewhat more personal to its own members. During the April-June session of 1715, Governor Hart sent to the Council a copy of an instruction from King George I (1714-1727), and the Council forwarded a copy to the House. It was Article 21 of a long series of "Royal Instructions," issued in view of the straitened condition of public finances in the Province. It provided in part that "You shall reduce the Sallary of the members of the Assembly to a moderate Proportion as may be no Aggrievance to the Country wherein nevertheless you are to use Your Discretion so as no Inconvenience may arise thereby."

The indecision of the royal document was matched by the indecision of concerned parties in Maryland. A week after sending Article 21 to the Council, the Governor inquired in a message to the House whether reducing the size of the county delegations in the House from four to three members would meet the need. The House, in reply, with the concurrence of the Council, told the Governor it had "considered and debated" Article 21. "The matter therein being new," it said, "We are desirous that the same be referred to the Consideration of next Session of the Assembly by which time We shall better inform Ourselves of the Conveniency or Inconveniency that will attend such an Alteration."

## PROCEDURES AND POLICIES

Most of the actual or projected changes in legislative procedure were routine and not sensational during these early years of the eighteenth century. Two of them seem mildly inconsistent, and others are of interest for a continuing show of independence by the House of Delegates.

In the spring of 1708, the House, in a message to the Governor and the Upper House, inquired whether the Legislature would meet on Good Friday. It is a day, said the

House of Delegates, "Perticularly Devoted to Allmighty God by all good Christians; but inasmuch as this house being mett upon the Publiq Affaires of the Province, and would make what dispatch thereof they could, Therefore desire to know" if the Upper House would sit on that day. The House said it would follow whatever the Upper House was doing, but somewhat pointedly added to the message a note of its desire to finish the session on the following day, by Saturday evening. The Upper House replied that on Good Friday it "will after the Duty of the morning Service is over Sitt in Councill the rest of the day."

In contrast, perhaps some question could be raised about the decision of the House, some years later, in taking part of a day's session to observe the anniversary of Guy Fawkes Day, a vestige of the famous Gunpowder Plot of 1605, when there was an ill-managed and abortive attempt to blow up the Parliament Building in London, and members therein.[27] The House *Journal* for November 5, 1712, informs that "This being the Anniversary Day of Thanksgiving for the delivery from the Gunpowder Plot the Hon. Speaker attended by the whole House repaired to the Church and after Divine Service and Sermon ended the House met according to Adjournment."

During these years, the House of Delegates was appointing four regular committees at each session. As listed for the October-November session of 1709, they were the committees on Election and Privileges, Aggrievances, Public Accounts, and Lawse. House sessions sometimes were held from nine a.m. until four p.m.; and at other times were split, as from eight to eleven o'clock in the forenoon and two to five o'clock in the afternoon. The oath of office administered to

---

27. The event is still observed by the Parliament on the opening day of a session, when a perfunctory and ceremonial inspection is made of the cellars under the building.

employees of the House still recalled the former problem with "leaks" of House business; in 1708, for example, the oath to the sergeant-at-arms and the doorkeeper was that "You do swear you will not disclose or divulge to any Person whatsoever any of the Debates or Matters transacted in the House."

A matter of real substance arose in 1712, when there was an explicit statement of the long-time Maryland custom and rule that bills not passed at one session of the Legislature are dead and do not carry over to the following session. The bill here involved was routine, but its pathway wound through at least three sessions of the Assembly.

On October 31, 1711, the House passed and sent to the Upper House a bill "reinvesting lands in Sewards' Heirs." The Upper House, as frequently was done, referred it over to the next session; the reason given was that the Proprietor had "no Agent at present to be heard thereto." The bill was returned to the House, and that body concurred in putting off the matter until another session. Several days later, the Assembly was prorogued.

During the next session, on November 8, 1712, the House put the bill into its *Journal* as "read and endorsed," but this was its first appearance in the 1712 session. It was sent on to the Upper House, which immediately returned the bill. "It is conceived that the above Indorsement is no Ways Parliamentary," wrote the Upper House, "this not being the next Session of that Assembly to which the Bill was referred but another Assembly . . . and in this Case should this Bill be indorsed in like Manner . . . and past into a Law it would be debated, ordained and Enacted by two different Assemblies which must certainly be very irregular." In its message the Upper House also referred to the "well known" difference between adjournment and prorogation.

The House of Delegates in reply said it was "not unsensible" to the difference between adjournment and prorogation, but here it had been a dissolution, "and so this a new Assembly and if all Matters referred from the last to this should be discontinued it would be very inconvenient for then every Thing not then finished must begin anew." The argument of the House was obscure, to say the least. The word "dissolution" did not appear in the *Journals* for all this early period. At the conclusion of any day's work, each of the two Houses would "adjourn" to the next day, as in the modern usage. At the end of a session, the Assembly was "prorogued" by the Governor; this had the effect of a *sine die* adjournment, except that it came from the Governor and not from the Legislature.

In any event, the House did not pursue the argument further, and the bill was not passed in the session of 1712. Mr. Seward's heirs had more troubles ahead; the bill was in the June-July session of 1714, nearly two years later, and again it was put off until the following session.

Queen Anne's County was erected in 1706 and began thereafter to send four delegates to the House. The Queen for whom it was named died in 1714, and her death stirred the same profuse and flattering compliments that all the English monarchs received. She died without an heir, and under the Act of Settlement the eldest son of the Electress Sophia [28] succeeded as king. He became George I of England, and immediately was hailed by the Governor of Maryland as the paragon of all kingly virtues.

## THE RESTORATION

Of more immediate concern to the Province was the death in February, 1714/5, of Charles Calvert, third Lord Baltimore and second Proprietary of the Province of

---

28. Sophia was a granddaughter of James I of England, so the English bloodline was continued.

Maryland. He was succeeded by his son, Benedict Leonard Calvert. The news of Charles Calvert's death did not reach Maryland until about the end of May; and in the meantime, Benedict Leonard had died in April. The title then went in succession to another Charles, the 16-year-old son of Benedict Leonard.

During his lifetime, Benedict Leonard had embraced the Protestant faith, and his children (including young Charles) had been brought up in the Church of England. The late and elder Charles, Lord Baltimore, had belonged to the Church of Rome; and it was that fact in the 1690s that contributed to the government in Maryland's being taken from him, with the Province assuming royal status.

After the younger Charles assumed the title, there was an unexpected quirk in the legislative process in Maryland. A technical question arose whether in the enacting clauses of its bills, reference should be made to the minority of the Proprietary. The decision was that the minority status should not be mentioned, and the rationale was a lawyer's dream: while young Charles "in his natural capacity" was a minor, as "Lord Baltimore" he was a "Body Politick" and thus not liable to the incidence of minority.

The elder Charles, Lord Baltimore, had petitioned the Queen in 1710 to ask for the return of his Province; but the petition was denied. The matter involved was governmental and political; during the royal period, Lord Baltimore had his private rights and his revenues from the Province, but had no share in its government. During the royal period, accordingly, the legislative *Journals* continued to list Charles, Lord Baltimore, as Proprietary.

With the younger Charles, a Protestant, becoming the fifth Lord Baltimore, his guardian petitioned King George to restore the Province. This time the request was granted, and Maryland once more became a Proprietary colony.[29]

29. For a detailed account of the years of the Restoration period, *see* Bernard C. Steiner, *Restoration of the Proprietary in Maryland*, 8 AMERICAN HISTORICAL ASSOCIATION REPORT 229-307 (1899).

## Chapter 7

## THE PROPRIETARY RESTORED

## 1716-1732

The Province that was restored to Lord Baltimore in 1715 was some 80 years old and far different from the tiny colony of two or three hundred venturesome souls that had settled at St. Mary's in 1634.

By the middle 1710s, there were an estimated forty-five or fifty thousand people in Maryland, scattered among the 12 organized counties approximately as follows: [1]

| | |
|---|---|
| Anne Arundel | 4,999 |
| Baltimore | 2,923 |
| Calvert | 3,500 |
| Cecil | 2,097 |
| Charles | 4,007 |
| Dorchester | 3,475 |
| Kent | 2,886 |
| Prince George's | 3,790 |
| Queen Anne's | 3,850 |
| St. Mary's | 4,090 |
| Somerset | 6,352 |
| Talbot | 4,178 |

These figures added to about 46,000 people, and of course they did not include the sparsely populated "western" and unorganized lands stretching out from Baltimore and Prince George's counties. Another estimate of Maryland's

---

1. J. THOMAS SCHARF, 1 HISTORY OF MARYLAND 337 (Baltimore, 1879). These figures are for 1712 and are from the London Public Records Office. It should be remembered that the boundaries of some of these counties in 1715 were different from the modern boundaries. *See* J. Louis Kuethe, *A Gazetteer of Maryland, A.D. 1673*, 30 MARYLAND HISTORICAL MAGAZINE 310-25 (1935).

population in the year 1715 was a total of 50,200.[2]

The rapidly growing population did not seem particularly to affect the activities and the subject matter of the General Assembly. There was further revision of the laws and continuing friction with the Proprietary during the years ahead. Controversies between the two houses of the Assembly and with the Governor kept on without abatement; and the matter of a per diem allowance for members of the Council of State became one of perennial dispute. Another frequent topic of recurring interest was that of laying claim for the rights of the inhabitants to the benefits of the English common and statutory law.

## The Reinstatement of Lord Baltimore

The Governor announced to the General Assembly on April 24, 1716, the reinstatement of Lord Baltimore as Proprietary. The background, he explained, was that of the younger Lord Baltimore's "having Embraced the Protestant Religion which has ... removed that Umbrage which has long been wisely Conceived" against the administration of Maryland's government by Catholics. This session of the Assembly was held in the "Court house commonly called the Stadt house in the Citty of Annapolis" (the term "Stadt" house probably coming from the influence of King William, who before going to England had been Prince of Orange). The oaths of office for members during that session were the "Oath of Allegiance Supremacy and Abjuration" and the Test, the latter being an attestation of one's Protestant religion. The total membership in the House continued to be the same, being four for each county and two from Annapolis. The special representation for St. Mary's City had been discontinued after the capital was moved to Annapolis.

---

2. MATTHEW PAGE ANDREWS, 1 TERCENTENARY HISTORY OF MARYLAND 419 (Chicago-Baltimore, 1925). The source was Chalmers' AMERICAN COLONIES.

Very early in the session of July-August, 1716, the question of a proper enacting clause was discussed in serious detail. Already in 1715, the Assembly had decided how best to treat the minority of the new Lord Baltimore in framing an enacting clause. In 1716, the Governor in his opening address brought up the entire subject. A joint committee was appointed to consider it, being called a "conference" committee in the usage of the times. The committee reported at some length and gave a historical summary of the style of enacting clauses in Maryland:

> On Consideration of the Subject Matter It is observed that the Stile of the Laws which were made before the Revolution when this Government was wholly in his Lordship's Hands was Generally in these Words Be It Enacted by the Right Honorable the Lord Proprietary by & with the Advice & Consent of the Upper & Lower Houses of this present General Assembly & the Authority of the same
>
> It is likewise observed that after the Crown took the Administration of this Government the Stile was generally in these words
>
> Be It Enacted by the King's most Excellent Majesty by & with the Advice & Consent of this present General Assembly & the Authority of the same
>
> But for that about the years 1710 & 1711 Sundry Laws of this Province were dissented to by her late Majesty for want of mentioning her Majesty's President as a distinct Body in these Laws since which the Stile of the Laws has run in his present Majesty's name thus Be It Enacted by the Kings most excellent Majesty by & with the Advice and Consent of his Majesty's Governour Council and Assembly of this Province & the Authority of the same ....
>
> It is proposed that the Stile be (at least till his Lordship's Pleasure shall be further known) by the Right Honorable the Lord Proprietary by & with the Advice & Consent of the Upper & Lower Houses of this present General Assembly

The House of Delegates concurred in the recommendation of the joint conference committee. The House had before it also a recommendation from Lord Baltimore that all the laws which had been enacted since George I became king should be reenacted in his (Lord Baltimore's) name; but the House did not agree with that suggestion. The House wrote to the Governor and Council that "Re-Enacting them for the sake of a Stile would look like Questioning the Authority by which they were made (which we cannot admitt ought even to be doubted) and Whereas by Re-Enacting them a great Charge will fall on the publick And that the continuing them in the Stile they are now in Can be no Derogation to his Lordship's Honour or Right of Government or prejudice to any Person we hope your Excellency & Honours will excuse us from Re-Enacting any other Laws than those that appear deficient." The Council (Upper House) concurred with the Lower House.

## REVISION OF THE LAWS

The big legislative task of the middle 1710s was the completion of an entire revision of the laws in force in the Province and the publication of a "code." The subject had been discussed for years. For some time the House had been engaged in preliminary efforts by studying what laws of England prevailed in Maryland. That work was still in progress in 1714. In the June-July session of that year, the Governor and Council, in a message to the House, cited the uncertainty as to what English laws were effective here, "which renders the Law in this Province very dubious and uncertain." The suggestion was that eminent opinion be obtained from England, "to the End her Majesty's Subjects here may know by what Rule they walk and the several Courts of Law how to render their Judgments thereon." The House thought this to be "a Thing worthy of our

216

Consideration but as we are desirous to put an End to the present Sessions the Time of year being very inconvenient for revising our Laws," proposed it all be deferred until the next session. To this the Governor and Council agreed.

At the next session in 1714, in October, the Governor in his address notified the Assembly that "I am commanded by her Majesty to revise the Laws of this Province to which I desire your assistance in the most expeditious manner conveniently may be in order to render so useful a work of as little Expence as possible to the Country . . . ."

Queen Anne had sent detailed instructions for the work, "to take Care that all Laws now in force be revised & considered And if there be any thing in the matter or Stile of them which may be retrenched or altered you are to represent the same unto us." The House in reply promised to apply itself with "utmost diligence" and to do the job with "as little Expence as possible." This message was dated October 7, 1714. On the next day, October 8, the Governor called the two houses together to announce the death of Queen Anne and to suggest "It is thought fitt you do not proceed to any other Business save that of Settling the Publick Levys . . . ." Both Houses acceded, and the session was ended the following day, October 9.

The task of revision was continued in 1715, when the Governor again presented the instructions of the late Queen Anne; he suggested that the legislators "pursue it with application . . . long & frequent Assemblys are grievous Burthens to the people." Again the House promised "utmost diligence." Forty-eight bills were enacted at the April-June session in 1715. In 1716, a joint committee continued the work.

The process of revising the laws was essentially finished in 1716 and 1717, including an act of 1715 repealing all laws except those specifically enacted that year. This did not quite do the job, however, and another act was passed at the

217

May-June session in 1719 "explaining and declaring particularly what laws were repealed" in 1715. In the 1719 bill a long list of statutes was included, to provide with particularity what laws were meant to be repealed.

After revising the laws, the next task was that of publication. Chapter 25 of the Acts of 1715 was passed for that purpose, to require that all laws of that and of the succeeding session should be "fairly transcribed on parchment," with copies going out to the sheriffs of the several counties. For the session of 1715, "because there is not parchment now to be had in the province" it would be acceptable to use "good paper." It was not until 1725, however, that the issue of printed session laws became regular.

While the availability of the session laws was helpful, another need was for a code which at least would purport to show all the laws in force at a given time, and such a publication appeared in 1718. There had been such efforts earlier, to be sure; *A Complete Body of the Laws of Maryland* dated from 1700, and *All the Laws of Maryland,* from 1707.

The code of 1718 assuredly was not a "code" in the modern sense. It contained copies of a series of statutes dating from 1692 to 1718. The arrangement was chronological and not topical. It did, however, have a rudimentary index, marginal notes, and 220 pages devoted to copies of the laws. It was published in Philadelphia, by Andrew Bradford. Distribution was handled by Evan Jones.[3]

The Code of 1718 had an amazing variety of acts of the Assembly, illustrating well the broad legislative interests in

---

3. A facsimile copy of the 1718 code was published in 1978, by Michael Glazier, Inc., Wilmington, Delaware. It is in THE COLONY LAWS OF NORTH AMERICA SERIES, (John D. Cushing, ed.) (Wilmington, 1978). *See also* LAWRENCE C. WROTH, A HISTORY OF PRINTING IN COLONIAL MARYLAND, 1686-1776, at 41-43 (Baltimore, 1922).

Maryland. For the March-April session of 1707, for example, five acts were included in the code, with partial titles as follows:

> Against forging and counterfeiting of foreign coins, gold, or silver.
>
> For preventing the exportation of tobacco out of this Province by land, before the duties payable are paid . . . .
>
> For suspending (during the Queen's pleasure) the prosecution of the priests of the Romish communion . . . .
>
> Explaining some doubtful expressions in the act for limitation of officers' fees.
>
> Requiring the agents of the Lord Baltimore to certify into the Secretary's office the instructions and conditions of plantations . . . .

### RELATIONSHIPS WITH LORD BALTIMORE AND THE GOVERNOR

Lord Baltimore's veto of several bills in 1721 sparked a controversy on legislative powers which was of greater importance than the bills themselves. They all were special acts in the name of one or more persons and designed to provide relief in property matters; and they were of a type which in later years would be handled individually by the courts or as a class by way of general statutes. Their titles, in brief, were to invest an estate in fee, to make good a survey, to dispose of remaining parts of personal estate, to settle the value of a decedent's lands, to dispose of personal and real property to settle damages, and to supply defects in a conveyance. Almost from the beginnings of the Province, the Assembly had been passing numerous and varied bills on such matters of private property.

"I have formerly made known to you," wrote Lord Baltimore, that the Legislature of Great Britain does not take upon them, among their Parliamentary Proceedings to Decide matters of Meum and Tuum; The Peoples Properties are ruled by the known Laws of the Land, however Extraordinary their Cases may be, unless for the joynt Relief, And upon the united Application of all Parties Concerned . . . .

The Upper House (together with the House of Delegates in a separate and similar message) agreed with Lord Baltimore; but, it said, there must be occasional special acts to bring justice in particular cases. Without using the term, the two houses were arguing for a kind of equity jurisdiction to be vested in the Legislature:

> We shall According to your Lordships Just and kind Intimations use our Endeavours to Discourage the Decision of Matters of Private Controversy Otherwise than by the known Establisht Laws and Confess our Parliamentary Proceedings here have sometime been too much Interrupted by such Private Disputes but begg leave with the Greatest Submission to your Lordships Opinion & all due Difference to theirs that have the honour personally to Advise your Lordship, to Declare our Sentiments that it is highly Necessary in Some Extraordinary Cases where Justice is due but Cannot Otherwise be had, That an Especiall Act should Pass Even betwixt Contending Parties, to prevent a Defect of Justice And that such Proceeding unless we much mistake is or at least of late years has been Agreeable to the Practice of the English Parliament but in Other Cases we shall neither Doubt your Lordships kind Endeavours nor be slack in our own that the Province may flourish in an unbyass'd Administration of the Law in the Establish'd Courts of Justice . . . .

At the same session of the General Assembly, on August 4, 1721, the Upper House commented on a bill to confirm the will of William Bozman of Somerset County, and in so doing well illustrated the point made by Lord Baltimore in his veto message:

On reading the Annexed bill & hearing the Evidence thereon we Esteeme it a thing of most Dangerous Consequences to Admitt any Evidence to Alter the Effect of a will made so many years since and besides the Evidence produced us on this Occasion is so short that we Can lay no weight upon it but on perusal of the words of the Will we are Clearly of opinion that the Devisor has Sufficiently Explained his Intentions to Devise a Tenancy in Common in fee simple to the Devisees on the Conditions in the Will mentioned for that the word Inherit can Only relate to an Inheritance and shall by Implication as well Extend to the Immediate Devisees as to those that are to take by Survivorship on Condition And that therefore tis plain that what the Devisor intended by words of Devise to the Devisees was an Inheritance which must be a fee and therefore to avoid makeing a Law for the relief of a Person that seems already relievable by the Laws in force And the more Strictly to Conform to the Directions in his Lordships Speech we reject the bill and referr the Parties Petitioninng for it to the Comon Law for their Relief.

The comment on this bill from the Upper House read more like a judicial opinion than a legislative debate; and after going through all that, it was determined the bill should be rejected.

In a related context, while considering a bill for confirming lands devised for the use of churches, the House of Delegates, in 1722, reported that "... we esteem it Unparliamentary and not fit to be drawn into Practice that while any Contest is depending an Act should be made to alter the Law on which the Contending Parties Grounded their Suits which indeed would be to make the Act have a Retrospect."

The General Assembly stepped into another area at this time which would be considered impolitic to later generations, in passing legislation concerning appointment of an acting governor in the event of a vacancy in the governor's position. The concern was prompted by Governor Hart's health; ultimately his abrasive and contentious personality led to his recall by Lord Baltimore.

As early as July, 1716, Governor Hart notified the Council that he was asking Lord Baltimore to remove him from office, though at that time giving no reason. A few weeks later, on August 2, 1716, in a message from the Upper House to the House of Delegates, it was proposed that an act of the Assembly cover the possibility of need for an acting governor. The message cited first that Lord Baltimore had sent neither instructions nor authority for filling the position in case of the death or absence of a governor and that because "his Excellency the present Governour has been formerly in great danger of his Life by Several Fitts of Sickness there may happen great prejudice & Confusion among the people upon his death If it should please God he should die . . . ." The message continued that the failure of Lord Baltimore to send any powers or instructions into the Province "cannot be otherwise provided for than by an Act of Assembly." Acting upon this suggestion, the Legislature passed an act in 1716 to establish a line of succession. The first person named by the Proprietary as a member of the Council was to be acting governor, and, in his absence, the second person named to the Council was to be the successor. Both of these possibilities would continue until the return of the governor, if he simply were absent, or until the Proprietary might direct otherwise.

Again, in 1720, Governor Hart notified members of the General Assembly that he intended to go to England soon, for reasons of health. This never occurred, however, and he was peremptorily recalled a few months later. The first message he had from Lord Baltimore "permitted" him to go to England for a period of a year and to appoint the first-named member of the Council in his stead. Later, in a letter dated in London on December 30, 1719, and appearing

222

in the legislative *Journal* for the October session in 1720, there was a direct and unmistakable order from Lord Baltimore ("I positively command and require") that he leave the Province not later than the following May. The final order also spoke ominously of "a most unadvised (to give it no worse a Term) Declaration of yours ...."

Two of the disputatious encounters involving Governor Hart had legislative overtones. They concerned Charles Carroll and Thomas Macnemara; and the heat and vehemence with which Governor Hart entered into both frays may have been part of his downfall. Whatever the merits of the controversies otherwise, they certainly were exacerbated in the Governor's mind by the religious preference of Carroll and Macnemara; both were Roman Catholics.

This Charles Carroll was the grandfather of Charles Carroll of Carrollton; he came into the Province in 1688, as "agent and receiver general of the Lord Proprietary." [4] His exact status and powers in the Province were obscure. He claimed to hold offices of "Escheater General" and "Navall Officer" in the Province, and he cited statutes of Charles II and William III in his support. Two of the certainties were that he represented private business interests of Lord Baltimore and as a Roman Catholic had not taken the Oath of Abjuration.

His particular problems began in July, 1716, when he was summoned to appear before the House of Delegates to explain his collection and receipt of a number of fines and forfeitures for the criminal convictions of others, which he was holding for Lord Baltimore. The House voted without dissent that the fines belonged to Lord Baltimore "by his

---

4. 4 TERCENTENARY HISTORY OF MARYLAND 9 (Henry Fletcher Powell ed.) (Chicago-Baltimore, 1925). This Charles Carroll, the first of a confusing number of famous personages to hold that name, sometimes is identified as "Charles Carroll (the immigrant)."

Prerogative" and were not a part of his private estate; and also that "the said Charles Carroll receiving the said fines without takeing the oaths is contrary to the known laws of this Province and an Inroade upon our Constitution."

A few weeks later, on August 9, Carroll sent a letter to the Governor requesting that he (the Governor) give orders to several officers concerned in collecting revenues for Lord Baltimore, "deducting thereout 1000 pounds for your Excellency's Sallary," in order that the remainder of the funds might be sent to England by the next mailing. Carroll included, on the subject of Lord Baltimore's revenues, this piece of unsolicited advice to the Governor:

> I most humbly recommend to your Excellency that Caution be used in assenting to some Laws which I understand are prepared And whereby his Lordship's Interest will evidently suffer detriment without a Salvo at least of their not taking Effect till his Lordship's pleasure be known that his Lordship may have time if his Lordship shall think it proper to square his proceedings to the Tenour of such Laws.

The fact that Charles Carroll ended his letter with the traditional "I am your Excellency's most humble Servant" did not in the slightest allay the Governor's wrath. He sent copies of the letter to both houses, terming it "Insnareing and Insolent," and "Considering the Circumstances of my health it is very Inhumane . . . ." The two houses appointed a joint or "conference" committee to consider the matter.

The joint committee decided first that the fines and forfeitures should not have been collected by Carroll, and that they should not have been turned over to any person "disaffected" with King George's government "or the Protestant Interest." Next, said the committee, the recommendation of caution in assenting to some laws was "an unintelligible Direction" designed on purpose "to disturb his Excellency in that weak Condition of Health he is in or for

some other Secret Ends which Mr Carrol ought to explain."
Continuing, "He says Caution is to be used in assenting to
some Laws but says not which and seems to take it for
granted Caution is not used in any." Finally, "Mr Carrol
seems not very kind to his Lordship in being privy to a
proceeding that may be to his Lordship's Detriment without
detecting it that It may be now prevented by the
Legislature."

Carroll, the committee concluded, had used "a very
indecent Way & Freedom" with the Governor and "is guilty
therein of great Arrogance unless He has some superior
Authority." Both houses concurred that Carroll should be
reprimanded.

The case of Thomas Macnemara involved an attorney who
had been disbarred by the General Assembly after a long and
checkered career in the Province. Years earlier, in 1707, he
had protested an order from then Governor Seymour that all
attorneys who were not members of one of the Inns of Court
in England must appear before the Council for an
examination as to their fitness.[5] Macnemara petitioned for
examination, protesting that the order deprived him of his
livelihood. The petition was denied, with the Council citing his
"many misdemeanors" and his frequently affronting the
courts.

Later, for failure to pay alimony to his wife, he was jailed;
and his subsequent release on *habeas corpus* so angered the
Council that the judge in the case was summarily removed
from office. Still later, on a charge of practicing law while
disbarred, he was ordered placed in the stocks "bare
breeched" for one hour; the time was reduced because of a
heavy rain storm.

---

5. One of the private attorneys who commented on the case said that
Macnemara was a barrister of the Society of Gray's Inn in London. There
is other evidence that Macnemara had "entered" Gray's Inn in 1711. *See*
AUBREY C. LAND, THE DULANYS OF MARYLAND 33 (Baltimore, 1955).

After other troubles, his fortunes took a turn for the better when he was elected Clerk of the House of Delegates in 1714, 1715, and 1716. Also, he was restored to the practice of law but he repeatedly enraged the courts by his unruly behavior. At some time he incurred Governor Hart's strong dislike; the Governor asked for his disbarment, and such a provision was incorporated into a general act concerning magistrates in the Province. As the next development, the reason for which is obscure, a number of local attorneys were asked to comment on the bill for disbarment; their comments appeared in the *Journal*. They all agreed (as Macnemara had claimed) that the Assembly passed the act without giving him a chance to defend himself, and that this "secrecy" was a denial of rights and of justice. There was the further question whether a particular action of this kind was properly included in a general bill.

Lord Baltimore vetoed the bill, for reasons similar to those in the opinions of the attorneys. The veto message was delivered to the Assembly at the May-June session in 1719. The bill, it was said, was "against a Particular Person without hearing the Party, which is the undoubted Right of every one of his Majesty's Subjects." Also, "Laws made against persons ex post facto have been Rarely passed in England but always Esteemed severe and We hope such a Generall Act may be made as will so Effectually Reach all particular Persons for the future that there may be no more Occasion to have Resort to the like Extraordinary means."

Both houses protested against the veto and the claim of Macnemara that he had been the victim of "secret" proceedings. The Upper House in a message to the Governor said that

> we have but Just Reason to Suspect that the party therein Charged having a Just Apprehension of his own Demeritts forbore makeing any application in our house, lest it had been condemn'd here ..., which Design

226

Manifestly Appears by his Artful Management in Deferring his Petition to the lower house untill after the bill had been engrossed there.

Similarly, said the Lower House,

we are under some concern to find the Justice of the Legislature Questioned under the Private Opinion of some Gent of the Law .... We had Good Reason to Believe he had notice of the final Vote that Pass't for it yet he made no Application to be heard till after the Engrosst Bill Come from the Upper House Assented to at which Time we Adjudged his proper Application law to your Excellency it seeming unparliamentary to Call in Question a bill Solemnly past by us.

The Legislature also reacted to the veto by passing another bill at that session for disbarring Macnemara.

There was yet another episode tc the Macnemara affair, appearing in the *Journal* for the April session in 1720. Lord Baltimore wrote to the Governor that Macnemara had made "a Satisfactory Submission to us the Lord Proprietarie," and his suspension from practicing law was removed. The Governor, in sending this information to the Assembly, wrote that he was "surprised" at the manner of Lord Baltimore's action. Macnemara, wrote the Governor, made no "due submission to me who was personally affronted." To find him "to be Restored without so much as a Letter from them to me (on an Occasion which surely was not Triffling) does indeed Amaze me."

Macnemara had died in the interim, a fact which the Governor noted by adding to his message to the Legislature that "It is true the Person is removed by the impartial hand of Providence from further Disturbance, but the Example may be laid hold of by other Practitioners." It may have been this blunt criticism of Lord Baltimore that led to the swift recall of Governor Hart.

The new Governor was a cousin of Charles Calvert, fifth Lord Baltimore, though the exact chain of relationship is uncertain. The Governor also was a Charles Calvert, and for a time the title pages of the *Journal* carried the identical names for both offices. One of his accomplishments was to allay the constant antagonism to the Hart regime; shortly after assuming his post, Governor Calvert expressed to the Assembly the hope "that those little heats which lately disturbed you are now happily at an end."

The doctrine of separation of powers, to become much more evident in later decades of the eighteenth century, was mentioned briefly during the October session in 1720. The House sent a message to the Upper House about a bill to ease the handling of bonds of administration in cases before the courts, and mentioned the "abusive prosecution" of such bonds by provincial judges who also were members of the Council. The Council in its reply assured that judges of the Court of Appeals who had been on a case in the Provincial Court would not sit in the same case on appeal; and as a *non sequitur* added a word for the value of judicial service to the membership of the Upper House and Council.

## LEGISLATIVE ROUTINE

Changes and innovations in legislative procedure were routine in the 1720s. The rules of the House were printed in the *Journal* for the October-November session of 1722, but they differed little from those last printed in 1698. Both sets of rules contained the prohibition against the use of tobacco in the "Barr or Gallerys of this House." Another, and an unusual, mention of the basic product of the Province came from the House Committee on Aggrievances in 1722, concerning legislation about fencing in fields. "It is offered to this Committee as an Agrievance," it was reported, that "most or all Horses at this Time have taken to eating Tobacco . . . ." Still another mention of tobacco is in the *Journal* for the February session of 1721, and it might better not have been preserved for posterity. It was a short session of only nine days, and the main purpose of it as announced was that very few of the tobacco growers conscientiously could comply with the oath required against the export of "trashy" tobacco.

A question of privilege of members of the House arose from a grievance filed in 1718 by Delegate John Brannock of Dorchester County. He questioned at what time a member of the House could have an execution served against him. A House committee voted that the Delegate "be not taken till after this Session."

The House continued to enforce strictly the requirements for attendance and decorum at its sessions. In July, 1721, the Sergeant was ordered to bring in two members "for their not Attending this Assembly." At the same session, a delegate was fined ten shillings "to be paid immediately to the Sergeant for his Absence at Calling over the House & Contempt thereon."

The House Committee of Aggrievances, in 1722, was directed also to serve as a Committee for Courts of Justice.

At the time it was announced in 1722 that the House would hold its daily session from nine a.m. until four p.m., the Rev. Mr. Samuel Skipper asked to "read Divine Services" at eight a.m. and again at four p.m. during the Assembly. The Rev. Mr. Skipper also was Clerk of the Upper House.

A bill passed at the April-May session of 1718 denied the right of suffrage to Roman Catholics. All "profest Papists whatsoever" were to be included in the ban, and the prohibition applied to all elections for delegates to the General Assembly.

Compensation for members of the Assembly was continued at 150 pounds of tobacco daily for members of the Upper House and 140 pounds for delegates. The two delegates from Annapolis now were to receive compensation equal to the others, instead of the half-pay that had been determined for them earlier.

229

In 1720 a petition was presented by John Peter Zenger for printing the laws of each session, with copies to go to both houses and to the Provincial Court. Again in 1721, he was to do the printing, for compensation of five hundred pounds of tobacco.

A bill was considered in 1722 to erect a school "at some Convenient Place in every County." Each was to have a good school master "capable of Teaching Grammar and the Mathematicks if such can be Conveniently got." Compensation was to be 20 pounds per annum.

The House in 1721 made an incisive comment upon a bill concerning incestuous and clandestine marriages. In a later year, the remark might simply have been that "we already have too many laws," but in the decorous language of the eighteenth century the comment was longer and less direct:

> By the Lower house of Assembly
> *August the 3d 1721*
> May It Please your Honours
> Having duely Considered and fully Debated the reasons in the within bill we cannot consent to the Passing thereof in regard we Conceive the Law now in force Sufficiently Provides against the Evills Complained of there being but one Instance to the Contrary fresh in our memorys. And we are humbly of Opinion the Business of the Legislature is rather Intended to punish Crimes frequently Comitted than to make laws upon one such Transgression which may not again happen in many Ages here And we are fearfull the Difficulties laid down in the within bill are left more Insuperable than the Evills It Designed to prevent

On the same day this message was sent, the House of Delegates in like vein commented on a bill "laying a fine on Pedlars and petty Chapmen Tradeing into this Province." The House said it was "no proper time" to discourage the importation of merchandise into the Province and again concluded "the Evil thereof might be Greater than that Proposed to be remedyed by the Bill . . . ."

## COMPENSATION OF THE COUNCIL OF STATE

For a time during the several years before and after 1720 it seemed that vigorous and often acrimonious debates were on the wane between the Upper House and the House of Delegates. Over a period of six or seven years there were only two disagreements serious enough to reach the *Journals,* but then a couple of colossal controversies restored the normal acerbity.

There was a mild occurrence in 1716, when the Council ordered its Secretary to allow no copies of the legislative *Journals* to be taken from his office, except by the Governor or a member of the Council; the Delegates, it was said, had made a practice of getting copies from the Secretary, "And that often the said Journals are mislaid."

The next encounter was more heated, concerning the official copy of Lord Baltimore's message at the beginning of a session. Eight days after the start of the July-August session in 1721, both houses wanted the message for "perusall," but the House tartly reminded the Upper House that it already had furnished to the Upper House a copy of the original as attested by the House Clerk. Also, added the House, "the original Speech ought to be lodged in this house according to the Antient Custom & Privilege."

The claim for an "Antient Custom and Privilege" predicably stirred a quick answer from the Upper House. Beginning with the promise that it was "waveing all Disputes about the Antient Custom and Priviledges of your house" the Upper House still could not accept that it should not have the original copy of the speech. "If we had required it as being a branch of the Legislature to whom it was in the first place Addressed," wrote the Upper House, "we should not in our Oppinion have Exceeded that measure of Right which is justly due the prehemancy both in the order and Dignity of our house."

The next controversy began during the September-October session in 1723, and it continued for many years and over a great number of sessions. It precipitated perhaps a new high in the intensity and heat of vituperation between the two houses and in the violence and insulting tone of the debate. Both sides argued from law, custom, and "right" principles of government; and both sides long held to the extremity of their positions with little hint of the gradual moves toward compromise which usually marked their differences.

The trouble began when the House of Delegates refused to approve payment of per diem compensation to the members of the Upper House when they were engaged in their duties as the Council of State. The Council, usually known as the Upper House while performing legislative duties, doubled also as the Board or Council of State for extensive administrative and executive duties. Here it was following the pattern of the old English curia regis or king's council, after its original administrative character was expanded to make it also the Upper House of the Parliament. Also, and again following the English example, the Council of State sometimes was called the privy council.[6]

The members of the Council received a per diem compensation of 150 pounds of tobacco while engaged in their legislative work as the Upper House; this was specifically set in the acts successively regulating the election and summoning of members of the General Assembly. It was the claim of the House of Delegates that Lord Baltimore received regular grants for operating the government, and that the expense of the Council for its administrative work properly should come from that

6. *See generally,* David W. Jordan, *Maryland's Privy Council, 1637-1715,* LAW, SOCIETY, AND POLITICS IN EARLY MARYLAND (Aubrey C. Land, Lois Green Carr, and Edward C. Papenfuse eds.) (Baltimore, 1977).

allowance. There were conflicting claims about whether or not an act of the Legislature required payments to the Council; or whether, apart from law, the payments had been established by custom. Lord Baltimore entered the debate only indirectly, but effectively, by refusing to make payments to the Council from funds appropriated to him for administrative expenses.

Both houses had to approve any such payments if they were to be made by "the public." The appropriations would have to be in what then was termed the Journal of the Committee on Accounts; in modern terms, the Budget Bill. From this simple beginning, the arguments, personal vilification, and threats became more and more shrill. Certainly, as with all legislative encounters, they were less mortal than they sounded; but for years the fracas continued, mutually derogatory and discrediting. Even with a discount for forensic exaggeration, it must have bruised some egos.

When the excitement began during the September-October session of 1723, it was the House of Delegates which raised the issue. The public should not be burdened, it said, with paying compensation to members of the Upper House while acting as members of the Council of State. In citing an act of 1670 it concluded that Lord Baltimore should pay "the many great and Necessary Expences of Government" and that the House, if it permitted the payments, "should be esteemed but bad Husbands of their Mony, and Little deserving the Trust Reposed in us."

But, said the Upper House, ". . . to have Recourse to a Law made forty or fifty years ago to Explain a Law lately made without having Regard to several Laws intervening relating to the same Duty but under different Applications must certainly be an erroneous way of Proceeding . . . ." Having made this point, the Upper House went on to say that the act of 1670 had been modified by an act of 1691, and the latter required the payments. So, continued the Upper House, if its members were to be expected to serve at their own private expense, "we cannot but think it reasonable that you should do the same, and therefore we propose that if Your House will remit your allowances this year for your attendance, we will remit ours. . . ."

In one sentence, the House answered that it could not recede. The Upper House then found another act, this one from 1692, which gave the Council an allowance from an act imposing a duty on liquors; and the Upper House repeated the recommendation that both houses serve without compensation. We think, it wrote, "we have as much Reason to refuse your Allowances, as you have to refuse ours."

The Lower House then made a single concession. It agreed to permit the allowances for service up to that time, "with a Resolution never to Agree to the Like Allowances Again . . . ." The Upper House answered with some heat to this disingenuous offer of a Pyrrhic victory: "we think Unbecoming your House and which we reject with Indignation . . . the terms you propose we shall never Agree to."

The House then shifted its strategy, asking for the return of the Journal of the Committee on Accounts (i.e., the Budget Bill) from the Upper House. It was not returned as requested, and the Upper House warned again it would not consent to the bill without the extra payments included. The House of Delegates countered with a notification to the Governor that it had no further business before it. In modern terms, that was a threat to allow the Legislature to adjourn without passing the Budget Bill.

The Upper House was "much surprised" at this threat. Even if the two houses cannot agree about the allowances, it reasoned, it is "absolutely necessary" to provide all other appropriations. Again the Upper House proposed that payments to both houses be removed from the bill; and, "If

234

you refuse this, the Blame will be laid on those who deserve it and we shall be Excused." Promptly this reply came back from the House:

> There being no Law now in force, nor Custom that has any Reasonable foundation that we know of, we Cannot recede from our former Resolutions, nor agree to put our Allowances which are founded on a Law in Force upon the same Foot as that which has none to Support it . . . . Your Honours make much use of your Power in this Case, as we hope this House never will of theirs.

At this the Upper House softened its position a trifle, saying it had not refused to consent to the Allowances for the House of Delegates but simply had "proposed" this settlement, and that it was the House that was making an "ill use" of power. The only answer from the House was that the law provided for an allowance to the Upper House only for its legislative work. Again the House said it had no more "Publick Busieness" for the session and asked the Upper House either to return the Journal of Accounts or to conclude the session without a budget bill. The Upper House remained indecisive:

> The Journal of Accounts now lies before us, and Requires some Time for our Consideration; and we conceive it not Consonant to the Wisdom of publick Assemblies to do things in a hurry. We desire therefore that you wou'd not be Impatient at a small delay, which may prevent great Mistakes.

But, said the House, you recommended yourselves as "Servants of Consequence to the Country," so "please to exert yourselves" to "putting a period to the present and increasing Charge of this Session." To this the Upper House wrote that it "in a Little Time shall send you our Thoughts." But why take more time, asked the House, when five days ago you were ready to assent to all the allowances in the bill "Except Your own and Ours."

The "thoughts" promised by the Upper House came finally in a message of five pages. It called for a "good understanding" and "good manners," and then goaded the House of Delegates with this prod:

> But Gent. give us Leave to tell you with a Plainness that becomes the Superiority of Our House, that we have a great Deal to complain of upon that Head . . . . You, we must be free to tell you, for want of those good Dispositions, with an Uncharitable Construction upon the Manner of our Claims, load us with the sin of Calumny . . . .

Once more there was a brief and decisive answer from the House, that the five-page message

> seems rather to require a coment than an Answer and consists as we understand it of no matter other than
> 1  The same pretended Reasons you gave us in your former Messages
> 2  Of Rhetorical florid Expressions to grace those pretended Reasons &
> 3  Of Reproaching us with your own mistaken manner of treating us.

The Upper House countered with a two-page message "to explain" the five-page document. By this time, however, it was October 26, 1723, and the session already had continued for a full week longer than necessary for the other business of the Province. The Governor sent a message to the Upper House, hoping that the differences could be resolved, because he planned to end the session by the evening of that day. The House of Delegates immediately asked him to end the session, either by prorogation, dissolution, or adjournment. The House also sent another message to the Upper House, regretting the prolongation of the session and the extra expense, all "in favor of your small personal interest in a temporary Claim."

The Upper House, even on this last day of the session, seized upon a claimed admission in an earlier message from the House, that its position might have some merit. At this point the Upper House brought the argument down to a very personal level. "We shall not enter into the Debate with you," it told the House of Delegates, "whether you be in your Senses or no but this we may very Justly Affirm, that any man in his Wits may read in plain English your Message of Yesterday" as supporting the contention of the Upper House. Also, continuing the personal attack, "As we have the Superiority in our House, we are Resolved by a disregard of your Abuses, to Intitle ourselves to it in Good manners also, and so shall refer all further Debate on the Head of our Allowances to another Session."

Accordingly, the Upper House returned to the House of Delegates the Journal of Accounts "read and assented to . . . saving to ourselves all Rights to Claim the Usual Allowances made to us as a Council of State and Omitted in this Journal or any other Thing past in this Session to the contrary Notwithstanding."

As he prorogued the General Assembly, the Governor took an open part in the debate, saying in a final message to the House that Lord Baltimore "will be surprized at your Endeavouring to load his Revenue with the Charge of maintaining the Council after his Lordship has so generously Sacrificed his private Interest for the Public Good . . . ." Thus ended the first episode.

A year later, at the session of October-November, 1724, the Upper House reminded the House of Delegates of the "reproach" from the Governor and again asked for its allowances as the Council of State; and it made two or three other requests to the same effect during that session. Again the House said "No," referring the Upper House back to its messages of 1723. The House also denied that the Governor's message at the end of the prior year had been a "reproach," and hoped the Upper House would give "no further Trouble" about the per diem payments. The Upper House, still

237

insisting upon the rightness of its position, said it would postpone further debate, always reserving the liberty of renewing the request "as a just and indubitable Right."

The first renewal of the controversy came in the fall session of 1725. Again the reply of the House was "No," with these embellishments:

> His Lordship who employs you is paid by the people. . . . We cannot guess to what degree of Unhandsome and insulting usage you would grow to in your message to us. . . . You now seem resolved to lay us under the Dilemma of Spending time in Shewing you how you derogate from your sometimes boasted Superiority in good manner. . . . You reproaching us with being Obstinate shall never divert us from being resolute in our Duty, nor Maintaining the Character due to our Station.

The predictable answer from the Upper House was that the House was "inflammed . . . to such a Degree of Unhandsomeness as to fill a long message with reflections upon the Subject of Useing the word Obstinate which we think however to have been very properly applyed to the Substance of Your message." Then, from the House, "If you were resolved to stirr dissensions you could not well have Chosen rougher to Express your Sense in."

Once more the Upper House capitulated, near the end of the fall session of 1725, with a final rejoinder that "Rather than delay the Publick business at this time by Contending (tho for an Equitable Right) with an Obstinate people, we shall Refer further debates thereon to another Opportunity."

Lord Baltimore came into the controversy by a message to the July session in 1726, emphasizing the hardship upon him if the allowances for the Council of State were taken from his revenues. This inspired the Upper House once more to take up the cudgels with the House of Delegates; but again to no avail. The House would say only that the reasons advanced by Lord Baltimore "are not sufficient to Induce us to receede from our former resolutions We therefore desire you will insist no longer on our doing it." The best the Upper House could salvage from this session in 1726 was a message of its own to Lord Baltimore, that it returns "our bounden thanks to your Lordship for so strenuously recommending to the Lower House of Assembly the payment of our severall Claims . . . and have no reason to doubt (should those Gentlemen persist in their Denial of our just Claim) but that your Lordship will Discover some other effectual Method for Discharge thereof."

There the matter rested for two years, but it was back in a different guise in 1728. On October 21 of that year, the House proposed that "in future Assemblyes" its per diem allowance be reduced from 140 to 100 pounds of tobacco, and it inquired whether the Upper House would agree to a similar reduction. The Upper House, noting "that for some years past we have been denied any Allowance as a Council of State . . .," made a counter offer to accept a reduction in the same proportion as the House if it also would be given an allowance for its administrative work on the council.

This offer, said the House of Delegates, "is indeed an extraordinary Proposal . . . ." The understanding of the House was that the Upper House was willing to accept a reduction in its legislative allowance, but that it wished to have the full allowance of 150 pounds for the administrative work. These terms, so "very advantageous to yourselves as you propose," the House would not accept, being "so prejudicial and unjust with regard to ourselves . . . ." The Upper House quickly answered, objecting to "the reflecting and ridiculing Expressions and misconstructions therein contained" which "are not agreable to that modesty and wisdom which ought to rule in Parliamentary proceedings."

This ended the perennial controversy for 1728; it was to surface again, dramatically, in 1735 and 1736.

## OTHER LEGISLATIVE CONTROVERSIES

During the long quarrel between the two houses on the issue of an allowance for the administrative work of the Council of State, the two houses were engaged in other lesser problems of controversy. One, in 1724, stemmed from the form of amendments to a bill. The House amended a bill by interlineation, after it had been returned from the Upper House. This procedure, said the Upper House in asking that the bill be returned for corrections, made an "entire alteration" of the bill and was "a Practice unheard of till now in Parliamentary Proceedings." The House insisted it was but trying to make the bill conform to what it believed the Upper House wanted.

The Upper House, in part as a general comment, replied that "We are sorry to find such a disposition in your House to Clamour and Asperse ours as appears almost in all your messages." At another time in 1724, the Upper House complained that ". . . you turn everything into Banter and Ridicule a method of proceeding unbecoming that Gravity and wisdom which ought to be a Rule to every part of a Legislature." As if to confirm the charge, the House during the same session in 1724 sent a message to the Upper House that "We desire to know your Honours Sentiments of our Resolves Communicated to you in the Year 1722 if yet Your Honours have had time to consider the same." The enigmatic reply of the Upper House was that "we approve of them so far as they relate to the constitution of this Province."

About the same time, in 1722, the Upper House criticized the House for seeming, alone, to conclude an agreement to pay monies to Major Nicholas Sewall, for an interest his family had in lands below the Choptank River being turned back to the Indians. The message from the Upper House reminded the House of Delegates "of the privileges of our House which is invested with a right & equall share of power in raising and Appropriating the publick Money" and of "the

240

evil consequences of making such positive Agreements . . . without having first Conferred with our House Thereupon in a Parliamentary way." Here the difference was considerable, for the House would have allowed Major Sewall more than ten times as much as would the Upper House. The House protested that it had set a figure only as an estimate, and this matter was settled quickly.

Another dispute beginning in 1725 was more serious than a routine squabble, though it was neither so long nor so serious as the one about allowances for the Council. It concerned a rather trivial variation in the manner of returning engrossed bills from one House to the other.

It began during the October-November session of 1725, when the House inquired of the Upper House whether it had returned to the House a number of engrossed bills, in order that "your Honours assent may appear to this House in the Same Manner our Assent Appears to your Honours According to the Ancient practice of the Legislature of this Province which has never been Interrupted till very lately and which as the most Parliamentary Course by which the priviledge of this House is best Secured we pray may be restored." In an immediate message, the Upper House did not agree:

> . . . the three Engrost Bills . . . are assented to by this House which we hope will be sufficient for your Satisfaction and for the future shall Endorse the Original Bills sent down That we cannot Conceive the detaining of the Engrost bills can be any Injury to the Priviledge of your House for we think it proper they shou'd remain in this House for his Honour the Governours perusal and Affixing the Seals as Chancellor by which means they will be ready for the Assent at the Conclusion of the Session and the publick Business be Expedited.

This reply in turn did not satisfy the House. It cited that until 1715 the practice had been as the House desired, "at which time we find the practice was first altered but for what Causes does not appear. . . . We entreat your Honors not to enter into debates with us concerning it." But, the Upper House rejoined, the only difference since 1715 is that the assent formerly was done verbally, and since that year it has been done in writing by an endorsement upon the original bill. "It appears to be most Agreeable to reason that as your House have in possession the Originall bills with our Assent thereon, so the Engrost bills should remain in our House which will give each house the opportunity of perusing and Considering them."

The House agreed with the summary by the Upper House of what had happened, but "we only insist upon the Renovation of an Antient practice." The Upper House persisted there should be no change, "and as we are a part of the Legislature we think we ought to have one part of the Bills in our house for our perusall . . . ." At this point the contention of the House became philosophical:

> . . . every Innovation contrary to a good Constitution is an Injury to it and the practice we pray a Renovation of has been the constant practice Used and Approved during the Government of his Lordships Ancestors and of the Crown . . . . Alterations of Antient Customs thus made Sub Silentio are never accounted of weight Sufficient to Sanction them Every Innovation is to be carefully watched . . . . We therefore think it our Duty to interpose in time that this young obstacle to old experience, may not it self grow stiff through Age and Obstinate by Use. . . .

With this introduction, the House of Delegates continued with what assuredly would vastly irritate the Upper House:

> Your Honours give us Occasion to remark that tho you be an Acting Body in this Legislature, Yet it is We that are the Peoples Representatives for whom all Laws are made and human Government Establisht Your Honours seem to be assistants to Prerogative and dependant on

it rather than a State in which the people place a Confidence Dependant on it . . . .

The House went on to stress the different status of the Upper House, whereby its members (as being also the Council) could be discharged by Lord Baltimore at any time; and the House asked the Upper House to "trust" its Speaker to present the bills to the Governor.

"Notwithstanding the inviduous remark you are pleased to make of our being only Assistants to the prerogative," the Upper House rejoined, "we Suppose ourselves to be an intermediate Estate between the prerogative and the Liberties of the people . . . free to act for the good of both. . . ."

There was an inconclusive ending to the debate on returning engrossed bills. Near the end of the session the House sent four such bills to the Upper House, "with our Assent Subscribed in Confidence of your returning them and all others in like Case . . . we rely on it accordingly always saving to this House its due and Accustomed Priviledges."

## ENGLISH STATUTORY AND COMMON LAW

The great legislative debate of the 1720s was that of the applicability and use of the English statutes and common law in the Province of Maryland. This controversy differed from most of the others in that it was not between the two houses of the Assembly. Instead, it was between the entire Assembly (with the House of Delegates in the lead) on the one side, and the Governor and Proprietary (together with English officials) on the other. A major period for the debate was in the decade from 1722 to 1732,[7] but the argument had

---

7. The debates during the 1720s were notable for the active role of Daniel Dulany. He had come to the Province very early in the 1700s, from Ireland. He was virtually penniless and would have been an indentured servant except for the kindness of an attorney in St. Mary's who took the

heavy overtones for decades both earlier and later. The question was not to be settled finally until the Constitution of 1776 provided (in Article 3 of the Declaration of Rights) "That the inhabitants of Maryland are entitled to the common law of England . . . and to the benefit of such of the English statutes, as existed at the time of their first emigration, and which by experience have been found applicable to their local and other circumstances, and of such others as have been since made in England. . . ." Other than the final issue of revolution and freedom from England, there was no question before the Provincial Assembly more basic and more vital than that of the English statutes and common law.

The importance of having the statutes and common law of England also effective in the Province of Maryland, and this was particularly true for the members of the House of Delegates, lay in the security the English laws provided against possible arbitrary power and uncertain policies of the Proprietary and of the Governor (and in the final analysis, of the King). It was a period in England of rising importance of the legislative branch and of landmark decisions by the judiciary, both offering a degree of potential certainty to government in Maryland.[8]

---

young man into his office to read law. He was admitted to the Bar in 1709, in Charles County; and in the same year he became clerk to the Committee on Laws in the House of Delegates. In 1722 he was elected to the House as a representative from Annapolis, serving there for 20 years and then going into the Upper House for a long tenure. When he entered the House, he was assigned to the Committee on Laws, and within several years he was chairman and spokesman for this important committee. Because he had a son of the same name, he usually is referred to as Daniel Dulany the elder. *See* AUBREY C. LAND, THE DULANYS OF MARYLAND (Baltimore, 1955).

8. *See generally,* ST. GEORGE LEAKIN SIOUSSAT, THE ENGLISH STATUTES IN MARYLAND (Baltimore, 1903).

Though the issue of English statutes became highly active in the 1720s, it had been a recurring one for many years; and the proponents took it back all the way to the Charter of Maryland, granted in 1632. That document had given the Proprietary, with the advice, assent, and approbation of the freemen of the Province, or their deputies, a power to enact laws, with the injunction they "be consonant to reason, and be not repugnant or contrary, but (so far as conveniently may be) agreeable to the laws, statutes, customs and rights of this our Kingdom of England." This language did not actually settle the question of the effect of the English statutes, but it was evidence that laws in the Province were to be generally similar to those in England.

The members of the House also might have cited their decision during the 1630s, when they literally faced a complete absence of laws locally enacted. Lord Baltimore vetoed those they passed in 1634/5, and the Assembly rejected the proposals made by the Proprietary in 1637/8. The Assembly then determined informally that in the absence of other laws they should be governed by "the lawes of England." Presumably, though it was not specific, it meant the English common law as well as statutory law.

The House of Delegates also might have cited a piece of collateral evidence in a bill apparently passed by the Assembly long before, during its February-March session of 1638/9, as to the role it envisaged for the legislative process in Maryland. The language of that proposed statute translated into an intent that the Assembly itself, as representative of the inhabitants of the new Province, should hold the same status as the Parliament was guaranteed in the common and statutory law of England. It was "An Act For the Establishing the house of Assembly and the Laws to be made therein." It provided for elections and "that the said Severall Persons so elected and returned as aforesaid shall be and be called Burgesses and shall supply the places of all the freemen consenting or subscribing to such their election in the same manner and to all the same intents and purposes as the Burgesses of any burrough in England in the Parliament of England useth to Supply the place of the Inhabitants of the Burroughe whereof he is Elected Burges...." [9]

A bill discussed in the Province in 1662 had declared that in all cases where laws of the Province were silent, justice should be administered "according to the laws and statutes of England, if pleaded and produced." This seemed to claim that the courts of the Province could apply both statutory and common law from England.

Charles Calvert, third Lord Baltimore, once said in 1678 that "Where the necessity and exigencyes of the Province Doe not enforce them to make any Particular Lawes They use no other Lawe than the Lawe of England." [10] Later, in the 1680s, he said that "when the laws of this Province are silent, justice may be administered according to the laws of England, if the Governor or Chief Judge and the justices of my court shall find such laws consistent with the conditions of my Province."

The latter statement left much to the individual construction and perhaps whim of both the Governor and the judiciary. The Assembly in 1696 tried to bring certainty to the question by inserting into a bill it passed a declaration that

---

9. *Archives,* 1 at 81-82. This bill was followed by bracketed language that "The freemen have assented to this Bill that it be engrossed and published under the great Seale" and that "The Lieutenant Generall in the behalf of the Lord proprietarie willeth that this be a Law." However, it also was one of a number of bills printed in full under the "Memorandum that these bills were engrossed to be read the third time but were never read nor passed the house." The memorandum was signed by John Lewger, Secretary of the Province.

10. *Archives,* V at 264-5.

the people of the Province should have the benefit of the laws of England in all cases where the laws of the Province were silent. This bill mainly concerned religion, and the title spoke only of that subject. The bill accordingly was vetoed, because the title was silent on the other subjects in the bill.

In the first two decades of the eighteenth century, some excellent laws were enacted and a rudimentary code was published, but these accomplishments did nothing to settle the question of the English statutes.[11] Added to this was the continued uncertainty whether the term applied only to statutory law or both to common and statutory law. All these questions were active in a number of other American colonies and in Jamaica.[12]

In 1722 the House of Delegates began to sharpen the issue. It adopted a resolution, which was forwarded to Lord Baltimore, declaring that the inhabitants of Maryland had a right to the benefits and protection of the English law. This

---

11. There was some thought in England during this period that Maryland and other colonies should be under more strict surveillance by the home government, and that they should be obliged to submit their laws to revision in England. *See* J. THOMAS SCHARF, 1 HISTORY OF MARYLAND 378 (Baltimore, 1879).

12. "It is significant that the colonists always endeavored to be in a position to fall back, *in general,* upon English common law in protection of their prerogatives; although they *specifically* sought shelter, as occasion best suited, in the terms of the charter or in their own local precedents, laws, and customs. The Burgesses desired an allowance for salaries for public service, in contradistinction to English custom; they were willing to admit the alleged 'superior' social rank of the Council; but they proposed, in return for that acknowledgment, that the members of the Council, when not in session, should not receive any pay out of the 'publick leavy.' In this matter, the members of the Council, while desirous of maintaining their position of superior ranking, showed a decided tendency to abandon English custom for what may be called 'the American plan' of getting regular salaries." Matthew Page Andrews, 1 TERCENTENARY HISTORY OF MARYLAND 425 (Chicago-Baltimore, 1925).

247

resolution, adopted on October 25, 1722, came to have a continuing importance as a statement of Maryland's position; and it frequently was repeated and cited during coming decades. It provided in part:

> ... This Province is not under the Circumstance of a Conquered Country, that if it were the present Christian Inhabitants thereof would be in the Circumstances not of the Conquered but of the Conquerors, It being a Colony of the English Nation encouraged by the Crown to transplant themselves hither for the sake of improving and enlarging its Dominions. . . .
> This Province hath always hitherto had the Common Law and such general Statutes of England as are not restrained by words of local Limitation in them, and such Acts of Assembly as were made in the Province to suit its particular Constitution . . . such Statutes and Acts of Assembly being Subject to the like Rules of Common Law or equitable Constructions as are used by the Judges in Construing Statutes in England. . . . Whoever shall advise his Lordship or his Successours to govern by any other Rules of Government, are Evil Counsellors Ill-wishers to his Lordship and to his present happy Constitution, and intend thereby to infringe our English Liberties and to frustrate in great measure the Intent of the Crown by the Original Grant of this Province to the Lord Proprietary. . . .

The then Lord Baltimore had a contrary opinion, which was included in a veto message written in London on March 19, 1722/3 and printed in the *Journal* of the Upper House on September 25, 1723. The vetoed bill concerned limitations on actions for trespass and ejectment; and Lord Baltimore in his veto message said that the bill

> is not only Explanatory of an English Statute not in force in our Province, but seems by implication to introduce English Statutes to operate there, which Statutes have been always held not to extend to the Plantations unless by Express Words Located thither and you are upon all Occasions so to Conduct yourself on my behalf as not only not to admitt any such practice

to take Place in Maryland but even to discountenance any Doubts concerning the same and when any of the English Statute Laws are found Convenient and well Adapted to your Circumstances you ought specially to Enact them De Novo, or such part of them as you find proper for you; and not by any Act of the Province Introduce in a Lump (as it were) any of the English Statutes and these Sentiments you may instil and make known as you see Cause.

As part of its continuing studies on English law, the House in the session of September-October, 1723, gave to a committee the task "to Inspect the Ancient Records of this Province and Examine how farr the Laws and Generall Statutes of England have been received in the Courts of Judicature here." The assignment emphasized a closely related dispute with the Proprietary as to the wording of the oath of office to be taken by members of the judiciary, which was based upon their acceptance and enforcement of the English common and statutory law.

The matter of the oath was pursued at the October-November session of 1724. The Attorney General then was recommending an oath for judges of the Provincial Court that "you shall do equal Law and Right . . . according to the Laws Statutes & reasonable Customs of England and the Acts of Assembly & Useage of the Province of Maryland. . . ."

The Upper House proposed a change in the recommendation of the Attorney General, with respect to the word "reasonable." Its proposal was that instead of the "reasonable Customs of England," the oath should refer to the "reasonable Laws Statutes and Customs of England." But, said the House of Delegates, this change would "leave room for the Judges to be Arbitrary what Statutes were reasonable. . . ." The House asked the Upper House to adopt the Attorney General's version of the oath.

The bill on judges' oaths did not pass in 1724, and nothing further was done in that year on the larger question of English statutes. The session in 1725 brought on that controversy again.

The 1725 session began on October 6. On opening day the Governor communicated to a joint meeting of the two houses a long message received from Lord Baltimore. The best lawyers in England, said the Proprietary, have been against extending the English statutes to Maryland. He cited a statute on habeas corpus that had been adjudged in England not to apply to the colonies; an act about servants passed during the reign of Elizabeth that would be "destructive" here; and a statute on usury frequently held not to apply to the "plantations." Next, he cited the restrictions in the Charter, that the statutes passed here be "as near as Conveniently may be Agreeable to the Laws, Statutes, Customs and Rights of England." It would be to the "happiness" of the Province, he said, "if the Statutes of England not Expressly located thither, are not in the Gross in force amongst you. . . ."

Continuing, said the Proprietary, "when any of the English Statute Laws are found Convenient and well adapted to your Circumstances you ought specially to Enact them de novo, or such part of them as you think proper for you: and happy would it be for you all to Conduct Yourselves accordingly." In support of the Proprietary, the Governor suggested that a committee of both Houses make a "collection" of the English laws, and that the Assembly enact here those "suited to our Constitution."

In replying to Lord Baltimore, the Upper House agreed that extending some of the English laws to Maryland would be unwise, and it was appreciative of the privileges already accorded to the citizens here under the Charter of 1632. The Upper House asked for a "Seasonable end" to the "Animosities and Cruel Jealousies which almost Universally prevail in every County within this province."

250

The House of Delegates was not convinced. Its resolutions, it said, were "to well Grounded to be departed from, for any the Reasons that yet appear to us." It followed with a detailed quotation from the resolutions earlier adopted by the House in 1722. To this the House added a long statement to Lord Baltimore that covered its case in detail. The English laws mentioned by the Proprietary as not suited for Maryland were described, and the House cited a case from the Court of King's Bench holding that in the case of an "uninhabited Country newly found by our English Subjects, all Laws in force in England are in force there, so it seems to be agreed...." What, asked the House, is the difference in Maryland, inhabited first "by a Rude Savage & unpolished people Ignorant of Arts and of the use of Letters, having no knowledge of the true God, nor any known Laws or Rules of Civill Government, Save what they have Learnt Since the English Settlement."

Finally, said the House, "We only Contend for the Preservation of our Constitution and to be Govern'd According to the same Rules of Government as our Predecessors were, and if this be not opposed we shall give your Lordship no Cause to think us Turbulent or Troublesome."

The Assembly passed a bill in 1725 on the form of the oath required of the judiciary, of interest in the arguments for the English Statutes for the effect it could have upon judicial decisions; it was vetoed by Lord Baltimore.

In the fall of 1727 the House again took up the argument, and once more as to a bill concerning judicial oaths. In a message to the Governor, it stressed that the benefits of the English laws could not be secured to the Province unless the magistrates were under the "tie of an oath" to act consistently with the laws.

Also, in 1728, at the October-November session, the House of Delegates returned to press for the English statutes, specifically on the matter of the judicial oath. Daniel Dulany, as chairman of the Committee on Laws, presented a long report from the Committee to the House. The opening paragraph follows:

> We take it as a truth not to be denied, with any Shew of reason that the Benefit of the Laws of England as well Statute as Common is the undoubted Right of the People of Maryland and that their Representatives could not be Guilty of anything more Destructive to the Rights and Liberties of those who have entrusted them, more inconsistent with their own Duty or more base and treacherous Than to give up or Consent to impair or Lessen that Right and that as the best of Laws without being duly executed are insignificant and useless so the benefit of the good & wholesome English laws will be of none Advantage to the Brittish Subject residing in Maryland unless all possible Care be taken that Justice be equally, justly and impartially administred according to the Directions of the said Laws and that the Judges be under the Tie of an Oath to discharge so essentiall and necessary Part of their Duty.

There followed in the report from Delegate Dulany a reasoned debate against the specific provisions which the Governor had suggested for the judicial oath, and then the report marshaled a series of historical references testifying to the scholarship of the Committee (and of its chairman): [13]

> Your Committee beg leave to observe that the words of the Statute of eighteenth of Edward the third which was made near four hundred Years Since and has continued ever since without Alteration are, That ye deny to no man Common Right by the Kings Letters nor none other mans, & in the twentieth year of the same King it is observed that the King had commanded all his judges that they should thenceforth do Equall Law and Execution of Right to all his Subjects rich and Poor

---

13. *See also,* DANIEL DULANY, THE RIGHT OF INHABITANTS OF MARYLAND TO THE BENEFIT OF THE ENGLISH LAWS (Annapolis, 1728).

without having regard to any Person and without omitting to do Right for any Letters or Commands that might come from the King himself or from any other or by any other Cause and that if any, Letters, Writs or Commandments should go to the Justices or other deputed to do Law and Right according to the Usage of the Realm in Disturbance of the Law or of the Execution of the same or of right to the Parties, That the Justices should certify the King and his Councill of such Letters and Writs contrary to Law and Proceed to Execute the Law, and by the Sixteenth of Charles the first for taking away the Star Chamber in the fifth paragraph of it which is declaratory of the subjects right in his Property, It is declared and Enacted that neither his Majesty nor his Privy Councill have or ought to have any jurisdiction Power or Authority by English Bill, Petition, Articles Libell, or any other Arbitrary way whatsoever to Examine or draw into Question determine or Dispose of the Lands Tenements Hereditaments Goods or Chattles of any the Subjects of this Kingdom but that the same ought to be tryed and Determined in the Ordinary Courts of Justice and by the Ordinary Course of the Law, the Kings Letters are mentioned in the Oath Prescribed by the first Act and Sir William Thorpe chief Justice of the Kings Bench in the 25th year of Edward the third was Condemned to be hanged for taking Bribes contrary to that Oath which Judgment was confirmed in Parliament. . . .

The quotations from Daniel Dulany and from scores of other members of the House and of the Council over the years give abundant evidence of scholarly learning and ability. With few opportunities for education and little time for self-improvement, the legislators and other officials set high standards for able and imaginative writing. The *Journal* for the times is no dry-as-dust compendium, but has much of scholarship and vitality.

Note, as an example, a brief portion of the message in 1725 from Governor Calvert to the Assembly. He was lamenting the possible effect of some criticism against him, in causing enmity from the members; and he concluded:

I am afraid some Evil Spirits walk among us, and it
would be matter of Great pleasure to such, to have your
house and me att Variance, but for my own part, I defye
the Devill and his Works to do it, and Shall use those
most Excellent Words in the Litany, 'Abate their pride,
Asswage their Malice, and Confound their Devices.'

Another instance, combining grace and practicality, was in
a message from the Upper House to the Governor in 1734,
responding to his address to the Legislature: "Next to the
Happiness which immediately results from the well digested
Councils of a Legislature is the little Expence and Charge a
County may be burthened with on that account...."

Both houses joined in a cogent and effective message to
George II in 1727, after his accession to the throne,
combining nicely the themes of "the King is dead, long live
the King!" Following the laudatory remarks about the late
George I, the message assured George II that the Assembly
"after haveing paid this Duty to his Glorious Memory,
Joyfully ... offer our most Sincere Congratulations for your
Majestys Accession.... None of your Majesty's Subjects can
have a more Awfull and Just regard for your Majesty then
the People of this Province...."

## PROCEDURES AND JURISDICTION

There were 50 members of the House of Delegates in the
early 1730s, with four coming from each of the 12 counties
and two from Annapolis. Those levels of representation had
been set for several decades, and there seemed no strong
disposition to change them. A petition was received in 1725
from "inhabitants" of Talbot County, asking that the county
delegation be reduced to two members; it was rejected, with
no reported discussion.

Compensation for members of the House remained at 140
pounds of tobacco as a per diem; and for the Upper House,
150 pounds. All received "itinerant" charges. These figures

remained without change during all the long and bruising debates over possible allowances for the members of the Council of State. In the House of Delegates, for a session in 1730 extending from May 21 to June 16, most of the members from the respective counties received compensation as follows (in pounds of tobacco) for their per diems and itinerant charges:

| | |
|---|---|
| Annapolis | 2,520 |
| Anne Arundel | 2,520 |
| Baltimore | 2,760 |
| Calvert | 2,760 |
| Cecil | 3,000 |
| Charles | 2,760 |
| Dorchester | 3,000 |
| Kent | 2,880 |
| Prince George's | 2,760 |
| Queen Anne's | 2,880 |
| St. Mary's | 2,880 |
| Somerset | 3,015 |
| Talbot | 2,880 |

In addition, a separate portion of the budget lists other payments for "ferreges," and there is another supplementary allowance of one pound or more for each. Payments to members of the Upper House ranged from 2378 to 3068 pounds of tobacco. Clerks, doorkeepers, and "sergeants" were listed, also in pounds of tobacco, from 1260 to 3450. Also, to the sexton of St. Anne's Parish "for tolling the Bell to this Assembly," 450; to the rector of St. Anne's, for "reading" prayers for the Assembly and the Provincial Court, 1,500; and for "beating drum" and cleaning the State House for one year, 1,200.

At the very end of the *Journal* for the Upper House for the session in March, 1725, there appears the laconic memorandum that "The Gentlemen of the Upper and Lower

Houses had one days allowance too much in the Journall of this Sessions."

Legislative procedures continued without basic change in the late 1720s and early 1730s. The House of Delegates at the beginning of each session adopted substantially the rules of the preceding session. The rule on attendance was expanded in 1728. Earlier it had required only that "no bill be read but in full house." The change in 1728 was that "No Bill shall be read at any time dureing this Sessions till all the Members in Town be called in except in Case of Sickness or other reasonable Excuse to be Permitted by the Speaker." The *Journal* of the Upper House never listed any rules; formal rules were hardly necessary with only eight or ten members.

Daily hours for the sessions continued, either from nine a.m. to five p.m., or a split session from eight until eleven or twelve in the forenoon and from one to five or two to six in the afternoon. Provision always was made for divine services, either during the daily hours or perhaps at seven a.m.

Perhaps the most important innovation of this period occurred at the session of 1732, when for the first time the names of delegates were listed for yea and nay votes, under "for the affirmative" or "for the negative." It was done only if the vote was split, being omitted for unanimous votes. The change itself was put to a recorded vote in the House, being carried by a vote of 39 to 19. A further feature of the innovation was that, during the roll call, the delegates' names were called by counties and in the order of their formation; and within a county, the individual names were listed in order of the members' respective seniority of service. The order of counties for roll calls in 1732 was as follows (but note that in several instances, counties were not in the order now accepted for the date formed):

St. Mary's
Kent
Anne Arundel
Calvert
Talbot
Dorchester
Cecil
Baltimore
Prince George's
Charles
Somerset
City of Annapolis
Queen Anne's

In 1734 the House ordered that "the Yeas and Nays be taken of the Resolutions of all Questions, if demanded."

A possible change of remarkable magnitude never went beyond that of a proposal. During the July-August session in 1729, members of the House of Delegates conceived that the veto power of Lord Baltimore might be abolished, and they accordingly wrote to the Upper House:

> By the Lower house of Assembly 5th August 1729
> May it please your Honours
> This house having taken into Consideration that the Right Honorable the Lord Proprietary hath frequently dissented to Laws pass'd in this Province by the Legislature thereof, which We conceive to be an Aggrievance to his Majesty's Subjects therein & not warranted by the Charter, and as it is an Affair of the greatest Importance to the People to be at a Certainty about their Laws: Wee desire your Honours to join with this house in applying to his Lordship, or in taking such other Steps as may be necessary to settle a matter of so great Consequence

A few days later the Upper House, in what likely was a remarkably restrained answer and with something less than enthusiasm, returned a quietly negative message:

We declare that We shall always be ready to joyn with you in a proper Application to Our Proprietor to redress any Aggrievance his Majestys Subjects within this Province may labour under, but as you now question a Power that the Proprietarys of this Province have exercised from the beginning of their Government, & We believe with good Reason, We therefore do not think fit to joyn with you as proposed by your Message.

Without explanation of the provocation, the Governor in his message to the Assembly at the July-August session in 1729 recommended care in the drafting of legislative proposals, suggesting "Great Care and Caution in the Penning of Laws since it little availeth to be cautious and circumspect in Our Consultations, if we are not equally such in forming Our Resolutions into Laws."

Also without further explanation than appeared in its title, a bill was passed in 1732 "for preventing Bribery and Corruption in the Elections of Citizens or Delegates to serve in Assembly for the City of Annapolis." It would have been a most stringent measure, except that it was vetoed. Under the proposal, every person before voting had to take an oath (or for Quakers, make an affirmation) that he had not received, directly or indirectly, any money, office, place, employment, gift, or reward for his vote. Officials of Annapolis were to administer the oath, under a penalty of 20 pounds in current money. The officials also had to take oath that they had not accepted any bribe or falsified the election returns. All oaths were to be under penalty of perjury. Civil penalties also could be recovered for any violation, up to 50 pounds in current money.

An unusual emergency during the summer session in 1731 required no further explanation. There was a suspected outbreak of smallpox on a ship anchored in Annapolis harbor, and the session was quickly prorogued and postponed. Actually, there was some doubt about the truth of the story. An Annapolis merchant and the master and mate of the ship

petitioned to be allowed to land their cargo. The Upper House
suggested they be given a license to unload, but the House
of Delegates was afraid to allow the cargo to be landed and
apprehensive of "the Crews Roving about the Towne." An
act was passed hurriedly, requiring that the ship be
quarantined for four months and required to anchor at least
one mile from the shore. The fear of the Assembly was not
helped by a report that there was a "rage" of smallpox in
Joppa, Baltimore County, and that the sessions of court to be
held there in June had been cancelled. The Assembly was
prorogued on July 29, and it returned on August 19 to
complete the session.

A small tempest occurred between the two houses in 1729,
when the House of Delegates discovered an original way to
amend a bill. It was a routine measure "preventing the
untimely killing of Deer," returned with amendment from
the House of Delegates to the Upper House. However,
instead of adding the amendments to the original bill, as was
the custom, the House drafted a completely new bill and sent
it to the Upper House. The first suspicion of the Upper House
was that its bill "had been designedly suppressed or
concealed" in the House. The Upper House continued that "if
you thought this to have been a harsh Censure, We answer,
that it was very unparliamentary, to send Us another Bill of
your own drawing, instead of Amendments to our Bill sent
down to you." The House protested that this had seemed the
easiest way to handle the amendments. Whether by design
or simply by accident, the House only three days later
invented another variation in the amending process. This
time the bill sent down from the Upper House was not
returned, and the House suggested instead that amendments
be made to former acts of the Assembly. Again the Upper
House complained, saying that its bill had been "laid asleep
as it were in your House, & another Bill sent up with your
message." Here also the House of Delegates had a

beguilingly simple explanation, that the substitution had been "for the sake of Dispatch."

Printing procedures were regularized and improved during this period, and there was concern about the preservation of records and of the *Journals* of the Assembly. In an address to both houses in 1727, the Governor spoke of the *Journals* being recorded only in "Loose Paper and Seperate Journalls Ruin and annihilation will sooner attend them in such Parcells than if they were transcribed into large and strong books without this precaution our Transactions in Assembly will be hereafter known only by uncertain Traditions." Following this suggestion, the House ordered in 1727 that "the Severall Ancient Journals of this House be bound into Books . . . and that for the Future the Clerk of this House have a Sufficient Margin in the Record Book of the Journals of this House and make Marginal Notes of the Occurrences therein."

Also, by Chapter 8 of 1727, the Assembly provided for the "speedy and effectual Publication of the Laws of the province and for the Encouragement of William Parks, of the City of Annapolis, Printer." Parks was to receive two thousand pounds of tobacco from each county, for providing to each a copy of the acts of the current session. His fee covered printing, stitching, and delivering. Parks earlier had proposed that if the Assembly would use "proper means to Establish me for a certain number of Years; that I may think myself settled amongst you in regard to the Country which perhaps I may live and dye in (if so Established here) I will undertake to Ease the publick of that Charge and Content my self with running the Hazard of Subscriptions for it." He was appointed to "have the Character of Publick Printer to the Province."

During the following year, 1728, the Upper House complained that without its concurrence the House of Delegates had settled upon a fee for work done by Parks.

The House replied that this work was particularly in its service, but this to the Upper House was "a Method we do not remember we ever came into" and that it desired only "to prevent any Encroachment on each others rights."

As may be seen from the minor contentions on the form and procedure of amendments and printing, the members of the General Assembly of Maryland remained jealous and combative about their mutual rights and privileges, and they were even more sensitive in their relationships with the general public. A number of such incidents are recorded in the *Journals* of the time.

Thus, in 1725, the Sheriff of Cecil County (for a reason not known) arrested Delegate Ephraim August Herrmann of that county. The sheriff was called before the House, which resolved unanimously that the arrest was "a Violent Breach of the priviledges of this House . . . and Contrary to the Law of parliaments." He was fined and also required to pay damages to Col. Herrmann.

In 1728, as part of an altercation with the Upper House, its members were tartly reminded by the House of Delegates that "we are the Deputys, Representatives or Delegates of all the Freemen of Maryland not excepting even your Honours in this Assembly. . . ."

In 1726, Charles Carroll was brought before the House and charged with contempt, "it appearing that he has Challenged Mr James Hollyday a Member of this House during the Sitting thereof." The details of the "challenge" were not revealed, but Carroll asked the pardon of the House and was required to give security that he would keep the peace; he preferred to remain in custody rather than to furnish security.[14]

---

14. This was a son of the original Charles Carroll, the Immigrant, who had died in 1720. This one, therefore, was the father of Charles Carroll of Carrollton. In later years, after Charles Carroll of Carrollton had become famous in his own right and had adopted that distinguishing cognomen,

The House was disturbed in 1732 over the contents of an anonymous letter sent to several of its members, to the general effect that a "Mr Tittle Tattle hath Sworn he would make the Lower House Drunk," with some obscure results upon revenues and tobacco taxes, and "whether the fate of Maryland doth not Depend upon the wisdom & Integrity of the Lower House of Assembly." All this sounds somewhat innocuous to later generations, but to the House it was "pernicious," and it asked the Governor to propose a reward for discovering the author.

In 1731, Delegate John Hall of Prince George's County "represents" to the House that Michael Taylor, also of Prince George's, "used him in a very opprobious & indecent manner." The Sergeant-at-Arms was directed to bring Taylor before the House "to resolve to what shall be Objected to him." Nothing further appears in the *Journal* on this matter.

A somewhat similar episode in 1728 was described as "scandalous & seditious." Posted "on a Gentlemans Gate in Prince George's County" was this paper, which, if sincere, sounded like minor revolt:

> Countrymen and Friends
> Tis past doubt that the present State of the Country might with facility be remedied (that is) by suing for a Tobacco Law tis miserably known how much tis wanting were honesty used as it is pretended now a sincere and hearty attachment to our selves and posterity cant be better demonstrated than by pushing Vigorously while the Gap is open therefore as an Expedient (my honest Countrymen) let us meet at Queen Ann Town on Monday the 28th Instant to assert our Rights armed in a Suitable manner to our good and Honourable Pretensions we desire it may be Published
> 20 October 1728

---

his father frequently was identified as Charles Carroll of Annapolis. The three of them, in order, thus were Charles Carroll the Immigrant, Charles Carroll of Annapolis, and Charles Carroll of Carrollton.

The threat was deemed serious enough to warrant its communication to both houses by the Governor, and each house also sent a message of thanks to the Governor for his alert warning.

## A CENTURY OF PROGRESS

As the Province neared the end of its first century, there were many indications of its growth and development. In part, its development was a movement toward the west. The *Journal* for 1732 lists a patent for land "in fork of Monocassy on Potomack Side"; and another "on Potomack River at that place Commonly called Conegosheigoe."

Statutes were being enacted to lay out and "erect"towns throughout the more settled areas. Baltimore Town was in a bill in 1729. In 1730 there was one for Chester Town. An act was passed for Marlborough in 1731, and another in that year separated New Benedict Town from the earlier Benedict Leonard Town. A number of towns were erected in 1732. Fells Point was separated from Baltimore, "on a creek Divided on the East from the Town lately laid out in Baltimore County called Baltimore Town on the Land whereon Edward Fell keeps Store." A town was erected at the bridge near the head of Great Choptank River, to be called Bridge Town. Also on the Eastern Shore, a town was erected "at the head of Wiccomoco River, in Somerset County ... at the Landing commonly called Handy's, or Carr's Landing ... the town aforesaid be called by the Name of Salisbury Town."

A petition went to the Upper House in 1733 to erect a town at Elk Ridge Landing; and in the same year Princess Anne was erected "near the Head of Manokin River." Other towns were erected in 1736. One was George Town, to come from part of a tract called Tolchester on the Sassafras River, "at the Place where the ferry is now kept." Another in 1736 was

Piscattaway Town in Prince George's County, at the head of Piscattaway Creek. Prince Fredericktown and Leonardtown, already laid out, were made county seats in 1728.

The bills to "erect" towns differed materially from the later and more familiar laws to create municipal corporations as separate entities of local government.[15] The early bills were only to provide for an organized sale of land and the rental payments to the Proprietary. In the Salisbury bill, for example, commissioners were appointed by name to acquire a tract of land and have it surveyed into lots. The lots then could be purchased, with a time preference given to residents of the home county. Owners would get a title in fee, on the condition they build houses upon their lots within 18 months; and each owner was obligated to pay "One Penny, Current Money of Maryland per Annum, for each Lot, to the Right Honourable the Lord Proprietary, and his Heirs forever. . . ."

From time to time in the *Journal,* also, one sees names which in later years become geographical names. In 1726 the House received a petition from Josias Sunderland of Calvert County; and by an act of 1727 a deed was validated for John Bowen of Calvert County. A member of the Dorchester County Delegation in the same year was Henry Hooper; John Brome was a delegate from Calvert County in 1740.

---

15. For many years prior to 1954, when Article 11E was added to the Constitution of Maryland to provide municipal home rule, new municipal corporations were created in Maryland by special and local acts of the Legislature.

## Chapter 8

## INTO THE SECOND CENTURY
## 1733-1748

In the years from 1732 leading to the middle of the century, the Province and the General Assembly dealt with a variety of old and new problems of government. Some were financial: taxes, revenue, purchases, fines, forfeitures, fees, and the perennial issue of compensation for the Council of State. Other problems were a continuation of political controversies between the two houses of Assembly and with the Governor and Lord Baltimore. Confrontations with the Indians persisted. The right of a member of the House of Delegates to hold another public office became one of the long-time issues of governmental concern.

Perhaps the greatest problem of all was that of the chronically depressed condition of the market for tobacco. The colony long had had virtually a one-crop economy, and when that market failed, the settlers were in trouble. For years the problem had been well recognized. In his message to the July session in 1726, the Governor had given two causes for the then low market prices for tobacco: "the sending Home Trash Tobacco, and the Uncertainty of Shipping our Crops." Continuing,

> To prevent the first, it would undoubtedly be the Interest of the Countrey to destroy the Trash here, for no body but a Madman would Ship bad Tobacco to bring himself in Debt. This would in a great Measure lessen the quantity Especially if tending of Seconds was prohibited; and if the good Tobacco was Ship'd at a time certain the Merchants might regulate the Market at home very much to our Advantage.

Over the years, other possibilities were discussed for controlling the quantity and the prices of the tobacco crop. They included both limiting the size of the crop planted by each grower and the destruction of growing crops.

265

The spring session beginning in March, 1732/3, was marked by the presence of Lord Baltimore, and it was to be the last time a Proprietary ever visited the Province. On the opening day of the session, taking place of the usual message from the Governor, Lord Baltimore addressed the members as "my Faithfull Tenants legislatively assembled"; and in the traditional return messages from the Assembly, the Upper House assured him that "your lordships presence amongst us ... might Animate our Endeavours for the good of the Province...."

Two notable pieces of legislation were discussed at this session of 1732/3. One was a paper currency bill, for the Province to use coin and paper money in the modern sense as a substitute for tobacco as the medium of exchange. This bill was unusual also in listing a number of capital projects to be constructed; the bill proposed to appropriate (all in terms of the new currency) 500 pounds for a new house for the Governor, 500 pounds for repairing public buildings, and 6,000 pounds for building jails in the counties. This was akin to a "bond construction bill" in the modern sense; such bills earlier had been limited to one specific project and financed by pounds of tobacco. A supplementary bill in 1735 provided that officers' fees were to be paid in current money and at a stated price. Another bill in the same session required payments for hogsheads of tobacco to be in sterling money or in gold or silver.

A second bill of note at the session in 1732/3 was a form of bankruptcy law, although of limited application. The new legislation set up procedures for adjusting and paying off debts, without need for continued confinement in jail. Up to this time the colony had been following the traditional old English practice of putting debtors in jail, and it was a self-defeating device whereby the offender could not possibly pay off the debt. The only curative procedure used in the past had been that of petitions addressed to the

266

Assembly, from persons "languishing" in jail until their debts were paid, seeking freedom. Following these petitions, a number of bills would be passed each session, sometimes combined in an omnibus bill. The bills were all fairly uniform. Under them the prisoners would be released from custody and made subject to an early form of composition of creditors.[1]

The new bill of 1732/3 established the procedure in advance, and possibly for any prisoner in debt. It was to be initiated by the prisoner after he was in jail, by petition to the county court having jurisdiction. Included was the equivalent of a pauper's oath. The court then was to notify creditors, schedule a hearing of interested parties, and at the end could discharge the debtor from custody. If the debtor had any assets, a trustee was to handle their division among all creditors. Debts due the Crown or the Proprietary were not to be subject to the new law.

It may be noted, in passing, that in 1735 the House considered a bill "Restraining Infamous persons from Carrying Guns."

## MEMBERS HOLDING TWO OFFICES

The years of the 1730s and early 1740s were remarkable for the extent and virulence of controversy within and between the branches of government in Maryland. Much of it was between the two houses of Assembly; and as in earlier years, there was sharp conflict also between the House of Delegates and the Governor, extending sometimes to Lord Baltimore.

---

1. *See generally* Tommy R. Thompson, *Debtors, Creditors, and the General Assembly in Colonial Maryland*, 72 MARYLAND HISTORICAL MAGAZINE 59-77 (1977).

The first legislative-executive encounter came in the spring session of 1734; it was temporarily settled, but not solved, by the Governor. The House, by a vote of 37 to 4, expelled delegates Daniel Dulany and John Beale of Anne Arundel County, Levin Gale of Somerset County, and Robert Gordon of Annapolis, "they being Disqualified to Sit as Members of this House having received Places of Trust and Profit from the Government Since their Election."

Immediately following the vote in the House, the Speaker called the four delegates before him and "acquainted them they were Discharged from any further Attendance." The full House then ordered the sheriffs of the two affected counties and the Mayor, Recorder, and Aldermen of the City of Annapolis to issue new writs of election to fill the vacancies.

The action of the House of Delegates would have been perfectly clear to legislators and other public officials in later generations, under the familiar Constitutional requirement that no person may hold more than one office of profit or trust created by the Constitution or laws of the State.[2] In the eighteenth century, the answer was not that obvious. Governor Ogle promptly and peremptorily dissolved the General Assembly, though the session was only six days old. The action of "dissolving" was much more precipitous and drastic than the "prorogation" that normally ended a session. Prorogation involved only the ending of a particular session, until a day certain; dissolution called for an ending of the legislators' term of office and a general election to choose another House.

Governor Ogle pointedly directed his message of dissolution only to the House of Delegates:

---

2. In the Maryland Constitution of 1867, *see,* in the Declaration of Rights, Article 35.

Gentlemen of the Lower House of Assembly

It is with very great Concern that I find myself under a Necessity of taking Notice of your expelling several of the Members of your House, for only accepting of Offices under the Government since their Election, although there is no Law of this Province to render them unqualified, or incapable to sit for that Reason: Had the Gentlemen you have been pleased to expel, been guilty of, or charged with any Misdemeanor in their Duty as Members of Your House; You would have been the proper Judges how to proceed; and I would not pretend to interpose; but when you have proceeded to so great a Length, as Either to make a Vote, or Resolution of your own house equally valid and binding to an Act of Assembly, or else to form a violent & unreasonable Construction upon Laws, so as to make them agreeable to your Purpose; I could not without being wanting in my Duty to His Majesty, His Lordship the Lord Proprietary, as well as the Discharge of the Obligation I am under to preserve the Rights and Liberties of His Majesty's Subjects under my Government, delay exercising that Authority with which I am intrusted in preserving Our Constitution, and hindering One Branch of Our Legislature from engrossing the same Power and Authority which is vested and only vested in the whole

It has always been the Custom of Our Mother Country to keep up, and Support that necessary Dependance, which One Part of the Legislature has and ought to have upon Others, to the End that Publick Interest may be carried on by the united Endeavours of all the Parts of the Legislature: It is by observing these wise Maxims, that Our happy Constitution is so firmly established; and nothing can in all Probability tend more to weaken that Establishment, than the overthrowing that Dependance I have been mentioning; and It is evident to any Considering impartial Man, that your expelling your Members in the Manner you have done, is assuming a Power to your selves entirely independent, and indeed destructive of the other Parts of the Legislature; and of the Liberties and Properties of His Majesty's Subjects; which, not only as a Governor but as a Subject to His Majesty King George, I am obliged to support and

269

maintain to the Utmost of my Power; And therefore, with the Advice of His Lordship's Council of State I Dissolve this present General Assembly, and It is accordingly dissolved.

Following the old English custom of affixing distinctive descriptive terms to sessions of the Parliament, this session in Maryland has been called the Addled Parliament.

Later in 1734, writing from London, Lord Baltimore approved the action of Governor Ogle in dissolving the General Assembly, though clearly hoping such action would not again be necessary:

> Additional Instruction to Samuel Ogle Esquire Lieutenant Governor of the Province of Maryland Dated August the 10th 1734
>
> As to the Dissolution of the last Assembly I cannot but approve of it, & think you was under an unavoidable Necessity of Acting as you did; but as I would Avoid all Occasions of unnecessary Uneasiness, so I would not have you take any farther notice of what happen'd in that matter, & I wou'd not have places bestow'd on any persons (if it can in prudence be avoided) during the sitting of an Assembly, so as to give a Handle to the same Complaints; but if such a Necessity should happen, as that any place must be given to a Person after his Election or During the Sitting of the Assembly; & the Lower House shou'd again insist on the Supposed Authority of Expelling such Members, I Enjoyn you to Act with the same Resolution you did before in Dissolving them.

The voters, with a strong assist from the House of Delegates, combined their efforts to reverse the earlier decision to expel the four members because they had accepted other positions. At the elections in 1734 for members to serve in the Assembly, Messrs. Dulany, Gale, and Gordon were reelected; it is not known whether former Delegate Beale tried for reelection. The House, for its part, elected Daniel Dulany as its Speaker when the Assembly met for its spring session of 1735. His name was presented to the Governor for approval, as was routine. However, breaking the routine, Dulany excused himself from the office for "want of Health, which Excuse the Governour is pleased to admitt . . . ." Another Speaker accordingly was chosen, but Dulany continued his membership in the new House.

Several years later, in 1740, the House again expelled members for having accepted positions under the executive branch. Governor Ogle responded by proroguing the session, choosing that as an alternative to the earlier dissolution. In a long message to the House, he set forth the constitutional and political arguments against the power of the House of Delegates to expel members for also holding executive positions, and he explained his limiting the penalty to prorogation:

> Gentlemen of the Lower House of Assembly
> I was in great hopes after what passed in the year 1734 about the Lower House expelling some of their Members, for having accepted Places under the Government after their Election that no other dispute of the like nature would have been brought upon the Carpet again, as you have now done by expelling one of your members for having accepted the Place of Deputy Commissary of Dorchester County since it is very certain, that there is no Law in this Province that puts the least Restraint upon any man as to his accepting of any Place after his Election or that makes him liable to any Penalty for his so doing: And indeed it appears manifestly from Our own Act of Assembly for directing the manner of electing and Summoning Delegates and Representatives to serve in succeeding Assemblies &c that the Legislature of this Province had no such Intention, since they very plainly and clearly express their Sense how far the Laws of England in relation to Elections are to be binding here, Viz. 'that no Ordinary Keeper within this Province, during the time of his Ordinary Keeping, or any other Persons disabled by any Laws of England from sitting in Parliament, shall be

elected, chosen or serve as a Deputy or Representative in any general Assembly to be hereafter called' And this has been the Universal Opinion and Judgment of all Assemblies since that time, without any one Exception that I have ever heard of till lately to the Contrary; till lately that some Gentlemen seem to have been led away with an Opinion, that the Lower House of Assembly ought to be bound by no Rules but that of their own Will and Pleasure, which they seem to perswade themselves is much for the Advantage of the People they represent, and accordingly it is but a too common Question Cannot the Lower House do what they please with their own Members. But if such a Doctrine was once to be established as Law, the Time may come when the People of this Province will not think themselves much obliged to the first Promoters and Establishers of it.

Every Man of understanding who has a thorough knowledge of the English Constitution, cannot but know that the peculiar Priviledges which Englishmen enjoy above all other nations is, that no man can be disseized of the least of his Rights, but either by the known Rules of the Common Law, or a clear and possitive Law to which the People have given their Assent by their Representatives, and which is equally binding upon the Legislators themselves, as upon the meanest of the People: And indeed Our whole Constitution is so entirely established upon this Principle, that was there any arbitrary Power to be lodged in any of the several Branches of the Legislature it would be unjustifiable in them to act any otherwise than by the known Rules of Law, as they ought to be a pattern of Moderation, Justice and Equity to all Inferior Courts and Magistrates, who may be in any manner concerned in judging of the Rights and Properties of their Fellow Subjects.

But it is happy for the People of this Province, that their Rights and Liberties are not left at the Mercy of any one part of the Legislature, who are severally, by the Frame of Our Constitution, reasonable and proper Checks upon one Another

In the present Case I am now taking notice of, it is very certain that the Government has a legal and

necessary Check upon the Lower House of Assembly, as
It can, upon their sending any of their members to a new
Election without any legal Cause, do him Justice by
putting the whole House in the same condition by
Ordering a General Re Election, as it has a legal and
indisputable Right to do, And indeed it is a Right so
necessary to be executed that no Governor can be
thought to do his Duty to his Majesty, or the Lord
Proprietary, or to take a proper care of the just Liberties
of the People if he does not put it in Execution, as often
as a proper Occasion Offers for it, And I make no Doubt
but your House expected I should have thought my self
obliged to have dissolved you immediately upon the
present Occasion, however as I have a sincere Desire to
do everything in my Power for the real Advantage and
Satisfaction of the good People of this Province and am
unwilling that any honest and well meaning men should
be in any Danger of being led away with notions of the
Assembly being dissolved out of any private or sinister
view, or to prevent in any manner the hearing of any of
their complaints either here, or before the Proprietor or
finally before his Majesty at home I have thought it
proper to pass over this Occasion and only to Prorogue
you as usual, you are therefore by the Advice of his
Lordships Council of State prorogued to the first
Tuesday in November next, and you are to take notice
you are prorogued to that day accordingly.

The Governor's two reactions in response to the expulsion
of House members for accepting other positions, by
dissolving the Assembly in 1734 and proroguing it in 1740,
expressed his disapproval but did not finally settle the
constitutional question. That question was to continue
during the following decades, with the House of Delegates
persisting in expelling its members for accepting other
positions. The constitutional issue finally was resolved in the
Constitution of 1776, being variously treated by Article 32 of
the Declaration of Rights and sections 9, 21, and 37 of the
Constitution. The early argument of the House, that
delegates could not hold a second office of profit under the

Province, ultimately prevailed; and it has continued through the years of State government.

## COMPENSATION FOR COUNCIL OF STATE

The matter of compensation for members of the Council again came to the fore in the middle 1730s. It involved, as in the 1720s, the claim of the Upper House to per diem compensation for the time it spent as a Council of State. The House of Delegates had argued, and so far successfully, that in this role the Council was a part of the executive establishment, and that if any payments were made they should come from the allowances to the Governor or to Lord Baltimore, rather than from "the publick." The issue had dominated a number of sessions during the prior decade, and then for a time the Upper House dropped its public discussion of the claim.

The Upper House briefly mentioned compensation during the spring session in 1733, though in a somewhat camouflaged vein. It proposed to the House of Delegates that the compensation of *all* legislators "be Either taken away, or reduced to halfe by an Act of Assembly." In reply, on April 10, 1733, the House gravely voted on the issue, in an informal poll meant only to get a sense of the members' reactions. The members decided first, apparently by unanimous vote, that there should be a reduction in compensation. Secondly, on a recorded roll call, 17 of the members voted to reduce their compensation, while 30 of them held that per diem payments should be eliminated entirely. This, of course, was only a straw-vote kind of device, and no legislation resulted.

In the March-April session of 1735, the Upper House returned directly to the issue, and for a time the quarrel had all the fire and bitterness of the 1720s. The claim of the members of the Council, wrote the Upper House on April 22,

274

1735, up to this time was "through Mistake & prejudice hitherto unjustly denied." Members of the Upper House hoped that the "Prejudices and passionate heats" in the House of Delegates were subsiding, and they requested the same allowances for their executive and administrative work as for their legislative duties. The House in reply denied that "heats passion or prejudice" had influenced or would influence their proceedings; the House still could not "now" agree to making the payments and "therefore desire your Honours will not insist upon it." There the matter rested for 1735.

On April 7, 1736, at the next session, the Upper House, in a message to the House of Delegates, noted that in the legislative budget there were no per diem allowances for it as a Council of State. With the message the Upper House sent the Journal of Accounts (the Budget Bill) "in Order to insert the Allowances claimed by us without which it will not pass." Here again was the threat, renewed after a lapse of ten years or more, to reject the entire budget for the Province if allowances for the Council were not included.

The Upper House followed with another message on April 8. "Our very great Regard" for the members of the House of Delegates, it wrote, "easily prevails with us to endeavour to put the best Construction on what comes from your house," but it still was "at a loss" to understand the House. This time the Upper House did not repeat in detail the arguments of past years. Instead, it cited the message from the House a year earlier, in 1735, in which the House said it could not "now" agree to the payments. This, deduced the Upper House, was a plain intimation the House of Delegates would "be willing at some other time to make those Allowances."

At this point the two houses began mutual recriminations. The Upper House inquired about a tobacco bill which had been sent to the House and not returned, and it asked for satisfaction on that bill before it could agree to send down to the House some engrossed bills it was holding. The House of Delegates, in turn, styled it "irregular and unparliamentary" for the Upper House to inquire about the tobacco bill, and it again asked for the engrossed bills being held in the Upper House.

With legislative proceedings in a seemingly hopeless snarl, the Governor prorogued the session for ten days. "It is with infinite Regrett," he said to both houses assembled, "I see the present misunderstanding between the two houses of Assembly, which has put so full a stop to all Our Proceedings: I wish with all my heart you could have found some Way amongst your selves to have reconciled all Differences, but since that cannot be, nothing remains for me to do, but to put an End to these unhappy Disputes by a Prorogation."

Ten days later, on April 20, 1736, the Assembly began a new session. It was to continue until May 6 and was able to pass a considerable amount of legislation. When the Governor addressed the two houses on April 20, he recalled the recent prorogation with "a good Deal of Concern." Continuing, "As I was obliged to make Use of my Authority then, to prevent the Continuance of a Misunderstanding between the Two Houses, I must hope you will for the future carefully avoid putting me under the like Necessity."

The new session began, however, much as a replica of the earlier one. The Upper House renewed its claim for compensation as a Council of State. The House of Delegates replied that its omitting the allowances from the Journal of Accounts "did not proceed from any mistake but from a Resolution of this house never to burthen Our Constituents with anything which We think not strictly regular"; and the House returned the Journal of Accounts to the Upper House in order that it might be passed without the disputed allowances. This was on May 4. On May 5 the Upper House reiterated "Our Resolution never to agree to the Journals unless You will be pleased to consent to what is strictly regular with Regard to those Allowances."

Suddenly, and in the staid language of the Journal inexplicably, the long dispute seemingly ended on a note of compromise. On May 5, the day the Upper House was vowing never to pass the Budget Bill without the extra allowances, the House of Delegates agreed to paying the allowances for the future, "from the laying the last publick Levy," but to stay with its resolution not to give allowances for any prior service.

The Upper House on the same day agreed to this solution, adding graciously

> As on the One hand we have the greatest Satisfaction in being assured that the Claims of Councillors of State will not meet with any Opposition hereafter; so on the other hand we do assure you Gentlemen of not less Joy on Our Part, that we shall not charge the Country with any Claims since the time of paying the last publick Levy to this Session.

With equal felicity, the House of Delegates welcomed the agreement of the other:

> and as the putting so happy an End to all Disputes concerning the Councillors Allowances, as is proposed in your last Message must contribute to keep up that harmony between the two Houses which is so absolutely necessary to dispatch the Publick business, so it cannot be but very advantageous to the People as it will certainly prevent the Charge which would unavoidably attend unnecessary Disputes, and therefore this house concurs with what Your Honours propose and We now send you the Journals desiring your Concurrence thereto.

On these amicable notes, the protracted controversy ended for a time. It was to arise again.

## Taxes and Finance

There were general matters of public finance of interest to the House of Delegates, in addition to the particular question about compensation for the Council of State. They all were part of the perennial interest of the House to establish its part, and its importance, in determining the taxes and controlling the expenditures of the Province.

Thus, in the March-April session if 1735, there was a bill to levy three pence per hogshead on exports of tobacco, with the proceeds to go to the purchase of arms and ammunition. The House wished to add an amendment giving it some controls over the collection and distribution of the proceeds. The Upper House struck out these provisions by amendment, and it sent a mild reprimand and lecture to the House about the proper division of governmental functions between the executive and legislative branches of government:

By the Upper House of Assembly 16th April 1735

Gentlemen

Having sent you the Bill for raising 3 pence per hogshead for purchasing Arms & Ammunition with an Amendment which is absolutely necessary to prevent confounding the Legislative Part of our Constitution with the Executive part of it, we think it incumbent on us to Express ourselves so fully and clearly upon that Head as may if possible prevent all mistakes and Misunderstandings between the two houses about things of this Nature which we shall always endeavour to avoid as far as lies in our power

All mony raised by the Parliament of Great Brittain is constantly appropriated to some particular use, and the Commons think it their Duty in regard to those they represent to call for Accounts from Time to Time to see that the mony is disposed of according to the Appropriation of it, but are never concerned in the actual laying of it out which indeed in the nature of the Brittish Constitution is impracticable

This Privilege Gentlemen has never been denied the Representatives of the good People of this Province, but all Accounts of the publick Mony have been constantly laid before them when called for to go further & break in upon the executive Part of our Constitution is so far from being for the Advantage of those you represent that it can only tend to throw us into Confusion and put a Stop to all Sorts of publick Business whatsoever, all these things will appear so very plain & obvious to you upon the least Enquiry that we cannot but flatter ourselves that you will see no reason to depart from the old way in which the 3 pence per hogshead has been always hitherto raised for the necessary Defence of the Province.

The bill passed (Chapter 22 of 1735) as the Upper House suggested, with the proceeds of the tax to be paid over to the Governor, adding that they "shall be paid out and applied as soon as conveniently may be, in the purchase of such Arms and Ammunition, as his said Excellency shall think necessary and wanting for the Defence of this Province."

A few days later, however, on April 22, 1735, the Governor complained to the House about an attempted diversion of the proceeds of this tax for a prior year. The House was proposing, he said, to use these funds for the general purposes of the Province and not particularly for defense. By a vote of 27 to 16, the House promptly determined that the proceeds of this tax, from the earlier year between September 29, 1732 and September 29, 1733, should *not* be used for the purchase of arms and ammunition.

The special tax for defense remained a sore subject with the House, leading to attempts to monitor the spending of the proceeds, and sometimes to a refusal to impose the tax. In the spring of 1738, the House asked the Governor for a report on the purchase of arms and ammunition, and he complied. In a message of appreciation, the House assured him that "Our desiring the Account of the said money did not proceed from any Apprehension that you had misapplied any of it, but because we conceived it to be our Duty to enquire how any money assessed on the people we represent, has been disposed of." To this the Governor responded that "it is certainly your Duty to enquire."

There was another prorogation to end an abbreviated session in the spring of 1739, following contention based partly upon taxes and finances and partly upon procedures between the two houses. This time, also, the Governor refused to sign any bills, so that the meeting was called a "convention" and not a "session." The houses differed sharply on a bill concerning officers' fees and on the appropriation bill; with the bill on officers' fees, the argument was whether it should be a "perpetual" or a "temporary" act; and with the appropriation bill, the Upper House would not accept language inserted in the preamble by the Lower House. Not calling the meeting a "session" meant that it would have no effect upon temporary laws to expire after three sessions of the Assembly.

The session in 1739 was illuminated, as had become usual, by open criticism between the two houses. On May 30 the Upper House wrote to the Lower House that "you seem now after sitting above four Weeks to shew a Disposition to proceed." This insinuation, to the Lower House, was "a real Surprize," for it said it had been "assiduously employed" during those weeks. "However surprizing the Truths mentioned in our message," replied the Upper House, "yet they are not the less Truths for that Reason."

Also in the 1739 session, and except for not using a strong word, the House of Delegates directly accused Lord Baltimore of wrongful acts. In a message dated June 9, 1739, the House wrote that the Proprietary "hath possessed himself of a considerable annual Sum" amounting to at least 2200 pounds sterling, "arising on the shiping trading into, and Staple Export of this Province, without any Law that appears to Us to levy the same, and which, were it legal to raise, was intended to support the Government here."

Taxes for defense again were in dispute in 1740. This time it was no academic matter; England and Spain were at war, and funds were needed for maintaining forces to be sent to the West Indies. As part of this discussion, the House wrote to the Upper House that "the granting of Money was well as raising the proper Fund, for the repaying it is the peculiar Privilege and Right of this House." The Upper House disclaimed any intent to invade the prerogatives of the House of Delegates and wrote about the respective duties of the two Houses:

> We cannot find anything in Our former Message that has the least Tendency to deny your House the priviledge of forming Bills to raise money, and proposing proper Funds for that Purpose, and therefore are at a Loss to know, why you should make Your Message more Prolix in endeavouring to Assert that Right; but we hope, you will be so Ingenious as to allow, that when you have formed such Bills providing such Funds and sent them to Our House we have a Right and Priviledge of reading and considering them, and if We find them deficient or inconvenient, have a Negative upon them, or may propose Amendments to them and Alterations in them, or else why do you send them to us.

The Upper House had some suspicion, also, that the recalcitrance of the House of Delegates with respect to imposing a defense tax lay partly in an effort to trade off action between that bill and others in which the House was interested. During the July session in 1740, the Upper House charged directly that the refusal of the House to pass the defense tax at the preceding session was based upon a "bare suggestion" that the Upper House would not return certain bills to the House of Delegates.

The House engaged in controversy with the Governor about its action, and lack of action, on another tax bill. Two related taxes were involved. One was a tax of 12 pence upon every hogshead of tobacco exported; the other was a tax of 14 pence for every ton of burden on all foreign vessels trading in or to the Province. The House claimed these taxes (then being collected) were not supported by any legislation, and that they should not have been imposed and collected over the years.

Parts of the argument were taken back to an act of 1704;[3] whether it was one of those having "perpetual" effect, and what was the legal result of omitting to repeal an earlier act. The Governor, for his part, also cited an Order of the King in Council during the year 1692. Another act cited in upholding the tax was one enacted in 1732. In 1740, however, the House stoutly maintained that the taxes were "not warranted by any law of this Province." Further, it said, the tax is an "Incroachment on our Liberties and priviledges, as British Subjects and what Our Sovereign Lord the King doth not do in any of his Realms."

At one point during this involvement, the House wrote directly to the King, broadening the controversy to complain that "the Inhabitants of the Province of Maryland daily suffer many Aggrievances Extortions and Oppressions under the Proprietary Government."

However, most of the contention about the 12-pence and 14-pence taxes was between the House of Delegates and the Upper House, the latter being joined by the Governor. The usual long messages and citations to history and political theory passed back and forth. The Governor listed nine acts

---

3. Export taxes on tobacco were imposed as early as 1647. That tax was for ten shillings on every hogshead, on the condition that the Proprietary would pay the costs for any war involving Maryland. The act of 1647 had an involved history, including the question whether or not it was later repealed. *See* DONALD MARQUAND DOZER, PORTRAIT OF THE FREE STATE — A HISTORY OF MARYLAND 105-06, 131, 156-59. (Cambridge, 1976).

of the Assembly in support of his position that the taxes were valid, ranging all the way from 1671 to 1717, plus the Order of the King in Council in 1692.

Debates on the two taxes grew heated during the session from April to June, 1740. Further legislative action seeming out of the question, and following a request from the House, the Governor prorogued the session on June 5. He said that the Assembly had done nothing "to strengthen the Hands of the Government."

Another session was called a few weeks later, to last from July 7 to July 29, 1740, and again to be cut off with an unscheduled prorogation.

The Upper House opened the hostilities at the July session, with a message that the House of Delegates had fallen "far short" of what "reasonably" might have been hoped. The House countered with a message to the Governor, going on the offensive to charge that its bills had been held in the Upper House without action or return, "contrary to the constant usage of Assemblies." Continuing,

> who can blame the representatives of a free People for guarding against A Practice which in its Consequences must affect their Rights in their tenderest parts Which must render their House of Delegates a name only or mere Shadow, by depriving them of that Freedom of Action, that share in Legislature, which by their Charter and Birth Right the People are entitled to which must prostitute them to the Sole Power of an Upper House and Subject them at all times to the Absolute Will of their Governments.

Concluding, said the House, "we will not Introduce the practice of bargaining for what of Right, as British Subjects, the People ought to Enjoy."

The Governor, in reply, wrote that he felt the proceedings of the Upper House had been "just and reasonable," and he could not understand why the House had not passed the defense bill. The Province had been deprived of an Assembly for almost three years, he wrote further.

After another message from the House to the Governor, his final suggestion was that he wanted to finish the session and would dismiss the Assembly "whenever you acquaint me that no Business lies before you." The reply from the House was swift and succinct: "It is the Sense of this House that the Laws already passed ... are sufficient..... We pray your Excellency will be pleased to put an End to this Session." For the second time in 1740, therefore, there was an untimely prorogation of the General Assembly. On the latter occasion, in addition to the procedural impasse and the seeming impossibility of accomplishing any work, the House was contending with the Governor over its right to expel members for having accepted executive positions in addition to their legislative offices.

The long-continuing debates over the tobacco taxes underscored a basic and important distinction in the public finances of the Province. It had two major types of revenues, those to provide income to the Proprietary and those for the normal activities and administrative expenses of the Province. The line between the two was not quite that clear, however. The successive Lords Baltimore frequently cited the moral claim they had for remuneration for their expenses in first establishing the colony in the 1630s; these expenses have been estimated at some forty thousand pounds sterling. A result was that the House of Delegates constantly had to weigh whether a particular tax for the Proprietary was for remuneration or profit.[4] The perennial argument was to be ended only by the Revolution and the end of Proprietary government.

---

4. *See* Gust Skordas, *Maryland Government, 1634-1866,* in THE OLD LINE STATE — A HISTORY OF MARYLAND 314 (Morris L. Radoff ed.) (Annapolis, 1971).

## OTHER CONTROVERSIES

There were other routine quarrels between the two Houses during these years of the 1730s, not involving taxes and finance. All of them served to enliven the *Journals* and to continue the chronic state of disagreement and sarcasm in the Legislature.

In the March session of 1733, as to a bill for regulating ordinaries, the Upper House observed that it could act more clearly "If the Rules of Parliamentary proceedings Could have been found by us ever to have been given Countenance to an intercourse of Messages between the two Houses."

During the March-April session of 1736, after an inquiry from the Upper House about why a bill had not been returned to it, the House of Delegates answered scoffingly that "as your honours did not see the Bill ... sent back to your house Engrossed we think that you might have reasonably presumed that it was the Opinion of this house that the same should not be past into a Law."

The tenderness of sensibilities in both houses shows in a rather inconsequential argument in 1738, about an alleged slight during an exchange of messages between them. The complaint consumed five or six pages in the *Journals,* all devoted to exchanging further messages, until the Governor saw the futility of the dispute and prorogued the Assembly.

This episode began when a messenger from the Upper House in delivering a message to the House of Delegates was not immediately admitted, but was asked to wait. This, wrote the Upper House, "obliges us in Vindication of the Respect due to this house & to prevent unnecessary debates to the delay of the Publick Business and the like Indignity hereafter to send our Messages by our Clerk." But, answered the House, the Speaker when told of the messenger had gone himself to the door to receive the message. Further, the House protested, "we had no intention to treat your House or any member of it with but the greatest decency and Good manners." In the same message, however, the House hardened its stance by demanding "immediate Reparation" from the Upper House.

"We hope you will permit us to think it somewhat unusual," replied the Upper House, "as well in Publick Bodies as Private for the Party who Offers an Affront to demand Reparation from the Injured." Other complications followed, as when the Clerk of the Upper House was kept waiting an hour to deliver another message, only to be refused, and (as an amazing climax) to be asked instead to be the bearer of a message from the House of Delegates.

The culmination of it all came when the Upper House sent a long message to the Governor to complain of the treatment accorded to it, concluding that the House seemed content to put a stop to public business, and asking the Governor to take action to prevent further expense to the Province. This, in the jargon of the Assembly, was a request for prorogation; and the Governor promptly obliged. The affair so rankled the Upper House that when the Assembly came into session again the following year, in May of 1739, another long message from the Upper House to the Governor again went through the involved history of this complaint.

Not to be outdone, the House of Delegates also, at the beginning of the 1739 session, sent a long message to Governor Ogle. Expressing the House "at a loss" to understand the reason for the prorogation in 1738, it blamed the "misunderstanding" on a "misapprehension" of a member of the Upper House. However, said the House, it was willing to "pass by" the treatment it and its Speaker had received, "as also the manner of the then Prorogation and that at a time when the representative Body of the People were in the Execution of their Duty." The prorogation, concluded the House, resulted in "great Charge and Trouble to his Majesties Liege Subjects the good People of Maryland."

The Governor, in reaction to the message from the House, objected that it contained "Charges against the Government in General and my self in Particular which I am Confident are without a Foundation." The prorogation was necessary, he said, as there had been "a Stop to all publick Business, and Even to Intercourse by Messages."

The years of the late 1730s and 1740 were certainly one of the tumultuous periods in the history of the General Assembly. From 1734 through 1740, six sessions were ended on a discordant note, either by dissolution or by early prorogation. In sum, the sessions, the action, and the causes were as follows:

| | | |
|---|---|---|
| 1734 | Dissolution | Expulsion of House members |
| 1736 | Prorogation | Council's compensation; business stalled |
| 1738 | Prorogation | Exchange of messages; business stalled |
| 1739 | Prorogation | Finances; procedure |
| 1740(1) | Prorogation | Defense taxes; business stalled |
| 1740(2) | Prorogation | Expulsion of House members; procedural impasse |

## OPERATIONS AND PRIVILEGES

These years of the late 1730s and early 1740s were marked also by less dramatic changes in legislative procedure and by other matters of legislative interest.

Thus, in 1734 the rules of the House were changed to require that a bill be read twice before going to the Upper House and "once after before it is Engrossed." The earlier procedure was to read the bill three times before it was engrossed. House roll calls in 1735 continued to be by county in the order of priority of formation, and within a county by seniority of membership. In 1737 the House determined that the printer must complete the session laws "more promptly" if he expected to be paid for the job. About this time Jonas Green of Annapolis became the public printer.

The House during the late 1730s frequently considered and decided matters of elections. Some of these cases came properly under the heading of judging the elections and qualifications of its members, but others were on matters of general procedure which in later years would be for judicial determination.

The House ordered in 1734 that as to "all Complaints concerning Elections [5] the Enquiry be made at the bar of the House" and that "no Members of this House appear at the bar of this House as an Advocate." In 1734 the House voted that an election of delegates, taken before an under-sheriff in the absence of the sheriff, was not illegal; the vote was close, however, the question carrying by a count only of 22-19. In 1735 the House voted "No" on a question whether the oath of a person who at an election swears to have a visible estate sufficient to qualify him as a voter, is sufficient against all other evidence to entitle him to vote. This tally also was close, the question being defeated on a vote of 22-23. Also in 1735, several persons were held not to be residents of Annapolis and not entitled to take part in its elections; and without details the House voted "No" on questions whether there had been "undue" elections in St. Mary's County and in Dorchester County.

The House continued to protect the privileges of its members. It called before it during the May-June session of 1739 the former sheriff of Dorchester County, who had caused a judgment to be entered against Delegate John Brannock of that county, for an unpaid debt. However, the House determined that "the said Brannock had prepared Tobacco to pay the said fees a Considerable time before the said March Court and Actually Tendered the same. . . ." This,

---

5. For a general description of procedures for elections in the Province, *see* Robert J. Dinkin, *Elections in Proprietary Maryland,* 73 MARYLAND HISTORICAL MAGAZINE 129-36 (1978).

together with other charges against the sheriff, was held to be "Illegal Cruel and Inhuman, and tend to the aggrievance and oppression of the good People of this province."

The year before, in 1738, the House had called before it one John Leeds, who as a magistrate in Talbot County was accused of a lack of proper respect for the House. He received this charge:

> You have been charged here with having said that you know not by what Authority this House called you before Them. That you thought as a Magistrate You were for any Misdemeanour in your Office only answerable to the Government, and not to this House: And that you valued not a button or fart what this House could do to you, and were it not, you thought people wou'd think you were fearful of appearing here, you would not attend Them on their Summons; and that you further said, this House had no more Authority to call you before Them than your horse had; also that you have grosly abused Mr. Nicholas Goldsborough a member of this House by calling Him a Son of a bitch, and Saying 'twas by his means you were called here. Which matters have been fully proved against you.
>
> And Forasmuch as this house ordered you amongst other Magistrates of Talbot County to pay your proportionable part of certain Fees, that have accrued on an Accusation made here against you and Them, and that you have refused the payment of your part thereof.
>
> This House therefore have ordered that the Sheriff of Ann Arundell County receive you into his Custody from the Serjeant at Arms attending this House, in whose custody you are at present, and that you remain in that Sherifs custody until you make a proper Submission to this House, and in particular to Mr. Nicholas Goldsborough for your Contempt aforesaid, and also until you pay your proportionable part of the Fees aforesaid.

In 1740 the Governor was asked for an opinion on the question of activity by a House committee during an interim between sessions. In reply, he cited an opinion by the Council of State, dated August 1, 1739,[6] holding that interim activity was "unwarrantable and illegal" and would have a "mischievous consequence":

> It is there declared to be the opinion of the Board, That no Members of the Lower House could be qualified by virtue of any Order made in the last Convention of Assembly, to act as a Committee of the said House, after the Prorogation, and during the Interval of the Assembly, and that the Exercise of any such Authority or Power is not only Unwarrantable and Illegal, but is an Encroachment on, and has a Tendency to overthrow the Authority, which every Governor in his Majestys Dominions is invested with, of Proroguing and Dissolving Assemblies, and that therefore it might be of very mischievious Consequence to give the least Countenance to such a Proceeding, even by Overlooking it, or not taking a due notice thereof. Wherefore the Board was of Opinion That every Officer should be cautioned and directed, not to Submit to or Comply with, any Commands, Request or Application, made, or to be made, by or under the pretended Authority of any such Committee.

After holding that a House committee could not meet between sessions of the Assembly, Governor Ogle softened the ruling by directing officers throughout the Province to supply copies of official papers to "any person whatsoever," and adding that persons appointed by the House might get the copies without fee.

The Assembly continued its long-time claim for the benefit of the English common law and statutes. At the May-June session in 1739, the House Committee on Aggrievances and Courts of Justice, commenting upon the erection of a new chancery court without a specific law, reported that "Your Committee most humbly Conceive that according to the laws of our Mother Country (the Birth right of every Liege

---

6. *See Archives,* XXVIII at 174.

Subject here) that no offices can be created with new fees or new fees appointed to old Offices without our Common Assent in Assembly." Also, the House frequently, as in 1739, repeated its adoption of the resolutions of 1722, which had included the well-known phrases that "this Province is not under the Circumstances of a Conquered Country," the settlers have not forfeited any part of "their English Liberties," and the Province has "the Common Law, and such General Statutes of England as are not restrained by words of Locall Limitation in them."

Some historians in commentaries on this period have written in terms of political parties, somewhat in the modern sense. Most commonly the mention is of a "Proprietary" party and an "Anti-Proprietary" party, and the latter sometimes was called the "Country" party. A more unusual mention was of an "Eastern Shore" party, though that cannot be completely surprising in later centuries. The editors of the Maryland *Archives,* for example, cite the vote in 1738 on a bill to prevent the further importation of horses into the Province; the tally showed 14 negative votes from the Eastern Shore and 14 affirmative votes from the Western Shore.

With all the quarrels and travail of its legislative work, the General Assembly upon occasion could rise to heights of social grace, sometimes accompanied by a boldness of expression that hardly would be ventured in a later time. In 1737 the Governor and both houses of the Assembly joined in this message of congratulations to the Prince of Wales, upon the occasion of his marriage:

> May it please Your Royal Highness
> To Accept Our most Respectfull Congratulations which though late, yet not less Sincere than those of the rest of his Majestys Subjects on the Joyfull Occasion of Your Royal Highness's Happy Marriage
> Amidst all the Felicities and blessings which We, as Subjects to Your Great Father enjoy, We could not be

291

without Apprehensions, lest those Amiable qualities of Love and Benevolence for Mankind so Conspicuous in Your Royal Highness should not be transmitted from your own Royal Person in a Race of Princes who by the bright Example might Endear themselves to every Subject

This Auspicious Union, Great Sir, of the Illustrious Houses of Hannover and Saxe Gotha Dispells many of those fears, and Draws our Wishes nearer to a perfect Completion: A Prospect is opened, and Our View is Extended by the Strength of Our Hopes and Desires to a Succession of Princes, whose Virtues will Shew their Descent from Those Two who are now the Comfort and Delight of all his Majesties Dominions

May every joy attendant on the Marriage Bed be Redoubled on Your Royall Highness and Consort, and may Our repeated Occasions of Rejoyceing on the Births of a numerous Issue afford us a Pleasing Assurance of the throne of Great Britain never wanting an Inheriter of Your many Excellent Virtues.

Some years later, in 1744, the House of Delegates sent another candid message, this time to the King, upon the occasion of his daughter's marriage:

The Marriage of her Royal Highness the princess Louisa with the Prince Royal of Denmark, is, to us, matter of the Greatest Joy and Satisfaction, as it affords the Agreeable prospect of Encreasing your Royal Issue, and of our never wanting a Protestant Descendant of your Royal Line to fill your Throne to the latest Posterity.

Another testimony to their social graces was the participation of the Assembly, and probably a goodly number of the citizens of Annapolis, in a community celebration when the Assembly adjourned its 1747 session. As reported in *The Maryland Gazette* (Annapolis) for July 14, 1747, after the session was concluded, "The Gentlemen of the Upper House invited those of the Lower House into the Council Chamber, where all the Loyal Healths, Success to the Tobacco Trade,

292

etc. etc. were Drank; then the Members of both Houses went to the Stadt-House, where the Healths were repeated; mean time the Town Guns fired 10 or 11 Rounds, and the Populace having Punch and Wine distributed amongst them, made loud Acclamations of Joy...." [7]

After the almost constant dissension in the General Assembly from the middle 1730s through 1740, there was a period of unusual quiet from 1741 through 1744. The Assembly met for a May-June session in 1741, in September and October of 1742, and in May and June of 1744. There was no session in 1743. In 1742 the House reaffirmed its perennial claim to the benefits of the English statutes and common law.

One of the important pieces of legislation during these several years was Chapter 19 of 1742, which took the "seaboard" portions of Somerset County in order to create Worcester County. This gave the Province a total of 13

---

7. *The Maryland Gazette* was published as a weekly paper of general circulation beginning in 1745 (although there had been earlier and irregular publications in the late 1720s and in the 1730s). Its editor was Jonas Green, who became the official printer for the Province by printing the *Journals* and the *Laws*. Green doubled also as Postmaster for Annapolis. He was assisted by his wife, Anne Catherine Green, who took over the publication after Green died in 1767. When she died in 1775, their son Frederick assumed the publication. During Jonas Green's lifetime, his wife also had other pursuits; the advertising columns of the *Gazette* occasionally published notices she had inserted, that she was holding for public sale such items as "very good raisins of the sun" and "very good chocolate."

The *Gazette,* not blessed with regular and reliable sources of information, sometimes included materials coming to it from questionable contributors. One such was in the issue of June 3, 1746, in a report from two unidentified men "of repute" who had been fishing off Kent Island in the afternoon, with the weather clear and calm. They reported seeing a man about five feet in height walking on the water; he was said to have crossed from Kent Island to Talbot County, a distance of about four miles.

counties, little more than a century after its founding. Four delegates from Worcester County were present for the session in 1744.

One potential for trouble occurred in 1742, when the House charged Samuel Ogle with having sent an emissary to challenge a member of the House to a duel. Ogle was the former Governor, who was still in the Province. The House quickly reacted. The incident was "an absolute Violation of its Just Rights and Privileges," said the House by unanimous action, "and the said Samuel Ogle Esquire hath in a high Degree been guilty of the same." Governor Bladen appeared before both houses and asked the House of Delegates to drop its protest, in consideration of the high station Ogle held in Maryland and of his imminent departure for England. The House responded that "in Justice to the Rights and Priviledges of ourselves and those whom We represent" it had to take notice of the former Governor's action "in the most Public manner," but that in deference to the request from the new Governor, it "dropt the Affair."

## TROUBLES WITH AN INDIAN TREATY

An issue of some explosive possibilities arose during the May-June session of 1744. As events proved, it marked the end of amity among the House of Delegates, the Upper House, and the Governor. The matter concerned a message the Governor had sent to the House earlier, asking that it appoint two persons who with two members of the Upper House would join a group appointed by the Governor to conclude a treaty with the Indians of the Six Nations. The House appointed its two representatives and sent them off with a series of 19 "instructions" for treating with the Six Nations. The Governor vigorously objected to the set of instructions:

I little thought you would have Ventured at giving any Instructions to such Members for their Conduct.... The prerogative of making, or treating about Peace or War, is such an acknowledged and undoubted Right of the Crown, that either or both Houses of Parliament never pretended to authorize, or instruct any Minister employed in such negotiations .... It was impossible for you to conceive their Seats in your House intitled you to any such Authority.... I cannot but look on these Instructions as an Essay, to set up a power in your House, unknown to every Constitution and Government under the British Government....

The Governor was nettled also that while the instructions had been framed during the session two years earlier, nothing had been said or publicized about them until a few days before his protest. Concluding, "I must further say Plainly, you have taken upon your selves a Province which does not belong to you," and that the peace commissioners were to observe and pursue only the directives that came from him.

The House of Delegates stoutly defended its action in issuing the instructions. The Governor's message, it said,

being of an Extraordinary Nature, and containing very forced Accusations of the Intentions of this House, we choose to Attribute to the cavilling Temper and malevolent Disposition of others, rather than to your Excellency....

We can with great truth and sincerity assure your Excellency. that we never had, nor have it in our thoughts or Inclinations, to Attempt getting into our Hands any share or part of the Power of Government.... How Majesty itself has been drawn into the Present Case, we are at a loss to know, unless it was to Render the thing more Terrible and give the greater fforce to the designed accusation.... We readily acknowledge the Power of War and Peace to be in the Crown .... Upon the most Mature consideration of the said instructions, we cannot conceive that they contain any one Article or Matter,... but such necessary Travelling Charges only....

This rejoinder to the Governor was approved in the House by a vote of 24-21. To buttress its argument, the House inserted into the *Journal* for 1744 the 19 instructions issued to its appointees in 1742.

For the most part, actually, they seem rather innocuous. Thirteen of the 19 directives covered matters about which the House members were to "enquire" or to be "well informed"; they involved such questions and topics as the cause of the current uneasiness, whether there had been a previous treaty, the mood of the Shawans and the cause of their coming to Maryland in 1742, what Indians lived near the Susquehanna River, Indian complaints of injury, what lands were claimed, whether the King kept up a general peace, whether an Indian settlement with the French was imminent, the policies of the colony of Pennsylvania, and the value to Maryland of keeping peace with the Indians.

Two of the six remaining instructions were that the commissioners from Maryland were to make sure the Indians knew that the original inhabitants of Maryland had purchased their lands from the Indians, and that Maryland wanted peace with them. Another instruction was of no outside substance, simply enjoining the House representatives to keep a journal of the proceedings and to report them back to the House of Delegates. The three remaining directives, however, might conceivably have been interpreted as interfering with the prerogatives of the Executive. One was to insert into any articles of peace that the Six Nations procure information about why the Shawans came to Maryland in 1742; another, that an article go into the peace treaty stating the cause of the current uneasiness; and the third, that the Province of Maryland not be burdened with the terms of a treaty, holding the value of the negotiations to not more than three hundred pounds sterling.

Despite the rather inoffensive nature of most of the directives to the commissioners from the House, the

Governor remained unconvinced. His answering message to the House, also a long one, complained that the House "shewed such a willingness to treat in so indecent a manner, a Message Signed and sent" by him. He concluded with another review of the preemptive rights of the Executive in matters of foreign policy. Since the peace conference had long since been concluded, this controversy subsided.

Yet it had touched singularly close to the developing political philosophy of separation of powers. In part this had come from the English model for the powers of the executive and legislative branches, and in part it came from the recent writings of John Locke. This also was the mid-eighteenth century and the time of Montesquieu, whose writings, particularly *L'Esprit des Lois,* were to have such a profound influence upon the new American constitutions to be drafted a generation later.

## FINES, FORFEITURES, AND REVENUES

With the Indian Nations affair behind it, the House of Delegates went on to other matters of contention with the Upper House, the Governor, and Lord Baltimore; and it settled some basic matters of its own procedures and prerogatives. The substance of a number of these discussions and quarrels was to appear later in the Constitution of 1776.

The session of 1745 was called mainly to provide assistance for the garrison at Louisburg, on Cape Breton Island; it recently had been captured by the British fleet and troops from New England. The House agreed to make an appropriation, but with many a backward glance and diverting tactic.

The appropriation voted by the House was to be raised by an additional tax upon ordinaries, but the House added to it a provision for a Provincial agent in London. Having such a representative frequently had been discussed and argued; this time the Upper House suspected that the main purpose of the agent would be as a colonial voice against Lord Baltimore. Keeping the argument on a high plane, the Upper House protested it was improper to have two subjects in the bill. "On the subject of any Money Bill," it wrote, "no Clause was ever lookt on as relative to his Majestys Service, or proper for such Bill which did not either immediately grant Money to his Majesty or to his Use or was an Appendix to some other Bill which had before granted Money to his Majesty . . . ."

The House of Delegates utilized this occasion also to reiterate its frequent claim for an exclusive power in the introduction and amendment of money bills:

> It is the undoubted Right of the House of Delegates, to raise on the People of this Province, any Sum of Money, or other Tax, and for such Time, and in such Manner, and to such uses and Purposes, as to them shall seem meet, and . . . the Upper House have not any Right to propose any Alterations or Amendments, so as to alter or change the substantial or material Parts of any such Bill, sent up to them from this House.

This, of course, was a very sweeping claim; it covered not only the introduction of money bills but an exclusive power over their contents, with the Upper House to have no power to make material changes.

The Upper House was quick to reply: "This We conceive to be a most extraordinary Claim and such as no House of Commons ever made." With an evident reference back to the Cromwell period a century earlier, the Upper House spoke of "the most Violent Means" by which a part of the House of Commons had "usurped the whole Authority as well Legislative, as Executive," and it hoped the House of Delegates in Maryland had no such purpose. The Upper House made one concession, however:

Had You been pleased to have contented Yourselves with Asserting that it was your undoubted Right to begin a Money Bill in your House, we could at this time for the sake of dispatch, forborn to have made any Observation on such an Assertion, But we hope You will not think We act beside Our Duty, in letting you know what Objections We have to any Money Bills, so that you may if they are reasonable remove them and make the Bill proper for its passage here. . . .

Concluding, the Upper House admonished, "neither Ourselves or our Province are too Old or knowing not to be taught by the wise Legislature of Great Britain."

The House of Delegates, by this time thoroughly intransigent, fired three more salvos during this August-September session of 1745, directed to the Governor or to the Governor and Council combined. The Proprietary was involved in all three of the complaints.

One was to the Governor alone, requesting a general accounting for the collection of fines, forfeitures, and other amercements in the Province. In its message the House stressed that the people were burdened with many taxes and charges, "of which it requires our utmost Attention to find Ways and means to ease them." Further, there were "sundry Fines and Forfeitures which we humbly conceive ought to be appropriated to the Support of Government; as also Amerciaments in the Provincial Court, an Account of the Disposal whereof hath not for many years been rendered to the House of Delegates."

In reply, wrote Governor Bladen, fines and forfeitures appropriated by acts of Assembly had been accounted for to Lord Baltimore, "to whom only they were accountable." Fines and forfeitures by the common law "are as much his Lordship's Right, as any thing else can possibly be" and if those who received them honestly reported them to Lord Baltimore "they have fully discharged their Duty." Finally, he said, if there were any occasion to lay such accounts before the House, "which I think there is not, it would be a very difficult Task on me to procure such Accounts, because several of the Gentlemen who have been Agents are dead, and I am not acquainted with their Executors or Administrators. The same Reasons will reach the Amerciaments."

Three days after this exchange of messages, on August 24, 1745, the House Committee of Aggrievances and Courts of Justice reported to the House that the collection of these fees and penalties was not warranted by law and was contrary to the powers vested in magistrates, that assessing and levying such illegal fees was a grievance, and that such oppression "tends to alienate the Affections of the People from his Lordship's Government." The full House approved this report by a vote of 40-8. On August 27, the House voted unanimously "that the levying of the same is illegal and oppressive."

Following the report of its committee, the House again on September 2 asked Governor Bladen for an accounting of the fines and forfeitures, specifying the period from 1715 to 1745. The Governor's answer to its previous message, the House said, "we humbly beg leave to say is by no means satisfactory." The collections, it was continued, were "in Trust, and for the Benefit only of that People among whom they are levied." The House objected to taking it "for granted" that the agents had accounted for the funds, and "tho' they have done so, yet have not yet done their Duty: For if those Fines and Forfeitures be a part of the publick Treasure of this Province, as we humbly conceive they are, we think they are not to be paid to any Person out of it, but are to be retained in it, to support the Calls and Occasions of this Government."

Governor Bladen in reply wrote that the reasoning of the House was "very foreign" to the question. By analogy, he compared the right of Lord Baltimore to the common law fines to the disposition of such fines accruing to the King of England. As to the fines imposed by statute, the acts expressly declared them payable to the Lord Proprietary and made no mention of payment to a treasurer; "it will be Time enough to charge the officers with a non Compliance in their Duty, when they make such Payments to Persons not directed by the Acts to receive the same." All of this long exchange of messages on fines and forfeitures had no effect upon the procedures and accounting for them.

The second of the three complaints of the House in 1745 was an inquiry directed to the Governor about the quitrents received by the Proprietary, and their amounts.[8] The inquiry was coupled with a proposal to substitute a fixed annual payment to Lord Baltimore. The Governor seemed reluctant to be precise, saying at first only that a payment under five thousand pounds sterling would not be "reasonable." Later the figures were supplied, by counties, adding to about 5,100 pounds. For purposes of discussion, the House settled for the five thousand pounds. This complaint also was left hanging in abeyance.

The third and final of these controversies in 1745 was based upon the imposition and collection by the Governor and Council of a special tax at the rate of one pound of tobacco on every taxable person in the Province; i.e., a poll tax. All the sheriffs had a power of execution for collecting the tax. "In as much as it is not known to this House," wrote the House of Delegates, "by what Power and Authority your Excellency and their Honours have done the same, we humbly pray, your Excellency will please to order to be laid before this House, the Authority by which the said Tax hath been assessed, levied, and Execution issued for the same."

---

8. Quitrents were the annual rents paid to the Proprietary as owner and landlord of the Province. By payment of a quitrent, the tenant was "quit" or free from all other service. *See Generally,* Beverly W. Bond, Jr., *The Quit Rent in Maryland,* 5 MARYLAND HISTORICAL MAGAZINE 350-65 (1910).

The Governor's first answer was that the House was "resolved" to treat him "with the utmost Indecency and ill manners." He professed that he would willingly "lose the Remembrance of your extraordinary Behaviour towards myself, in the Pleasure I shall receive, when I see your Actions correspond with the Professions you make of Duty to his Majesty, and Affection for his Service."

The Governor then responded that the tax was levied by virtue of an act of Assembly for regulating the militia and for the defense and security of the Province, passed in 1715. This brought on from the House a long discussion of the act of 1715 and a number of subsequent acts, whether any of them had been "perpetual" in effect, and the meaning of the phrase so often appended to legislation that an act should be effective "for three years and to the End of the next Session of Assembly after the End of the said three years." The House contended the act of 1715 had long since expired, and that in any event the Governor and the Council had not acted agreeably to the letter and intent of that act.

The Governor at even greater length argued that the act of 1715 had not expired and that a later act of 1732 "looked upon" the act of 1715 as perpetual. He contended also that he and the Council had fully observed the meaning and intent of the act of 1715. Finally, "there is no Foundation for charging the Governor and Council with highly, or at all, infringing on the Liberties of the People of Maryland, which is a Thing I, for my own part, detest."

At one point in the long debate, on September 10, the House of Delegates said that as the act of 1715 "has long since expired, we must humbly hope, that neither your Excellency nor the Council, nor both together, for the Time being, will levy this 50,000 lb. of Tobacco on the People, not only not once in every year in the Interval of Assemblies, but not ever 'once in many years' nor at all in the future." To this the Governor made quick answer in his final message of September 28, "that for the sake, Defense, and Ease of the Province, I am determined, with the Advice of the Council, to put the same in Execution in all it's Parts, as often as Occasion requires; til I am satisfied by some better Reasons, that this Law of 1715 has been expired ever since 1725, contrary to that common Sense which I am master of."

The House linked together the extra tax for the Cape Breton campaign and the tobacco poll tax levied by the Governor and Council. When prodded by the Governor early in the session for having been in session for two weeks and still having no bill for Louisburg and Cape Breton, the House responded that

> a bill to that End is in as great Forwardness, as the subject matter would admit. . . . Were We inclined to think of any other than a fair and upright Behaviour in your Excellency, we conceive there is equal Room to suspect a Delay on your Part, as you have had before you our Address relating to the Authority by which your Excellency and his Lordship's Council have levied upon the People one Pound of Tobacco per poll, near as long as the Affair for Support of Cape Breton hath been under our Consideration. . . .

As he ended the 1745 session, the Governor wrote again of his disappointment in not getting legislation for the relief of Louisburg and Cape Breton. That failure, plus the several other tribulations he had with the House, led him, in under-statement, to tell the House that "Upon the whole Gentlemen Your Conduct through this Session takes from me the Liberty of meeting with this Lower House again."

In 1746, the House returned briefly to two other tobacco taxes, one a tax of 12 pence per hogshead on tobacco shipped from the Province, and the other a tax of 14 pence per ton on all foreign "bottoms" trading in Maryland. In a letter to the

Governor, the House said that both taxes had been "authenticated" by him. The Governor was assured that the House proposed "nothing in this matter but what is fair and honest." The Governor's answer was that both taxes had long been collected by Lord Baltimore and his ancestors, "by virtue of their Proprietaryship distinct from the Government."

Thus ended for a time the long and acrimonious debate on the annual tobacco taxes; the issues were to reappear in future sessions. In the meantime, the argument was notable for two other contributions, one to the folklore and the other to the laws and customs of Maryland.

Apparently as a "first" in the General Assembly of Maryland and a part of its legislative folklore, an action of the House on September 21, 1745, must be recorded. The Governor had just returned his next-to-last message on the tobacco tax, arguing in part that since the session was so far advanced and no provision had yet been made for the usual tax for arms and ammunition, the Assembly at the least should pass legislation for that tax. Upon receiving the message, the House entertained a motion "to refer the Consideration thereof to the first Day of November next." The motion carried by a vote of 32-18. While sessions in that time did not have to end upon a day certain, the already protracted duration of the session in 1745 and the six weeks' interval before November 1 make it rather obvious that here was an early use of the famous parliamentary device of making a bill a special order for some distant time after the end of the session.

The second by-product of the tobacco tax debate was to achieve a written characterization of the difference between a "temporary" and a "perpetual" act. The distinction seems rather simple, yet it was a point that had been argued intermittently for decades. The Governor and the House made separate statements of the differences, but they varied only in slight detail. As stated by the House, "there is no Time limited for the Duration, Operation, or Continuance" of a perpetual act, and therefore "it must continue in force 'til it is repealed." A temporary act, "having a fix'd or limited Time for it's Duration or operation, it must certainly expire, when the Time so fixed or limited expires, or the End for which it was made is fully answered, unless it is continued by another Law."[9]

## THE LATE 1740s

The Assembly met for a short session in March, 1746. There was little business, but the House of Delegates had an opportunity to express again its dissatisfaction with Lord Baltimore. The Assembly was adopting a testimonial to King George II upon the occasion of his defeating the efforts of Charles Stuart ("the Pretender") to seize the throne. A first draft of the testimonial was prepared in the Upper House, but the House of Delegates objected to a portion of it which alluded to the "Religion Liberties and Properties" enjoyed by the King's subjects. The objection of the House was that the Province was under Lord Baltimore, causing a grievance to the citizens "by means of which they apprehend themselves in some Measure deprived of that full and free Possession of their Civil Rights which they acknowledge they should otherwise enjoy." The House proposed alternate language for the testimonial.

There was another session in 1746, from June 17 to July 8. The House refused to take part in King George's War; and it would not support a tax for an expedition to Canada.

---

**9.** It was always difficult to distinguish between temporary and permanent acts, and to remember when the temporaries would expire. This problem brought a comment in the *Maryland Gazette* for November 1, 1749: "Early this Morning expired, much lamented by some, and rejoiced at by others, the Act of Assembly of this Province *For Tryal of all Matters of Fact in the several Counties where they have arisen or shall arise.*"

The House engaged the Governor in verbal combat over a rather inconsequential happening, and the usual flurry of messages resulted. This time the charge was that immediately after the prior session in March was prorogued, the Governor encountered Delegate Walter Smith of Calvert County and insulted the delegate with "warmth, Passion, scornful Looks and Gestures," as well as "opprobrious names and Language," rising to the climax that the delegate "was a sorry Fellow." The House found itself under an "indispensible necessity" to take notice of the "treatment" Delegate Smith had received.

The House wrote the Governor that the delegate was "a person of strict Honour and veracity," the "indignity" offered to him was "equally to this House," the Governor had impugned the great Parliamentary precept which guaranteed "Liberty of Speech on every Debate" in the Assembly, and the delegate should not be questioned on legislative matters "by Any Person whatsoever, or in Any manner of Place but by the House." These rights, it concluded, are the "Law of the Land, and our undoubted Birthright as British subjects and Englishmen."

About a week later, on July 3, the Governor answered the charge. The assertion that he called Smith "a sorry Fellow," he maintained, "is absolutely false and an Imposition on your House: Perhaps it is true that I might say, he was an ungrateful Fellow. . . . But pray Gentlemen, what is this, or any Thing else that is said in Conversation with any man, to the Privilege of your House? Assert your Rights in God's name; I shall never Attempt or desire to infringe them, but do not imagine, I am to take every Thing to be Privilege that you are pleased to call so."

The Governor went on to cite Parliamentary statutes and practices and the proper construction of the privileges of the Parliament. He intimated that the objections of the House may have been intended primarily to impress the voters.

Concluding, "in short, Gentlemen, take my advice as a Friend to the Rights of your House; what really are your rights insist on and preserve, so far my wishes shall always go along with you but do not, like the Vain Frog in the Fable, swell up and puff the Privilege 'til it burst."

The next move was up to the House, and by a vote of 28-17 it approved a four-page reply to the Governor. Your answer, wrote the House, "is so far from affording us a Prospect of a Forbearance of such Practices in the future, that your very Answer is a fresh Breach of the Privileges of this House. . . . Confession and Excuse is often better made than a Iustification, and particularly so, when a Fact charged is true." The House followed with its own account of history and precedent. In summation, "We really Sir would not have guess'd at the Little Regard you have shewn for our Privileges or Charactors which as Representatives of a Free People are in a Parliamentary sense sacred and which we are determined to preserve." It questioned whether the episode "proceeded from the Vanity of the Frog or the stupidity of a Certain Animal cloathed in a Lyons Skinn."

At the end, however, the House assured the Governor it would cause him "no Further Trouble on this head." The final word came from the Governor in an address to the House when the session was ended. He again assured the House he had no intention of infringing upon a privilege but added a hardly-veiled warning against a new doctrine, "the more Confusion the better," that was not covered within the privilege of freedom of speech. He hoped that he might "never be forced by the Duty of my Station, to the disagreeable Necessity of taking Notice of any Words spoken in your House which no Rule of Parliament can Privilege." This extravagant claim for privilege ended for the session, and it was further placed to rest when Samuel Ogle in the same year replaced Thomas Bladen in the Governor's office.

In one way or another, however, legislative privilege and prerogative remained strongly in the minds of members of the House of Delegates all through the 1740s. Most of the issues were minor and short-lived; others were of some importance, and one caused the Governor to prorogue the Assembly.

Two small problems arose in 1740. In the July session that year, the Upper House proposed sending jointly a congratulatory message to the King for the success of English arms in the war with Spain. The House of Delegates responded that it was "not unmindful" of the occasion, but that it could not give a "direct answer" until it ascertained the fate of a House bill that had been in the Upper House for almost a week. But, asked the Upper House, what relation is this bill to a congratulatory message? The House avoided the direct question but stepped around the problem by sending its own congratulatory message and notifying the Upper House it was "unnecessary" to participate in the joint message.

The dignity of its own proceedings was vigorously upheld by the House of Delegates in 1747. One Richard Snowden, "being permitted to come into this House with several other Gentlemen, to hear the debates, did, whilst a Member was Debating, accuse him of falsehood; which being a great Contempt of the Rights and privileges of this House, the Serjeant at Arms was ordered to take the said Richard Snowden into Custody." Snowden abjectly apologized, in a letter to the Speaker:

> Hurry'd by my passion, I inadvertently made use of an Expression, which I acknowledge was indecent, and contrary to the privileges of your Honourable House; for which I am sincerely sorry, and heartily beg pardon of your Honourable House, and of that worthy member in particular, for whom I have the highest Regard: and nothing but an Imagination, that my Credit as a Man of veracity, was at Stake, could have carried me to such a Pitch of Indiscretion. Therefore I am ready

308

to make such Submission, as your Honourable House will please to accept of. . . .

Snowden was ordered to attend the House, where the Speaker reprimanded him:

Inasmuch as you have offered an high Indignity to this House in a public Manner, and particularly to a Member thereof, in the Execution of his Duty; you are to ask pardon of this House. and that Member, and at the same time take notice, that the Consideration of your Age and Character, and that what you did is looked upon to be done thro' Inadvertency, hath induced the House to use you with great Indulgence.

Snowden then made "his Due Submission to the House, and to the Member in particular. Whereupon, he was discharged on payment of the ffees to the Serjeant at Arms."

During the August-September session in 1745, the House of Delegates met with tact and diplomacy a possible collision with the Governor and Council. It was a rather bizarre episode, with elements of international security and conflicting orders at home.

Governor Shirley of the Massachusetts Bay colony wrote to the Governor in Maryland in 1745, concerning the military campaign in Canada. Feeling that the letter might give valuable and prejudicial information to the enemy, the Governor and Council ordered the printer, Jonas Green, neither to print the letter nor to suffer it to be printed, "upon any Pretence whatsoever, as he shall answer the contrary at his Peril."

Unfortunately for the printer, the Order in Council came to him on a Friday evening, after the House had ordered the letter to be included in its *Journal* and then had adjourned for the day. Mr. Green wrote to the Speaker of the House with much concern, citing the order from the House to print the letter and the express prohibition from the Council:

As I am, Sir, solely dependent on the several Branches of the Legislature for a Living (for I can have no publick money except granted by your Honourable House, nor any, if so granted, except the other Branches should acquiesce thereto, and cannot live without it) I am in a most terrible Dilemma: Impending Danger, Ruin, Destruction, hanging over me, let me act as I will. In this desperate Case I am sure to err. If I print it I shall highly offend the Governour and Council, and must expect no Favour and Countenance from thence; if I do not, the Lower House of Assembly I may justly expect will be likewise offended: And I cannot live without the Favour and Protection of both. To obey two Orders, so diametrically opposite, is impossible; and to know how to act in this unhappy situation, perplexes and almost distracts me. I am Honourable Sir, with the utmost Deference, and in the greatest Distress.

Your Honour's most obedient humble Servant Jonas Green

The House in a resolution described the facts in some detail, proceeding to a strong statement in principle of the manner in which the action of the Council had interfered with the rights, privileges, and authority of the House of Delegates:

Resolved, That the making, issuing, and serving the aforementioned Order of the Governour and Council in the aforesaid manner, in Contradiction and Opposition to an Order of this House before then entered into, is an high Violation, and tends to subvert the fundamental Rights, Privileges, and Authority of this House. And that any Order or Resolve of this House, relating to their Proceedings, is not, nor ought to be, suspended or controuled by any Order of the Governour and Council.

Immediately thereafter, however, in the same resolution, the House recognized Green's problem, and "out of Compassion to the Circumstances of the Printer, and from no other motive whatever, do wave his printing that Letter as ordered by this House on Friday last."

In 1748 the House addressed Governor Ogle about a statement of accounts it had received from Edward Lloyd, signed by him as Treasurer of the Eastern Shore. The House voiced this concern:

> As this House have had no share in, or Knowledge of his Appointment to that office, which of right they ought; we hope we shall stand excused by your Excellency if we do not Acknowledge Any Authority he hath in that Station. . . . We cannot therefore consistent with our Duty as representatives of the people, give up this part of their Right; and as we have not had the least View of encroaching on the Prerogatives of the Government, so we humbly hope your Excellency will not attempt to deprive us of that right we have enjoyed in the Nomination of the Treasurers of this Province.

The House followed with a resolution, "That the Nomination of the Treasurers of this Province, is the undoubted right of this House."

In 1749, while considering a contested election for the delegates from St. Mary's County, the House made its decision and went on to be highly critical of one or more members of the Upper House for "intermeddling" in the election of members of the House of Delegates. This particular matter seems to have originated in Cecil County. The *Journal* does not explain the extent of the offense, but it leaves no doubt about the disapproval of the House:

> Resolved, That it is an high Infringement of, and a dangerous Attack upon, the Liberties and Privileges of the Freemen of this Province, and tends to subvert the Freedom of Elections of Delegates to serve in Assembly, for any Person who, in the Time of a General Assembly of this Province, doth, or hereafter shall, sit as a Member of an Upper House of Assembly, any way to interest, intermeddle, or concern himself in the Election of Delegates to serve in Assembly, so long as such House doth or shall claim or exercise a Negative on any of the Proceedings of the House of Delegates.

Resolved, That none of the Persons, who in the Time of a General Assembly of this Province do, or hereafter shall, sit as Members of an Upper House of Assembly, and do or shall, for the Time being, as such, claim or exercise a Negative on any of the Proceedings of the House of Delegates of the said Province, have any Right to vote at an Election of Delegates to serve in Assembly, so long as such Negative shall be claimed or exercised: And that any Vote given by such Person is and shall be deemed and taken to be absolutely void, and of no Effect, in such Election.

As the General Assembly reached the mid-point in the eighteenth century, there were unmistakable signs of a deepening and increasingly articulate spirit of controversy in the House of Delegates, toward the Upper House, the Governor, and the Proprietary. In the quarter century remaining before the Revolution, it was but a step toward including the King among the objects of complaint.

# Chapter 9

## DEEPENING CONFRONTATION WITH LORD BALTIMORE 1749-1756

As the General Assembly came to and then moved beyond the mid-eighteenth century, both its internal conflicts and those with the Governor and Lord Baltimore continued without abatement. Some were of the brush-fire variety, while others stirred the basic enmity between the two houses and with the Proprietary. Some observers of Maryland history sense a growing antagonism between the House of Delegates and Lord Baltimore by the early 1750s. The Preface for the *Archives* covering the legislative years from 1752 to 1754 notes that "the conflict of interests between people and Proprietary was responsible for a condition of the public mind which in the next decade was to render it specially intolerant of the measures employed by the British Government that brought about the American Revolution."

Along with these fundamentals of political philosophy, and sometimes as the vehicle for developing the philosophy, the Assembly in this decade of the early 1750s was continually concerned with some of its old matters of controversy: prerogatives as mirrored in powers of appointment; holding dual public employments; and even the compensation of the Council of State, supposedly settled in 1736. Perennial questions of taxes, revenues, fines, and fees arose again, aggravated by the pressures of the French and Indian War[1] and the supply bills to finance the war effort.

---

1. The American version of the Seven Years' War in Europe.

THE GENERAL ASSEMBLY OF MARYLAND

## Appointment of the House Clerk

The House of Delegates precipitated a power struggle with the Governor at an abbreviated session which began on March 9, 1749. It involved the appointment of the clerk of the House, and whether the Governor or the House had the right of appointment. Historically, the Governor had the better of the argument, and he finally prevailed; but he had to prorogue the session at the end of three days in order to win the encounter.

Standard procedure for appointing a clerk of the House over the years had been a nomination by the House, which was submitted to the Governor for his approval. In the very early years, there were occasions when the House simply asked the Governor to provide a clerk. In either case, of course, it had been the Governor who made the final decision.

As the session opened on May 9, 1749, however, the laconic information in the *Journal* was that two members of the House "acquaint his Excellency their house hath made choice of Mr. Michael Macnemara as their Clerk and that they attend to see him qualified." Immediately following in the *Journal* was the Governor's instant reply: "His Excellency is pleased to acquaint them, that Mr. Macnemara must be first Presented to him as their Clerk in the usual Manner for his approbation."[2]

Two members of the House notified the Governor at once that the House action "did not proceed from any design in the house to infringe the Rights of the Government or from any disregard of his Excellencys Person," but that they thought

2. Michael Macnemara was a son of Thomas Macnemara, who had been a protege of Daniel Dulany the Elder. Thomas died in 1720, after frequently bringing his own name in disrepute. Dulany sent Michael to England to get a legal education in the Inns of Court. Michael was Mayor of Annapolis during the 1750s. *See* AUBREY C. LAND, THE DULANYS OF MARYLAND 7, 8, 33, 41, 96, 236 (Baltimore, 1955).

themselves justified by precedent. In proof they cited the House *Journal* from the July session in 1732, which mentioned only that the House chose Macnemara (he actually had been clerk since 1728). He then "qualified" by taking the oath; and there was no mention of the Governor's approval or of a request for it. The Governor responded by quoting from the *Journal* of the Upper House for that same session. It specified that after the House chose Macnemara it "acquainted" the Governor of the choice "and hopes for his Excellencys Approbation who is pleased to approve...."

For good measure the Governor reviewed the manner of appointment from 1734 through 1746, which covered the period from his first arrival in the Province. Without exception, the record showed that the name was presented to the Governor for his "approbation." He then went back to the session of 1700, "when the Lower House seems first to have Chosen their Clerk." Continuing,

> you will not only see the Governors Approbation necessary but the Reason of it, the Lower House being satisfied that the appointment of their Clerk was realy in the Governor and only permitted to them out of his Condescension as they themselves Express it with this Express Condition of Presenting him for Approbation.

The *Journal* for 1700 showed, said the Governor, that the House asked him to appoint a clerk, to which he replied that the House might "nominate" one and present him for "approbation."

The House countered with the appointment of a committee to research the precedents. The committee came back with a report covering what it could find for the years from 1666 to 1746. The report showed that in most of these years the word "approbation" was used in describing the approval of the Governor.

The House of Delegates still refused to concede the appointment. On May 11, 1749, "The House having duly considered the Governor's Message of this Day, and the Report made by the Gentlemen appointed to search in the Offices for Precedents in the Journals, relating to the manner of choosing and appointing of Clerks to this House," went on by unanimous vote to qualify Macnemara as clerk, having the oath administered by one of the justices of the Provincial Court who also was a member of the House.

The Governor then acted with swiftness and certainty. He prorogued the Assembly at once, on May 11, with the cool statement that "I find myself under a Necessity for many Important Reasons to prorogue this Assembly." The three-day meeting is styled in the *Journal* as a "convention" and not a "session" of the General Assembly.

Thirteen days later, on May 24, 1749, the Assembly was back, this time for a "session" that was to last until June 24. The Governor had done his homework well during the interval. In his opening address to the Assembly, he presented a review of the procedure for appointing the House clerk, from 1637 through to the 1740s. Along with the history from Maryland he covered custom in the House of Commons in England:

> You must be sensible that the Clerk of the house of Commons holds his Place by an appointment from the King, and that the Power of making all officers within this Province is delegated by the Royal Charter to his Lordship, and consequently that the Power of Appointing a Clerk to the Lower house of Assembly, must be allowed to be vested in the Lord Proprietor unless the Representatives of this Province should be supposed to have a greater Authority in this Matter than the Representatives of Great Britain. . . . I therefore flatter myself, that you will not on your Part insist upon a Point, that every reasonable Man must be satisfyed my Duty will not permit me to agree to.

With this the House capitulated. It had no intention of "infringing" upon the rights of the Governor, it assured him, or to show any disregard to his Administration, but said that its actions had been from an opinion that it was supported by the *Journals* of the House. At this session, therefore, the clerk chosen by the House was presented for the "approbation" of the Governor, "to whom his Excellency is pleased to declare, that he doth approve of their choice." This time the House had made a poor choice of an issue for venting its hostility to the Governor and Lord Baltimore.

### ELECTION DISPUTES

The House continued, during these middle years of the century, to dispose of numerous and varied questions and petitions concerning elections; and as frequently occurred earlier, some of the cases would be considered in later centuries as more judicial than legislative.

In 1745 the House handled a petition contesting the election of Delegate George Steuart, of Annapolis. Without reported details, he was declared not elected and had to forfeit his seat. In 1749 the House disposed of a contested election concerning an "unfair election" of all the delegation from St. Mary's County.[3]

Two petitions involving matters of possible judicial import touched the part played by the sheriffs' offices in the electoral process; all the writs for the election of delegates provided that elections should be called and administered by the sheriffs. Both cases arose in 1745. One came from St. Mary's County; two candidates were tied in the voting, and the sheriff cast the deciding vote. In the House, by a vote of 31-17, it was held that the sheriff had no right to vote, and the "winner" was ousted. The other question was from

---

3. The four delegates from St. Mary's County all filed for reelection, and all were reelected "by a great majority." *Maryland Gazette* (Annapolis), July 19, 1749.

Dorchester County. An elected delegate was rejected by a vote of 30-17 because he had acted as under-sheriff during the election.

Perhaps the most unusual election appeal during these years was in 1753. It required almost the wisdom of a Solomon to unravel, but the House of Delegates of Maryland did it. The contestants were George Steuart and Alexander Hamilton. Both were physicians ("Doctor of Physic") of Scottish extraction; and Steuart was the same person who had been required to forfeit his office in 1745.

Steuart and Hamilton both claimed election from the City of Annapolis. The City had been created by the Assembly years earlier, under the corporate name of "The Mayor, Recorder and Aldermen of the City of Annapolis." In this instance, Steuart's writ was returned by the Aldermen and not signed by the Mayor. Hamilton's writ was signed by the Mayor and not by the Aldermen. Neither return was signed by the Recorder.

This puzzler was referred to the House Committee of Elections and Privileges, which in its report to the full House injected another complication into the facts. While the Committee's report is a bit obscure, it seemed to make the points that neither of the election returns specified that the delegate was to care for "the Good and Welfare of the Province in General," this exclusion made both writs different from the usual and traditional form, and the writs therefore were "disagreeable" to the City Charter:

> Your Committee beg Leave to observe, that by the Indentures annex'd to the said Writ, the said George Steuart and Alexander Hamilton are impowered to advise, debate, act, do, and consent to all such Things as by common Consent shall happen to be ordained and enacted, to the Honour and Glory of GOD, the Service of his Majesty, his Lordship, and the Citizens of the City aforesaid: Whereby the Good and Welfare of the Province in general, appears to be excluded from the

Care and Attention of the said Delegate; which your Committee find is not only different from the Writ aforesaid, but also, from former Indentures in such Cases made, and as they humbly conceive, disagreeable to the Charter of the said City, by which it is granted that Delegates returned for the said City, shall have full Power, and free Votes, in all and every of our General Assemblies touching or concerning all Matters, or Things, there to be discoursed and handled, as other the Deputies or Delegates of the several and respective Counties formerly have had, now have, or hereafter may have.

The House worked its way through this maze, and for some reason, not explained, it declared Dr. Hamilton to be elected. Dr. Steuart was not admitted to the House. The cost for witnesses in this hearing was more than seven pounds sterling. Dr. Steuart was expelled again in 1757 for an "undue election."[4]

Another unusual election case involved former Delegate William Rasin of Kent County, who became sheriff of that county after leaving the State House. While sheriff, he was called to the Bar of the House for his failure to issue a writ for the election of a delegate from Kent County. Sheriff Rasin came to the House on May 13, 1754, to say that he had directed his deputy to provide for the election, "which his said Deputy had neglected to do." He added that he himself now had brought a writ of election. The House considered the matter and ordered "That the Committee of Accounts do tax the Fees due to the Officers of the House, on the complaint against William Rasin. . . ." The Committee of Accounts issued its report, and the case was resolved:

---

4. There is some thought that his sympathies for the Proprietary party were the cause of his electoral problems.

By the Committee of Accounts, May 13, 1754.

In Pursuance to an Order of the House of Delegates, we have proceeded to tax the Fees and Charges due to the Officers of the House, on a Complaint against William Rasin, Sheriff of Kent County, for omitting to return the Writ of Election, and Indenture signed between him, as Sheriff aforesaid, and the Electors of the County aforesaid, at the last Election, viz

| | | | |
|---|---|---|---|
| To the Clerk, | £. 0 | 3 | 0 |
| To the Serjeant, for a Messenger, | 1 | 10 | 0 |
| To Ditto, for Ferriages and Expences, | 0 | 14 | 6 |
| To Ditto, for serving the Precept, | 0 | 3 | 0 |

£. 2 10 6

Which is humbly submitted to the Consideration of the honourable House.

Signed per Order, Beale Nicholson, Cl. Com.

Ordered, That Mr. Rasin do pay the Fees taxed in the said Report, and on Compliance therewith, he be discharged from his further Attendance on this House.

In all these cases, it was the House of Delegates alone which received and decided the election disputes. They involved House members only, of course, but also entailed orders, reprimands, and penalties against officers who were in no sense appointees or employees solely of the House, or even of the legislative branch. Also, as in the several following examples, decisions by the House in effect enacted laws applicable throughout the Province.

On two occasions the House made general pronouncements upon electoral matters. One concerned possible bribery or corruption, and the other was about what seemed to be a new practice of electioneering. The announced rule on bribery and corruption was in the *Journal* for October 18, 1753; it involved the adoption of an English statute as law for this Province. The order in this case also specified duties of the sheriffs or other returning officers:

Upon the Question being put, Whether the Statute made in the second Year of the present King, intituled, An Act for the more effectual preventing Bribery and Corruption, in the Elections of Members to serve in Parliament, ought to be received as a Law within this Province?

Resolved unanimously in the Affirmative.

Resolved also unanimously, That all the Statutes of England, made for the Security, Confirmation, or Advancement, of the Rights, Liberties and Privileges of the British Subject, for the Prevention or Detection of Bribery and Corruption, and the Maintenance and Preservation of Freedom in Elections, the Direction and Regulation of Returning Officers in their Duty, and the Qualification of Electors, except in such cases wherein sufficient Provision hath been or shall be established by Acts of Assembly, have the force of Laws within this Province, and as such ought uniformly and inviolably to be received and observed.

Resolved also, That it is, and hath been, a Duty incumbent on every Elector of a Delegate or Burgess, to serve in Assembly for this Province, to take the Oath of an Elector, prescribed to be taken by the Statute of the 2d of George the 2d, Chap. 24th, before he is admitted to vote, or be polled at any Election, if required, as is directed by the said Statute.

Resolved likewise, That it hath been, and is the indispensable Duty of every Sheriff, or other Returning Officer, or Officers, within this Province, to take and subscribe the Oath, directed to be taken in the said Statute, inserting the Word Assembly for Parliament, before he, or they, proceed to such Election; and that the Clerk of every Court, where the Election is made, record such Oath.

Resolved likewise, That it is the Duty of every Sheriff, or Returning Officer, or Officers, within this Province, to read the same, in an audible, clear, and distinct Manner, immediately after taking the Oath aforesaid, or cause the same to be read openly to the Electors, and before he, or they, proceed to take any Vote, or admit any to Poll, at such Election.

The second electoral pronouncement by the House which had the effect of enacting a law occurred in 1749. The House Committee on Elections and Privileges had complained to the House about electioneering by candidates for election; specifically, of their giving "uncommon Entertainments, and great Quanties of strong and spirituous liquors, to the Electors ... thereby engaging the Promises of the weaker Sort of the said Electors to vote for them." The Committee report continued with a recommendation for "eradicating these spreading Evils, which if suffered any longer to grow and spread, may in Time have a great Tendency to destroy the Freedom and Independence of the most valuable Branch of our Constitution." The House concurred with the report, but no further action was mentioned in the *Journal:*

By the Committee of Elections and Privileges, June 17, 1749.

Your Committee take Leave further to report to your Honourable House, That they are credibly informed, and have too much Reason to believe, that in several of the Counties of this Province, it has of late been very much the Practice of those who offer themselves to the People as Candidates in approaching Elections, for the Honourable Trust of Representatives in Assembly, not only at the immediate Time of such Elections, but for a long Time before, both by themselves and their Agents, to give uncommon Entertainments, and great Quantities of strong and spirituous Liquors, to the Electors of such Counties; thereby engaging the Promises of the weaker Sort of the said Electors to vote for them at such Elections: Which Engagements (tho' by sober Reflection convinced of the Folly, Imprudence, and ill Consequences of them) being publicly made, they want Resolution to break.

This practice, if not prevented for the future, your Committee humbly conceive, must tend to the destruction of the Health, Strength, Peace, and Quiet, and highly contribute to the Corruption of the Morals of his majesty's loyal Subjects, and his Lordship's faithful Tenants, within this Province, to the stirring up and promoting Envy, Strife, and Contention, amongst Friends and Neighbours, and to the creating and formenting Parties and Divisions, which must always be a Disadvantage both public and private; except to those few, the success of whose pernicious Schemes may in great Measure depend upon the formenting and keeping up such Parties and Divisions, and hindering an Union of Interests and Councils, the only sure Preservative of the common Good; and must be of the greatest ill Consequence, by encouraging the labouring Part of his Lordship's Tenants to idle away that Time at such Entertainments, and waste and exhaust that Spirit and Vigour with such strong and spirituous Liquors, which ought to be spent for the Benefit of themselves and their Families in particular, and employed for the Advantage of Society in general: But the Ways and Means for preventing these impending Dangers, and for eradicating these spreading Evils, which if suffered any longer to grow and spread, may in Time have a great Tendency to destroy the Freedom and Independance of the most valuable Branch of our Constitution, is humbly submitted to the mature Consideration and wise Determination of your Honourable House.

Signed per Order, Tho. Harwood, junior, Cl. Com.

On reading the said Report, the House concurs therewith.

A similar case was reported from Baltimore County in 1752, in a petition questioning the recent election of William Govane. As reported in the *Maryland Gazette* for February 13, 1752, it was charged that Govane "some Days before the Time appointed for the said Election, gave, or caused to be given, great Quantities of Rum, Punch, and other Strong Liquors, to the People in several Parts of the said County, in Order to secure the Votes of the said People, for himself and his Friends, at the said Election; and when the said People were warmed and intoxicated with strong Liquors, engaged their Promises to vote for him the said Govane, and his friends at the said Election."

## THE SEAMY SIDE OF POLITICS

There were instructive sidelights to the art of political preferment in letters within the executive branch during these years. One, in 1755, from Governor Sharpe to the Secretary of Lord Baltimore, spoke of the Governor's having given a commission to "a gentleman who has behaved very well in the Assembly." The Governor suggested also that members of the House of Delegates and their families might have a share of the Proprietary's "favours, as thereby their virulency may be abated." Several years earlier in a letter dated February 12, 1748/9, from Governor Samuel Ogle to Lord Baltimore, there was a broad reference to a "Mr. D.," which undoubtedly was to Daniel Dulany the Elder; he had been an outstanding member of the House of Delegates for many years and by this time was appointed as a member of the Upper House, or Council:[5]

> Mr. D. I hope will get both his sons into the Lower house & I cannot but flatter myself, that the gentle Rubs I have given him may have a good Effect. I gave him to understand, that your Lordship had Reason to expect from me, that those I gave the most considerable places to, should do your Lordship proportional Services, otherwise you might think I followed my own inclinations more than your real Interest, if his sons should both get in & behave well, I suppose he will think himself fully entitled to the favour he asks & indeed in such a Case I propose to oblige him, as your Lordship has left it to my Discretion. In your Lordships last Letter, your words seem to emply the whole office for the son, but half of it was all that has been asked for & as this will be enough to oblige them & to keep others

---

5. *Archives,* XLIV at 699.

likewise in Expectation, I hope your Lordship will never consent to more upon any future Application.

One of the Dulany sons referred to in this letter was Walter, who in 1748 was in the House of Delegates, representing Annapolis. In 1749, the other son, Daniel, Jr., was in the House delegation from the new county of Frederick. Walter left the House in 1750 to take another public position; and the younger Daniel quickly had his election challenged and was declared no longer a member. This occurred on June 8, 1749, following a petition from Frederick County as to "an undue Election and Return." As the question in this case was first put to the House, it was "Whether any Voter or Voters should be objected to, on Complaint of undue Election or Return, that were not objected to at the Poll on Scrutiny at the Time of Election." The House voted in the negative on this question, 11-42. Next, with no reason given in the *Journal,* the House unanimously declared the younger Daniel Dulany "not duly elected" and dismissed him from any further attendance in the House.

Some years later, in 1761, Governor Horatio Sharpe in a letter to his brother made revealing comments about Thomas Bladen, who had been Governor from 1742 to 1747:

> I have indeed heard that Mr. Bladen while he was Governor did often insist when he was bestowing Offices that the Persons about to enjoy them should previously give a considerable Sum of Money or quantity of Tobacco to a Man who served him in the double capacity of Scribe and Valet, part of which it is supposed was afterwards accounted for by the Valet to the Master, but Believe me nothing of this sort has been transacted during my Administration. . . .[6]

---

6. Sharpe to William Sharpe, August 4, 1761, *Archives,* IX at 533.

Earlier in that same year of 1761, a long and revealing letter of advice was sent to Governor Sharpe by Cecilius Calvert, Secretary of the Province and an uncle of Frederick, sixth Lord Baltimore. The letter set forth in naked detail an elaborate scheme to assure that the Province would be governed with a "proper attachment to his Lordships Just rights & prorogative." Secretary Calvert referred to his message as one of "Loaves & Fishes." The Government of Maryland, he said, "has within itself all the Materials & Powers proper for attaining the several Ends of Government. . ., but if a Man having within his Power all the springs, wheeles & Materials for a well regulated watch, will not adapt each to its proper place & Office, can he expect to find from it, the advantageous Effects of a regular movement?"

Continuing, said the Secretary, "to Me it seems extreamly easy, with the several advantages this Government has, to prevent for the future that Turbulent & Malevolent Spirit in the Lower House of Assembly." He recommended the same controls over the Judiciary "And so to Knit & Unite the several Branches of Power there, as to form one Grand Regular Movement, all tending to the Honour & prosperity of his Lordship, & the Happiness & Welfare of the whole Province, without leaving it in the Power of any Individual amongst them, either from Motives of Interest, Avarice or Ambition, to disturb its operations."

After having thus set forth his goals, Secretary Calvert wrote more particularly of his proposals for handling each part of the government. First, as to the Council (and Upper House), appointments would "Tickle the Vanity" of the recipients, with the aim of having the Council "as the chief Strength & Support not only of his Lordships rights, but of the whole frame of Government." If the Council is properly constituted, he concluded, "I think there cannot be much danger from the Noise & clamour that any Lower House of Assembly may raise."

Having thus assured the Council as a chief bulwark in the Province, the Secretary devoted some time and considerable scorn to the best way to manipulate the House of Delegates:

> Here give Me leave to observe & to lay it down as a Rule, that whatever Noise & Clamour may be raised under the appearance of consulting & promoting the Welfare & happiness of the people, by their Representatives, 19 in 20 of these in fact only consult & intend their own private interest; & therefore by throwing out a Sop in a proper manner to these Noisy Animals it will render them not only Silent but tame enough to bear Stroking & tractable enough to follow any direction that may be thought fit to be given to them. . . .

Here the Secretary cautioned that it was the followers and not the leaders in the Assembly who should receive the "sops." The leaders might "demand and expect a very considerable price" and even when "obtained" might be turned out by the House. "Instead of this I would take off their followers & leave the Leaders to Explain either alone or with so Slender a Train as to prevent their doing any Mischief, or obstructing any wise or Salutary Measure. . . ."

With this basis in philosophy, the Secretary turned his fine craftsmanship to the "followers" in the House of Delegates, with a close analysis of the composition of the House and the devices to appeal to the members:

> There are 58 Members of that House; 14 Counties send four each & the City of Annapolis sends two. Now the buissiness is to find Baits for 30 of these; which number is a clear Majority, Supposing they were all to attend; But it is very rare by information that above two thirds are present, & not above one Day in a Session that they Exceed 48. To answer therefore this purpose, I would appropriate the 14 Sheriffs places, which will undoubtedly secure 14 Members & may by good Management of their Comissions secure double that number; (But with this reserve against appropriation of

the Sheriffs in case it shall hurt the receipt of his Lordships Revenue) There are 14 Farmers of his Lordships Quit-Rents, 14 Deputy Comissioners and 14 Deputy Surveyours; all these places are considerable to the Middling sort of people, of whom the Lower House is composed, & might gain a great Majority of that House by being properly applied amongst them, their Brothers & Sons; besides Military Comissions & those of Justice of the Peace without number, for others who may be lead by their Vanity & fondness of making a figure & being Vested with Power amongst their Neighbors.

The timing for all these appointments, the Secretary continued, should be synchronized with the election of delegates, so as to be most productive. Finally, in return for the appointments given to their friends and relatives, the members of the House of Delegates should comply with "such hints and proposals" as might be given for their behavior in office; "for as at first obtaining those Comissions should depend on their behaviour in that House, so ought their continuance in their offices to depend on their behaviour under their Comissions, that neither his Lordship nor the Public may suffer by either a Negligent or oppressive discharge of their Duty."

After dealing in similar detail with the judiciary, Secretary Calvert concluded that "if this Plan or one something like it is laid down Inviolably adheard to & Speedily put in Execution, the Government will not only be carried on with Ease & quiet to itself, & Honour to his Lordship & all concerned; But also his Lordships rights & those of the people will meet with a fair Decision."

In a postscript to his letter, Calvert assured Governor Sharpe about his purpose in writing and the need for keeping secret the contents of his letter. "The purpose of this Epistle," he cautioned, "is on No Account designed towards corrupt Views, But as a Malignancy is prevalent, your Strict

Honour is relyed on, that you keap Secreet the Name to this Letter & against accident by Mortality after you have considered the Substance you are desired to Extinguish this Letter; keeping it till then in close privacy that none may see or get a Copy of it." [7] Secretary Calvert obviously did not foresee that Governor Sharpe would keep the "Epistle" in his letter book and that in the next century it would be published in the Maryland *Archives.*

## HOLDING TWO PUBLIC EMPLOYMENTS

The House of Delegates had two other pursuits which indirectly bore upon elections. One was the effort to enforce a rule, later to be in the Constitution of 1776, against any person's holding two public employments in the Province; and the other was a companion protest against any person's receiving compensation from two public positions for the same day.

The House earlier had argued against one person's holding two public positions, in the late 1730s. Also, in the late 1740s, it attempted to secure legislation against the practice, but the Upper House would not agree. The latter occurred in June, 1749, when the House voted 31-15 in favor of a bill "to prevent Persons holding Offices and Places of Profit and Trust, from serving in Assembly." Despite non-concurrence by the Upper House, the House frequently expelled its own members who while in the House accepted another position.

Thus, in the May-June session of 1747, Delegate William Stoughton of Somerset County accepted a position as Deputy Naval Officer of Pocomoke and so disqualified himself from the House. In May, 1750, Delegate Walter Dulany of Annapolis took another place in the Office of Deputy

---

7. Calvert to Sharpe, March 17, 1761. *Archives,* XIV at 1-13. Historians seem agreed that Secretary Calvert was "crafty."

Commissary of Anne Arundel County; and Delegate Edward Tilghman of Queen Anne's County accepted the office of Keeper of the Rent-Rolls for the Eastern Shore. Both were disqualified from the House, although one week later Walter Dulany was reelected and was accepted in the House. Also in 1750, Delegate Nathaniel Wright of Queen Anne's County became a Tobacco Inspector and lost his place in the House. In the middle 1750s, Delegate Lloyd Buchanan of Baltimore County was appointed by the Attorney General to the prosecutor's place in that county, and he was dismissed from the House.

The House had particular difficulty with the partially separate problem of a person's receiving double compensation after working at two public positions on the same day. This was a budgetary matter, and the House could not assume exclusive control of expenditures. It did make its opposition perfectly clear, however. Thus, on May 11, 1750, the House twice had recorded roll-call votes against double compensation. One posed the question whether a member of the House who served also as a Provincial Magistrate "on one and the same Day, should have a distinct Allowance in the Journal of Accounts." This vote was in the negative, 21-29. Immediately thereafter, there was a similar vote whether a member of the Upper House should sit as a Judge in the Court of Appeals on "one and the same Day," with an allowance for each service on that day. This vote also was in the negative, 18-34. On the first of these two votes, it is uncertain why the House did not solve the problem by dismissing the Provincial Magistrate from his seat in the House; the *Journal* does not speak to this question.[8]

---

8. "Probably no other colony was quite so strict on the subject of exclusion as Maryland, or disqualfied persons for such a wide variety of reasons." MARY PATTERSON CLARKE, PARLIAMENTARY PRIVILEGE IN THE AMERICAN COLONIES 161 (New Haven, 1943).

## The Province at Mid-Century

Frederick County was created in the late 1740s, by dividing Prince George's County. It was named for Frederick, sixth Lord Baltimore. Beginning in 1749, it sent four delegates to the House. The creation of the new county had been discussed for several years, with some division of opinion as to whether the eastern boundary line should be established at Eastern Branch or at Rock Creek. The House favored Rock Creek, and the bill as passed (Chapter 18 of 1748) used that boundary. This brought the number of counties to 14. There was a proposal at the time to create an additional county, using the mouth of Eastern Branch and the mouth of the Monocacy as boundary lines, thus dividing the new Frederick County.

Boundary commissions were established to fix definite lines between Prince George's and Baltimore counties, and between Dorchester and Worcester counties. Another proposal, which reached the form of a draft bill, was to establish a new Prince William County northward and eastward from the mouth of Tuckahoe Creek, covering part of the present Caroline County.

The Province was beginning to show what would be the proportions of the present State. Washington, Allegany, and Garrett counties still were to be added in the West; Montgomery, Howard, Carroll, and Harford were to be taken from existing counties in the central portion; and Caroline and Wicomico were yet to be carved from the already organized counties on the Eastern Shore. Baltimore City remained (until 1851) a part of Baltimore County.

There was an interesting summary in mid-century of the population and of the "gross national product" of Maryland. It is supposed that the summary came from Governor Horatio Sharpe: [9]

9. This summary was part of a series of questions and answers about the Province which appeared in the *London Chronicle,* September 16-19,

It may not be improper to inform those who having never been in the province are ignorant of the Numbers & Circumstances of the Inhabitants that by a particular & exact Account taken in the Year 1754 their Number was found to be 107963 white people, & 46225 Negroes who are Slaves; & that the Value of the Produce which the Inhabitants exported in the preceeding Year (consisting as appeared by the Custom House Books of 30634 Hogsheads of Tobacco 110567 Bushels of Wheat, 154741 Bushels of Indian Corn, 2500 Tuns of Pigg & 600 Tuns of Bar Iron, 6327 Barrels of Bread & Flour, 430 Barrels of Pork, 420 Bushels of Pease & Beans, 100 Hogsheads & 100 Bags of Flaxseed, 170 Barrels of Herrings, 1095500 Staves & Heading, 200000 Shingles, a large quantity of Wallnut & other Plank together with several Ships which having been built in the province were sent to G Britain loaded with Tobacco & there sold) amounted on a very moderate Calculation to the Sum of £ 350,000 Currency. . . . The whole Produce of Maryland Yearly might be called at least £ 1,053,480.

The *Journals* in this first half of the eighteenth century carry another indication of the developing State, in the proper names that would survive into later generations and legislative history. Taken almost at random, there were such names as Stevenson, Purnell, Smallwood, Ridgley, and Warfield; Sudler, Thomas, Hall, Tilghman, and Duvall; Dorsey, George, Fowler, Paca, and Matthews; Key, Holiday, Hammond, Gassoway, and Clayton; Hanson, Plater, Lee,

1758. It is thought the questions were propounded by Cecilius Calvert, Secretary of the Province and an uncle of Frederick, sixth Lord Baltimore. The answers, it is believed, were written by Governor Sharpe. *See State of the Province of Maryland in 1758,* 33 MARYLAND HISTORICAL MAGAZINE 228-47 (1938).

For a study of Maryland growth in population from 1631 to 1730, *see* Arthur E. Karinen, *Maryland Population: 1631-1730: Numerical and Distributional Aspects,* 50 MARYLAND HISTORICAL MAGAZINE 365-407 (1959).

Gresham, and Gale; Ghiselin, Hyatt, Howard, Tasker, and Henry; Goldsborough, Harris, Cockey, Aisquith, and Tench; Risteau, Hance, Darnell, Wilmer, and Rasin; Evans, Beall, Carroll, Gray, and Tolley; Ridout, Chase, Cresap, Pearis, and Waters; Boone, Hopkins, Towson, Cromwell, and Merryman; James, Parrish, Hooper, Weems, and Worthington; Sothoron, Joiner, Lowe, Brice, and Blades; Digges, Pumphrey, and Briscoe.[10]

By the mid-eighteenth century, the *Maryland Gazette* and other publications of Jonas Green were supplying varied materials about the General Assembly and its work. The *Gazette* for May 9, 1750, had this advertisement:

> The Votes and Proceedings of the Honourable Lower House of Assembly, now sitting, will be publish'd once or twice a Week during the Session, (and the whole completed soon after the Close of the Session). Any Gentlemen (not entitled to them by Law) who are inclinable to take them, either as they are publish'd, or all together after the Assembly breaks up, are desired to give in their Names to the Printer as soon as possible; for very few or none, will be Printed, but what shall be Bespoke: The Price is Three Pence per Day.

On April 24, 1751, the *Gazette* advertised an 80-page collection of all the tobacco laws for the years from 1747 to 1750. Copies of the Charter for the Province were advertised on May 29, 1751. In 1752 and 1753 the *Gazette* had full accounts of the House proceedings, as if copied from the *Journal.* On September 1, 1757, a hostelry was advertised for the members of the Assembly:

> Anne Howard, (living at the sign of the SHIP where her Mother formerly kept Tavern, in Annapolis, and)

---

10. In contrast, to show that not all the eighteenth-century names survived, note the account in the *Maryland Gazette* for November 21, 1750, of a fatal accident occurring to a resident of Talbot County. Captain Meshach Batfield was killed when he fell from a carriage. The deceased had two surviving brothers, named Shadrach and Abednego.

having a Number of very good Spare Beds and Bedding, and a convenient House for Entertainments, will take in Gentlemen of the Assembly, at the ensuing Session, at THREE SHILLINGS per day.

The *Gazette* had this news item on January 17, 1754: "Last Week arrived in Town, to regulate and settle the Affairs of the Post Office, Benjamin Franklin, Esq: of Philadelphia." Another news item (January 10, 1765) informed the public that "We now have a BRIDGE across Severn River, over which People pass."

Charles Calvert, fifth Lord Baltimore, died on April 24, 1751. He was succeeded by Frederick, sixth Lord Baltimore, still a minor and under a guardian with respect to Provincial affairs. Frederick would not reach his majority until February 6, 1753. He never visited Maryland, and much of the business of the colony was entrusted to his uncle, Cecilius Calvert, also resident in England. Frederick's main interest in the Province seemed to be as a source of revenue for his extravagant tastes.

Governor Samuel Ogle died on May 3, 1752. The new Governor, Horatio Sharpe, did not arrive in the Province until August 10, 1753; during the interim the duties of the governorship were handled by Benjamin Tasker, President of the Council. Sharpe was to remain Governor until 1769; he was a respected figure and served as a moderating influence among the growing controversies between the legislative branch, mainly the House of Delegates, and the executive branch of government. His conciliatory approach did not deter him, however, from taking a strong stand if he felt his own jurisdiction and prerogatives were threatened. He could and did take the House to task when he felt it was overreaching its limits.[11]

---

11. *See generally,* Paul H. Giddens, *Governor Horatio Sharpe and His Maryland Government,* 32 MARYLAND HISTORICAL MAGAZINE 156-74

By the same token, the House of Delegates frequently was critical of Sharpe, as it was of all incumbents in the Governor's position.

## TAXES, FEES, FINES, AND FORFEITURES

Much of the legislative history of Maryland during the late 1740s and into the 1750s closely concerned the international scene and the successive wars in which England was involved. There had been a war with Spain in the early 1740s; and later a war with France, which in the colonies was known as King George's War. In the 1750s the Seven Years' War developed, known generally in America as the French and Indian War. Many of the continuing and enlarging disputes between the House of Delegates and the Upper House, Governor, and Proprietary were on matters arising from relationships with the Indians and financing the military campaigns.

Of all these controversies, that of financing the war effort was perhaps the key item of contention. The Governor, on the urging of the Council, the Proprietary, and the King over a period of years, pressed the House for war appropriations; or as they became known, the Supply Bill. The House would allow the enlistment of Maryland citizens, but only with support and maintenance to come from elsewhere; it did not want to provide support except for defensive purposes, and that only for short periods.

One of the Governor's early and pressing importunities was in December, 1747. He had the Legislature in session on

(1937); Aubrey C. Land, (ed.), *The Familiar Letters of Governor Horatio Sharpe,* 61 MARYLAND HISTORICAL MAGAZINE 189-209; LADY EDGAR, A COLONIAL GOVERNOR IN MARYLAND — HORATIO SHARPE AND HIS TIMES, 1753-1773 (New York, 1912).

December 22 and 23, obviously an unseasonable selection. He acknowledged his difficulties in timing, but told the members that both men and money were needed for the campaign against the French in Louisburg and Nova Scotia. To make matters worse, the House *Journal* reports a condition of deep snow, with the Bay and rivers frozen. The House refused to levy any additional taxes. It wrote in a message to the Governor that the Province had been at great expense in encouraging the enlistment of some three hundred men, maintaining them here, transporting them to Albany, and later supplying them with provisions. The House refused to add to the taxpayers' burdens; and with that, told the Governor that "no further Business lies before us." The Governor prorogued the session.

Over the next several years, the Governor's requests for money for the Supply Bill, and for "a present" for the Six Nations of Indians, were interspersed with sharp questions raised by the House with respect to tobacco taxes collected by the Proprietary, the disposition of fees and forfeitures, and the panel of taxes devised to raise money for the Six Nations. The three latter items were not strictly connected with the Supply Bill, but the combination of all the several arguments made for an active financial history.

The gifts to the Six Nations were considered in 1754. At the same time, the Governor was requesting funds to help in a Virginia-sponsored campaign to the Ohio River Valley. The House agreed to provide money for the gifts to the Indians; but since an actual military campaign was not involved, it refused to grant maintenance funds for the Ohio campaign. This campaign, said the House, "does not require our immediate Aid or Assistance."

The tobacco tax and the disposition of revenues from fees, fines, and forfeitures involved political and legal questions stemming from the status of the Province under Proprietary government. The possible payment to the Six Nations was a political effort to placate them and keep them from French influence; it had no problems other than monetary. The House decision was to send 500 pounds sterling to the Indians and to include 150 pounds additional for the expense of two envoys to go to Albany, where the gifts were to be made. A number of excise taxes were proposed, but the final decision was to take the money from the Loan Office. This transaction literally was a loan, taken technically from the "Commissioners or Trustees for Emitting the Bills of Credit Established by Act of Assembly."

The dispute over the tobacco tax was a recurring grievance of the House of Delegates for years during the middle 1750s, and a continuation of the dispute of the 1740s. It was originally imposed as an export tax of two shillings a hogshead and was an important source of revenue for the Province. From the beginning, however, a portion of the tax went to Lord Baltimore as a quitrent; a partial share of 12 pence a hogshead was designated for the support of the government. Queen Anne, years earlier, had ordered that of this latter amount, a 3-pence portion be used for purchases of arms and ammunition. Then, after the Province was restored to the Proprietary, the entire 12-pence share was appropriated by Lord Baltimore. The House protested over the years, particularly as to the 3-pence share formerly spent for defense.

The issue was argued with some warmth during the May-June session of 1750. Referring to the entire 12-pence tax, the House in a message to Lord Baltimore insisted the levy was not warranted by law. Continuing, "We therefore humbly hope your Lordship will no longer Continue to levy the said sum, or lay us under the Disagreeable necesity of taking any other method of Application for Redress."

The use and disposition of monies derived from license fees, fines, and forfeitures also generated heated protests from the House. At first the issue centered upon the license fees from ordinaries, but it had expanded to include other license fees and also the fines and forfeitures. The fees from ordinaries originally had been claimed by the Proprietary, then turned over as a perquisite to his Provincial secretary; and by the middle 1700s, under Charles, fifth Lord Baltimore, these fees were used to pay for arms and ammunition. Frederick, sixth Lord Baltimore, claimed the fees for his personal use; and the House argued and protested the claim for years. The House wanted the fees, fines, and forfeitures for the use of the Province; and as part of its strategy, the House asked for reports of the receipts and proposed an alternate use for them.

Reports of the moneys received from fees, fines, and forfeitures were requested in October, 1753, for the years 1745 to 1752, and by year and county. A few days later, the House proposed in a message to the Upper House, accompanied by an attached bill, that these moneys go into a "school fund." Here the House argued that "As nothing can conduce more to the Advantage of any Country than Learning, which lays a Foundation for Virtue and Good Manners in Youth, and as the Schools already established within this Province for that Purpose have not a sufficient Maintenance for suitable Masters, so we hope you will agree to pass this Bill."

The Upper House would not agree, saying that the fees, fines, and forfeitures "are the undoubted Right of his Lordship." The Upper House agreed about the advantages of learning, but could not agree that under the circumstances "any such Advantage can accrue to them." Also, reminded the Upper House, support of the government is necessary.

Failing to get the school bill passed, the House retaliated on November 14, 1753, by refusing to include in the Journal of Accounts (budget) then being considered, an allowance for the cost to the Governor in advertising 15 proclamations concerning a tobacco inspection bill. The House vote was

338

21-22 on this decision, the negative majority asserting that the proclamations were not necessary for the bill's validity. The Upper House argued that the cost of the proclamations should be included in the Journal of Accounts:

> Without entering into any Discussion with you on that Point, we say, that the issuing these Proclamations, at that Time, was necessary to satisfy the minds of the People who had been made to believe, that the Inspection Law was, or would be, dissented to, and as this was a special Case, which may never probably happen again, we hope you will agree to allow the same.[12]

The response of the House was to reject the entire Journal of Accounts, on a vote of 16-25. Messages went back and forth during the next few days, with the House stating its case in this one:

By the Lower house of Assembly 17 November 1753

> May it Please your Honours.
> In answer to your Honours Message of the 31st of **October by Mr Chamberlain** in Relation to the License Money and Fines arising from the Hawkers and Pedlers Bill and all other fines being the undoubled Right of the Lord Proprietary, We can in no wise agree with you, for although all fines go to the King for this Reason that the Courts of Justice are Supported at his Charge for the Protection of his People, the People of Maryland and not his Lordship Support the Courts of Justice by an assessment and Charge on themselves and what fines are already transferred to, or given the Lord Proprietary are and have been applied to the private use of the Lord Proprietaries and not for the Support of the Courts of Justice or of the Government in any way that is known to this house, and although the Late Lord Proprietary has yearly taken and Received from the Trade and People of this Province very great Sums yearly for

---

12. Three years later, in 1756, the Upper House still was requesting compensation for the Governor for the cost of the 15 proclamations.

Support of Government, We know of no application of more than what is paid to the Governor for the time being so that the rest is put to a private use and not for Support of Government.

And We think it very hard that his Majestys Subjects of Maryland alone should be deprived of the Power of raising Money to be applied to such purposes as may be of General Service to them and we are apprehensive that such Refusal may withdraw the affection of the People from his Lordships Government, which from good offices from those presiding ought to be promoted, but as We expect this Session is drawing to a Conclusion We shall not again Send up that Bill, but hope at another time your honours will agree to what we have proposed in Relation thereto.

The last paragraph of this message from the House pointedly threatened that a refusal to allow it to raise money for the Province "may withdraw the affection of the People from his Lordships Government, which ... ought to be promoted." The House then suggested that, as the session was drawing to a close, the issue be dropped until another session.

The answer from the Upper House was to contest the claims of the Lower House for the use of these monies, but to agree to postpone the debate:

By the Upper house of Assembly 17 November 1753

Gentlemen

Your Message of this day, in answer to Ours of the 31st of October being We think of a very Extraordinary Nature, We shall make some Short Remarks thereon and leave them with you, for your further Consideration, if you think fit at another Session, and in the first Place We desire to know upon what foundation you have so Positively asserted that all Fines go to the King for this Reason that the Courts of Justice are Supported at his Charge, for the Protection of his People, if you intend thereby to assert that the Courts of Justice are Supported by the fines to the King, we may Venture to

Say You are Mistaken, and again we should be willing
to know, whether you think the applying the Fines to the
Proprietary is depriving his Majestys Subjects of
Maryland of the Power of Raising Money, to such
Purposes as may be of General Service to them; as for
the other Parts of your answer, We shall take no notice
thereof at present as the Session has continued already
too long and we are in hopes is near a Conclusion

Again at the session in the spring of 1754, the two houses
debated the proper use of fees, fines, and forfeitures. The
House of Delegates at this juncture asked for these monies
to supply the payment to the Six Nations of Indians, but the
Upper House would not agree. On these money issues, the
session was prorogued; the Governor expressing "great
Concern" at putting the Province to "a very considerable
Expence without doing the Business, which I conceived duty
prudence and good Policy obliged me so earnestly to
recommend."

The uncompromising stand of the House bore some
political fruit in the summer of 1754, when the Governor and
the Council suggested to Lord Baltimore that it would be
advisable to permit at least the license fees from ordinaries
to be used for arms and ammunition.[13]

## THE SUPPLY BILL

The financial difficulties and protracted controversies
continued during the mid-1750s, still closely connected with
the unusual needs and emergencies of the French and Indian
War. Repeatedly the Governor would request extra funds
from the General Assembly, sometimes for problems in
Maryland, but more often for campaigns in the North and
West. The usual reply of the House of Delegates was to
appropriate for the Maryland problems, but to refuse funds

---

13. *Archives,* XXXI, at 38.

for the out-of-Province campaigns. On a number of occasions, the Governor was forced to prorogue the Assembly without having gained his requests, and to try again at a following session.

Thus, in July of 1754, the Governor, apprehensive of "the Designs of the French," asked generally for funds to support the distant campaigns and also to care for the wives and children of friendly Indians, who were sent to Maryland while the men were in service. Funds were voted for care of the Indians, but at the end of the session the Governor once more had to voice his disappointment at the failure to send supporting funds elsewhere. At another session in December of that year, the Governor again was "disappointed." [14]

When the Assembly met next, for the February-March session of 1755, the House voted a Supply Bill in the amount of ten thousand pounds. This time it was the Upper House which refused to accede, for the reason (as stated by the House of Delegates) of "too near an Attachment of their Honours to his Lordship's Prerogative, as they have suffered the mere Shadow of a Claim to induce them to refuse the granting of Money, and to out-weigh the great Inconveniencies that must thereby attend our common Cause."

This charge against the Upper House was included in a message from the House of Delegates to the Governor. In reply the Governor again pressed for the Supply Bill, in part to meet the needs of Braddock's expedition into western Pennsylvania. A Supply Bill was not enacted, but two lesser

---

14. While Maryland contributed far less than was demanded of her for Supply bills during the French and Indian War, "it is equally true that the Lord Proprietor was still stingier. Baltimore never willingly allowed his ample revenues to bear a part of the common burden." Aubrey C. Land, *The Colonial Period,* THE OLD LINE STATE — A HISTORY OF MARYLAND 30 (Morris L. Radoff ed.) (Annapolis, 1971).

bills of war-time impact became law. One was to regulate rates of carriages for transporting military stores and equipment; this was to be, as a maximum, either 12 or 16 pence per mile, depending upon the weight of the load. The second bill was to fix maximum rates that might be charged by an ordinary; its purpose was "to prevent any Abuses or Impositions by Public-House-Keepers, in whose Houses any Officers or Soldiers may be quartered or billetted." This one was graduated by military rank:

> No Public-House-Keeper shall charge to, or receive from, any Officer, or private Soldier, quartered or billetted in his or her House, as aforesaid, more than the following Rates, viz. to a Commission Officer, under the Degree of a Captain, for his Diet of such good and wholesome Food as is usually provided by Ordinary-Keepers in this Province, with Small-Beer or Cyder, the Sum of Eighteen Pence Current Money per Diem, and Lodging; and to a private Soldier for his Diet, as aforesaid, with Small-Beer, the Sum of Twelve Pence Current Money per Diem, and Lodging.

Near the end of this spring session of 1755, the House of Delegates entered in its *Journal* the complete text of a resolution it had passed, stating and evidently wishing to preserve for posterity its reasons for not acceding to the Governor's repeated requests for a Supply Bill. The House then had finally passed one for ten thousand pounds, but it was rejected in the Upper House; the House of Delegates had included in the bill a provision taking away from the Proprietary the license taxes on ordinaries. These revenues, said the House resolution, always have been "the undoubted Right of the Country," and the Proprietary "can have no Right to impose or levy" any such funds "without the Consent of the Representatives in General Assembly." Continuing, the fees had been given to the Proprietary in 1717 "as a Gift from the People," and by accepting them for many years he had acquiesced in the right of the people to

343

dispose of them. On this note the session was prorogued, again without a Supply Bill.

In the summer of 1755 news came of the defeat of Braddock in western Pennsylvania. Along with this, and certainly because of the defeat, successive messages from Fort Cumberland in June and July of that year told of marauding Indians who had killed perhaps 25 settlers in the Wills Creek region and easterly; Indians had been seen crossing "Toonaloway Creek" and within 11 miles of "the Mouth of Conegogeek." The Governor immediately asked for a special military force to meet this threat.[15] The House concurred, proposing to grant two thousand pounds to maintain 80 men for four months. The Upper House refused to accept this bill, thinking it inadequate both as to the number of men and the time period.

The House of Delegates refused to change its bill. Again to preserve the record, it journalized the Fort Cumberland bill and another bill to provide five thousand pounds for a campaign along the Ohio River. The House did not press the matter further, notifying the Governor on July 8 "As we have sufficient Reason to despair of the Concurrence of the Upper House, at this Time, in such Measures as we think best adapted to those Purposes, we must repeat our Request . . . to put a speedy End to this Session." Accordingly, and repeating that the business of the session was "undone," the Governor prorogued the session on the same day.[16]

---

15. *Cf.* Mark J. Stegmaier, *Maryland's Fear of Insurrection at the Time of Braddock's Defeat,* 71 MARYLAND HISTORICAL MAGAZINE 467-83 (1976).

16. The seeming lack of concern for the Fort Cumberland area was a feeling that it was so far from the main settled areas of Maryland as to be a military responsibility for English troops rather than Americans and to be a part of the English campaign along the western frontier.

Also, the annual supply bills involved requests for forty or fifty thousand pounds, a major financial problem in the mid-eighteenth century.

The next session was a long one, extending from February 23 to May 20, 1756. The two houses spent weeks in considering a Supply Bill, culminating in another bitter dispute more procedural than substantive. The House of Delegates sent a total of three versions of the bill to the Upper House, leading to the complaint that there really were no essential differences among the bills. At one point, the Upper House returned a bill with amendments, instead of inquiring in advance if the House would accept the amendments; and the House determined it would not answer the objections of the Upper House. This precipitated a tart reply from the Upper House:

> By your Message of Yesterday it seems to us, that there can be no further Intercourse by Message between the two Houses, since you are now pleased to tell us in plain and express Terms, That to justify our own, or blame

---

By way of contrast, a committee specially appointed in 1758 to consider building a road from Fort Frederick to Fort Cumberland had no difficulty in recommending the expenditure of 250 pounds sterling for that purpose:

An Estimate of the Expence of Clearing a Road from Fort Frederick to Fort Cumberland, and the Several Different Stages.

| | |
|---|---:|
| For clearing a Road from Fort Frederick to Licking-Creek, 3½ Miles, . . . . . . . . . . . . . . . . . . . . . . . . . . . . . . . . £. | 000 |
| From Licking-Creek to Poake's Creek, 8½ Miles, . . . . . . . . . | 1200 |
| From Poake's Creek to the Mouth of Sidling-Hill-Creek, 12 Miles, | 1600 |
| For a Bridge over Sidling-Hill-Creek, . . . . . . . . . . . . . . . | 6000 |
| From Sidling-Hill-Creek to Fifteen-Mile Creek, 4 Miles, . . . . . | 2200 |
| From Fifteen-Mile Creek to Town-Creek, 15 Miles, . . . . . . . . | 14000 |
| From Town-Creek to Col. Cresap's a good Road 4 Miles, . . . . | 000 |
| From Col. Cresap's to Fort Cumberland wants no clearing 15 Miles, | .000 |

£.25000

your Conduct, can tend to nothing but to promote Controversy, we shall not therefore take the Trouble to do either. . . .

However, despite the seeming finality of this ultimatum, messages continued to pass between the two houses, and they finally passed a Supply Bill in the amount of forty thousand pounds. Again in the session of September-October, 1756, a Supply Bill was passed.[17]

## REVENUE AND FINANCE

Along with the major money matters of the Supply Bill, excise taxes on tobacco, gifts to the Six Nations of Indians, and the disposition of fees, fines, and forfeitures, there were lesser problems of financial import during the 1750s. One of them, the per diem compensation of members of the Council (Upper House) for time spent on administrative duties as the Council of State, seemingly had been settled in 1736, when the House of Delegates after years of furious bickering had agreed to approve the payments prospectively. The matter had been mentioned in following years, however, as evidence that the payments were not always made, but the Upper House did not pursue the matter strenuously. In 1753 it was discussed again, and the Upper House in its messages repeated verbatim the agreement reached in 1736.

The issue widened in 1754, when the Upper House called attention to the fact that it had no appropriations for building a home for the Governor, making per diem payments to the members of the Council for their administrative duties, and paying a salary to the Clerk of the Council. Again in April, 1756, the House of Delegates was notified (if that were

---

17. For general accounts of the Indian raids, military operations, and supply problems during the war, *see* Paul H. Giddens, *The French and Indian War in Maryland, 1753 to 1756*, 30 MARYLAND HISTORICAL MAGAZINE 281-310 (1935).

necessary) that there was nothing in the budget for per diems for the Council of State; once more the agreement of 1736 was cited, but the Upper House concluded that because of the length of the current session it would waive the claim for that year.

As a related financial matter, the Governor in his address to the Assembly in the spring session of 1754 complained of the "burthen" of payments required by the increase in the number of pensioners:

> The Excessive charge and burthen this Country is at present Subjected to by the great Increase of Pensioners in Several of Our Counties I believe might be hinted at, as calling for, and Capable of a Remedy; if it be truly Represented that the distribution of the great Sums annually collected for the Relief of the poor, as it is now made, instead of being an Encouragement to and a reward for Industry proves too frequently an Incitement only to Debauchery and Idleness.

The House in response to the Governor's message hoped for "some Methods to relieve ourselves from the excessive Charge and Burthen of Pensioners." There was no further mention of the matter.

As still another example of a developing interest in things financial, the House of Delegates began to exercise an auditing role. Perhaps the motivation came from the unusually high expenses of the military; an early instance is in an examination of the spending of a Supply Bill for six thousand pounds, passed in 1754. A particular object of criticism was Colonel Thomas Cresap, Jr.[18] The House

---

18. His father, Thomas, Sr., had been a noted explorer and a challenger of the Penns during the boundary controversies of the previous century. The elder Cresap is almost a legendary figure in the early history of the Province. He is reputed to have taken a second wife at the age of 80, to have travelled to Nova Scotia at the age of 100, and to have died at Oldtown at the age of 106. *See* Lawrence C. Wroth, *The Story of Thomas Cresap, A Maryland Pioneer,* 9 MARYLAND HISTORICAL MAGAZINE 1-37 (1914).

committee to study the accounts gave a long and meticulous report on expenditures made by him: [19]

> Your Committee having Examined the several Accounts and Papers relating to the Disposal of the £6000. granted by Act of Assembly for his Majesty's Service in July Last, take Leave to observe that in the **Accounts N° 1 and 2. given in by Colonel Cresap, there** is a Charge made of £16:19:3. for Carriage of 51. Bushels of Salt (from Blandensburgh to Old Town.) more than from any of the Accounts now before them appears to have been bought.
>
> That in the Same Account N° 1 there is a Charge made for 1500. Bushels of Wheat, 51. Bushels Whereof is said to be Damaged by Water of which we have No further Account, the remaining 1449. Bushels of that Account produces 42000 pounds of Flour, but Your Committee are of Opinion the same must Yield a much larger Quantity and they Conceive themselves Justified in that Opinion, by a Computation that 2½ Bushels of Wheat will afford 100. pounds of Flour Clear of Bran, the Truth Whereof is Confirmed by the Daily Experience of those Concerned in that Manufacture allowing the same to be Ground and Boulted for the Bran as Customary by which Computation it will appear that the aforesaid Quantity of Wheat produces 57960 pounds of Flour Exclusive of the Damaged Wheat, and that the said Cresap ought to Account for a further Quantity of 15960 pounds of Flour on 399. Bushels of Wheat and that the Addition of 15 p Cent (for Shrinkage & Loss in weighing) on the Wheat Beef and Pork Charged in the said Account is without Reason or any Just Foundation as they Conceive. That a Charge is Likewise made in the same Account of £59:6:7 for Carrying 29667. pounds of Flour from Conigocheeg to Old Town by Water, at 4/p Hundred and from thence by Land to the New Store at

---

19. Later, in 1757, the accounts submitted by Colonel Cresap were to escalate into a bitter controversy as "the Ridout affair." The main ⌐.iaracter then was John Ridout, the Governor's secretary. The prolonged dispute brought to the fore the developing philosophies of separation of powers.

1/6 p Hundred amounting to £22:5:0 and for Carrying 16400 pounds of Flour from Conigocheeg to New Store by Land at 7/6 p Hundred the Sum of £61:10:0. all which Charges and several other Articles for Carriage in the same Account Your Committee apprehend are Extravagant particularly the Charge of £8:0:0 for the Carriage of 100 Bushels of Wheat Your Committee also observe in Cresaps Account N$^U$ 3. he Charges for 37. Blankets Delivered Messrs. Fortye and Lynn at 16/-Each which (allowing to be of the Same Quality with those bought at Annapolis) are overcharged upwards of 100 p Cent and that sundry other Articles in the Said Account for Goods appear to them very unreasonable.

Your Committee also find in Colonel Cresaps said Account N° 3 the Sum of £22:12:0. Charged Cash paid for Slaughtering, cutting up and Salting the first time 226 Cattle at 2/. a Head yet by the same Account or any other now before them it Does not appear there were any More than 177 Live Cattle bought for the Present Expedition 60 Whereof as appears by the Same Account have not been Slaughtered in which Article there is an overcharge of £10:18:0. They are also of Opinion that the storage charged in that and the Account N° 1. and 2. are much too high, if not the same Article.

Your Committee further observe that in the abovementioned Accounts there are several sums of Money Charged as paid to Sundry Persons for Services some on Account of the present Expedition for which no Vouchers are Laid before them and they are of Opinion that the above Accounts Delivered in by Colonel Cresap are Stated in a Dark Confused and unintelligible Manner. . . .

Your Committee Likewise observe a Credit in Colonel Cresaps Account of £95:16:7 for 11499½ lb Raw Hides and £1:10:0 for 4 pair of Shoes which are not Deducted out of the Debet of said Account nor Credited in the General Account.

Similarly, but in less detail, a joint committee operating in 1756, to study the office and work of the Commissioners of the Paper Office, sent the Governor a set of suggestions for keeping books:

Your Committee also find that the Method of Book Keeping which has been and now is used in the Paper Currency Office and the Neglect of some of the Officers Impowered to Collect the Several funds payable into that Office is such that your Committee hath not been able to make such Estimates of what the funds Annualy Produce as is Required of them by the Honourable the Upper and Lower Houses of Assembly; And that if the present Method be Continued the said Books must Remain in the same Confused Manner

Your Committee thereof Humbly Proposes that the present method of Keeping the Books in that Office may be Changed into that which is Commonly called the Italian Method or double Entry and that the Commissioners be directed to Keep the Office Books for the time to come in that manner and form and that the Iron Chest Account may be made to Answer to a General Cash Account to all Intents & purposes

Your Committee further Propose that an Address be presented to His Excellency the Governor to order the Several officers Concerned in Collecting the money to be paid on the Several funds into the said Office to Return proper Accounts in due time and make payment accordingly

The reference in this quotation to the "Iron Chest Account" leads to an interesting bit of financial lore from the eighteenth century. The "Iron Chest" was in literal truth a large iron strong-box or chest, used after it was ordered by the Assembly in 1733 until approximately the time of the Revolution. After the monetary base of the Province changed from tobacco to currency and coin, the Iron Chest was the repository for the paper money issued by the Province.[20]

---

20. "About 1885, while repairs were being made to the old Council Chamber, or Treasury Building, near the State House, in cutting through a new window the Iron Chest was found walled up between the original outside wall of the building and a more recently constructed inner wall. In it was found a book of accounts and the woodcut block from which the

provincial money was printed .... The chest was turned over to the Maryland Historical Society, together with the beautifully bound contemporary manuscript volume of accounts, covering the period from 1734 to 1767, entitled 'Iron Chest Account Book No. I,' which apparently contains a complete record of the uses to which the chest was put during this period and the amount of money deposited and withdrawn from it." *Archives,* vol. XLVI at ix (Preface).

## Chapter 10

## LEGISLATIVE OPERATIONS AND PRIVILEGE
## THE 1750s

The decade of the 1750s was a strenuous time for the General Assembly, with demanding years of war, frenzied finance, and increasing acrimony toward the Governor and Lord Baltimore. Controversy with the Governor arose over the Ridout Affair, his handling of the militia, and the Supply Bill. The Upper House and the House of Delegates were at odds over their compensation; and with a call for the abolition of the Upper House, the House found a new source of irritation. Through it all, the House continued with its demands for attention and additional privilege.

COMPENSATION OF LEGISLATORS

There were several moves during the decade to reduce the compensation of both houses of the Legislature, but no final action was taken. Bills for that purpose were introduced into the June session of 1752 and the October-November session of 1753. In 1757 and again in 1758, the subject was up again; and these times it became a bit heated.

Introduction of the bills was an outgrowth of the controversy between the two houses, extending back several decades, over the payment of an extra allowance for those members of the Upper House who also held administrative positions in the Province. For the most part, the issue concerned additional per diem payments for members of the Council (Upper House) when they sat as members of the Council of State; and as a lesser issue the House also objected to payment of an extra salary to the clerk of the Upper House when he served as clerk of the Council of State. It was the Upper House which, as a retaliatory measure, had a chief interest in the bills to reduce the compensation of all members of the Assembly.

Both houses passed such bills during the session of December, 1757. Each amended the other's bill, and neither would accept the other's amendments. The bills became embroiled in parliamentary tangles which were more apparent than real, leading to charges of "unparliamentary" procedure and of rejecting a bill on a "slight" pretense. It was in understatement when the Upper House finally observed that in the House "a sincere Disposition" is lacking "to pass this very useful Bill."

During the February-March session of 1758, both houses again introduced bills for salary cuts. Again, each House passed its own bill and rejected the other.

The House of Delegates took one salary action which did not require concurrence by the Upper House. By resolution during the spring session of 1757, the House determined that any of its members absent without leave of the Speaker would forfeit all his allowance for attendance during the entire session. Two years earlier, in 1755, the House by a vote of 15-17 had rejected a motion to have the Sergeant-at-Arms sent to round up the absentees without leave.

## PROCEDURES AND OPERATIONS

In 1755 the House lost one of its famous names, but gained others; Dr. Charles Carroll died, but was succeeded by his son, Charles Carroll the Barrister; and Daniel of St. Thomas Jenifer was a new member from Charles County. Colonel Thomas Cresap became a delegate from Frederick County; he was the same Cresap whose war accounts and military expenditures were so closely examined and criticised in 1754 and 1755.

Both houses continued to receive all manner of petitions for redress of grievances. Most of them were on legislative or at least quasi-legislative problems, but the number and occasionally the content of petitions make unusual reading in later times. One of them to the Upper House during the May-June session of 1751 was "praying a Bounty to make public a Cure for the Bloody Flux; with several Testimonies of Cure performed, annexed to the said Petition." The Upper House handled that one with dispatch, sending it on to the House of Delegates. Another, in 1757, came from Joseph Wood of Frederick County, "praying a Reward may be given him for his Invention / as he says / of a Machine that will go perpetually without winding or Spring."

The first session of 1757, lasting from April 8 to May 9, was held in "Baltimore Town." It then was a village of perhaps 30 houses. The move was occasioned by an epidemic of smallpox in Annapolis. Most of the sessions of the House probably were held in the home of the Reverend Thomas Chase, rector of St. Paul's Parish; the Upper House seems to have met in an inn owned by William Buchanan, near the northeast corner of Market [1] and Calvert streets. For the December session in 1757, they were back in Annapolis; the House on December 15 asked for a "speedy End" to the session, as the "severity of the Weather may probably incommode us greatly in returning to our respective Homes."

The character of the legislative *Journals* was changing gradually over the years. By the 1750s, the wording was becoming "modern," though some of the words and phrases still were foreign to the twentieth century idiom. Punctuation was in greater vogue than earlier; at least some of the sentences and paragraphs would be ended with a period, and there was a greater, though certainly not a complete, use of commas. The frequent abbreviations used in the seventeenth century no longer appeared in the *Journals* for the mid-eighteenth century.

---

1. Now Baltimore Street. It is certainly only a coincidence that the Emerson Hotel later was constructed on that site.

The *Journals* of the Upper House were shorter in the 1750s than in the earlier decades. Frequently a daily session would have nothing more than "This house met again according to Adjournment," with the adjournment for that day noted. The *Journals* of the House of Delegates sometimes had only this brief notation of a day's meeting, but they often were in considerably more detail. For one thing, perhaps because of the contentious mood of the House, many more messages were printed than for the Upper House, and some of them would be from persons and officials other than those having to do strictly with the legislative business.

The House again was expressing some concern over the retention and preservation of the old *Journals*. As far back as the May-June session of 1739, the House Committee on Aggrievances and Courts of Justice reported that it found the *Journals* of the Assembly "in very great disorder," though noting that the cause might be that of recent repairs to the State House. The Committee had found no *Journals* dated earlier than 1688. Another committee report in 1744 discussed the condition of the *Journals.* This came during the May-June session of that year. It listed in some detail the *Journals* it had found, noting that some "want" binding and others were in loose sheets. The committee noted that earlier it had ordered the House Clerk, Michael Macnemara, to compile missing *Journals* for preceding sessions, "which order we do not find any ways comply'd with."

Political parties were forming in the modern sense, though in very rudimentary fashion. In great part they stemmed from the political facts of Provincial government. All the members of the Council, owing their appointments to the Governor, usually voted with him and Lord Baltimore; they came to be known as the Proprietary Party. By the mid-1750s a minority in the House of Delegates was counted in that party, but most members of the House were listed in an opposition group variously styled as the anti-Proprietary,

Popular, Country, or County Party. A summary in the *Archives* (vol. 55, preface) lists the main strength of the Proprietary Party in the House coming from St. Mary's, Somerset, and Worcester counties, with other members from Calvert and Queen Anne's counties. After the election of 1757, it is added, the County or Popular party picked up votes in the House, so that perhaps 40 out of the total of 58 members usually voted against Proprietary measures.[2]

The rules adopted for the House continued without particular change from those adopted earlier in the century. They still forbade "reviling" speeches, limited speeches to one per member at any reading of a bill, prohibited interruptions to another's speech, required a speaker to stand and address the chair, prohibited carrying a sword or other weapon while the House was in session, made misdemeanors on the floor punishable by the House, required three readings for every bill (two before and one after engrossing), and specified that no bill might be read until "all the Members in Town be called in." There were two rules against unexcused absence; one was the old one specifying a fine up to five shillings for every offense, and the other (a recent addition) required the offending member to forfeit all his allowances for the current session.

Normally, while adopting its rules for a session, the House also would adopt again the resolutions first passed in 1722, reaffirming its conviction that the inhabitants were not in the status of "a conquered" people and were to be treated as

---

2. The Revolutionary movement in Maryland was largely the work of the "Country" party, which for years led the organized opposition in the House of Delegates against the Proprietary. "The House of Delegates sought to relieve the financial burden which the proprietary system imposed on the Province by curbing the political powers and prerogatives of the Proprietors and enhancing those of their own body." PHILIP A. CROWL, MARYLAND DURING AND AFTER THE REVOLUTION — A POLITICAL AND ECONOMIC STUDY 20 (Baltimore, 1943).

Englishmen, including having the rights of the English statutory and common law.[3] For an extra measure, these resolutions also usually inveighed against the Proprietary for imposing and collecting the 12-pence per hogshead tax on exported tobacco; this, of course, had long been a complaint of the House.

## LEGISLATIVE PRIVILEGE

The House continued to insist upon a proper observance of its privileges and prerogatives as a legislative body, and some of its controversies discussed under other headings go back partly to this insistence. Upon occasion the House would act against persons of some standing in the community. Thus, in 1751, Charles Carroll (the father of Charles Carroll of Carrollton) was briefly imprisoned for an infringement of what the House deemed a reflection upon its proceedings. Carroll, a prominent Roman Catholic, was incensed over the constant legislative and social actions against persons of that faith. He posted an "advertisement" on the door of the House chamber, declared by the House to contain "matters scandalous and malicious, reflecting upon the proceedings of this House in general and a member thereof in Particular." The Sergeant-at-Arms was ordered to arrest him, and Carroll then was turned over to the Sheriff of Anne Arundel County. He was ordered kept in close confinement, and a motion to commit him to the public jail was defeated by a vote of only 22-28. The session ended a couple of days after Carroll was sent into "close confinement," and it is probable he then was quietly released.

---

**3.** "Maryland was more insistent on the complete extension of English law than any other colony; and at times demanded the application in the Maryland courts not only of common law but of statute law as well." MARY PATTERSON CLARKE, PARLIAMENTARY PRIVILEGE IN THE AMERICAN COLONIES 153 (New Haven, 1943).

Similarly, during the February-May session of 1756, the House ordered the arrest of the rector of a parish in Cecil County:

> It being moved to the House by a Member, that the Reverend Mr. John Hamilton, Rector of St. Mary Anne's Parish in Cecil County, in this Province, had uttered several reviling Speeches in his Presence, reflecting upon the Lower House of Assembly in general, and against some particular Members thereof:
> Ordered, That the Serjeant at Arms, attending this House, do take into his Custody the Body of the said John Hamilton, and him safe keep, so that he have him personally at the Bar of this House, to answer such Things as shall be objected against him, for having uttered several Speeches, reflecting on the Dignity and Proceedings of the Lower House of Assembly of the Province aforesaid.

Nothing further appears in the House *Journal* for that session about the transgression of the Reverend Mr. Hamilton.

Yet, while being elaborately punctilious in a strict observance of its own privileges (as it defined the term), the House frequently made what later generations would call wide incursions into the governmental domain of both executive and judicial officers in the Province. Its members did not hesitate to criticise and to direct others in the performance of duty, and the breadth of their interests and claims is now sometimes a matter of wonder. They involved the doctrine of separation of powers, which in the 1750s was but a developing principle and far from an exact science.

Thus, on May 27, 1751, William Eilbeck was brought before the Bar of the House. He was one of the justices of Charles County, and the charge concerned the nature of a verdict against Peter Dent. The precise facts were not recounted in the *Journal*. Eilbeck in effect pleaded guilty, and was given a stinging rebuke:

The House took into Consideration the Answer of Mr. Eilbeck, and Resolved, That his Behaviour proceeded from an Inadvertency, and not from any evil Design. Ordered, That Mr. Eilbeck be again called to the Bar, and that he be acquainted from the Chair, with the Sense that this House sustained of his Conduct; and that it be recommended to him to act with more Circumspection in his Station for the future.

Mr. Eilbeck was called to the Bar, and Mr. Speaker gave him the following Charge; viz.

Sir,

From what you yourself have declared at the Bar, as well as from the Report read to you, it plainly appears, that the Magistrates did not use that Caution which is absolutely necessary, in all Cases for the due Administration of Justice, which consists in hearing coolly, fully, and impartially, both Sides of the Question, before they proceed to Judgment; it being certain, that the Rule of doing Justice is violated, whenever a Determination is had upon hearing one Side of the Question only. Fines ought to be made agreeable to the Nature of the Crimes complained of; and are to be moderated, whenever a Breach of the Laws have arose by uncommon Aggravation: But of this you refus'd to enquire, and therein greatly erred; stretching your Power to the utmost Limits of the Law.

This Honourable House therefore recommends to you more Caution and Circumspection for the future, and hopes you'll give Occasion for no more Complaints of the like hereafter. There are some Fees which have arose by reason of this Enquiry, which it's expected you'll pay, and on which you are discharged from further Attendance.

In 1752, following the deaths of both Charles Calvert, fifth Lord Baltimore, and Governor Samuel Ogle, the session which began on June 3 was opened with an address of welcome from Benjamin Tasker, President of the Council and Acting Governor. The House abruptly inquired as to the basis for his authority to be President of the Council (and from that office to be Acting Governor). Tasker was in a difficult spot; all the commissions for membership to the Council had expired with the death of Charles Calvert. However, the new Proprietary, Frederick Calvert, had ordered the reinstatement of the former members of the Council, and this answer seemed to satisfy the House of Delegates.

There was another pronouncement by the House on a member of the judiciary, on March 8, 1755. The individual was John Rawlings, a justice from Frederick County. Again without summarizing the facts, he was adjudged by the House to have committed "manifest Error" in executing his office; and he was ordered, in all future judicial proceedings, "to direct yourself by the Right Rule of Law, and go no more by the crooked Cord of Opinion." The judgment of the House was sent on to the Governor for further action. He responded with a defense of Rawlings and a blunt suggestion that the House "forbear to meddle" in complaints which are "relievable elsewhere, and are the proper Objects for the Enquiry of another Jurisdiction":

> From the Papers that have been submitted to me, and his own Asseverations, I must confess, Gentlemen, and beg Leave to observe as much to you, that it does not, as I before hinted, appear to me, at present, that he has been guilty of any Misdemeanor whatever; although he must of Necessity have been a great Sufferer by being brought so far from his Home, and compelled to a long and expensive Attendance on your House. I assure you it is very far from my Intent or Design, to call in Question the Rights and Privileges of your House; but at the same Time, I shall regard it as my Duty, and must endeavour to preserve the Rights, Liberties and Privileges of the People, which are secured by and dependent upon, the due and legal Exercise of the Laws, under our present happy Constitution, and not suffer them to be called upon, or prosecuted out of the ordinary Course of Procedure: And I cannot help recommending to you, Gentlemen, as you sit here at a very considerable Expence to the Country, to forbear to meddle, for the

future, with such Complaints, as are (if not groundless) relievable elsewhere, and are the proper Objects for the Enquiry of another Jurisdiction.

The House made another excursion into non-legislative fields during the April-May session of 1757, with a general suggestion to the Governor that he file suit on the bonds of sheriffs, clerks, and other public officers "who have failed in their duty." "It is truly discouraging to us to find," wrote the House to Governor Sharpe, "that many of the Officers that have been, and now are employed in the Collection of the Public Money, should act in such a Manner as affords us too much Room to apprehend they think themselves secure under the notorious Fraud of Pocketing it; and in others (who can't plead Ignorance of the Laws) such an Omission of Duty as we could not suspect." The Governor's only reply was that he already had directed the Attorney General to proceed in some of the cases cited, and that he would verify this had been done.

The next infraction, reported in the *Journal* of October 8, 1757, was against Sheriff Hercules Couts of Kent County, charged with having been "absent and intoxicated with Liquor the greatest Part of the Time" during the last election for delegates to the Assembly. He was brought to the Bar of the House, where he confessed and was reprimanded by the Speaker as follows:

Mr. Couts,
You having at the Bar of this House confessed, that you, as Sheriff of Kent County, have been Guilty of a manifest Neglect of your Duty, in being absent and intoxicated with Liquor the greatest Part of the Time between the Opening and Closing of the Polls, at the late Election of Representatives to serve in this General Assembly for said County, it is the unanimous Opinion of this House, that you be Reprimanded by me at the Bar of the House, and that you ought to receive very severe Treatment, in order to deter other Sheriffs from being

Guilty of Breaches of their Duty in Affairs of so great Importance and Concern to the Community; but yet, in Consideration of your low Circumstances, and in Compassion to your numerous Family, this House is inclined to exercise Justice with the greatest Lenity, and in a Manner which will least affect your unhappy Relatives; and I do Reprimand you accordingly; in Hopes the mild Treatment you have received, will raise in you a proper Sense of the Gratitude you owe to this House, and have a happy Influence on your future Conduct. You are discharged from any further Attendance on this House, upon Payment of the Fees due to the Officers thereof.

Also in 1757, during the spring session, the House of Delegates sent a long message to the Governor on one phase of his conduct of the war. Governor Sharpe, in concert with the governors of other colonies, had agreed to treat by regulation the use of carriages and wagons for transporting men and materials, the quartering of troops, and the number of troops. It was with some asperity that the House framed its indictment of the Governor's handling of these war measures:

Now, May it please your Excellency, As we do not know of any Statute of England, or any Law of this Province, that impowers you, as Governor thereof, to form such Regulations as are above specified, or any Law, Statute, or Custom, for Quartering Troops of any Denomination whatever within this Province, either in Time of Peace or War, and as we cannot presume your Excellency would, without some Law, Statute, or Custom, to authorize it, enter into such Agreement as is abovementioned, we therefore most humbly Request the Favour of you to lay before us the Law or Statute, or inform us of the Custom by which you are Vested with such Authority.

The Governor's reply was conciliatory. Admitting he had no direct statutory authority to issue the regulations, either from England or Maryland, he pointed out that the governors in all the colonies were under a directive from the King to pursue the war with diligence; and he cited acts passed earlier in Maryland, at the Governor's request, to set maximum rates for carriage hire and for the quartering of troops.

The House persisted in its inquiry. "As we could not entertain an Opinion" that he would issue regulations without some statutory authority, it wrote, "so we are fully persuaded your Excellency will ... act in a Manner consistent with the Statutes of England, the Laws of this Province, and the Rights and Liberties of the good People thereof, committed to your Care and Protection." Having delivered its opinion upon a matter already concluded, the House dropped the problem of regulations for the conduct of the war.

## THE RIDOUT AFFAIR

The most abrasive encounter between the House of Delegates and the Governor during this period came during a long and bitter confrontation over "the Ridout affair." It began actively during late September, 1757, but also was an aftermath of criticism by the House of the military accounts and expenditures of Colonel Thomas Cresap, Jr., in 1754 and 1755. The accounts submitted by Cresap were found to be incomplete, and the Governor wished to return them to Cresap for correction. The original records were in the custody of the House, having been submitted to the House earlier by order of the Governor and having been sharply criticised by the House. On the Governor's order, his secretary, John Ridout,[4] removed the original papers from the custody of the House, though he left copies in place of

---

4. John Ridout had come to Maryland with Governor Sharpe in 1753, as the Governor's secretary; he remained in that post until Governor Sharpe left the Province in 1773. *See* Paul H. Giddens, *Governor Horatio Sharpe Retires,* 31 MARYLAND HISTORICAL MAGAZINE 215-25 (1936).

the originals. The House resented the removal of the original documents, and blamed its own clerk for permitting them to go. Most of all, however, the House seized upon the incident as a golden opportunity to castigate the Governor. It was a dispute stemming from the long-standing and growing enmity of the House toward the Governor, the Proprietary, and the executive authority they symbolized.

The first skirmish was an "order" by the House that John Ridout appear before it to explain the incident. Upon his non-compliance, the House on September 30, 1757, directed its sergeant-at-arms "to take into custody the body" of John Ridout, "for his Contempt in refusing to attend according to the Order of the House." [5] The next sequence in the developing drama came when the sergeant-at-arms attempted to "take" Ridout from the Governor's house, leading to an immediate but mildly worded protest from the Governor:

Gentlemen of the Lower House of Assembly,
I am sorry to inform you, that as I was this Day at Dinner, your Serjeant came into my House and demanded to see my Secretary; and on my asking him, Upon what Account He told me, That he had Orders from your House to take him into Custody. I could not help being at first much surprized at his Answer; but, recollecting that your Serjeant is but just appointed, and concluding that he must as yet be almost a Stranger to the Duty of his Office, I suppose he must have behaved in this Manner without any Orders for so doing: If that is the Case, I shall excuse him on the Consideration abovementioned; but if he acted in this Manner by any

---

5. Actually, Ridout had appeared informally before the House to explain that he had removed the Cresap papers for correction; but when further questioned on other matters, he declined to answer and referred members of the House to the Governor.

Order of your House, I can't but expect that the Reason of such an extraordinary Proceeding, without any previous Application, will be communicated to me.

Horatio Sharpe

The Governor's message of September 30 "was Read, and Ordered to lie on the Table." Three days later, on October 3, the House responded with an abrupt and quarrelsome rejoinder:

> To his Excellency Horatio Sharpe, Esq.: Governor and Commander in Chief in and over the Province of Maryland:
>
> The humble Address of the House of Delegates.
>
> May it please your Excellency,
> John Ridout having been Guilty of a Contempt of the Authority, and of a Breach of the Rights and Privileges of this House, at the Bar thereof, we did issue a Warrant to our Serjeant to take him into Custody: This we conceive to be a Right which we ought to exercise without any previous Application to your Excellency. If the Serjeant, in the Execution of his Duty, behaved in a Manner inconsistent with the Decorum that ought to be observed in your Excellency's House while you are at Dinner, it was not by any Direction from this House: and we hope, if he has been Guilty of the least Intrusion or Indecency, your Excellency will impute it to his being but just appointed to his Office.

On October 11 the Governor answered with some indignation. His first message, he said, was "not so much by Way of Charge against your House, as by Way, of Complaint of such Usage" and was purposely worded that an apology might easily have been made and an end put to the affair. Yet the House, he continued, countered with an assertion that it could issue such a warrant as "a Right which we ought to exercise without any previous Application to your Excellency."

Next, wrote the Governor, the House had referred to Ridout simply by name and not by his title as the Governor's secretary. This omission, combined with the warrant, made the whole affair in the judgment of the Governor an interference in executive affairs by the legislative branch. Furthermore, he said:

> I do not propose to enter into any Debate with you upon this Point, because, as I have hitherto avoided making any Incroachments on the just and constitutional Rights and Privileges of your House, as one of the Branches of the Legislature, so am I determined not to suffer mine, while I consider myself as the Chief Branch of that Body, to be brought into Dispute, lest you should construe such a Condescension in me into a vesting you with a Right to dispute them whenever you shall think fit.
>
> However, I would just observe to you, by Way of Information, with Regard to your Rights, that as you are one of the Branches of the Legislature, you, as well as the other Branches, have certain Rights and Privileges constitutionally annexed to you while together, which the other Branches may not interfere with, and you, as well as they, have likewise certain Servants to attend you in the Discharge of your Duty, tho' if the Matter was to be disputed, your Right to cloath that Servant, which you are pleased to call a Serjeant, with such great Authority, would not, I am apt to think, be easily made appear.

The Governor went on to say that sending for Ridout was "an Attempt by you to exercise an unconstitutional Authority, in sending for a Person to appear at your Bar, with whom you have nothing to do, and who is constitutionally under my Protection, and consequently of a Contempt of my Power, and of a Breach of the Rights and Privileges incident to my Station. And I must here take the Liberty to tell you, Gentlemen, that these Powers, Rights and Privileges, I am determined, whenever I shall leave this Government, to deliver up to my Successor, as full and entire, in all their several Branches, as they came into my Hands."

Finally, "having now given you a general View of the Rights of the several Branches of the Legislature, with Regard to each other, and my Sense of your late Treatment of me in the Person of my Secretary, I shall conclude with entreating you to give the Matters I recommended to your Consideration, an immediate Place in your Deliberations." You may best contribute to the good of the people, he advised, "by diligently attending the public Business, and carefully avoiding all such Steps, as can only tend to protract this Session."

The House of Delegates would not be deterred. The next day, October 12, it appointed a special committee of three members "to inspect the Records in the Provincial Office, and Report to the House, Whether any Commission, appointing Mr. John Ridout Secretary to his Excellency the Governor, be on Record there; and whether it there appears that he has taken the Oaths to the Government, to Qualify him on such Commission; and that they likewise inspect the said Records, and Report, whether it appears on Record in the said Office, that a Commission hath been granted by any former Governor of this Province, appointing any Person as his Secretary."

The purpose here, of course, was to ascertain how "official" was the status of the Governor's secretary; whether, in effect, he was a Secretary or a secretary. In appointing the committee, the House showed an awareness of the uses of the new device of political parties; all three of the members appointed were accounted as leaders in the County or anti-Proprietary party.

It was to be two months, in December, 1757, before the House had a report from its special committee and could again send a message to the Governor. It was a long report, covering more than six pages in the *Journal.* After covering in some detail the testimony Ridout made to the House and the exchanges between him and the sergeant-at-arms, the message came to the main point of interest for the House.

"We do not know," the Governor was told, "of any such Officer as a Governor's Secretary, nor ever heard of such in this Government; . . . and we hope a new Officer is not to be created within this Government by your Excellency's Messages informing us any Gentleman is such; and we cannot look upon Mr. Ridout as any Thing more than a Gentleman supported by your Excellency, or perhaps his Lordship, for your Convenience and Assistance in Writing." Also, "Whether we have a Right to order our Serjeant to take a Governor's Secretary into Custody, or not, it is Time enough to dispute, when there is one legally commissioned (which we apprehend cannot be without the Consent of the Legislature) and duly qualified." Finally, on this point, "We do not desire to bring your Excellency's just and constitutional Rights, while you are the Chief Branch of our Legislature, into Dispute; nor will we tamely suffer ours to be violated or infringed."

In his final message to the House of Delegates about the Ridout Affair, at the end of the 1757 session, the Governor wrote at some length about the work and status of John Ridout and of the Governor's entire household. The final observation of the House had been to state the "principle" that the Governor in his legislative capacity had no servant necessarily and constitutionally attendant upon him for the discharge of his duties; and that "we are satisfied we have as much Right to call him before us, as any other Gentleman that may reside in your Excellency's House, and as much Right to call one of your Family before us, as one of any Gentleman's Family in the Province."

Stung by the claim that the House of Delegates might freely call before it any member of the Governor's household, Governor Sharpe gave a spirited defense of his secretary and all members of his family, and of their privilege in being free from calls of the Legislature:

As I would willingly avoid all Enquiries into your Rights and Privileges, I have not taken any Notice of your Claim of an unlimited Power, to call one of any other Gentleman's Family before you, but have only denied your Right, to call before you any of mine. The Power of Protecting those that reside in my House, while they offend not the Laws, is a Right that I can neither part with, nor suffer to be disputed: and I will venture to pronounce, that none of my Predecessors, when they granted the Prayer of a new Speaker, by assuring him 'that the Members of the Lower House of Assembly should be free from Restraint, in their own Persons, and in their Attendants, during the Session,' designed thereby to invest him with a Power of stripping them of their Attendants, whenever he should think proper.

In concluding his long message at the end of the 1757 session, and his historical allusions in defense of his secretary and his household, Governor Sharpe told the House that while he would be guilty of a breach of trust if he permitted his rights and privileges to be "trampled on," yet "I shall ever think myself bound to support the Dignity of your House, as the Third Branch of our Legislature." With the session being prorogued on the following day, December 16, the status of the Upper House, the Ridout affair, and the larger question of separation of powers ended for the session. The latter shortly would resume in another context.

### ABOLITION OF THE UPPER HOUSE

In its last message about the Ridout affair, the House spoke of another facet of legislative power of which there had been prior hints, but which perhaps had never been so clearly articulated. In response to the Governor's message of October 11, 1757, in which he had described the relative positions and powers of the Governor and the two houses, the House of Delegates was stirred into asserting that the Upper

House had no "secure" constitutional existence. "What are the Rights and Privileges of those Gentlemen, that are said to constitute another Branch," said the House in its message, "we know nothing about; as it is a Branch undevised in our Charter, and unknown in it's original." For a time, the House supplemented the other controversies with its new contention that the Upper House should be abolished.

A day before the 1757 session ended, on December 15, the Governor submitted a long message to the House, He wrote with a strong defense of the Upper House, recounting in some detail the efforts by Governor Fendall a century earlier to abolish the Upper House and the ignominious downfall of that earlier governor:

> That Gentleman, having been opposed in some of his Measures by the Council, agreed, as it should seem, with some of the great Speakers and Leading Men among the Burgesses, to Destroy the Upper House, and Subvert the Constitution: To bring this about, it was so ordered, that the Speaker and the Members of the Lower House, should go in a Body to the Upper, and tell the Governor and Council that they could not allow them to be an Upper House, or a distinct Branch of the Legislature; but that, if they pleased, they might take Place in, and become a Part of the Lower; the Governor readily accepted the Offer, and was received as their President. The Secretary, and other Gentlemen of the Council, Protested against such a Step, as a manifest Breach of his Lordship's Rights, Royal Jurisdiction and Seigniory, and desired Leave to enter their Reasons; but they were not suffered. As soon as this Affair was known in England, proper Measures were taken to restore the Constitution and Government: Another Governor was appointed, the Upper House re-assumed their Authority, Rights and Privileges, and Mr. Fendall, and the Chiefs of the Faction, were apprehended, tried, and convicted of Rebellion; their Lives were with some Difficulty spared, but the Punishment inflicted on them, by Loss of Goods and Imprisonment, was thought sufficiently Exemplary, to deter all future Governors, and Leading Men, from imitating their Conduct.

The Governor added still more to the historical justification for an Upper House. The original Charter of 1632, he said, gave to the Proprietary a right to make laws and left it to his discretion how to convene the freeholders for that purpose. The first sessions of the Assembly had been combinations of the Governor's Council and of the freemen (or their representatives). One of the laws passed in 1638 had provided that the Council and the burgesses "shall be judged a General Assembly." The burgesses had sought in 1642 to separate the Assembly into two houses, a change which finally was made in 1649. So, said the Governor in summarizing this part of his history lesson, "the Upper House is Coeval with the Lower, and established on as firm a Basis; and . . . your Position of It's being unknown in it's Original, was too general, and ought to have been confined to Yourselves."

Continuing with a further excursion into history, the Governor recited that in 1681 the Lower House, feeling the need for a sergeant-at-arms, "humbly Requested his Lordship to appoint such a Person to attend them during that Session," but the request was denied. Before there was a sergeant-at-arms, the Governor wrote (and probably with a sense of irony), it would not have been possible for the House to order its man to take a Governor's secretary into custody; "and I believe it is a Question that was never started in any Lower House of Assembly, before the present Session." He cited also the time the Lower House had "humbly desired his Excellency would be pleased to permit" one of his staff to go into the House to furnish some information.

The extended and extreme controversies about John Ridout and also concerning the possible abolition of the Upper House, partly combined at the end of the 1757 session, left scars and memories. Governor Sharpe in a personal letter dated January 1, 1758, said that the House of Delegates was undertaking to assume all the powers of the House of

Commons.[6] Several days earlier, in a letter to Cecilius Calvert dated December 26, 1757, he wrote of the practice of the House in calling persons before it for real or imagined offenses, and of the pretense that "the Upper House is no part of our Constitution." [7] The same theme was touched upon several months later by Benjamin Tasker, President of the Council. This occurred at the end of the March-May session of 1758, when the two houses were locked in a dispute about that year's Supply Bill; Tasker wrote about the spirit and claims of the Maryland House of Delegates: [8]

> If the Authority challenged by them had been acknowledged by us there would be little Occasion for an express Resolve that this House is an unnecessary Branch of the Legislature, and the next Step might be to controul the Supreme Magistrate in his Exercise of the executive Power measure out the Duty of Obedience to Government by the particular Convenience of each Individual, and awe and intimidate the ordinary Jurisdictions by resolving standing Laws to be null and void, or publishing Constructions of them to regulate the Conduct of the Subject, and the Determination of his Judges.

## THE SUPPLY BILL

The Supply Bill fared no better in early 1758 than in 1757. The Assembly met from February 13 to March 9, but without success. It was back again from March 28 to May 13, with the same result. The House of Delegates was furious over what it felt was unauthorized aid sent to Fort Cumberland on the

---

6. *Archives,* IX at 124.

7. *Archives,* IX at 119. Cecilius Calvert was Secretary of the Province and an uncle of Frederick, sixth Lord Baltimore.

8. The Assembly in Maryland has been called "more active" than any other colonial legislature in expanding claims of privilege to its own advantage and power. MARY PATTERSON CLARKE, PARLIAMENTARY PRIVILEGE IN THE AMERICAN COLONIES 153n (New Haven, 1943).

far frontier. That, together with its desire to be a unicameral legislature, continually made it unwilling to vote for Supply. Finally, when the Assembly elected in September, 1757, had met in four sessions without voting for Supply, the Governor determined on August 21, 1758, to dissolve the Assembly and call for new elections. However, the election failed to solve the problem; the Assembly which met in October, 1758, contained in the House most of the same anti-Proprietary group that had been in the Assembly the year before.

In the second session of 1758, from March to May, the Supply Bill was embroiled in the usual and sometimes irrelevent disputes between the two houses. The Upper House complained on April 18, for example, that the preamble of the bill "asserts that only the Delegates of the People give and grant, Whereas the Bill could not pass without the Proprietary's and our Concurrence." The bill also would have vested in the House of Delegates the "sole Nomination of the Officers" for administering its provisions; but the Upper House conceived that the appointment of civil and military officers was vested in Lord Baltimore. We must take the liberty to assure you, wrote the Upper House, "that we would not suffer our Estates to be taxed by Officers deriving their Power from your sole Nomination, and who naturally think themselves peculiarly accountable for their Conduct to yourselves."

The House of Delegates argued in return that in England the House of Commons had primary powers with respect to money bills. But, said the Upper House, there is no exact analogy: "that Money Bills have taken their Rise in the Upper House, that they have been framed in a Committee composed of Members of both Houses, and that they have been amended by us we presume need not be proved." The Upper House posed a set of pointed questions to the House of Delegates:

Whence do you derive the Power of making Laws but from the Charter? will you not contend that the King granted a Power by the Charter, which the Crown does not exercise or even attempt to exercise? whence would you derive the Power you now assume to appoint Commissioners? Do you claim it from Usage? you can't cite one Instance. Do you claim it under any and what Act of Assembly? you can't produce one. Do you derive it from the Charter with the Power of Legislation? By your own Argument you can't. The Perplexity you must be involved in by not attending to the true Origin of our Constitution ought to recommend that as much to your Consideration as the Learning of Land Tax Acts

All the Power as we apprehend that we have or can exercise flows from the Charter, and Power when granted should be exercised according to the Restrictions and Limitations imposed by the Grantor.

The House of Delegates, four days before the end of the session, countered by a vote of 28-9 that it had done "what was incumbent on them" toward the passage of a Supply Bill but "have been frustrated by the Non-Concurrence of the Upper House," a situation which "cannot be imputed" to the House. The Upper House, it was added in a long resolution stating the position of the House of Delegates, "laid down Positions tending to destroy the ancient and undoubted Rights and Privileges of this House, and have assumed Powers that do not Constitutionally or Reasonably Belong to them. . . ." [9]

---

9. During the winter of 1765-6, Benjamin Franklin was asked by a committee of the Parliament in England whether Maryland had refused to furnish a quota for the defense of the Province during the French and Indian War. With typical finesse, he replied that "Maryland has been much misrepresented in this matter. Maryland, to my knowledge, never refused to contribute or grant aid to the crown. The assemblies, every year during the war, voted considerable sums, and formed bills to raise them. The bills were, according to the constitution of that province, sent up to the Council, or Upper House, for concurrence, that they might be presented to the

The preamble of the Supply Bill, continued the House, follows a statement by the House of Commons in the reign of Henry IV (1399-1413), "That all Grants and Aids are made by the Commons, and only assented to by the Lords." The resolution went on to say that currently in England all supply bills were "the sole Gift of the Commons" and that the right of nominating all commissioners of this nature was constantly exercised by the Commons.

The matter of money bills and the proper procedures and priorities for them was argued in another context during the second spring session in 1758. That was the proposal to reduce the compensation of members of the General Assembly and perhaps of other officials in the Province as well. It had been bruited about in rather listless fashion for several years; in 1758, as had happened before, each house passed a bill of its own, but neither passed the other's bill. At one point the Upper House complained that its bill had gone to the House of Delegates more than two weeks earlier and that "you have not been pleased to take the least Notice to us." During the interval the House had sent to the other its own version of the bill; but, argued the Upper House, "we apprehend that the Bill sent from us ought first to be considered and the Method you have pursued is inconsistent with all Rules of proceeding." The House of Delegates responded with its typical squelch: "we think ourselves obliged now in Order to put a Stop to your sending down to this House any more Bills relative to the imposing or altering Taxes, to let you know that if any such shall hereafter be sent to us they shall be rejected upon a View of the Title, as it is

---

Governor, in order to be enacted into laws. Unhappy disputes between the two Houses, arising from the defects of that constitution principally, rendered all the bills but one or two abortive. The proprietary's council rejected them. It is true, Maryland did not then contribute its proportion, but it was, in my opinion, the fault of the government, not of the people." Quoted in ELIHU S. RILEY, A HISTORY OF THE GENERAL ASSEMBLY OF MARYLAND, 1635-1904, 287 (1905, republished in 1972).

the undoubted Right of this House that all Bills relative to Taxes should take their Rise here." The Upper House then asked for a conference committee on the subject, but even this proposal was rejected by the House of Delegates. The Supply Bill was lost again in a welter of procedural logistics; 1758 was another year that saw the bill introduced and considered, but not passed.

## POWER OVER THE MILITIA

The long controversies with the Governor over the Ridout affair, the locus of power between the executive and legislative branches, and the philosophy of separation of powers all ended inconclusively when the fall session of 1757 was prorogued. The House of Delegates returned to the fray in the spring of 1758. This time the argument stemmed from the power, unsupported by a legislative act, to order out and make dispositions of the Provincial militia.

This long exchange began on April 1 when, in a message to the Governor, the House requested "the Favour to be informed explicitly by what Law or Authority the Militia of Kent and Queen-Anne's County were ordered out and compelled to march." The question also extended to the militia of Calvert County, which, the House understood, was about to be ordered out. The Governor's reply, on April 4, was that previously, and with the assent of the House, he had ordered out units of county militia to protect the settlements in the Conococheague area and to "range on the Western Frontier." These enlistments were about to expire, and the Governor believed the orders for the Kent and Queen Anne's militia were covered by the earlier authorization. Immediately the House determined to bring in a "Remonstrance" on the subject.

The groundwork for the "Remonstrance" was set up with care and precision. The House sent the Governor an

377

"Address and Remonstrance" detailing its complaints; next it passed a series of seven propositions, framed as resolutions, and each with a recorded roll call; and finally it combined the seven propositions into one document, which was entered on the *Journal* as "the Resolves" of the House. All of it was done with the elaborate ceremonial trappings of the time.

The "Address and Remonstrance" was addressed "To his Excellency Horatio Sharpe, Esq; Governor and Commander in Chief in and over the Province of Maryland." It was titled "The humble Address and Remonstrance of the House of Delegates." The salutation was "May it please your Excellency." When it had been read to the House, and assented to, and the Speaker had signed it, two members of the House were appointed to "acquaint his Excellency, That this House hath prepared an Address and Remonstrance, to be presented to him, and desires to know when and where he will receive it." That matter of protocol settled, on April 17, 1758, 13 members of the House were appointed to make the actual presentation.[10]

"We beg leave to assure your Excellency," the House began, "that nothing less than the Regard we owe to the Preservation of the Lives, Liberties and Properties of the good People of this Province, could induce us to trouble you with a Representation so disagreeable to us, as what we are obliged to make to you."

The gravamen of the complaint, of course, was the sending of two companies of militia toward the western frontier, one from Queen Anne's County and the other from Kent County.

10. All this was time-honored custom, no matter how critical and harsh the terms of the address. One wonders about the demeanor of the participants in one of these ceremonies, with the House delegation knowing the contents of the message and the Governor from long experience expecting the worst.

This stated, the House pressed on without even beginning a new sentence to relate a fortuitous mishap which had occurred to the company from Kent County, which, "in an Attempt to cross the Bay in their Way thither, were drove back from Patapsco, by a violent Storm, into Chester River, their Vessels forced ashore, great Quantities of their Provisions lost, and the Men exposed to the most extreme Hardships." The Governor's action "at the most severe Season of the Year" was "unnecessary," "extremely grievous," "ruinous," and "unreasonably burthensome to the Country."

The House next disputed the Governor's claim that he was supported by law in calling out the two companies of militia, saying that the law covered only the mustering and training of troops in the counties of their residence. In this instance, the Province was not under any invasion. "We really are at a Loss to conceive what could induce your Excellency to be of Opinion, that you had a Power, under that Law, to march the Militia beforementioned, unless you supposed you had an Authority under it, to march the Militia of this Province whenever and wheresoever you pleased." The House was clearly sensible, it said, of the "slavish Condition we and our posterity must be reduced to" by establishment of such a power.

About three weeks later, on May 8, 1758, the House proceeded to consider the seven "Resolves prepared to be Entered on the *Journal*." The first was carried by a vote of 30-9, reading as follows:

> Resolved, That no Person is Punishable for obstinately Refusing to appear and serve in Arms for the necessary Defence of this Province, by Virtue of that Clause of the Act for Ordering and Regulating the Militia of this Province, for the better Defence and Security thereof (admitting it were in Force) which vests a Power in the Justices of the Provincial Court to fine and imprison, after a Procedure according to the due

Course of Law, and Conviction of such obstinate Refusal and Disobedience as aforesaid, except upon a Foreign Invasion.

The second resolution was carried by a vote of 31-8. It read as follows:

Resolved, That agreeable to a reasonable Construction of the said Act, there was not a Foreign Invasion of this Province in December last, when his Excellency the Governor, with the Advice of his Council, ordered the Companies of Militia of Queen-Anne's and Kent Counties to march to the Western Frontier, nor was there one when the Companies were ordered out from Calvert and Cecil Counties in March last.

Thirdly, and carried by a vote of 31-7, was this resolution:

Resolved, That the marching the said Militia of Queen-Anne's and Kent Counties, was not only Illegal, but not Necessary for the Security of the Western Frontier of this Province; and however promising the Aspect might be at the Time of issuing the Orders for their March, yet, as in the ordinary Course of the Seasons, Storms and the most severe Weather could not but be then expected, it was Oppressive and Cruel; and the Impressing Provisions for those Companies, in those Counties so far distant from the Frontier, was Inconvenient and unnecessarily Expensive.

Resolution No. 4, carried by a vote of 33-6, read as follows:

Resolved, That upon a Foreign Invasion (supposing there is not any Act of Assembly to Compel them) every loyal Subject in this Province, who is capable (or as many as may be necessary) ought, and it is the Opinion of this House would, take up Arms, with the Approbation and Consent of the Governor or Commander in Chief of the Province for the Time being, for the necessary Defence thereof; but that no Person is Compellable to serve in Arms after such Invasion is suppressed.

Resolution No. 5 passed on a vote of 31-8, as follows:

> Resolved, That the Governor of this Province setting up an Authority under the Act aforesaid, with the Advice of his Council, to march the good People of his Province to the Frontiers thereof, whenever he and they may be apprehensive of a foreign Invasion, is not warranted by the said Act; and that if such a Power should be exercised, the People might be Enslaved, by being Marched as often to, and Compelled to remain as long on, the Frontiers, as the Governor and his Council might think fit, while their helpless Families were perishing at home.

Next, Resolution No. 6, passed by a vote of 32-7, was:

> Resolved, That that Part of his Excellency's Message of the 5th Instant, which is in the following Words, 'Should the Issue of this Session be such as I most earnestly hope it will, I shall immediately Countermand the Orders that have been sent to Captain Brome and to the Captain of a Company of Militia in Cecil County; but if you should unhappily break up again, without making Provision for the Support of any Troops, either to act under the Command of Brigadier Forbes, or to be left on our Frontiers, I apprehend the Gentlemen of the Council will think it absolutely necessary that Two or Three Companies of Militia should immediately, &c.' seems to be calculated to intimidate and influence the Representatives of the People to agree to a Bill for making Provision for his Majesty's Service, and the Defence and Security of this Province, upon a Mode of Taxation unreasonable, unequal, and grievous to his Majesty's faithful Subjects, and which must, in the End, be destructive of their common Interest.

Finally, Resolution No. 7 carried on a vote of 33-6, as follows:

> Resolved, That the said Part of his Excellency's Message, so far as it was intended to serve the Purpose abovementioned, appears to be a Violation of the Liberty and Freedom that ought to be preserved in all the Proceedings and Determinations of this House.

The seven resolutions then were combined into one, preceded by a declaration that

> It is the undoubted Right and indispensable Duty, of the Representatives of the Freemen of this Province in Assembly convened, to enquire into, represent, and remonstrate against, every Measure in the Administration, or Exercise of the Executive Powers of Government, within this Province, which, in their Opinion, may tend to affect the Lives, Liberties, or Properties of the People, in any Manner not clearly warranted by the known Laws or Customs thereof.

The end product was a remarkable and extraordinary set of legislative resolutions. Granted that in some of them there was a reasoning after the fact, and that some were partly repetitive; a more serious question remains whether in sum they were an invitation to civil disobedience and military insubordination. It was to this low estate that relationships had deteriorated between the Governor and the House of Delegates of Maryland.

## Chapter 11

## TOWARD THE FINAL BREAK WITH ENGLAND

### 1757-1764

As the General Assembly moved into the late 1750s and early 1760s, it was less than 20 years before the final break with England, the Proprietary, and the Governor. Some of the issues became repetitive. The actors changed and the provocations varied, but basically there was a sameness in the philosophical arguments. The main contentions continued as for years past; the parties argued over supply bills, tax bills, financial powers, and decorum. The House of Delegates strove for power and security of position; and in the process it opposed adamantly the prerogatives and processes of executive power vested in the Proprietary and the Governor and the shared legislative powers and obvious executive sympathies of the Upper House of the Assembly.

### SUPPLY AND ASSESSMENT BILLS

The perennial issue of supply and assessment bills continued without abatement until the end of the French and Indian War in 1763. The House of Delegates remained wary of expending the men and the capital of Maryland for what it regarded as a frontier war waged by and for England, except when the close interests of Maryland were concerned. It proposed something very like an income tax in order to meet what it considered the necessary expenditures. The King, the Proprietary, and the Governor, joined by the Upper House, took a broader view of the interests of the Province and the way to impose the extra taxes. The supply and assessment issue was a perfect vehicle for the House of Delegates to face together both its executive and its legislative antagonists.

383

The House of Delegates was in a strong position in the late 1750s. It passed a supply bill in 1757 and then defeated four successive attempts, in as many sessions, to pass another; and when the Governor in exasperation dissolved the Assembly and called for a new election, the continued strong anti-Proprietary representation in the new House assured that passage of supply bills would remain difficult.

The new Legislature met in October, 1758. The Governor in his opening address made a particular effort to prod the House, speaking of the "odious distinction" between Maryland and its neighboring colonies with respect to participation in the war effort. The Upper House in its message replying to the Governor noted its sorrow for the "odious distinction," but the House of Delegates would say only there was "no Occasion for the odious Distinction." At this session there was not only a failure to pass the Supply Bill, but no other legislation was enacted, and the Governor prorogued the Assembly before two weeks had passed.

The pattern continued. Eight supply bills failed during successive sessions through April-May, 1761.

The tax proposed by the House of Delegates (whether or not the term was used) was an income tax of from 7½ percent to 10 percent upon earnings from the professions, benefices, public offices, and various occupations; and the House suggested also a tax upon the assessed value of personal and real property. The House bill proposed in addition, much to the discomfiture of the Upper House, that the House of Delegates should have an exclusive power to appoint commissioners to enforce the taxes.

There was another short session, from April 4 to 17, in the spring of 1759. Again, upon the failure of the Supply Bill, the session was prorogued in less than two weeks. It was at this session that as an added exhortation the Governor had a message from William Pitt the Elder, but to no avail. The House passed its bill, but it was quickly returned from the

384

Upper House with this peremptory message: "We this morning upon a single reading sent it down to you with a negative." As he issued the order of prorogation, the Governor wrote to the House that from "the Miscarriages of the Same Bill five times, in as many Successive Sessions, I have not the least Glimmering of hope, however Expressive of Zeal your professions have been, and interesting the Occasion, that you will entertain any Disposition to make amends for your former failures."

The Supply Bill proposed by the House in 1759 was for sixty thousand pounds sterling, but its title showed the presence of a controversial provision that the cost was to be met "by an equal Assessment on all Estates, Real and Personal, and Lucrative Offices and Employments." The bill passed the House on a 24-12 vote. After it was returned from the Upper House so precipitously, the House of Delegates notified the Governor that "we shall not receive any that may be proposed by any other Branch."

In 1760 the House vented its dislike for supply bills upon the administration of one passed some years earlier. The complaint was that the commissioners under the bill had not properly met to rate and ascertain the tax; and that they had wrongly directed the sheriffs, rather than the tax collectors, to collect the tax. In a resolution the House directed that the proceedings of the commissioners were void and of no effect, and that "no Sheriff or Collector hath any Power or Authority to Collect, Levy, Demand or Receive the said additional Land-Tax." [1]

---

1. *Maryland Gazette,* October 9, 1760.

## THE TAX BILL FROM THE HOUSE OF DELEGATES

The Governor tried an innovation for the spring session of 1760. This time he submitted to the Assembly a written opinion from the King's Attorney General, commenting on several phases of the Maryland tax bill of 1759. In a special message to the House of Delegates, the Governor in 1760 called particular attention to the opinion from the Attorney General in England, telling the House that "I think it my Duty to intreat you in Particular Cautiously to avoid at this time the rock on which you have heretofore split."

The long opinion from the King's Attorney General, Charles Pratt, was submitted originally to Lord Baltimore. It was a curious combination of law and politics. Some parts of the bill he treated purely as political questions. The proposed tax on the earnings of sheriffs "my Lord will leave to be Debated by the two Houses." As to the "narrowness" of the exemption of persons to be assessors, "my Lord has nothing to do with this." On the tax on tenants for life, he said, "my Lord will leave this to be settled by the two Houses." As to the tax on "plate and ready money, my Lord has Nothing to do with this."

On some of the other questions, the Attorney General had only cryptic words of advice. On the taxes required from Lord Baltimore's private officers, "Here my Lord ought to interpose; for it is a great indignity to compel his Lordships Agents into a Publick Service without making them a Liberal allowance and Compensation for their Trouble." As to the tax on uncultivated lands, "This seems to me a very unreasonable Tax, and ought to be resisted by the Proprietary because it seems principally to be at his Estates." Finally, as to the proposed tax to be imposed on the Governor, "This is rather an uncivil than an unjust Tax and therefore the Upper House would do well to Oppose it in so far as they may in reason."

386

In three areas, however, the Attorney General's opinion had provisions of some substance. The first concerned the proposal by the House of Delegates that it have the exclusive right to nominate commissioners for the enforcement of the new tax laws:

> In my Opinion the Sole Nomination of these Commissioners, who are new officers Appointed by this Bill belongs neither to the Proprietary nor to the Lower House Stricto Jure; but like all other new regulations must be Assented to by both, but can be claimed by neither, the Proprietarys Charter intitles him to nominate all Constitutional Officers, and all others which by the Laws are not otherwise provided for but I do not Conceive my Lord has any Original Right to nominate new Officers Appointed for the Execution of a new Law without the Consent of the two Houses; nor on the other hand have the Lower House any such independent Authority; and therefore I think the Upper House are right notwithstanding this claim in which they ought to be Supported by the proprietary, because it is unreasonable for one Branch of the Legeslature to Assume a Power of Taxing the Other by Officers of their Single Appointment

Secondly, the ruling covered the general power of the Upper House to examine claims and accounts, and spoke to the claim of the House of Delegates to have powers similar to those of the House of Commons in England:

> The Upper House are right in making a stand to this Clause in the Bill and should take care how they Admit Encroachments of this kind where they are Supported by Arguments drawn from the Exercise of Like rights in the House of Commons here: The Constitution of the two Assemblies differ ffundamentally in many respects. Our House of Commons stands upon its own Laws, The Lex Parliamenti, Whereas assemblies in the Colonies are regulated by their respective Charters, Usages and the Common Law of England, and will never be Allowed to Assume all those Priviledges which the House of

Commons are intitled to Justly here upon Principals that neither can nor must be applied to the Assemblies of the Colonies

Finally, the King's Attorney General added another general word of advice about the claims of the House of Delegates in Maryland to be comparable to the House of Commons in England:

> Having given my sense upon each of the Objections so far as they have been Taken up and maintained by the Upper House in the Margin of that part of the Case, I shall only add here a General peice of Advice to Lord Baltimore; that in this Disposition of the Lower House to Assume to themselves any priviledge which the English House of Commons enjoy here his Lordship should resist all such Attempts where they are unreasonable with firmness and should never Allow any Encroachment to be Established upon the weight of that argument singly; for I am satisfied neither the Crown nor the parliament will ever suffer these Assemblies to erect themselves into the power and authority of the British House of Commons

The House of Delegates found all this something less than impressive. Speaking to the plea of the Governor to avoid "the rock on which you have heretofore split," the House on March 25, 1760, said to him in a special message that "We have observed your Excellency's pathetic and particular Admonition" about the Supply Bill. As for the opinion from the King's Attorney General, the House "presumed" it was given only as private counsel to the Lord Proprietary, and "being desirous to pay it all due Regard, we cannot but wish that Opinion had been accompanied with the State of the Case upon which it was founded. . . ."

## OTHER EFFORTS FOR A SUPPLY BILL

The Upper House for its part was unimpressed with the Supply Bill sent to it by the House of Delegates at the spring session of 1760. The bill appears to be "defective," it said, and recommended to the consideration of the House "a Tax long experienced in this Province and more equal and less grevious to the People than a Land Tax...." Not surprisingly, the Supply Bill failed once more, and the session was quickly prorogued.

The Assembly met again in April and May of 1761, but once more there was no Supply Bill. This was the sixth session of the legislators elected in September, 1758. When he prorogued the Legislature on May 6, 1761, the Governor set a return date for October 3 of the same year. Before that time, however, and upset with "the obstinate behavior" of the House, the Governor called for a new election; it was held during the months of October and November. The first session of the new Assembly was held in March and April, 1762.

The new House of Delegates was not materially different from the one dissolved in 1761. Many of the prominent anti-Proprietary delegates were back, and they continued to control proceedings. A compilation in the *Maryland Gazette* showed that 43 of the 58 members in the House had prior legislative experience (most of them having been in the Assembly immediately preceding).

The House in 1762 passed and sent on to the Upper House the same supply bill as in past years, and it was as obnoxious to the Upper House as the others. Perhaps as some small inducement to persuade the Upper House to accept the bill, the House of Delegates said it would be "willing to depart from a Strict parliamentary course, and for the present to waive our Right respecting the Mode of proceeding upon Money Bills." The simple meaning of this obscure language was that for the moment the House would at least consider amendments proposed in the Upper House. This offer was preceded by an elaborate rationalization, that in a bill "of Such a Length, and of an Intricate a nature some parts may possibly be found liable to Objections, which may have escaped us."

The Upper House had never conceded that its powers were so limited with respect to money bills, and it did not succumb to the disingenuous approach of the House of Delegates. Repeating a favorite phrase of the times, the Upper House wrote that "We cannot but lament . . . you have offered Us such a bill as you must have been satisfied this House would never agree to . . . ." At the end of the short session in 1762, for the information of the Governor, the Upper House wrote a six-page exposition of the history of the several supply bills. The current version, it said, "was framed on the same vicious Plan" as the one which the King's Attorney General had said several years earlier "ought not to have been passed into a Law."

In addition, wrote the Upper House, if no supply bill is passed, "it will be intirely owing to the perseverance of that House in Measures which nothing but a Determined Resolution to Evade a Compliance with his Majesty's Requisitions or to deprive this House of their Constitutional Rights and Share in the Legislature of this Province could have induced them pertinaciously to adhere to."

Toward the end of this March-April session in 1762, the two houses again exchanged long and futile messages on the supply and assessment bill. "We are confident," said the Upper House, "it would not have been irregular or contrary to the established Mode of Proceeding for this House to have proposed amendments to the Bill you were pleased to send us." But, answered the House, "we cannot but express our Sorrow, that an occasional waiver of our Rights in respect to the Mode of Proceeding on Money Bills, intended more speedily to bring about a Termination of the differences that have unhappily subsisted between your Honours and the late Lower Houses on that Matter, instead of having the good Effect desired by us, should serve only to put your Honours upon assuming a Right, not only of proposing, but also of preparing and sending down Money Bills, for the Concurrence of this House . . . A Right which the House of Lords in our Mother Country, independent as they are, have rarely, if ever, asserted to be in them, or attempted to exercise. . . ." This assumption, concluded the House, "deprives us of all Hopes" for an agreement on the bill. Also, "if his Majesty's Requisitions, which have occasioned our Meeting, are not complied with, let those answer for it, who will not consent to raising the necessary Supplies, when the most suitable Means for doing it, are offered them."

This latter message, rejoined the Upper House, "is of so Extraordinary a Nature both in Language and Sentiment, and so unbecoming the Representative of the People of Maryland . . . that but for the Salutary Motive of Obviating those groundless pretentions we most certainly should not have paid the Least regard to it." Concluding, the Upper House threw in this clencher: "We cannot for one Hour trust you with the powers you would by this Bill acquire over the People."

The Supply Bill before the House during the March-April session of 1762 contained, as for years before, the equivalent of a modern income tax. As the principle was expressed that year, it was to levy "a Yearly Tax on Lawyers, Physicians, hired clerks acting without Commission, Factors, Agents, or Managers, Trading or using Commerce within this Province, as such. . . ." They would have been required to pay for each of the following three years a tax of "Eight pence for every Twenty Shillings of the clear annual Amount of their Profit."

## FINANCIAL POWERS OF THE HOUSE OF DELEGATES

Despite the offer of the House in 1762, temporarily "to depart from a Strict parliamentary course" and to permit the Upper House to propose amendments to the Supply Bill, the House of Delegates was moving otherwise to tighten its powers and prerogatives over money bills in general. It received a message from the Upper House on May 6, 1761, from the Committee to Examine the Journal of Accounts, that the Committee could not proceed with its work "without having the same Publick Accounts laid before them which were laid before the Committee of Accounts of the lower House." The House in reply, through the Clerk of its Committee of Accounts, said that "he was not permitted to deliver the Papers." The Upper House then unanimously resolved that "for the future no Accounts be allowed by this House" unless it had the same accounts and copies as the House of Delegates. For emphasis, and to put everyone on notice, the Upper House ordered the public printer, Jonas Green, to publish its resolution in "his Six Succeeding Gazettes."

On another matter likewise involving the public funds, the House of Delegates continued its unimpressive efforts to reduce the daily allowance to members of the Assembly. A bill for this purpose was considered during the November-December session of 1758, but postponed to the following session. Then, at the April session in 1759, a bill passed its second reading in the House by a vote of 18-17. Several preliminary votes were taken in working out the details of the bill. Eighteen delegates voted for establishing the allowance at 80 pounds of tobacco daily, while 17 delegates voted it should be "less." Twenty delegates voted it should be "more" than 40 pounds of tobacco daily, and 16 delegates voted for a figure of 40 pounds. After these monumental but unconvincing decisions, the bill was recommitted "for Amendments."

392

In the realm of finances, also, the House continued its decades-long effort to secure the proceeds of the license fees on ordinaries for the public expenses of the Province. This controversy stemmed from the year 1715, and it is recounted in many pages of the *Journals.* In that year, when the Calverts were restored as Proprietors, they laid claim to the license fees for their own use; and with minor exceptions they retained the fees over the years. The several exceptions came during the years from 1740 to 1760, when public opinion on a number of occasions led the Calverts to pledge these monies to the sinking funds used to support supply bills during the successive military campaigns. Even while temporarily acquiescing in a diversion of the license fee revenues, the Lords Baltimore continued to assert their right to them.

In the 1761 session the House passed a bill to use the license fees for the support of a college in Annapolis, but the bill did not pass the Upper House. In 1762 the House considered but did not approve a proposal to dedicate the license fees for the Supply Bill. In 1763 the House again proposed to use the funds for support of a college in Annapolis; and that failing, to use them for defending the frontiers against Indian attacks. All these bills failed to be enacted; and it was not until 1766 that the Proprietary finally gave up his claim for the license fees from ordinaries.

A final financial episode of these years involved principally Henry Darnall, Naval Officer of the Patuxent District; and this one had overtones of executive prerogative and the separation of powers. The House of Delegates on a number of occasions during the 1750s had urged the Governor to file suit on the surety bonds of public officials suspected of embezzling public funds.[2] In 1758 this effort concentrated

---

2. As early as 1755, the House had urged Darnall's removal, but at the time this was felt by some to be a reaction against his Catholic sympathies. After that time he had "conformed," and by the late 1750s he was nominally at least a member of the Established Church.

upon Darnall. On April 19 of that year, without naming the suspect other than as a "naval officer," the House in a long message to the Governor suggested Darnall's bond be put into suit. The House added a general word of complaint to the Governor, that "we cannot dismiss this Subject without lamenting to your Excellency, that want of Confidence, undeserved we think on our Part, with which you seem, of late, to entertain every Remonstrance of the Representatives of the People, however just and well founded. . . ."

It finally was established that Darnall had embezzled some two thousand pounds; the discovery was made by a joint legislative committee to examine the accounts of the Loan Office.

There was an unusual sequel to the Darnall incident. At one point during the exchange of messages between the Governor and the House in 1761, the Governor requested that the House publish in its *Journal* copies of all the materials and messages the Governor had sent to the House concerning Darnall. The House refused, or at least failed to comply. Thereupon, the Governor and the Council, acting together, ordered Jonas Green, the printer to the Province, to print these materials separately and distribute them with another publication, the *Votes and Proceedings of the Lower House.*

## DIGNITY AND DECORUM

Along with its concerns about supply bills, powers of the executive branch, separation of powers, and lessening the prerogatives of the Upper House, the House of Delegates continued its regard for the dignity and decorum of the House and for preserving public respect for it and its members.

One disciplinary action in 1758 was purely in-house in its origin, and after receiving a proper explanation, the House "waved" any further proceedings:

> On Motion, the Question was put, Whether Mr. Edmund Key, in Debate Yesterday, on Appointment of a Committee for Draught of a Supply Bill for his Majesty's Service, made Use of the Word Indolent reflecting on some Gentlemen appointed by the House to that Duty, or Not? Resolved in the Affirmative.
>
> Mr. Key being called upon to explain himself with Relation to the Word reflecting on the Gentlemen appointed, confessed that the Word dropped from him thro' Inadvertency, without any Design to reflect upon the House, or any Member thereof. Which Submission the House consented to accept, and waved all further Proceeding thereon.

This slight offense settled, the House was faced with the Wilson-Hammond affair. Unaccountably, it was much more serious, and it continued for a longer time than its facts warranted. It arose from what legislators of later generations would conceive to be no more than normal banter among members, but from the time the incident occurred in December, 1758, it was a major incident.

Hammond was a former Speaker of the House, and an aggressive member of the popular or country party. Wilson was a delegate from Somerset County, and a member of the Proprietary party. This situation, of course, was the key to the affair; in the main, it was punishment meted out to a member of the Proprietary group by the dominant popular party.

It all started during the House session on the afternoon of Saturday, December 9, 1758:

> On Motion,Ordered, That the following Discourse and Words be entered on the Journal, viz. It being related by a Member, That whilst the Supply Bill was Reading this Morning, Mr. Speaker ordered the Serjeant to desire the Gentlemen in the Porch to walk in, and Mr. Wilson, one

of the Members then in the Porch, desired the Serjeant to give his Service (or Compliments) to Mr. Speaker, and tell him, That I am Tired with hearing so much Nonsense.

On Motion, Ordered, That the Consideration of the Words spoken by Mr. Wilson be Referred till Tuesday next.

On Motion, Ordered, That the following Discourse and Words be entered on the Journal, viz. It being related by a Member to the House, That on the first Reading of the Supply Bill, Mr. Speaker asked the Patience of the House a few Minutes and left the Chair, upon which Mr. Wilson, one of the Members of this House, entered into a bantering Conversation with Mr. Sulivane, another Member, about taking the Chair; at the Close of which, he turned towards Mr. Hammond, a Member of this House, and said, Here's Mr. Hammond had the Chair once, and Forfeited it; upon which Mr. Hammond said to Mr. Wilson, Forfeited it! how? which Expression he repeated; to which Mr. Wilson replied smilingly, I suppose you don't want me to explain myself.

There were two conceivable incidents in this account. One was between Delegate Wilson and the Speaker, no more serious than that he (Wilson) was tired of the Speaker's "nonsense." The other was evidently more serious, though never fully explained; it was an implication that there was some questionable or reprehensible conduct connected with the time Hammond was Speaker, although pertaining to a private matter.

The first incident was settled quickly enough. Three days after it occurred, on December 12, Delegate Wilson was called to explain. He "addressed himself to Mr. Speaker, and confessed that he had no Intention to Reflect upon Mr. Speaker, or any Member of the House, by those Words." Wilson then was ordered to withdraw, after which "the Question was put, That Mr. Wilson be admonished by the Speaker, to be for the future more guarded and circumspect in his Expressions and Conduct relative to the Orders from

the Chair, and the Proceedings of the House." This was
resolved in the affirmative, by a vote of 25-22. Wilson then
was called in: "Mr. Speaker acquainted Mr. Wilson, That the
House accepted his Submission, and admonished him
according to the Resolution of the House."

Later the same day, Delegate Wilson was called upon
again, to explain his remarks or implication concerning
Delegate Hammond. "The Question was put, That Mr.
Wilson be allowed to justify the Words he had spoken of Mr.
Hammond, a Member of this House, by relating a private
Transaction between the said Hammond and another Person,
in Relation to their private Affairs." This was resolved in the
negative, by a vote of 15-30. It meant, of course, that Wilson
was not to be afforded an opportunity to explain his remark.

After a short adjournment of the House, "till Half an Hour
past Two of the Clock," Wilson was ordered to withdraw. A
question then was put to the House which seemed only an
elaboration of the first question: "Whether this House will
suffer any of its Members to mention the State of the Case,
in considering of the Words, viz. (Here's Mr. Hammond had
the Chair once, and forfeited it), spoke by Mr. Wilson, against
Mr. Hammond, to make good the Truth thereof, or Not?"
This was resolved in the negative, 11-34.

Later the same afternoon, as to the words spoken by
Wilson, the House put the question "That Mr. Wilson ask the
Pardon of the House, and that of Mr. Hammond, the Member
they Particularly Reflected on." The House divided 23-23 on
this question, and the Speaker voted in the affirmative to
break the tie. Delegate Wilson then was called in to be told
of the decision. He refused to apologize to Hammond; the
House persisted in its order; and Wilson was committed to
the custody of the Sergeant-at-Arms. This part of the episode
was accompanied by some frank and colorful language:

> Mr. Wilson was called in; and on his Appearance Mr.
> Speaker acquainted him with the Resolution of the
> House.

Upon which Mr. Wilson addressed himself to Mr. Speaker, and said, That he would readily ask the Pardon of the House; but that Mr. Hammond was a Person of so very infamous a Character, and guilty of so many Vices, that he could not suffer his Lips to belie his Heart, and therefore hoped the House would excuse him from asking his Pardon; which Words were ordered to be taken down by the Clerk.

Mr. Wilson was ordered to withdraw; which he accordingly did.

Ordered, That Mr. Wilson be again called in; who being asked by Mr. Speaker, if he would comply with the Resolve of the House, he desired the Indulgence of the House, with Time to consider upon the Matter, and to have a Copy of the Resolution of the House thereon; which was accordingly given him, and the Time he prayed for granted.

Mr. Wilson was again called in, and was asked by Mr. Speaker, if he would comply with the Resolution of the House, with which he had before been acquainted; who replied, he had Reflected upon what he had before acquainted Mr. Speaker be determined to submit to, and that he could not recede therefrom.

Mr. Wilson desired the Indulgence of the House to retire; and that he would return again in a few Minutes.

The House gave him Leave to retire.

Mr. Wilson again appeared, and delivered the following Words in Writing, viz.[t]
Mr. Speaker,

I am obliged to you for informing me of the Determination of the House upon this Occasion, and am sorry that any Expression of mine should give either Trouble or Offence to the House. I observe, that Part of the Censure is, that I should ask the Pardon of the House, with which I could readily comply; but as to asking the Pardon of Mr. Hammond, I look upon him to be a Person of so very infamous a Character, and charged with so many Vices, that I cannot suffer my Lips to belie my Heart, and therefore hope the House will excuse me from asking his Pardon.

Mr. Wilson was ordered to withdraw.

Thereupon it was moved, That the Resolution of the House be enforced; and the Question was put, That Mr. Wilson be committed to the Custody of the Serjeant at Arms attending this House, and to remain in his Custody until he comply with the Order of the House. Resolved in the Affirmative.

Ordered, That Mr. Wilson be again called; who appeared.

Ordered, That Mr. Wilson be committed to the Custody of the Serjeant at Arms attending this House; who accordingly was committed to the custody of the Serjeant at Arms, to remain in Custody until he complies with the Order of the House.

This last part of the Wilson-Hammond affair occurred on December 12, 1758. Wilson continued to refuse an apology to Hammond. He remained in the custody of the Sergeant-at-Arms (although there are no details as to how onerous were the terms of his custody). The matter was brought up again six days later, on December 18, with a motion to remit that part of the censure concerning Hammond; the motion failed by a 12-30 vote. The session ended after another five days, on December 23. The "custody" evidently ended at that time; the House had no jurisdiction over its members when it was not in session.

In a little more than three months, however, the General Assembly was in session again, and once more the Wilson-Hammond affair was before the House. The new session extended from April 4 to April 17, 1759, and the House waited until April 16, the day before the session was prorogued, before it took any official action. On that day a question was put to the House whether it would admit Wilson "to make his Submission." By a vote of 16-19 the question was determined in the negative. Immediately after, another question was put to the House:

On Motion, the Question was put, That the following Question be put, viz. That this House do Resolve, That it is beneath the Dignity of this House to call upon any

399

Member, committed for a Breach of an Order of the House, to comply with the Order, till he had previously signified his Inclination to the House to comply with and obey the same; and that Mr. Samuel Wilson had not signified to the House his Inclination to comply with their Order, before or at the Time of putting the aforegoing Question. Resolved in the Affirmative.

This latter motion was carried by a vote of 20-15. The House then incorporated the gist of the motion into a resolution to be entered on its *Journal.* Perhaps the House was trying only to emphasize its action against Wilson, but it here put itself into the anomalous position of terming it "beneath the Dignity of the House" to call upon a member to comply with an order of the House unless previously the member had said he would do so. Whatever the fine-drawn logic of its position on the question of compliance with an order, the House proceeded next to add fresh confusion to the whole situation. It put the question "That as this House will not admit of the Submission of Mr. Samuel Wilson, that he be Expelled this House, that the Country may have the Benefit of being Represented by a due Number of Members." This question was determined in the negative, by a vote of 15-20; and exactly the same members who respectively had voted for and against the earlier motion about compliance with the order now voted against and for the motion for expulsion. The riddle of all this left Wilson in limbo: he could not take his seat in the House, but he also was not expelled. Fortunately for him and his uncertain status, the session was prorogued on the following day.

The House in 1761 engaged in a curious bit of parliamentary maneuvering following the death of King George II and the accession of George III. The Governor had proposed that he, the Upper House, and the House of Delegates join in an address of condolence for the passing of George II and an expression of welcome for the new King, George III. Such an address was formulated to the satisfaction of the Governor and the Upper House, but the House wanted to add an amendment on what the others felt was an extraneous matter. The House sought to add to the combined address of condolence and congratulation a request of the new King that he help in what long had been a pet project of the House, to provide for an agent in England to represent the Assembly and the Province. Specifically, the House proposed to amend the address by inserting a proposal that "the People shall be permitted to raise a Support for an Agent, who may lay all the Grievances which they suffer under the Government of their Lord Proprietary properly before your Majesty. . . ." The Governor and the Upper House, of course, would not join in a statement that the Province was suffering grievances under the administration of Lord Baltimore, so they refused to join with the House in any such address. The sequel was a decision that two addresses be sent from Maryland, one by the Governor and Upper House and the other by the Lower House.

In explaining its refusal to join in the House amendment trying to secure an agent in London, the Upper House wrote to the Governor that the proposed amendment was "extremely improper and foreign to the subject of the Address," and that it was "apparently intended to cast an injurious Blemish upon his Lordships Government, and Shift from the real Authors of it, the Disgrace which has been brought upon this Province by the Singular Disregard Shewn to the Requisitions of Aid frequently urged in the most pathetick manner by the Kings Ministers, and the Strongest terms recommended by your Excellency."

Before sending its Address to King George III, in 1761, the House asked the Governor to affix the Provincial seal to it. Governor Sharpe refused, thinking that procedure improper under the circumstances. There is some uncertainty whether the Address from the House actually was sent to London in 1761. Perhaps it was for this reason the House had another address prepared during the March-April session in the following year, 1762. That proved to be a rather extensive address. There was the matter of condolences for the departed King and also the other matter of the accession of the new King. In addition, George III had been married recently, so there was a need to congratulate him for his marriage to an "illustrious Protestant princess." To the latter was appended, in the earthy frankness of the times, a hope for the "Prospect that our Posterity will be subjects to your Royal Offspring." However, the matter of the agent in London was dropped from the House address of 1762. The House address was not to be presented to the King through Lord Baltimore as an intermediary; instead, it was to be transmitted "to Mr. Benjamin Franklin in London to be by him presented to His Majesty."

There was a contest of mild proportions between the Upper House and the House of Delegates during the October-November session of 1763. The House passed a bill to establish a college in the Province and sent it on to the Upper House. Three weeks later (having no word about the bill during that time) the House inquired about the "delay" in the Upper House. During the inevitable exchange of messages the House observed that the bill was not complicated; which, in its return message, the Upper House translated into a House claim that the bill was "plain, simple, and perfect." The House protested it had not anywhere expressed such an opinion. However, thus provoked, the House did admit that "plain and Simple it does appear to us, but we have not alledg'd to be perfect. . . ." Also, continued the House in general complaint about the reaction of the Upper House:

> These are disingenuous Arts, inconsistent with the dignity which Should be maintained in a Parliamentary Intercourse between the Several Branches of the Legislature. If the only Reason of your keeping the bill is, that you might have an Opportunity of Considering

it. We think that end might have been as well an answer by sending it down to us, first Ordering your Clerk to keep a Copy of it for your Selves, but since you seem to be of a different Opinion We . . . must take care for the future not to Subject ourselves to a like Inconvenience. . . .

The Upper House, of course, would not allow the subject to be dropped with the House having the final word. It sent off another long and more or less patient reply:

We did not mean to give you any Offence by the Message You have been pleased to chuse for the Subject of your Animadversions, nor can we, on the Strictest Review, discover in it any Provocation for all that Asperity of Language, and Acrimony of Resentment of which it seems to have been the unfortunate Occasion

The Practice of retaining Bills sent to this House is founded upon Numerous Precedents, as those were upon Reason when a Measure is proposed, are we to be compelled at all Events either to give an Assent, or Dissent to it, when we have not Sufficient time to deliberate and determine upon the Propriety or Impropriety of it. . . .

But the Bill, it seems, is in your Opinion as Simple and plain, as the Object of it, is usefull and necessary, although it should appear by your Votes and Proceedings that a very great Majority, or even every Member of your House may be of that Opinion, must it therefore be a matter of such absolute Certainty as to exclude all possibility of any real Diversity of Sentiment among other People if not, why should our Hesitation provoke so great resentment? you are pleased to observe that you did not in your Message of the 22nd Instant desire us to come to any Determination upon the Bill, but that it might be returned to you with such Propositions for amendments as we might think Expedient, But surely, if you will stop One Moment to Consider, You can't fail to discover that we could not make any Propositions for Amendments till we had first determined, what was Proper to be rejected, and what fit to be adopted, or in other words, till we could come to a

full and comprehensive Determination upon the Plan of
the Bill & every part of the execution of it. . . .

## HOUSE RULES AND PROCEDURES

Along with its contentions and disputes with the Governor,
the Upper House, and Lord Baltimore, the House of
Delegates continued its regular activities in policing and
controlling its own members and in changing and improving
its procedures.

During the March-April session of 1762 there appeared,
seemingly for the first time, the time-honored introductory
phrase on a bill, "A Bill, entitled an Act. . . ." The general
introductory language earlier had been "An Act entitled," or
simply "An Act for. . . ." Occasionally, and in 1762 this was
of recent origin, one finds "An Act entitled an Act." The new
phrase could become a bit complicated when the purpose of
the bill was to amend an earlier act, as "A Bill, entituled, An
Act continuing an Act, entituled, An Act for destroying
Wolves in Frederick County. . . ."

The Assembly continued in the 1760s its long-time practice
in making most laws effective for only three years; a regular
ritual during each session was to inquire what laws were due
to expire within the near future.

The rules adopted by the House for each session during
this time were essentially the same as for many years, and
frequently the adoption of rules was accompanied by the
long set of resolutions first adopted in 1722, affirming that
the residents of Maryland were not a "conquered" country,
but that they enjoyed the rights and privileges of
Englishmen everywhere, including the benefits of the
English statutory and common law.

The matter of the English statutes, and the extent of their
applicability in Maryland, continued in the discussions of the
1760s. The usual insistence of the House of Delegates was
that both the statutory and the common law of England

applied in this Province, but only to the extent they had not been modified here. This convenient philosophy could be confusing to the average citizen,[3] and not all of the learned authorities agreed with it fully. One such instance occurred in 1763. The Assembly was considering an inspection act, containing, among other things, a provision relating to the regulation of coins. This, declared Governor Sharpe in a special message, was inconsistent with an English statute, and he was bound to comply with that law. "I am by the Kings Instruction," he wrote,

> required to pay Strict Obedience to the Statute, which was made in the Sixth year of the Reign of Queen Anne for Ascertaining the Rates of foreign Coins in these Plantations, & that as I find by several Cautions which have been given me Since I assented to a Continuance of the Inspection Law, that the Clause inserted therein relative to the Regulation of Coin hath been deemed at home repugnant to the above mentioned Act of Parliament, & that was I to Assent hereafter to any Act rating the Coins Specified in that Statute higher than they are thereby rated I Should run the greatest Risk of incurring both his Majestys & the Lord Proprietary's Displeasure

A slight change in the House rules was made by resolution early in the 1760s; and perhaps because it was not actually incorporated into the rules, it was not observed in the daily procedure. It occurred on October 15, 1763, providing "On Motion of Colonel Tilghman Resolved that for the future the

---

3. Such a result was reported in the *Maryland Gazette* on September 18, 1751: "On Thursday last, came on the trial of Thomas Bevan, for attempting to rob the House of Mr. Coke, on the 2d of July last; at first he pleaded, Not Guilty, but when his Comrade came to be Sworn, he objected to him, as being unqualified by the Laws of England, to give Evidence; but when he was told, that there was an Act of Assembly of this Province, which made one Convict's Oath good against another, he ask'd for Pardon of the Court for giving them so much Trouble, and pleaded Guilty."

name of every Gentleman who may make a Motion in the house be incerted in the Entry that may be made in consequence thereof." Such a resolution had been adopted on a number of prior occasions, but for some unaccountable reason it was never observed.

The House had before it a number of questions concerning the election of its members. Two of them involved the writs of election issued by the county sheriffs, supposedly in conformance with a directive from the General Assembly, but occasionally defective in one respect or another. The House Committee on Elections and Privileges submitted a report on one of these defects in 1762; it involved a variation of the troublesome "shall" and "may," so confusing to later generations of bill-drafters:

> Your Committee beg Leave to observe, that they find in the Form of the Writ of Election, directed by the Act of Assembly, the following Sentence: 'And during the Courts sitting, the said Freemen are required to appear, or the major Part of such of them as shall then appear, shall and may, and are hereby authorized, &c.' and that the Writ of Election for Charles County does vary from the said Form, by the Words shall and may being left out in the said Paragraph of the said Writ. And that in the Writ of Election for Frederick County, the Words affixed to these Presents, expressed in the latter Part of the Form of the Writ directed by the Act of Assembly of this Province, is also omitted. Both which Variances we take to be Omissions of the Clerk in making out the said Writs.
>
> All which is humbly submitted to the Consideration of your Honourable House.
>
> Signed p Order, Richard Tilghman, junior, Clerk.

The unfortunate Dr. George Steuart, of Annapolis, continued his sorry record of being expelled from the House of Delegates, allegedly because of irregularities in his election. His greatest sin probably was his active record in support of the Proprietary party in the House. Regularly he would be expelled (one commentator said by methods "fair or foul") and just as regularly the City of Annapolis would return him to office. During the October-November session in 1758, the House devoted most of its time to attempts to unseat him. The efforts failed; but there is suspicion that when the Governor rather hurriedly prorogued the session, it was because of the attempt in the House to invalidate the votes for Dr. Steuart, which came from the Aldermen in Annapolis.

All this was to no avail. At a later session in 1758, the House directed the Mayor, Recorder, and Aldermen of the City of Annapolis to elect a delegate to serve "in the Room of Dr. George Steuart, who is dismissed from any further Attendance of this House." Following what was becoming almost a custom,[4] Delegate Steuart was back for the session in April, 1759, only to encounter another challenge.

The session in 1758, which was prorogued in order to block a move to expel Delegate Steuart, had an instance of an expulsion because of holding two offices. Delegate Benjamin Handy of Worcester County had accepted the office of sheriff, and he was dropped from the House of Delegates.

The Clerk of the House during these years was Michael Macnemara; his father, Thomas, had been Clerk for years during the earlier part of the century. Michael, after 1760, spent two years in England, but he returned and again became Clerk for the October-November session in 1763.

---

4. The voters in the counties frequently reelected delegates who for one reason or another had been expelled by the House. The *Maryland Gazette* reported such an instance in 1757. On October 13 there was a note that Edmund Key, a member from St. Mary's County, "had Treated several of the Electors, between the Date of the Writ and the Day of Election, the House was pleased to dismiss Mr. Key. . . ." On November 10 the *Gazette* recorded that there had been an election in Mary's County to fill the vacancy, and that "Mr. EDMUND KEY was Re-chosen by a very great Majority."

Governor Sharpe grudgingly consented to his reinstatement. He was an active partisan of the anti-Proprietary members (which likely explains his holding the Clerk's position for so long); in the estimation of the Governor he was "a most turbulent spirit."

## JONAS GREEN, PRINTER

The Assembly during the early 1760s was able to improve and regularize the printing and publication of the laws, journals, and other legislative materials in the Province. One aspect of the improvement concerned the work of Jonas Green, who served as the "official" printer; and the other development involved extended discussion leading to the publication of Bacon's *Laws,* a milestone in legislative publication and codification in Maryland.

Jonas Green had been the legislative printer for many years, beginning in 1738.[5] Many acts had been passed for his "encouragement" as printer, some of which probably were unfair to him with respect to remuneration. In any event, payments more or less promised to him sometimes were not made, so that Green's compensation was irregular and insufficient. In 1762 he finally presented a petition to the Assembly, detailing his plight. The House appointed a special committee to review his work and needs. The committee report reviewed the entire period of his work, with this summary for the past ten years:

> That in October 1753, a new Act passed, to continue till the 20th of December, 1755, giving the like Allowance to the said Jonas Green, subject to the like Abatement when no Session, as the Act of 1749, and laying a further Duty on him to Print the Inspection Law, passed that

---

5. For an account of the printing and community activities of Jonas Green and his family, *see* LAWRENCE C. WROTH, A HISTORY OF PRINTING IN COLONIAL MARYLAND, *1686-1776* at 75-94 (Baltimore, 1922).

Session, for the Vestries and Inspectors, without giving any further Reward for that new Duty: That in February 1756, an Act passed to continue till the 20th of December, 1757, apportioning the said Jonas Green's Allowance by the Number of Taxables in the respective Counties, which was continued in September 1757, to the 20th of December, 1758, and which expired on that Day, tho' the Session, begun in November 1758, ended but a few Days before the Expiration of that Law: That in March 1760, an Act passed, to continue to the 2d Day of April, 1761, giving the like Allowance, and under the like Conditions, as the last mentioned Act, and also impowering the Justices of the respective Counties to levy in the Whole, £210 for his Salary in 1759, there not having been any Session in that Year.

That the said last mentioned Act expired the 2d of April, 1761; since which there has not been any Session, and there hath been no Salary or Allowance to the said Jonas Green for the Year 1761. That the said Jonas Green hath at several Times Printed long Bills, Records and Papers, inserted in the Journals and Proceedings of the Lower House of Assembly, too numerous to particularize, for which he has not received, as your Committee can find, any Reward, more than his yearly Allowance, tho' the Votes and Proceedings have been swelled to a great Size, by the Insertion of such Bills and other Matters.

That since the Duties of Printing the Laws, and Votes and Proceedings, have been Blended, including May Session, 1747, and excluding the present Session, there have been Twenty-two Sessions, and Six Conventions of the Assembly, so that there have been Thirteen Meetings of the Assembly in and since 1747, more than at the Rate of one for each Year.

It was small wonder that Jonas Green needed "encouragement." A new act, in 1762, attempted to correct the problems. Some of his unpaid arrearages were paid off, and a schedule of payments from the several counties was included. The payments were for copies of the laws delivered to the counties. The act also repeated some of the

409

requirements upon him, such as living in Annapolis, printing with marginal notes, and details of binding. Even with the new bill, he discovered that insufficient time had been allotted for completing his work after a session; and another act in 1763 extended that period. Green's printing and publishing work extended also, privately, to the *Maryland Gazette.*[6]

## BACON'S LAWS

The publication of Bacon's *Laws* was a long and arduous process. Discussion began in 1753, and the publication finally was available in 1766. An advertisement in the *Maryland Gazette* (August 21, 1766) spoke of the publication as a "masterly performance."

At the November-December session in 1758, the Reverend Thomas Bacon submitted to a committee of the House of Delegates a proposal for printing the laws.[7] It was reported to the House, together with a recommendation of the committee for the content and effect of the new volume:

> Mr. Bacon proposed to the Committee, to deliver the said Eighteen Bodies of Laws, for the Use of the Public, for £. 300 Currency.
> The Price of each Copy to Subscribers advancing one Half as usual in such Cases to be Forty Shillings Currency.
> Upon Consideration of which Proposals, and the whole Matter referred to them by the Honourable House, your

---

6. Jonas Green has been described as a "civic leader, church officer, and poet, punchmaker, and punster to the popular Tuesday Club of local gentlemen." David C. Skaggs, *Editorial Policies of the Maryland Gazette, 1765-1783,* 59 MARYLAND HISTORICAL MAGAZINE 341-49 (1964).

7. For a general account of Bacon and his work, *see* LAWRENCE C. WROTH, A HISTORY OF PRINTING IN COLONIAL MARYLAND, 1686-1776 at 95-110 (Baltimore, 1922).

Committee humbly Report it as their Opinion, that the Publication of a Body of Laws of this Province, in the Manner proposed by the Petitioner, would be of great and general Utility.

That three Gentlemen be nominated and appointed by Law (of whom any two, with the Assistance of the Petitioner, and all his Abstracts and Papers relative to the Matter, to act), to inspect carefully all the Records of the Laws of this Province, and to consider what are in Force, or proper to be inserted, or any Way to be taken Notice of in the said Body.

That the Petitioner's Proposals to deliver Eighteen Copies of the said Body, for £300 Currency, is, in the Opinion of your Committee, reasonable, provided they be delivered within 18 Months from the Time the Original may receive the Approbation of the Gentlemen to be nominated as aforesaid.

That the Price to Subscribers wou'd be better ascertained when the Work is compleated, as the Number of Sheets it may contain can at present be only guessed at.

Your Committee humbly crave Leave further to Report it as their Opinion, That there be a Clause in any Bill which the Honourable House may think proper to have fram'd, for the carrying on and compleating the aforesaid Design, declaring, that all Laws heretofore made, and more especially such, the Force or Existence whereof have been any Ways questioned or disputed, shall remain, continue, and be in the same State and Condition, to all intents, Constructions, and Purposes whatsoever, as if the said Body had not been collected, compiled and published; and that no Law whatever, or any Part thereof, shall be repealed, abrogated, or made null or void, or receive any additional Force or Strength, thereby.[8]

---

8. Note this final recommendation of the Committee, "that no Law whatever, or any Part thereof, shall be repealed, abrogated, or made null or void, or receive any additional Force or Strength" by virtue of having been included and printed in the new code. Except when a code is actually "adopted" as a law, this rule has remained as a permanent part of the law of codification in Maryland.

The Assembly did nothing further on the project in 1758, and nothing occurred in 1759. At the 1760 session, a bill passed the House but died in the Upper House. Even though the bill was not passed, the House of Delegates ordered its terms printed in the *Maryland Gazette.* The reason for its rejection in the Upper House is easy to find. In the bill, the House named a committee of ten members to supervise the work, five from each House. The five members of the Upper House actually were named in the bill (which had been drafted in the House of Delegates). Also, another committee of three members was named in the bill, all to be from the House, "to supervise and correct the Press." The Upper House would not agree to such a one-sided arrangement.

The whole matter came up again in the April-May session in 1761. Bacon's proposals for the work were entered in the *Journal* of the House:

Ordered, That the Proposals for Printing a Collection of the Laws of this Province, made by the Mr. Thomas Bacon, be Entered on the Journal of this House. Agreeable to the said Resolve the following is entered.

Proposals.

1. That all the Acts of Assembly of this Province in Force or Use, shall be Printed at large, at the Expence of the Proposer, on such Paper and Letter, and in such Form, as any Laws of the Plantations have heretofore been Printed, which this General Assembly shall best approve of.

2. That the several Sessions shall be distinguished by their proper Dates, Names of Governors, &c. The Titles of all the Acts passed in each, inserted in their due Order, with Reference to the Records where they may be found; and an Account of the several Continuations, and Time of Expiration or Repeal of such as are expired or abrogated. Each Session shall be divided into Chapters, and the Chapters into Sections with Numbers, for the easier Quotation of any Laws in Being.

3. That ample marginal Notes shall be Printed, with Reference to any subsequent Law, whereby a Paragraph may in any wise be affected or altered; and a compleat Common-Place, or short Alphabetical Abridgement of the Laws, shall be added, whereby the Whole, relating to any one Article, may easily be seen, and turned to in the several Acts at large.

4. That a Copy of the Whole shall be laid before the General Assembly, which shall meet next after the 25th Day of August next, for the Inspection and Approbation of his Excellency the Governor, and of the Upper and Lower Houses; which, after the said Approbation is received, shall be Printed with all possible Expedition.

5. That the said Proposer shall deliver Three Printed Copies of the said Work neatly Bound and Lettered; one for the Use of his Excellency the Governor, one to the Clerk of the Council for the Use of the Upper House, and another to the Honourable the Speaker for the Use of the Lower House of Assembly, on Condition that the said Proposer be allowed Two Hundred Pounds Current Money of this Province in the Public Journal; and for any farther Reimbursement of his Labour and Expence therein, is willing to depend on the Benefit arising from the Sale of his remaining Printed Copies.

The House of Delegates appointed a committee to prepare a bill for publication of Bacon's *Laws,* based upon the proposal he had submitted. The bill then was subjected to a typical series of motions in the House. The first motion was to signify the "desire" of the House that it nominate seven and the Upper House nominate three members, whose names would go into the bill "for Encouraging a Collection and Publication of the Laws of this Province." This motion failed, without a recorded vote.

Next, the House voted on a proposal that it would nominate seven members of the House for the committee, and desiring "to know" what members of the Upper House would be "pleased" to join those from the House. This motion passed, 18-17.

413

The House then proceeded to other motions which would have assured active political interference with the editorial content of the new code. The first motion to deal with editorial policy concerned codification of the much-disputed law imposing the 12-pence per hogshead tax on exports of tobacco. By a vote of 29-6, the House voted "That a Proviso be added to the said Bill, ordering the Committee Nominated for Revising and Examining the Collection of the Laws made by Mr. Thomas Bacon, to Report the Laws which are in Use in this Province, tho' not in Force, in an Appendix to the said Collection, and not in the Body of the said Collection." This motion, of course, was an obvious reference to the "12-pence law."

The next motion referred to it specifically, with a directive to be added to the bill that the 12-pence law not be inserted in the collection of laws but placed in an appendix "and distinguished as a Law not in Force." This motion was rejected, by a vote of 5-30. Next was a very similar question, that the proviso in the bill be that the 12-pence law not be included in the collection of laws but that it be placed in an appendix. This motion dropped the language in the next previous one, that in the appendix the disputed law be distinguished "as a Law not in Force." The latter motion carried by a vote of 24-11.

When the bill passed the House and went to the Upper House, it was there amended to require that the 12-pence law be included in Bacon's collection, and as "a law now in force." The House of Delegates would not agree with the amended version, and once again the bill failed. No further attempt was made to enact legislation supporting Bacon's *Laws,* although perhaps the extended discussion in the Assembly contributed to public awareness of and interest in the project. With the help of private subscriptions, it finally was published in 1766.

Bacon's *Laws,* dated in 1765, was formally titled *Laws of Maryland, with Proper Indexes.* The title page identified the editor as "Thomas Bacon, Rector of All-Saints Parish in Frederick County and Domestic Chaplain in Maryland to the Right Honourable Frederick Lord Baltimore." It contained the Charter of Maryland, from the original Latin and also an English translation. In chronological order it had the laws enacted in the Province from 1637 through 1763. Some were by short title only, others had a combination of short title and a condensed version of text, and still others were printed in full. There was a long index, prepared in explanatory style; and there was a separate index to "private, parochial, and town laws." For the times and with the facilities available, it was a tremendous and a monumental job. It contained no pagination, but library reference cards to the original publication list it with 730 pages, with large folios approximately 10 x 15 inches. More than two centuries later it remains a basic tool in seventeenth and eighteenth century legal research.[9]

---

9. Bacon in a prefatory note describes the earlier compilations then available. The earliest was a coverage of the laws from 1704 to 1707, with others included from the 1690s; even in Bacon's time the only copy available had no title page, so one could not ascertain when and by whom it was published.

The second source was *The Laws of the Province of Maryland, Collected into one Volume,* published in Philadelphia by Andrew Bradford. It covered the period from 1692 to 1718. The laws were printed in full, and the volume ran to 218 pages, plus a topical index. A facsimile copy of this publication was printed in 1978, as part of "The Colony Laws of North America Series." Except for the limited period it covers, the 1978 reprint is a useful, informative, and well-edited source for early Maryland laws.

The third of the several collections listed by Thomas Bacon was issued in 1726 by William Parks, then printer to the Province. It is described as having 118 pages and was published in Annapolis by Thomas Reading.

An editorial note in the 1978 publication of Bradford's Code lists also a collection of laws published in the year 1700, possibly a forerunner of the

## The Impending Stamp Act

There was no session of the General Assembly in 1764. The Governor delayed his call, so that the next session did not begin until September 23, 1765. The Governor announced that a smallpox epidemic in Annapolis in the spring of 1765 was responsible for the decision to postpone the session until September. This decision, however, and more certainly the failure to call a session in 1764, stemmed from the anticipation of possible unrest in the Province if and when the Parliament passed the Stamp Act. That finally occurred in February, 1765. The final turn toward revolution began in 1765; and the General Assembly of Maryland was an active participant.

---

1707 collection. In Bacon's time it usually was referred to as the "Old Body of Laws."

For a general biographical sketch of Thomas Bacon, see William E. Deibert, *Thomas Bacon, Colonial Clergyman,* 73 MARYLAND HISTORICAL MAGAZINE 79-86 (1978).

## Chapter 12

## THE STAMP ACT
## 1765-1767

The Stamp Act was enacted by the English Parliament in February, 1765. It changed the course of American history; and in the Province of Maryland it brought a new thrust to the motivations and the conflicts of legislative life.

To many of the English, and particularly the English taxpayers, the Stamp Act seemed eminently fair and reasonable. Both England and its American colonies were still in financial straits from the long and costly French and Indian War, ended only in 1763. The taxes levied upon American taxpayers were those long borne by the English. The revenues were to be devoted to "defending, protecting, and securing" the colonies in America.[1] Why shouldn't the colonies be required to pay a portion of the cost? Why shouldn't they be charged for a war which, though international in scope, had a prime incidental effect of assuring the life and livelihood of the colonies?

So ran much of the English thinking. To many in England, the answers were so obvious that the Stamp Act passed both Houses of the Parliament with little discussion.[2] It was a long piece of legislation, imposing taxes and fees upon a great variety of legal, commercial, and even social transactions: deeds, mortgages, licenses, college diplomas, playing cards, dice, pamphlets, newspapers, calendars, advertisements . . . . It affected every part and every class of

---

1. It has been estimated that revenues from the Stamp Act would cover only about one-seventh of the cost of maintaining English troops in America. Paul H. Giddens, *Maryland and the Stamp Act Controversy,* 27 MARYLAND HISTORICAL MAGAZINE 82 (1932).

2. The Parliament passed the Stamp Act "with a yawn. . . . The yawn could be forgiven for it looked reasonable, even routine, to tax the colonists in order to pay for protecting their frontiers." CARL BODE, MARYLAND — A BICENTENNIAL HISTORY 41 (New York, 1978).

America; and it was imposed directly upon many thousands of individuals.[3] The taxes were highly unwelcome to the colonists, and they were frightening for their implications of possible future exactions. "Last, but not least, the tax fell heavily upon two classes skilled in controversy, loquacious in expressing themselves, and accustomed to fish in troubled waters — lawyers and editors." [4]

There were other aggravating circumstances. All the colonies were suffering to some extent from economic woes in the after-war period, and other pieces of English legislation also fanned the controversies. There was an act for the benefit of English creditors, which restricted the use of paper money. Another, for the benefit of English fur traders, curtailed Americans' access to the western lands.

---

3. The Province of Maryland may have had the strongest claim of all the American colonies against the legality of the taxes imposed by the Stamp Act. The 20th section in the Charter granted by Charles I in 1632, on behalf of the King, provided "that we, our heirs and successors, at no time hereafter, will impose, or make or cause to be imposed, any impositions, customs, or other taxations, quotas or contributions whatsoever, in or upon the residents or inhabitants of the province aforesaid, for their goods, lands, or tenements within the same province, or upon any tenements, lands, goods or chattels within the province aforesaid, or in or upon any goods or merchandizes within the province aforesaid, or within the ports or harbours of the said province, to be laden or unladen...." *Cf.* J. Moss Ives, The Ark and the Dove — The Beginnings of Civil and Religious Liberties in America 86 (New York, 1936).

Some secondary sources cite Riley as evidence that a Provincial court in Maryland held the Stamp Act to be unconstitutional, as in contravention of the 20th section of the Charter. However, no such statement appears in Riley at the place cited. *See* Elihu S. Riley, A History of the General Assembly of Maryland, 1635-1904 at 277 (1905, reprinted in 1972).

4. Charles A. Beard and Mary R. Beard, 1 The Rise of American Civilization 209 (New York, 1930).

There was the Sugar Act of 1764, levying duties upon imports into England and adding to the list of articles which the colonists could export only to England. For England it was a classic application of the mercantile system, except for the unexpected result of losing its American colonies.

## PROTEST IN MARYLAND

In Maryland, the House of Delegates was the focal point of the ensuing discontent and protest. For a century and a quarter it had been striving to improve its relative importance in the legislative scheme of things in this Province. Many times its issues had been exaggerated; its arguments, misguided; its motives, not always pure; but it never gave up the effort. Its barbs had been directed toward the King, the Proprietary, the Governor, the Council and Upper House, and members of both the administrative bureaucracy and the judiciary. Since the King, Proprietary, and Upper House-Council were a political triumvirate, with interlocking obligations and loyalties, the popular side of the argument vested in the House of Delegates. Much of the focus of Maryland leadership in the developing revolution was in the House.

Questions were raised by legislators from time to time during 1764 about why the Assembly was not called into session. Without doubt, under the Charter, it was solely a function of the Governor to issue a call. It is evident from private correspondence of the Governor that he was aware of the clamor, and that his failure to call the session was a calculated effort to keep legislative protests at a minimum. The House members continued in 1765 their informal questions about a session, until by late summer the Governor (again in private correspondence) was concerned that unless he issued the call for a session the members might meet for a sort of unofficial rump session.

419

Nationally, the Stamp Act, the Sugar Act, and the accumulations of English mercantilism brought a swift and unprecedented unity to the American colonies. Not even the emergency of the French and Indian War had been so unifying; and in Maryland, as evident from the long list of unenacted supply bills, that struggle had been no more than a necessary nuisance. There were riots and general turmoil in many of the colonies during the spring and summer of 1765. Much of the emotion of the protests was concentrated upon King George III, but that unfortunate gentleman was then in one of his periods of temporary insanity and seems to have been an innocent bystander to the stirring events of 1765.

In other colonies, stamp agents had their offices attacked; the homes of enforcement officers were invaded; and the "Sons of Liberty" were organized. Calls went out for concerted action among all the colonies.

As early as June 8 the Massachusetts House of Representatives issued a call for a general colonial assembly to meet in New York City in October. A particular reason for the wish of Maryland legislators to have a legislative session called quickly was to make possible a formal response to the invitation from Massachusetts. Finally the Governor acted, calling a session to meet on September 23, 1765. Writing to Lord Baltimore about his decision, he said that "so earnestly did the Inhabitants of this Province desire that some of their Representatives should be present at such meeting that I am convinced the Members would have been obliged by their Constituents to meet here even if I had not called them, & that in such Case there would have been a great Outcry raised throughout the Province against the Council & Myself which might have been productive of Disorder & ill Consequences." [5]

---

5. *Archives,* XIV at 231-232.

Already, in fact, there had been "Disorder & ill Consequences" in Maryland. On August 25, in Annapolis, a mob moved against Zachariah Hood, who had been appointed as distributor of stamped paper for the Province. He was burned in effigy, his office was destroyed, and he was driven from town.[6]

The pages of the *Maryland Gazette* during this period had frequent and spirited references to the Stamp Act. The *Gazette* discontinued publication for several weeks, because of "the *intolerable . . . and unconstitutional* STAMP ACT." [7] Issues during the spring of 1766 had numerous notices of activities of the Sons of Liberty. When word came of the repeal of the Stamp Act, the news "diffus'd a general Joy in every Countenance. The Afternoon was spent in Mirth; and all Loyal and Patriotic Toasts were Drunk." [8] Later in the spring a day of celebration was observed in Annapolis, "as a Day of Rejoicing and Festivity . . . and in the Evening the City was beautifully Illuminated. . . ." [9]

## DANIEL DULANY THE YOUNGER

One of the most powerful voices to protest the Stamp Act from Maryland, and indeed from all of America, was Daniel Dulany the Younger. He had been a member of the General Assembly and was a leading barrister.[10] He wrote and published a long and reasoned pamphlet which ranks as one

---

6. For an account of Hood and his problems, *see* Paul H. Giddens, *Maryland and the Stamp Act Controversy,* 27 MARYLAND HISTORICAL MAGAZINE 83-86 (1932).

7. *Maryland Gazette,* January 30, 1766.

8. *Id.,* April 30, 1766.

9. *Id.,* June 12, 1766.

10. Dulany the Younger was an elected member of the House from Frederick County for several years during the early 1750s. In 1756 he was

of the great political disquisitions in American history. It was entitled *Considerations on the Propriety of Imposing Taxes in the British Colonies for the Purpose of Raising a Revenue by Act of Parliament.* It marshaled the arguments of history and of law against the Stamp Act; and in its logical progression and meticulous clarity, it was a beautifully written essay: [11]

## CONSIDERATIONS, & c.

In the constitution of *England,* the three principal forms of government, monarchy, aristocracy, and democracy, are blended together in certain proportions; but each of these orders, in the exercise of the legislative authority, hath its peculiar department, from which the others are excluded. In this division, the *granting of supplies,* or *laying taxes,* is deemed to be the province of the house of commons, as the representative of the people. — All supplies are supposed to flow from their gift; and the other orders are permitted only to assent, or reject generally, not to propose any modification, amendment, or partial alteration of it.

---

elected from Annapolis, and in 1757 he was appointed to the Council. *See* Richard Henry Spencer, *Hon. Daniel Dulany, 1722-1797,* 13 MARYLAND HISTORICAL MAGAZINE 143 (1918).

11. Reprinted in 6 MARYLAND HISTORICAL MAGAZINE 374-406 (1911), and 7 MARYLAND HISTORICAL MAGAZINE 26-59 (1912).

Although the Dulanys certainly were well above the average in education and background, many historians have commented upon the wide reading and historical perceptions of colonial Americans. Thomas Jefferson is reputed to have remarked, albeit somewhat humorously, that "American farmers are the only farmers who can read Homer." GILBERT CHINARD, THOMAS JEFFERSON — THE APOSTLE OF AMERICANISM 175 (Boston, 1939). For a Maryland comment, *cf.* "Many of the most ardent club men and horse fanciers owned excellently chosen libraries whose contents they knew from critical reading." Aubrey C. Land, *The Colonial Period,* THE OLD LINE STATE — A HISTORY OF MARYLAND 28 (Morris L. Radoff, ed.) (Annapolis, 1971).

THIS observation being considered, it will undeniably appear, that, in framing the late *Stamp Act,* the commons acted in the character of representative of the colonies. They assumed it as the principle of that measure, and the *propriety* of it must therefore stand, or fall, as the principle is true or false: for the preamble sets forth, That the commons of *Great Britain* had resolved to *give* and *grant* the several rates and duties imposed by the act; but what right had the commons of *Great Britain* to be thus munificent at the expense of the commons of America? — to give property, not belonging to the giver, and without the consent of the owner, is such evident and flagrant injustice, in *ordinary cases,* that few are hardy enough to avow it; and therefore, when it really happens, the fact is disguised and varnished over by the most plausible pretences the ingenuity of the giver can suggest. But it is alledged that there is a *virtual,* or *implied representation* of the colonies, springing out of the constitution of the British government; and it must be confessed on all hands, that as the representation is not actual, it is virtual, or it doth not exist at all; for no third kind of representation can be imagined. The colonies claim the privilege, which is common to all British subjects, of being taxed *only* with their own consent given by their representatives; and all the advocates for the *Stamp Act* admit this claim. Whether, therefore, upon the whole matter, the imposition of the *Stamp Duties* is a proper exercise of constitutional authority or not, depends upon the the single question, Whether the commons of *Great Britain are virtually* the representatives of the commons of *America,* or not?

THE advocates for the *Stamp Act* admit, in express terms, that 'the colonies do not choose members of parliament:' but they assert that 'the colonies are *virtually* represented in the same manner with the non-electors resident in *Great Britain.'*

. . . .

THERE is not that intimate and inseparable relation between the *electors of Great Britain* and the *Inhabitants of the colonies,* which must inevitably involve both in the same taxation: on the contrary, not a single *actual* elector in *England* might be immediately affected by a taxation in *America,* imposed by a statute which would have a general operation and effect, upon the properties of the inhabitants of the colonies. The latter might be oppressed in a thousand shapes, without any sympathy, or exciting any alarm in the former. Moreover, even acts, oppressive and injurious to the colonies in an extreme degree, might become popular in *England,* from the promise or expectation, that the very measures which depressed the colonies, would give ease to the inhabitants of *Great Britain.* It is indeed true, that the interests of *England* and the colonies are allied, and an injury to the colonies, produced into all its consequences, will eventually affect the mother country; yet these consequences being generally remote, are not at once foreseen; they do not immediately alarm the fears and engage the passions of the *English* electors; the connection between a freeholder of *Great Britain* and a *British American,* being deducible only thro' a train of reasoning, which few will take the trouble, or can have opportunity, if they have capacity, to investigate: wherefore the relation between the *British American* and the *English electors,* is a knot too infirm to be relied on as a competent security, especially against the force of a present, counteracting, expectation of relief.

IF it would have been a just conclusion, that the *colonies* being exactly in the *same* situation with the *non-electors* of *England,* are *therefore* represented in the same manner, it ought to be allowed, that the reasoning is solid, which, after having evinced a total *dissimilarity* of situation, infers, that the representation is *different.*

IF the commons of *Great Britain* have no right by the constitution to GIVE AND GRANT property *not* belonging to themselves but to others, without their consent actually or virtually given; if the claim of the colonies, not to be taxed *without their consent,* signified by their representatives, is well founded; if it appears that the colonies are not actually represented by the commons of *Great Britain,* and that the notion of a double or virtual representation, doth not with any

424

propriety apply to the people of *America;* then the principle of the *stamp act* must be given up as indefensible on the point of representation, and the validity of it, rested upon the *power* which they who framed it have to carry it into execution.

THE *English* subjects who left their *native* country to settle in the wilderness of *America,* had the privileges of *other Englishmen.* They knew their value, and were desirous of having them perpetuated to their posterity. They were aware, that as their consent, whilst they should reside in *America,* could neither be asked nor regularly given in the national legislature, and that if they were to be bound by laws without restriction, affecting the property they should earn by the utmost hazard and fatigue, they would lose every other privilege which they had enjoyed in their native country, and become mere tenants at will, dependent upon the moderation of their lords and masters, without any other security; — that as their settlement was to be made under the protection of the *English* government, they knew, that in consequence of their relation to the mother country, they and their posterity would be subordinate to the supreme national council, and expected that obedience and protection would be considered as reciprocal duties.

CONSIDERING themselves, and being considered in this light, they entered into a compact with the crown, the basis of which was, *that their privileges, as* English *subjects, should be effectually secured to themselves, and transmitted to their posterity.* As for this purpose, precise declarations and provisions, formed upon the principles, and according to the spirit of the *English constitution,* were necessary, CHARTERS were accordingly framed and conferred by the crown, and accepted by the settlers, by which all the doubts and inconveniences which might have arisen from the application of general principles to a new subject were prevented.

BY these charters, founded upon the unalienable rights of the subject, and upon the most sacred compact, the colonies claim a right of exemption from taxes *not imposed with their consent.* — They claim it upon the principles of the constitution, as once *English,* and now

425

*British* subjects, upon principles on which their compact with the crown was originally founded.

THE origin of other governments is covered by the veil of antiquity, and is differently traced by the fancies of different men; but, of the colonies, the evidence of it is as clear and unequivocal as of any other fact.

BY these declaratory charters the inhabitants of the colonies claim an exemption from *all* taxes not imposed by their own consent, and to infer from their objection to a taxation, to which their consent is not, nor can be given, *that they are setting up a right in the crown to dispense with acts of parliament, and to deprive the* British *subjects in* America *of the benefits of the common law,* is so extremely absurd, that I should be at a loss to account for the appearance of so strange an argument, were I not apprized of the unworthy arts employed by the enemies of the colonies to excite strong prejudices against them in the minds of their brethren at home, and what gross incongruities prejudiced men are wont to adopt.

Dulany's conclusions were credible and rational, that the colonies should conduct an orderly protest against the Stamp Act and that they should exert continued economic pressure against England.

### PREPARATION FOR THE STAMP ACT CONGRESS

Leadership in the campaign against the Stamp Act, among all the colonies, came mainly from the House of Representatives of the General Court of Massachusetts. A committee of that body, with James Otis as one of its members, wrote to the House of Delegates of Maryland in proposing unified action among the colonies. Referring to the Stamp Act and the Sugar Act, "and other Taxes proposed to be laid on the British Colonies," the committee "were humbly of Opinion that these Measures have a Tendency to deprive the Colonists of some of their most essential Rights as British Subjects and as Men Particularly the Right of Assessing their own Taxes, and being free from any Impositions but such as they Consent to by themselves or Representatives." Continuing,

426

Our Agent informs us that in a Conference he had with Mr. Greenville on these Subjects he was told that the Ministry were desirous of Consulting the Ease the Quiet and Goodwill of the Colonies. Such Expressions induce us to hope that there is nothing punitive in these Measures and that humble Dutiful Remonstrations may yet have their Effect, But if while these things are thus Publickly handled no Claim is made no Remonstrance is preferred on the part of the Colonies Such Silence must be interpreted a Tacit Cession of their Rights and an humble Acquiescence under all their Burdens.

The message from the committee in Massachusetts was accompanied by another from the Speaker of the House in that State. Massachusetts, he said, had appointed a committee of three to attend the meeting in New York City, and he was proposing that the group convene on the first Tuesday in October.

The gravity of the Stamp Act controversy in Maryland was evidenced when the Upper House approved sending commissioners from this State to the assembly in New York City, adding that it would "Chearfully Concur" in providing five hundred pounds for expense money. The Upper House did advise against "unlimited Credit" for the commissioners and for an accounting of their expenditures after they returned. After some minor disagreements on details, both houses agreed to this plan.

The Upper House, without a contest so far as appears in the *Journals,* concurred also in the appointment of the commissioners solely by the House of Delegates. This session of the Legislature in late September, 1765, lasted only six days; it had been convened for the sole purpose of considering the colonial assembly in New York City. Before the session was prorogued on September 28, the two houses (and note, with the approval of Governor Sharpe) agreed upon the terms of an ordinance for the attendance of the Maryland commissioners:

427

It is Ordained, by his Excellency and the Upper and Lower Houses of Assembly that the Sum of £ 500 Current Money be paid by the Treasurer of the Western Shore into the hands of William Murdock Edward Tilghman and Thomas Ringgold Esquires a Committee appointed by the Lower House of Assembly to meet the Committees from the Houses of Representatives or Burgesses of the several British Colonies on this continent at the City of New York on the first Tuesday of October next to consult together on the present Circumstances of the Colonies and the Difficulties to which they are and must be reduced by the Operation of the late Acts of Parliament for levying Duties and Taxes on the Colonies and to Consider of a general and United dutiful Loyal and humble Representation of their Condition to his Majesty and the Parliament and to implore Relief, be by them applyed in and towards the Expenses attendant thereon, and that they lay an Account of their Disbursements before the General Assembly of this Province as soon as Conveniently may be and that the Ballance if any be by them returned into the hands of the Treasurer.

Horatio Sharpe.

27 September 1765. Read and assented to by the Upper House of Assembly

Signed per order. Benjamin Tasker President

27th September 1765. Read and assented to by the Lower House of Assembly

Signed per order Robert Lloyd Speaker

Two other actions by the House of Delegates testified to the priority of its control over the Maryland commissioners attending the New York City meeting. First, the House drafted and sent with the commissioners a set of instructions to guide them in their work:

Instruction from the Honourable the Lower House of Assembly of the Province of Maryland to William Murdock Edward Tilghman and Thomas Ringgold Esquires a Committee Appointed to join the several

428

Committees from the several Colonies in America at New York.

Gentlemen you are to repair immediately to the City of New York in the Province of New York and there join with the Committees from the Houses of Representatives of the other Colonies in a General and united dutiful loyal and humble Representation to his Majesty and the British Parliament of the Circumstances and Condition of the British Colonies and Plantations and to pray relief from the Burthens and restraints lately laid on their Trade and Commerce and especially from the Taxes imposed by an Act of the last Session of Parliament Granting and Applying Certain Stamp Duties and other Duties in the British Colonies and Plantations in America whereby they are deprived in some Instances of that invaluable privilege of Englishmen and British Subjects Tryals by Juries that you take care that such Representation shall humbly and decently but expressly contain an Assertion of the Rights of the Colonists to be exempt from all and every Taxations and Impositions upon their Persons and Properties to which they do not consent in a Legislative way either by themselves or their Representatives by them freely Chosen and Appointed

Which were read Approved and Signed by the Honourable Speaker

As a second indication to guide the commissioners in New York City, the House of Delegates at the September session in 1765 adopted unanimously a set of "resolves declarative of the Constitutional Rights of the Freemen of this Province." The document was phrased simply as a resolution of the House, and it was passed without the visible assent or consideration of the Upper House. Its principles were based upon Magna Carta and "all the Liberties privileges Franchises and Immunities that any time have been held enjoyed and possessed by the People of Great Britain." It recited at length the understanding of the House of Delegates about the contents and guarantees of Maryland's Charter; and it claimed specifically for the citizens of

429

Maryland the right of trial by jury, the right to enact their own laws, and the "Sole Right to lay Taxes and Impositions on the Inhabitants of this Province or their Property and effects . . . ." It was a serious and imposing document and a strong addition to the pre-Revolutionary literature of the Province of Maryland:

> 1st. Resolved Unanimously that the first Adventurers and Setlers of this Province of Maryland brought with them and transmitted to their Posterity and all other his Majestys Subjects since Inhabiting in this province all the Liberties privileges Franchises and Immunities that any time have been held enjoyed and possessed by the People of Great Britain
>
> 2d. Resolved Unanimously that it was Granted by Magna Charta and other the Good Laws and Statutes of England and Confirmed by the Petition and Bill of Rights that the Subject should not be Compelled to Contribute to any Tax Tallage Aid or other like Charge not set by common Consent of Parliament
>
> 3d. Resolved Unanimously that by a Royal Charter Granted by his Majesty King Charles the first in the eighth Year of his Reign And in the Year of our Lord One thousand Six hundred and thirty two to Caecilius then Lord Baltimore it was for the Encouragement for People to Transport themselves and families in to this Province amongst other things Covenanted and Granted by his said Majesty for himself his heirs and Successors as followeth And we will also and for our more Special Grace for us our heirs and Successors we do Strictly enjoin Constitute Ordain and Command that the said Province shall be of our Allegiance and that all and Singular the Subjects and liege People of us our heirs and Successors transported or to be Transported into the said Province and the Children of them and of such as shall descend from them there already born or hereafter to be born be and shall be Denizens and lieges of us our heirs and Successors of our Kingdoms of England and Ireland and be in all things held treated reputed and esteemed as the liege faithfull People of us our heirs and Successors born within our Kingdom of England and

likewise any Lands Tenements Revenues Services and
other Hereditaments whatsoever within our Kingdom of
England and other our Dominions may inherit or
otherwise purchase receive take have hold buy and
possess and them may Occupy and enjoy give Sell Alien
and bequeath as likewise all Libertys Franchises and
privileges of this our Kingdom of England freely quietly
and peaceably have and possess Occupy and enjoy as our
liege people born or to be born within our said Kingdom
of England without the Let Molestation Vexation
trouble or Grievance of us our heirs and Successors Any
Statute Act Ordinance or provision to the Contrary
thereof Notwithstanding

And further our pleasure is and by these presents for
us our heirs and Successors We do Covenant and Grant
to and with the said now Lord Baltimore his heirs and
Assigns that we our heirs and Successors shall at no
time hereafter Set or make or cause to be Set any
Imposition Custom or other Taxation Rate or
Contribution whatsoever in or upon the Dwellers and
Inhabitants of the aforesaid Province for their Lands
Tenements Goods or Chattels within the said Province or
in or upon any Goods or Merchandizes within the said
Province to be laden or unladen within any the Ports or
Harbours of the said Province And our Pleasure is and
for us our heirs and Successors We Charge and
Command that this our Declaration shall be hence
forward from time to time received and allowed in all our
Courts and before all the Judges of us our heirs and
Successors for a Sufficient and lawfull Discharge
Payment and Acquittance Commanding all and Singular
our Officers and Ministers of us our heirs and
Successors and enjoyning them upon pain of our high
Displeasure that they do not presume at any time to
Attempt any thing to the Contrary of the Premisses or
that they do in any Sort withstand the same but that
they be at all times Aiding and Assisting as is fitting
unto the said now Lord Baltimore and his heirs and to
the Inhabitants and Merchants of Maryland aforesaid
their Servants Ministers factors and Assigns in the full
use and Fruition of the Benefit of this our Charter

4th. Resolved that it is the Unanimous Opinion of this House that the said Charter is Declaratory of the Constitutional Rights and Privileges of the Freemen of this Province

5th. Resolved Unanimously That Tryals by Juries is the Great Bulwark of Liberty the undoubted Birthright of every Englishman and Consequently of every British Subject in America and that the Erecting other Jurisdictions for the Tryal of Matters of fact is unconstitutional and renders the Subject insecure in his Liberty and Property

6th. Resolved That it is the Unanimous Opinion of this House that it cannot with any truth or Propriety be said that the Freemen of this Province of Maryland are Represented in the British Parliament

7th. Resolved Unanimously that his Majestys liege People of this Ancient Province have always enjoyed the Right of being Governed by Laws to which they themselves have consented in the Articles of Taxes and internal Polity and that the same hath never been forfeited or any other way Yielded up but hath been Constantly recognized by the King and People of Great Britain

8th. Resolved that it is the Unanimous Opinion of this House that the Representatives of the Freemen of this Province in their Legislative Capacity together with the other part of the Legislature have the Sole Right to lay Taxes and Impositions on the Inhabitants of this Province or their Property and effects And that the laying imposing levying or Collecting any Tax on or from the Inhabitants of Maryland under Colour of any other Authority is Unconstitutional and a Direct Violation of the Rights of the Freemen of this Province

## DISTRIBUTION OF STAMPS

With the commissioners to the Congress in New York City appointed and financed, their instructions prepared, and the resolution adopted to state Maryland's principles of government, a few other details remained to be settled before the short session of September, 1765, could be completed. They also dealt with the Stamp Act, for no other subject was considered in that session.

As a topic of some governmental difficulty, the Governor asked both houses about the policy to follow if some of the stamped paper should arrive in the Province. "It being Probable," wrote Governor Sharpe, that some of the stamped paper would soon arrive and that the master of the ship would ask how to dispose of his cargo, "I should be glad to know how You would Advise me to Act on Such Occasion."

The Upper House responded with a suggestion that if the stamped paper arrived in Maryland, it should be held on board the ship until arrangements could be made for its distribution. The treatment already accorded to Zachariah Hood in Maryland and "the Behaviour of Numbers of the Inhabitants" of other colonies "Affords great Room to apprehend" that attempts would be made to destroy the paper if it were brought ashore. "In Order to prevent such an Indignity being Offered to the Legislature of Great Britain," the Upper House recommended that arrangements be made to house the stamped paper aboard an English ship until it could be landed without risk.

The House of Delegates was more reticent than the Upper House, and it tactfully declined to give advice to the Governor about the handling and distribution of the stamped paper. "We should think ourselves extremely happy," wrote the House in obvious hyperbole, "were we in Circumstances to Advise your Excellency on so new a Subject." The House said only that it was not able to proffer the requested advice "without the Instructions of our Constituents which we cannot now Obtain we hope your Excellency think us excusable for declineing to offer you any Advise upon the Occasion." [12]

12. Later in the fall of 1765, the Stamp Tax paper became an immediate problem. HMS Sardeine, "at anchor off Newcastle in the Delaware River," notified Governor Sharpe that it had stamp paper on board and asked

## The Stamp Act Congress

Nine of the colonies were represented at the Stamp Act Congress in New York City in early October, 1765. The Congress passed a set of resolutions generally similar to those adopted by the House of Delegates in Maryland: that Englishmen cannot be taxed without their consent; the colonists cannot be represented in the Parliament, and so may be taxed only by their own legislatures; and the Stamp Act subverts the rights and liberties of the American colonists. Of perhaps more practical importance, the Congress initiated a general boycott of English goods, leading to quick demands from English merchants that the Stamp Act be repealed.

## Repeal of the Stamp Act

The next session of the General Assembly convened on November 1 and lasted until December 20, 1765. It was a full and general session, yet the Stamp Act continued to dominate the proceedings. High on the list of priorities in the House of Delegates was a "Remonstrance" addressed to Governor Sharpe for having so long delayed calling the session for the past September, allowing the Province to go without a session from November, 1763, until September, 1765. "We are truly concerned," wrote the House, "that the Duty we owe our Constituents lays us under the indispensible Necessity of Observing that every Power lodged in the Hands of Government is there intrusted by the Constitution to be exercised for the Common Good." The

directions for its disposition. Again the House replied, on receiving another request from the Governor, that it was "not agreeable" to the sentiments from constituents that it give any advice to him.

House could understand that the Governor had not called the session from March to September in 1765 because of the "unhappy Prevalence of the small Pox," it told the Governor, but it could not agree with the long interval of no session after the month of November in 1763. In the absence of an expression against the Stamp Act, it was said, a political writer in England had construed that the Province acquiesced in its enactment.

The House also sent a long letter of arguments and instruction to Charles Garth, Maryland's agent in London, for presentation to the House of Lords and the House of Commons. Included were copies of documents from the Stamp Act Congress in New York City and other colonies. The letter went back historically to the Maryland charter, amounting to "a strong Declaration and Promise that its Inhabitants should not by their Removal be stript of the Rights of Englishmen . . . ." This letter, in addition to its philosophical arguments, had also a number of practical commercial arguments. Thus, the usual practice of English commerce had been to give an "Indulgence of Time" in collecting duties and imposts on goods in trade, but there was no such indulgence in the Stamp Act. "Equally severe and Impolitick are the Prohibitions" against exporting to countries other than England, stressing that the costs of transshipping harmed normal trade with "the Sweeds Danes & Hamburghers." Finally, the letter to Garth protested against jurisdictional provisions for prosecutions under the Stamp Act; it seems to Americans "as if the Parliament esteemed it criminal to be an American."

The protests, remonstrances, riots, and boycotts from America, together with the plight of English merchants resulting from the boycotts and non-intercourse programs, led the Parliament in 1766 to repeal the Stamp Act. Welcome as was that action, it proved quickly to be for the Americans a matter of winning the battle but losing the war. Repeal of the Stamp Act was accompanied by a Declaration of the Parliament rejecting the philosophy that the colonists had an exclusive right of regulating their own taxes without controls by the Parliament. Instead, said the Declaration, the Parliament has a right to enact laws for the colonies "in all cases whatsoever."

Repeal of the Stamp Act, thus, which for a time seemed to restore harmonious relations between England and its colonies in America, did not at all settle the issue of taxation without representation.

## OTHER PROBLEMS OF 1765

Meanwhile, in late 1765, the General Assembly of Maryland had its usual host of domestic legislative and political problems. On that list was the Journal of Accounts, a perennial source of conflict between the two houses of Assembly. The relative period of harmony between them while opposing the Stamp Act quickly gave way to the traditional enmities and disagreements on other topics; it was the typical case of quarreling brothers who unite temporarily against an outside foe.

Two main matters of detail for years had caused an open split between the houses in considering the Journal of Accounts (or budget bill), with its appropriations for the operations of Provincial government. One was that of compensating the Governor for the cost of seals on proclamations issued by his office; the House insisted that many of the proclamations were not necessary, and that the inhabitants of the Province perfectly well knew of the contents of laws without being reminded by proclamation.

The other, and main, controversy had raged for years without solution. The House refused to include in the Journal of Accounts a separate per diem payment for the Clerk of the Council, who also doubled as the Clerk of the Upper House.

The Council and Upper House comprised the same persons, and the distinction rested upon the executive and legislative functions they performed. It was the contention of the House that the compensation of the Clerk of the Council was a proper executive expense, to be met from revenues of the Lord Proprietary and of the Governor and not charged to "the people."

These protracted differences were important to the Governor and to the Clerk of the Council, of course, who were not receiving remuneration and compensation they felt was owing; and they were important to the Upper House as a matter of principle. By 1765, however, the controversy had escalated into a far more pressing and dangerous situation. The years of impasse on the Journal of Accounts had resulted in the public debt's not being paid and in a steadily increasing number of creditors who were demanding payment. Included in the latter were a considerable number of soldiers with unpaid claims from the French and Indian War. The soldiers were indignant and pressed their claims with much fervor. The issue of war claims moved toward a climax in late 1765, with the Governor apprising the House of a threatened march on Annapolis. He had information, he wrote to the House, of a party of three or four hundred men assembled in Frederick and armed with guns and tomahawks. It was their intention, he was told, "to march hither in Companies in Order (as they express themselves) to settle the Disputes betwixt the two Houses of Assembly in Relation to their passing the Journal." Also, said the Governor, he had been informed that the march was originated by Delegate Thomas Cresap, who was said to have returned to Frederick from Annapolis and told the people "nothing would be done unless the People did come down . . . ."

The House in reply said it was "very sensible of the bad Consequences of large Bodies of People coming hither with

437

a View to intimidate either Branch of the Legislature or to lay them under any Restraint." The House asked the Governor for whatever evidence he had of the projected march. In particular, it said, it desired evidence of any complicity on the part of Delegate Cresap. Writing as of December 11, the House said that the delegate from Frederick County had not attended the House since November 22, but other delegates supposed he had left in expectation that the war claims would be paid without difficulty.

The Governor then sent to the House such information as he had about what part Delegate Cresap might have had in the proposed march on Annapolis. He had depositions from two persons in Frederick County who had heard remarks implicating the delegate. One of them was about nothing being done unless the people did go to Annapolis, but to that it was added that "the People did say they would come down in a Civil Manner to see if the Business was done."

There was a motion in the House in December, 1765, to send a list of the unpaid war claims to the Upper House, so they could be added to the Journal of Accounts. The motion was closely rejected, by a vote of 15-16. Again in that year the Journal of Accounts failed to pass, and the war claims and other items in the public debt remained unpaid.

On the other pending financial problem in 1765, that of a salary for the Clerk of the Upper House covering his duties with the Council of State, the House in its messages concerning the Journal of Accounts pointed out that even without the extra salary he would be paid some 139,000 pounds of tobacco that year, so he was not exactly uncompensated. Also, the House went back to another of its old complaints, the tonnage tax and the 12-pence per hogshead tax on exports of tobacco, both being paid to Lord Baltimore and (in the House view) unlawfully so. While again refusing to approve the extra compensation for the Clerk, the House asked the Governor to end the session quickly; one of its members was sick with smallpox, it said; and in the fear that others would catch it, the House was having trouble keeping a quorum. A later message to the Governor added a sequel. This time, the House said that one of its members already was dead from smallpox, and there was the same difficulty of maintaining a quorum. It was a year later, in 1766, that the Houses agreed to submit to the King in Council the thorny question of the Clerk's compensation, and in that year the Assembly finally was able to pass a Journal of Accounts.

Delegate Walter Dulany, representing the City of Annapolis, established a record of sorts in 1765 by twice being expelled from the House. He was a son of the famous Daniel Dulany the Elder and a brother of the equally well-known Daniel Dulany the Younger. During the short September session in 1765, Walter had to give up his seat in the House because of his having accepted an appointive office under the Proprietary government. In the special election which followed, he was again elected as a delegate in the Assembly; and that election was challenged during the November-December session. The question was further complicated by his being also the Mayor of Annapolis, and by some evidence of his having used that position to promote his reelection to the House of Delegates. The situation became even more questionable when his brother Daniel, as Recorder of Annapolis, was absent during the election and also failed to sign the election return.[13]

---

13. "Annapolis had long been run almost as a rotten borough for the Proprietary. The top officials in the Maryland government of the Lords Baltimore were also the top officials of Annapolis." Daniel Dulany also was Deputy Secretary of the Province. Walter also was Naval Officer of Patuxent. Included among the aldermen of Annapolis from time to time were Dr. George Steuart, a judge of the Land Office and member of the House; Upton Scott, clerk of the Council and of the Upper House; John

The House solved all this in one of its inimitable series of three propositions or questions, submitted to successive votes. All this occurred on November 12, 1765. The first and most involved question was:

> The Question was put whether the following Entry Viz
>
> It appearing to this House that Mr Walter Dulany the Sitting Member was Mayor of the City of Annapolis at the Time of his Election and qualified as returning Officer under the Statute 2 Geo 2d. That he sat and continued in the Chair on the Bench during the Time of the Election and in his Seat did Object to the Qualification of some of the Voters who offered to vote against him That there was no Adjournment by Order of the Court which Order was signified to the proper Officer by Mr Macnemara the Senior Alderman And further it appearing to the House that the Sitting Member is returned by four Aldermen of the said City which Return is not signed by the Recorder who was absent at the Time of the Election
> be entred on the Journal or not.

This issue was decided in the affirmative, by a vote of 26-21. For all its convoluted text, the question seemed to settle nothing more than having it entered on the *Journal*, so that the House could move on to the more simple and decisive questions. Next, "The previous Question being determined the Question was put whether the Mayor of the City of Annapolis be eligible to serve as a Delegate in Assembly or not." This also received an affirmative vote, 29-17. Thirdly came the clencher, "Whether Mr. Dulany was duly elected or not." Here there was a negative vote, 20-27; and Delegate Walter Dulany accordingly again was removed from the House of Delegates.

---

Brice, Chief Justice of the Provincial Court; Benjamin Tasker, Sr., Surveyor and also president of the Council; and Michael Macnemara, clerk of the House (although the latter was not one of the favorites of the Proprietary). *See* Neil Strawser, *Samuel Chase and the Annapolis Paper War,* 57 MARYLAND HISTORICAL MAGAZINE 177-94 (1962).

With all the matters of national and Provincial import before the Assembly in 1765, two counties raised a seemingly unimportant and local issue during the November-December session. The Upper House received and passed on to the House of Delegates separate petitions from both Baltimore and Worcester counties, saying their inhabitants desired to be relieved from "the great and heavy Charge, arising from the Allowances made for the Support and Maintenance of the Poor." Continuing, "Whether the Erection of Work-houses or Houses of Correction, in all the Counties, would not give great Relief to the Inhabitants in the annual Levies, afford a more regular and better applied Provision for the Poor, check the disorders committed by common Beggars & idle Vagabonds, and lay a Foundation for useful Industry, we refer to your Consideration."

## Compromise on Disputed Issues

The General Assembly met twice in 1766, in May and November. The sessions were partly notable for the compromises reached in some of the areas of power struggle which for years had concerned and aggravated the House of Delegates. One of the controversies involved the right of the Proprietary, rather than the Province or "public," to collect and dispose of monies collected as fines, forfeitures, and license fees.

With respect to the fines and forfeitures, a committee of the House had been appointed during the previous session, on November 15, 1765, to study and report upon whether these funds properly should be applied to general governmental expenses, rather than be paid to the Proprietary. The committee was instructed to inquire also whether an account of the application of the funds should be stated "for the Satisfaction of the publick" and to determine the entire amount of all duties, imposts, and sums received

441

and collected by the Proprietary and his officers. At the same time, another committee was formed "to enquire into the several lucrative Offices in this Province and of the Annual profits from each Office." The financial inquiries of the House of Delegates had a wide range.

One phase of the issue of fines, forfeitures, and license fees concerned particularly the license fees collected from ordinaries, together with the penalties for their violation. These monies had been a thorny issue for three quarters of a century. For years in seventeenth-century Maryland they had been collected by the Proprietary, but during the years from 1689 to 1715, when the Province was not under the Lords Baltimore, the collections from ordinaries had been claimed by both the Province and the Crown. After the Restoration in 1715, the Lords Baltimore again made exclusive claim for them. The House of Delegates never acquiesced to this claim, and time after time following 1715 it tried to recapture the funds for public use. The argument was so intense that sometimes, as in 1765, it was impossible to pass any legislation at all about ordinaries.

At the session in May, 1766, the House passed a regulatory bill for ordinaries, but with somewhat different provisions for licenses and penalties. Following a stratagem familiar two centuries later, it changed the proposed recipients for the monies collected; this time the funds were to go to the respective counties in which the ordinaries were located. The bill was passed by a very close vote in the House, 20-19. There followed an unexpected set of circumstances, leading ultimately to the recovery for the Province of the fines and fees from ordinaries.

When the Upper House received the bill in 1766, with its proposal to distribute the monies to the counties, it promptly and surprisingly amended the bill to give the disposition of the ordinary monies to the Assembly. This, of course, was a sharp shift in policy for the Upper House; always before it

442

had staunchly supported the Governor and the Proprietary in assuring that these funds would continue to go to the Lords Baltimore. Again this year the Council (comprising the same membership as the Upper House) already had received "Instructions" from the Lord Proprietary to the Governor, directing the Governor not to consent to any bill taking these monies away from the Proprietary.

At this point, a new element was added to the perennial controversy. The "Instructions" were submitted to a committee of the Council, and one of its members was Daniel Dulany, recognized as one of the outstanding lawyers in the Province. The committee held that the Proprietary was not entitled to the fees and forfeitures from ordinaries, and that neither the Charter nor any act of the Assembly had provided for the monies to go to him. By common law, continued the committee, any person was entitled to follow the trade of an innkeeper without license. To the extent of requiring licenses, the Assembly in Maryland had overruled the common law, but the inability of the Assembly since 1763 to renew and pass the licensing statute meant that for three years the trade of innkeeper or ordinary keeper in Maryland had reverted to a common law occupation. The Council unanimously adopted the report of the committee [14] and suggested to the Governor that further insistence on the Proprietary's claim would be counter-productive. So ended one dispute which for decades had rocked the legislative and executive brances in the Provincial government.

Two years later, in 1768, a change was made as to the disposition of license fees from hawkers and peddlers. The Proprietary long had claimed them as part of his prerogatives, and the House of Delegates had insisted they belonged to the public. A proposal in 1754 for licensing these

---

14. *Archives,* XXXIII at 143 ff.

trades passed the House but failed in the Upper House; and the same result occurred to another bill in 1766. The latter bill passed the House by a 27-19 vote, aided by the votes of a few members of the Proprietary party. This time, also, the House varied its strategy, proposing to give the licensing proceeds to the public schools. Again the Upper House countered with an amendment to leave the disposition of the proceeds with the Assembly. This should have been agreeable to the House of Delegates, but for the interposition of another long-term tenet of House philosophy, that the House should not permit the Upper House to make a change in a money bill. Finally, in 1768, a bill passed for licensing hawkers and peddlers, being incorporated with the provisions for licensing and regulating ordinaries. The reasoning of the Dulany committee report obviously applied equally to hawkers and peddlers and to ordinaries.

There was a third area of compromise between the Upper and Lower Houses during these years of the latter 1760s. This was on another long-time disagreement, that concerning the compensation for the Clerk of the Upper House in his role as Clerk of the Council; the Lower House had adamantly refused to include an item for such payment in the Journal of Accounts, or budget bill, maintaining that the payment should be made from the executive budget and not from general funds of "the public." As a recurring action each year, the Upper House protested the omission; and this had occurred as late as the November session in 1765.

There was only brief mention of the payment for the Clerk in the Journal of Accounts at the May session in 1766, but the attendant problem of the public debt and the war claims, both unpaid, was more pressing every year. A solution of sorts finally was reached during the November-December session in 1766.

The Journal of Accounts met its usual disputes at that latter session. The two houses did agree, however, to put it before a conference committee, where it could remain alive and open for argument. Each House issued long and detailed instructions to its conferees; and although the instructions staked out strong positions, as always, they still had innovative provisions suggesting a possible ending to the negotiations.

The instructions of the Upper House were sent to its conferees on November 20, 1766. Two alternatives were advanced for settlement of the compensation for the Clerk. One was that the issue be sent on appeal to the King in Council, for a ruling from that source. The second was that the claims of the Clerk, other public creditors, and the war debtors all be paid up to the present time. If necessary, the money was to be secured by the sale of bills of credit. For the future, no salary would be paid the Clerk from "public" funds; instead, he would be allowed fees as an officer, and the regulation of the fees would be given to the Governor and Council.

The House of Delegates, in turn, issued instructions to its conferees on the following day, November 21. The House repeated its firm opposition to the principle that the Clerk should be paid from general funds, but it also was aware that there seemed to be "no Probability of a speedy Concurrence of both Houses in this Sentiment." The distressed condition of the Province and of many of the claimants, it continued, called for a solution. The House recommended, therefore, the sale of bills of credit to care for payments to the late and the present Clerk, and also for those on the list of debts (with alternative possibilities for making the actual payments).

A few days later the House of Delegates agreed to the proposal to refer the Clerk's compensation to the King in Council and then passed a bill for the sale of bills of credit and payment of the public claims. The bill went on to the

Upper House, which in turn suggested some minor changes. These suggestions, although not vital to the bill, bestirred the House to its frequent thesis that the Upper House had no part in money bills except to pass them unchanged in the form proposed by the House:

By the Lower House of Assembly 4th December 1766.

May it please your Honours

This House Claim, as their inherent undoubted and fundamental Right, the Sole and exclusive Formation of all Mony Bills, and therein to limit the matter, manner, measurer and time of all Grants and Dispositions of Public Money whatsoever. A Right so essential to the Liberties and Propertys of those We represent that we are determined never to give it up, or Wave or Weaken it any Manner

We therefore return to your Honours, the Bill for the Payment of the Public Claims, for emitting Bills of Credit and for other Purposes therein mentioned, whereon to indorse your Assent or Negative, according to the established mode of Parliamentary Proceedings, But hope from the Evident Utility of the Bill, and to relieve the Extreme Distress of the People, your Honours will give your Assent, as we clearly of Opinion it may in its present frame, be well Carried into Execution, and that if any of the small matters pointed out by your Message should be thought Imperfections, they may be aided at a Time of more Leisure, as well as those material Defects you intimate to be in the Bill but which we are not at present able to discover.

The House of Delegates also incorporated its thoughts on money bills into a series of "resolves." The Upper House, for its part, expressed surprise that the House of Delegates "have taken Offence at our Message" and insisted it had no intent to make what "you Consider as an Attack upon / as you are pleased to call it / an inherent undoubted and fundamental Right Claimed by your House." The message of the Upper House cited instances in 1732 and 1733 when

446

suggestions made by the Upper House had been incorporated into acts for the sale of bills of credit. Without at all conceding the claims of the House with respect to money bills, the Upper House approved the bill in order to settle the immediate problem, adding this explanation and statement of future intentions:

> However, Gentlemen, tho' we are persuaded that the Bill is extremely defective, that the Pretensions you have advanced can't be supported by any Just reasoning, yet from a pure motive of Compassion, a Tenderness for the Public Creditors, and indeed the People in General, and from our most earnest desire to have an End put to the long Subsisting Controversy on the Subject of the Clerks of the Councils Claims, we have endorsed our Assent on the Bill, but we do deny that you are intituled, solely, and exclusively, to form Money Bills, and insist that this Claim is inconsistent with Our Constitution, as well as repugnant to the Usage of the Province, and as we foresee that this Claim, and your very extensive Application of it, may probably obstruct the Course of Public Business, unless some Expendient be fallen upon to settle and explain it, We now give you Notice that we shall lay this Subject before his Majesty in Council, at the same time with our Representation on the affair of the Clerks of the Council, in order that both Points may be settled.

As a somewhat sour footnote to these instances of partial cooperation and limited forbearance upon the issue of the Clerk's salary, it comes as an anti-climax to read in the *Journal* three years later, on December 15, 1769, a message from the Upper House to the House of Delegates that "We further observe that you have not make the usual Allowance to the Clerk of the Council, and therefore cannot Pass the Journal of Accounts as it now Stands, but if you shall think proper to make a Provision for his eventual Payment, in the same manner as was done in November Session 1766, we shall give Our Assent to the Passage thereof."

The power to legislate money bills and the proper procedure for making appropriations arose in another context in the November-December session of 1766, and this time the two houses could not strike an agreement. After the repeal of the Stamp Act, the House of Delegates passed a resolution of gratitude directed to two members of the Parliament who had led the effort for repeal. They were William Pitt, Earl of Chatham, and Charles Pratt, Lord Cambden; they were cited by the House for "defending and supporting the Rights and Liberties of their fellow Subjects." As an expression of thanks, the House proposed that "a sufficient Sum of Public Money be appropriated to purchase an elegant Marble Statue of the said Earl of Chatham, to be set up in such Place within the City of Annapolis, as the Lower House of Assembly shall direct" and that a portrait of Lord Cambden be made to be placed in the Provincial Court. Both the statute and the portrait, when completed, were to be "consigned" to the Speaker of the House.

The Upper House returned a firm "No" to this proposal. You have thereby assumed, it wrote to the House of Delegates in explanation, "the exclusive Right of appropriating or applying a sum of the Public Money, expressly by Law subject to the Disposition of the General Assembly; if you will frame a Bill for the purposes of that which we have rejected, in a manner Consistent with our Rights, We shall be willing to give our Assent to it."

The subordinate item of friction over the years, concerning the Governor's proclamations, could not be resolved in the late 1760s. The two houses refused to compromise upon placing an item in the Journal of Accounts to compensate the Governor for the expense of providing seals for proclamations of laws issued by him years earlier. The House of Delegates persisted in its argument that all the citizens knew of the laws and it was not necessary to proclaim them further.

## PROCEDURES

The House in 1766, by resolution, placed two controls upon the filing of petitions or "redress of grievances." This was the much-used device of the seventeenth and eighteenth centuries, and literally dozens of them would be submitted to the House during any session. A favorite subject was the release of a prisoner held for debt, his having, of course, few possibilities of meeting his obligations while in jail. The Assembly in 1732 had passed what seemed to be a rudimentary act for bankruptcy proceedings, permitting prisoners their freedom after filing an agreement to satisfy their creditors. Even this process had to be initiated by petition; and in the decades following 1732, hundreds of petitions for release had been filed. Accordingly, to regulate their numbers, the House on May 27, 1766, put a resolution in its *Journal* that it would not receive a petition for release from debt unless the prisoner previously had posted notice in the county where he was confined, having the fact of posting certified by justices of the county court.[15]

Other favorite subjects for petitions were from groups wanting new public buildings, such as jails or court houses, the division of church parishes, and other public facilities. These petitions also were restricted during the May session in 1766, by requiring public notice for at least two months before filing a petition.

The House of Delegates of Maryland had a visiting neighbor on May 25, 1766, one Thomas Jefferson of Virginia. He was at this time a young man of 23, on his first trip "north" from his native state. It was then three years before

---

15. Among all the American colonies, the practice of legislative petitions from insolvent debtors was seen most frequently in Rhode Island, Maryland, and New Jersey. *See* MARY PATTERSON CLARKE, PARLIAMENTARY PRIVILEGE IN THE AMERICAN COLONIES 52 (New Haven, 1943).

he was first elected to the House of Burgesses in Virginia. In writing to a cousin in Virginia, Jefferson left this description of proceedings in the Maryland House:[16]

> I will now give you some account of what I have seen in this metropolis. The assembly happens to be sitting at this time. Their upper and lower house, as they call them, sit in different houses. I went into the lower, sitting in an old courthouse, which, judging from it's form and appearance, was built in the year one. I was surprised on approaching it to hear as great a noise and hubbub as you will usually observe at a publick meeting of the planters in Virginia. The first object which struck me after my entrance was the figure of a little old man dressed but indifferently, with a yellow queüe wig on, and mounted in the judge's chair. This the gentleman who walked with me informed me was the speaker, a man of a very fair character, but who by the bye has very little the air of a speaker. At one of the justices' bench stood a man whom in another place I should from his dress and phis have taken for Goodall the lawyer in Williamsburgh, reading a bill then before the house with a schoolboy tone and an abrupt pause at every half dozen words. This I found to be the clerk of the assembly. The mob (for such was their appearance) sat covered on the justices' and lawyers' benches, and were divided into little clubs amusing themselves in the common chit chat way. I was surprised to see them address the speaker without rising from their seats, and three, four, and five at a time without being checked. When a motion was made, the speaker instead of putting the question in the usual form, only asked the gentlemen whether they chose that such or such a thing be done, and was answered by a yes sir, or no sir: and tho' the voices appeared frequently to be divided, they never would go to the trouble of dividing the house, but the clerk entered the resolutions, I supposed, as he thought proper. In short everything seems to be carried without the house in general's knowing what was proposed.

16. Quoted in *Archives,* LXI at xv, xvi (Letter of Transmittal).

The "little old man dressed but indifferently" in the Speaker's chair in Maryland would have been the Hon. Robert Lloyd of Queen Anne's County; the clerk "with a schoolboy tone and an abrupt pause at every half dozen words" was Turbutt Wright, then Clerk of the House. The "mob" would have been the august members of the House of Delegates of Maryland. When Jefferson was elected to the House of Burgesses in Virginia three years later, he either was more circumspect in his language, more accustomed to the ways of the world, or aware that his words might live to posterity. That body, he declared, was "the most distinguished body of men ever assembled to legislate."

# Chapter 13

## THE TOWNSHEND ACTS

### 1768-1772

The several years at the end of the 1760s were marked by a spirited dispute following the enactment of the Townshend Acts, together with the customary concerns over the prerogatives, procedures, and decorum of the House of Delegates and the usual legislative problems and issues. The long-time disagreements over the fees of officers exploded into the Steuart case. The building of a new State House brought to Maryland the famous building which two centuries later was to be extolled as the oldest State House in continuous legislative use.

### Enactment and Provisions

The series of laws known collectively as the Townshend Acts were enacted by the English Parliament in the late 1760s, to replace the Stamp Act. They were named for Charles Townshend, Chancellor of the Exchequer under William Pitt. They seem to have been rooted in an elaborate rationalization by Townshend, designed to meet the complaint of the American colonies that the Stamp Act was an exercise of "taxation without representation." However, except for a change in form and impact, the Townshend Acts equally represented "taxation without representation," so the protests from America continued in much the same vein as earlier.

The Stamp Act was enacted in 1765 and repealed in 1766. Units in the series of Townshend Acts were enacted by the Parliament in 1767, to be met with spirited protest in America and to be repealed in 1770.

Stamp taxes, in the jargon of tax people, were "internal" taxes, so called because they were applied and collected inside the colonies. The Townshend taxes, on the contrary, technically were "external" ones, to be collected as import duties on taxable goods being moved into the colonies. The Americans came quickly to identify them as "taxes," and whether they were "internal" or "external" seemed of little importance. As they were enacted by the Parliament, in which Americans were not and could not be represented, they were deemed also to be "taxation without representation." [1]

The Townshend Acts levied duties upon a number of products imported into the American colonies, including lead, glass, and tea. The taxes were not particularly high; and, as there had been such a tax upon molasses for a number of years, there was some reason to suppose the additional duties would not meet opposition.

Perhaps there would have been no unusual protest, as was the case with the tax on molasses, if the Parliament had stopped at this point. However, the English added provisions for enforcement which caused violent unrest in America. Collection of the duties was vested in British commissioners who were not under local control; British troops and revenue cutters were stationed in the colonies, and the device of "writs of assistance" was employed to help monitor collections.

---

1. "During the pre-Revolutionary debate, Americans gradually came to believe they alone remained uncorrupted and capable of defending the last vestiges of English liberty. Ideologically, the debate was between advocates of orthodox and opposition theories of the constitution; in fact, the debate was the inevitable result of the failure to extend parliamentary sovereignty to America.... Americans first sought salvation in slavish imitation of the British original, which led the assemblies dangerously toward similar pretensions of legislative supremacy." PETER S. ONUF (ed.), MARYLAND AND THE EMPIRE, 1773 — THE ANTILON-FIRST CITIZEN LETTERS 9 (Baltimore, 1974).

The latter was perhaps most heinous of all, in the American view. It authorized the issue and use of general search warrants by customs officers searching for prohibited or smuggled goods, in and for any premises whatever.

The outcry in the colonies was strong and quick. English customs officials and American informers were tarred and feathered; an English revenue sloop was burned; mobs attacked customs collectors and stole goods from them; the "Boston Massacre" in 1770 developed from taunts to English troops by American youngsters. The Province of Maryland was a part of the general unrest and, as had occurred in the protests against the Stamp Tax, the House of Delegates took a leading part in the excitement.

## REACTION IN MARYLAND

The first strong repercussions in the General Assembly of Maryland came during the May-June session of 1768. They were sparked by a circular letter from the Massachusetts House of Representatives, addressed to the lower house in each of the American colonies. The letter proposed that all the colonies join in concerted action against the Townshend Acts; it was read to the delegates in Maryland during this session in the spring of 1768.

Governor Sharpe, perhaps unintentionally, helped to precipitate legislative action in Maryland.[2] On June 20 of that year, he addressed to the House of Delegates a warning of the King's displeasure over the Massachusetts letter:

---

2. As the leading representative of the Proprietary and the King in the Province, Governor Sharpe naturally was not sympathetic to most of the contentions of the House. He once was quoted as having referred to the delegates as "flaming Patriots or rather inflaming Demagogues." DAVID CURTIS SKAGGS, ROOTS OF MARYLAND DEMOCRACY, 1753-1776 at 89 (Westport, Conn., 1973).

The governor communicates to Mr. speaker, the following message

Gentlemen of the lower house of assembly,

The King, our most gracious sovereign, having been informed, that a circular letter, a copy of which hath been communicated to his ministers, was, in February last, sent by the speaker of the house of representatives, of the colony of Massachusetts to the speakers of other houses of assembly in North America, hath been pleased to order it to be signified to me, that he considers such measure to be of a most dangerous and factious tendency calculated to inflame the minds of his good subjects in the colonies to promote an unwarrantable combination, to excite and encourage an open opposition to, and denial of the authority of parliament, and to subvert the true principles of the constitution; but while I notify to you his majesty's sentiments, with respect to this matter; I am also to tell you, that the repeated proofs which have been given by the assembly of this province, of their reverence and respect for the laws, and of their faithful attachment to the constitution, leave little room for his majesty to doubt of their shewing a proper resentment of such unjustifiable attempt to revive those distractions which have operated so fatally to the prejudice of both the colonies, and the mother country. And I flatter myself that in case such letter has been addressed to the speaker of your house, you will confirm the favorable opinion, his majesty at present entertains of his Maryland subjects, by taking no notice of such letter, which will be treating it with the contempt it deserves

20th June 1768.                    Horatio Sharpe

The Governor's message was phrased so strongly as to create rather than to allay a harsh reply. The answer came on the following day, June 21, in such detail and depth that it must have been in contemplation for some time. The House message was directed to King George III. Grounded in general political philosophy, Magna Carta, and the Charter of the Province, it argued the Maryland protest against the Townshend Acts:

To the Kings most Excellent Majesty,

Most gracious Sovereign
... Your Majesty's people of this province, conceive it a fixed, and unalterable principle in the nature of things, and a part of the very idea of property; that whatever a man hath honestly acquired cannot be taken from him without his consent: This immutable principle they humbly apprehend, is happily ingrafted as a fundamental into the english constitution, as is fully declared by Magna Charta and by the petition, and bill of rights: Hence it is that your Majesty's most distant subjects are justly entitled to all the rights, liberties, privileges, and immunities of your subjects born within the kingdom of England.

The letter to the King continued that in granting the Charter to Lord Baltimore, Charles I had promised that every Englishman "transplanted or hereafter to be transplanted" into the Province, and their children and descendants, should have "all privileges, franchises, and liberties of this our kingdom of England, freely, quietly, and peaceably to have and possess . . . ." Further, quoting from the Charter, inhabitants of the Province were assured that neither Charles I nor any successor would tax them with "any impositions, customs or other taxations, quotas, or contributions whatsoever ... upon any tenements, lands, goods or chattels within the same province . . . ."

The settlers in Maryland, it was continued, had worked and struggled to create and maintain the Province, thinking themselves secure in the principle that they would not be taxed except with their own consent:

Our ancestors firmly relying on the royal promise, and upon these plain and express declarations of their inherent, natural, and constitutional rights, at the hazard of their lives and fortunes, transported

457

themselves and families to this country, then scarcely known, and inhabited only by savages: The prospect of a full and peaceable enjoyment of their liberties and properties, softened their toils, and strength'ned them to overcome innumerable difficulties. Heaven prospered their endeavors and has given to your Majesty a considerable increase of faithful subjects, improved the trade, and added riches to the mother country. Thus happy in the enjoyment of the rights and privileges of natural born subjects, have they, and their posterity lived and been treated as freemen; and thus hath the great fundamental principle of the constitution, that no man shall be taxed but with his own consent, given by himself or by his representative been ever extended, and preserved inviolate in this remote part of your Majesty's dominions, until questioned lately by your parliament

The letter ended "with the deepest sorrow" and "all humility" that this great fundamental principle of the constitution had been "infringed." Concluding,

The people of this province, royal sire, are not in any manner, nor can they ever possibly be effectually represented in the british parliament; while therefore your Majesty's commons of Great Britain continue to give and grant the property of the people in America, your faithful subjects of this, and every other colony must be deprived of that most invaluable privilege, the power of granting their own money; and of every opportunity of manifesting by chearful aids, their attachment to their King, and zeal for his service, they must be cut off from all intercourse with their sovereign, and expect not to hear of the royal approbation, they must submit to the power of the commons of Great Britain, and, precluded the blessings, shall scarcely retain the name of freedom

Within moments after the letter to the King was approved by the House of Delegates, the *Journal* records receiving a letter from the Speaker of the House of Burgesses in Virginia, about "the late acts of parliament imposing duties

458

to be collected in America for the sole purpose of raising a revenue." Also, there was received a copy of "the late act of parliament conditionally suspending the legislative power of New York." In each instance, the Speaker was requested to write a "respectful answer in the name of the House." The penalty upon New York was the Parliament's response to the refusal of the Assembly in that colony to make provisions for the English troops sent there for law enforcement.

On the next following day, June 22, 1768, the House replied directly to Governor Sharpe concerning his message of June 20 about the King's displeasure over the letter from Massachusetts. It was said first that the House of Representatives of Massachusetts in framing the circular letter "have asserted their rights, with a decent respect to their Sovereign, and a due submission to the authority of parliament." The remainder of the letter to Governor Sharpe had some critical and biting comments about the Governor's role in the controversy:

> To his excellency Horatio Sharpe Esquire governor and commander in chief in and over the province of Maryland
> The humble address of the house of delegates.
> May it please your excellency,
> ... It is very alarming, to find, that at a time when the people of America think themselves aggrieved by the late acts of parliament, imposing taxes on them, for the sole and express purpose of raising a revenue, and in the most dutiful manner are seeking redress from the throne, any endeavors to unite in laying before their Sovereign, what is apprehended to be their just complaint, should be looked upon 'as a measure of most dangerous and factious tendency, calculated to inflame the minds of his Majesty's good subjects in the colonies, to promote an unwarrantable combination, excite and encourage an open opposition to, and denial of, the authority of parliament, and to subvert the true principles of the constitution;' we cannot but view this, as an attempt, in some of his Majesty's ministers, to

suppress all communication of sentiments between the colonies, and to prevent the united supplications of America, from reaching the royal ear. We hope, the conduct of this house, will ever evince their reverence and respect for the laws, and faithful attachment to the constitution; but we cannot be brought to resent an exertion of the most undoubted constitutional right of petitioning the throne, or any endeavors to procure, and preserve, an union of the colonies, as an unjustifiable attempt, to revive those distractions, which, it is said, have operated so fatally to the prejudice of both the colonies and the mother country. We have the warmest, and most affectionate attachment to our most gracious Sovereign, and shall ever pay the readiest and most respectful regard to the just and constitutional power of the british parliament; but we shall not be intimidated, by a few sounding expressions, from doing what we think is right

... What we shall do upon this occasion, or whether in consequence of that letter, we shall do any thing is not our present business to communicate to your excellency ....

Your excellency may depend, that whenever we apprehend the rights of the people to be affected, we shall not fail boldly to assert, and steadily endeavor to maintain and support them, always remembering what we could wish never to be forgot, that by the bill of rights, it is declared, 'That it is the right of the subject to petition the King, and all commitments and prosecutions for such petitioning, are illegal.'

Having thus expressed its disdain for the acts of the Parliament and the efforts of Governor Sharpe to withhold its criticism, the House proceeded in a series of formal resolutions to cover much of the philosophy and history already contained in the letter to the King. In a related set of eight resolutions the House made these points:

1. The settlers in Maryland brought with them the liberties, privileges, franchises, and immunities of the people of England.

460

2. By Magna Carta "and other the good laws and statutes of England, and confirmed by the petition and bill of rights" subjects are not to contribute to any tax not set by common consent of Parliament.

3. The Charter of Maryland guaranteed the inhabitants of this Province equality with Englishmen in matters of property and taxes.

4. The Charter is declaratory of the constitutional rights and privileges of the freemen of this Province.

5. Trial by jury is the grand bulwark of liberty; the erection of "other jurisdictions, for the tryal of matters of fact is unconstitutional, and renders the subject insecure in his liberty and property."

6. It cannot be said with any truth or propriety that the freemen of Maryland are represented in the British Parliament.

7. The people of Maryland have always enjoyed the right of being governed by laws to which they have consented, and this right has not been forfeited or given up.

8. The freemen of this Province in their legislative capacity have the sole right to lay taxes and impositions upon the inhabitants of the Province, or their property and effects; and laying a tax under any other authority is unconstitutional.

The Governor, in swift retaliation, notified the House that even without its prior notification it had no remaining business, his duty would have been to put an end to the session:

> The governor communicates to Mr. Speaker the following message:
> Gentlemen of the lower house of assembly,
> I am extremely sorry to find, by your address just now presented to me, that what I recommended to you, by his Majesty's express command, hath not had more weight

and influence in your house. Had you not instantly, on presenting your address, informed me, by a message, that no more business is before you, I should have been obliged, in obedience to his Majesty's commands, immediately to put an end to this session, in order to prevent any proceedings of your house, in consequence of the sentiments declared in your address.

Horatio Sharpe

Again in 1769 the House of Delegates returned to the issue of the Townshend Acts. At the November-December session that year, a set of resolutions was received from Peyton Randolph, Speaker of the Virginia House of Burgesses. They were generally on the pattern of the earlier resolutions from Maryland: that the right of imposing taxes in Virginia was vested solely in the House of Burgesses; the inhabitants had a right to petition for the redress of any grievance; trials for any crimes committed within Virginia should be tried by courts in that colony; and a "humble, dutiful, and loyal address" would be presented to the King, covering these several matters.

The House of Delegates in Maryland then passed another set of resolutions, substantially similar to those from Virginia. The Speaker was directed to notify Peyton Randolph of the Maryland resolutions and to send copies of them also to the several lower houses among the American colonies.

Another phase of the controversy with England occurred outside the Legislature, under the leadership of legislators and of merchants in the Province.[3] This was the development

---

3. "After Parliament imposed the Townshend duties the delegates to the Assembly even more definitely assumed leadership of the resistance to imperial centralization. As the elected representatives of the people of the Province they petitioned the king for repeal of the obnoxious duties. As private citizens they launched the non-importation association, which pledged the associators to import none of the taxed articles nor any of 125 other commodities on pain of being branded enemies of the liberties of

of so-called non-importation associations and agreements, calling for a complete cessation of some items among the import trade with England. A number of incidents arose under these agreements. The ship *Good Intent,* complete with cargo, was returned from Annapolis to England, in 1769; and similar refusals of admission were made on shipments to Baltimore Town and to ports in the counties of Anne Arundel, Charles, Dorchester, Prince George's, Queen Anne's, St. Mary's, and Talbot.

The non-importation agreements adopted throughout the Province had strong and decisive language. The one adopted by merchants in Annapolis declared that violators would be considered "Enemies to the Liberties of America." [4] A news item in the *Gazette* for October 12, 1769, reported that a vessel from England was refused admission in Philadelphia and had sailed for Maryland "where, when she arrives, it is hoped she will meet with the like reception." [5] Another report, published on June 7, 1771, was that the town of Newport, Rhode Island, had violated its non-importation agreement; the merchants' group in Annapolis resolved to have no further commercial intercourse with the colony of Rhode Island. There were other defections, including some of the merchants in New York City, Boston, and Philadelphia. A group of six merchants in Baltimore Town sought to have the non-importation agreements ended.

---

America. Of 43 signers, 27 were either already or else soon to be members of the Lower House. Association meetings were very nearly extra-cameral gatherings of the House of Delegates." Aubrey C. Land, *The Colonial Period,* in THE OLD LINE STATE — A HISTORY OF MARYLAND 31 (Morris L. Radoff, ed., Annapolis, 1971).

*See also,* EDWARD C. PAPENFUSE, IN PURSUIT OF PROFIT: THE ANNAPOLIS MERCHANTS IN THE ERA OF THE AMERICAN REVOLUTION, 1763-1805 (Baltimore, 1975).

4. *Maryland Gazette,* June 29, 1769.

5. *Id.,* February 15, 1770. The *Gazette* "both influenced and reflected local thought." *See* David C. Skaggs, *Editorial Policies of the Maryland Gazette, 1765-1783,* 59 MARYLAND HISTORICAL MAGAZINE 341-49 (1964).

When the *Good Intent* was turned away from Annapolis and sent back to England, the decision received combined consideration by the committees on non-importation from Anne Arundel, Baltimore, and Prince George's counties. Some difficult questions were raised during the discussion. Since the *Good Intent* was already engaged for another cargo, in what ship should its original cargo be returned? What would be the disposition of that part of the cargo which was admissible and not covered by the non-importation agreements? Would the owner's attorney receive compensation for his work in the case? The committees from the three counties held firm on the decision that the vessel and its entire cargo must go back to London; and nothing was said about the attorney or his compensation. The ship was ordered to lay in provisions and water and to be ready to sail, "Wind and Weather serving, on a Day's Notice." The Captain later reported that the ship "only waits to take on Board a Quantity of Bread sufficient for his Voyage, and will then proceed back to London." [6]

The Townshend Acts were repealed by the Parliament in 1770, so once more the immediate provocation was removed between the English government and the colonies. The next serious confrontation was caused by the Tea Act of 1773, when the controversies over colonial rights and prerogatives continued under the new heading. Meanwhile, there were other occasions for dispute, also involving rights of self-government and the respective spheres of legislative and of executive authority.

**6.** *See The Case of the Good Intent,* 2 and 16 MARYLAND HISTORICAL MAGAZINE (1908, 1921).

464

## Prerogatives, Procedures, and Decorum

During the latter 1760s, the usual array of questions and differences arose, having to do with the powers and prerogatives of the House of Delegates, decorum in the House chamber, and matters of rules, procedure, and elections.

Included on this list was the claim of the Governor for reimbursement for the cost of affixing seals on 15 proclamations to advertise acts of the Assembly. Though the claim was years old, the new Governor in 1769, Robert Eden,[7] filed it as usual. This was during the November-December session of 1769. Eden, for the "harmony" of the session, did not then press the matter; but he also made clear he did not intend to relinquish the "indubitable" right of a governor to receive these fees. During the September-November session in 1770, the House returned to this claim, reiterating unanimously that an allowance for it would not be granted.

Another perennial issue was that of money bills and the priorities between the two houses in their introduction, consideration, and amendment. The House of Delegates again stated its claims during the October-November session in 1771. In a message to the Upper House, the House was "much concerned" that the Upper House had proposed amendments to virtually all the money bills. The House of Delegates, it said, would always claim "as their undoubted and fundamental Right the sole and exclusive formation of all Money Bills, as well for the application, and disposition as

---

7. *See* Rosamond Randall Beirne, *Portrait of a Colonial Governor: Robert Eden,* 45 Maryland Historical Magazine 153-75, 294-311 (1950). Eden was married to Caroline Calvert, a daughter of Charles Calvert, fifth Lord Baltimore. A descendent of the Edens, Anthony Eden, was a member of the English Cabinet during World War II. While in America during the war, he spoke to a joint session of the two houses of the General Assembly of Maryland.

for the granting and raising of all Public Money, nor will we ever give up, or wave or weaken that Right in any manner."

The Upper House, as for many years, did not at all agree with the House in its claims for exclusive power over money bills. The *Journals* illustrate, it said, that for many years there had been "abundant Instances" of money bills amended in the Upper House, of such bills framed in a joint committee, and of their "having taken their Rise in the Upper House." "We must think," concluded the Upper House, "your Complaint of Innovation, and claim of privilege to be most extraordinary .... We trust that whilst we act upon these principles Candour will acquit us of all Designs to multiply the Topics of Controversy which indeed are already too many." [8]

The House decisively resolved an individual question of legislative decorum, during the May-June session of 1768. The question was submitted to the House whether one of its members might have leave to attend a session of the Upper House as counsel for a bill on which he had voted in the House of Delegates. The bill concerned a petition to erect a court house and prison in Baltimore County. By a vote of 2-40 the House decided that its member could not appear before the Upper House.

The dignity of the House was at stake, or so it claimed, in an incident arising from Baltimore County. Late in the year 1769, because of a coming election for the Assembly, a

---

8. A compromise could not be reached in the struggle between the two houses "because it was rooted in an irreconcilable difference of claim. When the Upper House spoke of its privilege, honor, and dignity, it was referring to a charter the terms of which are traceable to the fourteenth century; when the Lower House spoke of its privileges, it had in mind the precedents and practices of the House of Commons in the seventeenth century which it used as guides of its own organization and conduct." 2 Charles M. Andrews, The Colonial Period of American History 327 (New Haven, 1936).

number of residents of that county petitioned to have a polling place at Joppa as well as in Baltimore Town. They cited in explanation the smallpox prevailing in Baltimore Town. A bill for the purpose was passed at the November-December session in that year, but with the extra polling place scheduled for Bush Town, rather than at Joppa.

The trouble arose after another petition received from Baltimore County protested the enactment of this bill. The second petition said that the bill had been sought and passed to please a few individuals and was of no benefit to the public; that it was repugnant to the laws and customs of the Province; and that the original petition was "devoid of Truth."

When the Assembly came back into session in September, 1770, the House of Delegates ordered its Sergeant-at-Arms to take into custody those who had signed the second petition, saying it reflected on the "Honour, Justice and Impartiality" of the House and was "derogatory of it's Rights and Privileges."

Although in retrospect the offense seems trivial, the House of Delegates gave it the complete treatment. The alleged signers appeared before the House, and the *Journal* tells in some detail of the judgments upon them. One John Smith said he never signed the petition "or was privy of assenting to the same," and that he was in Carlisle at the time he understood the petition was signed. He was reprimanded, but that was because he "misbehaved" himself when the order of the House was served upon him.

John Purviance testified he never signed the petition, nor was he "privy to or assenting to the same." He was discharged from further proceedings. James Sterrett said he was ill in bed when those distributing the petition visited his home. His wife told him what the visitors wanted, and he said they might put his name on the petition; but "he never saw the said Petition, or was acquainted with the language

467

thereof, or was otherwise privy or assenting to the same."
He was discharged.

Next came the case of six persons who responded to the
order to appear before the House only by a letter, jointly
signed. They had no thought of any "Reflection or Indignity
. . . on the Conduct of the House," they said. "Whatever
exceptionable Expressions" were in the petition "were rather
the Effect of Inadvertency and Hurry, than any
premeditated Design, to insult the House. . .," it continued.
Finally, "We flatter ourselves, the House will accept this
Apology, for our Conduct, and excuse our Personal
Attendance which we omit, not from Disrespect, to the
Process of the House, but from the inconveniency of such
Numbers as signed that Petition being absent from their
respective Homes."

The six petitioners might have been "flattered," but not
the House of Delegates of Maryland: "This House, on Order
to attach the body," it immediately resolved, "will receive no
Apology by Letter, and . . . the Subscribers of the above
Letter are guilty of a Contempt of the Order of this House
in not appearing." The Sergeant-at-Arms was ordered to take
all six into custody, for "reflecting on the Honour, Justice
and Impartiality of this House, and highly derogatory of its
Rights and Privileges; and also to answer for their Contempt
in not obeying the former Order of this House."

One of this group of six petitioners was a physician, who
cited that his absence "might prove fatal to several
Patients." Also, he said, the only reason he was in Baltimore
Town, where he signed the petition, was to attend a meeting
about the smallpox then prevalent; when asked to sign, he
saw many respectable names on it and supposed the signers
knew "what ought to be done as they are Natives of this
Country." The House accepted his excuse.

Two others of the six appeared and said they signed the
petition in ignorance of its contents; charges against them

were dismissed, with costs. The complaints against the remaining three signers (including two who were alleged to have answered the summons by saying they would attend the House "if it suited them") were voided by circumstance. The Governor abruptly prorogued the Assembly a few days later.

## "Treating" the Voters

An election problem in the form of "treating" the voters came before the House in 1768. It involved an election in Baltimore County, in late 1767. John Ridgely, Thomas Cockey Deye, John Moale, and Robert Adair had been declared elected and had taken seats in the House. The following spring, however, two petitions challenged the election of all four delegates and lodged a complaint against the sheriff of the county for "mal-conduct" in the election. The charge was that all four of the Baltimore County delegates had engaged in "treating" voters. After its hearings, the House voted that all four delegates had not been properly elected, and they were "excused" from further attendance in the House. A warrant was issued for another election, which was held on July 5, 1768; three of the four expelled delegates were reelected, although (and for another reason) the sheriff later was censured for having conducted this second election in an "irregular" manner.[9] On July 14, a few days after the special election, the *Maryland Gazette*

---

9. A year and a half later, on December 14, 1769, the sheriff of Baltimore County was admonished by the House to be "more circumspect" in handling elections; it is uncertain whether this complaint involved the special election of July 5, 1768, or another election. The offense was that he had closed the polls on the second day of a scheduled election, against the consent of one of the candidates and when the sheriff had reason to believe a number of persons were on their way to the polls and that others might be expected the next day. The sheriff's admonition was accompanied by an assessment of some ten pounds for costs.

THE GENERAL ASSEMBLY OF MARYLAND

noted dryly that "We are informed the above Gent. carefully avoided Treating both before and after the Election to prevent the least colour for a second complaint on that account."

Following the Baltimore County election of late 1767, and the decision that all four delegates involved had been engaged in "treating" voters, the House of Delegates by resolution attempted to set up uniform rules to prohibit the practice. Treating is "highly injurious, tends to corrupt and debauch the People" and may destroy freedom, the House declared. Without regard to "the greatness or smallness" of any treat, any person so elected should have his election declared void. The severity of language in the resolution much exceeded that found in ethics legislation some two centuries later:

> Resolved, That treating electors is highly injurious, tends to corrupt and debauch the people, and may, if not timely prevented, be destructive of that freedom, intended to be maintained in elections, by our excellent constitution
>
> It is therefore unanimously resolved, that on any petition for treating, this house will not take into consideration, or regard the greatness or smallness of any treat, but will, in all cases, in which any person or persons, hereafter to be elected to serve in assembly for any county within this province, at any time after the test or issuing of the writ of election, or after the place of any member becomes vacant hereafter, in the time of this present or of any other assembly, shall hereafter, by himself, or themselves, or by any other ways or means, on his, or their behalf, or at his, or their charge, or with his, or their privity or consent, before his, or their election, directly or indirectly give, present, or allow to any person having a voice or vote in such election, any money, meat, drink, entertainment, or provision, or make any present, gift, reward, or entertainment, or any promise, agreement, obligation, or engagement, to give or allow any money, meat, drink, provision, present,

reward, or entertainment, whatsoever, in order to be elected, or for being elected, will declare the election of such person void

At the same time, by an amendment to the original resolution, the House attempted to reach the problem of treating by a person other than the candidate, if done on behalf of or with the privity or consent of the candidate. The friend of the candidate was to be prevented from treating voters and in any way rewarding a voter in return for his vote for the candidate. The amendment also was very broad in its language and application:

> The question was put whether the following resolve, vizt. Also resolved, that if any person whatsoever, shall hereafter, after the test or issuing of the writ of election, or after the place of any member becomes vacant, directly or indirectly, on the behalf of, or with the privity or consent of any person, or persons, hereafter to be elected to serve in assembly, give, present or allow, to any person having a voice or vote, any money, meat, drink, entertainment or provision, or shall make any present, gift, reward, or provision, or make any promise, agreement, obligation, or engagement, to give, or allow, any money, meat, drink, provision, present reward, or entertainment whatsoever, in order to procure the election, or for the election of any person, or persons, hereafter to be elected to serve in assembly; such person shall be deemed guilty of bribery, and of a breach of the privileges of this house, and this house will punish the same accordingly; be agreed to? Resolved in the affirmative.

The amendment carried only by a vote of 15 to 14. Then, having adopted the original proposal to prohibit treating by the candidate and the amendment to prohibit treating for or on behalf of the candidate, the House declared "that the above resolves be standing rules in this house, and that they be printed in the Maryland gazette."

These orders against "treating" during election campaigns led to several disciplinary cases. Two Charles County delegates were so involved in 1771. Josias Hawkins was declared "guilty of treating at the late election," and Francis Ware also was declared in violation of the order of 1768.

## THE STEUART CASE

The Steuart case led into a sharp and prolonged disagreement during the late 1760s and early 1770s, between the House of Delegates and the Governor (including some of his executive officers). It went far beyond the actions and problems of William Steuart, being a curious and powerful amalgam of issues concerning such disparate topics as the Tobacco Inspection Act, the fees of officers, and the salaries of ministers of the gospel. The whole combination touched the basics of the legislative-executive power struggle.

The fight stemmed from the Tobacco Inspection Act of 1763, which the Assembly permitted to expire in 1770. The so-called "inspection" act actually was much broader than the inspection of tobacco, for it included provisions about the fees of officers and the salaries (fees) of ministers. The expiration of the act of 1763 was not simply a matter of forgetfulness. The matter was considered in 1770, but the two houses could not agree upon a bill. The House of Delegates wanted to reduce some of the fees, and the Upper House wanted to keep them at the current levels.

In the estimation of the House of Delegates, there was a fatal flaw in the arguments of the Upper House. Some members of the Upper House, in addition to being members of the Council of State, held other lucrative offices in the Province and therefore had a personal interest in a high level of fees for officers. Two of them who figured prominently in the ensuing debates were Benedict Calvert, a brother of the

472

Proprietary, and George Steuart; both were judges of the Land Office, and both were members of the Upper House and the Council.

To add to the confusion, there was a heated debate over the precise effect of the failure to renew the act of 1763 (Chapter 18). It was clear that it had expired, and in effect was repealed; but some made the additional argument that expiration of the act of 1763, which had superseded the original act of 1702, had the incidental effect of renewing the act of 1702.[10] The majority opinion in the early 1770s seemed to be, however, that expiration of the act of 1763 had left the Province with no law fixing officers' fees and ministers' salaries. However, those holding to this view then had the problem of determining what these fees and salaries should be, and how they should be fixed.

A further complicating factor lay in the long-time practice of setting compensation of ministers in terms of a tobacco poll tax. Use of the poll tax frequently was criticised, and it had accompanying effects of distinguishing inequitably among ministers in the amounts of their compensation, without regard to abilities and service.[11] Some extreme

---

10. Such an argument probably could not be made in the twentieth century. *See* Art. 3, sec. 29 in the Constitution of 1867, providing that "no Law, nor section of Law, shall be revived, or amended by reference to its title, or section only; . . . and it shall be the duty of the General Assembly, in amending any article, or section of the Code of Laws of this State, to enact the same, as the said article, or section would read when amended. And whenever the General Assembly shall enact any Public General Law, not amendatory of any section, or article in the said Code, it shall be the duty of the General Assembly to enact the same, in articles and sections, in the same manner, as the Code is arranged . . . ."

11. Although the poll tax controversy involved local, and not imperial, taxation, it has been argued that "the rhetoric and tactics tested and refined in the proprietary context could be, and were, readily transferred to imperial problems." *See* Jean H. Vivian, *The Poll Tax Controversy in*

examples were cited. One "bizarre case" involved a "heavy drinker" who was rector of St. Anne's Parish in Annapolis until he was "packed off" to All Saints Parish in Frederick; he had complained that his income in Annapolis was "hardly sufficient to keep him in liquor." [12] Opposition to the poll tax was evident in the Constitution of 1776, drafted only a few years later. Article 13 of the Declaration of Rights in that document provided "That the levying taxes by the poll is grievous and oppressive, and ought to be abolished." Elsewhere in the Declaration of Rights (Article 33), however, it was said that "the legislature may in their discretion levy a general and equal tax for the support of the christian religion . . . ."

After the Inspection Act of 1763 expired and there no longer was a law fixing applicable fees, Benedict Calvert and George Steuart instructed their clerk, William Steuart, to continue charging the same fees as had been specified in the former law. Under this authorization, William Steuart charged and accepted fees and notes in these former amounts, and he thereby won himself a spot of immortality in the legislative annals of Maryland.

---

*Maryland, 1770-76: A Case of Taxation with Representation,* 71 MARYLAND HISTORICAL MAGAZINE 151-76 at 176 (1976).

**12.** *See* James Haw, *Maryland Politics on the Eve of the Revolution: The Provincial Controversy, 1770-1773,* 65 MARYLAND HISTORICAL MAGAZINE 105 (1970).

"The Anglican Church in America fell somewhat short of its promise. Secure and self-satisfied, like the parent establishment in England, it clung to a faith that was less fierce and more worldly than the religion of Puritanical New England. Sermons were shorter; hell was less scorching; and amusements, like Virginia fox hunting, were less frowned upon. Most of the Anglican clergy were earnest and devout men, but some were indolent and worldly, and occasionally a scoundrel would appear who was more interested in winning at cards than in winning souls for the Lord." THOMAS A. BAILEY, THE AMERICAN PAGEANT — A HISTORY OF THE REPUBLIC 75 (Boston, 2nd ed. 1961).

During the September-November session of 1770, the House Committee on Grievances and Courts of Justice reported these facts to the House, "Which Proceedings and Doings in the said Land Office your Committee are of Opinion are in no wise warranted by Law and are oppressive and grievous to the People of this Province." On November 1 the House voted unanimously to concur with the committee report. Part of the report was the inclusion of an earlier report from the same committee, dated May 28, 1739: "Your Committee humbly observe that by the Royal Charter, the Resolves of your Honourable House, and the Common Custom of this Province, the Subjects here are entitled to the Customs, Common Law, and the securitive Statutes of the Rights and Liberties of the Subjects in our Mother Country, Great Britain, by which Custom of Great Britain, such like ffees ... have been settled by Acts of Parliament...."

The House acted immediately on November 1, 1770, to claim its right to impose and establish all taxes and fees, It ordered Steuart (William, that is) before the Bar of the House for an explanation:

> Resolved, unanimously, That the Representatives of the ffreeman of this Province have the sole Right with the Assent of the other Part of the Legislature to impose and establish Taxes or ffees; and that the imposing, establishing, or collecting, any Taxes, or ffees, on or from the Inhabitants of this Province under Colour, or Pretence of any Proclamation issued by, or in the Name of the Lord Proprietary, or other Authority, is arbitrary, unconstitutional, and oppressive—
>
> Resolved, unanimously, That in all Cases where no ffees are established by Law for Services done by Officers the Power of ascertaining the Quantum of the Reward for such Services is constitutionally in a Jury upon the Action of the Party.
>
> Resolved, unanimously, That the Notes taken by William Steuart, Clerk of the Land Office, from William Hamlin, Thomas Elliott, and John Brooker Meek, are illegal and void; and the ffees intended thereby to be secured, are excessive and not warranted by Law.

Resolved, unanimously, That the imposing any Oath, not appointed and required by Law, is illegal and of dangerous Tendency.

Ordered, That the said Resolves, with the Report, be immediately printed in the Maryland Gazette

Ordered, That the Serjeant at Arms, attending this House, do forthwith take into his Custody the Body of William Steuart, and have him immediately at the Bar of this House, to answer at the Bar of this House for taking Notes of Hand for the Payment of excessive ffees in the said Office, not warranted by Law; and also for imposing an Oath not appointed and required by Law.

When Steuart appeared before the House, his only defense was that he "acted in Obedience to the Orders of his Principals, and that he must continue so to act until otherwise ordered by them." The Speaker immediately issued a warrant to the Sheriff of Anne Arundel County to hold Steuart "for a high Contempt of this House; and keep him safe and close in the publick Gaol until he shall be thence discharged by Order of this House." This was the last piece of business recorded in the *Journal* for November 1, 1770. On the next day, November 2, Governor Eden prorogued the General Assembly, with a call to meet again on November 5. With the prorogation, Steuart was no longer within the jurisdiction of the House, and he was released from jail. Although the Governor did not so state at the time, there was no doubt in anyone's mind that the prorogation was directly for the purpose of freeing Steuart from jail.

When the Assembly met again on November 5, following the prorogation, the Governor in his usual opening address to the members assembled said that he hoped they would complete the business recommended by him at the opening of the prior aborted session. Although he certainly did not intend such a result, the House of Delegates neatly turned the phrase upon him: "We shall therefore take up that Business as nearly as can be done, in the same State it was dropt by the late abrupt Prorogation." Continuing, the House complained about the prorogation:

We should be wanting in Duty to your Excellency, to the People and to ourselves, were we to pass over in Silence a Measure, from which so many ill Consequences flow. When we view, as its Effects, a considerable Charge to the Province; a total Stagnation of Business for several Days; Bills of Importance before both Houses unfinished, that must be taken up anew; the Journal of Accounts laying before the Upper House; the Petitions of many People defeated, or with Expense and Difficulty renewed; an Enquiry into the Grievances of others stopped, and the Parties laid under the Necessity either of attending at a heavy Expence, or going away unheard; a publick Offender released, and publick Justice evaded; we cannot but complain of the prorogation as an undue and illadvised Exertion of Power: That Power with which your Excellency, as supreme Magistrate, is constitutionally invested for the Good of the People. Whatever might have been your Excellency's Motive, we may be allowed to conjecture, that as the immediate Releasement of Mr. William Steuart was to be the certain Effect, his Commitment was the true Cause of the Prorogation. . . .

The House of Delegates then furnished the Governor with a list of Steuart's offenses, being in total "such a violation of the law, such an Invasion of the Rights of the Subject, as cannot be submitted to by a free People." Also, said the House:

The Proprietor has no Right, Sir, either by himself, or with the Advice of his Council, to establish or regulate the ffees of Office; and could we persuade ourselves, that you could possibly entertain a different Opinion, we should be bold to tell your Excellency, that the People of this Province ever will oppose the Usurpation of such a Right.

We will not suppose that your Excellency had any Knowledge of or could possibly countenance these Transactions; and, therefore, we can with the greater ffreedom remonstrate against the Conduct of the Honourable Benedict Calvert and George Steuart, Esquires, who have thus daringly insulted the whole

Legislature at that Time assembled for the very Purpose of regulating Officers ffees, by attempting to introduce a Regulation of ffees by Proclamation; a Measure odious to the whole Province.

About two weeks later in the session, on November 20, 1770, Governor Eden addressed a long reply to the House of Delegates. He was blunt in disputing the House version of the affair; and he argued strongly that if William Steuart had committed the offenses charged, he should have been tried by the judiciary:

> Pretences for Censure are so easily framed that the most circumspect Behaviour can't prevent them. When they unhappily excite Animosity, give rise to querulous Expostulation, tend to promote popular Discontent, and obstruct the Course of publick Business, tho' the Mischiefs they produce, are much to be lamented, yet I can't but derive great Consolation from Reflection, when they spring from Passions I am not answerable for. Your positive Assertion, that the last Prorogation was an undue and ill advised Exertion of Power, permit me, Gentlemen, to observe, carries with it no Reasoning to convince my Judgment, nor any Authority to preclude a Vindication, especially as the Motives, which influenced me to apply for the Advice of those who are appointed by the Constitution to give it, and the Reasons by which they evinced the Propriety of their Opinion, have not been explained to you. . . .
>
> It can hardly, I presume, be a Question, whether when a Subject in this Government is illegally deprived of his personal Liberty, it is the Duty of the executive Power to relieve him. Whether, where the Authority to afford Relief is placed, there the Application for it is regular. Where this is cognizable, there the Propriety of it is determinable? The Right of Petition is established for Purposes so important, and secured, and enforced by Sanctions so interesting, that the Representatives of a free People, can never, on any Occasion, dispassionately wish to impair, or discountenance it. They would rather be inclined to connive at Improprieties in the Manner of

478

exercising the Right, than scan it with a View to censure. . . .

I required the Consideration, and Advice of the Council upon all the Circumstances of the Case, and their Opinion was, that you had assumed an unwarrantable Jurisdiction, which, if admitted, would cancel all the Guards, and Securities, provided by a wise, and free Polity for the Protection of the Subject, and that, having been illegally deprived of his Personal Liberty, Mr. Steuart was entitled to the Relief, which an Exertion of the Prerogative might afford him. In Consequence of this Opinion, and the Reasons by which it was supported, I interposed by proroguing the General Assembly from ffriday, till the Monday next following; after having passed all the Bills ready for my Assent, and flattered myself, that a short Recess (as it had been on other Occasions) would rather be productive of sedate Reflection, than of the heavy Charge that I had effectually dismissed a publick Offender from Confinement, obstructed publick Justice, and in Terms of very indefensible Exaggeration, occasioned a considerable Expence to the Province, and a total Stagnation of important Business for several Days. In Vindication, as well of the Gentlemen of the Council, as of myself, I shall succinctly rehearse the Reasons they advanced in Support of their Advice. They observed that, where the Legislature and executive Authorities, the Will to ordain, and the power to enforce it, are lodged in the same Person, or persons, there a Tyranny is established; That under this free Constitution, these Authorities are therefore, distributed into different Apartments; That the Executive being in the supreme Magistrate; neither House of Assembly can undertake the Administration of existing Laws without a dangerous Infringement of the Constitution: That, of the Legislative, you are but one of the component Parts; That a Right to Determine the ffees charged were excessive, implies the Right to settle the exact Compensation due for the Services performed, because without the Standard what ffees are adequate, what are more, or less than the just Proportion can't be ascertained; That your rigorous Commitment was bottomed on the Principle that, to you belongs the Authority of Punishing any Deviation from the Line of your Opinion . . . .

The Governor also sent to the House a copy of a letter he had from Benedict Calvert and George Steuart, explaining their joint action in adopting a set of officers' fees for William Steuart. Neither the Governor's message nor the letter from Benedict Calvert and George Steuart would at all convince the House of Delegates. On the last day of the session, the House adopted a series of resolutions adamantly insisting upon its right for legislative prerogatives to prevail over the executive and administrative decisions:

> On Motion, Resolved, unanimously, That this House is constitutionally invested with a Power to commit to the publick Gaol by Way of Punishment any Person for Breach of Privilege or Contempt, there to remain till discharged by Order of this House.
>
> Resolved, nemine contradicente, That this House as the grand Inquest of the Province has an unquestionable Authority founded on Precedent, and long uninterrupted Usage to hear and enquire into all Complaints and Grievances; and as incidental to that Authority has constitutionally a Power to commit any Person for any Crime whatsoever to the publick Gaol there to remain till he be discharged by due Course of Law.
>
> Resolved, That . . . his Lordship has no Right to settle and regulate the ffees or Reward to the Registers or Officers of the Land Office for Services performed by them therein.

This second session during the fall of 1770 also was abruptly prorogued by the Governor, evidently fearful that the House once more would attempt to imprison William Steuart.

Three days after the second prorogation, on November 24, an order was issued in the name of the Proprietary regulating the fees that could be charged by the Land Office.

Also, in a proclamation issued on November 26, it was directed that no fees should be charged greater than those fixed by the expired act of 1763. The proclamation was worded adroitly, to cite the need to prevent the charging of extortionate fees; its practical effect, of course, was to continue the fees in the act of 1763 (which in turn had continued the fees set in an amending act of 1747 and which some members of the Assembly thought were too high). After the extended dispute covering two sessions in the fall of 1770, the Legislature was out of session, and neither party had changed its stance.

There were incidental and side effects to the long controversy over fees and prerogatives. One occurred in Charles County. Feeling the need for some sort of tobacco inspection act, without regard to fees, planters in that county organized a private inspection system, to prevent the sale of "Virginia trash for Maryland tobacco." Other counties did the same, in an extra-legal attempt to maintain standards for the export trade.[13]

Another incidental effect came in a claim from the clergy as to the proper amount of their tobacco polls, and that brought on its own legal ramifications. The tobacco inspection act of 1763 had set each clergyman's poll in the amount of 30 pounds of tobacco annually for each resident; and the same figure had been set in the earlier act of 1747. Referring back to the original act of 1702, and citing the theory that the expiration of the act of 1763 and its earlier version of 1747 had caused a revival of the act of 1702, some of the clergy claimed the poll of 40 pounds of tobacco established by that original act. That claim, in turn, sparked a further argument about the possible invalidity of the entire act of 1702. It had been passed at a spring session in 1702, on the call of King William, and the act in question cited him

---

13. *See* Haw, *op. cit.,* at 107.

as being on the throne. He died while the 1702 session was in progress, however, and perhaps not only that act but the entire product of the 1702 session were completely void. That question never was settled legally.

It was almost a year until the Assembly met again, in October and November of 1771. The House of Delegates had not forgotten its quarrel with William Steuart, and once more it summoned him to appear. Also, the House had an additional report from its committee:

> By the Committee of Aggrievances and Courts of Justice
>
> October 10th 1771
>
> Your Committee humbly beg Leave to report to the Honourable House that the ffees of several of the Officers and Ministers of this Province their deputed Ministers and Servants are in themselves as now paid excessive great and oppressive to the Subject; and that the said ffees are under no Regulation of any Law of this Province. That your Committee were informed that several Officers do charge and receive ffees for Services performed by them in their respective Offices under and by Virtue of some Proclamation issued and published in the Name of his Excellency as Lieutenant General and Chief Governor of this Province. . . .

Next came the inevitable set of resolutions, stating the prerogatives of the House and criticising both the Governor and the Proprietary. The resolutions were adopted by the House on October 18, 1771, by a vote of 32-3:

> Ordered, That the following be entered as the Resolves of this House
>
> Resolved unanimously, That the Representatives of the Freemen of this Province have the sole Right, with the Assent of the other Part of the Legislature, to impose and establish Taxes or Fees; and that the imposing, establishing or collecting any Taxes or Fees on or from the Inhabitants of this Province under Colour or Pretence of any Proclamation issued by or in the

Name of the Lord Proprietary or other Authority is arbitrary unconstitutional and oppressive

Resolved, unanimously, That in all Cases where no ffees are established by Law for Services done by Officers the Power of ascertaining the Quantum of the Reward for such Services is constitutionally in a Jury upon the Action of the Party

Resolved, unanimously, That the Proclamation issued in the Name of his Excellency Robert Eden the Governor with the Advice of his Lordship's Council of State on the 26th Day of November 1770 is illegal, arbitrary, unconstitutional and oppressive

Resolved, unanimously, That the Paper Writing under the Great Seal of this Province issued in the Name of the Lord Proprietary on the 24th Day of November 1770 for the ascertaining the Fees and Perquisites to be received by the Registers of the Land Office is illegal, arbitrary, unconstitutional and oppressive.

The Question was put That the following be entered as the Resolve of this House

Resolved, That the Advisers of the said Proclamations are Enemies to the Peace, Welfare and Happiness of this Province and the Laws and Constitution thereof?

Resolved in the Affirmative.

Predictably, the adoption of resolutions to be sent to the Governor required a message to accompany them. It was dated November 22, 1771:

.... Having, as we hope, evinced to your Excellency's entire Satisfaction, that the Land Office is not a mere private, but a public Office, in which the Subjects here have a fixed and legal Interest; and stripping your Excellency's Proclamation of the ostensible Reason for issuing it, that it stands in it's Intention and Construction, as an implied Affirmative Allowance for the charging of Officers ffees, agreeable to the late Regulation; permit Us, Sir, to lay before you some of the Grounds and Reasons, which induce us to think your Excellency has attempted to exercise the Power, which can be constitutionally exercised only by the Legislature. By the Common Law, the Officers of

Justice were not intitled to any Reward from the Subject
for their Services; they were originally paid by the King
out of the Crown Revenues. In Process of Time, Statutes
were made for the Establishment and Regulation of
Fees. But in our Researches, we do not find a single
Instance of any Proclamation for levying the Salaries or
ascertaining the ffees of Officers.

"Property, in the very Nature of it, is an exclusive right,"
the House message continued. "Under this Idea, our happy
Constitution, anterior to any Statute extant, equitably and
justly provided, that the People only should be capable of
giving their own Property; and therefore no Tax could be
imposed upon them, but with their own Consent, given
personally, or by their Representatives." A number of
commentaries and statutes then were cited in support of this
right of property and of its disposition. One was a statute of
Edward I (1272-1307), and another was a commentary by
Lord Coke. In his enthusiasm, the author of the message
stepped partly out of anonymity and continued his prose in
the first person:

This Proclamation ought to be regarded with
Abhorrence; for who are a free People? Not *those* over
whom Government is reasonably and equitably
exercised, but *those* who live under a Government so
constitutionally checked and controuled that proper
Provision is made against its being *otherwise exercised.*
This Act of Power is founded on the Destruction of this
constitutional Security. If Prerogative may rightfully
regulate the ffees agreeable to the late Inspection Law,
it has a *Right* to fix any other Quantums; if it has a *Right*
to regulate to one *Penny,* it has a *Right* to regulate to
a Million; for where does its Right stop? At any given
Point? To attempt to limit it's Right, after granting it to
exist at all, is as contrary to Reason, as granting it to
exist at all is contrary to Justice; if it has any Right to
tax Us, then whether our own Money shall continue in
our own Pockets, or not, depends no longer on Us, but
on the Prerogative; there is nothing we can call our

own. . . . I repeat it again. I will maintain it to my last
Hours Taxation and Representation are inseparable.
This Position is founded on the Laws of Nature; it is
more it is itself an eternal Law of Nature; for whatever
is a Man's own, is absolutely his own; no Man hath a
Right to take it from him without his Consent, either
expressed by himself or his Representative; whoever
*attempts* to do it attempts an *Injury;* whoever *does* it,
commits a *Robbery.* He throws down the Distinction
between Liberty and Slavery. The Forefathers of the
Americans did not leave their native Country, and
subject themselves to every Danger and Distress, to be
reduced to a State of Slavery. They did not give up their
Rights; for should the *present Power* continue, there is
nothing which they can call their own: Or in the Words
of Mr. Locke, *"What Property* have *they* in that which
*another* may by *Right* take when he pleases, to
himself?"

Concluding the message, the House tied it nicely to the
resolutions that had preceded it. The resolutions had ended
by terming the *advisers* of the Governor's proclamation
"Enemies to the Peace, Welfare and Happiness of this
Province and the Laws and Constitution thereof." On the
same note of avoiding a direct confrontation with the
Governor, the message ended by telling the Governor "you
will be pleased to make known to us the Names of those ill
Advisers who have daringly presumed thus to tread on the
invaluable Rights of the Freemen of Maryland." The House
of Delegates approved the message by a vote of 31-3.

The Governor prorogued this session a few days later, on
November 30, 1771. His message of prorogation criticised
the House for "The vast Loss of Time to yourselves, and the
great Expence of Money to the Country which has accrued
this Session, and the very little Business that has been done
at it." He charged that the House in 1771 was completely
reversing its attitude toward a bill for fees that had been
considered in 1755; and he wrote of "the fflame you were

blown into at the Opening of the Session, by the mistaken Construction or Explanation of a Proclamation issued by me, solely for the Benefit of the People of this Province."

Even prorogation in 1771 did not end the matter; it was, indeed, one that only the Revolution could settle. At the June-July session in 1773, the House was back with another set of resolutions, substantially repeating its resolutions and messages of 1771.

One side phase of the Steuart case, the allowances to the clergy, continued for a number of years apart from the legal and technical aspects of the main argument. The House was particularly interested in solving the problem of uniformity of compensation without regard to individual duties and performance. On one occasion during the October-November session of 1771, that issue was in a conference committee; and the House conferees observed that while there was inequality in compensation, the lowest pay "is too good for the worst Clergymen." After extended arguments and disagreement within the conference committee, its work collapsed, leaving for posterity this disparaging exchange of mutual compliments between the two sets of conferees:

> The Conferees of the Lower House deliver to those of the Upper House the following.
> We are instructed to inform your Honours that a particular Answer to your illeberal Language cannot be productive of any Publick Good; and not being disposed to attempt a Rivalship with your Honours in the Talents for petulance and impertinent invective the Lower House have ordered an End to be put to this Conference.
> Whereupon the Conferees of the Upper House deliver to those of the Lower House the following.
> The Style of the Paper now delivered by the Conferees of the Lower House is so consistent with the Spirit of their other Proceedings that we are not Surprised at it, and most willingly Consent an End may be put to an Intercourse so extremely disagreeable.

486

So Ends this Conference, the 26th day of November Anno Domini 1771.

Late in 1773 a group of clergymen wrote directly to Governor Robert Eden about their "unhappy situation." If there is any well-founded objection to the system of fees, they said, "we think it is, in some Instances, it gives too large Salaries." They proposed a sliding scale of compensation, based upon the number of taxable persons in each parish. They concluded with tolerance and good humor that if any plan could be devised acceptable to the people, not injurious to the Church, and "not shaking the Foundation of our present Establishment . . ., we shall be happy."

The Steuart case was the longest and most bitterly contested of those involving fees, but there were others. Sometimes the question involved "excessive" fees rather than fees *per se.* Surveyors throughout the Province frequently were charged with having collected exorbitant fees, and a number of them were before the Bar of the House in October, 1771. One of them was Theophilus Hanson. In his case, the House determined that "he seemed rather to have followed the Charges of others than to have had any real Intention of Extortion," and he was discharged from further action. Another fortunate one was Arnold Elzey, Deputy Surveyor of Somerset County. In his case, "The House having heard what Mr. Elzey had to say, discharged him without payment of ffees."

John Frederick Augustus Priggs, Deputy Surveyor of Prince George's County, was less fortunate. The House issued him a reprimand and offered to discharge him upon payment of some 15 pounds in fees and allowances. Priggs refused to pay any such penalties, "alledging that he ought not to pay them." Accordingly, the House ordered its Sergeant-at-Arms to take him into custody as "guilty of a Contempt of the Authority of this House"; and he was ordered to remain in custody "until he be discharged therefrom by Order of this House."

## LEGISLATIVE PROBLEMS AND ISSUES

The sheriff of Charles County, Richard Lee, Jr., was the central figure in a 1769 case involving chastisement of an administrative officer. He was charged with cruel treatment of two prisoners in his custody. The House referred the problem to its Committee of Grievances, which asked to have the complainants called in for personal testimony. Sheriff Lee did not appear for the hearing, the word being that he was absent in Virginia. The Committee was told that the sheriff kept his prisoners for debt in a room some 15 feet square with no facilities for heat, and that one of the prisoners had been whipped. In the absence of the sheriff the only recourse for the House was to ask the Governor for his removal. This the Governor refused to do. The only punishment that could be meted out by the House was to force Lee to pay the costs for the complaint.

The House had to settle two problems of electoral procedure during its session of October-November, 1771. One was an easy matter concerning Sheriff Robert Hollyday of Baltimore County, for a mild infraction in returning the results of the current election. Four delegates were elected, but the sheriff sent in their names under a single indenture, instead of multiple and separate copies. The sheriff was admonished and directed to make individual returns; costs for some four pounds were assessed against him.

There was a more serious problem concerning Delegate Jonathan Hagar of Frederick County.[14] His problem was that he was neither a natural-born subject nor descended

---

14. Frederick County was the most westerly of all organized counties, then including the present Montgomery and Washington counties. It had long been unofficially organized into the lower, middle, and upper districts. Jonathan Hagar came from the upper district. He was the founder of Hagerstown, for a time called Elizabeth Town. After being expelled from the House in 1771, he was reelected to the Assembly meeting in June-July, 1773. *See* Basil Sollers, *Jonathan Hagar, The Founder of Hagerstown,*

from one; he had been naturalized in Maryland in the year 1747, and there was a serious question whether under existing statutes he qualified for membership in the General Assembly.[15]

The House held long and weighty deliberations on the Hagar case, including the study of a number of earlier English and Maryland statutes. On motion of House members, the earlier laws read included an English enactment under William III (1694-1702), and a Maryland act of 1716, two English statutes under George II (1727-1760), and a Maryland act of 1753. By a close vote of 23-24, Hagar was declared not a member and discharged from further attendance in the House. The question is described in the House *Journal* for October 8, 1771:

> Then the House took the several Statutes, the Act of Assembly, and the Resolves abovementioned into consideration, and after some Debate thereon, Mr. Hagar withdrew, and Mr. Speaker, by the Direction of the House, put the following Question: "That Jonathan Hagar, returned as a Representative for Frederick County, not being a natural born Subject, nor descended from a natural born Subject, but naturalized in the Year 1747, since the Stat of 13, Geo. 2. agreable to said Stat. long before said Election; hath been a Resident of this Province ever since, and hath a Freehold of fifty Acres of Land, be eligible?"
> Resolved in the Negative.

The Hagar case was to be discussed again in the House of Delegates on October 28, 1773, immediately prior to an unprecedented motion of the House for declaring its session adjourned.

---

Second Annual Report of the Society for the History of the Germans in Maryland, 1887-1888 at 21-28 (Baltimore).

15. In a growing country, with constant immigration, it may be wondered that the question did not arise more often.

When Robert Eden succeeded to the office of Governor of the Province, in 1769, as the replacement for Horatio Sharpe, the House of Delegates sent a special message to the Proprietary as a welcome for the new Governor. The House also seized the opportunity to comment upon the former Governor, with whom it had a long record of contention. "A Retrospection upon the Proceedings of this House," said the House with admirable delicacy, "will not permit us to say that Mr. Sharpe always paid a due regard to the Interests of the Province; yet we must acknowledge it is our Opinion, that his own Inclination led him very much towards that desirable Object." [16]

Some unidentified members of the Assembly suffered a time of frustration and uncertainty in 1772, when a person or persons unknown circulated a handbill about the Legislature written in Latin. The incident possibly would have been mentioned in the *Journal,* but for the fact that the Assembly was in a time of prorogation. The perturbed members took the next available alternative and went to the tolerant pages of the *Maryland Gazette* (March 12, 1772):

> To the Printer of the Maryland Gazette.
> Whereas we have seen a printed Paper now in Circulation, (written in *Latin,* and addressed to the General Assembly of *Maryland,* as we are told) which we do not understand; and which therefore most probably

---

16. While still Governor, Sharpe had constructed a new home at Whitehall. He was a bachelor, and the tradition is that he built the new home in the hope of marrying Mary Ogle, daughter of former Governor Samuel Ogle. Miss Ogle, however, married John Ridout, the long-time secretary for Governor Sharpe. When Sharpe returned to England in the early 1770s, he left Whitehall in the custody of John Ridout; and when Sharpe died some twenty years later, Ridout succeeded to full ownership in the property. Advocates of the tradition may note that Mary Ogle lived in Whitehall for many years, though not as the bride of Horatio Sharpe. *See* Charles Scarlett, Jr., *Governor Horatio Sharpe's Whitehall,* 46 MARYLAND HISTORICAL MAGAZINE 9 (1951).

contains Suggestions and Insinuations highly derogatory to the Honour of said General Assembly: We whose names are underwritten, being Members, and having the dignity thereof at Heart, request the Author of said Paper to put into our own vulgar Tongue, in order that we may have a fair Opportunity of confuting any false and scandalous Charges therein contained.[17]

A E I M Q V Y

B F J N R U Z

C G K O S W &

D H L P T X

### Rules and Petitions

During the September-October session in 1770, the House of Delegates added another item to its rules. It enjoined the officers of the House to be "particularly attentive that no Person do lean on, or converse with any Member, across the Bar of the House, or make any Sign to any Member to come out." Instead, "application" was to be made to the doorkeeper, but even that was forbidden "during the Reading of, or Debate and Deliberation upon any Matter or Thing whatever."

On the same day, October 18, 1770, two other orders in the form of rules were adopted, but without specifying they were actually to be added to the rules. One was a routine prohibition against a member leaving the House during proceedings. The other could have had a potential for trouble and possible embarrassment. With no exception whatever, it directed that if a letter or packet directed to the Speaker should come to the "hand or knowledge" of the Speaker (or to the person who last was Speaker if it occurred during a

---

17. The symbology of the letters of the alphabet is not explained; and the transposition between the "v" and the "u" was in the original. Query: was it all an elaborate hoax?

time of dissolution), "he do immediately take up and open the same and communicate the Contents thereof to this House at the next Session."

Having earlier restricted the right of filing petitions for appropriating public funds for construction projects and for release from jail for non-payment of debt, the House in 1768 fixed a time limit for submitting petitions questioning election returns. All such petitions were to be presented to the Speaker within five days from the first day of a session. Later, in 1774, a restriction was added for petitions for laying out new roads. Such a petition, it was said, must be advertised for one month before signatures might be sought for it, at a public place in the area and giving details about the direction and extent of the road.

A petition of some historical interest was received in the Upper House on October 17, 1771, from "Frances Colvill George Washington and John West Jun. Executors of Thomas Colville late of Fairfax County in Virginia."

Perhaps by all odds the most unusual petition of this or any other period came into the House of Delegates on May 31, 1768:

> The Humble Petition of Henry Darnall Junior, of Rachel Darnall Wife to the said Henry Darnall Junior, of Mary Darnall aged Nineteen Years, Daughter of the aforesaid Henry Darnall Junior and Rachel Darnall, and of Robert Darnall Uncle to the aforesaid Mary Darnall. Sheweth
>
> That an Advantageous offer of Marriage hath been made to the aforesaid Mary Darnall, and the Sum of three hundred Pounds Sterling a Year is proposed to be settled on the said Mary Darnall, during her natural Life in Lieu, and in Bar of Dower, and the Right she may have to the third part of the Personal Estate, which Settlement your Petitioners approve of, judging it to be for the Benefit of the said Mary, and are willing to execute the same on their parts, but Whereas the Petitioners are informed, that a Settlement to Bar the

492

said Marys Claim of Dower in the Lands, and the Share she might Claim of the Personal Estate, cannot be made effectual and binding in the Law upon the said Mary, she being yet an Infant under the Age of Twenty One Years, And as the Marriage aforesaid is deferred on Account of the apprehended invalidity of the Settlement, intended to be made should it be executed at this time.

Your Petitioners thereof humbly pray, that, in Order to remove all Doubts, about the force and validity of such a Settlement, A Bill may be brought in and passed into a Law, to impower the said Mary Darnall, by and with the Advice of your Petitioners, to enter into and assent to the aforesaid Marriage Settlement, or Articles for the Securing the said Jointure to the said Mary, and in bar of her Right of Dower, and the Share She might Claim of the personal Estate, by the Law or Usage of this Province

And that the said Settlement or Marriage Articles be made, to all Intents and purposes, as binding upon the said Mary Darnall, and of as full force and Virtue in Law as if she were of full Age.

And your Petitioners as in Duty bound will pray etc.

> Henry Darnall Junior
> Robert Darnall
> Rachel Darnall
> Mary Darnall.

The petition (as well as the bill quickly passed by the Assembly) did not in any manner identify the gentleman to whom Miss Darnall was to be wed. Actually, as certainly was known to all, it was Charles Carroll of Carrollton. The effect of the bill, in the event of Carroll's death, was to bar his widow from her dower and one-third interest in his personal estate; she and her family obviously thought the annual settlement of three hundred pounds sterling would be advantageous to her.[18] In any event, a bill was soon enacted,

18. Though it may be puzzling why the richest man in the Province should be concerned with barring his potential widow from her right of

being signed by the Governor only six days after the House received the petition.[19]

---

dower, the reason rather clearly was Carroll's desire to keep the family estate within the Carroll family, if he should die before his wife. Some years earlier, while Carroll was in England for his studies, he had courted an English girl and with marriage in mind had engaged in protracted negotiations with her father. The long negotiations and the questions they raised, plus doubts in Carroll's mind as he came to know her family better, led finally to his returning to America unmarried. *See* THOMAS O'BRIEN HANLEY, CHARLES CARROLL OF CARROLLTON: THE MAKINGS OF A REVOLUTIONARY GENTLEMAN (Washington, 1970). Carroll's marriage to Mary Darnall obviously was delayed, because of her minority, until the special act was passed by the Legislature.

Before the engagement to Mary Darnall, Carroll was engaged to another girl after his return from England. The marriage was postponed because of his serious illness; but she subsequently became ill and died before the ceremony.

While courting the English girl, Carroll wrote to his father that for his wife he hoped and expected "A chearful sensible virtuous good natured woman," though admitting that "not one in ten thousand is endowed with all these good qualities." His father's laconic reply was in a question: "Pray How many chearful sensible virtuous good natured men do you reckon" in ten thousand. *See Extracts from the Carroll Papers,* 2 MARYLAND HISTORICAL MAGAZINE 327-28, 339 (1916).

**19.** Daniel Dulany, perhaps the most able attorney in the Province, objected to the bill while it was in the Upper House. His point was that it is a "Standing Rule of this House not to pass Acts in Consequence of private Petitions, where the remedy or purpose sought is sufficiently provided for by the general existing Laws." In his judgment, the combined effect of a statute enacted under Henry VIII (1509-1547), and a Maryland act of 1715 made it clear that a young lady of 19 or 20 years clearly would be barred of a claim for dower, under the present circumstances; that in any event the husband could by deed dispose of his personal estate. Dulany questioned whether it was necessary or proper for the Legislature to interpose a special act. The wedding took place on June 5, one day after the Governor signed the bill. *Maryland Gazette,* June 9, 1768. As a postscript: Charles Carroll of Carrollton long outlived his wife.

## THE NEW STATE HOUSE

The "first stone" of the present State House was laid in the early spring of 1772. The event was described in the *Maryland Gazette* for April 2, 1772: "On Saturday last about Twelve o'Clock, his Excellency the Governor, attended by a Number of the Principal Gentlemen of this City, was pleased to lay the First Stone of the Foundation of the Stadt House; on which Occasion a cold Collation was provided for the Company, and after a few loyal and constitutional toasts had circulated, the Gentlemen retired, the Workmen giving three cheers on their Departure." [20]

## THE EVE OF REVOLUTION

The years between the repeal of the Townshend Acts in 1770 and the enactment of the Tea Act in 1773 were ones of deceptive quiet in the Province of Maryland. There was a brief respite in the issues of controversy between the Province and the English government. However, contention continued between the two houses of the Assembly and between the House of Delegates and the Governor. Accordingly, while the King and the Parliament had several years of relative quiet (so far as concerned this Province), there was no cessation for the Governor, and through him, Lord Baltimore. Legislative leaders, particularly in the

---

20. There is no reason to suppose from the context that the workmen actually were cheering for the departure. For background on the new building, *see* MORRIS L. RADOFF, BUILDINGS OF THE STATE OF MARYLAND AT ANNAPOLIS (Annapolis, 1954) and THE STATE HOUSE AT ANNAPOLIS (Annapolis, 1972). Also, for interesting speculation on the origin of the design for the State House dome, *see* Winifred and Douglas Gordon, *The Dome of the Annapolis State House,* 67 MARYLAND HISTORICAL MAGAZINE 294-97 (1972). It is thought that the Maryland dome was copied from that of the Schlossturm, a free standing tower on the palace of Karl-Wilhelm, Markgraf of Baden in Karlsruhe.

House of Delegates, had taken part in two victories over the English government, accomplishing the successive repeals of the Stamp Tax Act and the Townshend Acts. The House continued through the early 1770s to pursue a number of local grievances, and on such issues proceeded without interruption its opposition to whatever it conceived was a possible threat to the liberties and developing powers of the Province.[21]

The preeminent part taken by the House of Delegates in Maryland, in the pre-Revolutionary years, was much like the development in other American colonies. In all of them, after the middle 1760s, one ultimate issue came to be the growing legislative aspirations of the lower houses. The efforts of the Parliament to tax the colonies led the popular branches of colonial legislatures to claim equality with the Parliament in matters of taxation; and opposition to the Parliamentary taxes led to efforts of officials of the Crown to increase their administrative efforts at collection. On both sides there were reevaluations of the imperial-colonial connection; and on both sides there was a hardening of attitudes that could lead only to a constitutional impasse.[22]

---

21. "But what do we mean by the American Revolution? Do we mean the American war? The Revolution was effected before the war commenced. The Revolution was in the minds and hearts of the people; a change in their religious sentiments, of their duties and obligations. . . . This radical change in the principles, opinions, sentiments, and affections of the people was the real American Revolution." John Adams to Hezekiah Niles, 1818. BERNARD BAILYN, 1 THE IDEOLOGICAL ORIGINS OF AMERICAN POLITICS 160 (Pamphlets of the American Revolution, 1965).

22. *Cf.* JACK P. GREENE, THE QUEST FOR POWER: THE LOWER HOUSES OF ASSEMBLY IN THE SOUTHERN ROYAL COLONIES, 1689-1776 at 438 (Chapel Hill, 1963). This study covers the colonies of Virginia, North Carolina, South Carolina, and Georgia.

Barker describes the impasse as one of political authority located in England, in the person of Lord Baltimore, with the political function

In Maryland and elsewhere in America, by 1773, the stage was ready for the dramatic changes of the next three years.

---

located in Maryland within the General Assembly and the voters. *See* CHARLES A. BARKER, THE BACKGROUND OF THE REVOLUTION IN MARYLAND 117 (New Haven, 1940). *See also* Charles A. Barker, *The Revolutionary Impulse in Maryland,* 31 MARYLAND HISTORICAL MAGAZINE 125-38 (1941).

# Chapter 14

## THE TEA ACT
### 1773-1774

The Tea Act of 1773 was the third in the trilogy of English statutes which fanned ideas of revolution in America. There is irony in its history and repercussions; for while it was harmful to the merchant class in the colonies, it is arguable that it potentially helped most of the people. Whatever the balance of its impact, it led to riot, the destruction of property, and armed conflict; and ultimately to a hardening of attitudes that brought revolution.

The burning of the "Peggy Stewart" and the famous newspaper debate between "First Citizen" and "Antillon" were two of the notable reactions in Maryland to the enactment of the Tea Act. During the sessions in the years 1773 and 1774, the Assembly handled other and more usual legislative matters. A tobacco inspection act was passed; two new counties were formed; the controversial matter of a salary for the Clerk of the Council of State was settled. At the end of its work as a General Assembly, in the spring of 1774, the Legislature initiated a series of conventions to control the Province until 1777.

### ENACTMENT AND RESPONSE

The colonists by spirited protest had seen two of the English statutes repealed. The Stamp Act was enacted in 1765 and repealed in 1766. It was replaced by the Townshend Acts in 1767, and they in turn were largely repealed in 1770. The Tea Act in 1773 was designed not only to continue taxes on that commodity, but to show England's imperialistic concern for the tea business.

A central purpose of the Tea Act was to rescue the East India Company from some serious financial problems. Parliament loaned money to the company (which did not

499

concern the colonies), but it also gave the company a monopoly for the sale of tea in America. Prior to the Tea Act, the East India Company had sold tea to middlemen in England, who in turn had sent it to merchants (other middlemen) in the colonies. The Tea Act provided for direct sales in America, from producer to consumer, eliminating both sets of middlemen. Probably the final sales price to the consumer thereby could be reduced, but merchants in America were outraged. The problem was not only with the tea trade, but with the precedent which also could spread to other commodities; and there was the possible projection that America would be little more than a consuming adjunct to the English economy.

The response in America was swift and violent. The "Boston Tea Party" in Massachusetts and the burning of the "Peggy Stewart" in Annapolis harbor were direct and overt protests. Parliament's answer, particularly to the episode in Boston, was a series of five measures dubbed in America as "the intolerable acts." They included closing the port of Boston, quartering English troops in Massachusetts, and removing to England the trials of capital cases concerned with law enforcement.

The American counter-reaction was equally blunt. In June of 1773 the Massachusetts Legislature invited all the colonies to send delegates to what became the Continental Congress, meeting in Philadelphia. More strongly than ever before it gave a "national" tone to the protests. The Congress drafted a statement of the American position, voted to support Massachusetts in its resistance to the English measures, established non-importation agreements, provided for committees of "safety and inspection" to enforce them, and authorized the convening of another such Congress in 1774. The actions taken in 1773 for the first time brought a time of decision to the "American" people, whether individually they would or would not support active and serious opposition to England.

By the fall of 1773, the "Committees of Correspondence" were in full operation in the colonies. The House of Delegates of Maryland acted to participate in them, voting on October 15, 1773, to accept "most cordially" the invitation "to a mutual Correspondence and Intercourse with our Sister Colonies." The House established a standing Committee of Correspondence and Enquiry, "whose Business it shall be to obtain the most early and authentick Intelligence of all such Acts and Resolutions of the British Parliament or Proceedings of Administration as may relate to, or affect the British Colonies in America, and to keep up and maintain a Correspondence and Communication with our Sister Colonies respecting these important Considerations, and the Result of such their Proceedings from Time to Time to lay before this House."

## MATTERS OF ROUTINE

In spite of the emerging problems of national and international scope during these years of the early 1770s, the General Assembly of Maryland was concerned also with the regular and routine proceedings of a colonial legislature.

A Tobacco Inspection Act finally was passed during the November-December session of 1773, after several years of acrimonious debates. It was a long and complicated bill, attesting again to the importance of tobacco in the economic life of the Province and to the robust political potential of the inspectors. The bill dealt with inspectors, hogsheads, shippers, warehouses, transporting, and "trashy" tobacco. In the politics of the bill, it was provided that an inspector, while holding that office and for one year thereafter, could not be elected to the House of Delegates; and that he should not "presume to intermeddle or concern himself with any Election of a Deligate or Deligates otherwise than by giving his Vote or shall endeavour to influence any Person or Persons to give his or their Vote or Votes . . . ."

On December 6, 1773, by separate petitions, requests were received for the formation of two new counties. One was Caroline, to be erected from the lower end of Queen Anne's County and the upper portion of Dorchester County; and the other was Harford,[1] to be established from the upper portion of Baltimore County. Bills for each county were enacted at this session. The two new counties brought the total to 16. With four delegates for each county, and two additional for the City of Annapolis, the total membership in the House of Delegates was 66 when the Assembly convened in the spring of 1774. At that time a quorum of the House was set at 34 members.

The session ending in December, 1773, was notable also for the final and successful conclusion of the long and bruising controversy about compensation for the Clerk of the Council, the question being whether he should be paid by "the people" or from funds held by the Governor and the Proprietary. The Upper House, as it had done so often, sent a message to the House of Delegates about an "omission" in the Journal of Accounts. The House, also as if by rote, answered that it had never included such an allowance and that we "apprehend it to be no Omission." The Upper House finally abandoned the long fight, with a compromise that the allowance was to be made up to that date and not sought for the future.

---

1. Caroline County was named for Lady Caroline Eden, daughter of Frederick, sixth Lord Baltimore, and wife of Sir Robert Eden, last Proprietary Governor of Maryland.

Harford County was named for Henry Harford, an illegitimate son of Frederick, Lord Baltimore. During the 1760s, Frederick tried to assure the succession of Henry Harford to the proprietorship by barring the entail and executing deeds of conveyance to Harford. Frederick's will assured Harford's succession, but the Revolution cut off the political succession. *See* VERA F. ROLLO, HENRY HARFORD: LAST PROPRIETOR OF MARYLAND (Maryland Bicentennial Commission, 1976).

The House of Delegates made history of a sort when it suddenly adjourned its session on October 28, 1773. It had no such power, of course, and in all the dozens of controversies over the years it had publicly broached this possibility only twice; these instances had occurred in the very early sessions of 1641/2 and 1642. It was a clear Charter prerogative of the Governor both to call the Assembly into session and to declare it prorogued. Nonetheless, about two weeks after the session began in mid-October, 1773, the House declared itself adjourned. The *Journal* does not record either an explicit reason or a specific motion. Instead, there is only a brief entry by the Clerk of the House: "The House adjourns till Wednesday the Tenth Day of November next, to consult their Constituents on the present distressed Circumstances of the Province."

Shortly before the action to adjourn, the House had been engaged in discussing its action two years earlier in expelling Jonathan Hagar, a delegate from Frederick County, because he was neither a natural-born subject nor descended from one. In reaching that decision, the House had considered a number of English and Maryland statutes. After Hagar was expelled, he ran in the next election and was sent again as a delegate from Frederick County. The second election was not improper, in the judgment of the House when it had considered the matter for a second time, because a statute enacted in Maryland in 1771 treated the subject and served to legalize Hagar's membership.[2]

On October 28, 1773, however, the House again expelled Hagar. Its reasoning was that the session of 1771, which enacted the new law on natural born citizens, convened on October 2; but that the Proprietary had died in September of that year. Because of the death of the Proprietary, the House

---

2. *See* T. J. C. Williams, *Washington County, Maryland,* 2 MARYLAND HISTORICAL MAGAZINE 347 (1907).

resolved "That the said General Assembly of this Province, became, and was thereby dissolved; and that therefore the said Act was not enacted by legal and constitutional Authority, and is therefore void."

The unprecedented action of the House of Delegates in adjourning its own proceedings literally created consternation in Annapolis. There was no mention that the adjournment was specifically tied to the Hagar case, but Governor Robert Eden clearly thought the two were related. On the day following the adjournment, Governor Eden referred the whole matter to the consideration of the Council of State (the members of the Upper House but in their executive capacity): "His Excellency the Governor was pleased to inform the Council that it having been reported to him the preceding evening that the Lower House of Assembly had thought fit to adjourn themselves for 13 or 14 days he had in consequence thereof Sent to their Clerk for their Votes and Proceedings . . . ." [3]

Among the "votes and proceedings" obtained by the Governor was an entire report of the House deliberations on the Hagar case, on October 28. Next, it is recounted in the proceedings for the Council of State, the Governor asked the Council for its recommendation on the best way to show displeasure to the House for its action of adjournment. He was disturbed that simply to ignore the adjournment would be to give up the dignity and prerogative of the Proprietary and the Governor, and also whether a prorogation would be "Sufficiently expressive of the resentment of the two other Branches of the Legislature": [4]

---

3. *Archives,* LXIV at 433-436.
4. *Id.*

His Excellency then remarked that the whole Conduct
of the Lower House was So Extraordinary and
extravagant, that he really was at a loss in what manner
to Conduct himself so as at the Same time to Preserve
the dignity and Authority of the Government and give
every oppertunity to the Representatives of the people
to join with the other branch of the Legislature in
enacting Such Laws as are immediately Necessary for
and Conducive to the Welfare of the Province.

His Excellency was pleased to observe, that at this
late Season of the year should he so far resent this
Conduct of the Lower House by Proclamation to dissolve
them the necessary time required by Law for the return
of the writts on a new Election would Carry the meeting
of the assembly (this year) So deep into the winter
Season that a regular attendance of many of the
Members Could not be expected and at the Same time
assured the Board that as it was impossible to pass over
this unprecedented adjournment without giving up the
Dignity and Prerogative of the proprietary and his
government he had his doubts whether a prorogation
would be Sufficiently expressive of the resentment of
the two other Branches of the Legislature to this very
Extraordinary behaviour of the Lower house.

His Excellency then requested the Council to take the
whole of this Matter both with regard to the
adjournment and dispensing power assumed by the
Lower house in the dismission of Mr. J. Hagar into their
Serious Consideration and was pleased to assure the
Board that he Should be happy in being governed by
their advice on this and every occasion of Such
importance to the Prerogative of the Proprietary and the
honour of the Government he was intrusted with.

The Council agreed that the House had no power thus to
declare itself adjourned; and with respect to the Hagar
incident the Council viewed with "the utmost
disapprobation" the House's "assuming a power to abrogate
an act of the Legislature." Accordingly, and to regularize at
least the ending of legislative proceedings in the House of

Delegates, the Council recommended that the Governor declare the Assembly prorogued: [5]

> Upon Consideration of his Excellency's representation, the Council Answered that they Could not without the utmost disapprobation and Concern reflect upon the very intemperate Proceedings of the Lower House of Assembly as well in respect of their assuming a power to abrogate an act of the Legislature by their Resolve in the Case of Mr. Hagar as of their unprecedented adjournment for 13 or 14 days without the Concurrence or Consent of any other person or previous intimation of their intention or desire to adjourn and Should not Scruple to advise an immediate dissolution of the assembly if the Present Circumstances of this Province were less peculiar than they are but as the Speedy enaction of Some Laws is Necessary for the general welfare and tranquility and a dissolution would prevent it, So they think a prorogation would be more expedient at this time than a dissolution, and it being their wish to promote these important purposes recommended to his Excellency a prorogation for 15 or 16 days and especially as there will be an opportunity of animadverting on the unconstitutional and violent Conduct of the Lower house when they again meet.

> In consequence whereof His Excellency was pleased to Issue Proclamation to the Several Counties within this province, proroguing the present General Assembly to Tuesday the Sixteenth day of November next in the words following, vizt. —

Maryland Sst:

> By His Excellency Robert Eden Esquire Lieutenant General and Chief Governor in and over the Province of Maryland.

### "A Proclamation"

> Whereas for many important reasons I find myself under a necessity of proroguing the Present General Assembly of this Province.

---

5. *Id.*

I do therefore by and with the advice of the Lord Proprietarys Council of State, Prorogue the Same to Tuesday the Sixteenth day of November next. And to the intent that all persons Concerned May have due notice thereof; I do Strictly Charge and require the Several Sherriffs of this Province to Make this my Proclamation Publick in their respective Counties in the usual Manner as they will Answer the Contrary at their peril.

Whatever the legalities of the situation, the prorogation was permitted to supersede the adjournment; and the matter quietly ended.

At its session in March and April, 1774, the House voted that "the Name of every Gentleman, who may make a Motion in the House, be inserted in the Entry that may be made in Consequence thereof." This motion carried by a tally of 37-6. Years earlier, on several occasions, the House had approved such a change in its procedure, but it never had been specifically included in the rules adopted thereafter.

The House was notified on April 7, 1774, that Charles Wilson Peale had completed his portrait of William Pitt, Earl of Chatham. The portrait had been commissioned after Pitt had taken a leading part in seeking the repeal of the Stamp Act.[6]

On April 16, 1774, the House of Delegates passed "An Act to preserve the Independence of the Members of the Lower House of Assembly of this Province." The bill also passed the Upper House, but with a long and involved set of amendments. When it was returned to the House for concurrence, that body took no present action but "referred" the bill for consideration on the "second Tuesday in July next." This, of course, was an obvious ploy to avoid a vote on the bill; the House had not the remotest idea whether it would be in session on a day nearly three months away.

6. This portrait has been on exhibition in the State House for many years. In the late 1970s, it was hung along the main staircase between the first and second floors. For an account of its history, see In Grateful

Since the bill failed, it was not included in the printed acts for the session; and it is uncertain how it would have preserved the "independence" of the House of Delegates. However, the *Journal* does give the amendments proposed and adopted in the Upper House. Understandably, they must have seemed unduly restrictive to the members of the House of Delegates and as more likely to hamper the freedom than to preserve the independence of the House. Thus, the first proposal from the Upper House was a lengthy oath of office, engaging elected members of the House to swear to vote their consciences, not to deceive the electors, and not to misrepresent their conduct or views:

> And be it enacted, by the Authority aforesaid, That every Person who hereafter be elected or chosen to serve in the General Assembly of this Province as a Delegate or Deputy, shall, at the Time of his taking the Oaths to the Government; and repeating and subscribing the Test, take also the following Oath, to wit, 'I, A. B. do solemnly swear, that I have made Use of no Means, directly or indirectly, to deceive any Elector in Order, or with the Intent or Design to obtain or procure his Vote, either for myself or any other Person, and that whilst I shall serve as a Delegate or Deputy in the General Assembly of this Province, I will truly and faithfully, upon all Occasions, consent and agree to the passing, ordaining, and enacting, of all such Resolves, Regulations, and Laws, as I shall believe in my Conscience to be just, and conducive to the Peace, real Welfare and Prosperity of this Province, without any other Regard or View whatsoever; and that I will oppose and dissent from all Resolves, Regulations and Laws, which shall be proposed by any Person, and which I shall in my Conscience believe to be unjust, or not conducive to the Peace, real Welfare and Prosperity of this Province; and that I will not, in any Manner, directly or indirectly, misrepresent my own Conduct or Views as a

---

*Remembrance...* 4, 5, 7 (Annapolis, Maryland Commission on Artistic Property, 1976).

Delegate or Deputy, or the Conduct or Views of any
other Delegate or Deputy in the General Assembly, in
Order to gain the Vote of any Elector for myself or any
other Person, or to persuade or incline any Elector not
to give his Vote for any Person who shall or may be a
Candidate at any Election.'

The second proposal of the Upper House was to deny
membership in the House of Delegates, for a period of seven
years, to any person who had held office in the Province or
even made application for office. It was phrased so broadly
as possibly to be construed to deny a member of the House
a right to be reelected to the same office:

And be it enacted, That no Person who hath held or
enjoyed any Office of Profit in this Province, or who
hath, by himself or any other Person, with his Privity
and Consent, applied for his Appointment to any such
Office, though the said Application failed of Effect, shall
hereafter, for the Term of Seven Years, be capable to be
or eligible as a Delegate or Deputy to serve in the
General Assembly of this Province; and in Case any
Person who hath held or enjoyed any such Office, or
hath applied for the same as aforesaid shall be elected
and returned as a Delegate or Deputy to serve in the
General Assembly aforesaid, and shall not give Notice of
his said Incapacity to the House of Representatives,
after his Election, and before his taking the Oaths to the
Government, repeating and subscribing the Test, and
taking the Oath aforesaid, such Person shall forfeit and
pay the Sum of One Thousand Pounds Sterling to be
recovered and applied as aforesaid, and be incapacitated
and rendered incapable thereafter of serving his
Country in the Capacity of a Representative, and also of
holding or enjoying any Post of Honour, Profit, or Trust,
within this Province, any Law, Usage, or Custom, to the
Contrary notwithstanding.

Finally, the third proposal of the Upper House was to
eliminate all per diem allowances and itinerant charges for
every "Counsellor, Delegate or Burgess of Assembly." This
proposal was to take effect at the end of the current session,

in 1774, and it was to continue until the end of the session next following a period of 14 years.[7]

The three proposals from the Upper House were so obviously artful and disingenuous that it is small wonder the House of Delegates ordered them to lie on the table for three months, when it was most doubtful the House would be in session.

This session in the spring of 1774 began on March 23 and ended on April 19. It was the last session of the Provincial General Assembly. For the remainder of 1774 and for all of 1775 and 1776, the General Assembly was to be succeeded by a series of nine "conventions."

## "First Citizen" and "Antillon"

The debates between "First Citizen" and "Antillon" were one of the classic rhetorical confrontations of American colonial history. Their subject was the legality and rightness of the Governor's proclamation of fees in 1770, after those in earlier legislation had been allowed to expire. The debaters were Charles Carroll of Carrollton and Daniel Dulany, using pseudonymns in the elaborate custom of the times. The debates were printed in the *Maryland Gazette* over a period of weeks in early 1773.

Carroll attacked the validity of establishing fees by proclamation of the Governor; Dulany defended the proclamation.[8] Both were outstanding lawyers and public officials, and their debates were filled with the wordy allusions and classical phrases so characteristic of that era.

---

7. This third proposal, in referring to any "Counsellor" and not to any member of the Upper House, on a literal interpretation of the terms could have been construed as continuing compensation and itinerant charges for the Upper House, while eliminating them for the House of Delegates. Such a result was not mentioned and possibly was not intended.

8. "Carroll saw the empire as a system of virtually autonomous governments, held together by their connection with the mother country,

Carroll is generally said to have won the debate, though there is little doubt that the "judges" already were slanted in his favor. The elections held in May of 1773 resulted in a decided majority for the anti-proclamation and anti-Proprietary group.[9]

The incisive perceptions and the scholarly drafting of the letters by "First Citizen" and "Antillon" were illustrative of the solid learning and familiarity with history and the classics that so marked the leaders in Maryland and throughout all the American colonies. Other examples abound, in the letters, public statements, and resolutions of legislators over the years of colonial development. "The most important leaders of colonial opinion used a large number and a wide assortment of classical allusions to bolster their claims. . . . The colonists used not only the ideas of classical writers but also parallels from the history of Greece and Rome, culled from ancient as well as contemporary historians. . . . In the realm of political ideas, the colonial agitator used classical sources to prove both the existence and the validity of a law superior to all positive law, and to laud again and again the high value of individual freedom." [10]

---

but not subject to the absolute authority of Parliament. Dulany saw the empire as a single unit with local rights and privileges flowing from the ultimate sovereignty of the Parliament." PETER S. ONUF, (ed.), MARYLAND AND THE EMPIRE, 1773 — THE ANTILLON — FIRST CITIZEN LETTERS (Baltimore, 1974).

9. H. H. WALKER LEWIS, THE MARYLAND CONSTITUTION — 1776 14-16 (Baltimore, The Maryland State Bar Association, 1976).

10. Charles F. Mullet, *Classical Influences on the American Revolution,* 35 THE CLASSICAL JOURNAL 92, 93, 94 (1939-40).

Among colonial leaders in neighboring Virginia, Richard Lee II is said to have made entries in his journal in Greek, Latin, and Hebrew; and William Byrd is reputed to have proposed to his spouse in Greek. RICHARD M. GUMMERE, THE AMERICAN COLONIAL MIND AND THE CLASSICAL TRADITION 9 (Cambridge, Mass., 1963).

## THE BURNING OF THE *PEGGY STEWART*

The brigantine *Peggy Stewart* was burned to the water's edge in Annapolis harbor, shortly after she arrived on October 15, 1774. In the folklore of American history, the incident is second only to the famous "Boston Tea Party."

The ship had been built in Maryland. It was owned by Anthony Stewart and his father-in-law, James Dick. Included among the varied items in its cargo were 17 chests of tea.

The news of the ship's arrival was circulated around Annapolis and Anne Arundel County for several days, arousing considerable public indignation. The *Maryland Gazette* for October 20, 1774, wrote in its news story of "that detestable weed tea." Stewart's image suffered also from being generally identified as a Tory who upon occasion had supported the Council rather than the House of Delegates.

A remarkable feature of the whole episode was the extent to which Stewart and the consignee expressed regret for having imported the tea and attempted to placate the public. Because the ship was leaky, Stewart recommended the cargo be unloaded, but then said he would make no further claim for the tea. At a public meeting to consider the affair, some favored exacting an apology from Stewart and the consignee; others recommended burning the entire vessel and cargo; and there even was talk of hanging Stewart. The affair was ended by Stewart and the consignee themselves setting fire to the ship and completely destroying it and the cargo.[11]

---

11. The incident is fully described in MATTHEW PAGE ANDREWS, HISTORY OF MARYLAND - PROVINCE AND STATE 296-303 (1929). *See also* the *Maryland Gazette* for October 20 and October 27, 1774; *The Burning of the 'Peggy Stewart,'* 5 MARYLAND HISTORICAL MAGAZINE 235-49 (1910).

There was a similar and less-publicized occurrence in Maryland the following summer, in August, 1775. The vessel "Totness" ran aground in West River, some miles below Annapolis. The captain said he would not attempt to unload the cargo (which included tea), but he also seemed to make no effort to re-float the vessel and remove it. An unidentified group went aboard the "Totness" and burned it.[12]

## JONATHAN BOUCHER AND WILLIAM EDDIS

The revolutionary bent of the General Assembly, and particularly of the House of Delegates, was by no means the unanimous opinion of all residents of the Province of Maryland.[13] Hundreds of them had loyalist sympathies, some of whom lost most or all their property in Maryland and emigrated either to Canada or to England. Of them all, Jonathan Boucher and William Eddis left for posterity vivid criticism of the prevailing thought in Maryland.

Jonathan Boucher was a minister, who finally left for England in September, 1775. He is known particularly for his doctrine of passive obedience, and he wrote extensively both before and after leaving America. "Obedience to government," he wrote from England, "is every man's duty, because it is every man's interest." Continuing,

> If the form of government under which the good providence of God has been pleased to place us be mild and free, it is our duty to enjoy it with gratitude and with thankfulness.

---

12. Calvert to Robert Eden, August 17, 1775. Quoted in *Correspondence of Governor Eden*, 2 MARYLAND HISTORICAL MAGAZINE 1, (1907).

13. In letters written years later, in 1813 and 1815, John Adams estimated that about one-third of the people in America were against or "adverse to" the Revolution. *See* 10 THE WORKS OF JOHN ADAMS. . . . 63, 110 (Boston, 1856).

Also, "if it be less indulgent and less liberal than in reason it ought to be, still it is our duty not to disturb and destroy the peace of the community by becoming refractory and rebellious subjects, and resisting the ordinances of God." [14]

William Eddis was an Englishman who was in Maryland for a number of years during the 1770s. An inveterate letter writer, he left behind a profuse collection of comments on the American scene and the visible comings of revolution. An idea of equality seems generally to prevail in America, he wrote in 1772, "and the inferior order of people pay but little external respect to those who occupy superior stations."

Again in 1772 Eddis wrote that "under pretense of supporting the sacred claims of freedom and of justice factious and designing men are industriously fomenting jealousy and discontent; and unless they are stopped in their progress by the immediate and determined exertions of the wise and moderate, they will aggravate the dissension, which is become but too evident, and involve this now happy country in complicated misery."

---

14. Philip Evanson, *Jonathan Boucher: The Mind of an American Loyalist,* 58 MARYLAND HISTORICAL MAGAZINE 132-33 (1963). The Rev. Mr. Boucher was rector of St. Anne's Church in Annapolis from 1770 to 1772.

He also, at least by his own account, was active in the affairs of the General Assembly and was a draftsman of legislative papers: "I was in fact the most efficient person in the administration of Government, though I neither had a post nor any prospect of ever having one. The management of the Assembly was left very much to me; and hardly a Bill was brought in which I did not draw or at least revise, and either got it passed or rejected. . . . All the Governor's speeches, messages, etc., and also some pretty important and lengthy papers from the Council were of my drawing up. All these things were, if not certainly known, yet strongly suspected; and of course, though I really had no views nor wishes but such as I believed to be for the true interest of the country, all the forward and noisy patriots, both in the Assembly and out of it, agreed to consider me as an obnoxious person." *See* JONATHAN BOUCHER (ed.), REMINISCENSES OF AN AMERICAN LOYALIST, 1738-1789 at 92-93 (Boston, 1925).

By 1774 he ventured that "not the least future taxation will ever be admitted here without what they conceive a legal representation." In 1775 he wrote that "I am heartily disgusted with the times. The universal cry is *Liberty!* to support which, an infinite number of petty tyrannies are established, under the appellation of committees, in every one of which a few despots lord it over the calm and moderate, inflame the passions of the mob, and pronounce those to be enemies to the general good who may pressure any way to dissent from the creed they have thought proper to impose."

Later in 1775, in commenting on the tenure of Governor Eden, Eddis said that "considering the unsettled times, he is uncommonly popular; but how long he may continue so is a matter of great uncertainty."

On June 11, 1776, Eddis was ordered to be out of the Province by the first of August.[15]

## THE END OF THE PROVINCIAL ASSEMBLY

Alexander Contee Hanson edited a publication of the laws enacted in Maryland from 1763 through the Revolutionary period, including the proceedings of the nine conventions in 1774, 1775, and 1776. At the end of the laws for the Provincial Assembly, after those of the March-April session of 1774, he inserted an appropriate editorial comment. In the prevailing sentiment of the time, he spoke of the "arbitrary acts" of the King and the Parliament, a "settled design" of enslaving the colonies of North America, and the "determined spirit of opposition." Furthermore, "from this period, notwithstanding the mere forms of the ancient governments were permitted a little longer to subsist, there was no real

15. WILLIAM EDDIS, LETTERS FROM AMERICA, 65, 83, 110, 117 (Aubrey C. Land ed.) (Cambridge, Mass., 1969).

authority except that derived immediately from the people. . . ." [16]

The nine conventions that followed, and the successful culmination of their work in a new Constitution and a new government, were a convincing display of the flexibility and durability of the democratic philosophy and legislative processes in Maryland. The achievement of a stable government after revolution was an extraordinary accomplishment.

---

16. *Laws of Maryland.* . . . (Annapolis, 1787), following Chapter 28 of 1774.

## Chapter 15

## GOVERNMENT BY CONVENTION

## 1774-1776

The transition from Provincial government to State government was accomplished between April 19, 1774, and February 5, 1777. These dates marked the end of the last Provincial General Assembly and the beginning of the new General Assembly of the State of Maryland. The change was centered mainly in nine conventions and in the governmental agencies and policies they devised. Membership in the conventions was informal and not rooted in the strict electoral processes of the House of Delegates in the old Provincial Assembly. Yet the several conventions of 1774 through 1776 had a legislative base and acted as legislative bodies. It was the legislative processes in Maryland which had the credit for holding the Province together, governing it with some show of firmness and equity, and finally drafting a State Constitution and a solid framework of constitutional government. Maryland drew upon the legacy of 140 years of legislative schooling in the Province and centuries of developing Parliamentary government and common law in England; and a rich legacy it was.

Acting through the nine Provincial conventions and their counterparts in the several counties, and with the administrative and judicial aid of the Council of Safety in the Province and the committees of observation in the counties, the people of the Province through these critical years successfully wielded and preserved legislative, executive, and judicial powers in Maryland. In a further editorial comment, Alexander Contee Hanson wrote of the problem, the solution, and the spirit of the people:[1]

---

1. *Laws of Maryland. . . .* (Annapolis, 1787), following Chapter 28 of 1774.

517

Such an administration, the immediate offspring of necessity, might have been reasonably expected to be subversive of that liberty which it was intended to secure. But in the course of more than two years, during which it was cheerfully submitted to by all, except the advocates for British usurpation, although many occasions occurred in which an intemperate zeal transported men beyond the just bounds of moderation, not a single person fell a victim to the oppression of this irregular government. The truth is, that during the whole memorable interval, between the fall of the old, and the institution of the new form of government, there appeared to exist among us such a fund of public virtue as has scarcely a parallel in the annals of the world. Without this, the opposition of a country unskilled in war, destitute of arms, inferior far in numbers, and wanting almost every thing for which it had before relied solely on its now inveterate enemies, the opposition of such a people to the efforts of the most powerful nation on the globe, would have been feeble indeed. There were, moreover, amongst us, men not fired by the general enthusiasm, men too of character, talents and influence, who, doubting the reality of that spirit and patriotic ardour which seemed to animate all other classes of men, and reasoning as they thought from sure principles, concluded, that the subjugation of America would be effected almost as soon as it should be attempted. These men took their measures accordingly.

There are occurrences in which it would be impious to suppose that Divine Providence does not interfere. Amongst these is the revolution of America, which has taken place contrary to all reasonable calculation.

## THE CONVENTION FORMAT

The most evident fact about the several conventions was their total and complete illegality,[2] amounting to treason.

---

2. *Cf.* Herbert E. Klingelhofer, *The Cautious Revolution: Maryland and the Movement toward Independence: 1774-1776,"* 60 MARYLAND HISTORICAL MAGAZINE 262 (1965).

The Province still was nominally under the Charter of 1632 and the control of the Proprietary; its legislative body theoretically had two houses; its executive functions were vested in a Governor and Council, under the Proprietary; its judiciary was established by law and subject to the appointive power of the Governor. Eight of the nine conventions were held before the Declaration of Independence, and even that document had a tenuous "legality" only in the eyes of America. There was grim truth in Benjamin Franklin's remark to John Hancock as they signed the Declaration of Independence, "We must all hang together, else we shall all hang separately."

The nine Provincial conventions began, respectively, on June 22, November 21, and December 8 in 1774; April 24, July 26, and December 7 in 1775; and May 8, June 21, and August 14 in 1776. Several of them were in session for only four or five days; others went from two to five weeks; and the final one, which produced the new Constitution, lasted for three months (including a mid-session recess). In number of members (sometimes referred to as deputies) they ranged from 42 to 141. These figures must be taken most tentatively, given the difficulty of combining and reckoning early and late daily arrivals, excused absences, and early departures from Annapolis.[3]

---

The conventions were "extra-legal devices for exercising legislative and executive powers of government during the Revolutionary period." Morris L. Radoff, *An Elusive Manuscript — The Proceedings of the Maryland Convention of 1774,"* 30 THE AMERICAN ARCHIVIST 59 (1967).

3. The proceedings and operations of the nine Provincial conventions may be found in PROCEEDINGS OF THE CONVENTIONS OF THE PROVINCE OF MARYLAND.... (Baltimore, James Lucas and Annapolis, Jonas Green), 1836.

The initiating genius of the nine conventions lay in a series of small conventions held in the several counties of Maryland and in the calls they made for convening Provincial conventions.[4] The local conventions were called by informal local groups, though the similarity of their pronouncements gave evidence of concerted activity. The local conventions expressed concern for the plight of Boston, with its harbor completely closed to commerce; agreed to set up local "committees of correspondence"; encouraged non-importation agreements; and opposed taxation of Americans by the Parliament. The first set of local conventions also approved calling a Province-wide convention in Annapolis.

During the spring of 1774, after the Provincial Assembly was prorogued on April 19, local conventions (among others) were held in Anne Arundel County on May 25 and June 4; Baltimore County on May 25 and 31; Queen Anne's County on May 30; Kent County on June 2; lower Frederick County on June 11; Harford County on June 11; Charles County on

---

These meetings were "conventions" in the true sense of the term. They are not to be confused with the occasional earlier use of that word for meetings of the Provincial Assembly which for one reason or another did not enact any legislation. There is no compunction upon the General Assembly to produce laws at one of its sessions, and it seems a doubtful usage to call a "session" a "convention" solely for that reason. Despite the use of the term "Conventions," however, these meetings frequently assumed the powers of, and acted as, the Provincial legislature.

During the 1977 session of the General Assembly, as part of the 200th anniversary of that body as a State Legislature, the Hall of Records Commission of Maryland issued a full copy of the proceedings of the Constitutional Convention of 1776. *See* THE DECISIVE BLOW IS STRUCK (Annapolis, 1977).

4. For accounts of the proceedings in two of the county conventions (present-day Frederick and Washington counties), see vols. 10, 11, and 12 of the MARYLAND HISTORICAL MAGAZINE (1915, 1916, and 1917).

June 14; Caroline County on June 18; middle Frederick County on June 20; and St. Mary's County on June 30. Calls for cooperative meetings among all the counties were included in the resolutions adopted by each. The local conventions were not part of any organized or specified scheme of government; but as an informal showing of democracy in action they had an unimpeachable base in "the people," even with the limited concept of that term in the eighteenth century.

The Provincial conventions operated as unicameral bodies; for the first time in 130 years there was no opportunity for inter-house bickering. To complete their function as the sole and exclusive source of power within Province, the Governor was inactive, awaiting some resolution of the uncertain situation. After he prorogued the last Provincial Assembly in April of 1774, he did not attempt to call another for more than two years. He did consider calling a session in the spring of 1776; but by that time the Province was very close to revolution, and he was rebuffed. From the spring of 1774 through the end of 1776, the nine Provincial conventions provided the unique and almost solitary exercise of governmental power in Maryland.

The one conceivable challenge to the powers of the conventions was in the continued presence of officers and agents of the Proprietary and of England. This duplication continued until Governor Eden finally left the Province in June of 1776. Seemingly by common consent, but certainly following the lead of Governor Eden, all these officers and agents seemed quietly to relax their controls and permitted the conventions to operate without serious opposition. There was a practical justification for their inaction, for they had no powers to enforce their former duties.[5]

---

5. There actually were two governments in the Province during these years of the 1770s. The legal government was in England, under the

## The Convention of June 22, 1774

The first Provincial Convention was held in Annapolis beginning on June 22 and ending on June 25, 1774. Its procedure and operations are not detailed in the *Proceedings;* not until the Convention of December 7, 1775, was day-to-day business covered in any detail. For this first Convention, the *Proceedings* consist mostly of a series of 12 resolutions which were adopted, plus a decision to vote by counties. Ninety-two members were present; Matthew Tilghman was chairman of the Convention, and John Duckett was clerk.

For voting, it was agreed that upon any division each county should have one vote, and that all questions would be settled by a majority of the counties. The Convention considered letters from Boston, Philadelphia, and Virginia, as well as the English acts closing Boston harbor and for sending offenders for trial to England or another colony, and a pending act in the Parliament that would be "subversive of the charter of Massachusetts bay."

The 12 resolutions were a mixture. Some dealt with matters of political principle in relation to England, others touched upon relationships among the colonies, and still others concerned government and policy within Maryland. They covered these points:

> 1. The three acts of the Parliament (two passed and one pending) "are cruel and oppressive invasions of the people of the Massachusetts bay as men, and of their constitutional rights as English subjects." They will lay a foundation for the utter destruction of British America.

---

Proprietary and having also the Governor and other administrative officers in Maryland. The actual or *de facto* government was in Maryland, headed by the Council of Safety and reaching down into the committees of observation in the counties. *Cf.* Rosamond Randall Beirne, *Portrait of a Colonial Governor: Robert Eden,* 45 MARYLAND HISTORICAL MAGAZINE 167 (1950).

2. It is the duty of the colonies to unite to obtain a repeal of these acts.

3. Stopping all importations from and exportations to Great Britain would be the most speedy and effectual means of obtaining a repeal of these acts and preserving North America and her liberties.

4. Maryland will join in an association of the colonies to stop all such importations and exportations, as may be agreed upon by a general congress of deputies from the colonies.

5. Deputies to the congress from Maryland are authorized to agree to restricting exports to the West Indies.

6. Deputies to the congress from Maryland are authorized to agree to the importation of articles thought indispensably necessary.

7. Merchants and vendors in Maryland should not take advantage of non-importation agreements; they should see goods on hand at the previous rates; inhabitants of the Province should not deal with merchants who do not follow this rule.

8. A subscription should be opened for a collection for the relief of the distressed inhabitants of Boston.

9. "Gratitude and most cordial thanks" are sent "to the patrons and friends of liberty in Great Britain."

10. Deputies were named to attend the congress "to effect one general plan of conduct" for the relief of Boston and the preservation of American liberty.

11. Maryland will break off trade and dealing with any colony or town which does not join the general plan adopted by the colonies.

12. Deputies to the congress from Maryland, upon their return, shall notify the committees of the several counties of the measures adopted.

In summary, the 12 resolutions adopted at this first

Convention in Maryland were concerned mainly with the English acts closing Boston harbor and otherwise punishing the Massachusetts Bay colony. As methods for American retaliation, they mentioned only policies of non-importation and non-exportation. Delegates were appointed to attend a general congress of deputies, given some instructions for the policies they should support, and told to notify the local conventions in Maryland of whatever measures might be adopted by the general congress. Merchants and vendors in Maryland were asked to use restraint in holding prices stable. The resolutions were notable, finally, for a complete absence of provisions for governing the Province and its counties; and for still referring to the colonies as *British* America.

## THE CONVENTION OF NOVEMBER 21, 1774

The second Convention was held on a single day, November 21, 1774. It referred to itself as a "Provincial Meeting of Deputies, chosen by several of the counties in Maryland...." A number of the counties were not represented, "for want of sufficient notice of the time of this meeting." The 57 deputies present limited their actions to one resolution and one recommendation. The resolution was "That every member of this meeting will, and every person in the province ought, strictly and inviolably to observe, and carry into execution, the association agreed on by the ... continental congress." The first meeting of the Congress had been held in September, during the interim between the first and second conventions in Maryland. The announced intention of the first Convention in Maryland to participate in and support the Continental Congress and its recommendations now had been actively supplemented by an actual endorsement of congressional policies.

The recommendation made by the second Convention was on a more mundane topic. It was "that, during the present time of public calamity balls be discontinued." With these two pieces of business completed, the second Convention adjourned for about three weeks.

## THE CONVENTION OF DECEMBER 8, 1774

The third Convention began on December 8, 1774, and continued through December 12. Eighty-five members were present. John Hall served as chairman, and John Duckett once more was clerk. The work of this Convention appears only in the text of a series of resolutions adopted, but the tone of these resolutions differed markedly from those of the earlier June Convention. As before, there were resolutions in support of Boston and of the Massachusetts Bay colony; otherwise the resolutions ranged more broadly than before and with the intent of a greater substantive effect.

The injunction of the November Convention was repeated, that the association agreed upon by the Continental Congress should be supported. Seven persons were appointed as representatives to the Congress, and another seven (most of whom were the same) as the committee of correspondence.

Some of the resolutions had to be devoted to pressing problems within Maryland. The non-importation and non-exportation agreements, designed to hurt England, also were adversely affecting the Province. Thus, to promote the manufacture of woolens, there was a resolution proposing that sheep under four years of age should not be slaughtered. To increase the manufacture of linen and cotton, it was recommended that every planter and farmer ought to raise as much flax, hemp, and cotton "as he conveniently can"; and that the current growth of flax seed should not be exported.

Merchants and traders were having their problems, also. Earlier, in the June resolution, they had been asked not to take advantage of the non-trading agreements by raising prices; now it seemed they themselves were suffering from inadequate prices for their sales. The December Convention, therefore, devoted two long resolutions to the problems of merchants, traders, and factors. It was declared in a preamble that many merchants had sold their goods at or below "prime cost," it was unjust to require them to sell at this price, and there should be one general rule allowing a reasonable profit to the trader and preventing him from taking advantage of a scarcity of goods. Accordingly, and in the expectation that another policy "would give great satisfaction to the merchants and people of this province," the Convention enacted a price-fixing arrangement. While the language of the resolution was brief and precise, the Convention obviously doubted its ability to use the mandatory "shall," and it had to settle for the persuasive "ought." So, said the Convention, "no merchant ought to sell his goods, at wholesale, for more than 112 one-half per cent. — at retail, for cash, for more than 130 per cent. — on credit, for more than 150 per cent. advance on the prime cost. . . ." It was added, that in case any question should arise about the prime cost of goods, the merchant or factor possessing or owning the goods "ought to ascertain the same on oath, if requested."

In the same resolution, after having exhorted the merchants and factors to hold the line on prices, the Convention called upon the attorneys in the Province to lend their support. In case of a breach of the price level, the resolution continued, "no gentlemen of the law ought to bring or prosecute any suit whatever for such offender"; and if the offender were a factor, "no gentlemen of the law ought to bring or prosecute any suit for any debt due to the store of which the said factor has the management."

In this resolution, even with use of the uncertain verb "ought," the Convention was venturing into a most difficult area of price fixing and the restraint of suits at law. It went on in another resolution to make suggestions in other troublesome areas of the law. The second resolution "earnestly recommended" that "the determination of the several county committees be observed and acquiesced in: That no persons, except members of the committees, undertake to meddle with or determine any question respecting the construction of the association entered into by the continental congress: And that the peace and good order be inviolably maintained throughout this Province."

Next, the Convention tackled the task of defending the Province and its people, potentially a problem of high priority. On the premise that "a well regulated militia. . . is the natural strength and only stable security of a free government, and that such militia will relieve our mother country from any expense in our protection and defence; will obviate the pretence of a necessity for taxing us on that account, and render it unnecessary to keep any standing army (ever dangerous to liberty) in this province," the Convention went on to recommend that all men in the Province from 16 to 50 years of age should be enrolled in militia companies. This resolution continued by recommending the type of military organization to be used and that each county, by subscription or other voluntary method, raise the necessary funds. For the latter problem, the Convention even included a proposed schedule of amounts to be raised, ranging from 358 pounds sterling in Caroline County to 1333 pounds in Frederick County. Here, in addition to its other efforts at persuasion, the Convention was recommending formation of militia units and the necessary "voluntary" taxes.

The final recommendation from the Convention meeting in December of 1774 was an appeal for unity among all ranks in the Province. "As our opposition to the settled plan of the British administration to enslave America," it declared in another resolution, "will be strengthened by a union of all ranks of men in this province, we do most earnestly recommend, that all former differences about religion or politics, and all private animosities and quarrels of every kind, from henceforth cease and be forever buried in oblivion; and we entreat, we conjure every man, by his duty to God, his country, and his posterity, cordially to unite in defence of our common rights and liberties." The entreaties of the third Convention covered a host of the foremost problems of mankind: the economy and the price level, the practice of law, decisions of the Continental Congress, military protection, taxes, religion, politics, "private animosities and quarrels of every kind."

Running as a strain throughout all these resolutions, however, was a note of firmness and an early hint of a willingness to force issues. The phraseology was mild and did not necessarily carry a threat of overt action, but there were veiled suggestions of vigor and action: This Province would support the Massachusetts Bay colony "to the utmost of their power"; the Maryland delegates to the Continental Congress were empowered to agree to all measures which the Congress "shall deem necessary and effectual to obtain a redress of American grievances"; and the other colonies in America were urged to enter into like resolutions "for mutual defence and protection."

The final action of this Convention was to call another meeting on April 24, 1775, "unless American grievances be redressed before that time."

## THE CONVENTION OF APRIL 24, 1775

The fourth Provincial Convention met in Annapolis on April 24, 1775, and continued until May 3. Again it was "a meeting of the Deputies appointed by the several counties of the province of Maryland." One hundred members were present. Matthew Tilghman once more was chairman, and Gabriel Duvall again was clerk. This Convention continued on the same note as the earlier one in December, except for receiving through the committees of correspondence fresh news about happenings elsewhere in America.

The opening resolution was conciliatory. George III was declared to be the "lawful and rightful King of Great Britain." Continuing, the dominions belonging to England and "the good people of this province do owe, and will bear faith and true allegiance to our said lawful and rightful King, as the sovereign, constitutional guardian, and protector of the rights of all his subjects."

Also in a strong gesture of conciliation, there was a resolution to set May 11 of that year "as a day of fasting and humiliation," and to suggest that the inhabitants of the Province "by prayer and supplications, humbly and devoutly, implore the blessing, support and protection of Almighty God, for the preservation of the rights and liberties of America, and the restoration of peace, union and happiness to the British empire."

Information received from Philadelphia, some being forwarded from New York City, had the news that English troops were cutting off all communications southward from New York. Correspondence from Newport, dated April 25, 1775, contained news of the battles of Concord and Lexington and of the determination of the Massachusetts Bay colony to raise an army of thirty thousand men in New England.

This Convention in Maryland did little by way of substance. It expanded the policy of non-exportation to include Quebec, Nova Scotia, and Newfoundland; and it urged the inhabitants of Maryland to continue "the regulation of the militia."

Delegates were reappointed to attend sessions of the Continental Congress, and the total sum of six hundred pounds was requested from the counties, "by subscription," to pay the expenses of the delegates to the Congress. The amounts requested from the counties were itemized, ranging from 21 pounds for Caroline County to 80 pounds for Frederick County.

Although the opening and closing resolutions of this Convention had been conciliatory, speaking of allegiance to George III and of a day of "fasting and humiliation" in the Province, there were other and more martial declarations in the convention. The letter from Newport spoke of "the bloody, savage massacre" in Concord and Lexington and of the reaction of the Americans in convincing the King's officers "that Americans can and will fight." We had hoped, continued the letter from Rhode Island, "that the dispute between Great Britain and these colonies would have been settled without bloodshed; but the parliament of Great Britain it seems have determined to push their iniquitous unconstitutional measures by dint of arms. The sword of civil war has been drawn by the King's troops, and sheathed in the bowels of our countrymen."

This Maryland Convention also recognized the possibility of war. In its instructions to the delegates to the Congress, it gave them leave, as before, to concur with those measures the Congress thought "indispensably necessary," even if they proceeded "to the last extremity . . . ."

Until about the middle or latter part of 1775, the public and official attitude in Maryland toward England and the Parliament seemed to be an unlikely mixture of continued friendliness and potential hostility. "Before that period, the declarations of the colonies present a striking contrast with their acts. The former breathes nothing but peace and the most ardent desire for reconciliation; the latter exhibited nothing but the preparations for war. Every new measure of hostility was accompanied by professions of allegiance. The renewal of these professions was rendered necessary, by the constant misrepresentations of their purposes. From the origin of the struggle, it had been the effort of the English ministry to fix upon them the character of rebels, whose aim was independence and whose grievances were pretexts . . . ." [6]

## THE CONVENTION OF JULY 26, 1775

The fifth Convention in the Province met on July 26, 1775, and continued to August 14. Much had happened since the fourth Convention in April and May. The Continental Congress had met again on May 10, and during that session recommended that "the colonies be placed in a state of defence." On June 15 George Washington had been appointed as commander-in-chief of the Continental forces; and on June 17 came the Battle of Bunker Hill. By the time the Maryland Convention met in late July, it was ready to begin lessening its ties with England and to make a start on a simple frame of government for the Province. The *Proceedings* cite the presence of 141 members; Matthew Tilghman again was chairman, and Gabriel Duvall was appointed as clerk.

The first task at this Convention was that of binding the people of the Province into a loose political organization. This was initiated on the first day of the meeting, July 26, when the Convention by unanimous resolution adopted an "Association of the Freemen of Maryland." It was to be signed by all members of the Convention "and by all other the freemen of this province."

---

6. JOHN V. L. MCMAHON, AN HISTORICAL VIEW OF THE GOVERNMENT OF MARYLAND . . ., 426 (BALTIMORE, 1831).

Governor Eden, writing to his brother, said that "We are at this Time . . . in a State of thorough Confusion." He recounted a conference he had recently held with six "gentlemen" of the Province, who were apprehensive of an uprising by their servants and slaves. However, the Governor assured his brother, "You need be under no Uneasiness about me: I am well supported, and not obnoxious to any unless it be to some of the infernal Independents, who are in League with the Bostonians." *Correspondence of Governor Eden,* 2 MARYLAND HISTORICAL MAGAZINE 1-3 (1909).

In a long preamble, the Association recited the complaints of the Province against England: the raising of revenue without the consent of the colonists; the "arbitrary and vindictive" statutes passed against Massachusetts; the unlimited powers assumed by the Parliament over all the colonies; the commencement of hostilities in America. Against these grievances, it was continued, the Congress had chosen to oppose "uncontrollable tyranny" and had voted that the colonies be put into a state of defense. Continuing, the Association declared, "it is necessary and justifiable to repel force by force .... And we do unite and associate as one band, and firmly and solemnly engage and pledge ouselves to each other, and to America, that we will, to the utmost of our power, promote and support the present opposition, carrying on, as well by arms, as by the continental association, restraining our commerce."

Immediately following this declaration of martial purpose, however, the Association expressed hope for a reconciliation with England, and it added a firm intent to preserve civil law and domestic order:

> And as in these times of public danger, and until a reconciliation with Great Britain, on constitutional principals, is effected, (an event we most ardently wish may soon take place) the energy of government may be greatly impaired, so that even zeal unrestrained may be productive of anarchy and confusion; we do, in like manner unite, associate and solemnly engage, in maintenance of good order and the public peace, to support the civil power in the due execution of the laws, so far as may be consistent with the present plan of opposition, and to defend, with our utmost power, all persons from every species of outrage to themselves or their property, and to prevent any punishment from being inflicted on any offenders, other than such as shall be adjudged by the civil magistrate, the continental congress, our convention, council of safety, or committees of observation ....

From this statement of purpose, the Association of Freemen proceeded to establish a rudimentary form of government for the Province and its counties. In this sense, the Association could be called the first written constitution of Maryland. With subsequent amendments, it served as a basis for government until the formal Constitution became effective in 1777.

The new government continued on a representative basis, now ingrained from 140 years under the Provincial Assembly. Voters were to be "the freeholders of each county in this province, and other freemen having a visible estate of forty pounds sterling, or qualified by law to vote for burgesses." These qualifications were the same as those last prevailing for the Provincial Assembly.

Ultimate and supreme representative power in the Province was to be vested in the Convention. It held, or sometimes delegated within its continuing control, a unique combination of all legislative, executive, and judicial power. As a unicameral legislature it was neither hampered by a restrictive upper house nor shackled by the veto power of an executive. "Its only limits were its discretion."[7] Its membership comprised five delegates from each county, to be elected annually by the county voters. The Convention initially was an extra-legal body, not sanctioned by any basic or controlling document of constitutional status. Yet it was rooted in a vote of the people, under tried and traditional rules of franchise; if in the first instance it seemed to "seize" power, the alternative was anarchy. The system worked in the face of some difficult decisions, and the judgment of history has to be that the Convention did indeed use its powers with "discretion."

Executive power was to be vested in a Council of Safety, with a statement to explain its need. "It is absolutely

7. McMahon, *op. cit.,* at 418.

necessary in this time of imminent danger, that there would be some power existing, which may superintend the execution of the orders and resolutions of the Convention, and occasionally, from time to time, promote the prudent and necessary preparations for defence, and in case of necessity, call forth a due proportion, or even the whole of the force of the province, in an orderly and regular manner, whereby the strength of the whole will be greatly increased in the common defence, and the rights and liberties of all better secured."

The Council of Safety was established with 16 members, eight to be from the Eastern Shore and eight to be from the Western Shore. Membership was to continue only from one convention to another, and half of the members from each "shore" were to be retired from office at each convention. The Council was to be the highest executive power, with authority even to call special meetings of the convention. Its two greatest areas of power were military and financial. It was in general charge of all military personnel and activity; and it could issue bills of credit to finance the Province and could require an accounting from the two treasurers (one from each "shore").[8]

The military powers of the Council of Safety were described in some detail, within specifications listed in the Association of Freemen.[9] The Association covered the enrollment of companies of militia, the election by ballot of

---

8. *See generally,* Jean H. Vivian, *Thomas Stone and the Reorganization of the Maryland Council of Safety, 1776,* 69 MARYLAND HISTORICAL MAGAZINE 271-78 (1974).

9. There was no question that legally the power to deal with the militia was vested in the Governor of the Province. In this instance, Governor Eden silently acquiesced. He believed in mild and conciliatory action, and in any event had no power to enforce an objection. *Cf.* Herbert E. Klingelhofer, *The Cautious Revolution: Maryland and the Movement*

officers within a company, the designation of some companies as "light infantry," and the drills and compensation of the members. The Association defined "militia" as comprising every able-bodied effective freeman between the ages of 16 and 50 years; but exceptions were made for clergymen, practising physicians, "the household of his excellency, the governor," and persons who from religious scruples would not bear arms. Each company was to have 68 privates and its officers. The penalty for not appearing at muster was a fine of five shillings.

Executive powers within the separate counties also were covered by the Association of Freemen. Such authority was vested in a committee of observation in each county. These committees were to be elected by popular vote, by the same persons as entitled to vote for members of a convention. Members of the committees of observation were to be "of the most discreet and sensible" of those qualified, to serve for one year each. The number of members of the several committees was specified in the Association, ranging from 55 in Frederick County to 14 in Caroline County. Each committee of observation was stated to have "full power and authority to carry into execution the association and resolves of the continental congress and conventions of this province, so far as the same relate to the commercial opposition to the measures of the British ministry, in which the united colonies are engaged."

Finally, a judicial power was given to the Council of Safety. It was empowered to "hear, determine, and punish high and dangerous offences, according to the resolutions of this convention." All persons were enjoined to "pay obedience to and to acquiesce in the determination of" the Council; and it was authorized to inflict any punishment for "breaches and offenses."

---

*toward Independence: 1774-1776,* 60 MARYLAND HISTORICAL MAGAZINE 262 (1965).

A limited judicial power within its county was given to each committee of observation. All persons in a county were enjoined to obey the committee. It could censure any person adjudged by it to be guilty of a breach of directives from the Congress and the Convention. A committee of observation, "on probable proof that any person has been guilty of any high and dangerous offence, tending to disunite the inhabitants of this province in their present opposition, or to destroy the liberties of America," was authorized to apprehend the person and to send him to the Council of Safety on that "shore." The Council, in turn, was instructed to examine into the charge, and if it be sufficiently proved, to imprison the offender for a time not beyond the ending of the next convention.

To this point, the Association of Freemen had given legislative power in the Province to the Convention. Executive power was given to the Council of Safety on the Provincial level and to the several committees of observation on the county level. Judicial power in criminal cases was given to the Council of Safety for "high and dangerous offences," and the several committees of observation were given what in effect was a power of indictment over such offenses. There remained the area of judicial power in cases of civil jurisdiction, and here the Association of Freemen was not precise. It is uncertain whether it was felt that matters of civil jurisdiction were of less importance than criminal cases or that they were too sensitive to handle. In any event, the terms of the Association of Freemen provided that there should be a postponement of civil cases. If "there is no real dispute," said the Association, the parties and the attorneys should resolve the dispute in some amicable way. If there were a "real dispute," the parties "during these times of public calamity" should temporarily hold their positions, "until otherwise ordered by act of assembly, or some future convention."

However, well aware that simple postponement of all judicial questions in civil law would not suffice, the Association of Freemen made two other provisions for cases of immediate importance. First, it said that depositions might be taken to preserve testimony for a future time. Secondly, while saying generally that "no civil original writ, suit, or action shall be commenced or renewed. . . .," the Association provided exceptions for a number of suits involving wrong done to person or property, attachments, and contracts.

The final matter of substance to be included in the Association of Freemen was that of debts and taxes. Here also, for reasons easy to understand, the results were not precise. The Council of Safety already had been empowered to borrow money, but of equal or greater importance was the matter of collecting tax revenues. Here the Association seemed to assume that existing tax structures would be continued. On the problem of enforcing the collection of debts and taxes, the Association "earnestly recommended" that all inhabitants make payment without compulsion when able, or give security. It was recommended particularly that everyone pay public taxes. The purpose of the recommendations was "to prevent oppression and imprisonment of poor debtors, but not to give any pretence of non-payment to those who are of sufficient ability to pay their just debts."

One further item of procedure was incorporated into the Association of Freemen. That was the arrangement for its approval by all the freemen in the Province. This task was entrusted to the county committees of observation. Copies of the Association were to be sent out to all the counties, and each committee of observation was to appoint persons "to offer or carry the said association to all freemen resident within their county (the household of his excellency the governor excepted) and require their subscription to the same." The name of any freeman not subscribing was to be sent to the Convention, "to the end that the Convention may take order therein." [10]

The Association of Freeman was the only recorded business in the Convention which began on July 26 and continued to August 14, 1775; it obviously was crucial to the organized political life of the Province.

## THE CONVENTION OF DECEMBER 7, 1775

The sixth of the nine conventions in the Province met on December 7, 1775, and continued to January 18, 1776. Its *Proceedings* were much more detailed than were those of the first five conventions and in format were much like those of the Provincial Assembly for many years past. Extending over a period of about six weeks, this Convention was much the longest of any of the conventions to that date. Fifty-three delegates were listed as present on the first day; and the offices of president and clerk again were filled by Matthew Tilghman and Gabriel Duvall.

On the second day of the Convention a motion for secrecy was adopted by the delegates. It was a stringent requirement, "that every member of this convention consider himself under the ties of virtue, honour, and love of his country, not to divulge, directly or indirectly, any matter or thing agitated or debated in convention, during the time of debate, or before the same shall be determined." It was to apply, however, only in limited circumstances, when "the mover thereof shall openly request" secrecy or when a majority of the convention ordered secrecy. The sanctions for a violation were harsh; they included expulsion from the Convention, and the offender was to be considered as an enemy to America and treated as such.

----

**10.** As a footnote to the tone and temper of the Convention and of the Association of Freemen, note that the Governor and his "household" were specifically exempt from being included within the militia and also from being solicited for a subscription to the Association.

A number of disciplinary cases came before the
Convention during this sixth meeting, all under the heading
of political offenses. Agreeably to the procedures established
in the Association of Freemen, six months earlier, the cases
came up from committees of observation in the counties.

One involved Francis Baker, a member of the Convention
from Talbot County. He had been "guilty of a breach of the
continental association." He acknowledged his offense,
"expressed great contrition and sorrow for the same, and
prayed a remission of the penalty annexed by the congress
to his crime." He was expelled from the Convention, but as
he was "not offering himself for any office of trust" it was
decided that his offense would not be further punished, and
there were no other proceedings against him.

Another offense concerned the Rev. Mr. John Patterson, of
Kent County. The charge was that he had "some time past
publicly spoken words which reflected upon the Convention."
When he appeared before the Committee of Observation of
Kent County, he acknowledged that he had spoken against
the last two conventions, saying they attempted to bar
outsiders from judging of the propriety of their proceedings
and deprived persons of their liberties. There was, he had
said, "more liberty in Turkey than in this province." After
hearing from Patterson, the Convention assured him that "it
is not the intention of this Convention to preclude the
inhabitants of this province from judging of their
proceedings," but that it must be done with decency and
temper. Patterson, it was concluded, had been "highly
indecent and intemperate." Upon his declaration that he
would do no act to oppose or impede measures necessary for
the preservation of American liberty, and upon his payment
of costs, he was discharged.

William Bartlett Townsend, of Worcester County, was
charged with taking part in hostilities against the colony of
Virginia and committing "depredations" against property in

Maryland. In his absence, the Convention ordered the Committee of Observation of Worcester County to hold his property and prevent any of it from being taken out of the Province, awaiting Townsend's return.

Robert Buchanan, of Kent County, was cited for having refused to enroll in the militia, and for causing 14 other persons also to refuse enrollment. He was told he should have applied to the Convention with any complaints against the order to enroll. He claimed to have been "not well treated" by the county committee, but the Convention "highly" disapproved of his behavior before the committee.

Isaac Atkinson was cited by the Eastern Shore Council of Safety, for an unexplained offense. He pleaded that he had never meant to injure America, his native country, and that he was sorry for what he had done. He was reprimanded by the Convention and required to give bond for his future good behavior. Finally, Benjamin Shockley, of Worcester County, was reprimanded, also for an unspecified offense, and discharged.

This Convention, by resolution, enacted several measures obviously intended to have the effect of law. One was to require any ship belonging in this Province not to leave without a license. Another was to provide "that all rents, other than rents for houses, may be hereafter paid, and shall be received in tobacco, and other country produce, at a reasonable value, to be set by the committees of observation." A third measure concerned judgments and their collection. A fourth, about assessments and the collection of taxes, was a curious combination of resolution and what the Convention clearly hoped would be law. It illustrated the dilemma of the convention-system of government in making and enforcing mandates.

This latter resolution began by saying that the Convention "do highly disapprove of the negligence of many of the people of this province, in not paying off their levies." Such conduct, it said, might throw the Province "into disorder, confusion and anarchy," as desired by "the inveterate enemies and dreaded by the real friends of American liberty." Next, in a positive vein, the resolution promised that the Convention, if necessary, would assist tax officers "with their utmost power, in the collection of the levies which ought to have been paid in the summer past." Next, it said, the people should be assessed as earlier provided by acts of the Assembly.

Having established this basis, the Convention in the resolution made negative points, in an evident effort to avoid harshness. Tax officers were requested "not to distrain the effects of those whose extreme poverty disables them from paying." Also, to avoid part of the problem, the resolution advised against incurring capital expenditures for a time. Having spoken on both sides of the tax question, the Convention completed the dichotomy by concluding that the fixed intention of the Convention was "to support order in the community, and ease the good people of this province as far as possible."

Another measure of this Convention, also phrased as a resolution, amended the Association of Freemen by changing the composition of the Council of Safety. As established six months earlier, it really was two councils, with eight members from each "shore." The change in this sixth Convention was to provide only one Council of Safety and to give it a total of seven members, of whom four would be from the Western Shore and three would be from the Eastern Shore. The members also were given per diem compensation of 14 shillings.

The big development of the sixth Convention was its innovation in sending instructions to the Maryland delegation in the Continental Congress. The practice up to this time had been to give the delegates a general authority to make their own decisions in the Congress, but two sets of instructions were forwarded to them from Annapolis during this winter Convention of 1775-1776. The first was on shipments of tea into the colonies, declaring that "all India teas imported into this continent before the first day of March last, may be sold and used without any prejudice to the cause of America." The delegates were instructed "that they endeavour to procure the same to be permitted by the congress."

The second set of instructions was in a formal message to the delegates from Maryland, from the Convention, "taking into their most serious consideration, the present state of the unhappy dispute between Great Britain and the united colonies." The instructions began with a strongly conciliatory hope for peaceful relations with England and for a continuation of the present form of government:

> The experience we and our ancestors have had of the mildness and equity of the English constitution, under which we have grown up to and enjoyed a state of felicity, not exceeded among any people we know of, until the grounds of the present controversy were laid by the ministry and parliament of Great Britain, has most strongly endeared to us that form of government from whence these blessing have been derived, and makes us ardently wish for a reconciliation with the mother country, upon terms that may insure to these colonies an equal and permanent freedom. To this constitution we are attached, not merely by habit, but by principle, being in our judgments persuaded, it is of all known systems best calculated to secure the liberty of the subject, to guard against despotism on the one hand, and licentiousness on the other.
>
> Impressed with these sentiments, we warmly recommend to you, to keep constantly in your view the avowed end and purpose for which these colonies originally associated, the redress of American grievances, and securing the rights of the colonists.
>
> As upon the attainment of these great objects, we shall think it our greatest happiness to be thus firmly

542

united to Great Britain, we think proper to instruct you, that should any proposition be happily made by the crown or parliament, that may lead to or lay a rational and probable ground for reconciliation, you use your utmost endeavors to cultivate and improve it into a happy settlement and lasting amity, taking care to secure the colonies against the exercise of the right assumed by parliament to tax them, and to alter and change their charters, constitutions, and internal polity, without their consent, — powers incompatible with the essential securities of the lives, liberties, and properties of the colonists.

Continuing in the vein of conciliation, the instructions to the Maryland delegates in the Congress specified "that you do not without the previous knowledge and approbation of the convention of this province, assent to any proposition to declare these colonies independent of the crown of Great Britain, nor to any proposition for making or entering into alliance with any foreign power, nor to any union or confederation of these colonies, which may necessarily lead to a separation from the mother country." But, and this was a strong exception, any such action might be taken in the judgment of the delegation, or any four members, or of a majority of the membership. As a middle position, if a majority of the Congress made such a decision against the judgment of the Maryland delegation, the delegation was instructed to report back at once to the Convention, "and this convention will not hold this province bound by such majority in congress, until the representative body of the province in convention assent thereto."

In the meantime, while desirous of peace with Great Britain, the Maryland delegation was further instructed to join with the other colonies in such military operations "as may be judged proper and necessary for the common defence." In explaining the rationale of its instructions, the Convention put its directives on a high concept of proper representative government:

At the same time we assure you that we have an entire confidence in your abilities and integrity in the discharge of the great trust reposed in you, we must observe to you as our opinion, that in the relation of constituent and representative, one principal security of the former is, the right he holds to be fully informed of the conduct of the latter: we can conceive no case to exist, in which it would be of more importance to exercise this right than the present, nor any in which we can suppose the representative would more willingly acquiesce in the exercise of it. We therefore instruct you, that you move for and endeavor to obtain a resolve of congress, that the votes given by the colonies on every question agitated in congress, shall appear upon the journals thereof; and if such resolve be obtained, that you, at the expense of this province, procure copies of the said journals, except such parts thereof as relate to military operations, and measures taken to procure arms and ammunition, and from time to time lay the same before the convention of this province, shewing the part you, as representatives of the province, take in such questions.

As a final word of instructions to the Maryland delegation in the Continental Congress, the Convention directed the delegation to work against possible conflicts of interest in the membership of the Congress. Thus, said the Convention, members of the Congress should not also hold military command in either the continental army or any provincial force; hold another office of profit under the Congress or other government, assumed since the controversy with England began; or receive the profits of any such command or office.

Finally, the Convention meeting in the winter of 1775-1776 adopted unanimously a declaration supportive of the instructions it was sending to the Maryland delegates in the Congress, stating the aims of the Province in working and hoping for peace while also being prepared for a more drastic contingency. The declaration was an answer to the address by George III on October 27, 1775, at the last opening of the

Parliament. The King at that time said that the preparations for defense made by the colonies were for the establishment of an "independent empire" in America. The Maryland Convention made its declaration in order to make clear "to the parliament, the people of Great Britain, and to the whole world, the rectitude of our intentions in the present opposition to the measures of the British ministry and parliament." The Convention declared:

> That the people of this province, strongly attached to the English constitution, and truly sensible of the blessings they have derived from it, warmly impressed with sentiments of affection for, and loyalty to, the house of Hanover, connected with the British nation by the ties of blood and interest, and being thoroughly convinced, that to be free subjects of the king of Great Britain, with all its consequences, is to be the freest members of any civil society in the known world, never did, nor do entertain any views or desires of independency.
>
> That as they consider their union with the mother country upon terms that may insure to them a permanent freedom, as their highest felicity, so would they view the fatal necessity of separating from her, as a misfortune next to the greatest that can befal them.
>
> Descended from Britons, entitled to the privileges of Englishmen, and inheriting the spirit of their ancestors, they have seen with the most extreme anxiety the attempts of parliament to deprive them of those privileges, by raising a revenue upon them, and assuming a power to alter the charters, constitutions, and internal polity of the colonies without their consent. The endeavors of the British ministry to carry those attempts into execution by military force have been their only motive for taking up arms, and to defend themselves against those endeavors is the only use they mean to make of them, entitled to freedom, they are determined to maintain it at the hazard of their lives and fortunes.

This sixth Convention, meeting from early December, 1775, until past the middle of January, 1776, clearly was one of the most important of all. It continued its efforts for peace and at the same time took a strong position in defense of its "rights." It took an equally strong stand, for the first time, in sending precise instructions to its delegation in the Continental Congress.

## THE CONVENTION OF MAY 8, 1776

The seventh Convention in the Province of Maryland began on May 8 and continued through May 25, 1776. It handled some of the routine business which earlier would have been cared for by the Provincial Assembly, such as receiving the usual group of petitions for release from prisoners "lanquishing" in the county jails because of debt. It also cared for other matters arising from the convention-type government, and it participated in the continuing debates and proceedings of the Continental Congress and the other American colonies. Charles Carroll (the Barrister) [11] was elected to be chairman of this Convention.

A change was made in voting procedure. Theretofore, in the conventions, the unit system had been followed, so that nothing was recorded for a county delegation except the decision of the majority. The unit vote was continued, but it was decided for this Convention to record also the vote of each individual delegate within the county.

A number of disciplinary cases were handled, though generally with so few details that the exact offenses were not explained. They arose under the Association of the

---

11. A cousin of Charles Carroll of Carrollton. *See* W. Stull Holt, *Charles Carroll, Barrister: The Man,* 31 MARYLAND HISTORICAL MAGAZINE 112-26 (1936).

Freemen, and in one way or another they evidently concerned allegations of disloyalty. Thus, Alexander Wickham of Talbot County was discharged from further proceedings, "being a person too insignificant and contemptible for the further notice of this Convention."

Two members of the militia brought charges against one of their officers, Captain John Gunby, saying that from his conduct "they had cause to suspect his zeal for the rights and liberties of America." The Convention dismissed the petition of complaint, saying that Captain Gunby "hath by his conduct manifested a laudable zeal in defence of the rights and liberties of America in general, and this province in particular." Another case involved the Rev. Mr. John Eversfield, of Prince George's County. In it, the *Proceedings* show only that "in consideration of the age and infirmities of the said John Eversfield, and his want of abilities to exert any dangerous influence, that he be discharged, on paying the expenses of his confinement."

One general problem of discipline was handled in very restrained fashion. Some of the officers appointed to serve under the Convention were loathe to undertake their duties, "alleging scruples to take the usual oaths to the government during the unhappy differences with Great Britain." Here the Convention by resolution decided to dispense with the oaths "during the said differences, and that the persons already appointed, or who may hereafter be appointed, do qualify themselves for their trusts, by taking the respective oaths of office to which they are or may be appointed." Also, it was added, all persons concerned could rest assured "that proper care shall be taken, upon the settlement of those differences, an event we most ardently wish for, to indemnify them against any penalties directed by any laws to be inflicted upon persons acting as aforesaid, without having first taken said oaths."

A difficult problem of discipline was brought by the Council of Safety against Samuel Purviance, Jr., chairman of the Committee of Observation in Baltimore County. One charge was that he had usurped a power of the Council of Safety in directing the operations of the militia in the Province. A second charge was that in a letter to the President of the Continental Congress he had "unjustly represented" the Convention and the Council of Safety as "irresolute and afraid to execute the trusts reposed in them." The Convention determined on the first charge that it "highly disapprove and condemn his conduct in usurping the power to direct the operations of the military force of the Province." On the second charge, the Convention disclaimed any intent to prevent any person from examining into the conduct of the Convention and to communicate his sentiments thereon; but noted "it is equally necessary for maintaining order, that the public bodies should not be wantonly and licentiously traduced by misrepresentations." Purviance was censured and reprimanded by the Convention. "Justice would well warrant a more exemplary punishment," it was said, but in consideration of his "active zeal in the common cause" and the expectation he would have better conduct in the future, he was discharged from further proceedings.

The Continental Congress moved a step toward independence during its session in the spring of 1776. By resolution, it cited the continued failure of the Parliament to respond to the petitions from the colonies; that "it appears absolutely irreconcilable to reason and good conscience" for the people in the colonies to take an oath to support the government of Great Britain; and that it was "necessary" to suppress English authority and to exercise the powers of government under the colonies. Its recommendation was that in any colony not having a government "sufficient to the exigencies of their affairs," one should be adopted. The

Convention in Maryland, on May 21, 1776, adopted a series of resolutions in response to those of the Congress.

There was one notable variation between the resolutions adopted by the Continental Congress and those of the Convention in Maryland. The Congress had recommended it was "necessary" to suppress English authority and to exercise the powers of government under the colonies. In Maryland, however, the Convention determined that it is "not" necessary that the exercise of every kind of authority under England should be totally suppressed in this Province.

Appended to the Maryland resolutions, also, were the usual hopes for reconciliation with England, stating the Convention's persuasion that "a reunion with Great Britain on constitutional principles would most effectually secure the rights and liberties, and increase the strength and promote the happiness of the whole empire." The Maryland delegates, accordingly, were instructed to continue working toward that end in the Congress.

A final policy decision at this Convention was directed toward the King. Citing his policies in prosecuting "a cruel and unjust war" against the colonies, a resolution of May 25, 1776, directed that "every prayer and petition for the King's majesty, in the book of common prayer and administration of the sacraments and other rites and ceremonies of the church, according to the use of the Church of England, except the second collect for the king in the communion service, be henceforth omitted in all churches and chapels in this province, until our unhappy differences are ended."

Before this seventh Convention was adjourned, further provision was made for the Council of Safety. Its membership was to be changed from seven to nine, with five from the Western Shore and four from the Eastern Shore.

One other problem facing the spring Convention in 1776 was that of Governor Eden. He had remained quietly in the Province after proroguing the last session of the Provincial

Assembly, two years earlier. The people and the Convention did nothing to infringe upon his dignity, but the growing spirit of independence and an indication that perhaps the Governor was not being so quiet after all, brought on a polite request that he leave the Province.

## THE DEPARTURE OF GOVERNOR EDEN

Governor Robert Eden had been in Maryland since June, 1769. He had been respected and as popular as a governor could have been in that troublous time. From 1774 on, he had been permitted to hold a secure position; he and his household had been exempt from being solicited to subscribe to the Association of the Freemen, and they also had been specifically excluded from membership in the militia.[12]

During his period of inactivity in governmental affairs, he was closely observing events in Maryland and in America, with some disapproval. In 1775, in a personal letter, he said that "all power is getting fast into the Hands of the very lowest of the People. Those who first encouraged the Opposition to Government, and set these on their licentious Behaviour will probably be amongst the first to repent thereof." [13]

During the summer of 1775, Governor Eden had considered addressing a message to the people of the Province, in mild reproach for their opposition to England. In a draft of the letter he wrote of "intemperate zeal"; as to their seeming approval of the use of arms he said that "I

---

12. *See* Bernard C. Steiner, *Life and Administration of Sir Robert Eden,* Johns Hopkins University Studies in Historical and Political Science, series XVI, pp. 397-402.

13. Quoted in DAVID CURTIS SKAGGS, ROOTS OF MARYLAND DEMOCRACY, 1753-1776 (Westport, Conn., 1973).

would not for the world see the name of man I esteem in the list of such subscribers." On the advice of the Council, the message was never sent; and wisely so. This was the period when Governor Dunmore of Virginia, having been driven from Williamsburg to the safety of an English war ship, retaliated by destroying the town of Norfolk and plotting active warfare against the colony. Nothing so drastic occurred in Maryland, but in early 1776, Governor Eden was involved in an episode which quickly led to a request that he leave the Province.

One of the war ships commissioned by the Continental Congress intercepted a loyalist from Maryland carrying correspondence between Governor Eden and Lord George Germaine in England. Lord Germaine was proposing that Governor Eden join in assistance to Governor Dunmore in Virginia. General Charles Lee of the Continental Army ordered the Chairman of the Committee of Observation in Baltimore County to arrest Governor Eden. The Maryland Council of Safety would not agree to this action, causing the passage of a resolution in the Congress approving the proposal to arrest the Governor.

The Convention was not in session in Maryland when all this occurred. When it convened, on May 8, 1776, it considered the whole affair and on May 24 endorsed the refusal of the Council of Safety to have the Governor arrested. It did not appear from the correspondence between Governor Eden and Lord Germaine, said the Convention, that Eden's letter "has been with an unfriendly intent, or calculated to countenance any hostile measures against America." Furthermore, the Convention said, Governor Eden from his position is bound to execute instructions from England "or hazard the displeasure of the king, which it cannot be expected he will do. . . ." Finally, even if the Governor were arrested, his duties would devolve upon the President of the Council, "and therefore the Governor's departure cannot occasion a dissolution or suspension of the present established form of government within this Province."

Accordingly, the Convention passed a resolution "That it be signified to the Governor, that the public quiet and safety, in the judgment of this Convention, require that he leave this Province, and that he is at full liberty to depart peaceably with his effects." In the tally by individuals, the resolution carried by a vote of 36-19; and by the unit system of voting then in effect, by a vote of 12 counties to four. The latter four counties were all on the Eastern Shore, where loyalist sentiment was strong; and except for one vote from Charles County, every member from the Western Shore voted in the affirmative.

The rather mild action of the Convention in only requesting the Governor to leave was strongly disapproved by John Hancock, president of the Continental Congress, and by the Virginia Convention. In reply to the latter, the Maryland Convention answered that "This Convention, and the Council of Safety for the time being, were the only proper and adequate judges of the propriety and expediency of suffering Governor Eden to depart out of this Province, and have proceeded in that matter upon evidence which was satisfactory to themselves, and to which the Convention of Virginia were strangers."

The Governor left the Province in June, on the ship *Fowey*, but there remained some bits of excitement in his departure. The Convention charged that Captain Montagu of the *Fowey* had taken along several servants of inhabitants of Maryland and also a deserter from the Maryland military, and "hath violated the truce and acted in manifest violation of his promise to preserve the same sacred." It was ordered by the Convention "That the commanding officer do not permit any baggage or effects belonging to Robert Eden, Esq. or any other person on board the *Fowey*, to be carried on board the said ship; and to take care that all communications with the said ship immediately cease." [14] Another order was that the *Fowey* be convoyed down the Bay to prevent "any plunder" being committed by Captain Montagu, "but it is the opinion of this Convention" that the convoy ships should not attack the *Fowey*. Detachments of militia also were to be stationed as necessary to prevent communication with the *Fowey*.

One final episode shows in the *Proceedings* for July 2, 1776, before Governor Eden was out of the Province. It appeared that four citizens of the Province had gone on board the *Fowey* with "12 sheep, 3 lambs, and 7 shoats . . . as a present to Governor Eden." They pleaded this had occurred before they had any knowledge of the truce having been broken. The Convention decided that the four citizens were not "in any way criminal," and they were discharged from further question.

## THE CONVENTION OF JUNE 21, 1776

The eighth session of the Convention met on June 21, 1776, and continued to July 6. It handled the usual array of procedural matters, directives for governing the Province, disciplinary problems, and relationships with the Congress. Most notably, it issued two statements of policy and called the ninth Convention to sit as a Constitutional Convention.

In procedure, this Convention made two changes in its voting requirements. Almost immediately after the vote by counties on the ejection of Governor Eden, the Convention voted on a motion "That all questions be determined by a

---

14. Eden's personal baggage and his wines were sent to him later in London. Stores that he left on the dock in Annapolis and the contents of his house in Annapolis were confiscated by the State of Maryland. *See* Rosamond Randall Beirne, *Portrait of a Colonial Governor, II — His Exit,* 45 MARYLAND HISTORICAL MAGAZINE 294 (1950).

majority of members." This motion (which was handled by counties, under the old rule) was approved by seven counties (Anne Arundel, Calvert, Charles, Frederick, Harford, Prince George's, St. Mary's). It was disapproved, either unanimously or by a majority of the delegation, in four counties (Dorchester, Queen Anne's, Somerset, Worcester). In three other county delegations (Cecil, Kent, Talbot) the individual votes were equally divided. The second change in voting procedures was that the yeas and nays would be entered in the Proceedings if required by any one of the delegates. Another procedural decision was "that the debates and proceedings of this Convention be public, unless in cases where it shall be otherwise directed."

There was a motion also that compensation for the members be reduced from 14 to ten shillings daily; the larger figure had been set in December, 1775. This motion failed by a vote of 16-33, and the compensation remained at 14 shillings.

Among the directives for managing day-to-day affairs, the Convention voted that no person might have a passport to leave America, except an inhabitant of this Province or a person having a passport from another colony of residence. A writ of election issued by former Governor Eden, shortly before leaving the Province, to call an election for members of the Assembly,[15] was summarily cancelled. A number of directives were issued for the needs and activities of the militia. The powers of the Council of Safety were renewed, including a provision that the Council might "on good ground for suspicion, cause any person to be arrested and put to security for his good behavior and appearance at the next Convention"; or that the Council "may order any such suspected person to remove to and continue within any particular place or limits within the Province they shall

---

15. *Maryland Gazette,* June 13, 1776.

assign, or commit him to close prison until the meeting of the Convention."

A number of persons living nominally within Pennsylvania, "desirous of being under the government and protection of Maryland," were declared to be within the jurisdiction of this Province. Interest owed by farmers and planters, accruing after September 10, 1775, and before July 10, 1777, was declared payable in "Indian corn, wheat, flax, hemp or cotton, or linen or woollen cloth."

In disciplinary action, William Yeldell of Anne Arundel County was fined one hundred pounds in current money, plus costs of his imprisonment, for refusing to sign the Association of the Freemen.

In its dealings with the Continental Congress and the delegates from Maryland, there was a significant change made on June 28, 1776. At the earlier Convention in December, 1775, the delegates had been instructed to obtain the approval of the Convention for votes on possible independence. These instructions were "recalled" in this eighth Convention, with the Maryland delegates authorized to vote "as shall be adjudged necessary for securing the liberties of America, and this colony will hold itself bound by the resolutions of a majority of the united colonies in the premises; provided, the sole and exclusive right of regulating the internal government and polity of this colony be reserved to the people thereof."[16]

---

16. This resolution was adopted on June 28, 1776. A week earlier, however, on June 21, the Convention adopted another resolution requesting the permission of the Continental Congress for the Maryland delegates temporarily to attend the Convention in Maryland; and this resolution asked further that questions of "independence, foreign alliance, and a further confederation of the colonies" be postponed until the deputies from Maryland could attend the Congress.

Within a week following the resolution passed in Maryland on June 28, 1776, the Continental Congress meeting in Philadelphia adopted the Declaration of Independence.

With the decisions completed on these comparatively routine problems, the Convention then proceeded to more dramatic events. First, on July 6, 1776, it issued "A Declaration of the Delegates of Maryland," which in effect was a declaration of independence for this Province. It began with this preamble: "To be exempted from the parliamentary taxation, and to regulate their internal government and polity, the people of this colony have ever considered as their inherent and unalienable right, without the former, they can have no property; without the latter, no security for their lives or liberties."

There followed a recital of complaints against the Parliament: its claimed right of binding the colonies "in all cases whatsoever"; oppression in pursuing this claim; "passing many impolitic, severe and cruel acts for raising a revenue from the colonists"; taking away the right of trial by jury; altering the Massachusetts charter; cutting off intercourse among the colonies; restrictions on fisheries; extending the limits of Quebec; confiscating property on the high seas; seizing the persons and property of colonists. Continuing,

> A war unjustly commenced hath been prosecuted against the united colonies with cruelty, outrageous violence, and perfidy; slaves, savages, and foreign mercenaries have been meanly hired to rob a people of their property, liberties and lives, a people guilty of no other crime than deeming the last of no estimation without the secure enjoyment of the former; their humble and dutiful petitions for peace, liberty and safety, have been rejected with scorn; secure of and relying on foreign aid, not on his national forces, the unrelenting monarch of Britain hath at length avowed, by his answer to the city of London, his determined and inexorable resolution of reducing these colonies to abject slavery.
>
> Compelled by dire necessity, either to surrender our properties, liberties and lives, into the hands of a British

king and parliament, or to use such means as will most probably secure to us and our posterity those invaluable blessings,

We the delegates of Maryland, in convention assembled, do declare, that the king of Great Britain has violated his compact with this people, and that they owe no allegience to him; we have therefore thought it just and necessary to empower our deputies in congress to join with a majority of the united colonies in declaring them free and independent states, in framing such farther confederation between them, in making foreign alliances, and in adopting such other measures as shall be judged necessary for the preservation of their liberties: provided, the sole and exclusive rights of regulating the internal polity and government of this colony be reserved to the people thereof. We have also thought proper to call a new convention, for the purpose of establishing a government in this colony. No ambitious views, no desire of independence, induced the people of Maryland to form an union with the other colonies. To procure an exemption from parliamentary taxation, and to continue to the legislatures of these colonies the sole and exclusive right of regulating their internal polity, was our original and only motive. To maintain inviolate our liberties, and to transmit them unimpared to posterity, was our duty and first wish; our next, to continue connected with, and dependent on Great Britain. For the truth of these assertions, we appeal to that Almighty Being who is emphatically styled the searcher of hearts, and from whose omniscience nothing is concealed. Relying on his divine protection and affiance, and trusting to the justice of our cause, we exort and conjure every virtuous citizen to join cordially in defence of our common rights, and in maintainance of the freedom of this and her sister colonies.

Supporting the decision for independence, this Convention acted also (on July 4, 1776) to establish penalties for any inhabitant or resident of Maryland who while here would perform acts of war against the Province or give aid or comfort to the enemy. The prohibition included levying war against the united colonies, adhering to any person bearing arms for Great Britain against the united colonies, or giving intelligence of the warlike preparations or designs of the united colonies. Offenders who were presented by a grand jury and convicted by a petit jury were to suffer death without benefit of clergy.[17] The usual right of pardon was preserved. Demonstrating the continuing ties with England, even in a time of revolution, the several offenses were to receive the same construction as provided in the Statute of Treasons passed during the reign of Edward III (1327-1377).

Finally, as a capstone to this important eighth Convention, the *Proceedings* for July 3 have a resolution "that a new Convention be elected for the express purpose of forming a new government, by the authority of the people only, and enacting and ordering all things for the preservation, safety, and general weal of this colony." Each county was to have four delegates to the Constitutional Convention; and Annapolis and Baltimore Town, two each. Except for those

---

17. "Benefit of clergy was a privilege which, by the seventeenth century, had evolved into a criminal procedure in the common law that qualified convicts of specified felonies at common law could employ to avoid execution of sentence of death. At both English and Maryland law, a convicted lay felon was entitled to a single grant of benefit of clergy. A second conviction of a clergyable felony resulted in the execution of the sentence according to the law." Peter G. Yackel, *Benefit of Clergy in Colonial Maryland,* 69 MARYLAND HISTORICAL MAGAZINE 383 (1974). The seventeenth century version of benefit of clergy had evolved from the custom claimed by the clergy centuries earlier, whereby members of the clergy would be tried by ecclesiastical and not secular courts for any criminal infraction. It was one of the causes of the break between Henry II and Thomas Becket in the twelfth century. Because of complaints that the privilege was abused, it was abolished in England during the reign of George IV (1820-1830). An act of the Congress in 1790 abolished the right of clergy for any capital crime against the United States. *See* BLACK'S LAW DICTIONARY 200 (1951).

elected to represent the City of Annapolis, members of the new Convention were to be freemen above 21 years of age, being freeholders of not less than 50 acres of land or having visible property in the colony of not less than 40 pounds sterling. The property qualification for those elected from Annapolis was to own "a whole lot of land in the said city of Annapolis, or having a visible estate of 20 pounds sterling at the least, within this province, or having served five years to any trade within the said city and being a housekeeper."[18] One year's residence in the county or city was required of all.

Elections for the Constitutional Convention were to be free, conducted *viva voce* in the traditional manner, and without regard to any act of the Parliament or other qualification. No person was to come armed to the election; a muster of the militia was not to be made on the day of election; a company of militia, or any ten men thereof, could not vote "immediately succeeding each other"; and soldiers in the pay of the Province were not to collect at the time and place of holding an election, "so as in any manner to impede the freely and convenient carrying on such elections." Persons holding commissions in the military, and persons who had been "published" as an enemy of the Province by a committee of observation or the Council of Safety, were not permitted to vote. The election was to be held on August 1, 1776.

## THE CONSTITUTIONAL CONVENTION OF AUGUST 14, 1776

The ninth Convention, being the Constitutional Convention, began on August 14, 1776; it concluded its work on November 11. Matthew Tilghman, of Talbot County, was elected chairman; and Gabriel Duvall again was clerk.

---

18. From the wording and punctuation in the series of property qualifications for those elected from the city of Annapolis, it appears that any one of the three listed qualifications would suffice for election.

The Convention on its second day adopted a set of rules to cover its deliberations. The rules were essentially the same as those used for many years in the Provincial Assembly, except that no rules were required for the procedure in passing bills; this was the only convention with a set of rules appearing in its *Proceedings.* The rules were as follows:

*Resolved,* That the hours for sitting for despatch of the public business during this session be from nine o'clock in the morning until one in the afternoon, and from three till six.

Ordered, That the following rules be observed during this session.

That no member of the house use any reviling speeches, or name any member by his proper name, but shall use some other distinction, as the gentleman who spoke last, or the like.

That none shall deliver his opinion, or speak to any debate, unless he shall stand up in his place, and reverently direct his speech to the president.

That no member speak above once on any debate without license of the house declared by the president; and if two persons or more shall rise up together, the president shall appoint who shall speak first; and no member shall interrupt any other until the gentleman speaking hath ended.

That no person come into the convention, while the same is sitting, with sword or other weapon, upon penalty of such fine as shall be imposed on them by the president not exceeding twenty shillings.

That if any member be absent at the hours and place appointed, after the president and fourteen of the members are met, according to the order for sitting, he shall be fined according to the discretion of the president, not exceeding five shillings for any offence, unless upon such excuse as the president shall admit.

All misdemeanors which shall happen in the house shall be censured or fined in the house.

That if any member of the convention depart without leave of the house, such member shall forfeit all his preceding allowances due to him for his attendance this session.

> That no question be determined the day on which it is debated, if any three members desire the determination to be postponed to another day.
> That no question be determined (except for adjournment from day to day) unless forty-five members with the president be present.

Another rule, or order, was added on the same day, that the name of the sponsor of every motion be inserted in the entry in the *Proceedings.* Also, two days later, on August 17, there was another addition. It concerned the manner of putting questions to the Convention: "the question was then put, That all questions to be agitated in this house be determined *viva voce,* and that balloting on any question whatsoever be exploded, except in the appointment of committees, as it has a tendency to deceive the good people of this state, and to conceal the conduct of their representatives from them?" This question was resolved in the affirmative, by a vote of 31-17.[19]

While the main task of this Convention was to draft a Constitution, the members also treated the usual list of regular legislative, administrative, and judicial subjects. There were a number of decisions on the organization and administration of the military. Several disciplinary cases were handled. One involved the Rev. Mr. John Scott, who was held to be a "dangerous influence" in Somerset County. He was removed to Frederick County and allowed to live there, elsewhere on the Western Shore, or on the Western Shore of Virginia; but he could not return to Somerset County or the Eastern Shore of Maryland. Scott also was required to give security in the amount of one thousand pounds and to avoid corresponding "upon public matters with any person whatever."

---

**19.** The meaning of the word "exploded" is obscure. From its context, it must have meant to be spread around or scattered; *i.e.,* publicized. Note the use of the word "state" in putting this question.

The Convention acted to remove persons in the "log jail" in Frederick County to the "public jail," in order to occupy the upper story and to have the use of the prison yard in common with those jailed for debt.

During this meeting, Francis Sanderson of Baltimore County was charged with "delivering sentiments tending to discourage the American opposition to the hostile attempts of Great Britain." He was reprimanded and required to give bond for one thousand pounds, "conditioned that he will not hereafter speak or do any matter or thing in prejudice or discouragement of the present opposition."

This Convention also proceeded to establish two new counties, creating Washington and Montgomery counties from the "upper" and "lower" districts of Frederick County; the "middle" district continued as the future Frederick County.

Late in October, the Convention engaged in the first boundary dispute of the emerging State of Maryland. It stemmed from a provision in the newly formed Constitution of Virginia, undertaking to define the charter boundaries of a number of that state's neighbors. The Virginia Constitution spoke of "the free navigation and use of the rivers Potowmack and Pocomoke." The Maryland Convention quickly met that contention, resolving unanimously "that the State of Virginia hath not any right or title to any of the territory, bays, rivers, or waters, included in the charter" granted to Maryland. Maryland, said the Convention, has sole and exclusive jurisdiction over the Potomac River and over the portion of the Pocomoke River "comprehended in the said charter."

On August 17, the Convention formally ratified the Declaration of Independence and pledged the cooperative efforts of this colony: "The Convention took into consideration the resolution of Congress declaring the united colonies free and independent states, and thereupon

562

*Resolved unanimously,* That this Convention will maintain the freedom and independence of the United States with their lives and fortunes."

Meanwhile, the work as a Constitutional Convention proceeded with dispatch. On August 17, on motion of Delegate Samuel Chase, it was decided to appoint a committee to prepare "a declaration and charter of rights, and a plan of government agreeable to such rights as will best maintain peace and good order, and most effectually secure happiness and liberty to the people of this State."

Much of the close work on the new Constitution was done in the drafting committee and in committee of the whole on the floor of the Convention, so that the details of arriving at the final product do not appear in the *Proceedings.* Obviously there must have been considerable work done in advance, added to the unreported work accomplished in the privacy of committee; the Convention adjourned with a completed document less than three months after appointment of the drafting committee.

The Declaration of Rights and the new Constitution were ordered printed, with copies to go to each county "by express." Other copies were to go to the members of the Convention, judges of the elections, and electors chosen for the Senate.

By further resolution, "all petitions, applications, and reports" then pending, "whereon no final order hath been made or shall be made," were referred to the new General Assembly.

The last Article of the proposed Constitution called for an election on November 25, just two weeks later, to choose the electors for the Senate; they then were to meet in Annapolis on December 9 to choose senators. The election for members of the House of Delegates and for county sheriffs was set for December 18. Election returns were to be sent to the Council of Safety, and the new General Assembly was to meet in

Annapolis on February 10, 1777. Then, or later, the General Assembly was to choose a governor and his council. This final Article also named judges of election for the several counties, and designated the places for holding elections.

The Constitution itself was not placed on referendum. Instead, "This form of government was assented to and passed in Convention of the delegates of the freemen of Maryland, begun and held at the city of Annapolis, the 14th day of August, anno domini 1776."

## THE END OF AN ERA

With the new Constitution drafted and full arrangements made for the beginnings of State government, the work of the Provincial General Assembly and its nine conventions was ended. The final action was a formal resolution of adjournment, passed on November 11, 1776. To cover a possible contingency of having to meet again, the adjournment was only to November 28; and the Council of Safety was given power to call the Convention back into session before that date. This was not necessary, and the final meeting of the Convention was on November 11.

From the first town meeting held at St. Mary's in February, 1634/35, until the ninth Convention in the fall of 1776, the General Assembly of the Province of Maryland met for a total of 169 sessions.[20] Over those turbulent years it forged the independence and the integrity of the legislative processes in Maryland; and as its final act it left a firm and secure foundation for a future State government supported in constitutional and statutory law.

---

20. This total includes the nine conventions in 1774, 1775, and 1776. Though officially termed "conventions" rather than "sessions," these meetings had (or at least assumed) full plenary powers for the conduct of Provincial government. As events proved, the conventions qualified in every sense to be counted as sessions. Also, the total of 169 sessions

## THE CONSTITUTION OF 1776

The Maryland Constitution of 1776 embodied the development and the wisdom (or lack there of) of eight hundred years of Anglo-American law and government, supplemented particularly to reflect the quarrels, aspirations, and complaints of the House of Delegates (or Lower House of Assembly) during the century and a quarter it was part of the Provincial government. Section after section was grounded upon some earlier facet of history or unresolved conflict.[21] The Constitution was peculiarly the product of an accumulated inheritance from England and an environment of legislative struggle in an American colony.

---

includes several in earlier years which sometimes have been termed "conventions" because they did not pass any legislation. However, this seems to be a dubious distinction; there is no essential or indispensable condition that a legislative body must actually produce legislation at every session. Another transient reason for the earlier use of the term "convention" rather than "session" was to avoid the expiration of temporary laws due to expire "at the end of the next session." However important that consideration was at the time, it quickly lost its relevance.

21. One potential for conflict was discussed but not included in the final version of the Constitution and Form of Government. There was a proposal in the Convention on November 3, 1776, to include in the document a provision that either "Shore" could separate from the other at its discretion. After being amended to make a separation possible only if all the counties on the particular "Shore" voted for the measure, it received 17 favorable votes. Sixteen of those delegates were from the Eastern Shore. *See* MATTHEW PAGE ANDREWS, 1 TERCENTENARY HISTORY OF MARYLAND 579 (Chicago-Baltimore, 1925).

Note, however, the proviso in Article 59 of the new Constitution "that nothing in this form of government which relates to the eastern shore particularly shall at any time hereafter be altered, unless for the alteration and confirmation thereof at least two thirds of all the members of each branch of the general assembly shall concur."

Thus, the first articles in the Declaration of Rights were to justify the American Revolution and the independence claimed by the colonies. Article 1 adopted the compact theory of the origin of government; Article 2 claimed for the people of Maryland a sole and exclusive right of regulating their internal government; Article 4 made legislative and executive officers "trustees of the public," assured a power to reform a government or establish a new government, and rejected the doctrine of non-resistance against arbitrary power and oppression.

A number of articles in the Declaration of Rights adopted for Maryland many of the rights and prerogatives of individuals that originally had been formulated in England. Article 3 gave to the inhabitants of Maryland the rights of the common law; Article 14 spoke against sanguinary laws and cruel and unusual penalties; Article 15 prohibited *ex post facto* laws; Article 16 barred bills of attainder; Article 17 assured the right of speedy justice; Article 18 covered the trial of facts where they arise; Article 19 related to jury trials and court procedure; Article 20 prohibited self-incrimination; Article 21, without using the term, covered the right of due process; Article 22 barred the requirement of excessive bail and the inflicting of cruel and unusual punishments; Article 23 related to warrants and prohibited general search warrants; Article 24 generally prohibited forfeiture of estates; Article 25 assured the right to have a "well regulated" militia; Article 26 required legislative consent for having standing armies; Article 27 put the military under civil control; Article 28 regulated quartering troops in private homes; and Article 29 restricted the use of martial law. Article 38 protected freedom of the press.

Another series of articles in the Declaration of Rights gave particular attention to the legislative processes of the new State. Article 5 called for frequent elections; Article 7 prohibited the suspension of laws, except by the Legislature;

Article 8 assured freedom of speech in the Legislature; Article 9 related to a meeting place for the Legislature, and Article 10 called for frequent sessions; Article 11 continued the traditional right to petition the Legislature for redress of grievances; Article 12 required legislative consent to the imposition of all taxes; Article 13 prohibited poll taxes and regulated the imposition of all taxes.

The other main portion of the Constitution, entitled "The Constitution and Form of Government," also dealt in detail with the Legislature. Section 1 created a bicameral body; sections 9 and 21 gave to the respective houses a right to judge of the elections and qualifications of their members. Sections 11 and 22 gave to the Senate a general power to participate in the consideration and passage of laws, but these sections and Section 10 assured the House of Delegates of a power to originate money bills. Section 12 gave both houses a general right to control their proceedings and privileges. Section 24 gave to each House a power to appoint its own officers and settle its own rules. Section 23 required annual sessions of the General Assembly.

There was an innovation for the Senate, however, in a procedure that the senators (nine from the Western Shore and six from the Eastern Shore) would be chosen by a set of electors from the several counties.

The Governor also was not to be chosen by popular vote. The two houses of the General Assembly, by joint ballot, were to elect him, and the legislators also were to elect five persons to comprise the Governor's Council. The Governor's term was for one year only; and Article 31 in the Declaration of Rights added that "a long continuance in the first executive departments of power or trust is dangerous to liberty." These controls over the Governor, and the fact he was not given a right of veto over legislative acts, showed the acute distrust of executive power after the troubles encountered by legislators in the Provincial government and also mirrored their criticism of George III before and during the Revolution.

For the judiciary, the Governor was given a power to appoint all judges and justices, and a number of articles in the Declaration of Rights and sections in the Form of Government covered the judicial processes.

Article 32 in the Declaration of Rights and Section 37 in the Form of Government gave extensive coverage to the prohibition against any person's holding more than one public office of profit within the State.

A final notable feature of the new Constitution was the strict requirement for property qualifications for voting and for holding office. Voters were to be freemen having a freehold of 50 acres or property above the value of 30 pounds. Members of the House of Delegates were to own property above the value of 500 pounds. Members of the Senate were to own property above the value of 1,000 pounds; this same figure applied to members of the Governor's Council, but the Governor was required to have property worth 5,000 pounds, of which 1,000 pounds had to be of freehold estate.[22]

In sum, while the new Constitution followed the prevailing philosophy of the times (as well as the experience of the Provincial House of Delegates) in establishing three branches of government and the principle of separation of powers, both the executive and the judicial powers were weak; and in the legislative branch, the balance of power clearly was in the House of Delegates.[23]

---

22. *See also,* Thornton Anderson, *Maryland's Property Qualifications for Office: A Reinterpretation of the Constitutional Convention of 1776,* 73 MARYLAND HISTORICAL MAGAZINE 327 (1978).

23. For an excellent account of the background, personalities, and progress of the Constitutional Convention of 1776, *see* H. H. WALKER LEWIS, THE MARYLAND CONSTITUTION — 1776 (Baltimore, The Maryland State Bar Association, 1976).

The Provincial Assembly and its nine conventions built well upon their legislative heritage from England. The Constitution of 1776 incorporated much of that heritage and of the accumulated traditions, strivings, and struggles of the Provincial period. It was on this wide base that the General Assembly of the State of Maryland began its post-Revolutionary development.

# Index

## A

Abhorrers, 19
Acting governor, *see* Governor
Adair, Robert, 469
Adams, John, 496, 513
Adams, Thomas, 67
Addled Parliament, 270
Adjournment,
  Assembly's consent, 70
  uncertainty in 1666, 106
  prorogation differs from, 208
  attempted in House, 503
  *See also* Dissolution, Prorogation
Agent in London, 297, 401, 402, 435
Aisquith, 333
Albany, 336
Alfred the Great, 3
Allegany County, 331
All Saints Parish, Frederick, 473
Amendments,
  1640s, 55, 66, 73
  1663, 100
  late 17th century, 136
  suggestions by Lord Baltimore, 136
  "killing bill with kindness," 143
  form in 1720s, 240
  controversy in 1729, 259
  House opposed, on money bills, 298
  delaying, 304, 507
  extraneous matter in, 401
Andros, Edmund, 157
Angles, 3
Anglo-Saxon England, 3, 4, 5
Ann Arundell Towne, *see* Annapolis
Annapolis,
  Battle of the Severn, 92
  capital moved to, 150, 158—162, 164
  former names, 160, 161, 162
  description in 1690s, 162
  port rules, 189
  problems of, 193—198
  representation in Legislature,
    193—197, 254, 407
  plan to burn buildings in, 201
  compensation of delegates, 229, 255
  order in roll call votes in 1732, 257

Annapolis—Cont'd
  corruption in elections, 258
  smallpox outbreak, 258, 355
  election of delegate, 317
  election dispute between two
    delegates, 318, 319
  repeal of stamp tax, 421
  threatened march on, 437
  Walter Dulany as mayor, 439—440
  mayor eligible as delegate, 440
  non-importation agreements, 462,
    463
  delegates to constitutional con-
    vention, 558, 559
Anne (Queen), 162, 175, 180, 186, 189,
  202, 209, 217, 337, 405
Anne Arundel County,
  speaker from in 1650, 85
  established, 90, 98
  1650/1 session, 91
  named Providence County, 94
  in 1650s, 95
  boundaries in 1673, 107
  delegates in 1669, 108
  ferry in, 143
  Mt. Zion, 147, 159
  listed, 157, 213
  road work in 1696, 165
  expense allowances, 173
  Annapolis delegates, 193
  sheriff investigated, 198
  population in 1712, 213
  delegates' compensation in 1730, 255
  roll call votes, 1732, 257
  non-importation agreements, 463,
    464
  convention in 1774, 520
  "Antillon" and "First Citizen," 499,
    510—511
    *see also,* Charles Carroll of Carrollton
    and Daniel Dulany the younger
Anti-Proprietary Party, 356
Apology, 16
Appointments, 313
Appropriation bills,
  1680s, 144

571

Appropriation bills—Cont'd
  House acts alone, 240, 260
  powers of House as to, 278—280, 281,
    298—299, 448
  support of government, 299
  procedures, 448
  see also Bills, money
Archbishop of Canterbury, 171
Ark and Dove, 1, 30
Arrests,
  Annapolis, 1696, 165
Assessors, 386
Association of Freemen, 531—538
  preamble, 532
  voters, 533
  powers of Convention, 533, 536
  Council of Safety, 533—537
  military power, 534, 535
  powers within counties, 535
  executive powers, 535
  committees of observation, 535, 536
  judicial powers, 535, 536
  postponement of judicial cases,
    536, 537
  debts and taxes, 537
  approval, 537, 538
  disciplinary cases, 539, 540, 546—548
  see also Committees of observation,
    Council of Safety, Convention
    period
Associators' Assembly, 149, 155—157
Atkinson, Isaac, 540
Attendance,
  1637/8, 40
  1638/9, 60, 62
  1650, 87
  permission from Governor, 110
  1696, 172
  1698, 184
  1721, 229
  1728, 256
  1755, 354, 357
  1757, 354, 357
  constitutional convention, 560
Attorney General,
  member of Lower House, 132
  message to support Governor, 179
Attorney General (England), 386—388
Attorneys,
  asked to interpret law, 169, 226
  disbarment proceedings, 225—227
  English, opinions of, 250
  enforce price resolution, 526

Audits, 347—350
Australia, 21
"Avalon," 24

B

Bacon's Laws, 408, 410—415
  see also Bacon, Thomas
Bacon, Thomas, 412, 414, 415
  see also Bacon's Laws
Baker, Francis, 539
Baker, James, 175
Baldridge, Thomas, 41, 44, 50
Baltimore City,
  erected in 1729, 263
  1757, 355
  non-importation agreements, 463
  delegates to constitutional con-
    vention, 558
Baltimore County,
  in 1650s, 95, 98
  boundaries in 1673, 107
  delegates in 1669, 108
  ferry in, 143
  listed, 157, 160, 213
  expense allowances, 173
  courthouse in 1711, 198
  population in 1712, 213
  delegates' compensation in 1730, 255
  order in roll call votes in 1732, 257
  smallpox in Joppa, 259
  electioneering in, 323
  boundary commission, 331
  petition against care of the poor, 441
  non-importation agreements, 464
  sheriff ordered to be "circumspect,"
    469
  divided, 502
  convention in 1774, 520
Baltimore Street, Baltimore, 355
Baltimore Town, see Baltimore City
Bankruptcy, 266, 449
Baron of Baltimore, see Lord Baltimore
Batfield, Abednego, 333
Batfield, Meshach, 333
Batfield, Shadrach, 333
Battle Creek, 147, 148, 159
Battle of the Severn, 92, 97
Beale, John, 268—270
Beall, 333
Becket, Thomas, 558
Benedict, 263
Benefit of clergy, 558

Bevan, Thomas, 405
Bicameralism,
  early beginnings, 8, 9, 52, 116, 168
  1640s, 55, 72, 77
  effective in 1650, 83, 85, 86, 87
  exception in 1654, 93
  exception in 1659, 60, 95
  House dispute about "two" houses, 124, 261
  oaths in 1688, 152, 153
  abolition of Upper House proposed, 95—97, 370—373
  defended by Governor, 372
  supported by Benjamin Tasker, 373
  discussed, in Steuart case, 479
  conventions in 1770s; unicameral, 521, 533
  Association of Freemen; unicameral, 533
Bill drafting,
  1640s, 43, 45, 67
  improvement proposed in 1729, 258
  "shall" and "may," 406
  Jonathan Boucher, 514, 515
Bill of attainder, 114
Bills,
  early, 11, 12
  carried over, 208
  engrossed, form of, 241
  money, to arise in House, 281, 283
  money, exclusive power in House, 297, 374—376, 389, 392—394, 444, 446—448, 465
  provisions in new Constitution, 565—569
Bladen, Thomas, 294, 299, 300, 307, 325
Bladen, William, 172, 200, 201
Bladensburg, 348
Blades, 333
Blakiston, Nathaniel, 184, 185
Bonds, see Surety bonds
Bookkeeping, 349—351
Boone, 333
Boston, 161, 520, 522, 523, 525, 531
"Boston Massacre," 455
"Boston Tea Party," 500, 512
Boteler, John, 57
Boucher, Jonathan, 513—515
Bowen, John, 264
Bozman, William, 220
Braddock's expedition, 342, 344
Bradford, Andrew, 218, 415
Brannock, John, 229, 288

Brent, Fulk, 57
Brent, Giles, 57, 62
Brent, Margaret, 77
Bretton, William, 40, 67, 85, 100
Brice, 333
Brice, John, 439
Bridgetown, 263
Bright, John, 2, 21
Briscoe, 333
Brome, 381
Brome, John, 264
Buchanan, Lloyd, 330
Buchanan, Robert, 540
Buchanan, William, 355
Budget, see Journal of Accounts;
  Bills, money; Appropriations
Bunker Hill, 531
Burgesses, see Delegates
Bush Town, 467
Byrd, William, 511


C

Calvert, Benedict, 472, 474, 477, 480
Calvert, Benedict Leonard, 210
Calvert, Caroline, 465
Calvert, Cecilius (1),
  son of George, 24
  charter granted to, 25, 430
  as Lord Baltimore, 32, 33, 34, 35, 51, 57, 149
Calvert, Cecilius (2), 326, 329, 332, 334, 373
Calvert, Charles (1), 102, 142, 149, 156, 157, 158, 172, 209, 210
Calvert, Charles (2), 210, 246, 334, 360, 361, 465
Calvert, Charles (governor), 227, 228, 253
Calvert Cliffs, 93
Calvert County,
  named Patuxent County, 94
  in 1650s, 95, 98
  boundaries in 1673, 107
  delegates in 1669, 108
  capital in, 148, 159
  listed, 157, 161, 357
  expense allowances, 173
  population in 1712, 213
  delegates' compensation in 1730, 255
  roll call votes in 1732, 257
  militia, 377—382

Calvert, George,
  biographical sketch, 23
  *see also* Lord Baltimore
Calvert, George, Jr., 24, 30
Calvert, Leonard,
  son of George, 24, 142
  trip to America, 30, 32
  commander of Province, 33, 37
  deputy for, 34
  1637/8 session, 38, 41, 42, 43, 45, 46,
    51
  1638/9 session, 55—64
  1640 session, 68
  government overthrown, 76, 79
  administration of estate, 78
  death in 1647, 78
Calvert, Philip, 97, 107, 109, 142
Calvert Street, Baltimore, 355
Calvert, William, 126, 142
Canada, 21
Cape Breton Island, 297, 303
Caroline County, 331
  erected, 502
  convention in 1774, 521
Carroll, 333
Carroll, Charles, of Annapolis, 261, 354,
  358
Carroll, Charles, the Barrister, 354,
  546
Carroll, Charles, the immigrant, 223,
  224, 261
Carroll, Charles, of Carrollton, 223,
  261, 493, 494, 510, 511
Carroll County, 331
Catholics, *see* Roman Catholics
Cecil County,
  boundaries in 1673, 107
  listed, 157, 160
  expense allowances, 173
  population in 1712, 213
  delegates' compensation in 1730, 255
  order in roll call votes in 1732, 257
  militia from, 380, 381
Celts, 2, 3
Cerville, Robert, 111
Chandler, Job, 93, 94
Chaptico Hundred, 75
Charles I, 17, 18, 70, 83, 91, 93, 149, 253,
  418, 430, 457
Charles II, 18, 83, 97, 223
Charles County,
  in 1650s, 95, 98
  boundaries in 1673, 108

Charles County—Cont'd
  delegates in 1669, 108
  listed, 157, 158, 406
  expense allowances, 173
  population in 1712, 213
  delegates' compensation in 1730, 255
  order in roll call votes in 1732, 257
  non-importation agreements, 463
  private tobacco inspection system,
    481
  convention in 1774, 520
Charles (fifth Lord Baltimore), 338
Charles' Gift, 93
Charter government, 25
Charter of Maryland,
  provisions of, 25, 42, 43, 49, 51
  legislative powers, 27—29
  civil rights under, 29
  right of prorogation, 70
  complaints of House, 117
  controlling force, 120
  suffrage provisions, 139
  basis for good laws, 191
  municipal charters issued under, 195
  guarantee of English statutes, 244,
    250
  copy of, advertised, 333
  Upper House defended, 372, 374, 375
  tax provisions cited, 387
  stamp taxes under, 418, 429,
    430—432
  governor's function to convene
    legislature, 419
  Dulany's Considerations, 421—426
  Stamp Act protests citing, 435
  House message in 1768, 456—458
  guarantees for citizens, 461
  adjournment not a legislative right,
    503
  used for boundary dispute, 562
Chase, 333
Chase, Samuel, 563
Chase, Thomas, 355
Checks and balances,
  early doctrine, 21
  cited in 1740, 272
Chesapeake Bay, 95, 379
Chester River, 143, 185, 379
Chestertown, 263
Choptank River, 143, 263
Civil disobedience, 382
Clarke, Philip, 177
Clarke, Richard, 201

Clayborne, William, 51, 76
Clayton, 332
Clemency,
  for person convicted, 142
Clencher, 1640, 66
Clerk of the Council,
  compensation in 1700, 174
  salary, 346, 353, 354, 436, 438, 439,
    444, 445, 447, 499, 502
  see also Council
Clerk of the House, 88
  keeping Journals, 104
  oath, 111
  compensation in 1700, 174
  controversy over appointment of,
    202—204, 314—317
  in 1714, 225
  Jefferson's description of, 450, 451
  see also Employees of the Legislature
Clerk of the Upper House, see Clerk of
  the Council
Clerke, Robert, 40, 59
Cockey, 333
Codes,
  1663 book of laws, 100
  request for, in 1671, 112
  absence of, in 1681, 128
  1718 edition, 216—219, 246
  1700 edition, 218
  1707 edition, 218
  Bacon's Laws, 408, 410—415
  earlier editions, 415
  see also Laws
Coke, 405
Coke, Lord, 484
Colonies in America, 189, 247,
  417-426, 427, 428, 433,
  455, 456, 458, 496—497, 499, 500,
  501, 511, 522, 528, 532, 558
Colvill, Frances, 492
Colvill, Thomas, 492
Committees,
  early, 15
  drafting, 43, 45
  1642 session, 73
  rules committee, 73
  on grievances, 1690s, 134
  listed for House, 1680s, 134
  "Grand Committee" of both houses,
    134
  Conference committees, 134
  Joint committees, 134
  use of ordinary by, 145

Committees—Cont'd
  list for House, 1709, 207
  1722 change, 229
"Committees of Correspondence," 501,
  520, 525, 528
Committees of observation, 517, 522,
  526, 539, 540, 548, 559
Common Law,
  beginnings, 5
  early application in Maryland, 32, 70
  debate on use, in 1720s, 243—254
  cited, 272, 291, 293, 357, 404, 443,
    461, 475
  Dulany's Considerations, 421—426
  officers' fees, 483
  benefit of clergy, 558
Commons, House of, see Parliament
Commonwealth, 18, 83, 149, 159
Compensation,     see     Delegates;
  Expenses; Salaries
Concord, 529, 530
Conference committees,
  use in 1680s, 134
Congress, see Continental Congress
Conococheague Creek, 263, 344, 348,
  349, 377
Constitution of 1776, 297, 565—569,
  Declaration of Rights, Art. 3, 244
  Declaration of Rights, Art. 32, 273
  Form of Government, secs. 9, 21, 37,
    273
  holding two public positions, 329, 330
  Declaration of Rights, Art. 13, 33, 474
  Convention period, 516, 517—569
  Association of Freemen, 531—538
  basis for provisions of, 565, 566
  provisions for secession, 565
  provisions of, 566—568
  Declaration of Rights, 566—568
  legislative processes, 566, 567
  governor and executive branch,
    567, 568
  judiciary, 568
  holding two offices, 568
  franchise, 568
  summary of provisions, 568, 569
Constitution of 1867,
  Article 11E, 264
  Declaration of Rights, Art. 35, 268
  Article 3, sec. 29, 473
Constitutional Convention of 1776, 520,
  558—564
  called, 558

Constitutional Convention of 1776
  members, 559
  elections, 559
  rules, 560, 561
  quorum, 561
  sponsors of motions, 561
  disciplinary questions, 561
  legislative work, 561, 562
  Washington, Montgomery counties
    created, 562
  boundary dispute, 562
  drafting committee, 563
  copies printed, 563
  elections provided for, 563
  new government initiated, 563
  adopted constitution, 564
  adjournment, 564
Constitutions,
  written, 20
  Association of Freemen as first, 533
Continental Congress, 420, 427, 428,
    432, 434, 500, 523, 552
  First, 524, 525, 528, 529, 530
  instructions sent to delegates,
    541—544
  policy toward, 555
Controversy between the houses,
  1660s, 89, 105—107, 110
  1669, 112
  1676, 114
  late 17th century, 116
  House grievances, 116—123
  1682, 124—127
  laws effective for three years, 127
  jurisdictional questions, 129—132
  expenses of senators, 129
  form of messages, 131
  filling vacancies, 132
  joint committee chairman, 134
  oaths in 1688, 152
  oath in 1696, 168—170
  membership for John Coode,168—170
  paper affixed to House door, 170
  House clerk arrested by sheriff, 176
  Indian negotiations, 180
  cooperation between two houses, 181
  time of adjourning in House, 204
  compensation of Council, see Council
  1720s, 240—243
  form of amendments, 240
  House appropriates money, 240, 260
  form of engrossed bills, 241
  form of amendments, 259

Controversy between the houses
    —Cont'd
  holding two offices, see Two offices
  division of financial powers,
    278—280
  tobacco taxes, 282—284
  1730s, 285—287
  "rights" of the two parties, 286
  Senate "meddling" in House election,
    311
  1750s, 313
  salary bills in 1750s, 354, 376
  supply bills, 381—385, 389—391
  "delay" in action in Upper House,
    402—404
  money bills, see Bills
  conference committees in Steuart
    case, 486
  1770—1772, 495
Controversy with the Governor, see
  under Governor
Convention period
  1774—1776, 515, 517—569
  transition period, 517—518, 519, 521,
    524
  convention format, 518—521
  legislative base, 517, 519
  illegality of, 518—519, 533
  dates of conventions, 519
  attendance at conventions, 519
  county conventions, 520—521
  exercised governmental powers, 521,
    564
  Association of Freemen, 531—538
  see also Sessions (conventions) for
    1774, 1775, and 1776
"Conventions," 280, 316
  see also Sessions; Convention period
Cood, John, see Coode, John
Coode, John, 124—127, 155, 168—170
Copley, Lionel, 157
Cornwaleys, Thomas, 34, 41, 42, 43, 44,
    45, 46, 49, 57, 62
Council,
  appointed, powers, 34, 35, 37
  1638/9, 63
  1650, 85
  member of Lower House, 132
  members, 168
  compensation in 1700, 174
  compensation in 1720s, 232—239,
    240, 241
  status of, 243

Council—Cont'd
  compensation in 1730s, 254, 265, 274—277
  compensation in 1750s, 313, 346, 353, 354
  recommendations to control, 326
  proposal to eliminate all compensation for, 509
  see also Clerk of the Council
Council of Safety, 517, 522, 533—537, 559
  powers listed, 533—537
  military power, 534—535
  powers within counties, 535, 548, 554
  judicial powers, 535—536
  number of members, 533, 541, 549
  new government, 563, 564
Council of State, see Council
Counterfeiting, 219
Country Party, 357
County Party, 357
Court Crier, 147, 163
Couts, Hercules, 362
Cowes, 30
Cowman, John, 142
Coxe, James, 85, 88
Crawford, James, 165
Cresap, 333
Cresap, Thomas, Jr., 347, 354, 364, 437, 438
Cresap, Thomas, Sr., 345, 347
Criminal jurisdiction, 71
  clemency for person convicted, 142
Criticism between the houses, see controversy between the houses
Cromwell, 333
Cromwell, Oliver, 18, 83, 298
Curia regis, 4, 9, 232

D

Dallam, Richard, 202—204
Darnall, Henry, 393, 394, 492
Darnall, Mary, 492
Darnall, Rachel, 492
Darnall, Robert, 492
Darnell, 333
Davis, John, 40
Debt,
  jail for, 266—267, 488, 492
  1774-1776, 537
Declaration of the Delegates of Maryland, 556—557

Declaration of Independence, 519, 555
  ratified in Maryland, 562
Declaration of Rights, see Constitution of 1776
Delegates,
  term first used, 57
  1638/9, 63
  weapons prohibited, 86
  number in 1673, 108
  writs not sent to, 111, 133, 137
  electing, 1682, 124, 140, 245
  hats prohibited, 127
  vacancies, how filled, 132, 158
  number of, 133, 139, 140, 144, 155, 158
  Senator wearing sword, 134
  elections in 1678, 137, 138
  qualifications for office, 1678, 139
  sheriffs not eligible, 140
  minister not eligible, 169
  election in 1696, 172
  secrecy imposed upon, 179
  election in 1704, 191, 192
  Annapolis, how chosen, 194
  reduce number or compensation, 206
  number in 1716, 214
  execution served against, 229
  suffrage denied to Catholics, 229
  Annapolis, in 1718, 229
  powers, 245—246
  1730s, 254—263
  Annapolis, 1732, 258
  two offices, see under that heading
  execution against, 288
  insult to, charged, 306
  member accused of falsehood, 308
  Senate "meddling" in House election, 311
  delegate acted as under-sheriff, 318
  electioneering prohibited, 322, 323
  mayor eligible as, 440
  Jefferson's description of, 450
  member in Senate hearing, 466
  eligibility of naturalized citizen, 488
  proposal that they vote their consciences, 508
  proposal to bar office-holders, 509
  see also Expenses; Salaries; Expulsions; Elections; House of Delegates; Legislative Prerogatives; Legislative Procedures
Dent, Peter, 359
Deye, Thomas Cockey, 469

Dick, James, 512—513
Digges, 333
Disciplinary cases,
　Erbery, Edward, 102
　Coode, John, 124—127
　Husbands, Edward, 142
　Snowden, Richard, 308, 309
　Key, Edmund, 395
　Baker, Francis, 539
　Patterson, John, 539
　Townsend, William Bartlett, 539
　Buchanan, Robert, 540
　Atkinson, Isaac, 540
　Shockley, Benjamin, 540
　Wickham, Alexander, 547
　Gunby, John, 547
　Eversfield, John, 547
　Purviance, Samuel, Jr., 548
　Yeldell, William, 555
　Scott, John, 561
　Sanderson, Francis, 562
Dissolution,
　1708, 196
　claimed to be, in 1712, 209
　1734, 268, 270, 271, 287
　effect of interim activity, 290
　1758, 374, 384
　1761, 389
　after death of Lord Baltimore, 503—
　　507
　see also Prorogation; Adjournment
Dorchester County,
　established, 107
　boundaries in 1673, 108
　delegates in 1669, 108
　writs not sent to delegates, 111
　ferry in, 143
　listed, 157, 271
　expense allowances, 173
　population in 1712, 213
　delegates' compensation in 1730, 255
　order in roll call votes in 1732, 257
　election dispute, 288
　non-importation agreements, 463
　divided, 502
Dorsey, 332
Dorsey, Edward, 200
Dove, see Ark and Dove
Dower, 492—494
Drunkenness, 102
Duckett, John, 522, 525
Duels, 294
Duke of Gloucester Street, Annapolis,
　162

Dulany, Daniel, the elder, 314, 439
　biographical sketch, 243—244
　committee report, 252, 253
　expelled, 268—271
　reference to, 324
Dulany, Daniel, the younger,
　325, 439, 443, 444, 494, 510—
　511
　"Considerations" on the stamp tax,
　　421—426
Dulany, Walter, 325, 329, 330, 439—
　440
Dunmore, 551
Duvall, 332
Duvall, Gabriel, 528, 531, 538, 559


E

Earl of Chatham, see Pitt, William
East India Company, 500
Eastern Branch, 331
Eastern Shore
　expenses of delegates, 173, 192
　party, in 1740, 291
Eastport, 92, 162
Eddis, William, 513—515
Eden, Anthony, 465
Eden, Caroline, 502
Eden, Robert, 186, 465, 476, 478, 483,
　487, 490, 495, 502, 504, 513, 515, 521,
　531, 549, 550—553, 554
Edward I, 484
Edward III, 12, 252, 253, 558
Edwards, Isaac, 50
Eilbeck, William, 359
Electioneering, see Elections
Elections,
　1682, 124, 140
　1678, 137, 138
　qualifications for House, 1678, 139
　1694, 158
　insufficient returns of, 172
　1704, 191
　basis for good elections, 191
　non-voting, penalty, 193
　Annapolis, for legislators, 194
　act of 1638/9, 245
　corruption in Annapolis, 258
　election complaints in 1730s, 288
　conducted by under-sheriff, 288
　visible estate of voter, 288
　residence of voter, 288
　"undue" elections, 288

Elections—Cont'd
Senate "meddling" in House election, 311
disputes in 1750s, 317—324
sheriff cast deciding vote, 317
delegate acted as under-sheriff, 318
two delegates from Annapolis, 318—319
sheriff failed to issue writ, 319—320
House acted alone on disputes, 320
electioneering, 320, 322, 407, 469—472
bribery and corruption in, 320
English statute "adopted" by House, 320
"undue" election in Frederick County, 325
objection not raised at polls, 325
recommendations to control, 326—328
sheriff rebuked as to, 362—363, 488
questions in 1760s, 406—408
Dulany elected after expulsion, 439—440
"treating" voters, 469—472
polls closed early, 469
petitions for questioning returns, 492
tobacco inspectors not to participate, 501
House members not to deceive electors, 508
proposal to bar office-holders, 509
convention period, 517
constitutional convention, 558
under new constitution, 563, 568
see also Voting
Electress Sophia, 209
Elizabeth I, 11, 15, 16
Elizabeth Town, 489
Elkridge, 263
Elliott, Thomas, 475
Elzey, Arnold, 487
Emerson Hotel, 355
Employees of the legislature,
1640, 67, 74
1650, 88
1662, 100
fees in 1666, 103
joint committee clerks, 134
compensation in 1700, 174
clerk arrested by sheriff, 176
secrecy imposed upon, 179
oath in 1709, 208
compensation in 1730, 255

Enacting clauses, 9
1650, 86
late 17th century, 135
1702, 186, 187
1715, technical question as to, 210, 215
historical account in 1716, 215
1762, 404
End-of-session "jam,"
1650, 87
1706, 202
England,
condition in 1630s, 1
history, 1—22
invasions of, 3—5
civil war and Commonwealth, 83—94
Dulany's description of government, 421—426
English Common Law,
see Common Law
English statutory law,
debate on use, in 1720s, 243—254
Lord Baltimore's opinion, 250
cited, 271, 272, 290, 293, 358, 364, 404, 461, 475
election statute adopted by House, 320
inconsistency with, 405
effect on Hagar case, 489
included in Constitution of 1776, 566—568
Entertainment,
1666 bill from ordinary, 103
senators questioned, 129
arbor party, 141
evening party, 176
community celebration in 1747, 292
electioneering prohibited, 322, 323
laying cornerstone of State House, 495
Erbery, Edward, 102
Evans, 333
Evelyn, George, 35, 41, 43, 45
Eversfield, John, 547
Expense allowances,
1640s, 55, 56, 74
Kent County, 75, 99
1662, 99
senators questioned, 129
concern in 1676, 144
study of, in 1688, 145
1696, 172—174
payment in money, 173
committee established for, 173

Expense allowances—Cont'd
amounts by county, 173
1716, 192
Eastern Shore allowance, 192
1730s, 254, 255
proposal to eliminate, 509
*see also* Delegates; Salaries
Expulsions,
House in 1650, 90
Annapolis delegates, 195—197
delegates holding two positions,
268—274, 284, 329
George Steuart, 195—197, 406
Walter Dulany in 1765, twice,
439—440
"treating" voters, 469—472
Jonathan Hagar, 488—489, 503
Francis Baker, 539

**F**

Fees, 219, 280
Officers, paid in currency, 266
accounting for, 299—301, 337—341,
343, 346, 393, 441—444, 453
officers, *see* Steuart case
legislative right to fix, 475, 477, 480,
484, 487
"First Citizen" and "Antillon,"
510—511
Fells Point, 263
Fendall, Josias, 95—97, 371
Fennick, Cuthbert, 59
Ferries, 143, 161, 164
Feudal system, 4, 5, 6, 26
Fifteen Mile Creek, 345
Finance,
House controls over, 278—280
Governor accused of
mis-appropriation, 280
public debt, 437, 438, 444
inquiries by House, 442
1774—1776, 537
Finch, Sir John, 10
Fines,
disposition of funds, 223, 224
accounting for, 299, 337—341, 346,
441—444
House levied on officers, 320
"First Citizen" and "Antillon," 499,
510—511
*see also* Charles Carroll of Carrollton
and Daniel Dulany the younger
Fitzallen, 103

Forfeitures, *see* Fines
Form of Government, *see* Constitution
of 1776
Fort Cumberland, 344, 345, 373
Fort Frederick, 345
Fowey, 552
Fowler, 332
Franklin, Benjamin, 334, 402, 519
Frederick County, 404
created, 331, 488
delegates, 331
cited, 406
conventions in 1774, 520, 521
divided, 562
Frederick (6th Lord Baltimore), 331,
332, 334, 338, 361, 373, 415, 502
Freedom of speech, *see* Legislative
immunity
"Freeman," 36, 139
Freemen, *see* Association of Freemen
French and Indian War, 313, 335, 341,
342, 343, 383, 417, 420, 437
Fuller, William, 92

**G**

Gale, 333
Gale, Levin, 268—271
Garrett County, 331
Garth, Charles, 435
Gassoway, 332
General Assembly, *see* Senate; House of
Delegates; Upper House; Lower
House; Delegates; Elections;
Legislative Prerogatives; Legislative
Procedures; Sessions, Vetoes;
Expulsions
George, 332
George I, 209, 210, 216, 224, 254
George II, 254, 269, 282, 291, 292, 305,
321, 400—402, 440, 489
George III, 291, 400—402, 420, 455,
456, 529, 530, 544, 549, 568
George IV, 558
Georgetown, 263
Gerard, Thomas, 68, 71
Germaine, George, 551
Ghiselin, 333
Gittings, John, 100
Goldsborough, 333
Goldsborough, Nicholas, 289
Good Friday, 206
*Good Intent*, 462, 464
Gordon, Robert, 268—271

# INDEX

Govane, William, 323

Governor,
Leonard Calvert as, *see* Calvert, Leonard
writs not sent to legislators, 111
controversies with, 107, 110, 111, 112, 116, 171, 201, 202
signing bills in 1671, 136
compensation in 1700, 174
repairs to residence, 174, 205
party for legislators, 176
delegate arrested for judgment, 177
attending House sessions, 178
seeking committee records, 178
cooperation with, 181
power to issue municipal charter, 195—197
House in contention with, 201—206
relationships, early 18th century, 219—228
acting Governor, appointment, 221
dismissed by Lord Baltimore, 223
Charles Carroll's advice to, 224
English statutory and common law, 243—254
powers of, 244, 246
proposal for bill drafting in 1729, 258
Journals criticised by, 260
new house for, 266
legislators with two offices, *see* Two offices
accused of mis-appropriations, 280, 282
negotiations with Indians, 294—297
powers in foreign policy, 294—297
insult to legislator charged, 306, 307
controversies with House, 313
appointment of House clerk, 314—317
supply bills, *see* under that heading
contributions during French and Indian War, 342
home for, 1754, 346
suggestions for keeping books, 349, 350
rebukes House, 361—362
House suggests suits on bonds, 362
House advised on conduct of war, 363—364
Ridout Affair, 364—370, 372
secretary of, status, 364—370
Upper House defended by, 370—373
militia, powers over, 377—382
tax on, opposed, 386

Governor—Cont'd
Darnall case, 393—394
request for insertion in Journal, 394
cost of proclamations issued by, *see* Proclamations
Steuart case, *see* under that heading
1770—1772, 495
power to adjourn legislature, 503—507
inactive during convention period, 521
exceptions for, in Association of Freemen, 538

Grand Inquest, 480

Gray, 333

Green, Anne Catherine, 293

Green, Frederick, 293

Green, Jonas, 287, 293, 309, 333, 392, 394, 408—410

Greene, Thomas, 57, 62, 72, 79, 83, 89, 91

Gresham, 333

Grievances,
House in 1669, 116—123
right to petition for redress, 462

"Grievances before supply," 11, 12

Gunby, John, 547

Gunpowder Plot, 207

Guns, 267, *see also* Weapons

Guy Fawkes Day, 207

## H

Hagar, Jonathan, 488, 503—507

Hagerstown, 489

Hall, 332

Hall, John, 262, 525

Hamilton, Alexander, 318, 319

Hamilton, John, 359

Hamlin, William, 475

Hammond, 332, 395—400

Hance, 333

Hancock, John, 519, 552

Handy, Benjamin, 407

Hanson, 332

Hanson, Alexander Contee, 515, 517—518

Hanson, Theophilus, 487

Harford County, 331
territory in 1673, 107
erected, 502
convention in 1774, 520

Harford, Henry, 502

# INDEX

Harris, 333
Hart, John, 205, 222, 223, 226, 227, 228
Harvey Hundred, 75
Hatton, Thomas, 93, 94
Hawkers, 339, 443—444
Hawkins, Josias, 472
Hawley, Jerome, 34
Henrietta Marie, 24
Henry, 333
Henry II, 5, 558
Henry III, 7
Henry IV, 376
Henry V, 12
Henry VIII, 14, 15, 494
Herrmann, Augustine, 98, 107, 148, 163
Herrmann, Casparus Augustine, 163
Herrmann, Ephraim August, 261
Hobbes, Thomas, 23
Holiday, 332
Hollyday, James, 261
Hollyday, Robert, 488
Hood, Zachariah, 421, 433
Hooper, 333
Hooper, Henry, 264
Hopkins, 333
Horn's Point, 92
House of Burgesses, *see* Delegates;
    House of Delegates
House of Delegates,
    refusal to send delegates to, 91
    name of, changed, 168
    paper affixed to door, 170
    powers on financial matters, 171, 186,
        278—274
    compensation of officers, 174
    criticism by Governor Seymour, 175
    fees for doorkeeper, 175
    Governor attending sessions, 178
    "pardon" on behalf of, 185
    members in 1704, 191
    electing and summoning in 1704, 192
    members from Annapolis, 193
    members from St. Mary's City, 193
    meeting on Guy Fawkes Day, 207
    sessions in 1709, 207
    description in 1730s, 254—263
    members holding two offices, *see* Two
        offices
    Governor accused by, 280, 282
    disrespectful language toward, 289
    interim activity denied, 290

House of Delegates—Cont'd
    took part in Indian negotiations,
        294—297
    powers on money bills, 298, 384
    House acted alone on controversies,
        320
    recommendations to control, 327
    audits by, 347—350
    Journal in 1750s, 356
    Ridout Affair, 364—370, 372
    Sergeant-at-arms, powers, 364—370,
        372
    powers criticised by Governor, 373
    criticised by Benjamin Tasker, 373
    militia resolutions, 377—382
    tax powers criticised, 386—388
    not comparable to House of
        Commons, 388
    financial powers of, 392—394
    Darnall case; embezzlement,
        393—394
    delegate called "indolent," 395
    Wilson-Hammond affair, 395—400
    banter among members, 395—400
    grievances in 1760s, 401, 419
    financial inquiries in 1766, 442
    visit from Jefferson, 449—451
    petition protesting enactment of bill,
        467—469
    decorum; being attentive to
        proceedings, 491
    letters directed to Speaker, 491
    legislative aspirations, 496
    tobacco inspectors not eligible, 501
    membership in 1774, 502
    adjournment attempted, 503
    act to preserve independence of,
        507—509
    under new constitution, 563
    *see also* Delegates; Disciplinary
        cases; Expulsions; Legislative
        Prerogatives; Legislative Pro-
        cedures; Vetoes; Sessions; Ex-
        pense allowances; Salaries; Lower
        House
Howard, 333
Howard, Anne, 333
Howard County, 331
Hundreds,
    civil divisions, 75
Hyatt, 333

582

## I

Impeachments,
  Thomas Truman, 113—115
  procedure, 115
Indians,
  relationships with, 31, 62, 76, 84, 97, 101, 133, 180, 265, 344, 393
  treaty with, 101
  Truman impeachment, 113
  trouble with treaty, 294—297
  House "instructions" to conferees, 294—297
  funds for, 342
Informers, 119
Ingle, Richard, 76
Inns, see Ordinaries
Interim committee, 290
"Intolerable Acts," 500
Iron Chest, 350, 351
Isle of Kent, see Kent Island
Isle of Wight, 30
Itinerant charges, see Expense allowances

## J

Jails, 266, 492
Jamaica, 247
James, 333
James I, 15, 16, 17, 23
James II, 149
Jamestown, 24, 161
Jefferson, Thomas, 422, 449—451
John (King), 5, 7
Joiner, 333
Joint committees,
  Chairman, how selected, 134
Jones, Evan, 218
Joppa, 198, 467
Joseph, William, 150, 153
Journal of Accounts, 233, 234, 275
  threat not to pass budget, 234, 235, 237, 275, 277, 338, 392, 436, 438, 439, 444
  payment for two positions, 330, 502
  cost of proclamations, 339
  threatened march on Annapolis, 437
  conference committee on in 1766, 445
Journals,
  early, 14
  1666, 104
  expunging votes, 119

Journals—Cont'd
  "mutinous" and "seditious" passages in, 123
  changes in form, 168, 172
  copies held by Council, 231
  preservation, 260
  conflicting orders to print, 309
  names in, 332
  copies advertised, 333
  1750s, 355, 356
  Governor's request for publication in, 394
  sponsor of motion named in, 507
Judicial functions, 49, 50, 70, 98
  1774—1776, see under Association of Freemen
Judiciary, 49, 77
  procedure in Chancery Court, 112
  House criticises appointments, 204
  judge removed, 225
  members of the Council, 228
  powers of, 246
  oath for, 249, 251
  interpretation of oath, 249
  smallpox in Baltimore County, 259
  creation of new court, 290
  recommendations for controlling, 328
  magistrate as Delegate, 330
  judge as senator, 330
  Magistrates, see under that heading
Jutes, 3

## K

Karl-Wilhelm, 495
Kent County,
  1642 levy, 75
  delegates in 1650, 85
  established, 90, 98
  in 1650s, 95
  boundaries in 1673, 107, 108
  delegates in 1669, 108
  writs not sent to delegates, 111
  ferry in, 143
  listed, 157, 158
  expense allowances, 173
  population in 1712, 213
  delegates' compensation in 1730, 255
  roll call votes, 1732, 257
  sheriff rebuked by House, 362—363
  militia, 377—382
  convention in 1774, 520

# INDEX

Kent Island
"hundreds" on, 38
1640s, 56, 99
delegates in 1650, 85
in 1650s, 95
Quakers on, 185
walking on the water, 293
Key, 332
Key, Edmund, 395, 407
King,
powers of, 244
disposition of fines by, 301
complaints about, in 1750, 312
King George's War, 305, 335
King William's School, 166
see also St. John's College

## L

Land Office, 163
Laws,
publication of in 1666, 104
effective for three years, 127—129, 130, 179, 186
furnishing copies of, 137
William Joseph's recommendations, 150
revision in 1690s, 156, 157, 186, 187, 189
improvement in language, 168
interpreted by private attorneys, 169
perpetual, 179, 186
revenues not to be impaired, 180
effective in 1699, 187
publication in 1700, 189
revision, 191, 216—219
basis of, 191
possible reenactment in 1716, 216, 246
publication in 1725, 218
enacted without hearing, 225
complaint against "too many," 230
examples of, in 1707, 219
retroactive effect, 221
ex post facto, 226
Council's compensation; controversy, 233—239
publication in 1727, 260
English statute "adopted" by House, 320
copies advertised, 333
Bacon's code, 408, 410—415

Laws—Cont'd
effect of expiration, 473, 481
invalidated after death of Lord Baltimore, 503—507
abrogated by House alone, 503—507
Laws,
see also Codes; Vetoes; Legislative Procedures
Lawyers, see Attorneys
Lee, 332
Lee, Charles, 551
Lee, Hannah, 99, 100
Lee, Richard, Jr., 488
Lee, Richard, II, 511
Leeds, John, 289
Legislative Council, 93
Legislative immunity,
1637/8, 44, 46, 48
1638/9, 63
1661, 97—98
1690s, request for, 181, 182
execution served against member, 229
Legislative intent,
Statement of, in 1650, 90
Legislative prerogatives,
House grievances, 1669, 116—123
lower House, 1682, 124—127, 150
expenses of senators questioned, 129
1688, 152
late 17th century, 176—185
directive not to impair revenues, 180
1690s, request for, 181
1638/9, 245
member not to be arrested, 261
member "challenged" during session, 261
anonymous letter received, 262
delegate "used" in "opprobrious" manner, 262
"seditious" behavior, 262
lack of "proper respect" for House, 289
insult to delegate charged, 306, 307
freedom of speech, 307
member accused of falsehood, 308
content of Journal, 309
House insistence upon, 358-364
"scandalous" reflections upon House, 358
"reviling" speeches against House, 359
magistrate rebuked, 359—360, 361—362
inquiry of president of Council, 360—361

584

Legislative prerogatives—Cont'd
  suggestions to Governor about bonds, 362
  sheriff rebuked, 362—363, 488
  Governor advised on conduct of war, 363—364
  Ridout Affair, 364—370
  militia, powers over, 377—382
  basis for claims of House and Senate, 466
  "treating" voters forbidden, 469—472
  handbill circulated, 490—491
  adjournment not included, 503—507
  provisions in new Constitution, 565—569
Legislative procedures,
  beginnings in England, 2, 12, 16, 22
  1637/8, 38—53
  1640s, 55, 58, 59, 62, 66
  1650, 86
  latter 17th century, 107, 110, 135—136
  approval of bills, 130
  form of messages, 131
  manner of repealers, 131
  time for daily sessions, 136
  name of House, 168
  Journal usage, 168
  printing, 172
  for holding sessions, 179
  temporary laws to be discontinued, 179, 188
  cooperation between two houses, 181
  1709 dispute with Governor, 204
  bills carried over, 207
  notice of pending bill, 225—227
  1720, 228—230
  tobacco barred in House, 228
  printing by John Peter Zenger, 230
  1730, 254—263
  printing in 1720s, 260
  money bills, 281
  printing in 1730s, 287
  petitions, see under that heading
  "delay" in action on a bill, 402—404
  1750s and 1760s, 404—408
  printing in 1760s, 408—410
  Jefferson's description of, 449—451
  provisions in new Constitution, 565—569
  see also Rules; Titles; Vetoes; Veto power; Sessions; Three readings
Lenthall, William, 11
Leonardtown, 148, 264

L'Esprit des Lois, 297
Lewger, John, 34, 37, 41, 46, 56, 57, 58, 62, 67, 246
Lexington, 529, 530
Licenses, see Fees
Licking Creek, 345
Lieutenant General, see Governor
Lloyd, Robert, 428, 451
Locke, John, 20, 23, 297, 485
Londontown, 159
Long Parliament, 18, 96
Lord Baltimore,
  powers of, in charter, 26
  advice from Legislature, 80—82
  relations with Cromwell, 83
  Governor's power to bind, 118
  approval of bills, 130
  vacancies in House, 132, 140
  number in House, 140
  in residence, 1680s, 142
  House acknowledges his control, 152, 153
  Province restored, 213—216
  Laws reenacted in name of, 216
  relationships, early 18th century, 219—228
  Governor dismissed by, 223
  right to public fees, 223
  custody of message from, 231
  compensation of Council, 233
  powers of, 244, 245
  effect of English statutes, 248
  present in 1732, 266
  taxes as remuneration, 284, 304, 443
  fines to be paid to, 301
  quitrents received by, 301, 337
  appointment of House clerk, 314—317
  letter from Governor Sharpe, 324
  "favors" solicited, 324
  tobacco taxes in 1750s, 337
  controversy with in 1750s, 353
  tax on agents, 386
  license fees from ordinaries paid to, 443
  impasse with, in 1770s, 496—497
  death of, held to invalidate session, 503
  see also Calvert, George; Sessions; Veto power; Vetoes
Lord Cambden, see Pratt, Charles
Lord Proprietary, see Lord Baltimore
Lords, House of, see Parliament

Louisburg, 297, 303, 336
Lowe, 333
Lower House,
  established in 1650, 85
  rules in 1650, 86, 88
  expulsion from, 90
  writs not sent to members, 111
  trial of John Coode, 124—127
  possible members of, 132
  see also, Bicameralism, Upper House,
    Senate, House of Delegates
Loyalists, 513—515, 518

**M**

Macnemara, Michael, 314—317, 356,
  407, 440
Macnemara, Thomas, 223, 225, 407
Magistrates, 289, 359—360, 361—362
Magna Carta, 4, 5, 11, 17, 48, 49, 96, 98,
  141, 429, 430, 456, 457, 461
Manokin River, 263
Market Street, Baltimore, 355
Marlboro, 263
Marriages, 230, 492—494
Maryland Gazette, 292, 293, 333, 421,
  490, 510—511
Maryland Historical Society, 351
Massachusetts, 309, 420, 426, 427, 455,
  456, 459, 500, 525, 528, 529
Mathews, Thomas, 89, 90
Matthews, 332
Mattapanian Hundred, 38, 56, 75
"May" and "shall," 406
Meek, John Brooker, 475
Members, see Delegates
Membership in General Assembly,
  1638/9, 63
  1646, 78
  Margaret Brent, 78
  delegates, see under that heading
  proposal to bar, for one who had held
    office, 509
Merryman, 333
Messages, 131, 285
  admission of messenger, 285
  congratulatory, 308
Metcalfe, John, 100
Militia, 353, 377—382, 527
Ministers' salaries, see Steuart case
Moale, John, 469
Money,
  paper currency bill, 266
  iron chest for, 349—351

Money bills, see Bills
Monocacy River, 263, 331
Montesquieu, Baron de, 20, 297
Montgomery County, 331
  created, 562
Morecroft, John, 115
Morris, Robert, 115
Mount Calvert, see Mount Pleasant
Mount Pleasant, 164
Mount Zion, 147, 159
Municipal corporations, see Towns
Murdock, William, 428
"Mutinous" practices, 123, 124

**N**

Nabbs, Thomas, 40
Nanticoke River, 143
New England Company, 24
New Style Calendar, 30
New York (state),
  possible consolidation with, 189
  English retaliation in 1760s, 459
New Zealand, 21
Newfoundland, 24, 529
Newtown Hundred, 75, 85
Nicholett, Charles, 108—109
Nicholson, Francis, 157, 160, 162,
  172, 177, 185
Niles, Hezekiah, 496
Non-importation agreements, 462—
  464, 500, 520, 523, 525, 529
Norfolk, 551
Norman Conquest, 2, 4
Notice, see Legislative procedure
Nova Scotia, 336, 347, 529
Nuthall, John, 101

**O**

Oaths,
  1649 requirements, 81
  Puritan period, 84, 88, 89, 93
  refusal to take, 93
  clerk of House, 111
  Royal period, 149, 152—155, 214
  refusal to administer to John Coode,
    168
  employees, 1709, 208
  Charles Carroll the immigrant, 223
  relation to English law, 249
  form of, for judiciary, 251
  for voting, 258

Oaths—Cont'd
  for clerk of the House, 313—315
  English election oaths "adopted," 321
  illegal, if not set by law, 476
  proposed for House in 1774, 508
  problems during conventions, 547
Ogle, Mary, 490
Ogle, Samuel, 490
  legislators holding two offices, 268—274, 286
  interim meetings, 290
  challenge to duel, 294
  new governor, 307
  letter to Lord Baltimore, 324
  died, 334, 360
Ohio River, 336, 344
Old Style Calendar, 30
Oldtown, 347
One-crop economy,
  1666, 106
  1730s and 1740s, 265
Orders,
  same force as law, 94
Ordinaries,
  1666 charges from, 103
  limited accommodations, 106
  operation in 1674, 112
  keepers, not eligible for Legislature, 140, 192
  1688 charges from, 145
  1733 bill, 285
  tax on, in 1745, 297, 338
  advertisement for, 333
  use of license fees, 341, 393, 442, 443, 444
  regulated, in 1755, 343
Otis, James, 426

**P**

Paca, 332
Parks, William, 415
Parliament,
  beginnings, 7—10, 12, 21, 191
  16th century, 16
  17th century, 17, 23, 120, 246
  freedom of speech in, 98
  writs to fill vacancies, 133
  Revolution of 1688, 149
  selection of Speaker, 181
  private bills, procedure, 220
  money powers of, 278, 298, 376, 387—388
  privileges of, 306

Parliament—Cont'd
  appointment of clerk for Commons, 316
  Benjamin Franklin's comment to, 375
  inconsistency with act of, 405
  Stamp Act, see under that heading
  Dulany's description of, 421—426
  Stamp Act protests sent to, 435
  repeal of stamp tax; declaration, 435—436
  Townshend Acts, see under that heading
  see also Short Parliament;
  Long Parliament; Rump Parliament
Parrish, 333
Parties, see Political parties;
  Entertainments
Patapsco River, 97, 143, 185, 379
Patterson, John, 539
Patuxent, 93, 94
Patuxent County, see
  Calvert County
Patuxent River, 93, 143, 147, 148, 159, 161, 164
Peale, Charles Wilson, 507
Pearis, 333
Peddlers, 230, 339, 443—444
"Peggy Stewart," 499, 500, 512—513
Pensions, 347
Per diem compensation,
  see Salaries; Expenses
Perpetual laws, 179, 186, 188, 280, 282, 302, 304, 404
Petition of Right, 17, 96, 430
Petitioners, 19
Petitions,
  early, 11
  late 17th century, 134, 175
  1750s, 354
  against care of the poor, 441
  regulated, 449
  1760s, 449
  protesting enactment of bill, 467—469
  right claimed in Steuart case, 478
  construction projects, 492
  release from jail for debt, 488, 492
  questioning election returns, 492
  from George Washington and others, 492
  for Mary Darnall, 492—494
  in bar of dower, 492—494
Piscataway, 264

Piscataway Creek, 264
Piscataways, see Indians
Pitt, William, 384, 448, 453, 507
Plater, 332
Poake's Creek, 345
Pocomoke River, 562
Poisoning, 142
Political Parties,
  early, 19, 21
  in 1740, 291
  Proprietary party, 319
  1750s, 356, 357
  Ridout committee, 368
  reprisal in Wilson-Hammond affair,
    395-400
"Politics," 324—329
Poll tax, 301—303
  ministers paid with tobacco poll tax,
    473
Poplar Hill Hundred, 75
Popular Party, 357
Population, see Province of Maryland
Ports,
  bill to create, 141, 159
  rules of, 189
  smallpox in Annapolis, 258
Potomac River, 95, 263, 562
Pratt, Charles, 386—388, 448
Prerogatives, see Legislative
  prerogatives
Preston, Richard, 93
Prices,
  stability of, 523, 524, 525
Prince Frederick, 264
Prince George's County,
  boundaries in 1673, 108
  listed, 157, 158
  expense allowances, 173
  population in 1712, 213
  delegates' compensation in 1730, 255
  order in roll call votes in 1732, 257
  divided, 331
  boundary commission, 331
  non-importation agreements, 463,
    464
Prince William County, 331
Princess Anne, 263
Priggs, John Frederick Augustus, 487
Prisoners,
  cruelty to, 488
Private acts,
  passed, 198
  vetoed in 1721, 219

Private acts—Cont'd
  indexed in Bacon, 415
  marriage settlement for Charles
    Carroll of Carrollton, 494
Privilege of Parliament, see Legislative
  immunity
Privy Council, see Council
Procedures, see Legislative Procedures
Proclamations,
  effect of law, 67
  cost of advertising, 338, 436, 448, 465
Proctors, see Annapolis
Proprietary, see Lord Baltimore
Proprietary government,
  Described, 24
Proprietary Party, 319, 356, 357
Prorogation,
  Assembly's consent, 70
  sessions ended by, 110
  1688, 153
  1696, 171
  1698, 177
  1712, 182
  1708, 203
  1711, 208
  adjournment differs from, 208
  1723, 237
  1731, 259
  1740, 271
  1736, 276, 285, 287
  1739, 280, 287
  1740, 283, 284, 287
  1738, 286, 287
  summary of 1730s, 287
  effect of interim activity, 290
  1745, 306
  1749, 314, 316
  1747, 336
  1754, 341, 342
  1755, 344
  1757, 370, 377
  1758, 384, 407
  1759, 384, 385, 399, 400
  1760, 389
  1765, 427
  1768, 461
  1770, 469, 476, 477, 478, 480
  effect of; House complaint, 477, 478,
    479
  1771, 485
  1773, 503—507
  1774, 521
  see also Adjournment; Dissolution

Protectorate, 18
Protestants, *see* Religion
Protestation, 17
Protocol, 132—142
Providence, *see* Annapolis
Providence County,
  *see* Anne Arundel County
Providence Hundred, 85
  *see also* Anne Arundel County
Province of Maryland,
  in 1650s, 95
  1666, 104
  in 1690s, 157—158, 160
  possible consolidation with New
    York, 189
  in early 1700s, 213—214
  population in 1712, 213—214
  rights stated in 1722, 248
  in 1730s, 263
  1730s and 1740s, 265
  cost of establishing, 284
  1750, 312, 313, 331—335
  1750s and 1760s, 383
  political bases of, 387—388
  background of Stamp Tax, 417—419
  final days, 564
  legislative heritage, 569
Proxies, *see* Representative
  government
Public debt, 437, 438, 444, 445, 447
Pumphrey, 333
Puritan regime, 83—94
  test oath required for, 91
  writs issued in name of, 91
  act of 1654 in favor of, 92
  transfer to, 92
  end of regime, 94
  capital during, 159
Purnell, 332
Purviance, John, 467
Purviance, Samuel, Jr., 548

**Q**

Quakers, 154, 185, 258
Quebec, 529
Queen Anne's County,
  erected in 1706, 209
  population in 1712, 213
  delegates' compensation in 1730, 255
  order in roll call votes in 1732, 257
  party, 357
  militia, 377—382

Queen Anne's County—Cont'd
  non-importation agreements, 463
  divided, 502
  convention in 1774, 520
Quigley, John, 147
Quitrents, 301, 337
Quorum
  1640s, 58, 66
  1650, 85
  1696, 171
  1766, 439
  1774, 502

**R**

Randolph, Peyton, 462
Rasin, 333
Rasin, William, 319, 320
Rawlings, John, 361
Reading, Thomas, 415
Readings, *see* Three readings
Records,
  moved to Annapolis, 164
  informal custody, 200
Religion,
  1638/9, 63
  Toleration Act, 79—80, 94
  William Joseph's address, 150
  Associators' Assembly, 155—157
  minister as delegate, 169
  1700, 185, 296
  establishment of churches in 1702,
    186, 189
  veto of bill, 187, 188
  St. Anne's Church, 167, 190
  Good Friday session, 206
  Calverts in early 18th century, 210
  Lord Baltimore in 1716, 214
  Rights of, in 1740s, 305
  ministers' salaries, *see* Steuart case
  benefit of clergy, 558
Religions tests, *see* Oaths
Religious Toleration Act, 55, 79—80, 94
Repealers
  form of, 131
  general, 189
Representative government,
  beginning, 36, 37, 40, 41, 52
  1640s, 55, 56, 57, 58, 59, 63, 65, 69, 71
  1650, 84, 85
  1670s, 110
  1704, 192
  Annapolis, 193—197
  St. Mary's City, 193

Representative government—Cont'd
1730s, 254—263
recommendations to control, 326, 327
Resolutions,
resting of servants, 50
resolution of 1722, 248, 251, 291, 296, 357, 404
"treating" voters prohibited, 470—472
Resurrection Hundred, 75
Revenues,
impairment, 180, 186
major types, 284
Revolution of 1688, 2, 149
Revolution of 1776,
Stamp tax, see under that heading
eve of revolution, 495—497
meaning of term, 496
impasse in 1770s, 496—497
Tea Act, see under that heading
Townshend Acts, see under that heading
Loyalists, 513—515
Convention period, 515—516, 517—521, 521—569
Ridge, 147, 148, 159
Ridgely, John, 469
Ridgley, 332
Ridout, 333
Ridout Affair, 353, 364—370, 372, 377
see also Ridout, John
Ridout, John, 364, 490
see also Ridout Affair
Rights of Englishmen, 48, 141, 196, 214, 243—254, 272, 283, 291, 305, 306, 321, 358, 364, 404, 426, 429, 430, 432, 434, 435, 446, 454, 457, 460, 461, 475, 522, 545, 566—568
Ringgold, Thomas, 428
Risteau, 333
Roads, 492
Roanoke Island, 24
Robinson, John, 37
Rock Creek, 331
Roll call votes,
beginning of, 36, 50
late 17th century, 136
names listed in 1732, 256
in order of counties in 1732, 256, 257, 287
see also Voting

Roman Catholics,
England, 14, 16
case involving, 71
Toleration Act, 79—80
James II, 149
Associators, 155—157
1700, 185
Charles Calvert (1), 210
Lord Baltimore in 1716, 214
prosecution of priests, 219
Charles Carroll, the immigrant, 223
Thomas Macnemara, 223
suffrage denied in 1718, 229
Roman invasions, 3
Royal government,
Description, 25, 172
Rules,
early, 12—14
1637, 8, 38
1640s, 55, 59, 65
1650, 85, 87
1666, 102
secrecy imposed upon clerks, 179
1698, 183
1722, 228
1730, 256
permitting exchange of messages, 285
1750s, 357, 358, 404
amendment in 1763, 405
"treating" voters forbidden, 470—472
being attentive to House proceedings, 491
letters directed to Speaker, 491
sponsor of motion named in Journal, 507
constitutional convention, 560—561
see also, Legislative procedures
Rules Committee, see Committees
Rump Parliament, 96
Runnymede, 6

S

St. Anne's Church, 167, 190, 255, 473, 514
St. Clement's Hundred, 68, 75, 85
St. Clement's Island, 31
St. George's Hundred, 38, 56, 75, 85
St. George's River, see St. Mary's River
St. Inigoes Fort, 77
St. Inigoes Hundred, 75, 85, 89
St. John's, 57, 65

St. John's College, 167, 393
St. Leonard's Creek, 93, 159
St. Mary's and Potomac River County, 93, 94
St. Mary's City,
  settlement, 1, 29, 95, 564
  references to, 115
  delegates from, 139, 192, 193
  State House in, 146, 163
  dissatisfaction with State House, 147, 148
  oaths in 1694, 155
  captured in 1689, 155
  charter for, 158
  opposes moving capital, 160, 161
  representation in legislature, 193, 214 see also St. Mary's County
St. Mary's County,
  settlement, 1, 29
  established, 38, 90, 98
  hundreds, 75
  delegates in 1650, 85
  in 1650s, 95
  boundaries in 1673, 108
  delegates in 1669, 108
  itinerant charges, 145
  listed, 157, 357
  opposes moving capital, 160—161
  Provincial Court, 167
  expense allowances, 173
  population in 1712, 213
  delegates' compensation in 1730, 255
  roll call votes, 1732, 257
  election dispute, 288, 317
  non-importation agreements, 463
  convention in 1774, 521
  see also St. Mary's City
St. Mary's Hundred, 38, 56, 74, 90
St. Mary's River, 31, 40
St. Michael's Hundred, 56, 75, 85
St. Thomas Jenifer, Daniel, 354
Salaries,
  started, 74
  1696, 172
  1716, 192
  Annapolis delegates paid one-half, 197
  reduction in, 206, 274
  1718, 229
  allowance desired, 247
  1730s, 254, 255, 274
  1750s, 353, 354, 376, 392

Salaries—Cont'd
  proposal to eliminate, 509
  see also Expenses
Salisbury, 263, 264
Sanderson, Francis, 562
Sassafras River, 263
Saxons, 3
Schlossturm, 495
Schools, 230, 338, 444
Scott, John, 561
Scott, Upton, 439
"Seditious" practices, 123, 124
Senate,
  electors in 1776, 563
  see under Constitution of 1776
Senecas, see Indians
Separation of powers,
  early doctrines, 20, 98
  not observed, 198
  1720, 228
  treaty with Indians, 294—297
  not observed by House, 359—364, 377
  Ridout Affair, 364—370
  1750s and 1760s, 383, 393, 464
  Steuart case, see under that heading
  discussed, in Steuart case, 479, 483, 484
  no separation under Association of Freemen, 533
Servants,
  resting, 50
  illegitimate children, 167
Session Laws, see Laws; Codes
Session of 1634/5, 1, 31, 51, 245, 564
Session of 1637/8, 34, 35, 36—53, 245, 316, 372
Session of 1638/9, 55—64, 245
Session of 1640, 65—68
Session of 1641, 68—69
Session of 1641/2, 70—71, 503
Session of July, 1642, 72—76, 372, 503
Session of September, 1642, 76
Session of 1644/5, 76
Session of 1646, 77—79
Session of 1647/8, 79
Session of 1649, 79—82, 372
Session of 1650, 84—90
Session of 1650/1, 91
Session of 1654, 93, 94
Session of 1657, 94
Session of 1659/60, 95
Session of 1661, 97
Session of 1662, 98—100, 246

# INDEX

Session of 1663, 100
Session of 1665, 146
Session of 1666, 99, 101—104, 139, 146, 315
Session of 1669, 107—110, 115
Session of 1670, 233
Session of 1671, 110, 112, 136, 143, 283
Session of 1674, 111—112, 146, 147
Session of 1676, 113, 128, 129, 130, 137, 144
Session of 1678, 137, 138
Session of 1681, 124—127, 129, 131, 140, 372
Session of 1682, 124—127, 134, 143
Session of 1683, 140, 159
Session of 1684, 134, 137, 141, 142, 160
Session of 1688, 134, 145, 147, 150, 152—155, 356
Session of 1689, 155
Session of 1691, 233
Session of 1692, 135, 136, 144, 146, 156, 157, 158, 161, 234
Session of 1694, 154, 158, 160, 161
Session of 1694/5, 161, 167
Session of 1695, 157, 158, 164, 167, 176
Session of 1696, 163, 166, 168, 170, 171, 172, 187, 246
Session of 1697, 164, 176
Session of 1697/8, 175, 178, 179, 181
Session of 1698, 168, 183
Session of 1699, 164, 165, 186, 187
Session of 1700, 174, 176, 187, 315
Session of 1702, 166, 186, 473, 481
Session of 1704, 157, 166, 181, 187, 189, 191, 194, 200, 201, 282
Session of 1705, 198, 200
Session of 1706, 202
Session of 1707, 205, 219
Session of 1708, 192, 193, 197, 202, 203
Session of 1709, 197, 201, 204, 207
Session of 1711, 198, 204
Session of 1712, 182, 208, 209
Session of 1714, 204, 209, 216, 217
Session of 1715, 205, 206, 217, 218, 241, 302, 303, 393, 494
Session of 1716, 192, 193, 214, 215, 217, 222, 223, 231, 489
Session of 1717, 217, 283
Session of 1718, 229
Session of 1719, 218, 226
Session of 1720, 222, 223, 227, 228, 230
Session of 1721, 219, 220, 228, 229, 230
Session of 1722, 221, 228, 229, 240, 244, 247

Session of 1723, 232, 233, 236, 237, 249
Session of 1724, 237, 240, 249, 250
Session of 1725, 218, 238, 250, 251, 255, 303
Session of 1726, 238, 239, 261, 265
Session of 1727, 260
Session of 1728, 239, 251, 256, 260, 262, 315
Session of 1729, 258, 259, 263
Session of 1730, 255
Session of 1731, 258
Session of 1732, 256, 257, 258, 262, 263, 282, 315, 446, 449
Session of 1732/3, 266, 267, 274
Session of 1733, 263, 285, 350, 446
Session of 1734, 257, 268—270, 271, 288, 315
Session of 1734/5, 274
Session of 1735, 239, 266, 267, 275—279, 287, 288
Session of 1736 (Spring), 276, 285
Session of 1736, 239, 263, 275, 346, 347
Session of 1737, 287, 291
Session of 1738, 279, 285, 289, 408
Session ("convention") of 1739 (Spring), 290, 356
Session of 1739, 280, 286, 288, 475
Session of 1740, 271, 281, 282, 283, 289, 308
Session of 1741 (Spring), 293
Session of 1742, 293
Session of 1744, 292, 293, 294, 296, 356
Session of 1745, 298, 299, 300, 303, 304, 309, 310, 317
Session of 1746, 303, 305, 315
Session of 1747, 292, 308, 329, 335, 409, 481
Session ("convention") of 1749, 311, 314—316, 322, 325, 329, 331, 408
Session of 1750, 330, 337
Session of 1751, 355, 358, 359
Session of 1752, 353, 360
Session of 1753, 318, 319, 320, 338, 346, 353, 408, 489
Session of 1754, 336, 341, 346, 354, 364, 443
Session of 1755, 342, 343, 354, 361, 364, 485
Session of 1756, 339, 345, 346, 359, 409
Session of 1757, 353, 354, 355, 357, 362, 363, 364—370, 370—373, 374, 377, 384, 409

Session of 1758, 345, 353, 354, 373, 374, 376, 377, 378, 379, 384, 392, 393, 395—400, 407, 409, 410, 412

Session of 1759, 384, 385, 392, 399, 412

Session of 1760, 385, 386, 388, 407, 409, 410

Session of 1761, 384, 389, 392, 393, 394, 401, 412, 414

Session of 1762, 389—392, 393, 401, 404, 406, 408, 409

Session of 1763, 393, 402, 405, 407, 434, 435, 472, 473, 481

Session of 1765, 416, 419, 420, 427, 433, 434, 435, 437, 438—440, 441, 442, 444

Session of 1766, 439, 441, 442, 444, 447, 448, 449

Session of 1768, 444, 455, 459, 469—472, 492

Session of 1769, 447, 462, 465, 466

Session of 1770, 465, 467, 472, 475, 476, 478, 491

Session of 1771, 465, 482, 485, 486, 503

Session of 1773, 486, 489, 501, 502, 503

Session of 1774, 492, 502, 507—509, 510, 515, 521

Session (convention) of June 22, 1774, 522—524

attendance, voting, 522

resolutions adopted, 522—524

Session (convention) of November 21, 1774, 524

agreement with Continental Congress, 524

public bills discontinued, 524

Session (convention) of December 8, 1774, 525—528

resolutions, 525—527

appeal for unity, 527

temper of resolutions, 528

Session (convention) of April 24, 1775, 528—531

resolutions, 529, 530

attitude toward England, 528, 530

Session (convention) of July 26, 1775, 531—538

temper of delegates, 531, 532

Association of Freemen, 531—538

Session (convention) of December 7, 1775, 522, 538—546

motion for secrecy, 538

disciplinary cases, 539—540

measures enacted as law, 540—541

tax collections, 540—541

Session (convention) of December 7, 1775—Cont'd

desire for reconciliation, 542—544

directives to delegates in Congress, 541—546

summary, 546

Session (convention) of May 8, 1776, 546—550

routine business, 546—548

voting procedure, 546

disciplinary cases, 546—548

resolutions of, 549

Session (convention) of June 21, 1776, 553—559

procedural matters, 553—555

voting, 553

passports, 554

Declaration of the Delegates of Maryland, 556—557

acts of war against the Province, 557

constitutional convention called, 558

Session (constitutional convention) of August 14, 1776, see Constitutional convention of 1776

Sessions,

when called, 63, 71

three-year intervals, 94

daily, in 1722, 229

interim activity forbidden, 290

Governor's function to convene, 419

total number, 564

see also Conventions

Seven Years' War, 313, 335

Severn River, 92, 185

Battle of, 92, 97

Sewards' Heirs, 208

Seymour, John, 174, 189, 205, 225

"Shall" and "may," 406

Sharpe, Horatio, 324, 325, 329, 331, 334, 362, 364, 366—370, 372, 378, 401, 405, 408, 427, 428, 433, 434, 455, 456, 459, 460, 462, 490

Sharpe, William, 325

Shawans, 296

Sheriffs,

not members of Lower House, 132, 140, 192

Anne Arundel County; investigated, 198

duties for elections, 317, 321, 362, 482

sheriff cast deciding vote, 317

delegate acted as under-sheriff during election, 318

Sheriffs—Cont'd
  William Rasin of Kent County, 319, 320
  tax on earnings, 386
  ordered to be "circumspect," 469
  closing polls early, 469
  cruel treatment of prisoners, 488
  Governor asked to remove, 488
Shockley, Benjamin, 540
Short Parliament, 18
Sidling Hill Creek, 335
Simon de Montfort, 7
Six Nations, 294-297, 336, 337, 341, 346
Skipper, Samuel, 229
Smallpox,
  Annapolis and Joppa, 259
  Annapolis, 355
  1765, 416, 435, 439
  1769, 467-469
Smallwood, 332
Smith, John, 467
Smith, Thomas, 50
Smith, Walter, 306
Smyth, William, 103
Snow, Justinian, 44
Snowden, Richard, 308
Somerset County,
  established, 107
  boundaries in 1673, 108
  delegates in 1669, 108
  writs not sent to delegates, 111
  ferry in, 143
  listed, 157, 357
  courthouse, 158
  expense allowances, 173
  population in 1712, 213
  delegates' compensation in 1730, 225
  order in roll call votes in 1732, 257
  Worcester County formed from, 293
Sons of Liberty, 420, 421
Sothoron, 333
South Africa, 21
South River, 159, 164
Spa Creek, 92
Speaker,
  beginnings of office, 10
  powers in single house, 96
  Governor's approval of, 110
  writs to fill vacancies, 133
  request to Governor for immunities, 181, 182
  selection of, 1704, 181
  routine of election, 181, 182

Speaker—Cont'd
  Daniel Dulany, 270, 271
  Wilson-Hammond affair, 395—400
  Jefferson's description of, 450, 451
  letters directed to, 491
Special acts,
  passed, 198
  for towns, 264
Special orders, delaying tactics, 304, 402—404
Stamp Act, 416, 417-436, 448, 453, 455, 496, 499
  Dulany's Considerations, 421—426
  description of, 453
  William Pitt's part in repeal, 453, 507
State House, Annapolis,
  building, 150, 158, 163—166
  lightning in 1699, 165—166
  repairs, 166
  fire in 1704, 199—201
  cleaning in 1730, 255
  "new" in 1770s, 453, 495
State House, St. Mary's,
  proposed in 1660s, 99
  need for in 1674, 112
  constructed in 1670s, 146, 147, 160, 163
  use after 1695, 164
Statute of Treasons, 558
Stente, Thomas, 41
Sterrett, James, 467
Steuart case, 472—487
  effect of expiration of law, 473
  ministers paid with tobacco poll tax, 473, 481, 486, 487
  fees authorized, 474
  House order for explanation, 475
  William Steuart ordered before House, 476, 482
  Steuart held for contempt, 476, 477
  Steuart's offenses, 477-478
  claim for judicial trial, 478
  Steuart held entitled to relief, 479
  House claims legislative prerogative, 480, 482, 483, 484, 485
  other fee cases, 487
Steuart, George, 317—319, 406—407, 439, 474, 477, 480
  see also Steuart case
Steuart, William, see Steuart case
Stevenson, 332
Stewart, Anthony, 512—513
Stockett, Thomas, 104

# INDEX

Stone, William, 83, 90, 91, 92
Stoughton, William, 329
Stuart, Charles, 305
Stuarts, 15, 16, 305
Sudler, 332
Sugar Act of 1764, 419, 420, 426
Sunderland, Josias, 264
Supply bills, 313, 335, 336, 341-346, 353, 373-377, 383-385, 389-391, 393
Surety bonds,
  House suggests suits on, 362
  Darnall case, 393, 394
Surveyors, 487
Susquehanna River, 296
Susquehannocks, see Indians
Sword, see Weapons

## T

Talbot County,
  established, 98
  boundaries in 1673, 108
  delegates in 1669, 108
  ferry in, 143
  listed, 157, 158
  expense allowances, 173
  population in 1712, 213
  delegates' compensation in 1730, 255
  order in roll call votes in 1732, 257
  walking on the water, 293
  non-importation agreements, 463
Tasker, 333
Tasker, Benjamin, 334, 360, 373, 428, 440
"Taxation without representation," see Stamp Act; Townshend Act; Tea Act; Steuart case
Taxes,
  late 17th century, 171
  diversion for arms, 175
  revenues not to be impaired, 180, 185
  1730s and 1740s, 278-284
  defense, 281
  on hogsheads of tobacco, 276—280, 282, 283, 284, 303, 357
  on tonnage of foreign vessels, 282, 303
  export, 282
  Proprietary taxes for remuneration or profit, 284
  on ordinaries, 297
  decrease recommended, 299
  poll tax, collection, 301—303
  support expedition to Canada, 305, 336

Taxes—Cont'd
  excise, in 1750s, 337
  tobacco taxes in 1750s, 337
  tax collectors appointed by House, 374, 387
  powers of Upper House, 376
  controversy over, 1750s and 1760s, 383—388
  income tax proposed in 1750s, 384, 391
  authority to collect, 385, 387
  tax bill of 1759, 386, 388
  tax bill of 1760, 389
  Stamp Act; items taxable, 417—436
  tobacco taxes in 1760s, 438
  stamp taxes described, 453
  Townshend taxes described, 454
  Charter provisions as to, 457—458
  equality of, 461
  legislative right to fix, 475, 484, 485, 496, 520
  1770s, 527, 529, 537, 540—541
  provisions in new Constitution, 565—569
Taylard, William, 176
Taylor, Michael, 262
Tea Act of 1773, 464, 495, 499—501
  enactment and response, 499—501
  purpose, 499—500
Tenants, 386
Tench, 333
Test Oath, see Oaths
Thomas, 332
Thomas, Philip, 143
Thorpe, William, 253
Three readings,
  early England, 13
  1637/8, 46, 51, 53
  1638/9, 60, 63
  1640, 66, 68
  1650, 86
  1680s, 136
  1698, 183
  1730s, 287
  1750s, 357
Tilghman, 332
Tilghman, Edward, 330, 428
Tilghman, Matthew, 522, 528, 531, 538, 559
Tilghman, Richard, 406
Titles,
  two subjects in bill, 187, 188, 246, 298
  subject not covered in, 187, 188

Titles—Cont'd
  House to reject bill from reading title, 376
  supply bill of 1759, 385
  1762, 404
Tobacco, 143, 151, 219, 228, 265, 266, 275, 499
  tax on hogsheads, 276—280, 282—284, 303, 337, 357, 438
  use of proceeds from tax, 278—280, 282, 336
  poll tax on individuals, 301, 302, 303
  copies of laws, 333
  proclamations of laws, 338, 339
  publication in Bacon's Laws, 414
  Inspection Act, see Steuart case
  ministers paid with tobacco poll tax, 473
  inspection act of 1773, 501
Tolchester, 263
Toleration Act, 55, 79 — 80, 94
Tolley, 333
Tonnage tax, 282, 303, 438
Tonoloway Creek, 344
Tories, 19
"Totness," 513
Town Creek, 345
Towns
  bills to create, 141, 197
  St. Mary's City established as, 193
  Annapolis established as, 194—197
  Governor's power to issue charters, 194—197
  effect of bills to create, 264
  laws indexed in Bacon, 415
Townsend, William Bartlett, 539
Townshend Acts, 453 — 464
  description of, 454
  enforcement provisions, 454
  "writs of assistance," 454
  repeal, 464, 495, 496, 499
Townshend, Charles, 453 — 464
  see also Townshend Acts
Towson, 333
Treasury Building, 350, 351
"Treating" voters, see Elections
Truman, Thomas, 113 — 115
Tuckahoe Creek, 331
Tudors, 15
Two offices,
  right to hold, 265, 267—274, 313, 329, 330

Two offices—Cont'd
  House members expelled 268—274, 407, 439
  compensation from two offices, 329, 330
  Steuart case, 472—487
  provisions in new Constitution, 568
Tyler, Robert, 182

U

Ungle, Robert, 182
Upper House,
  established in 1650, 85, 168
  rules in 1650, 86, 88
  abolition of, attempted, 95—97, 370—373
  criticism of Lower House, 105, 124—127
  expenditures of members, 129
  compensation as Council, 232—239
  compensation in 1730, 255
  rules not necessary, 256
  powers on money bills, 298, 387—388
  "meddling" in House election, 311
  recommendations to control, 326
  recommendation to abolish, 353, 370—373, 374, 375
  Journal in 1750s, 356
  appointments, participation in, 374
  member of House in hearing, denied, 466
  see also Senate; Bicameralism; Disciplinary cases

V

Vacancies,
  House, how filled, 132
  Filled after expulsions, 268
Van Sweringen, 129, 141
Vaughan, Robert, 69, 72
Veto power,
  checks and balances, 21
  1640s, 55
  complaint from House, 117, 118, 155
  1721 session, 219
  hearing on bill required, 226
  abolition proposed, 257
  provisions in new Constitution, 567
Vetoes,
  session of 1634/5, 34, 245
  session of 1637/8, 52

# INDEX

Vetoes—Cont'd
late vetoes in 1678, 137, 138
1696 and 1699 acts, 187, 188, 246
effect of, 188
1721 session, 219, 248
election bill in 1732, 258
Virginia, 161, 450, 458, 462, 551, 562
Voting,
early divisions, 14
unicameral totals, 72
expunging from Journal, 119
qualifications, 191
non-voting, penalty, 193
Jefferson's description of, 450, 451
House members to vote their consciences, 508
convention, 553
provisions in new Constitution, 568
see also Elections; Roll call votes

## W

Ware, Francis, 472
Warfield, 332
Washington County, 331
created, 562
Washington, George, 492, 531
Waters, 333
Weapons,
prohibited in House, 86, 183
Senator wearing sword, 134, 357
1750s, 357
constitutional convention, 560
Weems, 333
West, John, 492
West River, 513
Western Shore, 185

Whigs, 19
Whitehall, 490
Whole house, committee of the,
early beginnings, 15
see also Committees
Wickham, Alexander, 547
Wicomico County, 331
William III, 155, 156, 180, 186, 214, 223, 481, 489
William and Mary, 19, 149, 155, 156
William the Conqueror, 4
Wills,
veto message on, 221
Wills Creek, 344
Wilmer, 333
Wilson, Samuel, 395—400
Witan, 4, 9
Wood, Joseph, 355
Wooton, James, 190, 191
Worcester County,
established, 293
delegates from, 294
party, 357
petition against care of the poor, 441
Worthington, 333
Worthy, Jo, 71
Wright, Nathaniel, 330
Wright, Turbutt, 451
"Writs of assistance," 454, 455

## Y

Yeldell, William, 555

## Z

Zenger, John Peter, 230

597

9947